PLAYFAIR
CRICKET ANNUAL
1992
45th edition

EDITED BY BILL FRINDALL

All statistics by the Editor unless otherwise credited

PLAYFAIR CRICKET COMPETITION 1992
TEST CRICKET QUIZ
£1500 TO BE WON

PLUS NATWEST FINAL TICKETS AND HOSPITALITY
PLUS 25 CONSOLATION PRIZES

First Prize £500 + overnight accommodation (B and B) at the Regents Park Hilton Hotel (opposite Lord's) on 4 and 5 September + TWO tickets to the 1992 NatWest Trophy Final + NatWest hospitality

Second Prize £400 + TWO tickets to the 1992 NatWest Trophy Final

Third Prize £300 + TWO tickets to the 1992 NatWest Trophy Final

Fourth Prize £200

Fifth Prize £100

Consolation prizes

Senders of the next 25 correct entries will each receive a copy of JACK IN THE BOX by Jack Bannister and published by Queen Anne Press at £14.99

Closing date for entries is 12.00 noon on 29 July 1992

Winning entries will be drawn by the Man of the Match Adjudicator at one of the NatWest semi-finals on Wednesday 12 August.

2

PLAYFAIR CRICKET COMPETITION 1992

TEST CRICKET QUIZ

ENTRY FORM

Please PRINT your answers in the spaces provided and answer every question.

1 Who was the first batsman to score a hundred in each innings of a Test match? ....

2 In which season did Bramall Lane stage a Test match? ....

3 Who was the first wicket-keeper to make 200 dismissals in Test cricket? ....

4 Who first scored a hundred and took six wickets in an innings of the same Test? ....

5 Who was knighted for his services to cricket in the 1992 New Year's Honours? ....

6 Who was the first bowler to take 300 Test wickets? ....

7 Against which country did South Africa last play a Test match? ....

8 In which year did Dr W.G.Grace first play Test cricket? ....

9 Who is the only man to captain England in his only Test match? ....

10 Who was the first cricketer to represent more than one country at Test level? ....

Your name and address:

....

....

....

Your daytime telephone number: ....

Post to: PLAYFAIR CRICKET COMPETITION, Special Events, Corporate Affairs Department, National Westminster Bank PLC, 1st Floor, 2 Broadgate, London EC2M 2AD

Entries must be received before noon on 29 July 1992. All-correct entries will go into the prize-winning draw on 12 August and an announcement detailing all prize-winners will appear in the October edition of *The Cricketer* magazine. A list of winners is available on request by writing to Mrs B.J.Quinn at the above address and enclosing a stamped addressed envelope.

Rules: All entries must be on this official form. Proof of posting is not proof of entry. The decision of the editor regarding the answers to this quiz shall be final and binding; no correspondence may be entered into.

1991 PLAYFAIR CRICKET COMPETITION

TEST CRICKET QUIZ ANSWERS

1 Who is the only visiting captain to lead his team to victory in a Bridgetown Test? — **R.E.S. (Bob) WYATT**

2 Which was the 64th GROUND (not town/city) to stage a Test match? — **TRUST BANK PARK or SEDDON PARK**

3 Who is the only batsman to play over 100 consecutive Test innings without a duck? — **David GOWER**

4 Who holds the record for the most successive matches as a Test captain? — **Allan BORDER**

5 How many runs did Graham Gooch score in Test cricket during the calendar year of 1990? — **1,264**

6 Who was the first wicket-keeper to make five stumpings in a Test innings? — **Kiran MORE**

7 Who was the first batsman in Test cricket to hit four consecutive balls for six? — **KAPIL DEV**

8 The first triple century in Test cricket was scored in the West Indies – by whom? — **Andrew SANDHAM**

9 Who equalled the Test record by catching five batsmen in an innings in November 1989? — **Mohammad AZHARUDDIN**

10 Who is the only umpire to have stood in more Tests than 'Dickie' Bird? — **Frank CHESTER**

There were 431 sets of correct answers out of a total of 828 entries. The winners were drawn by Basil D'Oliveira (Worcestershire and England) at the 1991 NatWest Trophy semi-final between Warwickshire and Hampshire at Edgbaston.

First Prize: £500 + two nights accommodation + two tickets to include hospitality at the 1991 NatWest Trophy Final — **R.WATSON (Hartlepool)**

Second Prize: £400 + two tickets to the 1991 NatWest Trophy Final — **D.McGUIRE (Headingley)**

Third Prize: £300 + two tickets to the 1991 NatWest Trophy Final — **A.YOUNGMAN (Sutton)**

Fourth Prize: £200 — **A.PRIGMORE (Wellingborough)**

Fifth Prize: £100 — **J.BELL (Burnhope)**

25 Runners-up who each received a copy of *The Golden Age of Cricket*:

R.Appleby (Worcester)
Mrs R.J.Blanshard (Clevedon)
B.M.Bond (Glossop)
W.Bowen (Idole, Carmarthen)
M.J.Box (Reading)
K.W.Brown (Doncaster)
A.R.Bull (Egerton, Bolton)
S.Clarke (Hackney, London)
L.R.Delaridge (Torquay)
A.D.Green (Solihull)
C.Hayward (Raglan)
I.Hesketh (Accrington)
M.Leddy (Formby, Liverpool)
J.Luck (Newcastle upon Tyne)
D.I.McIntosh (Hull)
I.O'Brien (Merstham, Surrey)
D.Padley (Coventry)
D.Plested (Hazlemere, Bucks)
G.Roberts (Cardiff)
M.Scott (Berwick-upon-Tweed)
P.F.Sheppard (Rhondda)
N.Verlander (London SE13)
B.Wadley (West Norwood, London)
N.M.Williams (Neath)
P.G.Yaxley (Wymondham, Norfolk)

4

EDITORIAL PREFACE

It is good to be contemplating the delights of a new season with English cricket on a high. What a debt we owe to Graham Gooch, whose captaincy and batting skills so dominated 1991. Working in close harmony with Micky Stewart and Keith Fletcher, his policy of ruthless professionalism has borne rich fruit for England and Essex. Last summer's Test series against the West Indies side, which for a decade or more had so dominated the international scene, was one of the most enthralling in living memory. None of its dramatic ingredients could challenge the epic quality of Gooch's undefeated 154 at Headingley, a radial chart of which appears within.

My choice of Phillip DeFreitas for our cover is intended as a tribute to a cricketer who has matured into a magnificently consistent bowler; his sustained accuracy and aggression have played a vital part in England's transformation.

This annual will appear a few days before two cricket events of major significance, South Africa's first Test match for 22 years and Durham's first appearance in the County Championship. Rarely have the game's historic landmarks been so eagerly awaited or more energetically sought.

We welcome Pakistan. Their fortunes this summer will depend largely on the rehabilitation of Waqar Younis. His 113 first-class wickets of last season were claimed at the astonishing rates of one every 30.85 balls and at 6.27 per match.

Again, I want to record my gratitude to the county secretariats and scorers for their generous assistance, to Tony Brown, Tim Lamb and Kate Jenkins of the TCCB, to John Jameson of MCC, and to David Armstrong of the Minor Counties Cricket Association. Thanks are also due to all those newcomers to county cricket who have grappled with my 'biodata' form and to readers who have taken the trouble to offer comment and suggestions.

After many seasons of valued contributions, Geoffrey Saulez has retired to an advisory role. The important task of providing first-class career figures has been undertaken by Paul Cartwright, a young statistician from Hampshire, in association with Philip Bailey.

Playfair is fortunate to have such benign sponsors as NatWest and we are especially grateful to Barbara Quinn and her Special Events team for their continued support and encouragement. In addition to weathering a period of grave turmoil at Queen Anne Press, Ian Marshall has once again shepherded this Annual safely from manuscript to publication. Without his expertise and devotion, allied to the guardianship of Publishing Director Caroline North and the enthusiasm of our Yorkshire typesetters, J&L Composition Ltd, it might never have seen the light of day.

BILL FRINDALL
Urchfont

NEW ZEALAND v SRI LANKA (1st Test)

Played at Basin Reserve, Wellington, on 31 January, 1, 2, 3, 4 February 1991.
Toss: Sri Lanka.   Result: MATCH DRAWN.
Debuts: Sri Lanka – C.P.Senanayake.

‡ (S.T.Jayasuriya)
§ (A.W.R.Madurasinghe)

NEW ZEALAND

T.J.Franklin c sub‡ b Labrooy	3	lbw b Ramanayake	39
J.G.Wright c Gurusinha b Labrooy	15	c Tillekeratne b Ramanayake	88
A.H.Jones c Tillekeratne b Ratnayake	5	c sub§ b Ranatunga	186
*M.D.Crowe c Tillekeratne b Ramanayake	30	c Tillekeratne b Ranatunga	299
M.J.Greatbatch c Gurusinha b Labrooy	13	not out	14
K.R.Rutherford c Tillekeratne b Ratnayake	25		
G.E.Bradburn c Tillekeratne b Ramanayake	14		
†I.D.S.Smith c Senanayake b Ratnayake	28		
C.Pringle lbw b Labrooy	0		
D.K.Morrison b Ratnayake	13		
W.Watson not out	10		
Extras (B1, LB7, W1, NB9)	18	(LB9, W1, NB35)	45
Total	**174**	**(4 wickets)**	**671**

SRI LANKA

C.P.Senanayake c Smith b Watson	0
†H.P.Tillekeratne c Greatbatch b Morrison	21
A.P.Gurusinha c Crowe b Watson	70
P.A.De Silva c Bradburn b Morrison	267
*A.Ranatunga hit wkt b Morrison	55
E.A.R.De Silva c Smith b Morrison	26
G.F.Labrooy c Wright b Morrison	0
R.J.Ratnayake b Watson	26
C.P.H.Ramanayake not out	14
K.P.J.Warnaweera b Watson	3
R.S.Mahanama absent hurt	–
Extras (LB7, NB8)	15
Total	**497**

SRI LANKA	O	M	R	W	O	M	R	W	FALL OF WICKETS			
										NZ	SL	NZ
Ratnayake	18.2	6	45	4	30	1	101	0		1st	1st	2nd
Labrooy	23	5	68	4	26	1	88	0	Wkt			
Ramanayake	11	3	39	2	40	5	122	0	1st	5	8	134
Warnaweera	6	1	14	0	34	8	75	0	2nd	18	41	148
Ranatunga					19.3	4	60	2	3rd	33	184	615
E.A.R.De Silva					56	14	141	0	4th	75	362	671
P.A.De Silva					8	0	59	0	5th	78	449	–
Gurusinha					7	0	16	0	6th	108	449	–
									7th	124	454	–
NEW ZEALAND									8th	131	487	–
Morrison	44	6	153	5					9th	150	497	–
Watson	46.1	10	121	4					10th	174		–
Pringle	31	4	116	0								
Bradburn	26	5	83	0								
Rutherford	2	0	11	0								
Jones	2	0	6	0								

Umpires: B.L.Aldridge (8) and S.J.Woodward (24).

Test No. 1163/7

NEW ZEALAND v SRI LANKA (2nd Test)

Played at Trust Bank Park, Hamilton, on 22, 23, 24, 25, 26 February 1991.
Toss: Sri Lanka. Result: MATCH DRAWN.
Debuts: Sri Lanka – U.C.Hathurusinghe, S.T.Jayasuriya.   ‡ (M.J.Greatbach)

NEW ZEALAND

T.J.Franklin c P.A.De Silva b Gurusinha	15	b Ratnayake		69
J.G.Wright c Hathurusinghe b Labrooy	21	c Tillekeratne b Ramanayake		101
A.H.Jones c Tillekeratne b Ratnayake	122	(4) not out		100
*M.D.Crowe c Tillekeratne b Ranatunga	36			
K.R.Rutherford c Tillekeratne b Ramanayake	4	b E.A.R.De Silva		6
S.A.Thomson b Ramanayake	36	c Tillekeratne b E.A.R.DeSilva		55
D.N.Patel not out	26	not out		9
†I.D.S.Smith c Senanayake b Ratnayake	7	not out		6
D.K.Morrison c Tillekeratne b Ratnayake	0	(3) c Jayasuriya b Ramanayake		0
C.Pringle b Ratnayake	9			
W.Watson c Tillekeratne b Ratnayake	4			
Extras (B4, LB12, NB4)	20	(B3, LB9, W2, NB14)		28
Total	**296**	**(6 wickets declared)**		**374**

SRI LANKA

C.P.Senanayake c Smith b Pringle	5	c Jones b Watson		64
U.C.Hathurusinghe c Smith b Morrison	23	c sub‡ b Thomson		81
A.P.Gurusinha c Thomson b Morrison	119	(4) c Smith b Morrison		102
P.A.De Silva c Smith b Watson	1	(5) c and b Patel		6
†H.P.Tillekeratne c Smith b Pringle	12	(6) c sub (G.E.Bradburn) b Patel		26
S.T.Jayasuriya lbw b Patel	35			
C.P.H.Ramanayake run out	13	(3) c sub‡ b Watson		11
*A.Ranatunga c Smith b Morrison	21	(7) not out		20
E.A.R.De Silva c Smith b Watson	4	(8) not out		11
G.F.Labrooy c Smith b Watson	6			
R.J.Ratnayake not out	1			
Extras (LB4, NB13)	17	(B4, LB11, NB8)		23
Total	**253**	**(6 wickets)**		**344**

SRI LANKA	O	M	R	W	O	M	R	W	FALL OF WICKETS				
										NZ	SL	NZ	SL
Ratnayake	30.4	10	77	5	27	4	70	1		1st	1st	2nd	2nd
Labrooy	22	6	46	1	20	2	65	1	Wkt	1st	1st	2nd	2nd
Ramanayake	27	9	52	2	26	5	97	2	1st	40	8	161	95
Gurusinha	14.2	3	36	1	4	1	12	0	2nd	40	38	162	121
E.A.R.De Silva	14	2	35	0	24	6	89	2	3rd	125	41	209	238
Ranatunga	13.4	1	34	1					4th	126	83	222	245
Hathurusinghe					2	0	15	0	5th	239	163	327	300
P.A.De Silva					2	0	14	0	6th	239	185	359	320
									7th	258	240	–	–
NEW ZEALAND									8th	270	246	–	–
Morrison	26	6	77	3	25	4	85	1	9th	288	246	–	–
Pringle	20	5	64	2	12	2	46	0	10th	296	253	–	–
Watson	26.4	8	65	3	37	8	75	2					
Patel	15	4	33	1	39	13	90	2					
Thomson	6	1	10	0	8	3	18	1					
Jones					4	1	15	0					

Umpires: B.L.Aldridge (9) and R.S.Dunne (5).   Test No. 1164/8

NEW ZEALAND v SRI LANKA (3rd Test)

Played at Eden Park, Auckland, on 1, 2, 3, 4, 5 March 1991.
Toss: New Zealand. Result: MATCH DRAWN.
Debuts: Nil.

SRI LANKA

C.P.Senanayake	c Smith b Cairns	20	c Greatbatch b Cairns	8
U.C.Hathurusinghe	b Watson	13	c Smith b Cairns	74
A.P.Gurusinha	lbw b Cairns	50	c and b Cairns	29
P.A.De Silva	c Smith b Cairns	96	c Morrison b Thomson	123
*A.Ranatunga	c Smith b Cairns	34	c Thomson b Cairns	30
†H.P.Tillekeratne	lbw b Morrison	31	c Cairns b Thomson	3
S.T.Jayasuriya	c Smith b Watson	18	not out	12
E.A.R.De Silva	c Jones b Patel	2	(9) c Greatbatch b Thomson	0
G.F.Labrooy	not out	70	(8) c Morrison b Cairns	1
R.J.Ratnayake	c Greatbatch b Watson	18	c Greatbatch b Morrison	20
C.P.H.Ramanayake	c Smith b Morrison	1	b Morrison	0
Extras	(B2, LB15, W1, NB9)	27	(B1, LB5, NB13)	19
Total		**380**		**319**

NEW ZEALAND

T.J.Franklin	lbw b Ratnayake	13	c Tillekeratne b Labrooy	31
J.G.Wright	c Ranatunga b Ramanayake	84	c Tillekeratne b Ramanayake	20
A.H.Jones	c Ratnayake b E.A.R.De Silva	27	lbw b Labrooy	73
M.J.Greatbatch	lbw b Labrooy	65	b Labrooy	7
K.R.Rutherford	c Gurusinha b E.A.R.De Silva	15	lbw b Labrooy	6
S.A.Thomson	lbw b Ratnayake	1	not out	80
D.N.Patel	c Labrooy b Ramanayake	41	not out	16
*†I.D.S.Smith	b Ratnayake	3		
C.L.Cairns	c P.A.De Silva b Labrooy	17		
D.K.Morrison	lbw b Labrooy	7		
W.Watson	not out	5		
Extras	(B1, LB7, NB31)	39	(B1, LB9, NB18)	28
Total		**317**	**(5 wickets)**	**261**

NEW ZEALAND	O	M	R	W	O	M	R	W
Morrison	21	5	87	2	20	2	74	2
Cairns	32	5	136	4	27	6	75	5
Watson	31.5	11	81	3	9	1	23	0
Thomson	12.1	6	22	0	19	5	63	3
Patel	8	2	37	1	23	6	78	0

SRI LANKA	O	M	R	W	O	M	R	W
Labrooy	21.3	6	48	3	19	6	42	4
Ramanayake	26	7	96	2	19	4	62	1
Ratnayake	33	3	83	3	21	3	44	0
E.A.R.De Silva	29	8	67	2	25	4	61	0
Gurusinha	6	2	15	0	2	1	1	0
Ranatunga					7	1	23	0
Jayasuriya					6	1	18	0

FALL OF WICKETS

Wkt	SL 1st	NZ 1st	SL 2nd	NZ 2nd
1st	34	63	9	39
2nd	61	139	56	80
3rd	132	140	201	95
4th	223	170	276	117
5th	234	172	282	217
6th	255	247	282	–
7th	273	257	285	–
8th	325	299	288	–
9th	356	304	319	–
10th	380	317	319	–

Umpires: B.L.Aldridge (10) and R.L.McHarg (3).

Test No. 1165/9

NEW ZEALAND v SRI LANKA AVERAGES

NEW ZEALAND – BATTING AND FIELDING

	M	I	NO	HS	Runs	Avge	100	50	Ct/St
M.D.Crowe	2	3	0	299	365	121.66	1	–	1
A.H.Jones	3	6	1	186	513	102.60	3	1	2
S.A.Thomson	2	4	1	80*	172	57.33	–	2	2
J.G.Wright	3	6	0	101	329	54.83	1	2	1
D.N.Patel	2	4	2	41	92	46.00	–	–	1
M.J.Greatbatch	3	4	1	65	99	33.00	–	1	5
T.J.Franklin	3	6	0	69	170	28.33	–	1	–
W.Watson	3	3	2	10*	19	19.00	–	–	–
I.D.S.Smith	3	4	1	28	44	14.66	–	–	16
K.R.Rutherford	3	5	0	25	52	10.40	–	–	–
D.K.Morrison	3	4	0	13	20	5.00	–	–	2
C.Pringle	2	2	0	9	9	4.50	–	–	–

Played in one Test: G.E.Bradburn 14 (1 ct); C.L.Cairns 17 (2 ct).

NEW ZEALAND – BOWLING

	O	M	R	W	Avge	Best	5wI	10wM
C.L.Cairns	59	11	211	9	23.44	5-75	1	–
W.Watson	150.4	38	365	12	30.41	4-121	–	–
D.K.Morrison	136	23	476	13	36.61	5-153	1	–

Also bowled: G.E.Bradburn 26-5-83-0; A.H.Jones 6-1-21-0; D.N.Patel 85-25-238-4; C.Pringle 63-11-226-2; K.R.Rutherford 2-0-11-0; S.A.Thomson 45.1-15-113-4.

SRI LANKA – BATTING AND FIELDING

	M	I	NO	HS	Runs	Avge	100	50	Ct/St
P.A.De Silva	3	5	0	267	493	98.60	2	1	2
A.P.Gurusinha	3	5	0	119	370	74.00	2	2	3
U.C.Hathurusinghe	2	4	0	81	191	47.75	–	2	1
A.Ranatunga	3	5	1	55	160	40.00	–	1	1
S.T.Jayasuriya	2	3	1	35	65	32.50	–	–	1
G.F.Labrooy	3	4	1	70*	77	25.66	–	1	1
R.J.Ratnayake	3	4	1	26	65	21.66	–	–	1
C.P.Senanayake	3	5	0	64	97	19.40	–	1	2
H.P.Tillekeratne	3	5	0	31	93	18.60	–	–	15
E.A.R.De Silva	3	5	1	26	39	9.75	–	–	–
C.P.H.Ramanayake	3	5	1	14*	39	9.75	–	–	–

Played in one Test: R.S.Mahanama did not bat; K.P.J.Warnaweera 3.

SRI LANKA – BOWLING

	O	M	R	W	Avge	Best	5wI	10wM
G.F.Labrooy	131.3	26	357	13	27.46	4-42	–	–
R.J.Ratnayake	160	27	420	13	32.30	5-77	1	–
C.P.H.Ramanayake	149	33	468	11	42.54	2-39	–	–

Also bowled: E.A.R.De Silva 148-34-393-4; P.A.De Silva 10-0-73-0; A.P.Gurusinha 33.2-7-80-1; U.C.Hathurusinghe 2-0-15-0; S.T.Jayasuriya 6-1-18-0; A.Ranatunga 40.1-6-117-3; K.P.J.Warnaweera 40-9-89-0.

WEST INDIES v AUSTRALIA (1st Test)

Played at Sabina Park, Kingston, Jamaica, on 1, 2, 3, 5‡, 6 March 1991.
Toss: Australia.   Result: MATCH DRAWN.
Debuts: Nil.   ‡ (no play)

WEST INDIES

C.G.Greenidge c and b McDermott		27	c Healy b McDermott	35
D.L.Haynes b McDermott		8	c Healy b McDermott	84
R.B.Richardson c Healy b Hughes		15	not out	104
C.L.Hooper c Marsh b Hughes		0	b McDermott	31
*I.V.A.Richards c Hughes b McDermott		11	not out	52
A.L.Logie not out		77		
†P.J.L.Dujon c Marsh b Hughes		59		
M.D.Marshall lbw b McDermott		0		
C.E.L.Ambrose c and b Waugh		33		
C.A.Walsh lbw b McDermott		10		
B.P.Patterson b Hughes		4		
Extras (LB6, W1, NB13)		20	(B15, LB6, W1, NB6)	28
Total		**264**	(3 wickets declared)	**334**

AUSTRALIA

G.R.Marsh c Dujon b Ambrose	69
M.A.Taylor c Hooper b Patterson	58
D.C.Boon not out	109
*A.R.Border c Dujon b Ambrose	31
D.M.Jones c and b Hooper	0
M.E.Waugh lbw b Marshall	39
G.R.J.Matthews c Dujon b Patterson	10
†I.A.Healy lbw b Walsh	0
C.J.McDermott b Patterson	1
M.G.Hughes c Hooper b Patterson	0
M.R.Whitney b Patterson	2
Extras (B4, LB23, W4, NB21)	52
Total	**371**

AUSTRALIA	O	M	R	W	O	M	R	W	FALL OF WICKETS			
										WI	A	WI
McDermott	23	3	80	5	24	10	48	3	Wkt	1st	1st	2nd
Whitney	21	4	58	0	17	3	55	0	1st	33	139	118
Hughes	21.3	4	67	4	22	5	79	0	2nd	37	159	134
Matthews	11	3	28	0	25	2	90	0	3rd	57	227	216
Waugh	6	1	25	1	13	6	20	0	4th	69	228	–
Border					10	3	21	0	5th	75	329	–
									6th	75	357	–
WEST INDIES									7th	144	358	–
Ambrose	30	3	94	2					8th	166	365	–
Patterson	24	1	83	5					9th	234	365	–
Marshall	22	3	57	1					10th	264	371	–
Walsh	23	4	73	1								
Hooper	7	1	37	1								

Umpires: D.M.Archer (25) and S.U.Bucknor (3).   Test No. 1166/68
In West Indies' first innings, D.L.Haynes (4) retired hurt at 9-0 and resumed at 69;
A.L.Logie (9) retired hurt at 69 and resumed at 166-8.

WEST INDIES v AUSTRALIA (2nd Test)

**Played at Bourda, Georgetown, Guyana, on 23, 24, 25, 27, 28 March 1991.
Toss: Australia.   Result: WEST INDIES won by 10 wickets.
Debuts: Nil.**

AUSTRALIA

M.A.Taylor lbw b Patterson	0	lbw b Ambrose	15
G.R.Marsh c Hooper b Patterson	94	b Walsh	22
D.C.Boon c Dujon b Marshall	7	c Dujon b Marshall	2
*A.R.Border b Marshall	47	c Dujon b Marshall	34
D.M.Jones b Marshall	34	run out	3
M.E.Waugh c Dujon b Patterson	71	c Richards b Ambrose	31
G.R.J.Matthews c Dujon b Ambrose	1	c Dujon b Marshall	16
†I.A.Healy run out	53	run out	47
C.J.McDermott lbw b Patterson	1	c Dujon b Patterson	4
M.G.Hughes b Ambrose	0	c Patterson b Walsh	21
M.R.Whitney not out	1	not out	0
Extras (B6, LB8, W2, NB23)	39	(B17, LB6, W2, NB28)	53
Total	**348**		**248**

WEST INDIES

C.G.Greenidge lbw b McDermott	2	not out	5
D.L.Haynes c Waugh b Border	111	not out	23
R.B.Richardson lbw b McDermott	182		
C.L.Hooper c Waugh b Matthews	62		
*I.V.A.Richards b Matthews	50		
A.L.Logie c Healy b Border	54		
†P.J.L.Dujon lbw b Border	29		
M.D.Marshall not out	22		
C.E.L.Ambrose b Border	0		
C.A.Walsh b Border	1		
B.P.Patterson lbw b Matthews	15		
Extras (B5, LB13, NB23)	41	(LB2, NB1)	3
Total	**569**	**(0 wickets)**	**31**

WEST INDIES	O	M	R	W	O	M	R	W	FALL OF WICKETS				
Ambrose	31.4	9	64	2	24	5	44	2		A	WI	A	WI
Patterson	24	1	80	4	14	5	47	1	Wkt	1st	1st	2nd	2nd
Walsh	24	2	81	0	23	4	55	2	1st	3	10	32	–
Marshall	23	3	67	3	15	2	31	3	2nd	24	307	43	–
Hooper	13	3	37	0	18	6	35	0	3rd	124	353	67	–
Richards	1	0	5	0	4	2	13	0	4th	188	443	73	–
									5th	237	444	130	–
AUSTRALIA									6th	238	529	161	–
McDermott	36	2	114	2	4	1	10	0	7th	339	530	172	–
Whitney	28	4	103	0					8th	346	530	187	–
Matthews	37.5	6	155	3					9th	346	532	241	–
Hughes	20	4	93	0	3.5	0	19	0	10th	348	569	248	–
Waugh	2	0	18	0									
Border	30	11	68	5									

Umpires: C.E.Cumberbatch (11) and C.R.Duncan (1).   Test No. 1167/69

WEST INDIES v AUSTRALIA (3rd Test)

Played at Queen's Park Oval, Port-of-Spain, Trinidad, on 5, 6, 8, 9, 10 April 1991.
Toss: West Indies. Result: MATCH DRAWN.
Debuts: Nil.

AUSTRALIA

G.R.Marsh c Hooper b Ambrose	10	lbw b Marshall	12
M.A.Taylor c Walsh b Marshall	61	b Patterson	2
D.C.Boon c Logie b Patterson	27	b Walsh	29
*A.R.Border run out	43	(5) not out	27
D.M.Jones lbw b Patterson	21	(4) not out	39
M.E.Waugh lbw b Marshall	64		
S.R.Waugh c Dujon b Walsh	26		
†I.A.Healy c Dujon b Marshall	9		
C.J.McDermott c Richardson b Patterson	0		
M.G.Hughes lbw b Patterson	0		
B.A.Reid not out	0		
Extras (B6, LB14, NB13)	33	(B1, LB9, NB4)	14
Total	294	(3 wickets declared)	123

WEST INDIES

C.G.Greenidge c M.E.Waugh b Reid	12
D.L.Haynes b McDermott	1
R.B.Richardson c Taylor b Hughes	30
C.L.Hooper lbw b Hughes	12
A.L.Logie c M.E.Waugh b Hughes	1
*I.V.A.Richards c S.R.Waugh b Hughes	2
†P.J.L.Dujon lbw b McDermott	70
M.D.Marshall c McDermott b Border	12
C.E.L.Ambrose c Border b M.E.Waugh	53
C.A.Walsh not out	12
B.P.Patterson b McDermott	0
Extras (B6, LB7, NB9)	22
Total	227

WEST INDIES	O	M	R	W	O	M	R	W
Ambrose	29	7	51	1	10	4	11	0
Patterson	26	2	50	4	7	0	27	1
Marshall	18.1	3	55	3	10	3	24	1
Walsh	30	9	45	1	12	6	11	1
Hooper	25	5	73	0	13	3	38	0
Richardson					1	0	2	0

FALL OF WICKETS				
		A	WI	A
Wkt	1st	1st	1st	2nd
1st	24	16	3
2nd	93	18	49
3rd	116	46	53
4th	174	52	—
5th	210	56	—
6th	268	86	—
7th	293	110	—
8th	294	197	—
9th	294	225	—
10th	294	227	—

AUSTRALIA	O	M	R	W
McDermott	14.2	2	36	3
Reid	22	0	79	1
Border	19	5	28	1
Hughes	17	5	48	4
S.R.Waugh	5	0	10	0
M.E.Waugh	6	2	9	1
Jones	1	0	4	0

Umpires: D.M.Archer (26) and L.H.Barker (15).

Test No. 1168/70

WEST INDIES v AUSTRALIA (4th Test)

Played at Kensington Oval, Bridgetown, Barbados, on 19, 20, 21, 23, 24 April 1991.
Toss: Australia. Result: WEST INDIES won by 343 runs.
Debuts: Nil.

WEST INDIES

Batsman	1st innings		2nd innings	
C.G.Greenidge	c Reid b McDermott	10	lbw b Hughes	226
D.L.Haynes	c M.E.Waugh b Hughes	28	c Healy b M.E.Waugh	40
R.B.Richardson	c Boon b McDermott	1	(4) lbw b M.E.Waugh	99
C.L.Hooper	c Jones b Hughes	0	(5) c Healy b M.E.Waugh	57
*I.V.A.Richards	c Hughes b McDermott	32	(6) lbw b M.E.Waugh	25
A.L.Logie	c Taylor b Reid	11	(7) not out	33
†P.J.L.Dujon	c Healy b Hughes	10	(8) c M.E.Waugh b McDermott	4
M.D.Marshall	c Marsh b Reid	17	(3) c Healy b McDermott	15
C.E.L.Ambrose	not out	19	b Reid	2
C.A.Walsh	c M.E.Waugh b McDermott	10	c Marsh b Reid	0
B.P.Patterson	c M.E.Waugh b Hughes	1	not out	4
Extras	(LB3, NB7)	10	(LB19, NB12)	31
Total		149	(9 wickets declared)	536

AUSTRALIA

Batsman	1st innings		2nd innings	
M.A.Taylor	lbw b Ambrose	26	(2) lbw b Marshall	76
G.R.Marsh	c Logie b Ambrose	12	(1) lbw b Ambrose	0
D.C.Boon	c Hooper b Marshall	0	b Ambrose	57
*A.R.Border	b Marshall	29	c Dujon b Ambrose	0
D.M.Jones	lbw b Marshall	22	(6) b Hooper	37
M.E.Waugh	not out	20	(7) b Hooper	3
S.R.Waugh	c Dujon b Patterson	2	(8) not out	4
†I.A.Healy	c Dujon b Walsh	2	(9) b Marshall	0
M.G.Hughes	c Logie b Walsh	3	(5) c Dujon b Marshall	3
C.J.McDermott	b Walsh	2	c sub (R.I.C.Holder) b Walsh	2
B.A.Reid	b Walsh	0	b Walsh	0
Extras	(LB2, NB14)	16	(B3, LB5, NB18)	26
Total		134		208

AUSTRALIA	O	M	R	W	O	M	R	W
McDermott	22	6	49	4	37.3	8	130	2
Reid	21	8	50	2	30	4	100	2
Hughes	16.1	2	44	4	36	6	125	1
S.R.Waugh	2	0	3	0	28	6	77	0
M.E.Waugh					28	6	80	4
Jones					3	1	5	0
WEST INDIES								
Ambrose	16	5	36	2	19	7	36	3
Patterson	13	6	22	1	15	3	56	0
Marshall	16	1	60	3	17	4	35	3
Walsh	5.1	1	14	4	15.3	4	37	2
Hooper					18	4	28	2
Richards					3	0	8	0

FALL OF WICKETS

Wkt	WI 1st	A 1st	WI 2nd	A 2nd
1st	17	24	129	0
2nd	21	27	153	111
3rd	22	59	352	111
4th	72	95	454	122
5th	89	97	470	190
6th	96	100	512	200
7th	103	106	522	200
8th	125	121	525	200
9th	148	127	525	208
10th	149	134	–	208

Umpires: D.M.Archer (27) and L.H.Barker (16). Test No. 1169/71

WEST INDIES v AUSTRALIA (5th Test)

Played at Recreation Ground, St. John's, Antigua, on 27, 28, 29 April, 1 May 1991.
Toss: Australia. Result: AUSTRALIA won by 157 runs.
Debuts: Nil.

AUSTRALIA

G.R.Marsh c Richards b Patterson	6	(2)	c Dujon b Ambrose	1
M.A.Taylor c Dujon b Hooper	59	(1)	c and b Ambrose	144
D.C.Boon c Greenidge b Ambrose	0	(4)	b Walsh	35
*A.R.Border c Dujon b Hooper	59	(5)	b Walsh	5
D.M.Jones lbw b Marshall	81	(6)	b Walsh	8
M.E.Waugh not out	139	(7)	lbw b Walsh	0
†I.A.Healy c Dujon b Marshall	12	(3)	c Logie b Patterson	32
P.L.Taylor c Dujon b Ambrose	2		lbw b Marshall	4
M.G.Hughes b Ambrose	1		c Walsh b Ambrose	13
C.J.McDermott c Dujon b Walsh	7		c Dujon b Marshall	1
T.M.Alderman b Walsh	0		not out	0
Extras (B1, LB12, W6, NB18)	37		(B11, LB7, NB4)	22
Total	**403**			**265**

WEST INDIES

C.G.Greenidge lbw b McDermott	6	run out	43
D.L.Haynes lbw b McDermott	84	run out	33
R.B.Richardson b McDermott	3	c Jones b Waugh	41
C.L.Hooper lbw b Hughes	2	c Waugh b P.L.Taylor	35
*I.V.A.Richards lbw b McDermott	0	c Alderman b Border	2
A.L.Logie c Jones b P.L.Taylor	24	lbw b Alderman	61
†P.J.L.Dujon c Jones b Hughes	33	lbw b McDermott	4
M.D.Marshall c Healy b Waugh	28	lbw b Hughes	51
C.E.L.Ambrose c M.A.Taylor b Hughes	8	run out	0
C.A.Walsh not out	11	c Healy b Hughes	0
B.P.Patterson b Hughes	2	not out	7
Extras (LB2, NB11)	13	(B5, LB7, NB8)	20
Total	**214**		**297**

WEST INDIES	O	M	R	W	O	M	R	W
Ambrose	30	6	92	3	16	1	64	3
Patterson	12	1	44	1	1	0	11	1
Walsh	22	1	54	2	26	2	56	4
Marshall	22	1	72	2	13.1	4	36	2
Hooper	15	1	82	2	27	6	61	0
Richards	7	0	46	0	8	0	29	0
AUSTRALIA								
McDermott	15	4	42	4	17	2	55	1
Alderman	7	0	42	0	15.4	4	63	1
Hughes	17	2	65	4	19	5	49	2
P.L.Taylor	11	2	40	1	10	0	39	1
Waugh	5	0	23	1	5	3	8	1
Border					15	2	71	1

FALL OF WICKETS

	A	WI	A	WI
Wkt	1st	1st	2nd	2nd
1st	10	10	4	76
2nd	13	22	49	92
3rd	129	35	142	142
4th	158	46	168	145
5th	342	114	184	182
6th	370	136	184	193
7th	381	188	237	271
8th	385	195	258	271
9th	403	206	265	271
10th	403	214	265	297

Umpires: L.H.Barker (17) and S.U.Bucknor (4).   Test No. 1170/72

WEST INDIES v AUSTRALIA AVERAGES

WEST INDIES – BATTING AND FIELDING

	M	I	NO	HS	Runs	Avge	100	50	Ct/St
R.B.Richardson	5	8	1	182	475	67.85	2	1	1
A.L.Logie	5	7	2	77*	261	52.20	–	3	4
D.L.Haynes	5	9	1	111	412	51.50	1	2	–
C.G.Greenidge	5	9	1	226	366	45.75	1	–	1
P.J.L.Dujon	5	7	0	70	209	29.85	–	2	23
C.L.Hooper	5	8	0	62	199	24.87	–	2	6
I.V.A.Richards	5	8	1	52*	174	24.85	–	2	2
M.D.Marshall	5	7	1	51	145	24.16	–	1	–
C.E.L.Ambrose	5	7	1	53	115	19.16	–	1	1
C.A.Walsh	5	7	2	12*	44	8.80	–	–	2
B.P.Patterson	5	7	2	15	33	6.60	–	–	1

WEST INDIES – BOWLING

	O	M	R	W	Avge	Best	5wI	10wM
M.D.Marshall	156.2	24	437	21	20.80	3-31	–	–
B.P.Patterson	136	19	410	18	22.77	5-83	1	–
C.A.Walsh	180.4	33	426	17	25.05	4-14	–	–
C.E.L.Ambrose	205.4	47	492	18	27.33	3-36	–	–
C.L.Hooper	150	35	391	5	78.20	2-28	–	–

Also bowled: I.V.A.Richards 23-2-101-0; R.B.Richardson 1-0-2-0.

AUSTRALIA – BATTING AND FIELDING

	M	I	NO	HS	Runs	Avge	100	50	Ct/St
M.E.Waugh	5	8	2	139*	367	61.16	1	2	10
M.A.Taylor	5	9	0	144	441	49.00	1	4	3
A.R.Border	5	9	1	59	275	34.37	–	1	1
D.C.Boon	5	9	1	109*	266	33.25	1	1	4
D.M.Jones	5	9	1	81	245	30.62	–	1	4
G.R.Marsh	5	9	0	94	226	25.11	–	2	4
I.A.Healy	5	8	0	53	155	19.37	–	1	10
S.R.Waugh	2	3	1	26	32	16.00	–	–	1
G.R.J.Matthews	2	3	0	16	27	9.00	–	–	–
M.G.Hughes	5	8	0	21	41	5.12	–	–	2
M.R.Whitney	2	3	2	2	3	3.00	–	–	–
C.J.McDermott	5	8	0	7	18	2.25	–	–	2
B.A.Reid	2	3	1	0*	0	0.00	–	–	1

Played in one Test: T.M.Alderman 0, 0 (1 ct); P.L.Taylor 2, 4.*

AUSTRALIA – BOWLING

	O	M	R	W	Avge	Best	5wI	10wM
M.E.Waugh	65	18	183	8	22.87	4-80	–	–
C.J.McDermott	192.5	38	564	24	23.50	5-80	1	–
A.R.Border	74	21	188	7	26.85	5-68	1	–
M.G.Hughes	172.3	33	589	19	31.00	4-44	–	–
B.A.Reid	73	12	229	5	45.80	2-50	–	–

Also bowled: T.M.Alderman 22.4-4-105-1; D.M.Jones 4-1-9-0; G.R.J.Matthews 73.5-11-273-3; P.L.Taylor 21-2-79-2; S.R.Waugh 35-6-90-0; M.R.Whitney 66-11-216-0.

ENGLAND v WEST INDIES (1st Test)

Played at Headingley, Leeds, on 6, 7, 8, 9, 10 June 1991.
Toss: West Indies. Result: ENGLAND won by 115 runs.
Debuts: England – G.A.Hick, M.R.Ramprakash, S.L.Watkin.

ENGLAND

*G.A.Gooch c Dujon b Marshall	34		not out	154
M.A.Atherton b Patterson	2		c Dujon b Ambrose	6
G.A.Hick c Dujon b Walsh	6		b Ambrose	6
A.J.Lamb c Hooper b Marshall	11		c Hooper b Ambrose	0
M.R.Ramprakash c Hooper b Marshall	27		c Dujon b Ambrose	27
R.A.Smith run out (Ambrose/Dujon)	54		lbw b Ambrose	0
†R.C.Russell lbw b Patterson	5		c Dujon b Ambrose	4
D.R.Pringle c Logie b Patterson	16		c Dujon b Marshall	27
P.A.J.DeFreitas c Simmons b Ambrose	15		lbw b Walsh	3
S.L.Watkin b Ambrose	2		c Hooper b Marshall	0
D.E.Malcolm not out	5		b Marshall	4
Extras (LB5, W2, NB14)	21		(B4, LB9, W1, NB7)	21
Total (79.2 overs; 365 minutes)	**198**		(106 overs; 449 minutes)	**252**

WEST INDIES

P.V.Simmons c Ramprakash b DeFreitas	38		b DeFreitas	0
D.L.Haynes c Russell b Watkin	7		c Smith b Pringle	19
R.B.Richardson run out	29		c Lamb b DeFreitas	68
(Gooch/Malcolm/Russell)				
C.L.Hooper run out (Ramprakash)	0		c Lamb b Watkin	5
*I.V.A.Richards c Lamb b Pringle	73		c Gooch b Watkin	3
A.L.Logie c Lamb b DeFreitas	6		c Gooch b Watkin	3
†P.J.L.Dujon c Ramprakash b Watkin	6		lbw b DeFreitas	33
M.D.Marshall c Hick b Pringle	0		lbw b Pringle	1
C.E.L.Ambrose c Hick b DeFreitas	0		c Pringle b DeFreitas	14
C.A.Walsh c Gooch b DeFreitas	3		c Atherton b Malcolm	9
B.P.Patterson not out	5		not out	0
Extras (LB1, NB5)	6		(LB1, NB6)	7
Total (54.1 overs; 235 minutes)	**173**		(56.4 overs; 241 minutes)	**162**

WEST INDIES	O	M	R	W	O	M	R	W	FALL OF WICKETS				
										E	WI	E	WI
Ambrose	26	8	49	2	28	6	52	6	Wkt	1st	1st	2nd	2nd
Patterson	26.2	8	67	3	15	1	52	0	1st	13	36	22	0
Walsh	14	7	31	1	30	5	61	1	2nd	45	54	38	61
Marshall	13	4	46	3	25	4	58	3	3rd	45	58	38	77
Hooper					4	1	11	0	4th	64	102	116	85
Richards					4	1	5	0	5th	129	139	116	88
ENGLAND									6th	149	156	124	136
Malcolm	14	0	69	0	6.4	0	26	1	7th	154	160	222	137
DeFreitas	17.1	5	34	4	21	4	59	4	8th	177	165	236	139
Watkin	14	2	55	2	7	0	38	3	9th	181	167	238	162
Pringle	9	3	14	2	22	6	38	2	10th	198	173	252	162

Umpires: H.D.Bird (45) and D.R.Shepherd (12).   Test No. 1171/100

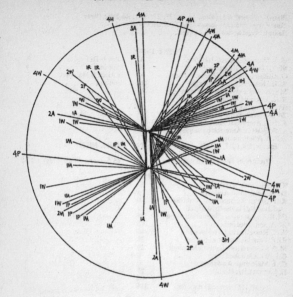

KIRKSTALL LANE END

MAIN STAND END

BOWLER	SYMBOL	BALLS	RUNS				TOTAL
			1	2	3	4	
AMBROSE	A	78	9	2	1	2	24
HOOPER	H	12	2	-	1	1	9
MARSHALL	M	89	15	1	-	6	41
PATTERSON	P	46	7	4	-	4	31
RICHARDS	R	15	3	-	-	-	3
WALSH	W	91	18	4	-	5	46
TOTALS		331	54	11	2	18	154

GRAHAM GOOCH

v. WEST INDIES (1ST TEST)

at HEADINGLEY. 8 & 9 JUNE 1991

154 NOT OUT
331 BALLS
449 MINUTES

© BILL FRINDALL 1991

ENGLAND v WEST INDIES (2nd Test)

Played at Lord's, London, on 20, 21, 22, 23 ‡, 24 June 1991.
Toss: West Indies.   Result: MATCH DRAWN.
Debuts: West Indies – I.B.A.Allen.   ‡ (no play)

WEST INDIES

P.V.Simmons c Lamb b Hick	33	lbw b DeFreitas	2
D.L.Haynes c Russell b Pringle	60	not out	4
R.B.Richardson c DeFreitas b Hick	57	c Hick b Malcolm	1
C.L.Hooper c Lamb b Pringle	111	not out	1
*I.V.A.Richards lbw b DeFreitas	63		
A.L.Logie b DeFreitas	5		
†P.J.L.Dujon c Lamb b Pringle	20		
M.D.Marshall lbw b Pringle	25		
C.E.L.Ambrose c and b Malcolm	5		
C.A.Walsh c Atherton b Pringle	10		
I.B.A.Allen not out	1		
Extras (B3, LB7, NB19)	29	(LB2, NB2)	4
Total (120.1 overs; 502 minutes)	**419**	(5.5 overs; 30 minutes)	**12-2**

ENGLAND

*G.A.Gooch b Walsh	37
M.A.Atherton b Ambrose	5
G.A.Hick c Richardson b Ambrose	0
A.J.Lamb c Haynes b Marshall	1
M.R.Ramprakash c Richards b Allen	24
R.A.Smith not out	148
†R.C.Russell c Dujon b Hooper	46
D.R.Pringle c Simmons b Allen	35
P.A.J.DeFreitas c Dujon b Marshall	29
S.L.Watkin b Ambrose	6
D.E.Malcolm b Ambrose	0
Extras (LB1, NB22)	23
Total (118 overs; 523 minutes)	**354**

ENGLAND	O	M	R	W	O	M	R	W	FALL OF WICKETS			
										WI	E	WI
DeFreitas	31	6	93	2	3	2	1	1	Wkt	1st	1st	2nd
Malcolm	19	3	76	1	2.5	0	9	1	1st	90	5	9
Watkin	15	2	60	0					2nd	102	6	10
ringle	35.1	6	100	5					3rd	198	16	–
Hick	18	4	77	2					4th	322	60	–
Gooch	2	0	3	0					5th	332	84	–
									6th	366	180	–
WEST INDIES									7th	382	269	–
Ambrose	34	10	87	4					8th	402	316	–
Marshall	30	4	78	2					9th	410	353	–
Walsh	26	4	90	1					10th	419	354	–
Allen	23	2	88	2								
Hooper	5	2	10	1								

Umpires: B.J.Meyer (23) and K.E.Palmer (19).   Test No. 1172/101

ENGLAND v WEST INDIES (3rd Test)

Played at Trent Bridge, Nottingham, on 4, 5, 6, 8, 9 July 1991.
Toss: England.   Result: WEST INDIES won by 9 wickets.
Debuts: England – R.K.Illingworth.

ENGLAND

*G.A.Gooch	lbw b Marshall	68	b Ambrose	13
M.A.Atherton	lbw b Ambrose	32	b Marshall	4
G.A.Hick	c Dujon b Ambrose	43	c Dujon b Ambrose	0
A.J.Lamb	lbw b Ambrose	13	lbw b Marshall	29
M.R.Ramprakash	b Ambrose	13	c Dujon b Ambrose	21
R.A.Smith	not out	64	c Richards b Walsh	15
†R.C.Russell	c Logie b Allen	3	b Walsh	3
D.R.Pringle	c sub (C.B.Lambert) b Allen	0	c Simmons b Walsh	3
P.A.J.DeFreitas	b Walsh	8	not out	55
R.K.Illingworth	c Hooper b Ambrose	13	c Simmons b Walsh	13
D.V.Lawrence	c Allen b Marshall	4	c Hooper b Allen	34
Extras	(LB17, W1, NB21)	39	(LB14, W3, NB4)	21
Total	(103.5 overs; 452 minutes)	300	(79 overs; 359 minutes)	211

WEST INDIES

P.V.Simmons	b Illingworth	12	c Russell b Lawrence	1
D.L.Haynes	c Smith b Lawrence	18	not out	57
R.B.Richardson	b Lawrence	43	not out	52
C.L.Hooper	c Russell b DeFreitas	11		
*I.V.A.Richards	b Illingworth	80		
A.L.Logie	c Ramprakash b DeFreitas	78		
†P.J.L.Dujon	c Hick b Pringle	19		
M.D.Marshall	c Illingworth b DeFreitas	67		
C.E.L.Ambrose	b Illingworth	17		
C.A.Walsh	lbw b Pringle	12		
I.B.A.Allen	not out	4		
Extras	(B2, LB13, W1, NB20)	36	(NB5)	5
Total	(118.1 overs; 518 minutes)	397	(32.2 overs; 148 minutes)	115-1

WEST INDIES	O	M	R	W	O	M	R	W
Ambrose	34	7	74	5	27	7	61	3
Marshall	21.5	6	54	2	21	6	49	2
Walsh	24	4	75	1	24	7	64	4
Allen	17	0	69	2	7	2	23	1
Hooper	6	4	10	0				
Richards	1	0	11	0				
ENGLAND								
DeFreitas	31.1	9	67	3	11	3	29	0
Lawrence	24	2	116	2	12.2	0	61	1
Illingworth	33	8	110	3	2	0	5	0
Pringle	25	6	71	2	7	2	20	0
Hick	5	0	18	0				

FALL OF WICKETS				
	E	WI	E	WI
Wkt	1st	1st	2nd	2nd
1st	108	32	4	1
2nd	113	32	8	–
3rd	138	45	25	–
4th	186	118	67	–
5th	192	239	100	–
6th	212	272	106	–
7th	217	324	106	–
8th	228	358	115	–
9th	270	392	153	–
10th	300	397	211	–

Umpires: J.H.Hampshire (8) and M.J.Kitchen (2).   Test No. 1173/102

ENGLAND v WEST INDIES (4th Test)

Played at Edgbaston, Birmingham, on 25, 26, 27, 28 July 1991.
Toss: West Indies.   Result: WEST INDIES won by 7 wickets.
Debuts: England – H.Morris.

‡(C.B.Lambert)

ENGLAND

*G.A.Gooch b Marshall	45	b Patterson	40
H.Morris c Dujon b Patterson	3	lbw b Patterson	1
M.A.Atherton lbw b Walsh	16	c Hooper b Patterson	1
G.A.Hick c Richards b Ambrose	19	b Ambrose	1
A.J.Lamb lbw b Marshall	9	c Dujon b Walsh	25
M.R.Ramprakash c Logie b Walsh	29	c Dujon b Marshall	25
†R.C.Russell c Richardson b Ambrose	12	c Dujon b Patterson	0
D.R.Pringle b Ambrose	2	c Logie b Marshall	45
P.A.J.DeFreitas c Richardson b Marshall	13	b Patterson	7
C.C.Lewis lbw b Marshall	10	c sub‡ b Ambrose	65
R.K.Illingworth not out	0	not out	1
Extras (B4, LB3, NB23)	30	(B5, LB21, NB14)	40
Total (70.4 overs; 330 minutes)	188	(105.4 overs; 469 minutes)	255

WEST INDIES

P.V.Simmons c Hick b Lewis	28	lbw b DeFreitas	16
D.L.Haynes c Russell b DeFreitas	32	c Hick b DeFreitas	8
R.B.Richardson lbw b Lewis	104	c Hick b DeFreitas	0
C.L.Hooper b Illingworth	31	not out	55
*I.V.A.Richards c Lewis b Pringle	22	not out	73
A.L.Logie c Atherton b Lewis	28		
†P.J.L.Dujon lbw b DeFreitas	6		
M.D.Marshall not out	6		
C.E.L.Ambrose c Hick b Lewis	18		
C.A.Walsh c and b Lewis	18		
B.P.Patterson b Lewis	3		
Extras (LB7, NB6)	13	(LB4, NB1)	5
Total (107.3 overs; 439 minutes)	292	(40.4 overs; 173 minutes)	157-3

WEST INDIES	O	M	R	W	O	M	R	W	FALL OF WICKETS				
										E	WI	E	WI
Ambrose	23	6	64	3	33	16	42	2		1st	1st	2nd	2nd
Patterson	11	2	39	1	31	6	81	5	Wkt				
Walsh	21	6	43	2	7	1	20	1	1st	6	52	2	23
Marshall	12.4	1	33	4	19.4	3	53	2	2nd	53	93	4	23
Hooper	3	2	2	0	12	3	26	0	3rd	88	148	5	24
Simmons					3	0	7	0	4th	108	194	71	–
									5th	129	257	94	–
ENGLAND									6th	159	258	96	–
DeFreitas	25.3	9	40	2	13	2	54	3	7th	163	266	127	–
Lewis	35	10	111	6	16	7	45	0	8th	163	267	144	–
Pringle	23	9	48	1	7	1	31	0	9th	184	285	236	–
Illingworth	17	2	75	1	4.4	0	23	0	10th	188	292	255	–
Gooch	6	1	11	0									
Hick	1	1	0	0									

Umpires: B.Dudleston (1) and D.R.Shepherd (13).   Test No. 1174/103

ENGLAND v WEST INDIES (5th Test)

Played at Kennington Oval, London, on 8, 9, 10, 11, 12 August 1991.
Toss: England. Result: ENGLAND won by 5 wickets.
Debuts: West Indies – C.B.Lambert.

ENGLAND

*G.A.Gooch lbw b Ambrose	60	lbw b Marshall	29
H.Morris c Lambert b Ambrose	44	c Dujon b Patterson	2
M.A.Atherton c Hooper b Walsh	0	c Hooper b Patterson	13
R.A.Smith lbw b Marshall	109	c Patterson b Walsh	26
M.R.Ramprakash c Lambert b Hooper	25	lbw b Lambert	19
†A.J.Stewart c Richardson b Patterson	31	not out	38
I.T.Botham hit wicket b Ambrose	31	not out	4
C.C.Lewis not out	47		
P.A.J.DeFreitas c Dujon b Walsh	7		
D.V.Lawrence c Richards b Walsh	9		
P.C.R.Tufnell c Haynes b Patterson	2		
Extras (B8, LB10, W1, NB35)	54	(B4, W1, NB10)	15
Total (151.1 overs; 664 minutes)	**419**	(31.4 overs; 168 minutes)	**146-5**

WEST INDIES

P.V.Simmons lbw b Lawrence	15	c Lewis b Botham	36
D.L.Haynes not out	75	lbw b Lawrence	43
R.B.Richardson c Stewart b Botham	20	(4) c Gooch b Lawrence	121
C.L.Hooper c Stewart b DeFreitas	3	(5) c Gooch b Tufnell	54
C.B.Lambert c Ramprakash b Tufnell	39	(3) lbw b Botham	14
†P.J.L.Dujon lbw b Lawrence	0	(7) c Stewart b Lawrence	5
M.D.Marshall c Botham b Tufnell	0	(8) b DeFreitas	17
*I.V.A.Richards c Stewart b Tufnell	2	(6) c Morris b Lawrence	60
C.E.L.Ambrose c Botham b Tufnell	0	lbw b DeFreitas	0
C.A.Walsh c Gooch b Tufnell	0	lbw b Lawrence	14
B.P.Patterson c Botham b Tufnell	2	not out	1
Extras (LB9, NB11)	20	(B7, LB5, W2, NB6)	20
Total (57.3 overs; 284 minutes)	**176**	(132.5 overs; 572 minutes)	**385**

WEST INDIES	O	M	R	W	O	M	R	W
Ambrose	36	8	83	3	8	0	48	0
Patterson	25.1	3	87	2	9	0	63	2
Walsh	32	5	91	3	9	3	18	1
Marshall	24	5	62	1	5	3	9	1
Hooper	34	1	78	1				
Lambert					0.4	0	4	1
ENGLAND								
DeFreitas	13	6	38	1	20	9	42	2
Lawrence	16	1	67	2	25.5	4	106	5
Tufnell	14.3	3	25	6	46	6	150	1
Botham	11	4	27	1	16	4	40	2
Lewis	3	1	10	0	25	12	35	0

FALL OF WICKETS				
	E	WI	WI	E
Wkt.	1st	1st	2nd	2nd
1st	112	52	53	3
2nd	114	95	71	40
3rd	120	98	125	80
4th	188	158	208	80
5th	263	160	305	142
6th	336	161	311	–
7th	351	172	356	–
8th	386	172	356	–
9th	411	172	378	–
10th	419	176	385	–

Umpires: J.W.Holder (10) and M.J.Kitchen (3).   Test No. 1175/104

ENGLAND v WEST INDIES AVERAGES

ENGLAND – BATTING AND FIELDING

	M	I	NO	HS	Runs	Avge	100	50	Ct/St
R.A.Smith	4	7	2	148*	416	83.20	2	2	2
C.C.Lewis	2	3	1	65	125	62.50	–	1	3
G.A.Gooch	5	9	1	154*	480	60.00	1	2	6
M.R.Ramprakash	5	9	0	29	210	23.33	–	–	4
P.A.J.DeFreitas	5	8	1	55*	134	19.14	–	1	1
D.R.Pringle	4	7	0	45	128	18.28	–	–	1
D.V.Lawrence	2	3	0	34	47	15.66	–	–	–
R.K.Illingworth	2	4	2	13	31	15.50	–	–	1
A.J.Lamb	4	7	0	29	88	12.57	–	–	7
H.Morris	2	4	0	44	50	12.50	–	–	1
G.A.Hick	4	7	0	43	75	10.71	–	–	8
R.C.Russell	4	7	0	46	73	10.42	–	–	5/–
M.A.Atherton	5	9	0	32	79	8.77	–	–	3
D.E.Malcolm	2	3	1	5*	9	4.50	–	–	1
S.L.Watkin	2	3	0	6	8	2.66	–	–	–

Played in one Test: I.T.Botham 31, 4* (3 ct); A.J.Stewart 31, 38* (4 ct);
P.C.R.Tufnell 2.

ENGLAND – BOWLING

	O	M	R	W	Avge	Best	5wI	10wM
P.A.J.DeFreitas	185.5	55	457	22	20.77	4-34	–	–
P.C.R.Tufnell	60.3	9	175	7	25.00	6-25	1	–
D.R.Pringle	128.1	33	322	12	26.83	5-100	1	–
S.L.Watkin	36	4	153	5	30.60	3-38	–	–
C.C.Lewis	79	30	201	6	33.50	6-111	1	–
D.V.Lawrence	78.1	7	350	10	35.00	5-106	1	–

Also bowled: I.T.Botham 27-8-67-3; G.A.Gooch 8-1-14-0; G.A.Hick
24-5-95-2; R.K.Illingworth 56.4-10-213-4; D.E.Malcolm 42.3-3-180-3.

WEST INDIES – BATTING AND FIELDING

	M	I	NO	HS	Runs	Avge	100	50	Ct/St
R.B.Richardson	5	10	1	121	495	55.00	2	3	4
I.V.A.Richards	5	8	1	80	376	53.71	–	5	4
D.L.Haynes	5	10	3	75*	323	46.14	–	3	2
C.L.Hooper	5	9	2	111	271	38.71	1	2	9
A.L.Logie	4	5	0	78	120	24.00	–	1	4
M.D.Marshall	5	7	1	67	116	19.33	–	1	–
P.V.Simmons	5	10	0	38	181	18.10	–	1	4
P.J.L.Dujon	5	7	0	33	89	12.71	–	–	17/–
C.A.Walsh	5	7	0	18	66	9.42	–	–	1
B.P.Patterson	3	5	3	5*	11	5.50	–	–	1
C.E.L.Ambrose	5	7	0	17	37	5.28	–	–	–
I.B.A.Allen	2	2	2	4*	5	–	–	–	–

Played in one Test: C.B.Lambert 39, 14 (2 ct).

WEST INDIES – BOWLING

	O	M	R	W	Avge	Best	5wI	10wM
C.E.L.Ambrose	249	68	560	28	20.00	6-52	2	–
M.D.Marshall	172.1	36	442	20	22.10	4-33	–	–
B.P.Patterson	117.3	20	389	13	29.92	5-81	1	–
C.A.Walsh	187	42	493	15	32.86	4-64	–	–
I.B.A.Allen	47	4	180	5	36.00	2-69	–	–

Also bowled: C.L.Hooper 64-13-137-2; C.B.Lambert 0.4-0-4-1; I.V.A.Richards
5-1-6-0; P.V.Simmons 3-0-7-0.

ENGLAND v SRI LANKA (Only Test)

Played at Lord's, London, on 22, 23, 24, 26, 27 August 1991.
Toss: England. Result: ENGLAND won by 137 runs.
Debuts: Sri Lanka – K.I.W. Wijegunawardene.   ‡(I.D.K.Salisbury)

ENGLAND

*G.A.Gooch c and b Ramanayake	38	b Anurasiri		174
H.Morris lbw b Ratnayake	42	c Mahanama b Anurasiri		23
A.J.Stewart not out	113	c De Silva b Anurasiri		43
R.A.Smith c Tillekeratne b Ratnayake	4	not out		63
M.R.Ramprakash c Mahanama b Hathurusinghe	0			
I.T.Botham c Mahanama b Ramanayake	22			
C.C.Lewis c De Silva b Anurasiri	11			
†R.C.Russell b Anurasiri	17	(5) not out		12
P.A.J.DeFreitas b Ratnayake	1			
D.V.Lawrence c and b Ratnayake	3			
P.C.R.Tufnell lbw b Ratnayake	0			
Extras (B9, LB8, NB14)	31	(B15, LB23, W1, NB10)		49
Total (95 overs; 395 minutes)	282	(85.1 overs; 356 minutes) (3 wickets declared)		211

SRI LANKA

D.S.B.P.Kuruppu b DeFreitas	5	lbw b Lewis	21
U.C.Hathurusinghe c Tufnell b DeFreitas	66	c Morris b Tufnell	25
A.P.Gurusinha lbw b DeFreitas	4	b Tufnell	34
*P.A.De Silva c Lewis b DeFreitas	42	c Russell b Lawrence	18
R.S.Mahanama c Russell b Botham	2	c Botham b Tufnell	15
S.T.Jayasuriya c Smith b DeFreitas	11	c Russell b Lewis	66
†H.P.Tillekeratne c Morris b Lawrence	20	b Tufnell	16
R.J.Ratnayake b DeFreitas	52	c sub‡ b Lawrence	17
C.P.H.Ramanayake lbw b DeFreitas	0	not out	34
K.I.W.Wijegunawardene not out	6	c Botham b DeFreitas	4
S.D.Anurasiri b Lawrence	1	lbw b Tufnell	16
Extras (LB15)	15	(B1, LB16, NB2)	19
Total (68.1 overs; 297 minutes)	224	(103.3 overs; 434 minutes)	285

SRI LANKA	O	M	R	W	O	M	R	W
Ratnayake	27	4	69	5	26	4	91	0
Ramanayake	24	5	75	2	20	2	86	0
Wijegunawardene	10	1	36	0	2	0	13	0
Hathurusinghe	17	6	40	1				
Anurasiri	17	4	45	2	36.1	8	135	3
Jayasuriya					1	0	1	0

ENGLAND								
DeFreitas	26	8	70	7	22	8	45	1
Lawrence	15.1	3	61	2	23	7	83	2
Lewis	10	5	29	0	18	4	31	2
Botham	10	3	26	1	6	2	15	0
Tufnell	7	2	23	0	34.3	14	94	5

	FALL OF WICKETS			
	E	SL	E	SL
Wkt	1st	1st	2nd	2nd
1st	70	12	78	50
2nd	114	22	217	50
3rd	119	75	322	111
4th	120	86	–	119
5th	160	105	–	159
6th	183	139	–	212
7th	246	213	–	212
8th	258	213	–	241
9th	276	220	–	253
10th	282	224	–	285

Umpires: H.D.Bird (46) and J.H.Hampshire (9).   Test No. 1176/4

AUSTRALIA v INDIA (1st Test)

Played at Woolloongabba, Brisbane, on 29, 30 November, 1, 2 December 1991.
Toss: Australia.   Result: AUSTRALIA won by 10 wickets.
Debuts: India – J.Srinath.

INDIA

R.J.Shastri c Waugh b McDermott		8	c Healy b McDermott	41
K.Srikkanth c Boon b McDermott		13	c Boon b Hughes	0
S.V.Manjrekar c and b Hughes		17	c Boon b Hughes	5
D.B.Vengsarkar c Waugh b Hughes		5	lbw b Hughes	0
*M.Azharuddin c Hughes b Whitney		10	c Boon b Hughes	12
S.R.Tendulkar b Whitney		16	c Healy b McDermott	7
Kapil Dev b McDermott		44	c Waugh b McDermott	25
M.Prabhakar not out		54	c Healy b Whitney	39
†K.S.More c Whitney b Hughes		19	lbw b McDermott	1
S.L.V.Raju c Healy b McDermott		12	c Healy b Whitney	2
J.Srinath c Healy b McDermott		21	not out	12
Extras (B1, LB6, NB13)		20	(LB4, NB8)	12
Total		**239**		**156**

AUSTRALIA

G.R.Marsh b Srinath		47	(2) not out	17
M.A.Taylor c Vengsarkar b Raju		94	(1) not out	35
D.C.Boon c More b Prabhakar		66		
*A.R.Border b Kapil Dev		28		
D.M.Jones b Kapil Dev		0		
M.E.Waugh c More b Srinath		11		
†I.A.Healy lbw b Prabhakar		12		
P.L.Taylor c Raju b Srinath		31		
M.G.Hughes b Kapil Dev		11		
C.J.McDermott c Azharuddin b Kapil Dev		8		
M.R.Whitney not out		7		
Extras (LB15, W1, NB9)		25	(LB4, NB2)	6
Total		**340**	(0 wickets)	**58**

AUSTRALIA	O	M	R	W	O	M	R	W		FALL OF WICKETS			
McDermott	28.1	11	54	5	25	7	47	4		*I*	*A*	*I*	*A*
Whitney	21	2	82	4	17.2	3	55	2	Wkt	1st	1st	2nd	2nd
Hughes	20	5	34	3	16	4	50	4	1st	21	95	0	–
Waugh	1	0	6	0					2nd	24	178	14	–
P.L.Taylor	18	3	56	0					3rd	50	244	14	–
									4th	53	244	32	–
INDIA									5th	67	265	47	–
Kapil Dev	34	9	80	4	9	0	23	0	6th	83	278	87	–
Prabhakar	37	10	88	2	2	1	3	0	7th	141	280	136	–
Srinath	24.4	4	59	3	9	5	6	0	8th	186	301	140	–
Raju	31	5	90	1	3	1	13	0	9th	206	316	142	–
Tendulkar	1	0	8	0	1	0	5	0	10th	239	340	156	–
Manjrekar					0.5	0	4	0					

Umpires: P.J.McConnell (20) and S.G.Randell (9).   Test No. 1177/46

AUSTRALIA v INDIA (2nd Test)

Played at Melbourne Cricket Ground, on 26, 27, 28, 29 December 1991.
Toss: India.   Result: AUSTRALIA won by 8 wickets.
Debuts: Nil.

‡(M.R.Whitney)

INDIA

R.J.Shastri c Healy b Reid	23		c Healy b Reid		22
K.Srikkanth c Boon b Reid	5		lbw Reid		6
M.Prabhakar b Reid	0	(9)	c Healy b Reid		17
S.V.Manjrekar c Waugh b Reid	25	(3)	c M.A.Taylor b McDermott		30
D.B.Vengsarkar c Reid b Hughes	23	(4)	c sub‡ b McDermott		54
*M.Azharuddin c Jones b McDermott	22	(5)	c M.A.Taylor b Reid		2
S.R.Tendulkar c Waugh b Reid	15		c Border b P.L.Taylor		40
Kapil Dev b Hughes b McDermott	19		c Healy b Reid		12
†K.S.More not out	67	(10)	lbw b Reid		12
S.L.V.Raju c Border b Hughes	31	(6)	c and b McDermott		1
J.Srinath c Border b Reid	14		not out		0
Extras (B1, LB8, W6, NB4)	19		(B1, LB6, NB10)		17
Total	**263**				**213**

AUSTRALIA

G.R.Marsh c Vengsarkar b Kapil Dev	86	(2)	lbw b Prabhakar		10
M.A.Taylor c Tendulkar b Prabhakar	13	(1)	st More b Raju		60
D.C.Boon c Srikkanth b Kapil Dev	11		not out		44
*A.R.Border b Kapil Dev	0		not out		5
D.M.Jones c More b Prabhakar	59				
M.E.Waugh c More b Shastri	34				
†I.A.Healy lbw b Kapil Dev	60				
P.L.Taylor c More b Prabhakar	11				
M.G.Hughes c Tendulkar b Kapil Dev	36				
C.J.McDermott not out	16				
B.A.Reid c Kapil Dev b Prabhakar	3				
Extras (LB9, NB11)	20		(LB3, NB6)		9
Total	**349**		(2 wickets)		**128**

AUSTRALIA	O	M	R	W	O	M	R	W	FALL OF WICKETS				
										I	A	I	A
McDermott	30	6	100	2	29	8	63	3		1st	1st	2nd	2nd
Reid	26.2	7	66	6	29	9	60	6	Wkt	1st	1st	2nd	2nd
Hughes	23	6	52	2	19	6	43	0	1st	11	24	13	16
Waugh	8	1	16	0					2nd	11	55	48	104
P.L.Taylor	6	0	20	0	11	3	40	1	3rd	61	55	75	–
									4th	63	162	78	–
INDIA									5th	109	211	79	–
Kapil Dev	35	9	97	5	12	1	30	0	6th	109	229	141	–
Prabhakar	34	7	84	4	11	0	38	1	7th	128	262	155	–
Srinath	25	3	71	0	8	0	28	0	8th	151	326	173	–
Raju	17	3	52	0	6	0	17	1	9th	228	337	210	–
Tendulkar	4	1	16	0					10th	263	349	213	–
Shastri	7	1	20	1	3	1	12	0					

Umpires: L.J.King (5) and T.A.Prue (4).

Test No. 1178/47

AUSTRALIA v INDIA (3rd Test)

Played at Sydney Cricket Ground, on 2, 3, 4, 5, 6 January 1992.
Toss: India.   Result: MATCH DRAWN.
Debuts: Australia – S.K.Warne; India – S.T.Banerjee.

AUSTRALIA

G.R.Marsh b Banerjee	8	(2) c Pandit b Kapil Dev	4
M.A.Taylor c Pandit b Banerjee	56	(1) c Kapil Dev b Shastri	35
D.C.Boon not out	129	c Azharuddin b Srinath	7
M.E.Waugh c Prabhakar b Banerjee	5	lbw b Prabhakar	18
D.M.Jones run out	35	c Pandit b Shastri	18
*A.R.Border c Pandit b Kapil Dev	19	not out	53
†I.A.Healy c sub (K.Srikkanth) b Prabhakar	1	c Prabhakar b Shastri	7
M.G.Hughes c Pandit b Prabhakar	2	c Prabhakar b Tendulkar	21
C.J.McDermott b Prabhakar	1	c Vengsarkar b Shastri	0
S.K.Warne c Pandit b Kapil Dev	20	not out	1
B.A.Reid c Tendulkar b Kapil Dev	0		
Extras (B4, LB14, W1, NB18)	37	(LB4, W1, NB4)	9
Total	**313**	**(8 wickets)**	**173**

INDIA

R.J.Shastri c Jones b Warne	206
N.S.Sidhu c Waugh b McDermott	0
S.V.Manjrekar c Waugh b Hughes	34
D.B.Vengsarkar c Waugh b McDermott	54
*M.Azharuddin c Boon b McDermott	4
S.R.Tendulkar not out	148
M.Prabhakar c Taylor b Hughes	14
Kapil Dev c Marsh b Hughes	0
†C.S.Pandit run out	9
S.T.Banerjee c Border b McDermott	3
J.Srinath run out	1
Extras (B1, LB4, NB5)	10
Total	**483**

INDIA	O	M	R	W	O	M	R	W		FALL OF WICKETS		
Kapil Dev	33	6	60	3	19	5	41	1		*A*	*I*	*A*
Prabhakar	39	12	82	3	27	10	53	1	*Wkt*	*1st*	*1st*	*2nd*
Banerjee	18	4	47	3					1st	22	7	9
Srinath	21	5	69	0	12	0	28	1	2nd	117	86	31
Shastri	13	1	37	0	25	8	45	4	3rd	127	197	55
Tendulkar					1	0	2	1	4th	210	201	85
									5th	248	397	106
									6th	251	434	114
AUSTRALIA									7th	259	434	164
McDermott	51	12	147	4					8th	269	458	171
Reid	4	0	10	0					9th	313	474	–
Hughes	41.4	8	104	3					10th	313	483	–
Waugh	14	5	28	0								
Warne	45	7	150	1								
Border	13	3	39	0								

Umpires: P.J.McConnell (21) and S.G.Randell (10).   Test No. 1179/48

AUSTRALIA v INDIA (4th Test)

Played at Adelaide Oval, on 25, 26, 27, 28, 29 January 1992.
Toss: India.   Result: AUSTRALIA won by 38 runs.
Debuts: Nil.

AUSTRALIA

G.R.Marsh	b Prabhakar	8 (2)	b Kapil Dev		5
M.A.Taylor	b Tendulkar	11 (1)	c Raju b Kapil Dev		100
D.C.Boon	b Kapil Dev	19	run out		135
*A.R.Border	c Pandit b Tendulkar	0	not out		91
D.M.Jones	c Azharuddin b Raju	41	c Pandit b Kapil Dev		0
M.E.Waugh	b Prabhakar	15	c Tendulkar b Kapil Dev		0
†I.A.Healy	c Pandit b Kapil Dev	1	c Srikkanth b Kapil Dev		41
M.G.Hughes	c Manjrekar b Kapil Dev	26	lbw b Srinath		23
S.K.Warne	st Pandit b Raju	7	c Pandit b Srinath		0
C.J.McDermott	b Raju	0	b Raju		21
M.R.Whitney	not out	0	c Srinath b Raju		12
Extras	(LB10, NB7)	17	(LB15, NB8)		23
Total		**145**			**451**

INDIA

K.Srikkanth	c Healy b McDermott	17	b McDermott		22
N.S.Sidhu	c Healy b Hughes	27	lbw b Hughes		35
S.V.Manjrekar	lbw b Hughes	2	run out		45
D.B.Vengsarkar	c Waugh b McDermott	13 (5)	lbw b Hughes		4
*M.Azharuddin	lbw b McDermott	1 (6)	c Taylor b McDermott		106
S.R.Tendulkar	lbw b McDermott	6 (4)	lbw b Waugh		17
Kapil Dev	c Border b Hughes	56	c Marsh b Hughes		5
M.Prabhakar	lbw b Whitney	33	lbw b McDermott		64
†C.S.Pandit	c Boon b McDermott	15	c Waugh b McDermott		7
S.L.V.Raju	not out	19	not out		8
J.Srinath	c Healy b Whitney	21	c Warne b McDermott		3
Extras	(LB5, NB10)	15	(B3, LB9, NB5)		17
Total		**225**			**333**

INDIA	O	M	R	W	O	M	R	W
Kapil Dev	23	11	33	3	51	12	130	5
Prabhakar	18	3	55	2	21	5	60	0
Srinath	10	2	26	0	37	13	76	2
Tendulkar	4	2	10	2	20	5	44	0
Raju	11.4	7	11	3	56	15	121	2
Srikkanth					1	0	5	0
AUSTRALIA								
McDermott	31	9	76	5	29.1	8	92	5
Whitney	26.2	6	68	2	17	3	59	0
Hughes	18	5	55	3	23	5	66	3
Waugh	2	1	3	0	12	2	36	1
Warne	7	1	18	0	16	1	60	0
Border					3	0	8	0

FALL OF WICKETS

	A	I	A	I
Wkt	1st	1st	2nd	2nd
1st	13	30	10	52
2nd	36	33	231	72
3rd	39	55	277	97
4th	50	64	277	102
5th	77	70	277	172
6th	81	70	348	182
7th	117	135	383	283
8th	141	174	383	291
9th	145	192	409	327
10th	145	225	451	333

Umpires: D.B.Hair (1) and P.J.McConnell (22).   **Test No. 1180/49**

AUSTRALIA v INDIA (5th Test)

Played at W.A.C.A.Ground, Perth, on 1, 2, 3, 4, 5 February 1992.
Toss: Australia.   Result: AUSTRALIA won by 300 runs.
Debuts: Australia – W.N.Phillips, P.R.Reiffel.

AUSTRALIA

M.A.Taylor c Srikkanth b Kapil Dev	2	(2)	lbw b Kapil Dev	16
W.N.Phillips c More b Prabhakar	8	(1)	c Kapil Dev b Srinath	14
D.C.Boon c Sidhu b Prabhakar	107		c Kapil Dev b Prabhakar	38
*A.R.Border c Srikkanth b Kapil Dev	59	(8)	not out	20
D.M.Jones c Srikkanth b Raju	7	(4)	not out	150
T.M.Moody c Vengsarkar b Prabhakar	50	(5)	c More b Kapil Dev	101
†I.A.Healy c More b Srinath	28	(6)	c More b Raju	7
M.G.Hughes c Srikkanth b Srinath	24	(7)	c Tendulkar b Srinath	11
P.R.Reiffel c More b Prabhakar	9			
C.J.McDermott c Srikkanth b Prabhakar	31			
M.R.Whitney not out	1			
Extras (B1, LB7, NB12)	20		(LB4, NB6)	10
Total	**346**		**(6 wickets declared)**	**367**

INDIA

K.Srikkanth c Boon b McDermott	34		c Jones b Whitney	38
N.S.Sidhu c Healy b Hughes	5		c Jones b Reiffel	35
S.V.Manjrekar c Jones b Hughes	31		c Healy b Whitney	8
S.R.Tendulkar c Moody b Whitney	114		c Moody b Reiffel	5
D.B.Vengsarkar c Taylor b Hughes	1		c Moody b Whitney	4
*M.Azharuddin c Healy b McDermott	11		lbw b Whitney	24
S.L.V.Raju c Taylor b Whitney	4	(10)	c Healy b Whitney	8
Kapil Dev c Hughes b Whitney	1	(7)	lbw b Whitney	0
M.Prabhakar c Reiffel b Whitney	1		c Healy b McDermott	3
†K.S.More c Healy b Hughes	43	(9)	c Taylor b Whitney	1
J.Srinath not out	5		not out	1
Extras (LB14, NB9)	23		(LB11, NB3)	14
Total	**272**			**141**

INDIA	O	M	R	W	O	M	R	W	FALL OF WICKETS			
										A	I	A	I
Kapil Dev	40	12	103	2	28	8	48	2		Wkt	1st	1st	2nd	2nd
Prabhakar	32.5	9	101	5	32	4	116	1		1st	10	25	27	82
Srinath	25	5	69	2	29.3	4	121	2		2nd	21	69	31	90
Raju	23	6	56	1	24	5	78	1		3rd	138	100	113	97
Tendulkar	5	2	9	0						4th	145	109	286	103
										5th	232	130	298	111
AUSTRALIA										6th	259	135	315	111
McDermott	21	6	47	2	20	8	44	1		7th	290	159	–	126
Hughes	26.5	5	82	4	12	2	25	0		8th	303	159	–	129
Reiffel	17	5	46	0	11	2	34	2		9th	339	240	–	134
Whitney	23	4	68	4	12.1	3	27	7		10th	346	272	–	141
Moody	2	0	15	0									

Umpires: A.R.Crafter (33) and T.A.Prue (5).   Test No. 1181/50

AUSTRALIA v INDIA AVERAGES

AUSTRALIA – BATTING AND FIELDING

	M	I	NO	HS	Runs	Avge	100	50	Ct/St
D.C.Boon	5	9	2	135	556	79.42	3	1	8
A.R.Border	5	9	4	91*	275	55.00	–	3	5
M.A.Taylor	5	10	1	100	422	46.88	1	3	7
D.M.Jones	5	8	1	150*	310	44.28	1	1	5
G.R.Marsh	4	8	1	86	185	26.42	–	1	2
M.R.Whitney	3	4	3	12	20	20.00	–	–	1
I.A.Healy	5	8	0	60	157	19.62	–	1	19
M.G.Hughes	5	8	0	36	154	19.25	–	–	4
M.E.Waugh	4	6	0	34	83	13.83	–	–	10
C.J.McDermott	7	1	1	31	77	12.83	–	–	1
S.K.Warne	2	4	1	20	28	9.33	–	–	1

Also played (2 Tests): B.A.Reid 3, 0 (1 ct); P.L.Taylor 31, 11; (*1 Test*): T.M.Moody 50, 101 (3 ct); W.N.Phillips 8, 14; P.R.Reiffel 9 (1 ct).

AUSTRALIA – BOWLING

	O	M	R	W	Avge	Best	5wI	10wM
B.A.Reid	59.2	16	136	12	11.33	6-60	2	1
M.R.Whitney	116.5	21	359	17	21.11	7-27	1	1
C.J.McDermott	264.2	75	670	31	21.61	5-54	3	1
M.G.Hughes	199.3	46	511	22	23.22	4-50	–	–

Also bowled: A.R.Border 16-3-47-0; T.M.Moody 2-0-15-0; P.R.Reiffel 28-7-80-2; P.L.Taylor 35-6-116-1; S.K.Warne 68-9-228-1; M.E.Waugh 37-9-89-1.

INDIA – BATTING AND FIELDING

	M	I	NO	HS	Runs	Avge	100	50	Ct/St
R.J.Shastri	3	5	0	206	300	60.00	1	–	–
S.R.Tendulkar	5	9	1	148*	368	46.00	2	–	5
K.S.More	3	6	1	67*	143	28.60	–	1	10/1
M.Prabhakar	5	9	1	64	224	28.00	–	2	3
S.V.Manjrekar	5	9	0	45	197	21.88	–	1	1
M.Azharuddin	5	9	0	106	192	21.33	1	–	3
N.S.Sidhu	3	5	0	35	102	20.40	–	–	1
Kapil Dev	5	9	0	56	165	18.33	–	1	4
D.B.Vengsarkar	5	9	0	54	158	17.55	–	2	4
K.Srikkanth	4	8	0	38	135	16.87	–	–	7
J.Srinath	5	9	4	21	78	15.60	–	–	1
S.L.V.Raju	4	8	2	31	82	13.66	–	–	2
C.S.Pandit	2	3	0	15	31	10.33	–	–	10/1

Played in one Test: S.T.Banerjee 3.

INDIA – BOWLING

	O	M	R	W	Avge	Best	5wI	10wM
R.J.Shastri	48	11	114	5	22.80	4-45	–	–
Kapil Dev	284	73	645	25	25.80	5-97	2	–
M.Prabhakar	253.5	61	680	19	35.78	5-101	1	–
S.L.V.Raju	171.4	42	438	9	48.66	3-11	–	–
J.Srinath	201.1	41	553	10	55.30	3-59	–	–

Also bowled: S.T.Banerjee 18-4-47-3; S.V.Manjrekar 0.5-0-4-0; K.Srikkanth 1-0-5-0; S.R.Tendulkar 36-10-94-3.

PAKISTAN v SRI LANKA (1st Test)

Played at Jinnah Stadium, Sialkot, on 12, 13, 14, 16, 17 December 1991.
Toss: Sri Lanka. Result: MATCH DRAWN.
Debuts: Sri Lanka – G.P.Wickremasinghe.

‡ (Ijaz Ahmed)

SRI LANKA

M.A.R.Samarasekera c Moin b Waqar	19	b Waqar		6
U.C.Hathurusinghe c Akram Raza b Aqib	17	c Ramiz b Wasim		7
A.P.Gurusinha b Aqib	33	lbw b Aqib		23
* P.A.De Silva b Waqar	31	c sub‡ b Akram Raza		19
A.Ranatunga lbw b Aqib	0	c Moin b Waqar		0
S.T.Jayasuriya b Akram Raza	77	not out		35
† H.P.Tillekeratne c Akram Raza b Waqar	49	not out		42
R.J.Ratnayake b Waqar	13			
C.P.H.Ramanayake b Akram Raza	0			
S.D.Anurasiri not out	3			
G.P.Wickremasinghe b Waqar	0			
Extras (B5, LB11, NB12)	28	(NB5)		5
Total	270	(5 wickets)		137

PAKISTAN

Ramiz Raja c Tillekeratne b Anurasiri	98
Shoaib Mohammad c and b Wickremasinghe	43
Zahid Fazal c and b Ratnayake	36
Salim Malik c Gurusinha b Anurasiri	101
Javed Miandad c Jayasuriya b Anurasiri	1
* Imran Khan not out	93
Wasim Akram not out	20
† Moin Khan	
Akram Raza	
Waqar Younis } did not bat	
Aqib Javed	
Extras (LB6, NB25)	31
Total (5 wickets declared)	423

PAKISTAN	O	M	R	W	O	M	R	W	FALL OF WICKETS		
										SL	P	SL
Wasim	32	7	47	0	13	4	31	1		_Wkt_	_1st_	_P_	_1st_	_SL_	_2nd_
Waqar	30.5	5	84	5	14.4	1	43	2	1st	21	128	6
Akram Raza	24	10	37	2	11	3	34	1	2nd	70	169	33
Aqib	23	4	70	3	7	3	22	1	3rd	89	232	58
Imran	9	1	16	0					4th	89	233	58
Salim					1	0	7	0	5th	128	365	58
									6th	229	–	–
SRI LANKA									7th	245	–	–
Ratnayake	31	4	100	1					8th	245	–	–
Ramanayake	33	9	75	0					9th	270	–	–
Wickremasinghe	27	3	120	1					10th	270	–	–
Hathurusinghe	1	0	3	0								
Anurasiri	61	21	106	3								
De Silva	4	0	13	0								

Umpires: Ikram Rabbani (1) and Khizer Hayat (26).   Test No. 1182/10

PAKISTAN v SRI LANKA (2nd Test)

Played at Municipal Stadium, Gujranwala, on 20, 21‡, 22‡, 24‡, 25‡ December 1991.
Toss: Sri Lanka. Result: MATCH DRAWN.
Debuts: Nil.

‡ (no play)

PAKISTAN

Ramiz Raja	not out	51
Shoaib Mohammad	c Tillekeratne b Ratnayake	1
Zahid Fazal	c Tillekeratne b Wickremasinghe	21
Javed Miandad	not out	20
Salim Malik		
* Imran Khan		
† Moin Khan		
Wasim Akram	did not bat	
Waqar Younis		
Aqib Javed		
Salim Jaffer		
Extras (LB10, NB6)		16
Total (2 wickets)		109

SRI LANKA

R.S.Mahanama
U.C.Hathurusinghe
A.P.Gurusinha
* P.A.De Silva
A.Ranatunga
S.T.Jayasuriya
† H.P.Tillekeratne
R.J.Ratnayake
C.P.H.Ramanayake
S.D.Anurasiri
G.P.Wickremasinghe

SRI LANKA	O	M	R	W
Ratnayake	13	3	39	1
Ramanayake	10	2	16	0
Wickremasinghe	7	2	27	1
Hathurusinghe	2	1	6	0
Anurasiri	1	0	2	0
Gurusinha	2	0	9	0
Ranatunga	1	1	0	0

FALL OF WICKETS

	P
Wkt	1st
1st	3
2nd	59
3rd	–
4th	–
5th	–
6th	–
7th	–
8th	–
9th	–
10th	–

Umpires: Athar Zaidi (3) and Khizer Hayat (27).   Test No. 1183/11

PAKISTAN v SRI LANKA (3rd Test)

Played at Iqbal Stadium, Faisalabad, on 2, 3, 4, 6, 7 January 1992.
Toss: Pakistan. Result: PAKISTAN won by 3 wickets.
Debuts: Nil.

‡ (M.S.Atapattu)

SRI LANKA

Batsman		1st	2nd innings	
R.S.Mahanama	c Moin b Salim Jaffer	58	lbw b Waqar	8
U.C.Hathurusinghe	b Waqar	49	c Zahid b Waqar	20
A.P.Gurusinha	c Zahid b Wasim	3	lbw b Aqib	14
* P.A.De Silva	c Moin b Salim Jaffer	12	lbw b Waqar	38
A.Ranatunga	lbw b Salim Jaffer	0	(8) c Miandad b Wasim	6
S.T.Jayasuriya	run out	81	c Salim Malik b Waqar	45
† H.P.Tillekeratne	c Shoaib b Waqar	11	c Moin b Aqib	14
R.J.Ratnayake	lbw b Waqar	4	(9) not out	5
S.D.Anurasiri	c Shoaib b Waqar	0	(10) b Wasim	0
K.I.W.Wijegunawardene	lbw b Wasim	2	(5) b Waqar	2
G.P.Wickremasinghe	not out	1	b Wasim	0
Extras	(B3, LB6, W2, NB8)	19	(LB3, NB10)	13
Total		**240**		**165**

PAKISTAN

Batsman		1st	2nd innings	
Ramiz Raja	lbw b Wickremasinghe	63	lbw b Wickremasinghe	8
Shoaib Mohammad	lbw b Wickremasinghe	30	(7) b Ratnayake	7
Zahid Fazal	lbw b Wijegunawardene	13	(2) c Anurasiri b Gurusinha	78
Javed Miandad	c Gurusinha b Wickremasinghe	14	(3) c Gurusinha b Wijegunawardene	2
Salim Malik	c Tillekeratne b Gurusinha	4	(4) c Gurusinha b Wijegunawardene	4
* Imran Khan	b Wijegunawardene	22	(5) lbw b Wijegunawardene	0
Wasim Akram	lbw b Gurusinha	13	(6) c De Silva b Wijegunawardene	54
† Moin Khan	lbw b Wickremasinghe	3	not out	22
Waqar Younis	lbw b Wickremasinghe	6	not out	1
Salim Jaffer	not out	8		
Aqib Javed	c sub‡ b Wijegunawardene	10		
Extras	(LB8, W1, NB26)	35	(B2, LB3, NB7)	12
Total		**221**	(7 wickets)	**188**

PAKISTAN	O	M	R	W	O	M	R	W
Wasim	22	8	62	2	18	2	71	3
Salim Jaffer	17	4	36	3	8	2	19	0
Waqar	21	1	87	4	17	3	65	5
Aqib	12.1	3	46	0	8	4	72	2

SRI LANKA	O	M	R	W	O	M	R	W
Ratnayake	13	2	40	0	9.3	0	43	1
Wijegunawardene	31.2	13	47	3	17.2	2	51	4
Wickremasinghe	32	9	73	5	26	6	53	1
Anurasiri	10	2	28	0	6	1	18	0
Gurusinha	15	9	19	2	12	5	18	1
Ranatunga	3	2	2	0				
Hathurusinghe	2	0	4	0				

FALL OF WICKETS

Wkt	SL 1st	P 1st	SL 2nd	P 2nd
1st	81	102	28	31
2nd	89	110	43	52
3rd	130	141	67	60
4th	130	146	72	60
5th	150	162	105	149
6th	179	186	136	156
7th	185	196	146	179
8th	193	197	160	—
9th	205	205	165	—
10th	240	221	165	—

Umpires: Khalid Aziz (3) and Shakoor Rana (16).　　　Test No. 1184/12

PAKISTAN v SRI LANKA AVERAGES

PAKISTAN – BATTING AND FIELDING

	M	I	NO	HS	Runs	Avge	100	50	Ct/St
Ramiz Raja	3	4	1	98	220	73.33	–	3	1
Imran Khan	3	3	1	93*	115	57.50	–	1	–
Wasim Akram	3	3	1	54	87	43.50	–	1	–
Zahid Fazal	3	4	0	78	148	37.00	–	1	2
Salim Malik	3	3	0	101	109	36.33	1	–	1
Moin Khan	3	2	1	22*	25	25.00	–	–	5
Shoaib Mohammad	3	4	0	43	81	20.25	–	–	2
Javed Miandad	3	4	1	20*	37	12.33	–	–	1
Waqar Younis	3	3	2	6	7	7.00	–	–	–

Also played: Aqib Javed (3 Tests) 10; Akram Raza (1 Test) did not bat (2 ct); Salim Jaffer (2 Tests) 8*.

PAKISTAN – BOWLING

	O	M	R	W	Avge	Best	5wI	10wM
Waqar Younis	83.3	10	279	16	17.43	5-65	2	–
Salim Jaffer	25	6	55	3	18.33	3-36	–	–
Akram Raza	35	13	71	3	23.66	2-37	–	–
Aqib Javed	50.1	14	145	6	24.16	3-70	–	–
Wasim Akram	85	21	211	6	35.16	3-71	–	–

Also bowled: Imran Khan 9-1-16-0; Salim Malik 1-0-7-0.

SRI LANKA – BATTING AND FIELDING

	M	I	NO	HS	Runs	Avge	100	50	Ct/St
S.T.Jayasuriya	3	4	1	81	238	79.33	–	2	1
H.P.Tillekeratne	3	4	1	49	116	38.66	–	–	4
R.S.Mahanama	2	2	0	58	66	33.00	–	1	–
P.A.De Silva	3	4	0	38	100	25.00	–	–	1
U.C.Hathurusinghe	3	4	0	49	93	23.25	–	–	–
A.P.Gurusinha	3	4	0	33	73	18.25	–	–	4
R.J.Ratnayake	3	3	1	13	22	11.00	–	–	1
A.Ranatunga	3	4	0	6	6	1.50	–	–	–
S.D.Anurasiri	3	3	1	3	3	1.50	–	–	1
G.P.Wickremasinghe	3	3	1	1*	1	0.50	–	–	1

Also played: C.P.H.Ramanayake (2 Tests) 0; M.A.R.Samarasekera (1 Test) 19, 6; K.I.W.Wijegunawardene (1 Test) 2, 2.

SRI LANKA – BOWLING

	O	M	R	W	Avge	Best	5wI	10wM
K.I.W.Wijegunawardene	48.4	16	98	7	14.00	4-51	–	–
A.P.Gurusinha	29	14	46	3	15.33	2-19	–	–
G.P.Wickremasinghe	92	20	273	8	34.12	5-73	1	–
S.D.Anurasiri	78	24	154	3	51.33	3-106	–	–
R.J.Ratnayake	66.3	9	222	3	74.00	1-39	–	–

Also bowled: P.A.De Silva 4-0-13-0; U.C.Hathurusinghe 5-1-13-0; C.P.H.Ramanayake 43-11-91-0; A.Ranatunga 4-3-2-0.

NEW ZEALAND v ENGLAND (1st TEST)

Played at Lancaster Park, Christchurch, on 18, 19, 20, 21, 22 January 1992.
Toss: New Zealand.   Result: ENGLAND won by an innings and 4 runs.
Debuts: New Zealand – B.R. Hartland; England – D.A. Reeve.

ENGLAND

*G.A. Gooch	c Smith b Morrison	2
A.J. Stewart	c Crowe b Morrison	148
G.A. Hick	lbw b Cairns	35
R.A. Smith	c Greatbatch b Pringle	96
A.J. Lamb	b Patel	93
†R.C. Russell	run out (Wright/Smith)	36
D.A. Reeve	c Jones b Pringle	59
C.C. Lewis	b Pringle	70
D.R. Pringle	c Greatbatch b Patel	10
P.A.J. DeFreitas	not out	7
P.C.R. Tufnell	did not bat	
Extras	(B5, LB10, W1, NB8)	24
Total	(163 overs; 648 minutes)	580-9 dec

NEW ZEALAND

B.R. Hartland	c Smith b Tufnell	22	c Smith b Tufnell		45
J.G. Wright	c Lamb b Tufnell	28	st Russell b Tufnell		99
A.H. Jones	lbw b Lewis	16	(4) c Russell b Pringle		39
M.J. Greatbatch	c Stewart b Tufnell	11	(6) c Smith b Tufnell		0
S.A. Thomson	b Tufnell	5	(7) lbw b Tufnell		0
D.N. Patel	run out (Pringle/Lewis)	99	(8) c Pringle b Tufnell		6
*M.D. Crowe	c Stewart b Pringle	20	(5) c Pringle b Tufnell		48
C.L. Cairns	c Hick b Reeve	61	(9) c Smith b Tufnell		0
†I.D.S. Smith	lbw b DeFreitas	20	(10) c Russell b Lewis		1
D.K. Morrison	not out	8	(3) c Russell b Lewis		0
C. Pringle	c Hick b DeFreitas	6	not out		5
Extras	(B1, LB7, NB8)	16	(B1, LB7, NB13)		21
Total	(127.4 overs; 498 minutes)	312	(132.1 overs; 495 minutes)		264

NEW ZEALAND	O	M	R	W	O	M	R	W
Morrison	33	5	133	2				
Cairns	30	3	118	1				
Pringle	36	4	127	3				
Thomson	15	3	47	0				
Patel	46	5	132	2				
Jones	3	0	8	0				

ENGLAND								
DeFreitas	32.4	16	54	2	23	6	54	0
Lewis	30	9	69	1	22	3	66	2
Pringle	15	2	54	1	21	5	64	1
Tufnell	39	10	100	4	46.1	25	47	7
Hick	3	0	11	0	14	8	11	0
Reeve	8	4	16	1	2	0	8	0
Smith					4	2	6	0

FALL OF WICKETS			
	E	NZ	NZ
Wkt	1st	1st	2nd
1st	6	51	81
2nd	95	52	81
3rd	274	73	182
4th	310	87	211
5th	390	91	222
6th	466	139	222
7th	544	256	236
8th	571	279	241
9th	580	306	250
10th	–	312	264

Umpires: B.L. Aldridge (11) and R.S. Dunne (6).   Test No. 1185/70

NEW ZEALAND v ENGLAND (2nd Test)

Played at Eden Park, Auckland, on 30, 31 January, 1, 2, 3 February 1992.
Toss: New Zealand.   Result: ENGLAND won by 168 runs.
Debuts: New Zealand – M.L.Su'a.

ENGLAND

*G.A.Gooch c Parore b Morrison	4	run out (Watson)	114
A.J.Stewart c Parore b Cairns	4	c Parore b Su'a	8
G.A.Hick b Cairns	30	lbw b Su'a	4
R.A.Smith c Parore b Cairns	0	b Morrison	35
A.J.Lamb b Su'a	13	c Watson b Patel	60
D.A.Reeve c Parore b Watson	22	lbw b Watson	25
C.C.Lewis c Cairns b Watson	33	run out (Patel/Parore)	23
†R.C.Russell c Parore b Cairns	33	c Hartland b Cairns	24
D.R.Pringle lbw b Cairns	41	lbw b Cairns	2
P.A.J.DeFreitas c Crowe b Cairns	1	c Wright b Morrison	0
P.C.R.Tufnell not out	6	not out	0
Extras (LB11, NB5)	16	(B8, LB16, NB2)	26
Total (83 overs; 359 minutes)	203	(98.4 overs; 413 minutes)	321

NEW ZEALAND

B.R.Hartland lbw b Lewis	0	c Russell b DeFreitas	0
J.G.Wright b Pringle	15	lbw b Lewis	0
A.H.Jones c Smith b DeFreitas	14	lbw b DeFreitas	5
*M.D.Crowe c Hick b Lewis	45	c Lamb b DeFreitas	56
K.R.Rutherford c Russell b DeFreitas	26	c Stewart b Pringle	32
D.N.Patel lbw b Lewis	24	c and b Tufnell	17
C.L.Cairns c Hick b Tufnell	1	c Russell b Tufnell	24
†A.C.Parore lbw b Pringle	0	lbw b Lewis	15
M.L.Su'a not out	0	lbw b DeFreitas	36
D.K.Morrison lbw b Lewis	0	run out (Stewart)	12
W.Watson b Lewis	2	not out	5
Extras (NB15)	15	(LB1, NB11)	12
Total (63 overs; 262 minutes)	142	(79 overs; 318 minutes)	214

NEW ZEALAND	O	M	R	W	O	M	R	W
Morrison	17	2	55	1	21.4	6	66	2
Cairns	21	4	52	6	19	6	86	2
Watson	24	13	41	2	26	10	59	1
Su'a	21	8	44	1	10	3	43	2
Patel					22	7	43	1
ENGLAND								
DeFreitas	16	2	53	2	27	11	62	4
Lewis	21	7	31	5	27	4	83	2
Pringle	15	7	21	2	7	2	23	1
Reeve	7	1	21	0				
Tufnell	2	2	16	1	17	5	45	2
Hick					1	1	0	0

FALL OF WICKETS

	E	NZ	E	NZ
Wkt	1st	1st	2nd	2nd
1st	9	2	29	0
2nd	9	35	33	0
3rd	9	91	93	7
4th	34	102	182	77
5th	72	123	263	109
6th	91	124	269	118
7th	128	139	319	153
8th	165	139	321	173
9th	171	139	321	203
10th	203	142	321	214

Umpires: B.L.Aldridge (12) and R.S.Dunne (7).   Test No. 1186/71
In New Zealand's first innings, Wright (5) retired hurt at 13-1 and resumed at 91-3.

NEW ZEALAND v ENGLAND (3rd Test)

Played at Basin Reserve, Wellington, on 6, 7, 8, 9, 10 February 1992.
Toss: England.   Result: MATCH DRAWN.
Debuts: New Zealand – R.T.Latham.

ENGLAND

*G.A.Gooch	b Patel	30	c Rutherford b Cairns	11
A.J.Stewart	b Morrison	107	c Smith b Patel	63
G.A.Hick	b Patel	43	c Smith b Su'a	22
R.A.Smith	c Rutherford b Patel	6	c and b Su'a	76
A.J.Lamb	c Smith b Patel	30	c Latham b Patel	142
D.A.Reeve	c Latham b Su'a	18	b Su'a	0
D.V.Lawrence	c Rutherford b Cairns	6		
I.T.Botham	c Cairns b Su'a	15	(7) lbw b Patel	1
†R.C.Russell	lbw b Morrison	18	(8) not out	24
P.A.J.DeFreitas	lbw b Morrison	3		
P.C.R.Tufnell	not out	2		
Extras	(B4, LB12, NB11)	27	(LB13, NB7)	20
Total	(118.1 overs; 463 minutes)	**305**	(119.3 overs; 469 minutes) (7 wickets declared)	**359**

NEW ZEALAND

B.R.Hartland	c Botham b Lawrence	2	lbw b Botham	19
J.G.Wright	c Reeve b Tufnell	116	c Russell b Botham	0
A.H.Jones	b Hick	143	(4) lbw b Reeve	9
*M.D.Crowe	b Tufnell	30	(3) not out	13
K.R.Rutherford	run out (Gooch/Hick)	8	not out	2
R.T.Latham	b Hick	25		
D.N.Patel	lbw b Hick	9		
C.L.Cairns	c Russell b Botham	33		
†I.D.S.Smith	b Hick	21		
M.L.Su'a	not out	20		
D.K.Morrison	not out	0		
Extras	(B1, LB15, W1, NB8)	25		
Total	(192 overs; 690 minutes) (9 wickets declared)	**432**	(24 overs; 95 minutes) (3 wickets)	**43**

NEW ZEALAND	O	M	R	W	O	M	R	W	FALL OF WICKETS				
Morrison	22.1	6	44	3	23	5	63	0		E	NZ	E	NZ
Cairns	25	3	89	1	22	4	84	1	Wkt	1st	1st	2nd	2nd
Su'a	36	10	62	2	33	10	87	3	1st	83	3	17	4
Patel	34	10	87	4	41.3	12	112	3	2nd	159	244	52	24
Jones	1	0	7	0					3rd	169	308	127	41
									4th	215	312	249	–
ENGLAND									5th	235	327	249	–
DeFreitas	8	4	12	0					6th	248	340	254	–
Lawrence	27	7	67	1	2.1	1	4	0	7th	277	369	359	–
Tufnell	71	22	147	2	9	5	12	0	8th	286	404	–	–
Hick	69	27	126	4					9th	298	430	–	–
Botham	14	4	53	1	8	1	23	2	10th	305	–	–	–
Reeve	3	1	11	0	4.5	2	4	1					

Umpires: B.L.Aldridge (13) and R.S.Dunne (8).   Test No. 1187/72

NEW ZEALAND v ENGLAND AVERAGES

NEW ZEALAND – BATTING AND FIELDING

	M	I	NO	HS	Runs	Avge	100	50	Ct/St
M.L.Su'a	2	3	2	36	56	56.00	–	–	1
J.G.Wright	3	6	0	116	258	43.00	1	1	1
M.D.Crowe	3	6	1	56	212	42.40	–	1	2
A.H.Jones	3	6	0	143	226	37.66	1	–	1
D.N.Patel	3	5	0	99	155	31.00	–	1	–
C.L.Cairns	3	5	0	61	119	23.80	–	1	2
K.R.Rutherford	2	4	1	32	68	22.66	–	–	3
B.R.Hartland	3	6	0	45	88	14.66	–	–	1
I.D.S.Smith	3	3	0	21	42	14.00	–	–	4
D.K.Morrison	3	5	2	12	20	6.66	–	–	–

Played in one Test: M.J.Greatbatch 11, 0 (2 ct); R.T.Latham 25 (2 ct); A.C.Parore 0, 15 (6 ct); C.Pringle 6, 5*; S.A.Thomson 5, 0; W.Watson 2, 5* (1 ct).

NEW ZEALAND – BOWLING

	O	M	R	W	Avge	Best	5wI	10wM
M.L.Su'a	100	31	236	8	29.50	3-87	–	–
D.N.Patel	143.3	34	374	10	37.40	4-87	–	–
C.L.Cairns	117	20	429	11	39.00	6-52	1	–
D.K.Morrison	116.5	24	361	8	45.12	3-44	–	–

Also bowled: A.H.Jones 4-0-15-0; C.Pringle 36-4-127-3; S.A.Thomson 15-3-47-0; W.Watson 50-23-100-3.

ENGLAND – BATTING AND FIELDING

	M	I	NO	HS	Runs	Avge	100	50	Ct/St
A.J.Lamb	3	5	0	142	338	67.60	1	2	2
A.J.Stewart	3	5	0	148	330	66.00	2	1	3
R.A.Smith	3	5	0	96	213	42.60	–	2	5
C.C.Lewis	2	3	0	70	126	42.00	–	1	1
R.C.Russell	3	5	1	36	135	33.75	–	–	8/1
G.A.Gooch	3	5	0	114	161	32.20	1	–	–
G.A.Hick	3	5	0	43	134	26.80	–	–	4
D.A.Reeve	3	5	0	59	124	24.80	–	1	1
D.R.Pringle	2	3	0	41	53	17.66	–	–	2
P.C.R.Tufnell	3	3	2	6*	8	–	–	–	1
P.A.J.DeFreitas	3	4	1	7*	11	3.66	–	–	–

Played in one Test: I.T.Botham 15, 1 (1 ct); D.V.Lawrence 6.

ENGLAND – BOWLING

	O	M	R	W	Avge	Best	5wI	10wM
P.C.R.Tufnell	186.1	69	367	16	22.93	7-47	1	1
C.C.Lewis	100	23	249	10	24.90	5-31	1	–
P.A.J.DeFreitas	106.4	39	235	8	29.37	4-62	–	–
D.R.Pringle	58	16	162	5	32.40	2-21	–	–

Also bowled: I.T.Botham 22-5-76-3; G.A.Hick 87-36-148-4; D.V.Lawrence 29.1-8-71-1; D.A.Reeve 24.5-8-60-2; R.A.Smith 4-2-6-0.

THE 1991 FIRST-CLASS SEASON
STATISTICAL HIGHLIGHTS

HIGHEST INNINGS TOTALS

621	Essex v Leicestershire	Leicester
575-8d	Worcestershire v Somerset	Worcester
572-7d†	Derbyshire v Nottinghamshire	Derby
566-6d	Essex v Middlesex	Chelmsford
544	Essex v Kent	Folkestone
543-8d	Essex v Derbyshire	Chelmsford
514-9d	Glamorgan v Gloucestershire	Abergavenny
504	Glamorgan v Hampshire	Southampton
501-6d	Yorkshire v Lancashire	Scarborough

† After following-on.

HIGHEST FOURTH INNINGS TOTALS

436†	Sussex v Kent (set 437)	Hove
403	Somerset v Warwickshire (set 409)	Taunton

† Highest total to tie any first-class match.

LOWEST INNINGS TOTALS

51	Middlesex v Essex	Chelmsford
68	Northamptonshire v Nottinghamshire	Wellingborough
83	Warwickshire v Kent	Tunbridge Wells
83†	Somerset v Worcestershire	Worcester
96	Middlesex v Kent	Canterbury
97	Sri Lankans v Gloucestershire	Bristol
99	Cambridge University v Glamorgan	Cambridge

† One man absent hurt.

LOWEST FIRST-CLASS TOTAL IN U.K. TO INCLUDE TWO HUNDREDS

258	Hampshire v Derbyshire	Chesterfield
	(C.L.Smith 114, K.D.James 101)	

MATCH AGGREGATES OF 1400 RUNS

Runs-Wkts

1578-37	Sussex v Kent	Hove
1442-29	Yorkshire v Lancashire	Scarborough
1415-25	Hampshire v Somerset	Southampton
1415-28	West Indies XI v World XI	Scarborough

FIRST TO INDIVIDUAL TARGETS

1000 RUNS	H.Morris	Glamorgan	June 20
2000 RUNS	S.J.Cook	Somerset	August 16
100 WICKETS	Waqar Younis	Surrey	September 4

DOUBLE HUNDREDS (18)

M.Azharuddin	212	Derbyshire v Leicestershire	Leicester
K.J.Barnett	217	Derbyshire v Nottinghamshire	Derby
M.R.Benson	257	Kent v Hampshire	Southampton
S.J.Cook (2)	210*	Somerset v Northamptonshire	Northampton
	209*	Somerset v Sri Lankans	Taunton
T.S.Curtis	248	Worcestershire v Somerset	Worcester
D.B.D'Oliveira	237	Worcestershire v Oxford University	Oxford
M.W.Gatting	215*	Middlesex v Derbyshire	Lord's

G.A.Gooch	259	Essex v Middlesex	Chelmsford
M.P.Maynard (2)	204	Glamorgan v Nottinghamshire	Cardiff
	243	Glamorgan v Hampshire	Southampton
T.M.Moody	210	Worcestershire v Warwickshire	Worcester
M.D.Moxon	200	Yorkshire v Essex	Colchester
Salim Malik	215	Essex v Leicestershire	Ilford
C.L.Smith	200	Hampshire v Oxford University	Oxford
N.R.Taylor	203*	Kent v Sussex	Hove
T.R.Ward	235*	Kent v Middlesex	Canterbury
A.P.Wells	253*	Sussex v Yorkshire	Middlesbrough

HUNDREDS IN THREE CONSECUTIVE INNINGS

N.H.Fairbrother	107* v Glam, 109 and 102* v Somerset	Liverpool/Taunton
N.R.Taylor	101 v Middlesex, 111 and 203* v Sussex	Canterbury/Hove

HUNDRED IN EACH INNINGS OF A MATCH (7)

A.R.Butcher	129	104	Glamorgan v Lancashire	Liverpool
S.J.Cook	197	115*	Somerset v Hampshire	Southampton
N.H.Fairbrother	109	102*	Lancashire v Somerset	Taunton
M.P.Maynard	129	126	Glamorgan v Gloucestershire	Cheltenham
C.L.Smith	145	101	Hampshire v Sussex	Hove
N.R.Taylor	111	203*	Kent v Sussex	Hove
T.R.Ward	110	109	Kent v Glamorgan	Maidstone

FASTEST HUNDRED (WALTER LAWRENCE TROPHY)

I.D.Austin	61 balls	Lancashire v Yorkshire	Scarborough

In 68 minutes, including 6 sixes and 13 fours – batting at number 10.

HUNDRED BEFORE LUNCH

		Day		
C.J.Adams	108*	3	Derbyshire v Cambridge University	Cambridge
D.B.D'Oliveira	157	2	Worcestershire v Oxford University	Oxford
A.J.Lamb	100*	2	Northamptonshire v Lancashire	Lytham
A.A.Metcalfe	104*	3	Yorkshire v Lancashire	Manchester
P.R.Pollard	108*	1	Nottinghamshire v Lancashire	Nottingham

CARRYING BAT THROUGH COMPLETED INNINGS

C.W.J.Athey (2†)	77*	Gloucestershire (186) v Somerset	Bristol
	103*	Gloucestershire (287) v Sussex	Hove
D.J.Bicknell	145*	Surrey (268) v Essex	Chelmsford
N.E.Briers	60*	Leicestershire (108) v Northamptonshire	Leicester
T.S.Curtis	186*	Worcestershire (382) v Glamorgan	Cardiff
G.A.Gooch	154*	England (252) v West Indies	Leeds
D.L.Haynes	75*	West Indies (176) v England	The Oval
P.M.Roebuck	91*	Somerset (224) v Middlesex	Taunton

† In successive innings.

FIRST-WICKET PARTNERSHIP OF 100 IN EACH INNINGS

274	129	V.P.Terry/C.L.Smith, Hampshire v Sussex	Hove
161	124	D.J.Bicknell/R.I.Alikhan, Surrey v Nottinghamshire	The Oval

Essex achieved first-wicket partnerships of 168* (G.A.Gooch/N.Shahid) and 118 (J.P.Stephenson/D.R.Pringle) v Cambridge University at Cambridge.

OTHER NOTABLE PARTNERSHIPS
First Wicket

300†	N.R.Taylor/M.R.Benson, Kent v Derbyshire	Canterbury

Second Wicket

265	P.R.Pollard/R.T.Robinson, Nottinghamshire v Derbyshire	Derby
264*	T.S.Curtis/T.M.Moody, Worcestershire v Essex	Ilford

Third Wicket

269	D.Byas/R.J.Blakey, Yorkshire v Oxford University	Oxford
258	M.W.Gatting/K.R.Brown, Middlesex v Derbyshire	Lord's
256	T.S.Curtis/D.A.Leatherdale, Worcestershire v Somerset	Worcester

Fourth Wicket

314†	Salim Malik/N.Hussain, Essex v Surrey	The Oval
287	G.A.Gooch/N.Hussain, Essex v Northamptonshire	Colchester

Fifth Wicket

316†	N.Hussain/M.A.Garnham, Essex v Leicestershire	Leicester
243	D.B.D'Oliveira/D.A.Leatherdale, Worcestershire v Oxford U	Oxford

Seventh Wicket

219*†	J.D.R.Benson/P.Whitticase, Leicestershire v Hampshire	Bournemouth

Eighth Wicket

184†	S.J.Rhodes/S.R.Lampitt, Worcestershire v Derbyshire	Kidderminster
178	A.P.Wells/B.T.P.Donelan, Sussex v Yorkshire	Middlesbrough

Tenth Wicket

133	S.P.Titchard/I.D.Austin, Lancashire v Nottinghamshire	Manchester

† County record.

EIGHT OR MORE WICKETS IN AN INNINGS

D.G.Cork	8-53†	Derbyshire v Essex	Derby
N.A.Foster	8-99	Essex v Lancashire	Manchester
D.R.Gilbert	8-55	Gloucestershire v Kent	Canterbury
D.J.Millns	9-37	Leicestershire v Derbyshire	Derby
T.A.Munton	8-89	Warwickshire v Middlesex	Birmingham

† Before lunch and on his 20th birthday.

TEN OR MORE WICKETS IN A MATCH (19)

D.G.Cork	10-78	Derbyshire v Essex	Derby
A.A.Donald (2)	10-96	Warwickshire v Yorkshire	Leeds
	10-74	Warwickshire v Glamorgan	Swansea
B.T.P.Donelan	10-136	Sussex v Gloucestershire	Hove
N.A.Foster	10-122	Essex v Middlesex	Chelmsford
M.Frost	11-143	Glamorgan v Gloucestershire	Cheltenham
M.J.Gerrard	10-60	Gloucestershire v Sri Lankans	Bristol
N.M.Kendrick	10-174	Surrey v Lancashire	Manchester
D.V.Lawrence	11-129	Gloucestershire v Hampshire	Bristol
K.T.Medlycott	11-134	Surrey v Cambridge University	Cambridge
D.J.Millns	12-91	Leicestershire v Derbyshire	Derby
T.A.Munton (2)	11-127	Warwickshire v Middlesex	Birmingham
	10-91	Warwickshire v Worcestershire	Birmingham
F.D.Stephenson	10-88	Nottinghamshire v Northamptonshire	Wellingborough
P.C.R.Tufnell	11-228	Middlesex v Hampshire	Lord's
Waqar Younis (3)	11-122	Surrey v Lancashire	The Oval
	11-136	Surrey v Hampshire	Bournemouth
	12-92	Surrey v Hampshire	The Oval
Wasim Akram	11-129	Lancashire v Middlesex	Uxbridge

SIX OR MORE WICKET-KEEPING DISMISSALS IN AN INNINGS

M.A.Garnham	6 ct	Essex v Warwickshire	Chelmsford
S.A.Marsh (2)	8 ct†	Kent v Middlesex	Lord's
	6 ct	Kent v Leicestershire	Leicester
C.P.Metson (2)	6 ct	Glamorgan v Oxford University	Oxford
	7 ct	Glamorgan v Derbyshire	Chesterfield

† Equalled world record and, uniquely, scored a hundred (108*).

NINE OR MORE WICKET-KEEPING DISMISSALS IN A MATCH

S.A.Marsh	9 ct	Kent v Middlesex	Lord's

MATCH DOUBLE (100 RUNS AND 10 WICKETS)

K.T.Medlycott	2, 109; 5-36, 6-98 Surrey v Cambridge U	Cambridge

100 RUNS AND 8 DISMISSALS IN AN INNINGS

S.A.Marsh	108*; 8 ct Kent v Middlesex	Lord's

NO BYES CONCEDED IN TOTAL OF 500 OR MORE

N.D.Burns	Somerset v Worcestershire (575-8d)	Worcester
S.A.Marsh	Kent v Essex (544)	Folkestone
W.K.Hegg	Lancashire v Yorkshire (501-6d)	Scarborough

FIFTY EXTRAS IN AN INNINGS

B	LB	W	NB		
65	8	32	1	24	Nottinghamshire v Derbyshire	Derby
56	14	22	1	19	Northamptonshire v Warwickshire	Northampton
54	8	10	1	35	England v West Indies	The Oval
52	9	8	1	34	Gloucestershire v Sussex	Hove

COUNTY CAPS AWARDED IN 1991

Derbyshire	M.Azharuddin
Essex	Salim Malik, P.M.Such
Glamorgan	M.Frost
Gloucestershire	–
Hampshire	J.R.Ayling, A.N.Aymes
Kent	–
Lancashire	–
Leicestershire	D.J.Millns
Middlesex	–
Northamptonshire	J.G.Thomas
Nottinghamshire	–
Somerset	R.P.Lefebvre
Surrey	G.P.Thorpe
Sussex	I.D.K.Salisbury, M.P.Speight
Warwickshire	D.P.Ostler
Worcestershire	T.M.Moody
Yorkshire	D.Byas

ESSEX WORTHY CHAMPIONS

Although a rejuvenated Warwickshire led the table for most of the summer, Essex always bore the hallmark of potential victors. With an inspired final burst, they overcame a 51-point deficit to end the longest-ever first-class season as worthy Britannic Assurance County Champions. Their fifth title in thirteen years ended a sequence of three near misses and was a tribute to a policy of ruthless efficiency. This was never more clearly demonstrated than in their annihilation of Middlesex in the final round of matches by an innings and 208 runs with a day and a half to spare. Having dismissed the reigning champions for 51, the season's lowest total, they crowned an astonishing first day by amassing 385 for 3, Graham Gooch having completed his ninth double hundred in first-class cricket.

Not often does a cricketer's devoted following include his team-mates but a very short time in the Essex camp would reveal that Gooch is not so much revered as worshipped by his players. He now wears the mantle of leadership with apparent ease and revels in the task of manipulating the team that means so much to him. Crucially he has managed to infuse a competitive edge into a side brimming with talent. Salim Malik proved an ample substitute for Mark Waugh, supplementing his delightful strokeplay with some wonderful catching and even snaring 15 Championship scalps with what became known on the county circuit as 'flighted filth'.

Nasser Hussain enjoyed his most prolific summer and shared in two record triple-century partnerships, one with the much-improved Mike Garnham, who, having waited 12 years for his first Championship hundred, scored two in successive innings. Bowlers win proper cricket matches (as opposed to the instant variation) and the contribution of Neil Foster was paramount to the county's success. Heroically, he overcame the pain from his ravaged knees and led the side astutely in his mentor's absence. As with the great Surrey team of the Fifties, it is hard to see Essex being toppled from their hard-won ascendancy.

Warwickshire came closest to doing so, recording 11 wins despite a fragile batting array which mustered just four hundreds. It was very much a team effort built around the exceptional pace of Allan Donald. Under Bob Woolmer's guidance, Andy Lloyd blossomed as a leader and instilled his side with new confidence.

Only 17 points separated the next three counties. Derbyshire ended an erratic summer by overcoming a 184-run deficit to beat Yorkshire and finish third. Nottinghamshire's innings victory over Worcestershire allowed them to gain fourth place by four points when Surrey suffered a one-wicket defeat at Old Trafford.

BRITANNIC ASSURANCE
COUNTY CHAMPIONSHIP 1991
FINAL TABLE

Win = 16 points. Tie = 8 points.

	P	W	L	T	D	Bonus Points Bat	Bowl	Total Points
1 ESSEX (2)	22	11	5	–	6	69	67	312
2 Warwickshire (5)	22	11	4	–	7	58	65	299
3 Derbyshire (12)	22	9	5	–	8	46	68	258
4 Nottinghamshire (13)	22	7	5	–	10	64	69	245
5 Surrey (9)	22	8	6	–	8	47	66	241
6 Kent (16)	22	6	3	1	12	50	55	209
7 Worcestershire (4)	22	6	4	–	12	54	59	209
8 Lancashire (6)	22	6	9	–	7	60	49	205
9 Hampshire (3)	22	5	7	–	10	57	56	193
10 Northamptonshire (11)	22	5	6	–	11	55	54	189
11 Sussex (17)	22	4	3	1	14	57	60	189
12 Glamorgan (8)	22	5	5	–	12	50	57	187
13 Gloucestershire (13)	22	5	10	–	7	42	53	175
14 Yorkshire (10)	22	4	6	–	12	58	37	159
15 Middlesex (1)	22	3	9	–	10	48	63	159
16 Leicestershire (7)	22	3	8	–	11	46	53	147
17 Somerset (15)	22	2	5	–	15	66	45	143

1990 final positions are shown in brackets.

SCORING OF POINTS

(a) For a win, 16 points, plus any points scored in the first innings.

(b) In a tie, each side to score eight points, plus any points scored in the first innings.

(c) If the scores are equal in a drawn match, the side batting in the fourth innings to score eight points, plus any points scored in the first innings.

(d) **First Innings Points** (awarded only for performances **in the first 100 overs** of each first innings and retained whatever the result of the match).

    (i) A maximum of four batting points to be available as under:–

        150 to 199 runs – 1 point
        200 to 249 runs – 2 points
        250 to 299 runs – 3 points
        300 runs or over – 4 points

    (ii) A maximum of four bowling points to be available as under:–

        3 to 4 wickets taken – 1 point
        5 to 6 wickets taken – 2 points
        7 to 8 wickets taken – 3 points
        9 to 10 wickets taken – 4 points

(e) If play starts when less than eight hours playing time remains and a one innings match is played, no first innings points shall be scored. The side winning on the one innings to score 12 points.

(f) A County which is adjudged to have prepared a pitch unsuitable for First-Class Cricket shall be liable to have 25 points deducted from its aggregate of points under the procedure agreed by the TCCB in December 1988.

(g) The side which has the highest aggregate of points gained at the end of the season shall be the Champion County. Should any sides in the Championship table be equal on points, the side with most wins will have priority.

ESSEX v VICTORIA

Played at Chelmsford, on 23, 24, 25, 26 September.
Toss: Essex. Result: MATCH DRAWN.

ESSEX

*G.A.Gooch c Berry b Fleming	31
J.P.Stephenson b Dodemaide	54
P.J.Prichard lbw b O'Donnell	2
N.Hussain c and b Dodemaide	5
N.V.Knight run out	53
J.J.B.Lewis b Jackson	25
†M.A.Garnham lbw b Fleming	33
D.R.Pringle lbw b Hughes	68
N.A.Foster st Berry b Jackson	37
J.H.Childs not out	8
P.M.Such did not bat	
Extras (B10, LB9, W4, NB4)	27
Total (9 wickets declared)	**343**

VICTORIA

D.J.Ramshaw lbw b Childs	11	c Garnham b Foster	0
W.N.Phillips c Pringle b Foster	2	lbw b Stephenson	11
D.M.Jones c Gooch b Childs	25	c Hussain b Such	9
D.S.Lehmann c Hussain b Such	15	lbw b Childs	8
*S.P.O'Donnell c Prichard b Such	12	b Childs	5
G.R.Parker b Childs	0	lbw b Childs	1
A.I.C.Dodemaide lbw b Foster	21	b Such	0
M.G.Hughes not out	60	not out	12
†D.S.Berry c Prichard b Childs	1	lbw b Such	4
D.W.Fleming c Garnham b Foster	8		
P.W.Jackson c Gooch b Foster	4		
Extras (LB9)	9	(B5, LB1)	6
Total	**168**	**(8 wickets)**	**56**

VICTORIA	O	M	R	W	O	M	R	W
Hughes	30.3	7	85	1				
Fleming	25	5	88	2				
O'Donnell	13	6	47	1				
Dodemaide	24	6	54	2				
Jackson	18	11	50	2				
ESSEX								
Foster	33.3	12	63	4	4	1	14	1
Pringle	3	3	0	0				
Childs	43	15	71	4	7	2	19	3
Such	17	7	25	2	6.1	2	7	3
Stephenson					4	1	10	1

FALL OF WICKETS			
	E	V	V
Wkt	1st	1st	2nd
1st	61	3	8
2nd	80	39	14
3rd	96	48	29
4th	103	70	33
5th	159	71	37
6th	206	71	40
7th	217	136	40
8th	277	137	56
9th	343	158	–
10th	–	168	–

Umpires: R.Julian and K.E.Palmer.

COUNTY CHAMPIONS

The English County Championship was not officially constituted until December 1889. Prior to that date there was no generally accepted method of awarding the title; although the 'least matches lost' method existed, it was not consistently applied. Rules governing playing qualifications were not agreed until 1873, and the first unofficial points system was not introduced until 1888.

Research has produced a list of champions dating back to 1826, but at least seven different versions exist for the period from 1864 to 1889 (see *The Wisden Book of Cricket Records*). Only from 1890 can any authorised list of county champions commence.

That first official Championship was contested between eight counties: Gloucestershire, Kent, Lancashire, Middlesex, Nottinghamshire, Surrey, Sussex and Yorkshire. The remaining counties were admitted in the following seasons: 1891 – Somerset, 1895 – Derbyshire, Essex, Hampshire, Leicestershire and Warwickshire, 1899 – Worcestershire, 1905 – Northamptonshire, 1921 – Glamorgan, and 1992 – Durham.

From 1977 to 1983 the Championship was sponsored by Schweppes. BRITANNIC ASSURANCE have been its benefactors since 1984.

1890	Surrey	1927	Lancashire	1964	Worcestershire
1891	Surrey	1928	Lancashire	1965	Worcestershire
1892	Surrey	1929	Nottinghamshire	1966	Yorkshire
1893	Yorkshire	1930	Lancashire	1967	Yorkshire
1894	Surrey	1931	Yorkshire	1968	Yorkshire
1895	Surrey	1932	Yorkshire	1969	Glamorgan
1896	Yorkshire	1933	Yorkshire	1970	Surrey
1897	Lancashire	1934	Lancashire	1971	Surrey
1898	Yorkshire	1935	Yorkshire	1972	Warwickshire
1899	Surrey	1936	Derbyshire	1973	Hampshire
1900	Yorkshire	1937	Yorkshire	1974	Worcestershire
1901	Yorkshire	1938	Yorkshire	1975	Leicestershire
1902	Yorkshire	1939	Yorkshire	1976	Middlesex
1903	Middlesex	1946	Yorkshire	1977 {	Kent
1904	Lancashire	1947	Middlesex		Middlesex
1905	Yorkshire	1948	Glamorgan	1978	Kent
1906	Kent	1949 {	Middlesex	1979	Essex
1907	Nottinghamshire		Yorkshire	1980	Middlesex
1908	Yorkshire	1950 {	Lancashire	1981	Nottinghamshire
1909	Kent		Surrey	1982	Middlesex
1910	Kent	1951	Warwickshire	1983	Essex
1911	Warwickshire	1952	Surrey	1984	Essex
1912	Yorkshire	1953	Surrey	1985	Middlesex
1913	Kent	1954	Surrey	1986	Essex
1914	Surrey	1955	Surrey	1987	Nottinghamshire
1919	Yorkshire	1956	Surrey	1988	Worcestershire
1920	Middlesex	1957	Surrey	1989	Worcestershire
1921	Middlesex	1958	Surrey	1990	Middlesex
1922	Yorkshire	1959	Yorkshire	1991	Essex
1923	Yorkshire	1960	Yorkshire		
1924	Yorkshire	1961	Hampshire		
1925	Yorkshire	1962	Yorkshire		
1926	Lancashire	1963	Yorkshire		

HAMPSHIRE'S CLASSIC FIRST WIN

The eleventh NatWest Trophy final provided a classic game of one-day cricket and a fitting climax to a summer of exhilarating big-match occasions. Overcoming the absence of their injured captain, Mark Nicholas, Hampshire gained their first title in this competition with two balls to spare. Surrey recovered from the early departure of their openers to set the highest target in this final since 1986. Paul Terry and Tony Middleton survived the opening onslaught from Waqar Younis, so paving the way for Man of the Match Robin Smith to treat a capacity Lord's crowd to his second major innings of the season.

Earlier, Hampshire had avenged seven semi-final defeats by cruising to their first September Lord's final with a nine-wicket win against Warwickshire, astonishingly losing only six wickets in reaching Mecca. That proved to be the farewell appearance of Chris Smith, who finished with 1474 runs (av 56.69), including a record seven hundreds and with a record-equalling eight match awards.

With the number of reserve days having been reduced from three to two, it was inevitable that the first round would be treated to the wettest conditions since the competition began in 1963. It led to the first use of the 'bowl-out' tie-break method, Derbyshire becoming its first victims when five bowlers from Hertfordshire proved more successful at hitting an unguarded wicket. They were swiftly followed by Oxfordshire who lost to Surrey in the new indoor school at The Oval's Ken Barrington Centre. Little did Tony Murphy realise that his last-ditch dual subterranean strike had paved the way for his team's appearance at Lord's.

GILLETTE CUP WINNERS

1963 Sussex	1969 Yorkshire	1975 Lancashire
1964 Sussex	1970 Lancashire	1976 Northamptonshire
1965 Yorkshire	1971 Lancashire	1977 Middlesex
1966 Warwickshire	1972 Lancashire	1978 Sussex
1967 Kent	1973 Gloucestershire	1979 Somerset
1968 Warwickshire	1974 Kent	1980 Middlesex

NATWEST TROPHY WINNERS

1981 Derbyshire	1985 Essex	1989 Warwickshire
1982 Surrey	1986 Sussex	1990 Lancashire
1983 Somerset	1987 Nottinghamshire	1991 Hampshire
1984 Middlesex	1988 Middlesex	

1991 NATWEST TROPHY FINAL

HAMPSHIRE v SURREY

Played at Lord's, London, on 7 September.
Toss: Hampshire. Result: HAMPSHIRE won by 4 wickets.
Match Award: R.A.Smith (adjudicator: M.C.Cowdrey).

SURREY	Runs	Mins	Balls	6s	4s	Fall
D.J.Bicknell b Ayling	13	60	50	–	1	1-25
J.D.Robinson not out	3	25	18	–	–	
†A.J.Stewart b Ayling	61	151	123	–	8	2-139
G.P.Thorpe c James b Connor	93	151	121	–	10	3-203
D.M.Ward c Maru b Connor	43	47	36	–	5	4-222
M.A.Lynch c Ayling b Connor	10	18	11	–	1	5-233
*I.A.Greig not out	7	13	5	–	–	
M.P.Bicknell						
J.Boiling						
Waqar Younis }did not bat						
A.J.Murphy						
Extras (B2, LB4, W3, NB1)	10					
Total (60 overs; 238 minutes)	240-5 closed					

HAMPSHIRE	Runs	Mins	Balls	6s	4s	Fall
V.P.Terry run out (Thorpe)	32	96	81	–	2	1-90
T.C.Middleton b Murphy	78	170	143	‡	5	2-160
R.A.Smith run out (Murphy)	78	127	94	–	7	5-231
*D.I.Gower lbw b Waqar	9	20	10	–	1	3-192
K.D.James c Stewart b M.P.Bicknell	0	3	2	–	–	4-193
J.R.Ayling not out	18	40	26	1	2	
†A.N.Aymes run out (M.P.Bicknell)	2	6	4	–	–	6-238
R.J.Maru not out	1	2	1	–	–	
S.D.Udal						
C.A.Connor }did not bat						
Aqib Javed						
Extras (LB17, W5, NB3)	25					(‡ one five)
Total (59.4 overs; 236 minutes)	243-6					

HAMPSHIRE	O	M	R	W	SURREY	O	M	R	W
Aqib Javed	12	2	54	0	Waqar Younis	12	0	43	1
Connor	12	4	39	3	M.P.Bicknell	11.4	1	32	1
Ayling	12	0	39	2	Murphy	12	0	56	1
James	9	3	33	0	Robinson	12	0	43	0
Maru	6	0	23	0	Boiling	12	1	52	0
Udal	9	0	46	0					

Umpires: M.J.Kitchen and K.E.Palmer.

J.D.Robinson retired hurt when 2 at 5-0 and resumed at 233-5.

THE NATWEST TROPHY

FIRST ROUND 26, 27 June	SECOND ROUND 11, 12 July	QUARTER-FINALS 31 July	SEMI-FINALS 14, 15 August	FINAL 7 September
LANCASHIRE				
Dorset	Lancashire			
HAMPSHIRE		HAMPSHIRE†		
Berkshire†	HAMPSHIRE†			
NOTTINGHAMSHIRE†			HAMPSHIRE	
Lincolnshire	NOTTINGHAMSHIRE	Nottinghamshire (£3,250)		
GLOUCESTERSHIRE†				**HAMPSHIRE (£26,500)**
Norfolk	Gloucestershire†			
WARWICKSHIRE†				
Yorkshire	WARWICKSHIRE†	WARWICKSHIRE†		
HERTFORDSHIRE†				
Derbyshire	Hertfordshire		Warwickshire† (£6,500)	
SOMERSET†		Somerset (£3,250)		
Buckinghamshire	SOMERSET†			
MIDDLESEX				
Ireland†	Middlesex			
ESSEX				
Devon†	ESSEX	Essex (£3,250)		
SUSSEX				
Scotland†	Sussex†		SURREY†	
KENT†				
Cambridgeshire	Kent	SURREY†		
SURREY†				Surrey (£13,000)
Oxfordshire	SURREY†			
WORCESTERSHIRE				
Bedfordshire†	Worcestershire†	Glamorgan (£3,250)		
GLAMORGAN				
Durham†	GLAMORGAN		Northamptonshire (£6,500)	
LEICESTERSHIRE†		NORTHAMPTONSHIRE†		
Shropshire	Leicestershire			
NORTHAMPTONSHIRE				
Staffordshire†	NORTHAMPTONSHIRE†			

† Home team. Winning teams are in capitals. Amounts in brackets show prize-money won by that county.

48

Congratulations Hampshire on winning the 1991 NatWest Trophy.

NATWEST TROPHY
PRINCIPAL RECORDS 1963-1991
(Including The Gillette Cup)

Highest Total	413-4	Somerset v Devon	Torquay	1990
Highest Total in a Final	317-4	Yorkshire v Surrey	Lord's	1965
Highest Total by a Minor County	305-9	Durham v Glam	Darlington	1991
Highest Total Batting Second	326-9	Hampshire v Leics	Leicester	1987
Highest Total to Win Batting 2nd	307-5	Hampshire v Essex	Chelmsford	1990
Lowest Total	39	Ireland v Sussex	Hove	1985
Lowest Total in a Final	118	Lancashire v Kent	Lord's	1974
Lowest Total to Win Batting First	98	Worcs v Durham	Chester-le-St	1968
Highest Score	206 A.I.Kallicharran	Warwicks v Oxon	Birmingham	1984
HS (Minor County)	132 G.Robinson	Lincs v Northumb	Jesmond	1971
Hundreds	198 have been scored in GC (93) and NWT (105) matches		
Fastest Hundred	36 balls – G.D.Rose	Somerset v Devon	Torquay	1990

Highest Partnership for each Wicket

1st	242*	M.D.Moxon/A.A.Metcalfe	Yorks v Warwicks	Leeds	1990
2nd	285	I.S.Anderson/A.Hill	Derbys v Cornwall	Derby	1986
3rd	259*	H.Morris/M.P.Maynard	Glam v Durham	Darlington	1991
4th	234*	D.Lloyd/C.H.Lloyd	Lancs v Glos	Manchester	1978
5th	166	M.A.Lynch/G.R.J.Roope	Surrey v Durham	The Oval	1982
6th	105	G.St A.Sobers/R.A.White	Notts v Worcs	Worcester	1974
7th	160*	C.J.Richards/I.R.Payne	Surrey v Lincs	Sleaford	1983
8th	83	J.Hartley/D.A.Hale	Oxon v Glos	Oxford	1989
9th	87	M.A.Nash/A.E.Cordle	Glamorgan v Lincs	Swansea	1974
10th	81	S.Turner/R.E.East	Essex v Yorkshire	Leeds	1982

Best Bowling	8-21	M.A.Holding	Derbys v Sussex	Hove	1988
	8-31	D.L.Underwood	Kent v Scotland	Edinburgh	1987
	7-15	A.L.Dixon	Kent v Surrey	The Oval	1967
	7-15	R.P.Lefebvre	Somerset v Devon	Torquay	1990
	7-19	N.V.Radford	Worcs v Beds	Bedford	1991
	7-30	P.J.Sainsbury	Hants v Norfolk	Southampton	1965
	7-32	S.P.Davis	Durham v Lancs	Chester-le-St	1983
	7-33	R.D.Jackman	Surrey v Yorkshire	Harrogate	1970
	7-37	N.A.Mallender	Northants v Worcs	Northampton	1984

Hat-Tricks	J.D.F.Larter	Northants v Sussex	Northampton	1963
	D.A.D.Sydenham	Surrey v Cheshire	Hoylake	1964
	R.N.S.Hobbs	Essex v Middlesex	Lord's	1968
	N.M.McVicker	Warwicks v Lincs	Birmingham	1971
	G.S.Le Roux	Sussex v Ireland	Hove	1985
	M.Jean-Jacques	Derbyshire v Notts	Derby	1987
	J.F.M.O'Brien	Cheshire v Derbys	Chester	1988

Most Wicket-Keeping Dismissals

6 (5ct, 1st)	R.W.Taylor	Derbys v Essex	Derby	1981
6 (4ct, 2st)	T.Davies	Glamorgan v Staffs	Stone	1986

Most Catches in the Field

4	A.S.Brown	Glos v Middlesex	Bristol	1963
4	G.Cook	Northants v Glam	Northampton	1972
4	C.G.Greenidge	Hants v Cheshire	Southampton	1981
4	D.C.Jackson	Durham v Northants	Darlington	1984
4	T.S.Smith	Herts v Somerset	St Albans	1984
4	H.Morris	Glam v Scotland	Edinburgh	1988

Most Match Awards: 8 – G.A.Gooch (Essex), C.H.Lloyd (Lancs), C.L.Smith (Hants)

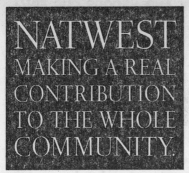

NATWEST
MAKING A REAL CONTRIBUTION TO THE WHOLE COMMUNITY.

This year as in previous years, NatWest is taking an active role in the community. And this support comes in various forms covering a wide range of environmental, social, arts and sporting projects all over the country.

Cash donations, and the secondment of around 100 of our senior staff to help with the day to day running of community projects are just two of the ways our resources are put to good use.

If our contribution helps the community in which we live and work, then we at NatWest believe it's money well spent.

NatWest

1991 BENSON AND HEDGES CUP FINAL

LANCASHIRE v WORCESTERSHIRE

Played at Lord's, London, on 13, 14 July.
Toss: Lancashire. Result: WORCESTERSHIRE won by 65 runs.
Match Award: G.A.Hick (adjudicator: D.C.S.Compton).

WORCESTERSHIRE	Runs	Mins	Balls	6s	4s	Fall
T.S.Curtis b DeFreitas	4	3	6	–	1	1-4
T.M.Moody b Allott	12	51	38	–	–	2-38
G.A.Hick c and b Allott	88	167	126	–	10	4-166
D.B.D'Oliveira c DeFreitas b Wasim	25	57	37	–	3	3-97
I.T.Botham c Fowler b Watkinson	19	73	46	–	–	5-172
*P.A.Neale c Watkinson b Austin	4	21	15	–	–	6-175
†S.J.Rhodes c Allott b Wasim	13	26	19	–	1	7-195
R.K.Illingworth not out	17	39	26	–	1	–
P.J.Newport c DeFreitas b Wasim	2	8	6	–	–	8-203
N.V.Radford not out	25	13	15	1	2	
G.R.Dilley did not bat						
Extras (LB8, W15, NB4)	27					
Total (55 overs; 236 minutes)	236-8	closed				

LANCASHIRE	Runs	Mins	Balls	6s	4s	Fall
G.D.Mendis b Radford	14	20	18	–	2	1-24
G.Fowler c Hick b Radford	54	140	106	–	7	6-111
M.A.Atherton c Rhodes b Radford	5	10	9	–	1	2-31
*N.H.Fairbrother run out (D'Oliveira)	1	2	2	–	–	3-32
G.D.Lloyd c Hick b Botham	10	45	39	–	1	4-64
M.Watkinson c Hick b Dilley	13	31	19	–	1	5-92
Wasim Akram run out (Rhodes/Illingworth)	14	44	38	–	–	7-134
P.A.J.DeFreitas c Neale b Newport	19	27	20	–	2	8-140
†W.K.Hegg not out	13	31	14	–	1	–
I.D.Austin c Illingworth b Newport	7	15	13	–	–	9-158
P.J.W.Allott c Neale b Dilley	10	7	8	–	2	10-171
Extras (LB5, W4, NB2)	11					
Total (47.2 overs; 195 minutes)	171					

LANCASHIRE	O	M	R	W	WORCESTERSHIRE	O	M	R	W
DeFreitas	11	1	38	1	Dilley	8.2	2	19	2
Allott	11	3	26	2	Radford	9	1	48	3
Watkinson	11	0	54	1	Botham	8	1	23	1
Wasim Akram	11	1	58	3	Newport	11	1	38	2
Austin	11	0	52	1	Illingworth	11	0	38	0

Umpires: J.W.Holder and D.R.Shepherd.

1991 BENSON AND HEDGES CUP

ZONAL POINTS TABLE

	P	W	L	Pts	Run Rate
GROUP A					
WORCESTERSHIRE	4	3	1	6	64.67
NORTHAMPTONSHIRE	4	3	1	6	63.57
Derbyshire	4	2	2	4	71.06
Gloucestershire	4	2	2	4	56.60
Combined Universities	4	–	4	0	43.71
GROUP B					
ESSEX	4	4	–	8	79.74
WARWICKSHIRE	4	3	1	6	77.19
Somerset	4	1	3	2	68.54
Surrey	4	1	3	2	65.90
Middlesex	4	1	3	2	59.79
GROUP C					
LANCASHIRE	4	4	–	8	74.13
KENT	4	3	1	6	76.25
Sussex	4	2	2	4	69.24
Leicestershire	4	1	3	2	64.31
Scotland	4	–	4	0	58.48
GROUP D					
YORKSHIRE	4	3	1	6	70.17
HAMPSHIRE	4	3	1	6	64.23
Nottinghamshire	4	2	2	4	76.13
Glamorgan	4	2	2	4	70.98
Minor Counties	4	–	4	0	63.63

FINAL ROUNDS

QUARTER-FINALS 29 May	SEMI-FINALS 12 June	FINAL 13, 14 July
WORCESTERSHIRE† Kent (£3,250)	WORCESTERSHIRE	**WORCESTERSHIRE** (£26,500)
ESSEX† Hampshire (£3,250)	Essex† (£6,500)	
LANCASHIRE† Northamptonshire (£3,250)	LANCASHIRE†	Lancashire (£13,000)
YORKSHIRE† Warwickshire (£3,250)	Yorkshire (£6,500)	

† Home team. Winning teams are in capitals. Prize-money in brackets.

BENSON AND HEDGES CUP
PRINCIPAL RECORDS 1972-1991

Highest Total	366-4	Derbys v Comb Us	Oxford	1991
Highest Total Batting Second }	303-7	Derbys v Somerset	Taunton	1990
Highest Losing Total				
Lowest Total	50	Hampshire v Yorks	Leeds	1991
Highest Score	198* G.A.Gooch	Essex v Sussex	Hove	1982
Hundreds	212 have been scored in Benson and Hedges Cup matches			
Fastest Hundred	62 min – M.A.Nash	Glamorgan v Hants	Swansea	1976

Highest Partnership for each Wicket

1st	252	V.P.Terry/C.L.Smith	Hants v Comb Us	Southampton	1990
2nd	285*	C.G.Greenidge/D.R.Turner	Hants v Minor C (S)	Amersham	1973
3rd	269*	P.M.Roebuck/M.D.Crowe	Somerset v Hants	Southampton	1987
4th	184*	D.Lloyd/B.W.Reidy	Lancashire v Derbys	Chesterfield	1980
5th	160	A.J.Lamb/D.J.Capel	Northants v Leics	Northampton	1986
6th	121	P.A.Neale/S.J.Rhodes	Worcs v Yorkshire	Worcester	1988
7th	149*	J.D.Love/C.M.Old	Yorks v Scotland	Bradford	1981
8th	109	R.E.East/N.Smith	Essex v Northants	Chelmsford	1977
9th	83	P.G.Newman/M.A.Holding	Derbyshire v Notts	Nottingham	1985
10th	80*	D.L.Bairstow/M.Johnson	Yorkshire v Derbys	Derby	1981

Most Wickets	7-12	W.W.Daniel	Middx v Minor C (E)	Ipswich	1978
	7-22	J.R.Thomson	Middx v Hampshire	Lord's	1981
	7-32	R.G.D.Willis	Warwicks v Yorks	Birmingham	1981
Hat-Tricks		G.D.McKenzie	Leics v Worcs	Worcester	1972
		K.Higgs	Leics v Surrey	Lord's	1974
		A.A.Jones	Middlesex v Essex	Lord's	1977
		M.J.Procter	Glos v Hampshire	Southampton	1977
		W.Larkins	Northants v Comb Us	Northampton	1980
		E.A.Moseley	Glamorgan v Kent	Cardiff	1981
		G.C.Small	Warwicks v Leics	Leicester	1984
		N.A.Mallender	Somerset v Comb Us	Taunton	1987
		W.K.M.Benjamin	Leics v Notts	Leicester	1987
		A.R.C.Fraser	Middx v Sussex	Lord's	1988

Most Wicket-Keeping Dismissals

8 (8ct)	D.J.S.Taylor		Somerset v Comb Us	Taunton	1982

Most Catches in the Field

5	V.J.Marks		Comb Us v Kent	Oxford	1976

Most Match Awards: 19 – G.A.Gooch (Essex); 11 – M.W.Gatting (Middx), T.E.Jesty (Hants/Surrey/Lancs), B.Wood (Lancs/Derbys); 10 – J.C.Balderstone (Leics).

BENSON AND HEDGES CUP WINNERS

1972	Leicestershire	1979	Essex	1986	Middlesex
1973	Kent	1980	Northamptonshire	1987	Yorkshire
1974	Surrey	1981	Somerset	1988	Hampshire
1975	Leicestershire	1982	Somerset	1989	Nottinghamshire
1976	Kent	1983	Middlesex	1990	Lancashire
1977	Gloucestershire	1984	Lancashire	1991	Worcestershire
1978	Kent	1985	Leicestershire		

REFUGE ASSURANCE LEAGUE 1991
FINAL TABLE

	P	W	L	T	NR	Pts	Away Wins	Runs/ 100 bl
1 NOTTINGHAMSHIRE (4)	16	13	3	–	–	52	7	83.47
2 Lancashire (2)	16	12	3	–	1	50	8	89.78
3 Northamptonshire (17)	16	10	4	–	2	44	3	86.26
4 Worcestershire (10)	16	9	4	1	2	42	4	95.16
5 Warwickshire (14)	16	8	4	1	3	40	4	82.53
6 Essex (12)	16	7	4	1	4	38	1	84.41
7 Yorkshire (6)	16	9	7	–	–	36	4	86.38
8 Somerset (8)	16	7	7	–	2	32	4	80.85
8 Surrey (6)	16	7	7	–	2	32	5	81.94
10 Kent (10)	16	6	8	1	1	28	2	87.46
11 Middlesex (3)	16	6	9	–	1	26	4	79.15
12 Gloucestershire (8)	16	5	9	–	2	24	4	77.68
12 Sussex (13)	16	5	9	–	2	24	3	81.42
14 Leicestershire (15)	16	5	10	–	1	22	3	78.29
15 Derbyshire (1)	16	5	11	–	–	20	2	84.38
15 Glamorgan (15)	16	4	10	–	2	20	1	82.61
17 Hampshire (5)	16	3	12	–	1	14	1	79.24

1990 final positions are shown in brackets.

When two or more counties finish with an equal number of points, the first four places are decided by (a) most wins, (b) most away wins, (c) runs per 100 balls.

The top four counties qualified for the Refuge Assurance Cup semi-finals.

REFUGE ASSURANCE CUP

SEMI-FINALS (1 September)

LANCASHIRE beat Northamptonshire by 4 wickets at Manchester
WORCESTERSHIRE beat Nottinghamshire by 14 runs at Nottingham

FINAL (15 September)

WORCESTERSHIRE beat Lancashire by 7 runs at Manchester

JOHN PLAYER LEAGUE CHAMPIONS

1969 Lancashire	1975 Hampshire	1981 Essex
1970 Lancashire	1976 Kent	1982 Sussex
1971 Worcestershire	1977 Leicestershire	1983 Yorkshire
1972 Kent	1978 Hampshire	1984 Essex
1973 Kent	1979 Somerset	1985 Essex
1974 Leicestershire	1980 Warwickshire	1986 Hampshire

REFUGE ASSURANCE LEAGUE CHAMPIONS

1987 Worcestershire	1989 Lancashire	1991 Nottinghamshire
1988 Worcestershire	1990 Derbyshire	

SUNDAY LEAGUE

PRINCIPAL RECORDS 1969-1991

Highest Total	360-3	Somerset v Glam	Neath	1990
Highest Total Batting Second	301-6	Warwicks v Essex	Colchester	1982
Lowest Total	23	Middlesex v Yorks	Leeds	1974
Highest Score	176	G.A.Gooch Essex v Glamorgan	Southend	1983
Hundreds	394 have been scored in Sunday League matches			
Fastest Hundred	46 balls G.D.Rose	Somerset v Glam	Neath	1990

Highest Partnership for each Wicket

1st	239	G.A.Gooch/B.R.Hardie	Essex v Notts	Nottingham	1985
2nd	273	G.A.Gooch/K.S.McEwan	Essex v Notts	Nottingham	1983
3rd	223	S.J.Cook/G.D.Rose	Somerset v Glam	Neath	1990
4th	219	C.G.Greenidge/C.L.Smith	Hampshire v Surrey	Southampton	1987
5th	185*	B.M.McMillan/Asif Din	Warwicks v Essex	Chelmsford	1986
6th	121	C.P.Wilkins/A.J.Borrington	Derbys v Warwicks	Chesterfield	1972
7th	132	K.R.Brown/N.F.Williams	Middx v Somerset	Lord's	1988
8th	105	W.K.Hegg/I.D.Austin	Lancashire v Middx	Lord's	1991
9th	105	D.G.Moir/R.W.Taylor	Derbyshire v Kent	Derby	1984
10th	57	D.A.Graveney/J.B.Mortimore	Glos v Lancashire	Tewkesbury	1973

Most Wickets

8-26	K.D.Boyce	Essex v Lancashire	Manchester	1971
7-15	R.A.Hutton	Yorkshire v Worcs	Leeds	1969
7-39	A.Hodgson	Northants v Somerset	Northampton	1976
7-41	A.N.Jones	Sussex v Notts	Nottingham	1986

Four Wkts in Four Balls   A.Ward   Derbyshire v Sussex   Derby   1970

Hat-Tricks (19): Derbyshire – A.Ward (1970), C.J.Tunnicliffe (1979); Essex – K.D.Boyce (1971); Glamorgan – M.A.Nash (1975), A.E.Cordle (1979), G.C.Holmes (1987); Gloucestershire – K.M.Curran (1989); Hampshire – J.M.Rice (1975), M.D.Marshall (1981); Kent – R.M.Ellison (1983); Leicestershire – G.D.McKenzie (1972); Northamptonshire – A.Hodgson (1976); Nottinghamshire – K.Saxelby (1987); Somerset – R.Palmer (1970), I.V.A.Richards (1982); Sussex – A.Buss (1974); Warwickshire – R.G.D.Willis (1973), W.Blenkiron (1974); Yorkshire – P.W.Jarvis (1982).

Most Economical Analysis

O	M	R	W				
8	8	0	0	B.A.Langford	Somerset v Essex	Yeovil	1969

Most Expensive Analyses

O	M	R	W				
7.5	0	89	3	G.Miller	Derbyshire v Glos	Gloucester	1984
8	0	88	1	E.E.Hemmings	Notts v Somerset	Nottingham	1983

Most Wicket-Keeping Dismissals

7 (6ct, 1st)   R.W.Taylor   Derbyshire v Lancs   Manchester   1975

Most Catches in the Field

5   J.M.Rice   Hampshire v Warwicks   Southampton   1978

MINOR COUNTIES CHAMPIONSHIP
FINAL TABLE 1991

		P	W	L	T	D	NR	Bonus Points Bat	Bowl	Total Points
EASTERN DIVISION										
Staffordshire	NW	9	5	–	–	4	–	17	17	114
Cumberland	NW	9	3	1	1	3	1	20	24	105
Durham	*NW	9	4	3	–	2	–	18	21	103
Cambridgeshire	NW	9	4	–	–	5	–	14	20	98
Norfolk	NW	9	3	3	–	2	1	22	21	96
Northumberland	NW	9	2	3	–	3	1	8	25	70
Lincolnshire		9	1	2	1	5	–	19	18	61
Hertfordshire		9	1	2	–	4	2	20	12	58
Suffolk		9	1	4	–	4	–	14	21	51
Bedfordshire		9	–	6	–	2	1	7	12	24
WESTERN DIVISION										
Oxfordshire	NW	9	3	–	1	3	2	15	19	100
Buckinghamshire	NW	9	3	1	1	3	1	15	22	98
Cheshire	NW	9	3	1	–	5	–	20	27	95
Devon	NW	9	3	2	–	2	2	20	15	93
Berkshire	NW	9	2	1	–	6	–	21	21	74
Dorset	NW	9	2	3	–	3	1	9	21	67
Shropshire	NW	9	2	1	–	6	–	11	22	65
Cornwall		9	1	4	2	1	1	5	18	60
Wiltshire		9	1	3	–	3	2	11	16	53
Wales		9	–	4	–	4	1	17	23	45

NW signifies qualification for the 1992 NatWest Trophy.
* Durham qualify in their own right as a first-class county.

Where points are equal, priority is given to the County winning the greater number of completed matches. Where this number also is equal, priority is decided according to the nett batting averages.

1991 CHAMPIONSHIP FINAL

Played at Wardown Park, Luton on 8 September.
Toss: Staffordshire. Result: STAFFORDSHIRE won by 10 wickets.

OXFORDSHIRE

			WKT	FALL
J.S.Hartley	b Hackett	4	1	5
†S.N.V.Waterton	c Humphries b Spiers	32	2	96
*P.J.Garner	c Hackett b Blank	75	3	138
T.A.Lester	c Humphries b Blank	23	4	151
P.M.Jobson	c Dean b Newman	14	5	176
G.P.Savin	c Humphries b Dutton	13	6	176
R.J.Cunliffe	c Humphries b Dutton	0	7	185
D.A.Hale	not out	13	8	215
K.A.Arnold	c and b Newman	15	9	–
R.A.Evans	} did not bat		10	–
I.J.Curtis				
Extras	(LB13, W12, NB1)	26		
Total	(55 overs; 8 wickets)	**215**		

STAFFORDSHIRE

			WKT	FALL
S.J.Dean	not out	117	1	–
D.Cartledge	not out	83	2	–
A.D.Hobson			3	–
D.A.Banks			4	–
A.J.Dutton			5	–
*N.J.Archer			6	–
P.G.Newman	} did not bat		7	–
†M.I.Humphries			8	–
R.A.Spiers			9	–
D.C.Blank			10	–
N.Hackett				
Extras	(B4, LB7, W4, NB1)	16		
Total	(37.5 overs; 0 wickets)	**216**		

STAFFS	O	M	R	W	OXON	O	M	R	W
Newman	11	1	33	2	Arnold	9	1	55	0
Hackett	11	0	43	1	Hale	5	0	20	0
Blank	11	0	40	2	Curtis	9	0	72	0
Spiers	11	0	35	1	Savin	2	0	19	0
Dutton	9	0	41	2	Evans	10.5	3	28	0
Cartledge	2	0	10	0	Hartley	2	0	11	0

Umpires: P. Adams and K. Bray.

P.J. Garner batted 154 mins, 126 balls, 7 fours
S.J. Dean batted 141 mins, 133 balls, 2 sixes, 13 fours
D. Cartledge batted 141 mins, 99 balls, 11 fours

MINOR COUNTIES CHAMPIONS

1895 {	Norfolk	1926	Durham	
	Durham	1927	Staffordshire	
	Worcestershire	1928	Berkshire	
1896	Worcestershire	1929	Oxfordshire	
1897	Worcestershire	1930	Durham	
1898	Worcestershire	1931	Leicestershire II	
1899 {	Northamptonshire	1932	Buckinghamshire	
	Buckinghamshire	1933	Undecided	
1900 {	Glamorgan	1934	Lancashire II	
	Durham	1935	Middlesex II	
	Northamptonshire	1936	Hertfordshire	
1901	Durham	1937	Lancashire II	
1902	Wiltshire	1938	Buckinghamshire	
1903	Northamptonshire	1939	Surrey II	
1904	Northamptonshire	1946	Suffolk	
1905	Norfolk	1947	Yorkshire II	
1906	Staffordshire	1948	Lancashire II	
1907	Lancashire II	1949	Lancashire II	
1908	Staffordshire	1950	Surrey II	
1909	Wiltshire	1951	Kent II	
1910	Norfolk	1952	Buckinghamshire	
1911	Staffordshire	1953	Berkshire	
1912	In abeyance	1954	Surrey II	
1913	Norfolk	1955	Surrey II	
1920	Staffordshire	1956	Kent II	
1921	Staffordshire	1957	Yorkshire II	
1922	Buckinghamshire	1958	Yorkshire II	
1923	Buckinghamshire	1959	Warwickshire II	
1924	Berkshire	1960	Lancashire II	
1925	Buckinghamshire	1961	Somerset II	

1962	Warwickshire II
1963	Cambridgeshire
1964	Lancashire II
1965	Somerset II
1966	Lincolnshire
1967	Cheshire
1968	Yorkshire II
1969	Buckinghamshire
1970	Bedfordshire
1971	Yorkshire II
1972	Bedfordshire
1973	Shropshire
1974	Oxfordshire
1975	Hertfordshire
1976	Durham
1977	Suffolk
1978	Devon
1979	Suffolk
1980	Durham
1981	Durham
1982	Oxfordshire
1983	Hertfordshire
1984	Durham
1985	Cheshire
1986	Cumberland
1987	Buckinghamshire
1988	Cheshire
1989	Oxfordshire
1990	Hertfordshire
1991	Staffordshire

1991 MINOR COUNTIES CHAMPIONSHIP

LEADING BATTING AVERAGES
(Qualifications: 8 innings, average 40.00)

		I	NO	HS	Runs	Avge
S.G.Plumb	Norfolk	16	5	150*	992	90.18
G.P.Savin	Oxon	10	7	62*	263	87.66
G.Miller	Cheshire	13	8	79*	355	71.00
A.J.Pugh	Devon	14	4	97*	646	64.60
A.Needham	Herts	10	3	84*	451	64.42
L.K.Smith	Wiltshire	14	2	200*	730	60.83
P.Burn	Durham	8	2	71	357	59.50
D.B.Storer	Lincs	16	3	112	747	57.46
S.C.Ecclestone	Cambs	9	4	72	286	57.20
A.J.Dutton	Staffs	10	4	63	336	56.00
D.W.Varey	Cheshire	10	2	91	446	55.75
N.T.Gadsby	Cambs	18	3	131	831	55.40
M.P.Briers	Durham	14	3	90	582	52.90
G.W.Cook	Durham	13	6	67*	366	52.28
S.M.Dutton	Cumberland	16	4	101*	625	52.08
G.E.Loveday	Berkshire	18	2	113*	820	51.25

		I	NO	HS	Runs	Avge
N.R.C.MacLaurin	Herts	12	2	89*	508	50.80
M.James	Herts	12	0	102	594	49.50
J.B.R.Jones	Shropshire	16	5	100*	540	49.09
R.I.Dawson	Devon	12	3	118	431	47.88
J.D.Love	Lincs	14	1	90	620	47.69
N.J.Adams	Cambs	16	4	91*	565	47.08
S.M.Clements	Suffolk	18	1	112	793	46.64
I.Cockbain	Cheshire	18	3	120	696	46.40
G.K.Brown	Durham	16	2	114*	633	45.21
S.J.Dean	Staffs	16	1	134*	678	45.20
M.D.Dale	Herts	10	6	40*	177	44.25
A.W.Harris	Wales	12	1	82	485	44.09
T.Parton	Shropshire	15	4	78	483	43.90
A.D.Hobson	Staffs	15	4	120*	481	43.72
N.A.Folland	Devon	14	1	95	565	43.46
R.J.Finney	Norfolk	15	4	101*	476	43.27
J.H.Edwards	Devon	11	2	92*	386	42.88
E.Nicolson	Cornwall	16	0	93	677	42.31
S.T.Crawley	Cheshire	18	0	104	761	42.27
S.N.V.Waterton	Oxon	14	2	100*	502	41.83
N.G.Folland	Beds	12	3	71	376	41.77
S.M.Willis	Devon	8	0	100	331	41.37
B.G.Evans	Herts	13	3	106*	407	40.70
D.R.Turner	Wiltshire	12	2	103*	406	40.60
M.J.Roberts	Bucks	16	2	113	565	40.35
R.Swann	Beds	15	1	130*	564	40.28
D.Cartledge	Staffs	14	0	109	562	40.14
M.L.Simmons	Berkshire	13	3	93*	520	40.00

LEADING BOWLING AVERAGES

(Qualifications: 20 wickets, average 30.00)

		O	M	R	W	Avge
A.Smith	Wales	170.5	53	423	23	18.39
P.J.Lewington	Berkshire	304	107	656	35	18.74
B.W.Reidy	Cumberland	153	48	437	23	19.00
S.Burrow	Bucks	159	42	421	22	19.13
D.A.Toseland	Cornwall	230	49	647	33	19.60
P.C.Graham	N'land	189.1	47	561	28	20.03
T.J.A.Scriven	Bucks	230.2	57	664	33	20.12
G.Edmunds	Shropshire	279.2	90	667	33	20.21
S.Greensword	N'land	176.3	50	487	24	20.29
S.Turner	Cambs	253	69	647	31	20.87
R.A.Evans	Oxon	217.2	61	565	27	20.92
P.A.Waterman	Herts	105.2	17	435	20	21.75
K.Donohue	Devon	170.4	40	442	20	22.10
A.P.Pridgeon	Shropshire	260.4	62	670	29	23.10
G.W.White	Devon	121.1	14	471	20	23.55
Ajaz Akhtar	Cambs	244.4	58	735	31	23.70
D.J.B.Hartley	Berkshire	125.5	16	511	21	24.33
G.G.Watts	Cornwall	204.2	49	658	27	24.37
J.P.Addison	Staffs	162	22	616	25	24.64
A.K.Golding	Suffolk	265.1	50	858	34	25.23
K.A.Arnold	Oxon	179.5	37	505	20	25.25
M.P.Briers	Durham	136	18	510	20	25.50

		O	M	R	W	Avge
N.P.Hackett	Staffs	205.4	52	658	25	26.32
P.D.McKeown	Lincs	202	40	694	26	26.69
G.Miller	Cheshire	337.2	82	996	37	26.91
N.D.Peel	Cheshire	254.4	49	862	32	26.93
M.D.Woods	Cumberland	182.2	40	598	22	27.18
R.Kingshott	Norfolk	280.3	79	827	30	27.56
G.S.Calway	Dorset	176	29	586	21	27.90
D.J.Makinson	Cumberland	243.1	58	698	25	27.92
S.J.E.Brown	Durham	185.2	38	574	20	28.70

SECOND XI CHAMPIONSHIP 1991
RAPID CRICKETLINE FINAL TABLE

		P	W	L	D	Bonus Bat	Points Bowl	Total Points
1	YORKSHIRE (17)	16	8	1	7	38	36	202
2	Warwickshire (7)	16	7	1	8	45	43	196
3	Somerset (15)	16	6	4	6	36	47	179
4	Hampshire (11)	16	5	–	11	44	40	164
5	Nottinghamshire (4)	16	5	2	9	38	33	151
6	Surrey (3)	16	4	4	8	33	46	143
7	Sussex (1)	16	4	3	9	37	41	142
8	Derbyshire (13)	16	3	5	8	34	50	132
9	Worcestershire (10)	16	3	5	8	36	45	129
10	Leicestershire (16)	16	3	6	7	34	41	123
11 {	Lancashire (8)	16	2	3	11	39	40	111
{	Middlesex (6)	16	2	4	10	36	43	111
13	Glamorgan (2)	16	2	2	12	36	40	108
14	Kent (5)	16	1	3	12	48	37	101
15	Essex (9)	16	1	6	9	34	37	87
16	Gloucestershire (14)	16	1	4	11	25	37	78
17	Northamptonshire (12)	16	–	4	12	33	39	72

Win = 16 points.
1990 final positions are shown in brackets.

RAPID CRICKETLINE CHAMPIONSHIP PLAYER OF THE SEASON:
A.R.Caddick (Somerset)

SECOND XI CHAMPIONS

1959	Gloucestershire	1970	Kent	1981	Hampshire
1960	Northamptonshire	1971	Hampshire	1982	Worcestershire
1961	Kent	1972	Nottinghamshire	1983	Leicestershire
1962	Worcestershire	1973	Essex	1984	Yorkshire
1963	Worcestershire	1974	Middlesex	1985	Nottinghamshire
1964	Lancashire	1975	Surrey	1986	Lancashire
1965	Glamorgan	1976	Kent	1987	Kent/Yorkshire
1966	Surrey	1977	Yorkshire	1988	Surrey
1967	Hampshire	1978	Sussex	1989	Middlesex
1968	Surrey	1979	Warwickshire	1990	Sussex
1969	Kent	1980	Glamorgan	1991	Yorkshire

CRICKET WORLD

SUBSCRIPTION OFFER

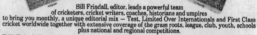

THE FIRST-CLASS COUNTIES
HONOURS, REGISTER, RECORDS
AND 1991 AVERAGES

Records are complete to the end of the 1991 English season (26 September).

ABBREVIATIONS

General

*	not out/unbroken partnership	f-c	first-class
b	born	HS	Highest Score
BB	Best innings bowling analysis	LOI	Limited-Overs Internationals
Cap	Awarded 1st XI County Cap	Tests	Official Test Matches
Tours	Overseas tours involving first-class appearances		

Awards

BHC	Benson and Hedges Cup 'Gold' Award
NWT	NatWest Trophy/Gillette Cup 'Man of the Match' Award
Wisden 1991	One of Wisden Cricketers' Almanack's Five Cricketers of 1991
YC 1991	Cricket Writers' Club Young Cricketer of 1991

Competitions

BHC	Benson and Hedges Cup
GC	Gillette Cup
NWT	NatWest Trophy
SL	Sunday League

Playing Categories

LB	Bowls right-arm leg-breaks
LF	Bowls left-arm fast
LFM	Bowls left-arm fast-medium
LHB	Bats left-handed
LM	Bowls left-arm medium pace
LMF	Bowls left-arm medium-fast
OB	Bowls right-arm off-breaks
RHB	Bats right-handed
RM	Bowls right-arm medium pace
RMF	Bowls right-arm medium-fast
RF	Bowls right-arm fast
RFM	Bowls right-arm fast-medium
RSM	Bowls right-arm slow-medium
SLA	Bowls left-arm slow-medium
WK	Wicket-keeper

Education

BHS	Boys' High School
BS	Boys' School
C	College
CE	College of Education
CFE	College of Further Education
CHE	College of Higher Education
CS	Comprehensive School
GS	Grammar School
HS	High School
IHE	Institute of Higher Education
LSE	London School of Economics
RGS	Royal Grammar School
S	School
SFC	Sixth Form College
SM	Secondary Modern School
SS	Secondary School
TC	Technical College
T(H)S	Technical (High) School
U	University

Teams (see also p 164)

Cav	Cavaliers	NSW	New South Wales
CD	Central Districts	OFS	Orange Free State
DHR	D.H.Robins' XI	PIA	Pakistan International Airlines
Eng Co	English Counties XI	RW	Rest of the World XI
EP	Eastern Province	SAB	South African Breweries XI
Int XI	International XI	SAU	South African Universities
IW	International Wanderers	Zim	Zimbabwe (Rhodesia)

DERBYSHIRE

Formation of Present Club: 4 November 1870
Colours: Chocolate, Amber and Pale Blue
Badge: Rose and Crown
Championships: (1) 1936
NatWest Trophy/Gillette Cup Winners: (1) 1981
Benson and Hedges Cup Winners: (0) Finalists 1978, 1988
Sunday League Champions: (1) 1990
Match Awards: NWT 29; BHC 50

Chief Executive: R.J.Lark, County Cricket Ground, Nottingham Road, Derby
DE2 6DA (☎ 0332-383211)
Captain: K.J.Barnett
Scorer: S.W.Tacey
1992 Beneficiary: K.J.Barnett

ADAMS, Christopher John (Repton S), b Whitwell, 6 May 1970. 6'0". RHB, OB.
Debut 1988. HS 134 v CU (Cambridge) 1991. BAC HS 112 v Yorks (Chesterfield)
1991. BB 4-29 v Lancs (Derby) 1991. **NWT:** HS 0. **BHC:** HS 44 Minor C (Wellington)
1990. **SL:** HS 71 v Lancs (Derby) 1991.

BARNETT, Kim John (Leek HS), b Stoke-on-Trent, Staffs 17 Jul 1960. 6'1". RHB,
LB. Debut 1979. Cap 1982. Captain 1983–. Boland 1982-88. Staffordshire 1976.
Wisden 1988. Benefit 1992. **Tests:** 4 (1988 to 1989); HS 80 v A (Leeds) 1989. LOI: 1.
Tours: SA 1989-90 (Eng XI); NZ 1979-80 (DHR); SL 1985-86 (Eng B). 1000 runs
(9); most – 1734 (1984). HS 239* v Leics (Leicester) 1988. BB 6-28 v Glam
(Chesterfield) 1991. Awards: NWT 2; BHC 9. **NWT:** HS 88 v Middx (Derby) 1983.
BB 6-24 v Cumberland (Kendal) 1984. **BHC:** HS 115 v Glos (Derby) 1987. BB 1-10.
SL: HS 131* v Essex (Derby) 1984. BB 3-39 v Yorks (Chesterfield) 1979.

BASE, Simon John (Fish Hoek HS, Cape Town), b Maidstone, Kent 2 Jan 1960. 6'2".
RHB, RMF. W Province 1981-84. Glamorgan 1986-87. Boland 1987-89. Border
1989-91. Derbyshire debut 1988. Cap 1990. HS 58 v Yorks (Chesterfield) 1990. 50 wkts
(1): 60 (1989). BB 7-60 v Yorks (Chesterfield) 1989. **NWT:** HS 4. BB 2-49 Gm v Sussex
(Hove) 1986. **BHC:** HS 15* v Somerset (Taunton) 1990. BB 3-33 v Minor C (Wellington)
1990. **SL:** HS 19 Gm v Kent (Swansea) 1987. BB 4-14 v Northants (Derby) 1991.

BISHOP, Ian Raphael (Belmont SS), b Port-of-Spain, Trinidad 24 Oct 1967.
Nephew of R.J. (Trinidad 1986-87). 6'5". RHB, RF. Trinidad 1986-91. Derbyshire
debut 1990. Cap 1990. **Tests** (WI): 11 (1988-89 to 1990-91); HS 30* v I (P-of-S); BB
6-87 v I (Bridgetown). LOI (WI): 29. Tours (WI): E 1988; A 1988-89; P 1990-91. HS
103* v Yorks (Scarborough) 1990. 50 wkts (1): 59 (1990). BB 6-39 WI v Kent
(Canterbury) 1988. De BB 6-67 v Leics (Leicester) 1989. **SL:** HS 16* and BB 1-51 v
Worcs (Worcester) 1989.

BOWLER, Peter Duncan (Educated at Canberra, Australia), b Plymouth, Devon 30
Jul 1963. 6'1". RHB, OB. Leicestershire 1986 – first to score hundred on f-c debut for
Leics (100* and 62 v Hants). Tasmania 1986-87. Derbyshire debut 1988 scoring 155*
v CU at Cambridge – first to score hundreds on debut for two counties. Cap 1989.
1000 runs (4); most – 1725 (1988). HS 210 v Kent (Chesterfield) 1990. BB 4-41 v Leics
(Leicester) 1991. Award: BHC 1. **NWT:** HS 46 v Cheshire (Chester) 1988. **BHC:** HS
109 v Somerset (Taunton) 1990. BB 1-15. **SL:** HS 77 v Leics (Leicester) 1991. BB
3-31 v Glos (Cheltenham) 1991.

BROWN, Andrew Mark (Aldercar CS; SE Derbyshire C), b Heanor 6 Nov 1964.
5'9". LHB, OB. Debut 1985 – no appearances 1987-88. HS 139* v Northants
(Chesterfield) 1990. **SL:** HS 2*.

64

CORK, Dominic Gerald (St Joseph's C, Stoke-on-Trent), b Newcastle-under-Lyme, Staffs 7 Aug 1971. 6'2". RHB, RFM. Debut 1990. Staffs 1989-90. HS 44 v Notts (Derby) 1991. 50 wkts (1): 57 (1991). BB 8-53 (before lunch on his 20th birthday) v Essex (Derby) 1991. **SL:** HS 30 v Warwks (Birmingham) 1991. BB 3-45 v Surrey (Chesterfield) 1991.

GOLDSMITH, Steven Clive (Simon Langton GS, Canterbury), b Ashford, Kent 19 Dec 1964. 5'10". RHB, RM. Kent 1987. Derbyshire debut 1988. 1000 runs (1): 1071 (1988). HS 127 v SL (Derby) 1991. BAC HS 89 v Kent (Chesterfield) 1988. BB 3-42 v Yorks (Scarborough) 1991. Award: BHC 1. **NWT:** HS 21 and BB 1-20 v Lancs (Derby) 1990. **BHC:** HS 45* and BB 3-38 v Minor C (Wellington) 1990. **SL:** HS 67* v Glos (Cheltenham) 1991. BB 3-48 v Surrey (Chesterfield) 1991.

GRIFFITH, Frank Alexander (Beaconsfield HS; Wm Morris HS; Haringey Cricket C), b Whipps Cross, Essex 15 Aug 1968. 6'0". RHB, RM. Debut 1988. HS 37 v Northants (Northampton) 1988. BB 4-47 v Lancs (Manchester) 1988. **BHC:** HS 10 v Notts (Nottingham) 1989. **SL:** HS 20 v Northants (Derby) 1991. BB 3-37 v Somerset (Derby) 1991.

JEAN-JACQUES, Martin (Aylestone SS, London), b Soufriere, Dominica 2 Jul 1960. 6'0". RHB, RMF. Debut 1986. Buckinghamshire 1983-85. HS 73 v Yorks (Sheffield) 1986 (on debut, sharing Derbys record 10th-wkt stand of 132 with A.Hill). BB 8-77 v Kent (Derby) 1986. **NWT:** HS 16 v Surrey (Derby) 1986. BB 3-23 v Cambs (Wisbech) 1987. **BHC:** HS 2*. BB 3-22 v Notts (Nottingham) 1987. **SL:** HS 23 v Lancs (Derby) 1991. BB 3-36 v Worcs (Worcester) 1986.

KRIKKEN, Karl Matthew (Rivington & Blackrod HS & SFC), b Bolton, Lancs 9 Apr 1969. Son of B.E. (Lancs and Worcs 1966-69). 5'9". RHB, WK. GW 1988-89. Derbyshire debut 1989. HS 77* v Somerset (Taunton) 1990. **SL:** HS 44* v Essex (Chelmsford) 1991.

MAHER, Bernard Joseph Michael (Abbotsfield CS; Bishopshalt GS; Loughborough U), b Hillingdon, Middx 11 Feb 1958. 5'10". RHB, WK. Derbyshire 1981-91 (cap 1987). HS 126 v NZ (Derby) 1986. BAC HS 121* v Leics (Derby) 1988. BB 2-69 v Glam (Abergavenny) 1986. **NWT:** HS 44 v Hants (Derby) 1988. **BHC:** HS 50 v Northants (Derby) 1987. **SL:** HS 78 v Lancs (Manchester) 1987.

MALCOLM, Devon Eugene (Richmond C, Sheffield), b Kingston, Jamaica 22 Feb 1963. 6'2". RHB, RF. Debut 1984. Cap 1989. **Tests:** 18 (1989 to 1991); HS 15* v I (Oval) 1990; BB 6-77 v WI (P-of-S) 1989-90. LOI: 4. Tours: A 1990-91; WI 1989-90. HS 51 v Surrey (Derby) 1989. 50 wkts (2); most – 56 (1988). BB 7-74 v Australian XI (Hobart) 1990-91. De BB 6-68 v Warwks (Derby) 1988. Award: BHC 1. **NWT:** HS 6. BB 3-54 v Lancs (Derby) 1990. **BHC:** HS 15 v Comb Us (Oxford) 1991. BB 5-27 v Middx (Derby) 1988. **SL:** HS 18 v Essex (Chelmsford) 1991. BB 4-21 v Surrey 1989 and v Leics 1990.

MORRIS, John Edward (Shavington CS; Dane Bank CFE), b Crewe, Cheshire 1 Apr 1964. 5'10". RHB, RM. Debut 1982. Cap 1986. GW 1988-89. **Tests:** 3 (1990); HS 32 v I (Oval) 1990. LOI: 8. Tour: A 1990-91. 1000 runs (6); most – 1739 (1986). HS 191 v Kent (Derby) 1986. BB 1-13. Award: NWT 1. **NWT:** HS 94* v Salop (Chesterfield) 1990. **BHC:** HS 123 v Somerset (Taunton) 1990. **SL:** HS 134 v Somerset (Taunton) 1990.

MORTENSEN, Ole Henrek (Brondbyoster S; Abedore C, Copenhagen), b Vejle, Denmark 29 Jan 1958. 6'3". RHB, RFM. Debut 1983. Cap 1986. Denmark 1975-82. HS 74* v Yorks (Chesterfield) 1987. 50 wkts (2); most – 58 (1991). BB 6-27 v Yorks (Sheffield) 1983. Hat-trick 1987. Awards: NWT 2. **NWT:** HS 11 v Surrey (Derby) 1986. BB 6-14 v Ire (Derby) 1989. **BHC:** HS 4*. BB 3-17 v Leics (Chesterfield) 1986. **SL:** HS 11 v Worcs (Worcester) 1989. BB 4-10 v Leics (Chesterfield) 1985.

O'GORMAN, Timothy Joseph Gerard (St George's C, Weybridge; Durham U), b Woking, Surrey 15 May 1967. Grandson of J.G. (Surrey 1927). 6'2". RHB, OB. Debut 1987. Comb US (BHC) 1988-89. HS 148 v Lancs (Manchester) 1991. 1000 runs (1): 1116 (1991). BB 1-17. **BHC:** HS 49 v Northants (Derby) 1991. **SL:** HS 49* v Surrey (Chesterfield) 1991.

SLADDIN, Richard William (Sowerby Bridge HS), b Halifax, Yorks 8 Jan 1969. 6'0". RHB, SLA. Debut 1991. HS 18 and BB 5-186 v Essex (Chelmsford) 1991.

WARNER, Allan Esmond (Tabernacle S, St Kitts), b Birmingham 12 May 1957. 5'7". RHB, RFM. Worcestershire 1982-84. Derbyshire debut 1985. Cap 1987. HS 91 v Leics (Chesterfield) 1986. BB 5-27 Wo v Glam (Worcester) 1984. De BB 5-51 v Essex (Colchester) 1985. Award: NWT 1. **NWT:** HS 32 v Kent (Canterbury) 1987. BB 4-39 v Salop (Chesterfield) 1990. **BHC:** HS 35* v Comb Us (Oxford) 1991. BB 4-36 v Notts (Nottingham) 1987. **SL:** HS 68 v Hants (Heanor) 1986. BB 5-39 v Worcs (Knypersley) 1985.

NEWCOMERS

RICHARDSON, Alastair William (Oundle S; Durham U), b Derby 23 Oct 1972. Son of G.W. (Derbys 1959-65); grandson of A.W. (Derbys 1928-36). 6'3". RHB, RFM.

TWEATS, Timothy Andrew (Endon HS; Stoke-on-Trent SFC), b Stoke-on-Trent, Staffs 18 Apr 1974. 6'3". RHB, RM.

WHITAKER, Paul Robert (Whitcliffe Mount S), b Keighley, Yorks 28 Jun 1973. 5'9". LHB, OB.

DEPARTURES

AZHARUDDIN, Mohammed (Nizam C; Osmania U), b Hyderabad, India 8 Feb 1963. 5'11". RHB, LB. Hyderabad 1981-91. Derbyshire 1991 (cap 1991). Wisden 1990. **Tests** (I): 41 (1984-85 to 1990-91, 7 as captain); HS 199 v SL (Kanpur) 1986-87. LOI (I): 112. Tours (I) (C=captain): E 1986, 1990C; A 1985-86; WI 1988-89; NZ 1989-90C; P 1989-90; SL 1985-86; Z 1983-84 (Young Ind). 1000 runs (1+2) inc 2000 (1): 2016 (1991). HS 226 S Zone v C Zone (Jamadoba) 1983-84. De HS 212 v Leics (Leicester) 1991. BB 2-33 Hyderabad v Andhra (Hyderabad) 1987-88. De BB 1-35. **BHC: HS 44* v Comb Us (Oxford) 1991.** BB 1-17. **SL:** HS 73 v Kent (Canterbury) 1991.

FOLLEY, Ian (Mansfield HS; Colne C), b Burnley, Lancs 9 Jan 1963. 5'9½". RHB, SLA. Lancashire 1982-90 (cap 1987). Derbyshire 1991. Tours: WI 1986-87 (Lancs); Z 1988-89 (Lancs). HS 69 La v Yorks (Manchester) 1985. De HS 17* v Kent (Canterbury) 1991. 50 wkts (2); most – 74 (1987). BB 7-15 (12-57 match) v Warwks (Southport) 1987. De BB 1-60. **NWT:** HS 3*. BB 2-10 La v Durham (Chester-le-St) 1983. **BHC:** HS 11* La v Notts (Nottingham) 1987. BB 4-18 La v Middx (Lord's) 1982. **SL:** HS 19 La v Northants (Tring) 1987. BB 3-23 La v Glos (Manchester) 1987.

McCRAY, Ewan (Poundswick HS), b Altrincham, Cheshire 29 Oct 1964. 6'1". RHB, OB. Derbyshire 1991. Cheshire 1989-90. HS 37 v Glos (Gloucester) 1991. **SL:** HS 18 v Northants (Derby) 1991. BB 4-49 v Glam (Checkley) 1991.

ROBERTS, Bruce (Peterhouse; Prince Edward S, Salisbury), b Lusaka, N Rhodesia 30 May 1962. 6'2". RHB, RM, WK. Transvaal 1982-89. Derbyshire 1984-91 (cap 1986). 1000 runs (3); most – 1643 (1987). HS 184 v Sussex (Chesterfield) 1987. BB 5-68 Transvaal B v N Transvaal B (Johannesburg) 1986-87. BAC BB 4-77 v Essex (Ilford) 1984. Awards: BHC 2. **NWT:** HS 64* v Worcs (Worcester) 1989. BB 2-73 v Leics (Leicester) 1984. **BHC:** HS 100 v Northants (Derby) 1987. BB 2-47 v Minor C (Shrewsbury) 1984. **SL:** HS 101* v Sussex (Hove) 1987. BB 4-29 v Lancs (Derby) 1984.

DERBYSHIRE 1991

RESULTS SUMMARY

	Place	Won	Lost	Drew
Britannic Assurance Championship	3rd	9	5	8
All First-class Matches		9	5	11
Refuge Assurance League	15th	5	11	
NatWest Trophy	1st Round			
Benson and Hedges Cup	3rd in Group A			

BRITANNIC ASSURANCE CHAMPIONSHIP AVERAGES
BATTING AND FIELDING

Cap		M	I	NO	HS	Runs	Avge	100	50	Ct/St
1991	M.Azharuddin	20	35	3	212	1773	55.40	6	9	23
1986	J.E.Morris	20	35	2	122*	1267	38.39	1	8	7
1982	K.J.Barnett	21	36	1	217	1318	37.65	2	8	23
1989	P.D.Bowler	22	40	3	104*	1270	34.32	2	9	15
–	T.J.G.O'Gorman	22	39	4	148	1060	30.28	2	4	21
–	C.J.Adams	12	19	2	112	436	25.64	1	–	15
–	K.M.Krikken	22	35	8	65	677	25.07	–	2	55/3
–	S.C.Goldsmith	15	25	3	73*	483	21.95	–	2	8
–	D.G.Cork	16	25	7	44	395	21.94	–	–	8
1987	A.E.Warner	14	20	3	46	289	17.00	–	–	3
–	R.W.Sladdin	7	8	3	18	68	13.60	–	–	6
1990	S.J.Base	13	16	3	36	136	10.46	–	–	14
1989	D.E.Malcolm	11	14	2	18	84	7.00	–	–	3
–	I.Folley	3	4	1	17*	20	6.66	–	–	2
–	M.Jean-Jacques	4	6	1	28*	33	6.60	–	–	–
1986	O.H.Mortensen	18	16	9	8	32	4.57	–	–	4

Also played (1 match each): F.A.Griffith 1; E.McCray 37 (1 ct).

BOWLING

	O	M	R	W	Avge	Best	5wI	10wM
O.H.Mortensen	535.1	138	1339	58	23.08	6-101	2	–
K.J.Barnett	162.1	33	393	17	23.11	6-28	1	–
D.G.Cork	457.3	76	1350	55	24.54	8-53	1	1
D.E.Malcolm	346.2	51	1271	39	32.58	5-45	1	–
S.C.Goldsmith	174	28	576	17	33.88	3-42	–	–
R.W.Sladdin	315.5	76	881	26	33.88	5-186	1	–
A.E.Warner	390.4	92	1066	31	34.38	4-42	–	–
S.J.Base	386	58	1248	31	40.25	4-34	–	–

Also bowled: C.J.Adams 12.4-1-48-5; M.Azharuddin 63.4-9-211-3; P.D.Bowler 104-18-412-9; I.Folley 106-12-350-2; F.A.Griffith 15-2-58-2; M.Jean-Jacques 113.4-18-437-9; E.McCray 25-10-53-0; J.E.Morris 2-0-30-0; T.J.G.O'Gorman 15-0-59-1.

The First-Class Averages (pp 164-179) give the records of Derbyshire players in all first-class county matches (their other opponents being the West Indians, the Sri Lankans and Cambridge U.), with the exception of D.E.Malcolm, whose full county figures are as above.

DERBYSHIRE RECORDS

FIRST-CLASS CRICKET

Highest Total	For	645		v Hampshire	Derby	1898
	V	662		by Yorkshire	Chesterfield	1898
Lowest Total	For	16		v Notts	Nottingham	1879
	V	23		by Hampshire	Burton upon T	1958
Highest Innings	For	274	G.A.Davidson	v Lancashire	Manchester	1896
	V	343*	P.A.Perrin	for Essex	Chesterfield	1904

Highest Partnership for each Wicket

1st	322	H.Storer/J.Bowden	v Essex	Derby	1929
2nd	349	C.S.Elliott/J.D.Eggar	v Notts	Nottingham	1947
3rd	291	P.N.Kirsten/D.S.Steele	v Somerset	Taunton	1981
4th	328	P.Vaulkhard/D.Smith	v Notts	Nottingham	1946
5th	203	C.P.Wilkins/I.R.Buxton	v Lancashire	Manchester	1971
6th	212	G.M.Lee/T.S.Worthington	v Essex	Chesterfield	1932
7th	241*	G.H.Pope/A.E.G.Rhodes	v Hampshire	Portsmouth	1948
8th	182	A.H.M.Jackson/W.Carter	v Leics	Leicester	1922
9th	283	A.Warren/J.Chapman	v Warwicks	Blackwell	1910
10th	132	A.Hill/M.Jean-Jacques	v Yorkshire	Sheffield	1986

Best Bowling	For	10-40	W.Bestwick	v Glamorgan	Cardiff	1921
(Innings)	V	10-47	T.F.Smailes	for Yorkshire	Sheffield	1939
Best Bowling	For	17-103	W.Mycroft	v Hampshire	Southampton	1876
(Match)	V	16-101	G.Giffen	for Australians	Derby	1886

Most Runs – Season	2,165	D.B.Carr	(av 48.11)	1959
Most Runs – Career	20,516	D.Smith	(av 31.41)	1927-1952
Most 100s – Season	8	P.N.Kirsten		1982
Most 100s – Career	34	K.J.Barnett		1979-1991
Most Wkts – Season	168	T.B.Mitchell	(av 19.55)	1935
Most Wkts – Career	1,670	H.L.Jackson	(av 17.11)	1947-1963

LIMITED-OVERS CRICKET

Highest Total	NWT	365-3		v Cornwall	Derby	1986
	BHC	366-4		v Comb Univs	Oxford	1991
	SL	292-9		v Worcs	Knypersley	1985
Lowest Total	NWT	79		v Surrey	The Oval	1967
	BHC	102		v Yorkshire	Bradford	1975
	SL	61		v Hampshire	Portsmouth	1990
Highest Innings	NWT	153	A.Hill	v Cornwall	Derby	1986
	BHC	123	J.E.Morris	v Somerset	Taunton	1990
	SL	134	J.E.Morris	v Somerset	Taunton	1990
Best Bowling	NWT	8-21	M.A.Holding	v Sussex	Hove	1988
	BHC	6-33	E.J.Barlow	v Glos	Bristol	1978
	SL	6-7	M.Hendrick	v Notts	Nottingham	1972

DURHAM

Formation of Present Club: 10 May 1882
Colours: Navy blue, yellow and maroon
Badge: Coat of Arms of the County of Durham
NatWest Trophy/Gillette Cup Winners: (0) Second round
1964, 1972, 1973, 1974, 1979, 1985
Match Awards: NWT 13

Chief Executive: M.E.Gear, McEwans Indoor Cricket Centre, Mercantile Road,
Rainton Bridge, Houghton-le-Spring, DH4 5PH. (☎ 091-512 0178)
Captain: D.A.Graveney
Scorer: B.Hunt

BAINBRIDGE, Philip (Hanley HS; Stoke-on-Trent SFC, Borough Road CE), b
Sneyd Green, Stoke-on-Trent, Staffs 16 Apr 1958. 5'10". RHB, RM. Gloucester-
shire 1977-90 (cap 1981; benefit 1989). Wisden 1985. Tours: SL 1986-87 (Glos); Z
1984-85 (EC). 1000 runs (8); most – 1644 (1985). HS 169 Gs v Yorks (Cheltenham)
1988. BB 8-53 Gs v Somerset (Bristol) 1986. Awards: NWT 1; BHC 2. NWT: HS 89
Gs v Leics (Leicester) 1988. BB 3-49 Gs v Scot (Bristol) 1983. BHC: HS 96 Gs v
Hants (Southampton) 1988. BB 3-21 Gs v Notts (Gloucester) 1981. SL: HS 106* Gs v
Somerset (Bristol) 1986. BB 5-22 Gs v Middx (Lord's) 1987.

BERRY, Philip John (Saltscar CS; Longlands CFE, Redcar), b Saltburn, Yorks 28
Dec 1966. 6'0". RHB, OB. Yorkshire 1986-90. HS 31* Y v Northants (Leeds) 1990.
BB 2-35 Y v CU (Cambridge) 1988. BAC BB 1-10.

BLENKIRON, Darren Andrew (Bishop Barrington CS, Bishop Auckland), b
Solihull, Warwks 4 Feb 1974. 5'10". Son of W. (Warwks 1964-74, Durham 1975-76).
LHB, RM. Awaiting f-c debut. NWT: HS 56 v Glam (Darlington) 1991.

BOTHAM, Ian Terence (Buckler's Mead SS, Yeovil), b Heswall, Cheshire 24 Nov
1955. 6'1". RHB, RM. Somerset 1974-86 (cap 1976; captain 1984-85; benefit 1984).
Worcestershire 1987-91 (cap 1987). Queensland 1987-88. Wisden 1977. YC 1977.
MCC Cricket Staff. Tests: 99 (1977 to 1991, 12 as captain). HS 208 v I (Oval) 1982;
BB 8-34 v P (Lord's) 1978. LOI: 99. Tours: A 1978-79, 1979-80, 1982-83, 1986-87; WI
1980-81 (capt), 1985-86; NZ 1977-78, 1983-84; I 1979-80, 1981-82; P 1977-78, 1983-
84; SL 1981-82; Z 1990-91 (Wo). 1000 runs (4); most – 1530 (1985). Hit 80 sixes 1985
(f-c record). HS 228 Sm v Glos (Taunton) 1980. Wo HS 161 v WI (Worcester) 1991.
Shared in 2 Somerset record stands: 310 (4th) with P.W.Denning and 172 (8th) with
I.V.A.Richards. 50 wkts (8) inc 100 wkts (1): 100 (1978). BB 8-34 (Tests). Wo BB
7-54 v Warwks (Worcester) 1991. Hat-trick 1978 (MCC). Awards: NWT 4; BHC 9.
NWT: HS 101 Wo v Devon (Worcester) 1987. BB 5-51 Wo v Lancs (Worcester)
1989. BHC: HS 138* Wo v Glos (Bristol) 1990. BB 5-41 Wo v Yorks (Worcester)
1988. SL: HS 175* Sm v Northants (Wellingborough) 1986. BB 5-27 Wo v Glos
(Gloucester) 1987.

BRIERS, Mark Paul, b Kegworth, Leics 21 Apr 1968. RHB, LB. Worcestershire
staff 1988. Awaiting f-c debut.

BROWN, Gary Kevin (Chace S, Enfield), b Welling, Kent 16 Jun 1965. Brother of
K.R. (Middlesex). 5'11". RHB, RM. Middlesex 1986 (1 match). HS 103 and BB 1-39
Minor C v Indians (Trowbridge) 1990. NWT: HS 42 v Lancs (Manchester) 1990.
BHC: HS 82 Minor C v Hants (Trowbridge) 1991.

BROWN, Simon John Emmerson (Boldon CS), b Cleadon 29 Jun 1969. 6'3". RHB, LFM. Northamptonshire 1987-90. HS 25* Nh v Glos (Northampton) 1988. BB 3-20 Nh v OU (Oxford) 1988. BAC BB 2-11 Nh v Glam (Swansea) 1987. **NWT:** HS 7*. BB 1-73. **SL:** HS 3*. BB 3-26 Nh v Leics (Leicester) 1990.

DALEY, James Arthur (Hetton CS), b Sunderland 24 Sep 1973. 5'10". RHB, RM. Awaiting f-c debut.

FOTHERGILL, Andrew Robert (Eastbourne CS), b Newcastle upon Tyne, Northumb 10 Feb 1962. 6'0". RHB, WK. Minor Co 1990. HS 3 Minor C v Indians (Trowbridge) 1990. **NWT:** HS 24 v Glam (Darlington) 1991. **BHC:** HS 45* Minor C v Somerset (Taunton) 1990.

GLENDENEN, John David (Ormesby SS), b Middlesbrough, Yorks 20 Jun 1965. 6'0". RHB, RM. Scored 200* for Durham v Victoria (Durham) 1991 (not f-c). Awaiting f-c debut. **NWT:** HS 109 v Glam (Darlington) 1991 – first 100 by Durham batsmen in NWT/GC.

GRAVENEY, David Anthony (Millfield S), b Bristol 2 Jan 1953. Son of J.K. (Glos 1947-64); nephew of T.W. (Glos, Worcs, Queensland and England 1948-72). 6'4". RHB, SLA. Gloucestershire 1972-90 (cap 1976; captain 1981-88; benefit 1986). Somerset 1991. Durham debut 1991-92. Captain 1992. Tours: SA 1989-90 (Eng XI – manager); SL 1986-87 (Glos – capt). HS 119 Gs v OU (Oxford) 1980. BAC HS 105* Gs v Northants (Bristol) 1981. 50 wkts (6); most – 73 (1976). BB 8-85 Gs v Notts (Cheltenham) 1974. Hat-trick 1983. Awards: NWT 2. **NWT:** HS 44 Gs v Surrey (Bristol) 1973. BB 5-11 Gs v Ire (Dublin) 1981. **BHC:** HS 49* Gs v Somerset (Taunton) 1982. BB 3-13 Gs v Scot (Glasgow) 1983. **SL:** HS 56* Gs v Notts (Bristol) 1985. BB 4-22 Gs v Hants (Lydney) 1974.

HENDERSON, Paul William (Billingham Campus S; Bede C); b Stockton-on-Tees 22 Oct 1974. 6'0". RHB, RFM. Awaiting f-c debut.

HUGHES, Simon Peter (Latymer Upper S, Hammersmith; Durham U), b Kingston upon Thames, Surrey 20 Dec 1959. 5'10". RHB, RFM. Middlesex 1980-91 (cap 1981; benefit 1991). N Transvaal 1982-83. Tours: I 1980-81 (Overseas XI); Z 1980-81 (Middx). HS 53 M v CU (Cambridge) 1988. BAC HS 47 M v Warwks (Uxbridge) 1986. 50 wkts (2); most – 63 (1986). BB 7-35 M v Surrey (Oval) 1986. Award: NWT 1. **NWT:** HS 11 and BB 4-20 M v Durham (Darlington) 1989. **BHC:** HS 22 M v Somerset (Taunton) 1990. BB 4-34 M v Somerset (Lord's) 1987. **SL:** HS 18* M v Surrey (Lord's) 1985. BB 5-23 M v Worcs (Worcester) 1989.

HUTTON, Stewart (De Brus S, Skelton; Cleveland TC), b Stockton-on-Tees 30 Nov 1969. 5'11". LHB, RM. Awaiting f-c debut.

JONES, Dean Mervyn, b Coburg, Victoria, Australia 24 Mar 1961. RHB, OB. Victoria 1981-91. **Tests** (A): 44 (1983-84 to 1990-91); HS 216 v WI (Adelaide) 1988-89; BB 1-5. LOI (A): 115. Tours (A): E 1987 (RW); 1989, 1991 (Vic); WI 1983-84, 1990-91; NZ 1989-90; I 1986-87; P 1988-89; Z 1985-86 (Young A). 1000 runs (1+2); most – 1510 (1989). HS 248 A v Warwks (Birmingham) 1989. BB 1-0.

LARKINS, Wayne (Bushmead SS, Eaton Socon), b Roxton, Beds 22 Nov 1953. 5'11". RHB, RM. Northamptonshire 1972-91 (cap 1976; benefit 1986). E Province 1982-84. **Tests:** 13 (1979-80 to 1990-91); HS 64 v A (Melbourne) 1990-91. LOI: 25. Tours: A 1979-80, 1990-91; SA 1981-82 (SAB); WI 1989-90; I 1979-80, 1980-81 (Overseas XI). 1000 runs (11); most – 1863 (1982). HS 252 Nh v Glam (Cardiff) 1983. BB 5-59 Nh v Worcs (Worcester) 1984. Awards: NWT 2; BHC 5. **NWT:** HS 121* Nh v Essex (Chelmsford) 1987. BB 2-38 Nh v Glos (Bristol) 1985. **BHC:** HS 132 Nh v

LARKINS – continued:
Warwks (Birmingham) 1982. BB 4-37 Nh v Comb Us (Northampton) 1980. **SL:** HS 172* Nh v Warwks (Luton) 1983. BB 5-32 Nh v Essex (Ilford) 1978.

McEWAN, Steven Michael (Worcester RGS), b Worcester 5 May 1962. 6'1". RHB, RFM. Worcestershire 1985-90 (cap 1989). HS 54 Wo v Yorks (Worcester) 1990. 50 wkts (1): 52 (1989). BB 6-34 Wo v Leics (Kidderminster) 1989. Hat-trick 1990. **NWT:** HS 6 and BB 3-51 Wo v Warwks (Birmingham) 1989. **BHC:** BB 2-53 Wo v Notts (Nottingham) 1990. **SL:** HS 18* Wo v Yorks (Worcester) 1990. BB 4-35 Wo v Derbys (Worcester) 1986.

PARKER, Paul William Giles (Collyer's GS; St Catharine's C, Cambridge), b Bulawayo, Rhodesia 15 Jan 1956. 5'10". RHB, RM. Cambridge U 1976-78 (blue 1976-77-78). Sussex 1976-91 (cap 1979; captain 1988-91; benefit 1988). YC 1979. **Tests:** 1 (1981); HS 13 v A (Oval) 1981. 1000 runs (8); most – 1692 (1984). HS 215 CU v Essex (Cambridge) 1976. Sx HS 181 v SL (Hove) 1981. BAC HS 140 Sx v Glos (Hove) 1984. BB 2-21 Sx v Surrey (Guildford) 1984. Awards: NWT 4; BHC 5. **NWT:** HS 109 Sx v Ire (Hove) 1985. BB 1-10. **BHC:** HS 87 Sx v Leics (Hove) 1991. BB 2-3 Sx v Minor C (Hove) 1987. **SL:** HS 121* Sx v Northants (Hastings) 1983. BB 1-2.

SCOTT, Christopher Wilmot (Robert Pattinson CS), b Thorpe-on-the-Hill, Lincs 23 Jan 1964. 5'8". RHB, WK. Nottinghamshire 1981-91 (cap 1988). HS 78 Nt v CU (Cambridge) 1983. BAC HS 69* Nt v Warwks (Nottingham) 1986. Held 10 catches for Notts in match v Derbys (Derby) 1988. **BHC:** HS 18 Nt v Northants (Northampton) 1988. **SL:** HS 26 Nt v Yorks (Nottingham) 1987.

SMITH, Ian (Ryton CS), b Chopwell 11 Mar 1967. 6'2". RHB, RM. Glamorgan 1985-91. Tour: Z 1990-91 (Gm). HS 116 Gm v Kent (Canterbury) 1989. BB 3-48 Gm v Hants (Cardiff) 1989. **NWT:** HS 33 Gm v Hants (Cardiff) 1989. BB 3-60 Gm v Durham (Darlington) 1991. **BHC:** HS 51 Gm v Hants (Southampton) 1991. BB 1-21. **SL:** HS 56* Gm v Warwks (Aberystwyth) 1989. BB 3-22 Gm v Hants (Cardiff) 1989.

WIGHAM, Gary (Barrington CS, Bishop Auckland), b Bishop Auckland 2 Mar 1973. 6'7". RHB, RMF. MCC Cricket Staff 1991. Awaiting f-c debut.

WOOD, John (Crofton HS; Wakefield District C; Leeds Poly), b Wakefield, Yorks 22 Jul 1970. 6'2¾". RHB, RFM. GW in Nissan Shield 1990-91. Awaiting f-c debut.

· DURHAM RECORDS

LIMITED-OVERS CRICKET

Highest Total	NWT	305-9		v	Glamorgan	Darlington	1991
Lowest Total	NWT	82		v	Worcs	Chester-le-St	1968
Highest Innings	NWT	109	J.D.Glendenen	v	Glamorgan	Darlington	1991
Best Bowling	NWT	7-32	S.P.Davis	v	Lancashire	Chester-le-St	1983

ESSEX

Formation of Present Club: 14 January 1876
Colours: Blue, Gold and Red
Badge: Three Seaxes above Scroll bearing 'Essex'
Championships: (5) 1979, 1983, 1984, 1986, 1991
NatWest Trophy/Gillette Cup Winners: (1) 1985
Benson and Hedges Cup Winners: (1) 1979
Sunday League Champions: (3) 1981, 1984, 1985
Match Awards: NWT 32; BHC 68

Secretary/General Manager: P.J.Edwards, County Cricket Ground, New Writtle Street, Chelmsford CM2 0PG (☎ 0245-252420)
Captain: G.A.Gooch
Scorer: C.F.Driver
1992 Beneficiary: D.R.Pringle

ANDREW, Stephen Jon Walter (Milton Abbey S; Portchester SS), b London 27 Jan 1966. 6'3". RHB, RMF. Hampshire 1984-89. Essex debut 1990. HS 35 v Northants (Chelmsford) 1990. BB 7-92 H v Glos (Southampton) 1987. Ex BB 5-55 v Yorks (Middlesbrough) 1990. Awards: BHC 2. **NWT:** HS 0*. BB 2-34 v Scot (Chelmsford) 1990. **BHC:** HS 4*. BB 5-24 H v Essex (Chelmsford) 1987. **SL:** HS 8. BB 4-50 H v Middx (Southampton) 1988.

BODEN, David Jonathan Peter (Alleynes HS, Stone; Stafford CFE), b Eccleshall, Staffs 26 Nov 1970. 6'3". RHB, RMF. Middlesex 1989. HS -. BB 4-11 M v OU (Oxford) 1989 – on debut. Awaiting BAC and Essex debut – joined staff 1990.

BUTLER, Keith Andrew (Dagenham Priory CS), b Camden Town, London 20 Jan 1971. 5'8". RHB, RM. Debut 1989. HS 10* v CU (Cambridge) 1989. Awaiting BAC debut. **SL:** HS 1.

CHILDS, John Henry (Audley Park SM, Torquay), b Plymouth, Devon 15 Aug 1951. 6'0". LHB, SLA. Gloucestershire 1975-84 (cap 1977). Essex debut 1985. Cap 1986. Devon 1973-74. Wisden 1986. **Tests:** 2 (1988); HS 2*; BB 1-13. HS 41* v Middx (Lord's) 1991. 50 wkts (6); most – 89 (1986). BB 9-56 Gs v Somerset (Bristol) 1981. Ex BB 8-58 v Glos (Colchester) 1986. Awards: BHC 1. **NWT:** HS 14* Gs v Hants (Bristol) 1983. BB 2-15 Gs v Ire (Dublin) 1981. **BHC:** HS 10 Gs v Somerset (Bristol) 1979. BB 3-36 Gs v Glam (Bristol) 1982. **SL:** HS 16* Gs v Warwks (Bristol) 1981. BB 4-15 Gs v Northants (Northampton) 1976.

FOSTER, Neil Alan (Philip Morant CS), b Colchester 6 May 1962. 6'3". RHB, RFM. Debut 1980. Cap 1983. YC 1983. Wisden 1987. **Tests:** 28 (1983 to 1989); HS 39 v P (Lahore) 1987-88 and v A (Manchester) 1989; BB 8-107 v P (Leeds) 1987. LOI: 48. Tours: A 1986-87, 1987-88; SA 1989-90 (Eng XI); WI 1985-86; NZ 1983-84, 1987-88; I/SL 1984-85; P 1983-84, 1987-88. HS 107* v Sussex (Horsham) 1991. 50 wkts (9) inc 100 wkts (2); most – 105 (1986). BB 8-99 v Lancs (Manchester) 1991. Awards: NWT 1; BHC 3. **NWT:** HS 26 v Worcs (Chelmsford) 1987. BB 4-9 v Northumb (Jesmond) 1987. **BHC:** HS 39* v Middx (Chelmsford) 1991. BB 5-32 v Surrey (Oval) 1985. **SL:** HS 57 v Northants (Northampton) 1991. BB 5-17 v Derbys (Derby) 1986.

FRASER, Alastair Gregory Gardner (Gayton HS, John Lyon S, Harrow; Harrow Weald SFC), b Edgware, Middx 17 Oct 1967. Brother of A.R.C. (Middlesex and England). 6'1". RHB, RFM. Middlesex 1986-89. Essex debut 1991. HS 52* v Sussex (Horsham) 1991. BB 3-46 M v NZ (Lord's) 1986. BAC BB 2-12 M v Lancs (Lord's) 1986. **SL:** HS 2*. BB 1-19.

GARNHAM, Michael Anthony (Camberwell GS, Melbourne; Scotch C, Perth; Barnstaple GS; N Devon SFC; East Anglia U), b Johannesburg, SA 20 Aug 1960. 5'10". RHB, WK. Gloucestershire 1979. Leicestershire 1980-85 and 1988. Essex debut 1989. Cap 1990. Cambridgeshire 1986-88. HS 123 v Leics (Leicester) 1991. Shared Essex record stand of 316 for 5th wkt with N.Hussain v Leics (Leicester) 1991. Awards: NWT 1; BHC 1. **NWT:** HS 110 Cambs v Warwks (Birmingham) 1988. **BHC:** HS 55 Le v Derbys (Leicester) 1982. **SL:** HS 79* Le v Lancs (Leicester) 1982.

GOOCH, Graham Alan (Norlington Jr HS), b Leytonstone 23 Jul 1953. 6'0". RHB, RM. Debut 1973. Cap 1975. Captain 1986-87, 1989-. Benefit 1985. W Province 1982-84. Wisden 1979. OBE 1991. **Tests:** 91 (1975 to 1991, 20 as captain); HS 333 and record match aggregate of 456 v I (Lord's) 1990; BB 2-12 v I (Delhi) 1981-82. LOI: 96. Tours (C=captain): A 1978-79, 1979-80, 1990-91C; SA 1981-82 (SAB); WI 1980-81, 1985-86, 1989-90C; I 1979-80, 1981-82; P 1987-88; SL 1981-82. 1000 runs (15+1) inc 2000 runs (4); most – 2746 (1990). HS 333 (Tests). Ex HS 275 v Kent (Chelmsford) 1988. Shared Essex record stand of 403 for 2nd wkt with P.J.Prichard v Leics (Chelmsford) 1990. BB 7-14 v Worcs (Ilford) 1982. Awards: NWT 8 (equal record); BHC 19 (record). **NWT:** HS 144 v Hants (Chelmsford) 1990. BB 3-31 v Warwks (B'ham) 1986. **BHC:** HS 198* v Sussex (Hove) 1982. BB 3-24 v Sussex (Hove) 1982. **SL:** HS 176 v Glam (Southend) 1983. BB 4-33 v Worcs (Chelmsford) 1984.

HUSSAIN, Nasser (Forest S, Snaresbrook; Durham U), b Madras, India 28 Mar 1968. Brother of M. (Worcs 1985). 5'11". RHB, LB. Debut 1987. Cap 1989. Comb Us (BHC) 1987-89. YC 1989. **Tests:** 3 (1989-90); HS 35 v WI (St John's) 1989-90. LOI: 2. Tours: WI 1989-90; P 1990-91 (Eng A); SL 1990-91 (Eng A). 1000 runs (1): 1354 (1991). HS 197 v Surrey (Oval) 1990. Shared in 2 record Essex stands 1991: 314 (4th) Salim Malik and 316 (5th) M.A.Garnham. Award: BHC 1. **NWT:** HS 97 v Sussex (Hove) 1991. **BHC:** HS 118 Comb Us v Somerset (Taunton) 1989. **SL:** HS 66* v Yorks (Middlesbrough) 1990.

ILOTT, Mark Christopher (Francis Combe S, Garston), b Watford, Herts 27 Aug 1970. 6'0½". LHB, LMF. Debut 1988. Hertfordshire 1987-88. Tour: SL 1990-91 (Eng A). HS 42* v Kent (Chelmsford) 1990. BB 5-34 v Derbys (Derby) 1990. **NWT:** BB 1-45. **BHC:** BB 3-34 v Surrey (Oval) 1991. **SL:** HS 6 and BB 2-24 v Yorks (Middlesbrough) 1990.

KNIGHT, Nicholas Verity (Felsted S; Forest Court C, Loughborough U), b Watford, Herts 28 Nov 1969. 6'0". LHB. Debut 1991. Comb Us (BHC) 1990-91 (captain 1991). HS 101* v Lancs (Manchester) 1991. **BHC:** HS 36 v Glos (Bristol) 1991. **SL:** HS 31* v Northants (Northampton) 1991.

LEWIS, Jonathan James Benjamin (King Edward VI S, Chelmsford; Roehampton IHE), b Isleworth, Middx 21 May 1970. 5'9½". RHB, RSM. Debut 1990 scoring 116* v Surrey (Oval). HS 116* (above). **SL:** HS 19 v Lancs (Manchester) 1991.

PRICHARD, Paul John (Brentwood HS), b Billericay 7 Jan 1965. 5'10". RHB. Debut 1984. Cap 1986. 1000 runs (4); most – 1407 (1990). HS 245 v Leics (Chelmsford) 1990, sharing Essex record stand of 403 for 2nd wkt with G.A.Gooch. BB 1-28. Awards: BHC 2. **NWT:** HS 94 v Oxon (Chelmsford) 1985. **BHC:** HS 107 v Scot (Glasgow) 1990. **SL:** HS 103* v Lancs (Manchester) 1986.

PRINGLE, Derek Raymond (Felsted S; Fitzwilliam C, Cambridge), b Nairobi, Kenya 18 Sep 1958. Son of D.J. (East Africa). 6'4½". RHB, RMF. Debut 1978. Cap 1982. Benefit 1992. Cambridge U 1979-82 (blue 1979-80-81; capt 1982). **Tests:** 25 (1982 to 1991); HS 63 v I (Lord's) 1986; BB 5-95 v WI (Leeds) 1988. LOI: 29. Tours: A 1982-83; SL 1985-86 (Eng B); Z 1989-90 (Eng A). HS 128 v Kent (Chelmsford) 1988. 50 wkts (6); most – 94 (1989). BB 7-18 v Glam (Swansea) 1989. Awards: NWT 2; BHC 4. **NWT:** HS 80* v Wilts (Chelmsford) 1988. BB 5-12 v Oxon (Chelmsford) 1985. **BHC:** HS 77* v Scot (Glasgow) 1990. BB 5-35 v Lancs (Chelmsford) 1984. **SL:** HS 81* v Warwks (Birmingham) 1985. BB 5-41 v Glos (Southend) 1985.

SHAHID, Nadeem (Ipswich S), b Karachi, Pakistan 23 Apr 1969. 6'0". RHB, LB. Debut 1989. Suffolk 1988. 1000 runs (1): 1003 (1990). HS 125 v Lancs (Colchester) 1990. BB 3-91 v Surrey (Oval) 1990. **BHC:** HS 42 v Hants (Chelmsford) 1991. **SL:** HS 36 v Glos (Cheltenham) 1991.

STEPHENSON, John Patrick (Felsted S; Durham U), b Stebbing 14 Mar 1965. 6'1". RHB, RM. Debut 1985. Cap 1989. Comb Us (BHC) 1987. Boland 1988-89. **Tests:** 1 (1989); HS 25 v A (Oval) 1989. Tour: Z 1989-90 (Eng A). 1000 runs (3); most – 1887 (1990). HS 202* v Somerset (Bath) 1990. BB 4-30 v CU (Cambridge) 1991. BAC BB 3-20 v Notts (Nottingham) 1991. Awards: BHC 2. **NWT:** HS 59 v Surrey (Oval) 1991. BB 1-24. **BHC:** HS 142 v Warwks (Birmingham) 1991. BB 3-22 v Northants (Northampton) 1990. **SL:** HS 109 v Lancs (Colchester) 1990. BB 4-17 v Warwks (Chelmsford) 1991.

SUCH, Peter Mark (Harry Carlton CS, Ex Leake, Notts), b Helensburgh, Dunbartonshire 12 Jun 1964. 5'11". RHB, OB. Nottinghamshire 1982-86. Leicestershire 1987-89. Essex debut 1990. Cap 1991. HS 27 v Middx (Ilford) 1990. BB 6-123 Nt v Kent (Nottingham) 1983. Ex BB 3-7 v Victoria (Chelmsford) 1991. **NWT:** HS 0*. BB 2-29 v Devon (Exmouth) 1991. **BHC:** HS 4. BB 3-50 Nt v Scot (Glasgow) 1985. **SL:** HS 8*. BB 4-30 v Derbys (Chelmsford) 1991.

TOPLEY, Thomas Donald (Royal Hospital S, Holbrook, Suffolk), b Canterbury, Kent 25 Feb 1964. Brother of P.A. (Kent 1972-75). 6'3". RHB, RMF. Surrey (v CU) and Essex debuts 1985. Cap 1988. GW 1987-88. Norfolk 1984-85. MCC Cricket Staff. HS 66 v Yorks (Leeds) 1987. 50 wkts (3); most – 77 (1989). BB 7-75 v Derbys (Chesterfield) 1988. Awards: NWT 1; BHC 2. **NWT:** HS 15* v Worcs (Chelmsford) 1987. BB 4-21 v Northumb (Jesmond) 1987. **BHC:** HS 10* v Notts (Chelmsford) 1990. BB 4-22 v Surrey (Chelmsford) 1988. **SL:** HS 38* v Lancs (Manchester) 1991. BB 6-33 v Notts (Colchester) 1988.

WAUGH, Mark Edward (E Hills, HS), b Canterbury, Sydney, Australia 2 Jun 1965. Younger twin of S.R. (NSW, Somerset and Australia). 6'1". RHB, RM. NSW 1985-91. Essex 1988-90 (cap 1989). Wisden 1990. **Tests** (A): 7 (1990-91); HS 139* v WI (St John's) 1990-91; BB 4-80 v WI (Bridgetown) 1990-91. LOI (A): 23. Tours (A): WI 1990-91; Z 1985-86 (Young A), 1987-88 (NSW). 1000 runs (2+2) inc 2000 (1): 2072 (1990). HS 229* NSW v WA (Perth) 1990-91, sharing Australian record stand of 464* for 5th wkt with S.R.Waugh. Ex HS 207* v Yorks (Middlesbrough) 1990. BB 5-37 v Northants (Chelmsford) 1990. Award: BHC 1. **NWT:** HS 47 v Hants (Chelmsford) 1990. **BHC:** HS 93 v Lancs (Chelmsford) 1989. BB 1-25. **SL:** HS 112* v Glam (Neath) 1989. BB 3-37 v Yorks (Middlesbrough) 1990.

NEWCOMERS

COUSINS, Darren Mark (Netherhall CS; Impington Village C), b Cambridge 24 Sep 1971. 6'2". RHB, RMF. Cambridgeshire 1990.

LOVELL, William Guy (Millom CS), b Whitehaven, Cumberland 16 Feb 1969. RHB, SLA. MCC Cricket Staff. Awaiting f-c debut. SL debut 1991.

RICHARDS, Alexander Charles (Forest S; Durham U), b Ilford 13 Sep 1971. 5'11". RHB, OB.

ROBINSON, Darren David John (Tabor HS, Braintree; Chelmsford CFE), b Braintree 2 Mar 1973. 5'10". RHB, RMF.

ROLLINS, Robert John (Little Ilford S), b Plaistow 30 Jan 1974. RHB, WK.

TENNANT, Lloyd (Shelfield CS), b Walsall, Staffs 9 Apr 1968. 5'11". RHB, RMF. Leicestershire 1986-91. HS 23* Le v Sussex (Hove) 1991. BB 4-54 Le v CU (Cambridge) 1991. BAC BB 3-65 Le v Notts (Nottingham) 1991. **SL:** HS 17* Le v Somerset (Leicester) 1988. BB 3-25 Le v Somerset (Leicester) 1986.

DEPARTURES – see p 153

ESSEX 1991

RESULTS SUMMARY

	Place	Won	Lost	Tied	Drew	Abandoned
Britannic Assurance Championship	1st	11	5		6	
All First-class Matches		12	5		8	
Refuge Assurance League	6th	7	4	1		4
NatWest Trophy	Quarter-Finalist					
Benson and Hedges Cup	Semi-Finalist					

BRITANNIC ASSURANCE CHAMPIONSHIP AVERAGES
BATTING AND FIELDING

Cap		M	I	NO	HS	Runs	Avge	100	50	Ct/St
1991	Salim Malik	22	33	9	215	1891	78.79	6	8	22
1975	G.A.Gooch	11	16	1	259	996	66.40	3	3	11
1982	D.R.Pringle	12	11	6	78*	328	65.60	–	2	4
1989	N.Hussain	22	29	7	196	1233	56.04	3	8	34
–	N.V.Knight	6	9	1	101*	388	48.50	1	2	5
1990	M.A.Garnham	22	25	6	123	831	43.73	2	5	58
1986	P.J.Prichard	21	33	5	190	1031	36.82	4	2	17
1989	J.P.Stephenson	22	36	2	116	1234	36.29	3	6	7
–	A.C.H.Seymour	9	16	1	157	454	30.26	1	2	7
1983	N.A.Foster	20	20	4	107*	474	29.62	1	1	11
1991	P.M.Such	11	5	4	23*	27	27.00	–	–	1
1988	T.D.Topley	19	19	4	50*	320	21.33	–	2	14
1986	J.H.Childs	20	13	6	41*	111	15.85	–	–	5
–	N.Shahid	7	8	1	22*	64	9.14	–	–	5
–	S.J.W.Andrew	14	8	2	13	30	5.00	–	–	4

Also played: A.G.J.Fraser (3 matches) 52*, 23; J.J.B.Lewis (1 match) 48 (1 ct).

BOWLING

	O	M	R	W	Avge	Best	5wI	10wM
N.A.Foster	693.5	163	2000	91	21.97	8-99	7	1
J.P.Stephenson	77.4	14	296	12	24.66	3-20	–	–
J.H.Childs	667.1	218	1702	58	29.34	6-61	4	–
D.R.Pringle	359.4	96	887	30	29.56	5-70	1	–
S.J.W.Andrew	366.3	72	1211	40	30.27	4-38	–	–
Salim Malik	118.2	10	473	15	31.53	3-26	–	–
P.M.Such	290	75	743	23	32.30	3-23	–	–
T.D.Topley	484.3	83	1720	53	32.45	5-58	3	–

Also bowled: A.G.J.Fraser 19-5-44-0; M.A.Garnham 4-0-39-0; G.A.Gooch 42.1-17-155-4; N.Hussain 8.3-0-50-0; N.V.Knight 5-0-32-0; P.J.Prichard 13.3-0-158-1; A.C.H.Seymour 4-0-27-0.

The First-Class Averages (pp 164-179) give the records of Essex players in all first-class county matches (their other opponents being the West Indians, Victoria and Cambridge U.), with the exception of:

G.A.Gooch 14-20-3-259-1219-71.70-4-4-16ct. 55.1-11-201-4-50.25-2/16.
N.Hussain 24-32-7-196-1307-52.28-3-8-37ct. 8.3-0-50-0.
D.R.Pringle 15-14-7-78*-479-68.42-0-4-8ct. 405.4-113-986-35-28.17-5/70-1-0.

ESSEX RECORDS

FIRST-CLASS CRICKET

Highest Total	For	761-6d	v	Leics	Chelmsford	1990
	V	803-4d	by Kent		Brentwood	1934
Lowest Total	For	30	v	Yorkshire	Leyton	1901
	V	14	by Surrey		Chelmsford	1983
Highest Innings	For	343* P.A.Perrin	v	Derbyshire	Chesterfield	1904
	V	332 W.H.Ashdown	for Kent		Brentwood	1934

Highest Partnership for each Wicket

1st	270	A.V.Avery/T.C.Dodds	v	Surrey	The Oval	1946
2nd	403	G.A.Gooch/P.J.Prichard	v	Leics	Chelmsford	1990
3rd	343	P.A.Gibb/R.Horsfall	v	Kent	Blackheath	1951
4th	314	Salim Malik/N.Hussain	v	Surrey	The Oval	1991
5th	316	N.Hussain/M.A.Garnham	v	Leics	Leicester	1991
6th	206	J.W.H.T.Douglas/J.O'Connor	v	Glos	Cheltenham	1923
	206	B.R.Knight/R.A.G.Luckin	v	Middlesex	Brentwood	1962
7th	261	J.W.H.T.Douglas/J.Freeman	v	Lancashire	Leyton	1914
8th	263	D.R.Wilcox/R.M.Taylor	v	Warwicks	Southend	1946
9th	251	J.W.H.T.Douglas/S.N.Hare	v	Derbyshire	Leyton	1921
10th	218	F.H.Vigar/T.P.B.Smith	v	Derbyshire	Chesterfield	1947

Best Bowling	For	10-32 H.Pickett	v	Leics	Leyton	1895
(Innings)	V	10-40 E.G.Dennett	for Glos		Bristol	1906
Best Bowling	For	17-119 W.Mead	v	Hampshire	Southampton	1895
(Match)	V	17-56 C.W.L.Parker	for Glos		Gloucester	1925

Most Runs – Season	2,559	G.A.Gooch	(av 67.34)	1984
Most Runs – Career	29,434	K.W.R.Fletcher	(av 36.88)	1962-1988
Most 100s – Season	9	J.O'Connor		1934
	9	D.J.Insole		1955
Most 100s – Career	71	J.O'Connor		1921-1939
Most Wkts – Season	172	T.P.B.Smith	(av 27.13)	1947
Most Wkts – Career	1,610	T.P.B.Smith	(av 26.68)	1929-1951

LIMITED-OVERS CRICKET

Highest Total	NWT	386-5	v	Wiltshire	Chelmsford	1988
	BHC	350-3	v	Comb Univs	Chelmsford	1979
	SL	310-5	v	Glamorgan	Southend	1983
Lowest Total	NWT	100	v	Derbyshire	Brentwood	1965
	BHC	100	v	Hampshire	Chelmsford	1987
	SL	69	v	Derbyshire	Chesterfield	1974
Highest Innings	NWT	144 G.A.Gooch	v	Hampshire	Chelmsford	1990
	BHC	198* G.A.Gooch	v	Sussex	Hove	1982
	SL	176 G.A.Gooch	v	Glamorgan	Southend	1983
Best Bowling	NWT	5-8 J.K.Lever	v	Middlesex	Westcliff	1972
	BHC	5-13 J.K.Lever	v	Middlesex	Lord's	1985
	SL	8-26 K.D.Boyce	v	Lancashire	Manchester	1971

GLAMORGAN

Formation of Present Club: 6 July 1888
Colours: Blue and Gold
Badge: Gold Daffodil
Championships: (2) 1948, 1969
NatWest Trophy/Gillette Cup Winners: (0) Finalists 1977
Benson and Hedges Cup Winners: (0) Semi-Finalists 1988
Sunday League Champions: (0) Fifth 1988
Match Awards: NWT 26; BHC 40

Secretary: G.R.Stone, Sophia Gardens, Cardiff, CF1 9XR (☎ 0222-343478)
Captain: A.R.Butcher
Scorer: B.T.Denning

BARWICK, Stephen Royston (Cwrt Sart CS; Dwr-y-Felin CS), b Neath 6 Sep 1960. 6'2". RHB, RMF. Debut 1981. Cap 1987. HS 30 v Hants (Bournemouth) 1988. 50 wkts (2); most – 64 (1989). BB 8-42 v Worcs (Worcester) 1983. Awards: BHC 1. **NWT:** HS 6. BB 4-14 v Hants (Bournemouth) 1981. **BHC:** HS 18 v Kent (Canterbury) 1984. BB 4-11 v Minor C (Swansea) 1985. **SL:** HS 48* v Worcs (Worcester) 1989. BB 4-23 v Yorks (Cardiff) 1987.

BASTIEN, Steven (St Bonaventure S, Forest Gate; Haringey Cricket C), b Stepney, London 13 Mar 1963 (of Dominican parents). 6'1". RHB, RMF. Debut 1988. Tour: Z 1990-91 (Gm). HS 36* v Warwks (Birmingham) 1988 (his first innings). BB 6-75 v Worcs (Worcester) 1990. **BHC:** HS 7. **SL:** HS 1. BB 2-42 v Kent (Maidstone) 1991.

BUTCHER, Alan Raymond (Heath Clark GS), b Croydon, Surrey 7 Jan 1954. Brother of I.P. (Leics 1980-87 and Glos 1988-90) and M.S. (Surrey 1982). 5'8½". LHB, SLA/LM. Surrey 1972-86 (cap 1975; benefit 1985). Glamorgan debut/cap 1987. Captain 1989-. Wisden 1990. **Tests:** 1 (1979); HS 20 v I (Oval) 1979. LOI: 1. Tours: WI 1982-83 (Int); I 1980-81 (Overseas XI); Z 1990-91 (Gm – captain). 1000 runs (12) inc 2000 (1): 2116 (1990). HS 216* Sy v CU (Cambridge) 1980. BAC HS 188 Sy v Sussex (Hove) 1978. Gm HS 171* v Warwks (Birmingham) 1989. BB 6-48 Sy v Hants (Guildford) 1972. Gm BB 3-35 v Middx (Cardiff) 1987. Awards: NWT 3; BHC 6. **NWT:** HS 104* v Middx (Lord's) 1990. BB 1-27. **BHC:** HS 127 v Yorks (Cardiff) 1991. BB 4-36 Sy v Middx (Lord's) 1985. **SL:** HS 113* Sy v Warwks (Birmingham) 1978. BB 5-19 Sy v Glos (Bristol) 1975.

COTTEY, Phillip Anthony (Bishopston CS, Swansea), b Swansea 2 Jun 1966. 5'4". RHB, OB. Debut 1986. Tour: Z 1990-91 (Gm). 1000 runs (1): 1001 (1990). HS 156 v OU (Oxford) 1990. BAC HS 125 v Leics (Hinckley) 1990. BB 1-49. **NWT:** HS 27 v Sussex (Cardiff) 1990. **BHC:** HS 68 v Hants (Southampton) 1989. **SL:** HS 92* v Hants (Ebbw Vale) 1991.

CROFT, Robert Damien Bale (St John Lloyd Catholic CS; W Glam IHE), b Morriston 25 May 1970. 5'10¾". RHB, OB. Debut 1989. Tour: Z 1990-91 (Gm). HS 91* v Worcs (Abergavenny) 1990. BB 5-62 v Warwks (Swansea) 1991. **NWT:** HS 26 v Middx (Lord's) 1990. BB 2-28 v Worcs (Worcester) 1991. **BHC:** HS 0. BB 2-49 v Minor C (Trowbridge) 1991. **SL:** HS 31 v Notts (Nottingham) 1990. BB 2-30 v Glos (Swansea) 1991.

DALE, Adrian (Chepstow CS; Swansea U), b Germiston, SA 24 Oct 1968 (to UK at 6 mths). 5'11¼". RHB, RM. Debut 1989. Comb Us (BHC) 1989-90. Tour: Z 1990-91 (Gm). HS 140 and BAC BB 2-33 v Glos (Abergavenny) 1991. BB 3-21 v I (Swansea) 1990. Award: NWT 1. **NWT:** HS 86 v Worcs (Worcester) 1991. BB 2-32 v Staffs (Cardiff) 1989. **BHC:** HS 40 Comb Us v Surrey (Oxford) 1990. BB 3-24 Comb Us v Surrey (Cambridge) 1989. **SL:** HS 67* v Derbys (Heanor) 1991. BB 3-35 v Worcs (Swansea) 1990.

FOSTER, Daren Joseph (Somerset S; Southgate TC; Haringey Cricket C), b Tottenham, London 14 Mar 1966. 5'9". RHB, RFM. Somerset 1986-89. Glamorgan debut 1991. HS 20 Sm v Hants (Southampton) 1988. Gm HS 13* v Derbys (Chesterfield) 1991. BB 6-84 v Somerset (Taunton) 1991. NWT: HS 0. BB 1-15. BHC: HS 0. BB 2-26 Sm v Yorks (Leeds) 1989. SL: HS 8*. BB 4-26 Sm v Glos (Bath) 1989.

FROST, Mark (Alexander HS, Tipton; St Peter's S, Wolverhampton; Durham U), b Barking, Essex 21 Oct 1962. 6'2". RHB, RMF. Surrey 1988-89. Glamorgan debut 1990. Cap 1991. Staffordshire 1987. Tour: Z 1990-91 (Gm). HS 12 v Warwks (Birmingham) 1990. 50 wkts (2); most – 65 (1991). BB 7-99 (11-143 match) v Glos (Cheltenham) 1991. Award: BHC 1. NWT: HS 3. BB 3-50 v Dorset (Swansea) 1990. BHC: HS 3. BB 4-25 v Worcs (Worcester) 1990. SL: HS 6. BB 4-30 v Northants (Northampton) 1990.

HEMP, David Lloyd (Olchfa CS; Millfield S; W Glamorgan C), b Bermuda 8 Nov 1970. UK resident since 1978. 6'0". LHB, RM. Debut 1991. Scored 4 successive hundreds for Wales U-19 1990. Scored 68 and 258* for Wales v MCC (High Wycombe) 1991. HS 8. SL: HS 7.

JAMES, Stephen Peter (Monmouth S; Swansea U; Hughes Hall, Cambridge), b Lydney, Glos 7 Sep 1967. 6'0". RHB. Debut 1985. Cambridge U 1989-90; blue 1989-90. Tour: Z 1990-91 (Gm). 1000 runs (1): 1000 (1990). HS 151* CU v Warwks (Cambridge) 1989. Gm HS 106 v OU (Oxford) 1987 – sharing Glam record stand of 249 for 2nd wkt with H.Morris. BAC HS 70 v Surrey (Oval) 1991. NWT: HS 26 v Cheshire (Cardiff) 1987. BHC: HS 65 Comb Us v Worcs (Worcester) 1989. SL: HS 23 v Glos (Swansea) 1991.

KIRNON, Samuel (Montserrat SS, West Indies), b Fulwood, Preston, Lancs 25 Dec 1962. 5'10". RHB, RMF. Awaiting f-c debut. SL: HS 0. BB 2-48 v Surrey (Oval) 1991.

MAYNARD, Matthew Peter (David Hughes S, Anglesey), b Oldham, Lancs 21 Mar 1966. 5'10½". RHB, RM. Debut 1985 scoring 102 out of 117 in 87 min v Yorks (Swansea), reaching 100 with 3 sixes off successive balls. Cap 1987. N Districts 1990-91. YC 1988. **Tests**: 1 (1988); HS 10 v WI (Oval) 1988. Tour: SA 1989-90 (Eng XI). 1000 runs (6); most – 1803 (1991). HS 243 v Hants (Southampton) 1991. BB 3-21 v OU (Oxford) 1987. BAC BB 1-25. Awards: NWT 1; BHC 4. NWT: HS 151* v Durham (Darlington) 1991. BHC: HS 115 v Comb Us (Cardiff) 1988. SL: HS 101 v Derbys (Checkley) 1991.

METSON, Colin Peter (Enfield GS; Stanborough S, Welwyn Garden City; Durham U), b Goffs Oak, Herts 2 Jul 1963. 5'5½". RHB, WK. Middlesex 1981-86. Glamorgan debut/cap 1987. HS 96 M v Glos (Uxbridge) 1984. Gm HS 84 v Kent (Maidstone) 1991. NWT: HS 9. BHC: HS 23 v Kent (Swansea) 1990. SL: HS 30* v Hants (Bournemouth) 1990.

MORRIS, Hugh (Blundell's S), b Cardiff 5 Oct 1963. 5'8". LHB, RM. Debut 1981. Cap 1986. Captain 1986-89. **Tests**: 3 (1991); HS 44 v WI (Oval) 1991. Tour: SL 1990-91 (Eng A). 1000 runs (5) inc 2000 (1): 2276 – inc 10 hundreds – both Gm records (1990). HS 160* v Derbys (Cardiff) 1990. Shared Glam record stand of 249 for 2nd wkt with S.P.James v OU (Oxford) 1987. BB 1-6. BAC BB 1-45. Awards: NWT 1; BHC 3. NWT: HS 154* v Staffs (Cardiff) 1989. BHC: HS 143* v Hants (Southampton) 1989. BB 1-14. SL: HS 100 v Derbys (Ebbw Vale) 1986.

RICHARDS, Isaac Vivian Alexander (Antigua GS), b St John's, Antigua 7 Mar 1952. 5'11". RHB, OB. Leeward Is 1971-91 (captain 1981-91). Somerset 1974-86 (cap 1974; benefit 1982). Glamorgan debut/cap 1990. Queensland 1976-77. Wisden 1976. **Tests** (WI): 121 (1974-75 to 1991, 50 as captain); HS 291 v E (Oval) 1976; BB 2-17 v P (P-of-S) 1987-88. LOI (WI): 187. Tours (WI) (C=captain): E 1976, 1980, 1984, 1988C, 1991C; A 1975-76, 1979-80, 1981-82, 1984-85, 1986-87C, 1988-89C; NZ 1986-87C; I 1974-75, 1983-84, 1987-88C; P 1974-75, 1980-81, 1986-87C; SL 1974-75. 1000 runs (13+3) inc 2000 (1): 2161 (1977). Only West Indian to score 100 f-c hundreds (111). HS 322 (Sm record) v Warwks (Taunton) 1985. Gm HS 164* v Hants (Southampton) 1990. Shared record Somerset stand of 172 for 8th wkt with I.T.Botham v Leics (Leicester) 1983. BB 5-88 WI v Queensland (Brisbane) 1981-82. BAC BB 4-36 Sm v Derbys (Chesterfield) 1986. Gm BB 2-27 v Sussex (Hove) 1990. Awards: NWT 6; BHC 6. **NWT:** HS 139* Sm v Warwks (Taunton) 1978. BB 3-15 Sm v Beds (Bedford) 1981. **BHC:** HS 132* Sm v Surrey (Lord's) 1981. BB 3-38 v Warwks (Birmingham) 1990. **SL:** HS 126* Sm v Glos (Bristol Imp) 1975. BB 6-24 Sm v Lancs (Manchester) 1983.

WATKIN, Steven Llewellyn (Cymer Afan CS; S Glamorgan CHE), b Maesteg 15 Sep 1964. 6'3". RHB, RMF. Debut 1986. Cap 1989. **Tests:** 2 (1991); HS 6; BB 3-38 v WI (Leeds) 1991 – on debut. Tours: P 1990-91 (Eng A); Z 1989-90 (Eng A), 1990-91 (Gm). HS 31 v Leics (Leicester) 1989. 50 wkts (3); most – 94 (1989). BB 8-59 v Warwks (Birmingham) 1988. **NWT:** HS 6*. BB 3-18 v Sussex (Cardiff) 1990. **BHC:** HS 15 v Hants (Southampton) 1991. BB 3-28 v Minor C (Trowbridge) 1991. **SL:** 31* v Derbys (Checkley) 1991. BB 5-23 v Warwks (Birmingham) 1990.

NEWCOMERS

COWDREY, Christopher Stuart (Tonbridge S), b Farnborough 20 Oct 1957. Brother of G.R., son of M.C. (Kent and England 1950-76), grandson of E.A. (Europeans). 6'1". RHB, RM. Kent 2nd XI debut when aged 15. Kent 1977-91 (cap 1979; captain 1985-90; benefit 1989). **Tests:** 6 (1984-85 to 1988, 1 as captain); HS 38 v I (Delhi) 1984-85; BB 2-65 v I (Madras) 1984-85. LOI: 3. Tours: SA 1989-90 (Eng XI); NZ 1979-80 (DHR); I/SL 1984-85; SL 1977-78 (DHR). 1000 runs (4); most – 1364 (1983). HS 159 K v Surrey (Canterbury) 1985. BB 5-46 K v Hants (Canterbury) 1988. Awards: NWT 3; BHC 7. **NWT:** HS 122* K v Essex (Chelmsford) 1983. BB 4-36 K v Hants (Canterbury) 1983. **BHC:** HS 114 K v Sussex (Canterbury) 1977. BB 4-14 K v Sussex (Canterbury) 1987. **SL:** HS 95 K v Worcs (Canterbury) 1983. BB 5-28 K v Leics (Canterbury) 1984.

SHAW, Adrian David (Neath Tertiary C), b Neath 17 Feb 1972. 5'11". RHB, WK. Wales 1990-91.

DEPARTURES

CANN, Michael James (St Illtyds C, Cardiff; Swansea U), b Cardiff 4 Jul 1965. 5'9". LHB, OB. Glamorgan 1986-91. Comb Us (BHC) 1987. OFS B 1989-90 (captain). GW 1990-91. HS 141 GW v Boland (Stellenbosch) 1990-91. Gm HS 109 v Somerset (Cardiff) 1988. BB 3-30 v Middx (Abergavenny) 1989. **NWT:** HS 2*. BB 3-40 v Staffs (Cardiff) 1989. **BHC:** HS 46 Comb Us v Somerset (Taunton) 1987. BB 1-1. **SL:** HS 5.

DAVIES, M. – see GLOUCESTERSHIRE.

DENNIS, Simon John (Scarborough C), b Scarborough, Yorks 18 Oct 1960. Nephew of F. (Yorkshire 1928-33) and Sir Leonard Hutton (Yorkshire and England 1934-55). 6'1". RHB, LFM. Yorkshire 1980-88 (cap 1983). Glamorgan 1989-91. OFS 1982-83. Tour: WI 1986-87 (Yorks). HS 53* Y v Notts (Nottingham) 1984. Gm HS 38 v Derbys (Derby) 1989. 50 wkts (1): 52 (1983). BB 5-35 Y v Somerset (Sheffield) 1981. Gm BB 5-76 v Leics (Cardiff) 1990. **NWT:** HS 14 Y v Salop (Telford) 1984. BB 2-45 Y v Northants (Leeds) 1983. **BHC:** HS 50 v Hants (Southampton) 1991. BB 3-41 Y v Northants (Bradford) 1984. **SL:** HS 16* (twice for Yorks). BB 3-19 Y v Hants (Middlesbrough) 1981.

Continued on p 153

GLAMORGAN 1991

	Place	Won	Lost	Drew	Abandoned
Britannic Assurance Championship	12th	5	5	12	
All First-class Matches		6	5	14	
Refuge Assurance League	15th	4	10		2
NatWest Trophy	Quarter-Finalist				
Benson and Hedges Cup	4th in Group D				

BRITANNIC ASSURANCE CHAMPIONSHIP AVERAGES
BATTING AND FIELDING

Cap		M	I	NO	HS	Runs	Avge	100	50	Ct/St
1986	H.Morris	17	30	7	156*	1601	69.60	5	8	13
1987	M.P.Maynard	20	32	5	243	1766	65.40	7	5	14
1988	R.J.Shastri	21	31	8	133*	1056	45.91	2	6	8
1987	A.R.Butcher	21	37	1	147	1558	43.27	4	12	13
–	A.Dale	15	23	3	140	711	35.55	1	3	7
–	S.P.James	10	17	3	70	429	30.64	–	2	8
1987	C.P.Metson	22	24	3	84	511	24.33	–	2	67/2
–	P.A.Cottey	11	16	5	55	259	23.54	–	1	9
–	I.Smith	8	11	2	39	196	21.77	–	–	7
1985	G.C.Holmes	6	8	1	54	136	19.42	–	1	1
1989	S.L.Watkin	18	15	8	25*	123	17.57	–	–	2
–	R.D.B.Croft	22	25	4	50	331	15.76	–	1	10
–	S.Bastien	11	6	3	22*	26	8.66	–	–	1
1987	S.R.Barwick	11	9	1	24*	64	8.00	–	–	1
–	D.J.Foster	8	9	3	13*	35	5.83	–	–	3
1991	M.Frost	18	11	4	8*	19	2.71	–	–	1

Also played (1 match each): M.J.Cann 29* (1 ct); S.J.Dennis 0, 3; D.L.Hemp 8, 4*.

BOWLING

	O	M	R	W	Avge	Best	5wI	10wM
R.J.Shastri	288.5	80	704	27	26.07	5-71	1	–
S.R.Barwick	286.5	79	726	26	27.92	4-46	–	–
S.L.Watkin	639.5	137	1848	66	28.00	6-55	4	–
M.Frost	497.2	84	1728	61	28.32	7-99	1	1
D.J.Foster	210.5	34	753	24	31.37	6-84	1	–
R.D.B.Croft	646.2	151	1777	34	52.26	5-62	1	–
S.Bastien	329.2	86	946	17	55.64	5-39	1	–

Also bowled: A.R.Butcher 2-1-1-0; M.J.Cann 8-0-37-0; A.Dale 106.1-22-380-7; S.J.Dennis 12-1-49-0; M.P.Maynard 4.5-0-34-0; I.Smith 36.1-7-132-3.

The First-Class Averages (pp 164-179) give the records of Glamorgan players in all first-class county matches (their other opponents being the West Indians, Cambridge U. and Oxford U.), with the exception of:
H.Morris 19-34-7-156*-1644-60.88-5-8-13ct. Did not bowl.
S.L.Watkin 19-16-8-25*-128-16.00-0-0-2ct. 662.5-144-1934-67-28.86-6/55-4-0.

GLAMORGAN RECORDS

FIRST-CLASS CRICKET

Highest Total	For	587-8d	v Derbyshire	Cardiff	1951
	V	653-6d	by Glos	Bristol	1928
Lowest Total	For	22	v Lancashire	Liverpool	1924
	V	33	by Leics	Ebbw Vale	1965
Highest Innings	For	287* D.E.Davies	v Glos	Newport	1939
	V	313* S.J.Cook	for Somerset	Cardiff	1990

Highest Partnership for each Wicket

1st	330	A.Jones/R.C.Fredericks	v Northants	Swansea	1972
2nd	249	S.P.James/H.Morris	v Oxford U	Oxford	1987
3rd	313	D.E.Davies/W.E.Jones	v Essex	Brentwood	1948
4th	306*	Javed Miandad/Younis Ahmed	v Australians	Neath	1985
5th	264	M.Robinson/S.W.Montgomery	v Hampshire	Bournemouth	1949
6th	230	W.E.Jones/B.L.Muncer	v Worcs	Worcester	1953
7th	195*	W.Wooller/W.E.Jones	v Lancashire	Liverpool	1947
8th	202	D.Davies/J.J.Hills	v Sussex	Eastbourne	1928
9th	203*	J.J.Hills/J.C.Clay	v Worcs	Swansea	1929
10th	143	T.Davies/S.A.B.Daniels	v Glos	Swansea	1982

Best Bowling	For	10-51 J.Mercer	v Worcs	Worcester	1936
(Innings)	V	10-18 G.Geary	for Leics	Pontypridd	1929
Best Bowling	For	17-212 J.C.Clay	v Worcs	Swansea	1937
(Match)	V	16-96 G.Geary	for Leics	Pontypridd	1929

Most Runs – Season	2,276	H.Morris	(av 55.51)	1990
Most Runs – Career	34,056	A.Jones	(av 33.03)	1957-1983
Most 100s – Season	10	H.Morris		1990
Most 100s – Career	52	A.Jones		1957-1983
Most Wkts – Season	176	J.C.Clay	(av 17.34)	1937
Most Wkts – Career	2,174	D.J.Shepherd	(av 20.95)	1950-1972

LIMITED-OVERS CRICKET

Highest Total	NWT	345-2	v Durham	Darlington	1991
	BHC	302-6	v Comb Univs	Cardiff	1988
	SL	277-6	v Derbyshire	Ebbw Vale	1984
Lowest Total	NWT	76	v Northants	Northampton	1968
	BHC	68	v Lancashire	Manchester	1973
	SL	42	v Derbyshire	Swansea	1979
Highest Innings	NWT	154* H.Morris	v Staffs	Cardiff	1989
	BHC	143* H.Morris	v Hampshire	Southampton	1989
	SL	130* J.A.Hopkins	v Somerset	Bath	1983
Best Bowling	NWT	5-13 R.J.Shastri	v Scotland	Edinburgh	1988
	BHC	5-17 A.H.Wilkins	v Worcs	Worcester	1978
	SL	6-29 M.A.Nash	v Worcs	Worcester	1975

GLOUCESTERSHIRE

Formation of Present Club: 1871
Colours: Blue, Gold, Brown, Silver, Green and Red
Badge: Coat of Arms of the City and County of Bristol
Championships (since 1890): (0) Second 1930, 1931, 1947, 1959, 1969, 1986
NatWest Trophy/Gillette Cup Winners: (1) 1973
Benson and Hedges Cup Winners: (1) 1977
Sunday League Champions: (0) Second 1988
Match Awards: NWT 35; BHC 41

Secretary: P.G.M.August, Phoenix County Ground, Nevil Road, Bristol BS7 9EJ (☎ 0272-245216)
Captain: A.J.Wright
Scorer: B.H.Jenkins
1992 Beneficiary: C.A.Walsh

ALLEYNE, Mark Wayne (Harrison C, Barbados; Cardinal Pole S, London E9; Haringey Cricket C), b Tottenham, London 23 May 1968. 5'10". RHB, RM. Debut 1986. Cap 1990. Tour: SL 1986-87 (Gs). 1000 runs (1): 1121 (1991). HS 256 v Northants (Northampton) 1990. BB 4-48 v Glam (Bristol) 1988. **NWT:** HS 45 v Notts (Bristol) 1991. BB 5-30 v Lincs (Gloucester) 1990. **BHC:** HS 36 v Derbys (Derby) 1987. BB 5-27 v Comb Us (Bristol) 1988. **SL:** HS 76* v Leics (Leicester) 1991. BB 3-25 v Essex (Chelmsford) 1990.

ATHEY, Charles William Jeffrey (Stainsby SS; Acklam Hall HS), b Middlesbrough, Yorks 27 Sep 1957. 5'9½". RHB, RM. Yorkshire 1976-83 (cap 1980). Gloucestershire debut 1984. Cap 1985. Captain 1989. Benefit 1990. **Tests:** 23 (1980 to 1988); HS 123 v P (Lord's) 1987. LOI: 31. Tours: A 1986-87, 1987-88; SA 1989-90 (Eng A); WI 1980-81; NZ 1979-80 (DHR), 1987-88; P 1987-88; SL 1985-86 (Eng B). 1000 runs (9); most – 1812 (1984). HS 184 Eng B v Sri Lanka (Galle) 1985-86. Gs HS 171* v Northants (Northampton) 1986. BB 3-3 v Hants (Bristol) 1985. Awards: NWT 4; BHC 5. **NWT:** HS 115 Y v Kent (Leeds) 1980. BB 1-18. **BHC:** HS 95 v Northants (Northampton) 1987. BB 4-48 v Comb Us (Bristol) 1984. **SL:** HS 121* v Worcs (Moreton) 1985. BB 5-35 Y v Derbys (Chesterfield) 1981.

BABINGTON, Andrew Mark (Reigate GS; Borough Road PE College), b Middlesex Hospital, London 22 Jul 1963. 6'2". LHB, RFM. Sussex 1986-90. Gloucestershire debut 1991. HS 58 v Sussex (Cheltenham) 1991. BB 5-37 Sx v Lancs (Liverpool) 1989. Gs BB 4-33 v Lancs (Bristol) 1991. Hat-trick 1986. **NWT:** HS 4*. BB 3-53 Sx v Leics (Hove) 1989. **BHC:** HS 9. BB 4-29 Sx v Surrey (Hove) 1988. **SL:** HS 11 v Essex (Cheltenham) 1991. BB 4-48 Sx v Worcs (Hove) 1989.

BALL, Martyn Charles John (King Edmund SS; Bath CFE), b Bristol 26 Apr 1970. 5'8". RHB, OB. Debut 1988. HS 28 v Surrey (Guildford) 1991. BB 5-128 v Kent (Canterbury) 1991. **NWT:** BB 3-42 v Lancs (Gloucester) 1989. **SL:** HS 5. BB 1-17.

De la PENA, Jason Michael (Stowe S; Bournside S), b London 16 Sep 1972. 6'4". RHB, RFM. Debut 1991. HS 1*. BB 2-69 v Leics (Hinckley) 1991.

GERRARD, Martin James (Grittleton House S; St Brendan's SFC; Wales Poly), b Southmead, Bristol 19 May 1967. 6'3". RHB, LMF. Debut 1991. HS 42 v Somerset (Bristol) 1991. BB 6-40 (10-60 match) v SL (Bristol) 1991. BAC BB 2-25 v Sussex (Cheltenham) 1991. **SL:** HS 7. BB 1-35.

HANCOCK, Timothy Harold Coulter (St Edward's S, Oxford; Henley C), b Reading, Berkshire 20 Apr 1972. 5'10". RHB, RM. Debut 1991. Oxfordshire 1990. HS 51 v Sussex (Hove) 1991. **SL:** HS 20 v Warwks (Birmingham) 1991.

HODGSON, Geoffrey Dean (Nelson Thomlinson CS, Wigton; Loughborough U), b Carlisle, Cumberland 22 Oct 1966. 6'1". RHB. Debut 1989. Cumberland 1984-88 (cap 1987 when aged 20 – county record). Warwickshire (SL only) 1987. 1000 runs (2); most – 1320 (1990). HS 126 v Z (Bristol) 1990. BAC HS 109 v Worcs (Bristol) 1990. **NWT:** HS 52 v Lancs (Manchester) 1990. **BHC:** HS 9. **SL:** HS 39 v Northants (Moreton) 1989.

HUNT, Alan Jeffrey (Dartmouth HS), b Birmingham 28 Dec 1968. 5'10". RHB. Debut 1991. HS 12 v SL (Bristol) 1991. Awaiting BAC debut.

LAWRENCE, David Valentine (Linden S), b Gloucester 28 Jan 1964. 6'2". RHB, RF. Debut 1981. Cap 1985. YC 1985. **Tests:** 4 (1988 to 1991) HS 34 v WI (Nottingham) 1991; BB 5-106 v WI (Oval) 1991. LOI: 1. Tours: SL 1985-86 (Eng B); 1986-87 (Gs). HS 66 v Glam (Abergavenny) 1991. 50 wkts (5); most – 85 (1985). BB 7-47 v Surrey (Cheltenham) 1988. Hat-trick 1990. Awards: NWT 2; BHC 2. **NWT:** HS 5*. BB 5-17 v Norfolk (Bristol) 1991. **BHC:** HS 23 and BB 6-20 v Comb Us (Bristol) 1991. **SL:** HS 38* v Yorks (Scarborough) 1991. BB 5-18 v Somerset (Bristol) 1990.

RUSSELL, Robert Charles (**Jack**) (Archway CS), b Stroud 15 Aug 1963. 5'8½". LHB, WK, occ OB. Debut 1981. Cap 1985. Wisden 1989. **Tests:** 25 (1988 to 1991); HS 128* v A (Manchester) 1989. LOI: 26. Tours: A 1990-91; WI 1989-90; P 1987-88; SL 1986-87 (Gs). HS 128* (Tests). Gs HS 120 v Somerset (Bristol) 1990. BB 1-4. Award: BHC 1. **NWT:** HS 42* v Lancs (Gloucester) 1989. **BHC:** HS 51 v Worcs (Worcester) 1991. **SL:** HS 108 v Worcs (Hereford) 1986.

SCOTT, Richard John (Queen Elizabeth S, Bournemouth), b Bournemouth, Hants 2 Nov 1963. 5'11". LHB, RM. Hampshire 1988-90. Gloucestershire debut 1991. Dorset 1981-85. HS 127 v Worcs (Worcester) 1991 – on Gs debut. BB 3-43 v Sussex (Hove) 1991. **NWT:** HS 22 H v Middx (Southampton) 1989. BB 4-22 v Norfolk (Bristol) 1991. **BHC:** HS 69 H v Sussex (Hove) 1989. BB 1-42. **SL:** HS 116* H v Yorks (Southampton) 1989. BB 2-8 H v Worcs (Worcester) 1990.

SMITH, Andrew Michael (Queen Elizabeth GS, Wakefield; Exeter U), b Dewsbury, Yorks 1 Oct 1967. 5'9". RHB, LM. Debut 1991. Comb Us (BHC) 1988-90. HS 22 v Warwks (Birmingham) 1991. BB 4-41 v Leics (Hinckley) 1991. **NWT:** BB 1-14. **BHC:** HS 15* Comb Us v Surrey (Oxford) 1990. BB 4-49 Comb Us v Somerset (Oxford) 1988. **SL:** HS 15* v Essex (Cheltenham) 1991. BB 3-16 v Sussex (Hove) 1991.

WALSH, Courtney Andrew (Excelsior HS), b Kingston, Jamaica 30 Oct 1962. 6'5½". RHB, RF. Jamaica 1981-91 (captain 1990-91). Gloucestershire debut 1984. Cap 1985. Benefit 1992. Wisden 1986. **Tests** (WI): 50 (1984-85 to 1991); HS 30* v A (Melbourne) 1988-89; BB 6-62 v I (Kingston) 1988-89. LOI (WI): 96. Tours (WI): E 1984, 1988, 1991; A 1984-85, 1986-87, 1988-89; NZ 1986-87; I 1987-88; P 1986-87, 1990-91; Z 1983-84 (Young WI). HS 63* v Yorks (Cheltenham) 1990. 50 wkts (5) inc 100 wickets (1): 118 (1986). BB 9-72 v Somerset (Bristol) 1986. Award: NWT 1. **NWT:** HS 25* v Berks (Reading) 1986. BB 6-21 v Kent (Bristol) 1990. **BHC:** HS 28 v Comb Us (Bristol) 1989. BB 2-19 v Scot 1985. **SL:** HS 35 v Glam (Cardiff) 1986. BB 4-19 v Kent (Cheltenham) 1987.

WILLIAMS, Ricardo Cecil (Ellerslie SS, Barbados; Haringey Cricket C), b Camberwell, London 3 Feb 1968. 5'9". RHB, RM. Debut 1991. HS 13 v Derbys (Gloucester) 1991. BB 1-81.

WILLIAMS, Richard Charles James (Millfield S), b Southmead, Bristol 8 Aug 1969. 5'8". LHB, WK. Debut 1990. HS 55* v Derbys (Gloucester) 1991.

WRIGHT, Anthony John (Alleyn's GS) b Stevenage, Herts 27 Jun 1962. 6'0". RHB, RM. Gloucestershire debut 1982. Cap 1987. Captain 1990-. Tour: SL 1986-87 (Gs). 1000 runs (4); most – 1596 (1991). HS 161 v Glam (Bristol) 1987. BB 1-16. Awards: NWT 1; BHC 1. **NWT:** HS 92 v Lincs (Gloucester) 1990. **BHC:** HS 97 v Worcs (Bristol) 1990. **SL:** HS 81 v Kent (Moreton) 1988 and v Leics (Leicester) 1989.

NEWCOMERS

DAVIES, Mark (Cwrt Sart CS; Neath Tertiary C), b Neath 18 Apr 1969. 5'6". RHB, SLA. Glamorgan 1990. MCC Cricket Staff. HS 5*.

DAWSON, Robert Ian (Millfield S; Newcastle Poly), b Exmouth, Devon 29 Mar 1970. 5'11". RHB, RM. Devon 1988-91. Awaiting f-c debut. **NWT:** HS 13 Devon v Essex (Exmouth) 1991.

HINKS, Simon Graham (St George's S, Gravesend), b Northfleet 12 Oct 1960. 6'2". LHB, RM. Kent 1982-91 (cap 1985). 1000 runs (3); most – 1588 (1990). HS 234 v Middx (Canterbury) 1990 sharing in Kent record stand of 366 for 2nd wkt with N.R.Taylor. BB 2-18 K v Notts (Nottingham) 1989. Awards: NWT 1; BHC 1. **NWT:** HS 95 K v Surrey (Canterbury) 1985. **BHC:** HS 85 K v Sussex (Canterbury) 1987. BB 1-15. **SL:** HS 99 K v Glam (Maidstone) 1986. BB 1-3.

HORRELL, Ryan (Pilton Community C), b Barnstaple, Devon 7 Apr 1973. 5'10". LHB, SLA. Devon 1991.

WINDOWS, Matthew Guy Newman (Clifton C), b Bristol 5 Apr 1973. Son of A.R. (Glos 1960-68). 5'7". RHB.

DEPARTURES

BARNES, Stuart Neil (Beechen Cliff S, Bath), b Bath, Somerset 27 Jun 1970. 6'1". RHB, RM. Gloucestershire 1990-91. HS 12* v I (Bristol) 1990. BAC HS 6. BB 4-51 v CU (Cambridge) 1990. BAC BB 2-10 v Derbys (Derby) 1990. **NWT:** HS 0. BB 1-64. **SL:** HS 11* v Sussex (Hove) 1989. BB 3-39 v Surrey (Cheltenham) 1990.

BELL, Robert Malcolm Hamilton (Truro S), b St Mary's, Isles of Scilly 26 Feb 1969. 6'5". RHB, RM. Gloucestershire 1990-91. Cornwall 1990. HS 0*. BB 2-38 v Worcs (Worcester) 1990.

GILBERT, David Robert (Marist Brothers S, Eastwood), b Darlinghurst, Sydney, Australia 29 Dec 1960. 6'1". RHB, RFM. NSW 1983-88. Tasmania 1989-91. Gloucestershire 1991. Lincolnshire 1984. **Tests** (A): 9 (1985 to 1986-87); HS 15 v NZ (Christchurch) 1985-86; BB 3-48 v NZ (Perth) 1985-86. LOI (A): 14. Tours (A): E 1985; NZ 1985-86; I 1986-87; Z 1985-86 (Young A), 1987-88 (NSW). HS 117 A v Delhi (Baroda) 1986-87. Gs HS 28* v Sussex (Cheltenham) 1991. 50 wkts (1): 64 (1991). BB 8-55 v Kent (Canterbury) 1991. **NWT:** BB 2-41 v Notts (Bristol) 1991. **BHC:** HS 16 v Worcs (Worcester) 1991. BB 1-31. **SL:** HS 10* v Worcs (Bristol) 1991. BB 2-27 v Surrey (Oval) 1991.

HARDY, Jonathan James Ean (Canford S), b Nakaru, Kenya 2 Oct 1960. 6'3¼". LHB. Hampshire 1984-85. Somerset 1986-90 (cap 1987). W Province 1987-91. Gloucestershire 1991. 1000 runs (1): 1089 (1987). HS 119 Sm v Glos (Taunton) 1987. Gs HS 52 v Hants (Southampton) 1991. Award: NWT 1. **NWT:** HS 100 Sm v Durham (Darlington) 1988. **BHC:** HS 109 Sm v Derbys (Taunton) 1990. **SL:** HS 94* Sm v Essex (Taunton) 1987.

Continued on p 154

84

GLOUCESTERSHIRE 1991

RESULTS SUMMARY

	Place	Won	Lost	Drew	Abandoned
Britannic Assurance Championship	13th	5	10	7	
All First-class Matches		6	10	9	
Refuge Assurance League	12th	5	9		2
NatWest Trophy	2nd Round				
Benson and Hedges Cup	4th in Group A				

BRITANNIC ASSURANCE CHAMPIONSHIP AVERAGES
BATTING AND FIELDING

Cap		M	I	NO	HS	Runs	Avge	100	50	Ct/St
1987	A.J.Wright	22	38	6	120	1477	46.15	3	9	16
1985	C.W.J.Athey	22	36	5	127	1350	43.54	4	9	15
1985	R.C.Russell	12	19	3	111	464	29.00	1	2	36/3
1990	M.W.Alleyne	22	35	3	165	921	28.78	1	4	10
–	G.D.Hodgson	21	37	1	89	990	27.50	–	7	7
–	R.J.Scott	17	30	1	127	763	26.31	2	3	6
1985	J.W.Lloyds	22	33	4	69	729	25.13	–	7	21
–	T.H.C.Hancock	3	5	1	51	83	20.75	–	1	5
–	J.J.E.Hardy	10	15	2	52	242	18.61	–	1	–
1985	D.V.Lawrence	15	22	1	66	383	18.23	–	1	4
–	A.M.Babington	15	19	7	58	176	14.66	–	1	7
–	D.R.Gilbert	20	26	6	28*	292	14.60	–	–	5
–	M.C.J.Ball	5	8	0	28	105	13.12	–	–	5
–	M.J.Gerrard	7	8	4	42	49	12.25	–	–	2
–	R.C.J.Williams	10	12	2	55*	95	9.50	–	1	18/3
1983	P.W.Romaines	3	5	0	28	35	7.00	–	–	1
–	A.M.Smith	13	13	2	22	60	5.45	–	–	–

Also played: J.M.de la Pena (2 matches) 1*, 0; R.C.Williams (1 match) 0, 13.

BOWLING

	O	M	R	W	Avge	Best	5wI	10wM
D.V.Lawrence	398.5	62	1296	60	21.60	6-67	3	1
M.C.J.Ball	178	34	547	18	30.38	5-128	1	–
D.R.Gilbert	602.2	129	1695	55	30.81	8-55	1	–
A.M.Smith	284.2	51	868	28	31.00	4-41	–	–
M.W.Alleyne	118.1	23	381	11	34.63	3-35	–	–
A.M.Babington	428.2	80	1300	35	37.14	4-33	–	–
R.J.Scott	175	38	545	14	38.92	3-43	–	–
J.W.Lloyds	510.2	121	1493	33	45.24	6-94	1	–

Also bowled: C.W.J.Athey 60-8-179-2; J.M.de la Pena 25-0-138-3; M.J.Gerrard 106.4-17-355-5; R.C.Russell 0.3-0-10-0; R.C.Williams 26-4-81-1; A.J.Wright 0.3-0-4-0.

The First-Class Averages (pp 164-179) give the records of Gloucestershire players in all first-class county matches (their other opponents being the West Indians, the Sri Lankans and Oxford U.), with the exception of D.V.Lawrence, whose full county figures are as above, and:
R.C.Russell 15-23-4-111-525-27.63-1-2-40ct/4st. 1.2-0-14-1-14.00-1/4.

GLOUCESTERSHIRE RECORDS

FIRST-CLASS CRICKET

Highest Total	For 653-6d		v Glamorgan	Bristol	1928
	V 774-7d		by Australians	Bristol	1948
Lowest Total	For 17		v Australians	Cheltenham	1896
	V 12		by Northants	Gloucester	1907
Highest Innings	For 318*	W.G.Grace	v Yorkshire	Cheltenham	1876
	V 296	A.O.Jones	for Notts	Nottingham	1903

Highest Partnership for each Wicket

1st	395	D.M.Young/R.B.Nicholls	v Oxford U	Oxford	1962
2nd	256	C.T.M.Pugh/T.W.Graveney	v Derbyshire	Chesterfield	1960
3rd	336	W.R.Hammond/B.H.Lyon	v Leics	Leicester	1933
4th	321	W.R.Hammond/W.L.Neale	v Leics	Gloucester	1937
5th	261	W.G.Grace/W.O.Moberley	v Yorkshire	Cheltenham	1876
6th	320	G.L.Jessop/J.H.Board	v Sussex	Hove	1903
7th	248	W.G.Grace/E.L.Thomas	v Sussex	Hove	1896
8th	239	W.R.Hammond/A.E.Wilson	v Lancashire	Bristol	1938
9th	193	W.G.Grace/S.A.P.Kitcat	v Sussex	Bristol	1896
10th	131	W.R.Gouldsworthy/J.G.Bessant	v Somerset	Bristol	1923

Best Bowling	For 10-40	E.G.Dennett	v Essex	Bristol	1906
(Innings)	V 10-66	A.A.Mailey	for Australians	Cheltenham	1921
	10-66	K.Smales	for Notts	Stroud	1956
Best Bowling	For 17-56	C.W.L.Parker	v Essex	Gloucester	1925
(Match)	V 15-87	A.J.Conway	for Worcs	Moreton-in-M	1914

Most Runs – Season	2,860	W.R.Hammond (av 69.75)		1933
Most Runs – Career	33,664	W.R.Hammond (av 57.05)		1920-1951
Most 100s – Season	13	W.R.Hammond		1938
Most 100s – Career	113	W.R.Hammond		1920-1951
Most Wkts – Season	222	T.W.J.Goddard (av 16.80)		1937
	222	T.W.J.Goddard (av 16.37)		1947
Most Wkts – Career	3,170	C.W.L.Parker (av 19.43)		1903-1935

LIMITED-OVERS CRICKET

Highest Total	NWT 327-7		v Berkshire	Reading	1966
	BHC 300-4		v Comb Univs	Oxford	1982
	SL 281-2		v Hampshire	Swindon	1991
Lowest Total	NWT 82		v Notts	Bristol	1987
	BHC 62		v Hampshire	Bristol	1975
	SL 49		v Middlesex	Bristol	1978
Highest Innings	NWT 158	Zaheer Abbas	v Leics	Leicester	1983
	BHC 154*	M.J.Procter	v Somerset	Taunton	1972
	SL 131	Sadiq Mohd	v Somerset	Bristol (Imp)	1975
Best Bowling	NWT 6-21	C.A.Walsh	v Kent	Bristol	1990
	BHC 6-13	M.J.Procter	v Hampshire	Southampton	1977
	SL 6-52	D.J.Shepherd	v Kent	Bristol	1983

HAMPSHIRE

Formation of Present Club: 12 August 1863
Colours: Blue, Gold and White
Badge: Tudor Rose and Crown
Championships: (2) 1961, 1973
NatWest Trophy/Gillette Cup Winners: (1) 1991
Benson and Hedges Cup Winners: (1) 1988
Sunday League Champions: (3) 1975, 1978, 1986
Match Awards: NWT 48; BHC 49

Chief Executive: A.F.Baker, County Cricket Ground, Northlands Road, Southampton
SO9 2TY (☎ 0703-333788/9)
Captain: M.C.J.Nicholas
Scorer: V.H.Isaacs
1992 Beneficiary: R.J.Parks

AYLING, Jonathan Richard (Portsmouth GS), b Portsmouth 13 Jun 1967. 6'4". RHB, RM. Debut 1988. Cap 1991. Took wicket of D.A.Polkinghorne (OU) with first ball in f-c cricket. HS 88* v Lancs (Liverpool) 1988. BB 4-47 v Surrey (Oval) 1991. **NWT:** HS 29 v Leics (Leicester) 1990. BB 3-30 v Yorks (Southampton) 1990. **BHC:** HS 14 v Yorks (Southampton) 1990. BB 2-22 v Lancs (Manchester) 1990. **SL:** HS 56 v Surrey (Oval) 1991. BB 4-37 v Notts (Southampton) 1990.

AYMES, Adrian Nigel (Bellemoor SM, Southampton), b Southampton 4 Jun 1964. 6'0". RHB, WK. Debut 1987. Cap 1991. HS 75* v Glam (Pontypridd) 1990. **NWT:** HS 2. **BHC:** HS 10 v Yorks (Leeds) 1991. **SL:** HS 33* v N'hants (Northampton) 1991.

BAKKER, Paul-Jan (Hugo De Groot C, The Hague), b Vlaardingen, Holland 19 Aug 1957. 5'11". RHB, RMF. Debut 1986. Cap 1989. HS 22 v Yorks (Southampton) 1989. 50 wkts (1): 77 (1989). BB 7-31 v Kent (Bournemouth) 1987. **NWT:** HS 3*. BB 3-34 v Worcs (Worcester) 1988. **BHC:** HS 7. BB 2-19 v Comb Us (Oxford) 1986. **SL:** HS 9. BB 5-17 v Derbys (Derby) 1989.

CONNOR, Cardigan Adolphus (The Valley SS, Anguilla; Langley C, Berkshire), b The Valley, Anguilla 24 Mar 1961. 5'9". RHB, RFM. Debut 1984. Cap 1988. Buckinghamshire 1979-83. HS 46 v Derbys (Portsmouth) 1990. 50 wkts (3); most - 62 (1984). BB 7-31 v Glos (Portsmouth) 1989. **NWT:** HS 13 v Yorks (Southampton) 1990. BB 4-29 v Warwks (Birmingham) 1991. **BHC:** HS 5*. BB 4-19 v Sussex (Hove) 1989. **SL:** HS 19 v Glos (Trowbridge) 1989. BB 4-11 v Derbys (Portsmouth) 1990.

COX, Rupert Michael FIENNES- (Bradfield C), b Guildford, Surrey 20 Aug 1967. 5'9". LHB, OB. Debut 1990. HS 104* v Worcs (Worcester) 1990 – in second match. **SL:** 13 v Surrey (Oval) 1991.

FLINT, Darren Peter John (Queen Mary's SFC), b Basingstoke 14 Jun 1970. 6'0". RHB, SLA. No 1st XI appearances – joined staff 1990.

GOWER, David Ivon (King's S, Canterbury; London U), b Tunbridge Wells, Kent 1 Apr 1957. 6'0". LHB, OB. Leicestershire 1975-89 (cap 1977; captain 1984-86, 1988-89; benefit 1987). Hampshire debut/cap 1990. Wisden 1978. YC 1978. **Tests:** 114 (1978 to 1990-91, 32 as captain); HS 215 v A (Birmingham) 1985; BB 1-1. **LOI:** 114. Tours (C=captain): A 1978-79, 1979-80, 1982-83, 1986-87, 1990-91; WI 1980-81, 1985-86C, 1989-90 (part); NZ 1983-84; I 1979-80, 1981-82, 1984-85C; P 1983-84; SL 1977-78 (DHR), 1981-82, 1984-85C. 1000 runs (11); most – 1530 (1982). HS 228 Le v Glam (Leicester) 1989. H HS 145 v Sussex (Southampton) 1990. Shared record Leics stand of 289* for 2nd wkt with J.C.Balderstone v Essex

87

(Leicester) 1981. BB 3-47 Le v Essex (Leicester) 1977. Awards: NWT 5; BHC 1. NWT: HS 156 Le v Derbys (Leicester) 1984. BHC: HS 114* Le v Derbys (Derby) 1980. SL: HS 135* Le v Warwks (Leicester) 1977.

JAMES, Kevan David (Edmonton County HS), b Lambeth, London 18 Mar 1961. 6'0". LHB, LMF. Middlesex 1980-84. Wellington 1982-83. Hampshire debut 1985. Cap 1989. 1000 runs (1): 1274 (1991). Shared record Hants stand of 227 for 8th wkt with T.M.Tremlett v Somerset (Taunton) 1985. HS 162 v Glam (Cardiff) 1989. BB 6-22 v A (Southampton) 1985. BAC BB 5-25 v Glos (Southampton) 1988. NWT: HS 42 v Glam (Cardiff) 1989. BB 3-22 v Dorset (Southampton) 1987. BHC: HS 45 v Essex (Chelmsford) 1989. BB 3-31 v Middx 1987 and v Glam 1988. SL: HS 66 v Glos (Trowbridge) 1989. BB 4-23 v Lancs (Southampton) 1986.

MARSHALL, Malcolm Denzil (Parkinson CS, Barbados), b St Michael, Barbados 18 Apr 1958. 5'11". RHB, RF. Barbados 1977-91 (capt 1987-88). Hampshire debut 1979. Cap 1981. Benefit 1987. Wisden 1982. Tests (WI): 81 (1978-79 to 1991); HS 92 v I (Kanpur) 1983-84; BB 7-22 v E (Manchester) 1988. LOI (WI): 121. Tours (WI): E 1980, 1984, 1988, 1991; A 1979-80, 1981-82, 1984-85, 1988-89; NZ 1979-80, 1986-87; I 1978-79, 1983-84; P 1980-81, 1986-87, 1990-91; SL 1978-79; Z 1981-82 (Young WI). HS 117 v Yorks (Leeds) 1990. 50 wkts (8+4) inc 100 wkts (2); most – 134 (1982). 2 hat-tricks: 1978-79 (Barbados), 1983 (4 wkts in 5 balls). BB 8-71 v Worcs (Southampton) 1982. Award: NWT 1. NWT: HS 77 v Northants (Southampton) 1990. BB 4-15 v Kent (Canterbury) 1983. BHC: HS 34 v Essex (Chelmsford) 1987. BB 4-26 v Kent (Canterbury) 1983. SL: HS 46 v Leics 1982 and v Middx 1990. BB 5-13 v Glam (Portsmouth) 1979.

MARU, Rajesh Jamandass (Rook's Heath HS, Harrow; Pinner SFC), b Nairobi, Kenya 28 Oct 1962. 5'6". RHB. SLA. Middlesex 1980-82. Hampshire debut 1984. Cap 1986. Tour: Z 1980-81 (Middx). HS 74 v Glos (Gloucester) 1988. 50 wkts (4); most – 73 (1985). BB 8-41 v Kent (Southampton) 1989. NWT: HS 22 v Yorks (Southampton) 1990. BB 3-46 v Leics (Leicester) 1990. BHC: HS 9. BB 3-46 v Comb Us (Southampton) 1990. SL: HS 33* v Glam (Ebbw Vale) 1991. BB 3-30 v Leics (Leicester) 1988.

MIDDLETON, Tony Charles (Montgomery of Alamein S, and Peter Symonds SFC, Winchester), b Winchester 1 Feb 1964. 5'10½". RHB, SLA. Debut 1984. Cap 1990. 1000 runs (1): 1238 (1990). HS 127 v Kent (Canterbury) 1990. BB 2-41 v Kent (Canterbury) 1991. NWT: HS 78 v Surrey (Lord's) 1991 (on debut). BHC: HS 60 v Notts (Southampton) 1991 (on debut). SL: HS 72 v Surrey (Southampton) 1990.

NICHOLAS, Mark Charles Jefford (Bradfield C), b London 29 Sep 1957. Grandson of F.W.H. (Essex 1912-29). 5'11". RHB, RM. Debut 1978. Cap 1982. Captain 1985-. Benefit 1991. Tours (C=captain): SL 1985-86C (Eng B); Z 1984-85C (EC), 1989-90 (Eng A). 1000 runs (7); most –1559 (1984). HS 206* v OU (Oxford) 1982. BAC HS 158 v Lancs (Portsmouth) 1984. BB 6-37 v Somerset (Southampton) 1989. Award: BHC 1. NWT: HS 71 v Surrey (Oval) 1989. BB 2-39 v Berks (Southampton) 1985. BHC: HS 74 v Glam (Southampton) 1985. BB 4-34 v Minor C (Reading) 1985. SL: HS 108 v Glos (Bristol) 1984. BB 4-30 v Glos (Trowbridge) 1989.

PARKS, Robert James (Eastbourne GS; Southampton Inst of Tech), b Cuckfield, Sussex 15 Jun 1959. Son of J.M. (Sussex, Somerset and England 1949-76) and grandson of J.H. (Sussex and England 1924-52). 5'8". RHB, WK. Debut 1980. Cap 1982. Benefit 1992. Tour: Z 1984-85 (EC). Held 10 catches in match v Derbys (Portsmouth) 1981. HS 89 v CU (Cambridge) 1984. BAC HS 80 v Derbys (Portsmouth) 1986. Award: BHC 1. NWT: HS 27* v Yorks (Southampton) 1990. BHC: HS 23* v Somerset (Taunton) 1988. SL: HS 38* v Essex (Portsmouth) 1987.

SHINE, Kevin James, (Maiden Erlegh CS), b Bracknell, Berkshire 22 Feb 1969. 6'2½". RHB, RFM. Debut 1989. Berkshire 1986. HS 26* v Middx (Lord's) 1989. BB 5-43 v Worcs (Portsmouth) 1991. **BHC:** HS 0. BB 4-68 v Surrey (Oval) 1990. **SL:** HS 2*. BB 2-35 v Lancs (Southampton) 1991.

SMITH, Robin Arnold (Northlands HS), b Durban, SA 13 Sep 1963. Brother of C.L. and grandson of Dr V.L.Shearer (Natal). 5'11". RHB, LB. Natal 1980-85. Hampshire debut 1982. Cap 1985. Wisden 1989. **Tests:** 28 (1988 to 1991); HS 148* v WI (Lord's) 1991. LOI: 31. Tours: A 1990-91; WI 1989-90. 1000 (6); most – 1577 (1989). HS 209* v Essex (Southend) 1987. BB 2-11 v Surrey (Southampton) 1985. Awards: NWT 5; BHC 2. **NWT:** HS 125* v Surrey (Oval) 1989. BB 2-13 v Berks (Southampton) 1985. **BHC:** HS 155* v Glam (Southampton) 1989. **SL:** HS 131 v Notts (Nottingham) 1989.

TAYLOR, Neil Raymond (Arnewood CS), b Boscombe 9 Feb 1964. 6'0". RHB, RMF. Debut for Minor Counties 1990. Middlesex 1990. Dorset 1987-91. HS 0. BB 3-44 M v Hants (Bournemouth) 1990. **NWT:** HS 7 and BB 2-25 Dorset v Lancs (Bournemouth) 1991. **BHC:** HS 3 and BB 3-52 Minor C v Derbys (Wellington) 1990. **SL:** HS 5*. BB 1-16. No 1st XI appearances for Hampshire (registered 1991).

TERRY, Vivian Paul (Millfield S), b Osnabruck, W Germany 14 Jan 1959. 6'0". RHB, RM. Debut 1978. Cap 1983. **Tests:** 2 (1984); HS 8. Tour: Z 1984-85 (EC). 1000 runs (8); most – 1382 (1987). HS 190 v SL (Southampton) 1988. BAC HS 180 v Derbys (Derby) 1990. Shared record Hants stand of 247 for 1st wkt with C.L.Smith v Warwks (Birmingham) 1987. Awards: NWT 4; BHC 3. **NWT:** HS 165* v Berks (Southampton) 1985. **BHC:** HS 134 v Comb Us (Southampton) 1990. **SL:** HS 142 v Leics (Southampton) 1986.

THURSFIELD, Martin John (Boldon CS), b South Shields, Co Durham 14 Dec 1971. 6'3". RHB, RM. Middlesex 1990. MCC Cricket Staff. HS -. BB 1-24. No 1st XI appearances for Hampshire (registered 1991).

TREMLETT, Timothy Maurice (Bellemoor SM; Richard Taunton SFC, Southampton), b Wellington, Somerset 26 Jul 1956. Son of M.F. (Somerset and England 1947-60). 6'2". RHB, RMF. Debut 1976. Cap 1983. Tours: SL 1985-86 (Eng B); Z 1984-85 (EC). HS 102* v Somerset (Taunton) 1985 – sharing record Hants stand of 227 for 8th wkt with K.D.James. 50 wkts (4); most – 75 (1985). BB 6-53 v Somerset (W-s-M) 1983. Awards: BHC 2. **NWT:** HS 43* v Leics (Leicester) 1987. BB 4-38 v Kent (Canterbury) 1983. **BHC:** HS 36* v Kent (Southampton) 1986. BB 4-30 v Surrey (Oval) 1986. **SL:** HS 35 v Worcs (Worcester) 1984. BB 5-28 v Kent (Canterbury) 1985.

TURNER, Ian John (Cowplain SS; Southdown C), b Denmead 28 Jul 1968. 6'1". RHB, SLA. Debut 1989. HS 39* v Glam (Swansea) 1991. BB 4-28 v Derbys (Chesterfield) 1991.

UDAL, Shaun David (Cove CS), b Farnborough 18 Mar 1969. Grandson of G.F. (Middx 1932 and Leics 1946). 6'2". RHB, OB. Debut 1989. HS 28* v Surrey (Southampton) 1990. BB 4-139 v SL (Southampton) 1990. BAC BB 4-144 v Sussex (Arundel) 1990. Award: NWT 1. **NWT:** BB 3-47 v Lancs (Southampton) 1991. **BHC:** HS 9 and BB 3-41 v Essex (Chelmsford) 1991. **SL:** HS 23 and BB 3-40 v Glam (Ebbw Vale) 1991.

WOOD, Julian Ross (Leighton Park S, Reading), b Winchester 21 Nov 1968. 5'8". LHB, RM. Debut 1989. MCC Cricket Staff. HS 96 v Northants (Northampton) 1989. BB 1-5. Award: BHC 1. **NWT:** HS 3*. **BHC:** 70* v Minor C (Trowbridge) 1991. **SL:** HS 66 v Notts (Nottingham) 1989.

NEWCOMER

MORRIS, Robert Sean Millner (Stowe S; Durham U), b Great Howard, Bucks 10 Sep 1968. 6'0". RHB, OB.

DEPARTURES – see p 154

HAMPSHIRE 1991

RESULTS SUMMARY

	Place	Won	Lost	Drew	Abandoned
Britannic Assurance Championship	9th	5	7	10	
All First-class Matches		5	7	12	
Refuge Assurance League	17th	3	12		1
NatWest Trophy	Winners				
Benson and Hedges Cup	Quarter-Finalist				

BRITANNIC ASSURANCE CHAMPIONSHIP AVERAGES
BATTING AND FIELDING

Cap		M	I	NO	HS	Runs	Avge	100	50	Ct/St
1981	C.L.Smith	15	26	3	145	1353	58.82	5	7	3
1989	K.D.James	22	35	9	134*	1216	46.76	2	6	8
1985	R.A.Smith	10	20	0	107	852	42.60	1	7	12
1983	V.P.Terry	18	32	2	171	1226	40.86	2	7	23
1990	D.I.Gower	22	37	5	80*	1132	35.37	–	8	13
1982	M.C.J.Nicholas	20	34	9	107*	723.	28.92	1	4	8
1990	T.C.Middleton	16	28	1	102	766	28.37	1	2	14
1991	A.N.Aymes	22	28	6	53	587	26.68	–	1	45/2
1991	J.R.Ayling	9	13	2	58	269	24.45	–	1	3
1986	R.J.Maru	20	25	3	61	369	16.77	–	1	29
–	I.J.Turner	8	10	4	39*	87	14.50	–	–	3
1988	C.A.Connor	14	15	0	30	148	9.86	–	–	3
–	K.J.Shine	15	17	8	25	80	8.88	–	–	2
	Aqib Javed	17	12	8	15*	25	6.25	–	–	–
1989	P-J.Bakker	9	6	2	6*	17	4.25	–	–	3

Also played: R.M.F.Cox (2 matches) 15, 26 (1 ct); T.M.Tremlett (1 match – cap 1983) 2; J.R.Wood (2 matches) 25, 0.

BOWLING

	O	M	R	W	Avge	Best	5wI	10wM
J.R.Ayling	185.5	36	555	21	26.42	4-47	–	–
Aqib Javed	485.1	81	1586	53	29.92	6-91	3	–
K.D.James	396.5	85	1219	37	32.94	4-32	–	–
P-J.Bakker	209.3	52	595	18	33.05	4-66	–	–
K.J.Shine	316.5	44	1350	37	36.48	5-43	2	–
C.A.Connor	331	58	1128	29	38.89	4-49	–	–
R.J.Maru	570.1	159	1534	34	45.11	5-128	1	–
I.J.Turner	238.5	65	637	14	45.50	4-28	–	–

Also bowled: D.I.Gower 0.1-0-4-0; T.C.Middleton 12-2-77-3; M.C.J.Nicholas 67.5-6-288-4; C.L.Smith 19-3-63-0; R.A.Smith 18-3-97-3; T.M.Tremlett 10-3-39-1; J.R.Wood 6-0-17-0.

The First-Class Averages (pp 164-179) give the records of Hampshire players in all first-class county matches (their other opponents being the West Indians and Oxford U.), with the exception of:

R.A.Smith 11-21-1-107-914-45.70-1-8-12ct. 18-3-97-3-32.33-2/20.

HAMPSHIRE RECORDS

FIRST-CLASS CRICKET

Highest Total	For 672-7d	v Somerset	Taunton	1899
	V 742	by Surrey	The Oval	1909
Lowest Total	For 15	v Warwicks	Birmingham	1922
	V 23	by Yorkshire	Middlesbrough	1965
Highest Innings	For 316 R.H.Moore	v Warwicks	Bournemouth	1937
	V 302* P.Holmes	for Yorkshire	Portsmouth	1920

Highest Partnership for each Wicket

1st	347	V.P.Terry/C.L.Smith	v Warwicks	Birmingham	1987
2nd	321	G.Brown/E.I.M.Barrett	v Glos	Southampton	1920
3rd	344	C.P.Mead/G.Brown	v Yorks	Portsmouth	1927
4th	263	R.E.Marshall/D.A.Livingstone	v Middlesex	Lord's	1970
5th	235	G.Hill/D.F.Walker	v Sussex	Portsmouth	1937
6th	411	R.M.Poore/E.G.Wynyard	v Somerset	Taunton	1899
7th	325	G.Brown/C.H.Abercrombie	v Essex	Leyton	1913
8th	227	K.D.James/T.M.Tremlett	v Somerset	Taunton	1985
9th	230	D.A.Livingstone/A.T.Castell	v Surrey	Southampton	1962
10th	192	H.A.W.Bowell/W.H.Livsey	v Worcs	Bournemouth	1921

Best Bowling	For	9-25 R.M.H.Cottam	v Lancashire	Manchester	1965
(Innings)	V	10-46 W.Hickton	for Lancashire	Manchester	1870
Best Bowling	For	16-88 J.A.Newman	v Somerset	Weston-s-Mare	1927
(Match)	V	17-119 W.Mead	for Essex	Southampton	1895

Most Runs – Season	2,854	C.P.Mead	(av 79.27)	1928
Most Runs – Career	48,892	C.P.Mead	(av 48.84)	1905-1936
Most 100s – Season	12	C.P.Mead		1928
Most 100s – Career	138	C.P.Mead		1905-1936
Most Wkts – Season	190	A.S.Kennedy	(av 15.61)	1922
Most Wkts – Career	2,669	D.Shackleton	(av 18.23)	1948-1969

LIMITED-OVERS CRICKET

Highest Total	NWT	371-4	v Glamorgan	Southampton	1975
	BHC	321-1	v Minor C (S)	Amersham	1973
	SL	292-1	v Surrey	Portsmouth	1983
Lowest Total	NWT	98	v Lancashire	Manchester	1975
	BHC	50	v Yorkshire	Leeds	1991
	SL	43	v Essex	Basingstoke	1972
Highest Innings	NWT	177 C.G.Greenidge	v Glamorgan	Southampton	1975
	BHC	173* C.G.Greenidge	v Minor C (S)	Amersham	1973
	SL	172 C.G.Greenidge	v Surrey	Southampton	1987
Best Bowling	NWT	7-30 P.J.Sainsbury	v Norfolk	Southampton	1965
	BHC	5-13 S.T.Jefferies	v Derbyshire	Lord's	1988
	SL	6-20 T.E.Jesty	v Glamorgan	Cardiff	1975

KENT

Formation of Present Club: 1 March 1859
Substantial Reorganisation: 6 December 1870
Colours: Maroon and White
Badge: White Horse on a Red Ground
Championships: (6) 1906, 1909, 1910, 1913, 1970, 1978
Joint Championship: (1) 1977
NatWest Trophy/Gillette Cup Winners: (2) 1967, 1974
Benson and Hedges Cup Winners: (3) 1973, 1976, 1978
Sunday League Champions: (3) 1972, 1973, 1976
Match Awards: NWT 41; BHC 64

Secretary: S.T.W.Anderson OBE, MC, St Lawrence Ground, Canterbury, CT1
3NZ (☎ 0227-456886)
Captain: M.R.Benson
Scorer: J.Foley
1992 Beneficiary: N.R.Taylor

BENSON, Mark Richard (Sutton Valence S), b Shoreham, Sussex 6 Jul 1958. 5'10".
LHB, OB. Debut 1980. Cap 1981. Captain 1991. Benefit 1991. **Tests:** 1 (1986); HS
30 v Ī (Birmingham) 1986. LOI: 1. 1000 runs (10); most – 1725 (1987). HS 257 v
Hants (Southampton) 1991. Shared Kent record stand of 300 for 1st wkt with
N.R.Taylor v Derbys (Canterbury) 1991. BB 2-55 v Surrey (Dartford) 1986.
Awards: NWT 2; BHC 3. **NWT:** HS 113* v Warwks (Birmingham) 1984. **BHC:** HS
118 v Glam (Swansea) 1990. **SL:** HS 97 v Surrey (Oval) 1982.

BRIMSON, Matthew Thomas (Chislehurst & Sidcup GS; Durham U), b Plumstead,
London 1 Dec 1970. 6'0". RHB, SLA. No 1st XI appearances – joined staff 1991.

COWDREY, Graham Robert (Tonbridge S; Durham U), b Farnborough 27 Jun 1964.
Brother of C.S., son of M.C. (Kent and England 1950-76), grandson of E.A. (Europeans). 5'11". RHB, RM. Debut 1984. Cap 1988. 1000 runs (2); most – 1576 (1990). HS
145 v Essex (Chelmsford) 1988. BB 1-5. Award: BHC 1. **NWT:** HS 37 v Glos (Bristol)
1990. BB 2-19 v Warwks (Canterbury) 1988. **BHC:** HS 70* v Leics (Canterbury) 1991.
BB 1-6. **SL:** HS 102* v Leics (Folkestone) 1989. BB 4-15 v Essex (Ilford) 1987.

DAVIS, Richard Peterr (King Ethelbert's S, Birchington; Thanet TC), b Westbrook,
Margate 18 Mar 1966. 6'3". RHB, SLA. Debut 1986. Cap 1990. HS 67 v Hants
(Southampton) 1989. 50 wkts (1): 73 (1990). BB 6-40 v CU (Cambridge) 1990. BAC
BB 6-59 v Sussex (Folkestone) 1990. **NWT:** HS 12 v Glos (Bristol) 1990. BB 3-19 v
Bucks (Canterbury) 1988. **BHC:** HS 1. BB 2-33 v Sussex (Hove) 1988. **SL:** HS 40* v
Northants (Canterbury) 1991. BB 5-52 v Somerset (Bath) 1989.

EALHAM, Mark Alan (Stour Valley SS, Chartham), b Willesborough, Ashford 27
Aug 1969. Son of A.G.E. (Kent 1966-82). 5'9". RHB, RMF. Debut 1989. HS 45 v
Lancs (Manchester) 1989. BB 5-39 v Sussex (Hove) 1991. **BHC:** HS 17* v Glam
(Swansea) 1990. BB 4-57 v Worcs (Worcester) 1990. **SL:** HS 29* v Glam (Llanelli)
1990. BB 3-26 v Derbys (Canterbury) 1989.

ELLISON, Richard Mark (Tonbridge S; Exeter U), b Willesborough, Ashford 21
Sep 1959. Brother of C.C. (Cambridge U 1982-83). 6'2". LHB, RMF. Debut 1981.
Cap 1983. Tasmania 1986-87. Wisden 1985. **Tests:** 11 (1984 to 1986); HS 41 v SL
(Lord's) 1984; BB 6-77 v A (Birmingham) 1985. LOI: 14. Tours: SA 1989-90 (Eng
XI); WI 1985-86; I/SL 1984-85. HS 108 v OU (Oxford) 1984. BAC HS 98 v Notts
(Nottingham) 1985. 50 wkts (4); most – 71 (1988). BB 7-33 v Warwks (Tunbridge W)
1991. Awards: NWT 1; BHC 5. **NWT:** HS 49* v Warwks (Birmingham) 1984. BB
4-19 v Cheshire (Canterbury) 1983. **BHC:** HS 72 v Middx (Lord's) 1984. BB 4-28 v

ELLISON – continued:
Glam (Canterbury) 1984. **SL:** HS 84 v Glos (Canterbury) 1984. BB 4-25 v Hants (Canterbury) 1983.

FLEMING, Matthew Valentine (St Aubyns S, Rottingdean; Eton C), b Macclesfield, Cheshire 12 Dec 1964. 5'11½". RHB, RM. Debut 1989. Cap 1990. HS 116 v WI (Canterbury) 1991. BAC HS 113 v Surrey (Canterbury) 1991. BB 3-28 v Yorks (Harrogate) 1991. **NWT:** HS 35* v Cambs (Canterbury) 1991. BB 2-4 v Oxon (Oxford) 1990. **BHC:** HS 52 v Scot (Glasgow) 1991. BB 2-52 v Leics (Canterbury) 1991. **SL:** HS 77 v Sussex (Hove) 1991. BB 4-45 v Somerset (Taunton) 1991.

FULTON, David Paul (The Judd S; Kent U), b Lewisham 15 Nov 1971. 6'2". RHB. No 1st XI appearances – joined staff 1991.

IGGLESDEN, Alan Paul (Churchill S, Westerham), b Farnborough 8 Oct 1964. 6'6". RHB, RFM. Debut 1986. Cap 1989. W Province 1987-88. Tests: 1 (1989); HS 2* and BB 2-91 v A (Oval). Tour: Z 1989-90 (Eng A). HS 41 and BB 6-34 v Surrey (Canterbury) 1988. 50 wkts (3); most – 56 (1989). **NWT:** HS 12* v Oxon (Oxford) 1990. BB 4-29 v Cambs (Canterbury) 1991. **BHC:** HS 26* v Worcs (Worcester) 1991. BB 3-24 v Scot (Glasgow) 1991. **SL:** HS 13* (twice). BB 5-13 v Sussex (Hove) 1989.

KERSEY, Graham James (Bexley & Erith Technical HS), b Plumstead, London 19 May 1971. 5'7". RHB, WK. Debut 1991. HS 27* v Surrey (Oval) 1991 – on debut.

LLONG, Nigel James (Ashford North S), b Ashford 11 Feb 1969. 6'0". LHB, OB. Debut 1990. HS 42* v Notts (Nottingham) 1991. **SL:** HS 23 v Yorks (Scarborough) 1991. BB 1-20.

LONGLEY, Jonathan Ian (Tonbridge S; Durham U), b New Brunswick, New Jersey, USA 12 Apr 1969. 5'7". RHB. Debut Comb Us (BHC) 1989-91. HS 17 v Essex (Southend) 1989. **BHC:** HS 49 Comb Us v Somerset (Taunton) 1989. **SL:** HS 57 v Middx (Lord's) 1989.

McCAGUE, Martin John (Hedland Sr HS; Carine Tafe C), b Larne, N Ireland 24 May 1969. 6'5". RHB, RFM. W Australia 1990-91. Kent debut 1991. HS 29 and BB 6-88 v Leics (Leicester) 1991. **NWT:** HS 9. **BHC:** HS 12 and BB 2-32 v Lancs (Manchester) 1991. **SL:** HS 17* v Leics (Canterbury) 1991. BB 4-51 v Derbys (Canterbury) 1991.

MARSH, Steven Andrew (Walderslade SS; Mid-Kent CFE), b Westminster, London 27 Jan 1961. 5'10". RHB, WK. Debut 1982. Cap 1986. HS 120 v Essex (Chelmsford) 1988. BB 2-20 v Warwks (Birmingham) 1990. Set world f-c record by holding eight catches in an innings AND scoring a hundred (v Middx at Lord's) 1991. **NWT:** HS 24* v Middx (Lord's) 1988. **BHC:** HS 71 v Lancs (Manchester) 1991. **SL:** HS 59 v Leics (Canterbury) 1991.

PATEL, Minal Mahesh (Dartford GS; Erith TC), b Bombay, India 7 Jul 1970. 5'9". RHB, SLA. Debut 1989. HS 43 v Leics (Leicester) 1991. BB 6-57 v Leics (Dartford) 1990. **NWT:** BB 2-29 v Oxon (Oxford) 1990.

PENN, Christopher (Dover GS), b Dover 19 Jun 1963. 6'1". LHB, RFM. Debut 1982. Cap 1987. HS 115 v Lancs (Manchester) 1984. 50 wkts (2); most – 81 (1988). BB 7-70 v Middx (Lord's) 1988. **NWT:** HS 20* v Surrey (Oval) 1991. BB 3-30 v Warwks (Canterbury) 1988. **BHC:** HS 24* v Northants (Northampton) 1989. BB 4-34 v Surrey (Canterbury) 1982. **SL:** HS 40 v Sussex (Maidstone) 1982. BB 4-15 v Glos (Maidstone) 1989.

PRESTON, Nicholas William (Meopham SS; Gravesend GS), b Dartford 22 Jan 1972. 6'1". RHB, RFM. No 1st XI appearances – joined staff 1991.

TAYLOR, Neil Royston (Cray Valley THS), b Orpington 21 Jul 1959. 6'1". RHB, OB. Debut 1979 scoring 110 and 11 v SL at Canterbury. Cap 1982. Benefit 1992. 1000 runs (8); most – 1979 (1990). HS 204 v Surrey (Canterbury) 1990. Shared in 2 Kent record stands: 300 (1st) with M.R.Benson and 366 (2nd) with S.G.Hinks. BB 2-20 v Somerset (Canterbury) 1985. Awards: BHC 8. **NWT:** HS 85 v Derbys (Canterbury) 1987. BB 3-29 v Dorset (Canterbury) 1989. **BHC:** HS 137 v Surrey (Oval) 1988. **SL:** HS 95 v Hants (Canterbury) 1990.

WARD, Trevor Robert (Hextable CS, nr Swanley), b Farningham 18 Jan 1968. 5'11". RHB, OB. Debut 1986. Cap 1989. 1000 runs (2); most – 1493 (1991). HS 235* v Middx (Canterbury) 1991. BB 2-48 v Worcs (Canterbury) 1990. Awards: NWT 1; BHC 1. **NWT:** HS 83 and BB 1-58 v Dorset (Canterbury) 1989. **BHC:** HS 94 v Worcs (Worcester) 1990. **SL:** HS 80 v Derbys (Chesterfield) 1990. BB 3-20 v Glam (Canterbury) 1989.

WREN, Timothy Neil, b Folkestone 26 Mar 1970. 6'3". RHB, LM. Debut 1990. HS 16 v Essex (Chelmsford) 1990. BB 3-14 v OU (Oxford) 1991. BAC BB 2-78 v Worcs (Canterbury) 1990. **SL:** HS 0*. BB 1-31.

NEWCOMER

HOOPER, Carl Llewellyn (Christchurch SS, Georgetown), b Georgetown, Guyana 15 Dec 1966, 6'1". RHB, OB. Debut (Demerara) 1983-84. Guyana 1984-91. **Tests** (WI): 32 (1987-88 to 1991); HS 134 v P (Lahore) 1990-91; BB 2-28 v A (Bridgetown) 1990-91. LOI (WI): 56. Tours (WI): E 1988, 1991; A 1988-89; NZ 1986-87; I 1987-88; P 1990-91; Z 1986-87 (WI B). 1000 runs (1): 1501 (1991). HS 196 WI v Hants (Southampton) 1991. BB 5-33 WI v Queensland (Brisbane) 1988-89.

DEPARTURES

COWDREY, C.S. – see GLAMORGAN.

DOBSON, Mark Christopher (Simon Langton GS), b Canterbury 24 Oct 1967. 5'10". RHB, SLA. Kent 1989-91. HS 52 and BB 2-20 v Glam (Canterbury) 1989. **SL:** HS 21 v Glos (Maidstone) 1989.

HINKS, S.G. – see GLOUCESTERSHIRE.

KELLEHER, Daniel John Michael (St Mary's GS, Sidcup; Erith TC), b Southwark, London 5 May 1966. Nephew of H.R.A. (Surrey 1955, Northants 1956-58). 6'1". RHB, RMF. Kent 1987-91. HS 53* v Derbys (Dartford) 1989. **NWT:** HS 21 and BB 3-16 v Oxon (Oxford) 1990. **BHC:** HS 11* v Notts (Nottingham) 1989. BB 1-23. **SL:** HS 19 v Notts (Nottingham) 1987. BB 2-25 (twice in 1987).

MERRICK, Tyrone Anthony (All Saints S, Antigua), b St John's, Antigua 10 Jun 1963. 6'1". RHB, RFM. Leeward Is 1984-89. Warwickshire 1987-89 (cap 1988). Kent 1990-91. Tour (WI B): Z 1986-87. HS 74* Wa v Glos (Birmingham) 1987. K HS 36 v Surrey (Oval) 1991. 50 wkts (3); most – 65 (1988). BB 7-45 (13-115 match) Wa v Lancs (Birmingham) 1987. K BB 7-99 v Sussex (Hove) 1991. Hat-trick 1988. **NWT:** HS 13 Wa v Cambs (Birmingham) 1987. BB 3-27 v Cambs (Canterbury) 1991. **BHC:** HS 22* v Lancs (Manchester) 1991. BB 4-24 Wa v Leics (Leicester) 1988. **SL:** HS 59 Wa v Northants (Birmingham) 1987. BB 4-24 v Essex (Chelmsford) 1990.

WELLS, V.J. – see LEICESTERSHIRE.

KENT 1991

RESULTS SUMMARY

	Place	Won	Lost	Tied	Drew	Abandoned
Britannic Assurance Championship	6th	6	3	1	12	
All First-class Matches		6	4	1	13	
Refuge Assurance League	10th	6	8	1		1
NatWest Trophy	2nd Round					
Benson and Hedges Cup	Quarter-Finalist					

BRITANNIC ASSURANCE CHAMPIONSHIP AVERAGES
BATTING AND FIELDING

Cap		M	I	NO	HS	Runs	Avge	100	50	Ct/St
1982	N.R.Taylor	22	34	3	203*	1647	53.12	6	7	14
1981	M.R.Benson	20	30	2	257	1329	47.46	4	6	9
1989	T.R.Ward	20	31	2	235*	1369	47.20	4	6	9
1979	C.S.Cowdrey	3	4	0	97	154	38.50	–	1	1
1988	G.R.Cowdrey	21	32	4	114	1064	38.00	2	5	17
1986	S.A.Marsh	21	29	5	113*	823	34.29	2	4	61/4
1990	M.V.Fleming	18	29	3	113	734	28.23	1	5	14
1985	S.G.Hinks	8	12	2	61*	236	23.60	–	2	6
1983	R.M.Ellison	16	24	7	61*	397	23.35	–	3	8
–	M.A.Ealham	3	5	0	36	96	19.20	–	–	3
1987	C.Penn	17	20	4	52	299	18.68	–	1	6
1990	R.P.Davis	18	23	4	44	338	17.78	–	–	22
–	M.J.McCague	8	10	2	29	142	17.75	–	–	1
–	M.M.Patel	5	7	2	43	76	15.20	–	–	2
–	N.J.Llong	3	6	2	42*	54	13.50	–	–	3
–	T.A.Merrick	18	22	6	36	198	12.37	–	–	3
1989	A.P.Igglesden	18	16	3	16*	100	7.69	–	–	3

Also played: G.J.Kersey (1 match) 27* (5 ct); V.J.Wells (2 matches) 1, 28, 0 (1 ct).

BOWLING

	O	M	R	W	Avge	Best	5wI	10wM
M.A.Ealham	98.1	20	274	15	18.26	5-39	2	–
C.Penn	407.4	79	1216	52	23.38	5-43	3	–
A.P.Igglesden	449	86	1288	48	26.83	5-36	1	–
T.A.Merrick	517	100	1688	58	29.10	7-99	1	–
M.J.McCague	153.3	23	481	16	30.06	6-88	1	–
R.M.Ellison	457.1	99	1375	45	30.55	7-33	2	–
M.M.Patel	183.2	43	458	13	35.23	3-33	–	–
R.P.Davis	455.2	126	1325	32	41.40	4-81	–	–
M.V.Fleming	184	41	498	12	41.50	3-28	–	–

Also bowled: M.R.Benson 13-0-44-0; G.R.Cowdrey 2-1-6-0; N.J.Llong 5-1-28-0;
S.A.Marsh 5-0-28-0; N.R.Taylor 3-0-26-0; T.R.Ward 17-4-40-1.

The First-Class Averages (pp 164-179) give the records of Kent players in all first-
class county matches (their other opponents being the West Indians and Oxford U.).

KENT RECORDS

FIRST-CLASS CRICKET

Highest Total	For	803-4d	v Essex	Brentwood	1934
	V	676	by Australians	Canterbury	1921
Lowest Total	For	18	v Sussex	Gravesend	1867
	V	16	by Warwicks	Tonbridge	1913
Highest Innings	For	332 W.H.Ashdown	v Essex	Brentwood	1934
	V	344 W.G.Grace	for MCC	Canterbury	1876

Highest Partnership for each Wicket

1st	300	N.R.Taylor/M.R.Benson	v Derbyshire	Canterbury	1991
2nd	366	S.G.Hinks/N.R.Taylor	v Middlesex	Canterbury	1990
3rd	321*	A.Hearne/J.R.Mason	v Notts	Nottingham	1899
4th	297	H.T.W.Harding/A.P.F.Chapman	v Hampshire	Southampton	1926
5th	277	F.E.Woolley/L.E.G.Ames	v New Zealand	Canterbury	1931
6th	284	A.P.F.Chapman/G.B.Legge	v Lancashire	Maidstone	1927
7th	248	A.P.Day/E.Humphreys	v Somerset	Taunton	1908
8th	157	A.L.Hilder/A.C.Wright	v Essex	Gravesend	1924
9th	161	B.R.Edrich/F.Ridgway	v Sussex	Tunbridge W	1949
10th	235	F.E.Woolley/A.Fielder	v Worcs	Stourbridge	1909

Best Bowling	For	10-30	C.Blythe	v Northants	Northampton	1907
(Innings)	V	10-48	C.H.G.Bland	for Sussex	Tonbridge	1899
Best Bowling	For	17-48	C.Blythe	v Northants	Northampton	1907
(Match)	V	17-106	T.W.J.Goddard	for Glos	Bristol	1939

Most Runs – Season	2,894	F.E.Woolley	(av 59.06)		1928
Most Runs – Career	47,868	F.E.Woolley	(av 41.77)		1906-1938
Most 100s – Season	10	F.E.Woolley			1928
	10	F.E.Woolley			1934
Most 100s – Career	122	F.E.Woolley			1906-1938
Most Wkts – Season	262	A.P.Freeman	(av 14.74)		1933
Most Wkts – Career	3,340	A.P.Freeman	(av 17.64)		1914-1936

LIMITED-OVERS CRICKET

Highest Total	NWT	359-4	v Dorset	Canterbury	1989
	BHC	319-8	v Scotland	Glasgow	1991
	SL	290-4	v Lancashire	Manchester	1987
Lowest Total	NWT	60	v Somerset	Taunton	1979
	BHC	73	v Middlesex	Canterbury	1979
	SL	83	v Middlesex	Lord's	1984
Highest Innings	NWT	129*	B.W.Luckhurst	v Durham	Canterbury	1974
	BHC	143	C.J.Tavaré	v Somerset	Taunton	1985
	SL	142	B.W.Luckhurst	v Somerset	Weston-s-Mare	1970
Best Bowling	NWT	8-31	D.L.Underwood	v Scotland	Edinburgh	1987
	BHC	5-21	B.D.Julien	v Surrey	The Oval	1973
	SL	6-9	R.A.Woolmer	v Derbyshire	Chesterfield	1979

LANCASHIRE

Formation of Present Club: 12 January 1864
Colours: Red, Green and Blue
Badge: Red Rose
Championships (since 1890): (7) 1897, 1904, 1926, 1927, 1928, 1930, 1934
Joint Championship: (1) 1950
NatWest Trophy/Gillette Cup Winners: (5) 1970, 1971, 1972, 1975, 1990
Benson and Hedges Cup Winners: (2) 1984, 1990
Sunday League Champions: (3) 1969, 1970, 1989
Match Awards: NWT 54; BHC 54

Secretary: Miss R. Fitzgibbon, Old Trafford, Manchester M16 0PX
(☎ 061-848 7021)
Captain: N.H.Fairbrother
Scorer: W.Davies
1992 Beneficiary: D.P.Hughes

ALLOTT, Paul John Walter (Altrincham GS; Durham U), b Altrincham, Cheshire 14 Sep 1956. 6'4". RHB, RFM. Debut 1978. Cap 1981. Benefit 1990. Wellington 1986-87. Cheshire 1976. **Tests:** 13 (1981 to 1985); HS 52* v A (Manchester) 1981 – on debut. BB 6-61 v WI (Leeds) 1984. **LOI:** 13. **Tours:** WI 1982-83 (Int), 1986-87 (La); I/SL 1981-82, 1984-85; Z 1988-89 (La). HS 88 v Hants (Southampton) 1987. 50 wkts (5); most – 85 (1981). BB 8-48 v Northants (Northampton) 1981. **Awards:** NWT 1; BHC 2. **NWT:** HS 19* v Worcs (Worcester) 1980. BB 4-28 v Leics (Leicester) 1986. **BHC:** HS 23* v Notts (Liverpool) 1989. BB 4-23 v Leics (Leicester) 1991. **SL:** HS 43 v Warwks (Manchester) 1988. BB 4-28 v Kent (Manchester) 1985.

ATHERTON, Michael Andrew (Manchester GS; Downing C, Cambridge), b Manchester 23 Mar 1968. 5'11". RHB, LB. Cambridge U 1987-89 (blue 1987-88-89; captain 1988-89). Lancashire debut 1987. Cap 1989. YC 1990. Wisden 1990. **Tests:** 18 (1989 to 1991); HS 151 v NZ (Nottingham) 1990; BB 1-60. **LOI:** 10. **Tours:** A 1990-91; Z 1989-90 (Eng A). 1000 runs (3); most – 1924 (1990). Scored 1193 in season of f-c debut. HS 191 v Surrey (Oval) 1990 sharing in Lancs record stand of 364 for 3rd wkt with N.H.Fairbrother. BB 6-78 v Notts (Nottingham) 1990. **Award:** NWT 1. **NWT:** HS 55 v Derbys (Derby) 1990. BB 2-15 v Glos (Manchester) 1990. **BHC:** HS 91 v Sussex (Manchester) 1991. BB 4-42 Comb Us v Somerset (Taunton) 1989. **SL:** HS 111 v Essex (Colchester) 1990. BB 3-33 v Notts (Nottingham) 1990.

AUSTIN, Ian David (Haslingden HS), b Haslingden 30 May 1966. 5'10". LHB, RM. Debut 1987. Cap 1990. **Tour:** Z 1988-89 (La). HS 101* v Yorks (Scarborough) 1991 (100 off 61 balls). BB 5-79 v Surrey (Oval) 1988. **NWT:** HS 13* v Derbys (Derby) 1990. BB 3-36 v Durham (Manchester) 1990. **BHC:** HS 80 v Worcs (Worcester) 1987. BB 4-25 v Surrey (Manchester) 1990. **SL:** HS 48 v Middx (Lord's) 1991. BB 5-56 v Derbys (Derby) 1991.

CRAWLEY, John Paul (Manchester GS; Trinity C, Cambridge), b Maldon, Essex 21 Sep 1971. Brother of M.A. (see NOTTS). 6'1". RHB, RM. Debut 1990. Cambridge U 1991 (blue 1991). HS 130 v Surrey (Manchester) 1991. **BHC:** HS 40 Comb Us v Northants (Northampton) 1991.

DeFREITAS, Phillip Anthony Jason (Willesden HS, London), b Scotts Head, Dominica 18 Feb 1966. 6'0". RHB, RFM. UK resident since 1976. Leicestershire 1985-88 (cap 1986). Lancashire debut 1989. Cap 1989. Wisden 1991. MCC Cricket Staff. **Tests**: 26 (1986-87 to 1991); HS 55* v WI (Nottingham) 1991; BB 7-70 v SL (Lord's) 1991. LOI: 62. Tours: A 1986-87, 1990-91; WI 1989-90; NZ 1987-88; P 1987-88; Z 1988-89 (La). HS 113 Le v Notts (Worksop) 1988. La HS 102 v OU (Oxford) 1990. 50 wkts (5); most – 94 (1986). BB 7-21 v Middx (Lord's) 1989. Awards: NWT 3; BHC 3. **NWT**: HS 69 Le v Lancs (Leicester) 1986. BB 5-13 v Cumberland (Kendal) 1989. **BHC**: HS 75* v Hants (Manchester) 1990. BB 4-13 v Scot (Perth) 1989. **SL**: HS 41* v Warwks (Birmingham) 1991. BB 4-20 Le v Middx and v Worcs 1986.

DERBYSHIRE, Nicholas Alexander (Ampleforth C; London U); b Ramsbottom 11 Sep 1970. 5'11¾". RHB, RFM. No 1st XI appearances – joined staff 1990.

FAIRBROTHER, Neil Harvey (Lymm GS), b Warrington 9 Sep 1963. 5'8". LHB, LM. Debut 1982. Cap 1985. Captain 1992. **Tests**: 7 (1987 to 1990); HS 33* v NZ (Lord's) 1990. LOI: 14. Tours: NZ 1987-88; P 1987-88, 1990-91 (Eng A); SL 1990-91 (Eng A). 1000 runs (8); most – 1740 (1990). HS 366 v Surrey (Oval) 1990, ground record including 311 in a day and 100 or more in each session, and sharing in Lancs record stand of 364 for 3rd wkt with M.A.Atherton. BB 2-91 v Notts (Manchester) 1987. Awards: NWT 5; BHC 5. **NWT**: HS 93* v Leics (Leicester) 1986. **BHC**: HS 116* v Scot (Manchester) 1988. **SL**: HS 116* v Notts (Nottingham) 1988.

FITTON, John Dexter (Redbrook HS; Oulder Hill S), b Littleborough 24 Aug 1965. 5'10". LHB, OB. Debut 1987. HS 60 v Northants (Lytham) 1991. BB 6-59 v Yorks (Manchester) 1988. **BHC**: BB 1-47. **SL**: HS 0. BB 1-25.

FOWLER, Graeme (Accrington GS; Durham U), b Accrington 20 Apr 1957. 5'9½". LHB, RM. Debut 1979. Cap 1981. Benefit 1991. **Tests**: 21 (1982 to 1984-85); HS 201 v I (Madras) 1984-85. LOI: 26. Tours: A 1982-83; WI 1982-83 (Int); NZ 1983-84; I/SL 1984-85; P 1983-84; Z 1988-89 (La). 1000 runs (8); most – 1800 (1987). HS 226 v Kent (Maidstone) 1984. BB 2-34 v Warwks (Manchester) 1986. Awards: NWT 2; BHC 3. **NWT**: HS 122 v Glos (Bristol) 1984. **BHC**: HS 136 v Sussex (Manchester) 1991. **SL**: HS 112 v Kent (Canterbury) 1986.

HEGG, Warren Kevin (Unsworth HS, Bury; Stand C, Whitefield), b Whitefield 23 Feb 1968. 5'8". RHB, WK. Debut 1986. Cap 1989. Tours: WI 1986-87 (La); SL 1990-91 (Eng A); Z 1988-89 (La). HS 130 v Northants (Northampton) 1987. Held 11 catches (equalling world f-c match record) v Derbys (Chesterfield) 1989. **NWT**: HS 29 v Glos (Gloucester) 1989. **BHC**: HS 31* v Worcs (Lord's) 1990. **SL**: HS 47* v Middx (Lord's) 1991.

IRANI, Ronald Charles (Smithills CS, Bolton), b Leigh 26 Oct 1971. 6'3". RHB, RM. Debut 1990. HS 31* v OU (Oxford) 1991. BB 1-12. Awaiting BAC debut.

LLOYD, Graham David (Hollins County HS), b Accrington 1 Jul 1969. Son of D. (Lancs and England 1965-83). 5'9". RHB, RM. Debut 1988. HS 117 v Notts (Worksop) 1988. BB 1-57. **NWT**: HS 39 v Hants (Southampton) 1991. **BHC**: HS 10 v Worcs (Lord's) 1991. **SL**: HS 100* v Kent (Maidstone) 1990.

MARTIN, Peter James (Danum S, Doncaster), b Accrington 15 Nov 1968. 6'4". RHB, RFM. Debut 1989. HS 29 v Yorks (Scarborough) 1991. BB 4-30 v Worcs (Blackpool) 1991. **NWT**: BB 2-19 v Dorset (Bournemouth) 1991. **SL**: BB 2-38 v Leics (Leicester) 1991.

MENDIS, Gehan Dixon (St Thomas C, Colombo; Brighton, Hove & Sussex GS; Durham U), b Colombo, Ceylon 24 Apr 1955. 5'9". RHB, RM. Sussex 1974-85 (cap 1980). Lancashire debut/cap 1986. Tours: WI 1982-83 (Int), 1986-87 (La); P 1981-82 (Int); Z 1988-89 (La). 1000 runs (12); most – 1756 (1985). HS 209* Sx v Somerset (Hove) 1984. La HS 203* v Middx (Manchester) 1987. BB 1-65. Awards: NWT 4; BHC 5. NWT: HS 141* Sx v Warwks (Hove) 1980. BHC: HS 125* v Northants (Manchester) 1991. SL: HS 125* Sx v Glos (Hove) 1981.

SHARP, Marcus Anthony (Clitheroe RGS; Edgehill CHE, Ormskirk), b Oxford 1 Jun 1970. 6'6¾". LHB, RM. Debut 1991. HS -. BB 1-21.

SPEAK, Nicholas Jason (Parrs Wood HS, Manchester), b Manchester 21 Nov 1966. 6'0". RHB, RM/OB. Debut v Jamaica (Kingston) 1986-87. Tour: WI 1986-87 (La). HS 153 v Surrey (Manchester) 1991. BB 1-0. SL: HS 27* v Leics (Leicester) 1991.

STANWORTH, John (Chadderton GS), b Oldham 30 Sep 1960. 5'10". RHB, WK. Debut 1983. Cap 1989. HS 50* v Glos (Bristol) 1985. NWT: HS 0. BHC: HS 8*. SL: HS 4*.

TITCHARD, Stephen Paul (Lymm County HS; Priestley C), b Warrington 17 Dec 1967. 6'3". RHB, RM. Debut 1990. HS 135 v Notts (Manchester) 1991. SL: HS 13 v Northants (Manchester) 1991.

WASIM AKRAM (Islamia C), b Lahore, Pakistan 3 Jun 1966. 6'3". LHB, LF. PACO 1984-86. Lahore Whites 1985-86. Lancashire debut 1988. Cap 1989. **Tests** (P): 37 (1984-85 to 1990-91); HS 123 v A (Adelaide) 1989-90; BB 6-62 v A (Melbourne) 1989-90. LOI (P): 99. Tours (P): E 1987; A 1988-89, 1989-90; WI 1987-88; NZ 1984-85; I 1986-87; SL 1984-85 (P U-23), 1985-86. HS 123 (Tests). La HS 122 v Hants (Basingstoke) 1991. 50 wkts (2); most – 63 (1989). BB 7-42 World XI v MCC (Scarborough) 1989. La BB 7-53 v Northants (Northampton) 1988. Hat-trick 1988. NWT: HS 29 v Hants (Southampton) 1991. BB 4-27 v Lincs (Manchester) 1988. BHC: HS 52 v Northants (Northampton) 1989. BB 5-27 v Scot (Perth) 1989. SL: HS 50 v Glam (Colwyn Bay) 1990. BB 4-19 v Yorks (Scarborough) 1990.

WATKINSON, Michael (Rivington and Blackrod HS, Horwich), b Westhoughton 1 Aug 1961. 6'1". RHB, RMF. Debut 1982. Cap 1987. Cheshire 1982. HS 138 v Yorks (Manchester) 1990. 50 wkts (3); most – 55 (1989). BB 7-25 v Sussex (Lytham) 1987. Awards: NWT 1; BHC 2. NWT: HS 90 and BB 3-14 v Glos (Manchester) 1990. BHC: HS 70* v Derbys (Liverpool) 1988. BB 5-49 v Yorks (Manchester) 1991. SL: HS 83 v Sussex (Manchester) 1991. BB 5-46 v Warwks (Manchester) 1990.

YATES, Gary (Manchester GS), b Ashton under Lyne 20 Sep 1967. 6'0". RHB, OB. Debut 1990. HS 106 v Notts (Nottingham) 1990 – on BAC debut. BB 4-94 v SL (Manchester) 1990. BAC BB 3-47 v Warwks (Birmingham) 1991. BHC: BB 2-50 v Sussex (Manchester) 1991. SL: BB 2-45 v Worcs (Worcester) 1991.

NEWCOMERS

BARNETT, Alexander Anthony (William Ellis S), b Malaga, Spain, 11 Sep 1970. Great nephew of C.J. (Glos and England 1927-54). 5'11". RHB, SLA. Middlesex 1988-91. HS 11* M v Surrey (Oval) 1991. BB 4-119 M v Derbys (Lord's) 1991.

CHAPPLE, Glen (West Craven HS), b Skipton, Yorks 23 Jan 1974. RHB, RM.

CORDINGLEY, Gareth (Queen Elizabeth GS, Blackburn), b Darwen 23 Jan 1973. RHB, RM.

FIELDING, Jonathan M. (Bury Metropolitan C).

FLETCHER, Stuart David (Reins Wood SS), b Keighley 8 Jun 1964. 5'10". RHB, RMF. Yorkshire 1983-91 (cap 1988). HS 28* Y v Kent (Tunbridge Wells) 1984. 50 wkts (1): 59 (1988). BB 8-58 Y v Essex (Sheffield) 1988. Award: NWT 1. **NWT:** HS 16* Y v Surrey (Oval) 1989. BB 3-20 Y v Berks (Finchampstead) 1988. **BHC:** HS 15* Y v Lancs (Leeds) 1990. BB 4-34 Y v Scot (Glasgow) 1987. **SL:** HS 11* v Essex (Chelmsford) 1991. BB 4-11 Y v Kent (Canterbury) 1988.

HARVEY, Mark

JACK, Steven Douglas (Glenwood HS; Witwatersrand U), b Durban, SA 4 Aug 1970. RHB, RF. Transvaal 1989-91. HS 26 and BB 8-51 Transvaal v E Province (Port Elizabeth) 1990-91.

DEPARTURES

HUGHES, David Paul (Newton-le-Willows GS), b Newton-le-Willows 13 May 1947. 5'11". RHB, SLA. Lancashire 1967-91 (cap 1970; captain 1987-91; benefits 1981, 1992). Tasmania 1975-77. Wisden 1987. Tours: SA 1972-73 (DHR); WI 1986-87 (La); Z 1988-89 (La). 1000 runs (2); most – 1303 (1982). HS 153 v Glam (Manchester) 1983. 50 wkts (4); most – 82 (1970, 1971). BB 7-24 v OU (Oxford) 1970. BAC BB 7-77 v Essex (Ilford) 1975. Awards: NWT 1; BHC 1. **NWT:** HS 71 v Durham (Chester-le-St) 1983. BB 4-61 v Somerset (Manchester) 1972. **BHC:** HS 52 v Derbys (Manchester) 1981. BB 5-23 v Minor C (W)(Watford) 1978. **SL:** HS 92 v Kent (Maidstone) 1984. BB 6-29 v Somerset (Manchester) 1977. Appointed assistant cricket manager Lancashire CCC.

JESTY, Trevor Edward (Privet County SS, Gosport), b Gosport, Hants 2 Jun 1948. 5'8½". RHB, RM. Hampshire 1966-84 (cap 1971; benefit 1982). Surrey 1985-87 (cap 1985; captain 1985). Lancashire 1988-91 (cap 1989). Border 1973-74. GW 1974-76, 1980-81. Canterbury 1979-80. Wisden 1982. LOI: 10. Tours: WI 1982-83 (Int); Z 1988-89 (La). 1000 runs (10); most – 1645 (1982). HS 248 H v CU (Cambridge) 1984. BAC HS 221 Sy v Essex (Oval) 1986. La HS 122* v OU (Oxford) 1991 – his final f-c innings. 50 wkts (2); most – 52 (1981). BB 7-75 H v Worcs (Southampton) 1976. La BB 1-20. Awards: NWT 6; BHC 11. **NWT:** HS 118 H v Derbys (Derby) 1980. BB 6-46 H v Glos (Bristol) 1979. **BHC:** HS 105 H v Glam (Swansea) 1977. BB 5-39 v Leics (Leicester) 1988. **SL:** HS 166* H v Surrey (Portsmouth) 1983. BB 6-20 H v Glam (Cardiff) 1976.

ORRELL, Timothy Michael (Bury Church HS; Stand C, Whitefield; Salford U), b Prestwich, Manchester 25 Nov 1967. 6'0". RHB, RM. Lancashire 1991. Comb Us (BHC) 1990. HS 16 v OU (Oxford) 1991. **BHC:** HS 15 Comb Us v Yorks (Leeds) 1990.

WARD, Michael John Paul (Manchester GS), b Oldham 12 Sep 1971. 5'11". RHB, OB. Lancashire 1991. HS -.

LANCASHIRE 1991

RESULTS SUMMARY

	Place	Won	Lost	Drew	Abandoned
Britannic Assurance Championship	8th	6	9	7	
All First-class Matches		7	9	8	
Refuge Assurance League	2nd	12	3		1
NatWest Trophy	2nd Round				
Benson and Hedges Cup	Finalist				

BRITANNIC ASSURANCE CHAMPIONSHIP AVERAGES

BATTING AND FIELDING

Cap		M	I	NO	HS	Runs	Avge	100	50	Ct/St
1989	M.A.Atherton	8	13	3	114*	603	60.30	2	2	6
–	J.P.Crawley	2	4	0	130	230	57.50	1	1	7
1985	N.H.Fairbrother	17	26	5	121	1011	48.14	5	3	18
–	S.P.Titchard	7	13	1	135	464	38.66	1	2	7
1986	G.D.Mendis	22	41	4	119	1223	33.05	3	3	7
1989	W.K.Hegg	21	31	7	97	758	31.58	–	3	39/3
1981	G.Fowler	18	31	2	113	865	29.82	2	2	1
–	N.J.Speak	17	31	2	153	806	27.79	1	2	7
1989	Wasim Akram	14	19	2	122	471	27.70	1	1	5
1990	I.D.Austin	12	16	4	101*	315	26.25	1	1	4
–	G.D.Lloyd	17	28	0	96	720	25.71	–	5	10
–	G.Yates	18	24	12	100*	292	24.33	1	–	8
1987	M.Watkinson	20	33	3	114*	713	23.76	1	3	8
–	J.D.Fitton	6	10	1	60	201	22.33	–	1	–
1989	P.A.J.DeFreitas	11	16	1	60	325	21.66	–	2	–
1970	D.P.Hughes	8	9	3	51	111	18.50	–	1	4
–	P.J.Martin	15	13	8	29	85	17.00	–	–	4
1981	P.J.W.Allott	8	8	2	26	63	10.50	–	–	4

Also played: J.Stanworth (1 match – cap 1989) did not bat (1 ct, 1 st).

BOWLING

	O	M	R	W	Avge	Best	5wI	10wM
Wasim Akram	429.3	99	1251	56	22.33	6-66	7	1
P.A.J.DeFreitas	394.2	95	1127	39	28.89	6-88	2	–
P.J.Martin	422.4	99	1262	33	38.24	4-30	–	–
P.J.W.Allott	173.1	43	489	12	40.75	4-56	–	–
M.Watkinson	603.2	106	2116	51	41.49	4-45	–	–
I.D.Austin	237.2	42	787	12	65.58	3-58	–	–
G.Yates	529.4	97	1770	26	68.07	3-47	–	–

Also bowled: J.D.Fitton 187.1-30-691-8; G.Fowler 7-0-41-1; D.P.Hughes 85.2-21-245-5; G.D.Lloyd 10-0-57-1; N.J.Speak 0.1-0-0-1.

The First-Class Averages (pp 164-179) give the records of Lancashire players in all first-class county matches (their other opponents being Cambridge U. and Oxford U.), with the exception of J.P.Crawley, whose full county figures are as above, and:

M.A.Atherton 9-14-3-138-741-67.36-3-2-6ct. Did not bowl.
P.A.J.DeFreitas 12-17-1-60-364-22.75-0-2-1ct. 423.2-102-1208-43-28.09-6/88-2-0.
N.H.Fairbrother 18-28-6-121-1059-48.13-5-3-18ct. Did not bowl.

LANCASHIRE RECORDS

FIRST-CLASS CRICKET

Highest Total	For 863		v Surrey	The Oval	1990
	V 707-9d		by Surrey	The Oval	1990
Lowest Total	For 25		v Derbyshire	Manchester	1871
	V 22		by Glamorgan	Liverpool	1924
Highest Innings	For 424	A.C.MacLaren	v Somerset	Taunton	1895
	V 315*	T.W.Hayward	for Surrey	The Oval	1898

Highest Partnership for each Wicket

1st	368	A.C.MacLaren/R.H.Spooner	v Glos	Liverpool	1903
2nd	371	F.B.Watson/G.E.Tyldesley	v Surrey	Manchester	1928
3rd	364	M.A.Atherton/N.H.Fairbrother	v Surrey	The Oval	1990
4th	324	A.C.MacLaren/J.T.Tyldesley	v Notts	Nottingham	1904
5th	249	B.Wood/A.Kennedy	v Warwicks	Birmingham	1975
6th	278	J.Iddon/H.R.W.Butterworth	v Sussex	Manchester	1932
7th	245	A.H.Hornby/J.Sharp	v Leics	Manchester	1912
8th	158	J.Lyon/R.M.Ratcliffe	v Warwicks	Manchester	1979
9th	142	L.O.S.Poidevin/A.Kermode	v Sussex	Eastbourne	1907
10th	173	J.Briggs/R.Pilling	v Surrey	Liverpool	1885

Best Bowling	For 10-46	W.Hickton	v Hampshire	Manchester	1870
(Innings)	V 10-40	G.O.B.Allen	for Middlesex	Lord's	1929
Best Bowling	For 17-91	H.Dean	v Yorkshire	Liverpool	1913
(Match)	V 16-65	G.Giffen	for Australians	Manchester	1886

Most Runs – Season	2,633	J.T.Tyldesley	(av 56.02)	1901
Most Runs – Career	34,222	G.E.Tyldesley	(av 45.20)	1909-1936
Most 100s – Season	11	C.Hallows		1928
Most 100s – Career	90	G.E.Tyldesley		1909-1936
Most Wkts – Season	198	E.A.McDonald	(av 18.55)	1925
Most Wkts – Career	1,816	J.B.Statham	(av 15.12)	1950-1968

LIMITED-OVERS CRICKET

Highest Total	NWT	372-5		v Glos	Manchester	1990
	BHC	330-4		v Sussex	Manchester	1991
	SL	276-6		v Derbys	Derby	1991
Lowest Total	NWT	59		v Worcs	Worcester	1963
	BHC	82		v Yorkshire	Bradford	1972
	SL	71		v Essex	Chelmsford	1987
Highest Innings	NWT	131	A.Kennedy	v Middlesex	Manchester	1978
	BHC	136	G.Fowler	v Sussex	Manchester	1991
	SL	134*	C.H.Lloyd	v Somerset	Manchester	1970
Best Bowling	NWT	5-13	P.A.DeFreitas	v Cumberland	Kendal	1989
	BHC	6-10	C.E.H.Croft	v Scotland	Manchester	1982
	SL	6-29	D.P.Hughes	v Somerset	Manchester	1977

LEICESTERSHIRE

Formation of Present Club: 25 March 1879
Colours: Dark Green and Scarlet
Badge: Gold Running Fox on Green Ground
Championships: (1) 1975
NatWest Trophy/Gillette Cup Winners: (0) Semi-finalists 1977, 1987
Benson and Hedges Cup Winners: (3) 1972, 1975, 1985
Sunday League Champions: (2) 1974, 1977
Match Awards: NWT 29; BHC 52

Chief Executive: F.M.Turner. **Administrative Secretary:** K.P.Hill, County Ground, Grace Road, Leicester LE2 8AD (☎ 0533-831880)
Captain: N.E.Briers
Scorer: G.R.Blackburn

BENJAMIN, Winston Keithroy Matthew (All Saints S, Antigua) b St John's, Antigua 31 Dec 1964. 6'3". RHB, RF. Debut (Rest of World XI) 1985. Leicestershire 1986-90 (cap 1989). Leeward Is 1985-91. Cheshire 1985. Tests (WI): 8 (1987-88 to 1988-89); HS 40* v P (Bridgetown) 1987-88; BB 4-52 v Eng (Oval) 1988. LOI (WI): 47. Tours (WI): E 1988; A 1986-87, 1988-89; I 1987-88; P 1986-87. HS 101* v Derbys (Leicester) 1990. 50 wkts (1): 69 (1989). BB 7-54 (inc hat-trick) v A (Leicester) 1989. Award: BHC 1. **NWT:** HS 17 v Sussex (Hove) 1988. BB 3-28 v Glos (Bristol) 1986. **BHC:** HS 21 v Northants (Northampton) 1987. BB 5-17 v Minor C (Leicester) 1986. **SL:** HS 41* v Essex (Chelmsford) 1989. BB 4-19 v Lancs (Leicester) 1986.

BENSON, Justin David Ramsay (The Leys S, Cambridge), b Dublin, Ireland 1 Mar 1967. 6'2". RHB, RM. Debut 1988. Cambridgeshire 1984-87. HS 133* v Hants (Bournemouth) 1991. Shared Leics record stand of 219* for 7th wkt with P.Whitticase v Hants (Bournemouth) 1991. BB 1-18. Award: NWT 1. **NWT:** HS 85 Cambs v Yorks (Leeds) 1986. **BHC:** HS 43 v Notts (Nottingham) 1990. BB 1-10. **SL:** HS 67 v Surrey (Oval) 1990. BB 3-37 v Warwks (Leicester) 1991.

BOON, Timothy James (Edlington CS, Doncaster), b Doncaster, Yorks 1 Nov 1961. 6'0". RHB, RM. Debut 1980. Cap 1986. Tour: Z 1980-81 (Le). 1000 runs (6); most – 1539 (1990). HS 144 v Glos (Leicester) 1984. Shared record Leics stand of 290* for 4th wkt with P.Willey v Warwks (Leicester) 1984. BB 3-40 v Yorks (Leicester) 1986. Awards: NWT 1; BHC 1. **NWT:** HS 76* v Salop (Leicester) 1991. **BHC:** HS 102 v Scot (Leicester) 1991. **SL:** HS 97 v Kent (Leicester) 1990.

BRIERS, Nigel Edwin (Lutterworth GS; Borough Road CE), b Leicester 15 Jan 1955. 6'0". RHB, RM. Debut 1971 (aged 16yr 103d – youngest Leicestershire player). Cap 1981. Captain 1990-. Benefit 1990. Tour: Z 1980-81 (Le). 1000 runs (8); most – 1996 (1990). HS 201* v Warwks (Birmingham) 1983. Shared record Leics stand of 233 for 5th wkt with R.W.Tolchard v Somerset (Leicester) 1979. BB 4-29 v Derbys (Leicester) 1985. Awards: BHC 3. **NWT:** HS 59 v Wilts (Swindon) 1984. BB 2-6 v Worcs (Leicester) 1979. **BHC:** HS 93* v Scot (Leicester) 1990. BB 1-26. **SL:** HS 119* v Hants (Bournemouth) 1981. BB 3-29 v Middx (Leicester) 1984.

COBB, Russell Alan (Trent C), b Leicester 18 May 1961. 5'11". RHB, SLA. Debut 1980. Cap 1986. Natal B 1988-89. Tours: NZ 1979-80 (DHR); Z 1980-81 (Le). 1000 runs (1): 1092 (1986). HS 91 v Northants (Leicester) 1986. Award: NWT 1. **NWT:** HS 66* v Oxon (Leicester) 1987. **BHC:** HS 22 v Warwks (Leicester) 1986. **SL:** HS 24 v Worcs (Leicester) 1981.

GIDLEY, Martyn Ian (Loughborough GS), b Leicester 30 Sep 1968. 6'1". LHB, OB. Debut 1989. OFS B 1990-91. HS 80 and Le BB 2-58 v Derbys (Leicester) 1991. BB 3-51 OFS B v WP B (Bloemfontein) 1990-91. **BHC:** HS 20[2] v Notts (Nottingham) 1990. **SL:** HS 14* v Worcs (Leicester) 1990. BB 3-45 v Surrey (Oval) 1990.

HAWKES, Christopher James (Loughborough GS; Durham U), b Loughborough 14 Jul 1972. 6'3". LHB, SLA. Debut 1990. HS 3.

HEPWORTH, Peter Nash, b Ackworth, Yorks 4 May 1967. 6'1". RHB, OB. Debut 1988. 1000 runs (1): 1119 (1991). HS 115 v CU (Cambridge) 1991 and v Essex (Leicester) 1991. BB 3-51 v Kent (Canterbury) 1991. **BHC:** HS 33 v Sussex (Hove) 1991. BB 4-39 v Scot (Leicester) 1991. **SL:** HS 38 v Sussex (Leicester) 1988. BB 2-33 v Notts (Leicester) 1991.

MILLNS, David James (Garibaldi CS), b Clipstone, Notts 27 Feb 1965. 6'3". LHB, RMF. Nottinghamshire 1988-89. Leicestershire debut 1990. Cap 1991. HS 44 v Middx (Uxbridge) 1991. 50 wkts (1): 63 (1991). BB 9-37 (12-91 match) v Derbys (Derby) 1991. **NWT:** BB 2-27 v Salop (Leicester) 1991. **BHC:** HS 11* v Sussex (Hove) 1991. BB 1-25. **SL:** HS 20* v Notts (Leicester) 1991. BB 2-20 v Warwks (Leicester) 1991.

MULLALLY, Alan David (Educated in Perth, Aus), b Southend-on-Sea, Essex 12 Jul 1969. 6'3½". RHB, LFM. W Australia 1987-90. Victoria 1990-91. Hampshire (1 match) 1988. Leicestershire debut 1990. HS 34 WA v Tasmania (Perth) 1989-90. Le HS 29 v Hants (Leicester) 1990. BB 4-59 v Yorks (Sheffield) 1990. **NWT:** BB 2-55 v Hants (Leicester) 1990. **BHC:** HS 5. BB 1-28. **SL:** HS 10* v Hants (Leicester) 1990. BB 2-19 v Somerset (W-s-M) 1991.

NIXON, Paul Andrew (Ullswater HS, Penrith), b Carlisle, Cumberland 21 Oct 1970. 6'0". LHB, WK. Debut 1989. Cumberland 1987. MCC Cricket Staff. HS 46 v Surrey (Oval) 1990. **NWT:** 12 v Hants (Leicester) 1990. **SL:** 17 v Worcs (Worcester) 1991.

PARSONS, Gordon James (Woodside County SS, Slough), b Slough, Bucks 17 Oct 1959. 6'1". LHB, RMF. Leicestershire 1978-85 and 1989 (cap 1984). Warwickshire 1986-88 (cap 1987). Boland 1983-85. GW 1985-87. OFS 1988-91. Buckinghamshire 1977. Tours: NZ 1979-80 (DHR); Z 1980-81 (Le). HS 76 Boland v W Province B (Cape Town) 1984-85. Le HS 69 v Glos (Leicester) 1989. 50 wkts (2); most – 67 (1984). BB 9-72 Boland v Transvaal B (Johannesburg) 1984-85. Le BB 6-11 v OU (Oxford) 1985. BAC BB 6-75 v Surrey (Oval) 1990. Awards: BHC 2. **NWT:** HS 23 v Northants (Northampton) 1984. BB 2-11 v Wilts (Swindon) 1984. **BHC:** HS 63* and BB 4-12 v Scot (Leicester) 1989. **SL:** HS 26* Wa v Derbys (Birmingham) 1987. BB 4-19 v Essex (Harlow) 1982.

POTTER, Laurie (Kelmscott HS, Perth, Aus), b Bexleyheath, Kent 7 Nov 1962. 6'1". RHB, SLA. Kent 1981-85. Leicestershire debut 1986. Cap 1988. GW 1984-86 (captain 1985-86). OFS 1987-88. 1000 runs (3); most – 1093 (1989). HS 165* GW v Border (East London) 1984-85. Le HS 121* v Notts (Leicester) 1989. BB 4-52 GW v Boland (Stellenbosch) 1985-86. Le BB 4-116 v Essex (Leicester) 1991. Award: BHC 1. **NWT:** HS 57 v Northants (Northampton) 1991. BB 1-28. **BHC:** HS 112 and BB 2-70 v Minor C (Leicester) 1986. **SL:** HS 105 v Derbys (Leicester) 1986. BB 4-9 K v Derbys (Folkestone) 1985.

ROSEBERRY, Andrew (Durham S), b Sunderland, Co Durham 2 Apr 1971. 6'0". Younger brother of M.A. (see MIDDLESEX). RHB, RM. No 1st XI appearances – joined staff 1990.

SMITH, Benjamin Francis (Kibworth HS), b Corby, Northants 3 Apr 1972. 5'9". RHB, RM. Debut 1990. HS 71 v Worcs (Worcester) 1991. BB 1-5. **NWT:** HS 6. **SL:** HS 33 v Middx (Uxbridge) 1991.

WHITAKER, John James (Uppingham S), b Skipton, Yorks 5 May 1962. 5'10". RHB, OB. Debut 1983. Cap 1986. Wisden 1986. YC 1986. **Tests:** 1 (1986-87); HS 11

WHITAKER – continued:
v A (Adelaide) 1986-87. LOI: 2. Tours: A 1986-87; Z 1989-90 (Eng A). 1000 runs (8); most – 1767 (1990). HS 200* v Notts (Leicester) 1986. BB 1-41. Awards: NWT 1; BHC 1. **NWT:** HS 155 v Wilts (Swindon) 1984. **BHC:** HS 100 v Kent (Canterbury) 1991. **SL:** HS 132 v Glam (Swansea) 1984.

WHITTICASE, Philip (Crestwood CS, Kingswinford), b Marston Green, Solihull 15 Mar 1965. 5'8". RHB, WK. Debut 1984. Cap 1987. HS 114* v Hants (Bournemouth) 1991. Shared Leics record stand of 219* for 7th wkt with J.D.R.Benson v Hants (Bournemouth) 1991. **NWT:** HS 32 v Lancs (Leicester) 1986. **BHC:** HS 45 v Notts (Nottingham) 1990. **SL:** HS 38 v Northants (Leicester) 1990.

NEWCOMERS

GOFTON, Robert Paul (Wolfreton S, Hull), b Scarborough, Yorks 10 Sep 1968. 5'10". RHB, RM. Worcestershire staff 1991.

PLENDER, Ian Foster (Oxclose S, Washington), b Gateshead, Co Durham 11 May 1969. RHB, RM.

WELLS, Vincent John (Sir William Nottidge S, Whitstable), b Dartford 6 Aug 1965. 6'0". RHB, WK. Kent 1988-91. HS 58 K v Hants (Bournemouth) 1990 and K v OU (Oxford) 1991. BB 5-43 K v Leics (Leicester) 1990. Award: NWT 1. **NWT:** 100* K v Oxon (Oxford) 1990. **BHC:** HS 25 K v Sussex (Canterbury) 1991. **SL:** HS 16 K v Worcs (Canterbury) 1990. BB 3-17 K v Somerset (Canterbury) 1988.

DEPARTURES

LEWIS, C.C. – see NOTTINGHAMSHIRE.

MAGUIRE, John Norman (Cavendish Road State HS; Queensland Institute of Technology), b Murwillumbah, NSW, Australia 15 Sep 1956. RHB, RFM. Queensland 1977-85. E Province 1989-91. Leicestershire 1991. **Tests** (A): 3 (1983-84); HS 15* v WI (St John's) 1983-84; BB 4-57 v WI (Kingston) 1983-84. LOI (A): 23. Tours (A): SA 1985-86 (Aus XI), 1986-87 (Aus XI); WI 1983-84. HS 65* EP v N Transvaal (Verwoerdburg) 1989-90. Le HS 44* v Derbys (Leicester) 1991. 50 wkts (1): 77 (1991). BB 7-46 Aus XI v EP (Pt Elizabeth) 1986-87 – inc hat-trick. Le BB 7-57 v Kent (Leicester) 1991. **BHC:** HS 35 v Sussex (Hove) 1991. BB 1-27. **SL:** HS 2* and BB 3-31 v Glam (Leicester) 1991.

MARTYN, Damien Richard, b Darwin, Australia 21 Oct 1971. 5'10". RHB, RM. W Australia 1990-91. Leicestershire 1991. Captained Australia U-19 v England 1991. HS 68* WA v Victoria (Melbourne) 1990-91. Le HS 60* v WI (Leicester) 1991. BB 1-22.

TENNANT, L. – see ESSEX.

WILKINSON, Craig William (Scotch C, Perth, W Australia), b Wardle, Lancs 19 Mar 1963. 6'0½". RHB, RM. Leicestershire 1991. HS 41 v Notts (Nottingham) 1991 – on debut. BB 4-59 v Derbys (Derby) 1991.

WILLEY, Peter (Seaham SS) b Sedgefield, Co Durham 6 Dec 1949. 6'1". RHB, OB. Northamptonshire 1966-83 (cap 1971; benefit 1981). Leicestershire 1984-91 (cap 1984; captain 1987). E Province 1982-85. **Tests:** 26 (1976 to 1986); HS 102* v WI (St John's) 1980-81; BB 2-73 v WI (Lord's) 1980. LOI: 26. Tours: A 1979-80; SA 1972-73 (DHR), 1981-82 (SAB); WI 1980-81, 1985-86; I 1979-80; SL 1977-78 (DHR). 1000 runs (10); most – 1783 (1982). HS 227 Nh v Somerset (Northampton) 1976 sharing record Northants stand of 370 for 4th wkt with R.T.Virgin. Le HS 177 v OU (Oxford) 1990. Shared record Leics stand of 290* for 4th wkt with T.J.Boon v Warwks (Leicester) 1984. 50 wkts (3); most – 52 (1979). BB 7-37 Nh v OU (Oxford) 1975. BAC BB 6-17 Nh v Sussex (Eastbourne) 1982. Le BB 6-43 v Hants (Leicester) 1985. Awards: NWT 7; BHC 7. **NWT:** HS 154 v Hants (Leicester) 1987. BB 3-33 v Derbys (Leicester) 1984. **BHC:** HS 88* v Northants (Leicester) 1984. BB 3-12 Nh v Minor C (E) (Horton) 1977. **SL:** HS 107 Nh v Warwks 1975 and v Hants 1976. BB 4-17 v Surrey (Leicester) 1991. F-c umpires reserve list 1992.

LEICESTERSHIRE 1991

RESULTS SUMMARY

	Place	Won	Lost	Drew	Abandoned
Britannic Assurance Championship	16th	3	8	11	
All First-class Matches		3	9	12	
Refuge Assurance League	14th	5	10		1
NatWest Trophy	2nd Round				
Benson and Hedges Cup	4th in Group C				

BRITANNIC ASSURANCE CHAMPIONSHIP AVERAGES

BATTING AND FIELDING

Cap		M	I	NO	HS	Runs	Avge	100	50	Ct/St
1981	N.E.Briers	22	40	5	160	1358	38.80	4	5	16
1986	J.J.Whitaker	22	26	3	105	1242	37.63	1	8	13
–	J.D.R.Benson	9	12	1	133*	393	35.72	1	1	9
–	B.F.Smith	13	20	3	71	585	34.41	–	3	3
1987	P.Whitticase	19	25	5	114*	620	31.00	1	4	42/2
1986	T.J.Boon	20	37	2	102	1057	30.20	1	6	8
–	P.N.Hepworth	21	35	4	115	915	29.51	1	3	17
1990	C.C.Lewis	12	15	1	73	413	29.50	–	2	4
1988	L.Potter	22	34	3	89	899	29.00	–	5	17
1984	G.J.Parsons	2	4	1	63	78	26.00	–	1	–
1991	D.J.Millns	19	24	8	44	306	19.12	–	–	9
1984	P.Willey	12	18	5	42*	217	16.69	–	–	6
–	L.Tennant	5	9	3	23*	94	15.66	–	–	–
–	M.I.Gidley	4	8	1	80	107	15.28	–	1	3
–	J.N.Maguire	22	24	7	44*	237	13.94	–	–	7
–	C.W.Wilkinson	13	13	2	41	138	12.54	–	–	7

Also played: P.A.Nixon (3 matches) 31, 5, 9 (6 ct, 1 st); A.D.Mullally (2 matches) did not bat.

BOWLING

	O	M	R	W	Avge	Best	5wI	10wM
C.C.Lewis	330.4	83	829	37	22.40	5-35	2	–
D.J.Millns	522.4	93	1815	62	29.27	9-37	3	1
P.N.Hepworth	102.2	20	404	13	31.07	3-51	–	–
J.N.Maguire	730.5	160	2222	69	32.20	7-57	3	–
L.Potter	418.2	93	1237	26	47.57	4-116	–	–
C.W.Wilkinson	293	56	974	20	48.70	4-59	–	–

Also bowled: J.D.R.Benson 35.1-7-145-1; T.J.Boon 10-3-21-1; M.I.Gidley 79.4-18-241-3; A.D.Mullally 37.4-10-99-1; G.J.Parsons 40-10-116-3; B.F.Smith 7-0-71-1; L.Tennant 69-12-296-5; J.J.Whitaker 1-0-14-0; P.Willey 157.4-36-441-5.

The First-Class Averages (pp 164-179) give the records of Leicestershire players in all first-class county matches (their other opponents being the West Indians and Cambridge U.), with the exception of:

C.C.Lewis 13-16-1-73-485-32.33-0-3-5ct. 364.4-88-952-40-23.80-5/35-2-0.

LEICESTERSHIRE RECORDS

FIRST-CLASS CRICKET

Highest Total	For	701-4d	v Worcs	Worcester	1906
	V	761-6d	by Essex	Chelmsford	1990
Lowest Total	For	25	v Kent	Leicester	1912
	V	24	by Glamorgan	Leicester	1971
		24	by Oxford U	Oxford	1985
Highest Innings	For	252* S.Coe	v Northants	Leicester	1914
	V	341 G.H.Hirst	for Yorkshire	Leicester	1905

Highest Partnership for each Wicket

1st	390	B.Dudleston/J.F.Steele	v Derbyshire	Leicester	1979
2nd	289*	J.C.Balderstone/D.I.Gower	v Essex	Leicester	1981
3rd	316*	W.Watson/A.Wharton	v Somerset	Taunton	1961
4th	290*	P.Willey/T.J.Boon	v Warwicks	Leicester	1984
5th	233	N.E.Briers/R.W.Tolchard	v Somerset	Leicester	1979
6th	262	A.T.Sharpe/G.H.S.Fowke	v Derbyshire	Chesterfield	1911
7th	219*	J.D.R.Benson/P.Whitticase	v Hampshire	Bournemouth	1991
8th	164	M.R.Hallam/C.T.Spencer	v Essex	Leicester	1964
9th	160	W.W.Odell/R.T.Crawford	v Worcs	Leicester	1902
10th	228	R.Illingworth/K.Higgs	v Northants	Leicester	1977

Best Bowling	For	10-18 G.Geary	v Glamorgan	Pontypridd	1929
(Innings)	V	10-32 H.Pickett	for Essex	Leyton	1905
Best Bowling	For	16-96 G.Geary	v Glamorgan	Pontypridd	1929
(Match)	V	16-102 C.Blythe	for Kent	Leicester	1909

Most Runs – Season	2,446	L.G.Berry	(av 52.04)		1937
Most Runs – Career	30,143	L.G.Berry	(av 30.32)		1924-1951
Most 100s – Season	7	L.G.Berry			1937
	7	W.Watson			1959
	7	B.F.Davison			1982
Most 100s – Career	45	L.G.Berry			1924-1951
Most Wkts – Season	170	J.E.Walsh	(av 18.96)		1948
Most Wkts – Career	2,130	W.E.Astill	(av 23.19)		1906-1939

LIMITED-OVERS CRICKET

Highest Total	NWT	354-7	v Wiltshire	Swindon	1984
	BHC	327-4	v Warwicks	Coventry	1972
	SL	291-5	v Glamorgan	Swansea	1984
Lowest Total	NWT	56	v Northants	Leicester	1964
	BHC	56	v Minor C	Wellington	1982
	SL	36	v Sussex	Leicester	1973
Highest Innings	NWT	156 D.I.Gower	v Derbyshire	Leicester	1984
	BHC	158* B.F.Davison	v Warwicks	Coventry	1972
	SL	152 B.Dudleston	v Lancashire	Manchester	1975
Best Bowling	NWT	6-20 K.Higgs	v Staffs	Longton	1975
	BHC	6-35 L.B.Taylor	v Worcs	Worcester	1982
	SL	6-17 K.Higgs	v Glamorgan	Leicester	1973

MIDDLESEX

Formation of Present Club: 2 February 1864
Colours: Blue
Badge: Three Seaxes
Championships (since 1890): (9) 1903, 1920, 1921, 1947, 1976, 1980, 1982, 1985, 1990
Joint Championships: (2) 1949, 1977
NatWest Trophy/Gillette Cup Winners: (4) 1977, 1980, 1984, 1988
Benson and Hedges Cup Winners: (2) 1983, 1986
Sunday League Champions: (0) Second 1982
Match Awards: NWT 47; BHC 48

Secretary: J.Hardstaff MBE, Lord's Cricket Ground, St John's Wood, London NW8 8QN (☎ 071-289 1300 and 071-286 1310)
Captain: M.W.Gatting
Scorer: H.P.H.Sharp
1992 Beneficiary: Middlesex Youth Development

BROWN, Keith Robert (Chace S, Enfield), b Edmonton 18 Mar 1963. Brother of G.K. (see DURHAM). 5'11". RHB, WK, RSM. Debut 1984. Cap 1990. MCC Cricket Staff. 1000 runs (2); most – 1505 (1990). HS 200* v Notts (Lord's) 1990. BB 2-7 v Glos (Bristol) 1987. Award: NWT 1. **NWT:** HS 103* v Surrey (Uxbridge) 1990. **BHC:** HS 56 v Minor C (Lord's) 1990. **SL:** HS 102 v Somerset (Lord's) 1988.

CARR, John Donald (Repton S; Worcester C, Oxford), b St John's Wood 15 Jun 1963. Son of D.B. (Derbyshire, OU and England 1945-63). 5'11". RHB, RM. Oxford U 1983-85 (blue 1983-84-85). Middlesex 1983-89 (cap 1987). Hertfordshire 1982-84 and 1991. 1000 runs (2); most – 1541 (1987). HS 156 v Essex (Lord's) 1987. BB 6-61 v Glos (Lord's) 1985. **NWT:** HS 83 v Hants (Southampton) 1989. BB 2-19 v Surrey (Oval) 1988. **BHC:** HS 67 Comb Us v Essex (Chelmsford) 1985. BB 3-22 Comb Us v Glos (Bristol) 1984. **SL:** HS 86 and 4-21 v Surrey (Lord's) 1989.

COWANS, Norman George (Park High SS, Stanmore), b Enfield St Mary, Jamaica 17 Apr 1961. 6'3". RHB, RF. Debut 1980. Cap 1984. YC 1982. MCC Cricket Staff. **Tests:** 19 (1982-83 to 1985); HS 36 v A (Perth) 1982-83; BB 6-77 v A (Melbourne) 1982-83. LOI: 23. Tours: A 1982-83; NZ 1983-84; I 1984-85; P 1983-84; SL 1984-85, 1985-86 (Eng B); Z 1980-81 (Middx). HS 66 v Surrey (Lord's) 1984. 50 wkts (6); most – 73 (1984, 1985). BB 6-31 v Leics (Leicester) 1985. Awards: NWT 1; BHC 1. **NWT:** HS 12* v Lancs (Lord's) 1984. BB 4-24 v Yorks (Leeds) 1986. **BHC:** HS 12 v Derbys (Derby) 1990. BB 4-33 v Lancs (Lord's) 1983. **SL:** HS 27 v Notts (Lord's) 1990. BB 6-9 v Lancs (Lord's) 1991.

ELLCOCK, Ricardo McDonald (Welches S, Combermere, Barbados; Malvern C), b Bridgetown, Barbados 17 Jun 1965. 5'11". RHB, RF. Barbados 1983-84. Worcestershire 1982-88. Middlesex debut 1989. HS 45* Wo v Essex (Worcester) 1984. M HS 26* v Somerset (Taunton) 1991. BB 5-35 v Yorks (Leeds) 1989. **NWT:** HS 6. BB 4-43 v Notts (Uxbridge) 1989. **BHC:** HS 12 and 2-45 Wo v Notts (Nottingham) 1984. **SL:** HS 13 v Somerset (W-s-M) 1989. BB 4-43 Wo v Kent (Canterbury) 1983.

EMBUREY, John Ernest (Peckham Manor SS), b Peckham, London 20 Aug 1952. 6'2". RHB, OB. Debut 1973. Cap 1977. Wisden 1983. W Province 1982-84. Benefit 1986. **Tests:** 60 (1978 to 1989, 2 as captain); HS 75 v NZ (Nottingham) 1986; BB 7-78 v A (Sydney) 1986-87. LOI: 58. Tours: A 1978-79, 1979-80, 1986-87, 1987-88; SA 1981-82 (SAB), 1989-90 (Eng XI); WI 1980-81, 1985-86; NZ 1987-88; I 1979-80, 1981-82; P 1987-88; SL 1977-78 (DHR), 1981-82; Z 1980-81 (Middx). HS 133 v

108

EMBUREY – continued:
Essex (Chelmsford) 1983. 50 wkts (13) inc 100 wkts (1): 103 (1983). BB 7-27 (12-66 match) v Glos (Cheltenham) 1989. Awards: NWT 1; BHC 6. **NWT**: HS 36* v Lancs (Manchester) 1978. BB 3-11 v Sussex (Lord's) 1989. **BHC**: HS 50 v Kent (Lord's) 1984. BB 5-37 v Somerset (Taunton) 1991. **SL**: HS 50 v Lancs (Blackpool) 1988. BB 5-23 v Somerset (Taunton) 1991.

FARBRACE, Paul (Geoffrey Chaucer S, Canterbury), b Ash, Kent 7 Jul 1967. 5'10". RHB, WK. Kent 1987-89. Middlesex debut 1990. HS 79 v CU (Cambridge) 1990. BAC HS 75* K v Yorks (Canterbury) 1987. BB 1-64. **NWT**: HS 17 v Berks (Lord's) 1990. **SL**: HS 26* v Lancs (Lord's) 1991.

FRASER, Angus Robert Charles (Gayton HS, Harrow), b Billinge, Lancs 8 Aug 1965. Brother of A.G.J. (see ESSEX). 6'5". RHB, RFM. Debut 1984. Cap 1988. **Tests**: 11 (1989 to 1990-91); HS 29 v A (Nottingham) 1989; BB 6-82 v A (Melbourne) 1990-91. LOI: 24. Tours: A 1990-91; WI 1989-90. HS 92 v Surrey (Oval) 1990. 50 wkts (3); most – 92 (1989). BB 7-77 v Kent (Canterbury) 1989. **NWT**: HS 19 v Durham (Darlington) 1989. BB 4-34 v Yorks (Leeds) 1988. **BHC**: HS 13* v Essex (Lord's) 1988. BB 3-39 (inc hat-trick) v Sussex (Lord's) 1988. **SL**: HS 30* v Kent (Canterbury) 1988. BB 4-28 v Glam (Lord's) 1990.

GATTING, Michael William (John Kelly HS), b Kingsbury 6 Jun 1957. 5'10". RHB, RM. Debut 1975. Cap 1977. Captain 1983-. Benefit 1988. YC 1981. Wisden 1983. OBE 1987. **Tests**: 68 (1977-78 to 1989, 23 as captain); HS 207 v I (Madras) 1984-85; BB 1-14. LOI: 85. Tours (C=captain): A 1986-87C, 1987-88C; SA 1989-90C (Eng XI); WI 1980-81, 1985-86; NZ 1977-78, 1983-84, 1987-88C; I/SL 1981-82, 1984-85; P 1977-78, 1983-84, 1987-88C; Z 1980-81 (Middx). 1000 runs (13+1) inc 2000 (2); most – 2257 (1984). HS 258 v Somerset (Bath) 1984. BB 5-34 v Glam (Swansea) 1982. Awards: NWT 6; BHC 11. **NWT**: HS 132* v Sussex (Lord's) 1989. BB 2-14 (twice). **BHC**: HS 143* v Sussex (Hove) 1985. BB 4-49 v Sussex (Lord's) 1984. **SL**: HS 124* v Leics (Leicester) 1990. BB 4-30 v Glos (Bristol) 1989.

HABIB, Aftab (Millfield S; Taunton S), b Reading, Berks 7 Feb 1972. 5'11". RHB, RMF. No 1st XI appearances – joined staff 1990.

HAYNES, Desmond Leo (Barbados Academy; Federal HS), b Holder's Hill, Barbados 15 Feb 1956. 5'11". RHB, RM/LB. Barbados 1976-91 (captain 1990-91). Middlesex debut/cap 1989. Scotland (BHC) 1983. Wisden 1990. Tests (WI): 102 (1977-78 to 1991, 4 as captain); HS 184 v E (Lord's) 1980; BB 1-2. LOI (WI): 182. Tours (WI): E 1980, 1984, 1988, 1991; A 1979-80, 1981-82, 1984-85, 1986-87, 1988-89; NZ 1979-80, 1986-87; I 1983-84, 1987-88; P 1980-81, 1986-87, 1990-91 (capt); Z 1981-82 (WI B). 1000 runs (2+4) inc 2000 (1): 2346 (1990). HS 255* v Sussex (Lord's) 1990. BB 1-2 (Tests). M BB 1-18. Awards: NWT 1; BHC 3. **NWT**: HS 149* v Lancs (Manchester) 1990. **BHC**: HS 131 v Sussex (Hove) 1990. **SL**: HS 107* v Lancs (Manchester) 1990.

HEADLEY, Dean Warren (Worcester RGS), b Norton, Stourbridge, Worcs 27 Jan 1970. Son of R.G.A. (Worcs, Jamaica and WI 1958-74); grandson of G.A. (Jamaica and WI 1927-54). 6'4". RHB, RFM. Debut 1991. HS 76 v Hants (Lord's) 1991. BB 5-46 v Yorks (Lord's) 1991 – on BAC debut. **NWT**: HS 11* v Somerset (Taunton) 1991. **BHC**: HS 26 v Surrey (Lord's) 1991. BB 1-34. **SL**: HS 6*. BB 1-70.

HUTCHINSON, Ian James Frederick (Shrewsbury S), b Welshpool, Montgomerys, 31 Oct 1964. 6'1". Brother of G.M. (Cambridge U 1990). RHB, RMF. Debut 1988. Shropshire 1984-86. MCC Cricket Staff. Scored 204 off 124 balls (14 sixes) before lunch for Cross Arrows 1985. HS 201* v OU (Oxford) 1989. BAC HS 177 v Kent (Uxbridge) 1989. BB 1-18. **NWT**: HS 23 v Ire (Dublin) 1991. **BHC**: HS 8. **SL**: HS 42 v Glam (Cardiff) 1991. BB 1-10.

KEECH, Matthew (Northumberland Park S), b Hampstead 21 Oct 1970. 6'0". RHB, RM. Debut 1991. HS 58* v Notts (Lord's) 1991. **BHC:** HS 47 v Warwks (Lord's) 1991. **SL:** HS 49* v Somerset (Taunton) 1991.

POOLEY, Jason Calvin (Acton HS), b Hammersmith 8 Aug 1969. 6'0". LHB. Debut 1989. HS 88 v Derbys (Lord's) 1991. **BHC:** HS 8. **SL:** HS 109 v Derbys (Lord's) 1991.

RADFORD, Toby Alexander (St Bartholomew's S, Newbury), b Caerphilly, Glam 3 Dec 1971. 5'10". RHB, OB. No 1st XI appearances – joined staff 1990.

RAMPRAKASH, Mark Ravin (Gayton HS; Harrow Weald SFC), b Bushey, Herts 5 Sep 1969. 5'9". RHB, RM. Debut 1987. Cap 1990. YC 1991. **Tests:** 6 (1991); HS 29 v WI (Birmingham) 1991. LOI: 2. Tours: P 1990-91 (Eng A); SL 1990-91 (Eng A). 1000 runs (3); most – 1541 (1990). HS 158 Eng A v SL A (Kandy) 1990-91. M HS 146* v Somerset (Uxbridge) 1990. BB 1-0. Award: NWT 1. **NWT:** HS 104 v Surrey (Uxbridge) 1990. BB 2-15 v Ire (Dublin) 1991. **BHC:** HS 78* v Somerset (Taunton) 1991. SL: HS 147* v Worcs (Lord's) 1990. BB 2-32 v Sussex (Hove) 1991.

ROSEBERRY, Michael Anthony (Durham S), b Houghton-le-Spring, Co Durham 28 Nov 1966. 6'1". RHB, RM. Debut 1986. Cap 1990. 1000 runs (2); most – 1593 (1990). HS 135 v Essex (Ilford) 1990. BB 1-1. **NWT:** HS 48 v Surrey and v Glam 1990. **BHC:** HS 38 v Somerset (Taunton) 1990. **SL:** HS 106* v Yorks (Lord's) 1991.

SIMS, Robin Jason (Vyners SS), b Hillingdon 22 Nov 1970. 5'8". LHB, WK. MCC Cricket Staff. Held catch as substitute to dismiss A.R.Border in Lord's Test 1989. Scored 278 (15 sixes) for Ickenham in 1990 Cockspur Cup. No 1st XI appearances – joined staff 1991.

SYLVESTER, Steven Antony (Wellesbourne SM; Buckinghamshire C; Goldsmiths' C, London U), b Chalfont St Giles, Bucks 26 Sep 1968. 5'11". RHB, LFM. Debut 1991. Buckinghamshire 1991. HS 0.

TAYLOR, Charles William (Spendlove S, Charlbury), b Banbury, Oxon 12 Aug 1966. 6'5½". LHB, LMF. Debut 1990. Oxfordshire 1986 and 1990. HS 21 v Kent (Lord's) 1991. BB 5-33 v Yorks (Leeds) 1990. **SL:** 3. BB 1-14.

TUFNELL, Philip Clive Roderick (Highgate S), b Barnet, Herts 29 Apr 1966. 6'0". RHB, SLA. Debut 1986. Cap 1990. MCC Cricket Staff. **Tests:** 6 (1990-91 and 1991); HS 8; BB 6-25 v WI (Oval) 1991. Tour: A 1990-91. HS 37 v Leics (Leicester) and v Yorks (Leeds) 1990. 50 wkts (3); most – 88 (1991). BB 7-116 (11-228 match) v Hants (Lord's) 1991. Award: NWT 1. **NWT:** HS 8. BB 3-29 v Herts (Lord's) 1988. **BHC:** HS 18 v Warwks (Lord's) 1991. BB 3-50 v Surrey (Lord's) 1991. **SL:** HS 13* v Glam (Merthyr Tydfil) 1989. BB 3-28 v Surrey (Lord's) 1991.

WEEKES, Paul Nicholas (Homerton House SS, Hackney), b Hackney, London 8 Jul 1969. 5'10". LHB, OB. Debut 1990. MCC Cricket Staff. HS 86 v Surrey (Oval) 1991. BB 3-57 v Worcs (Worcester) 1991. **NWT:** HS 7. BB 1-30. **BHC:** HS 0. **SL:** HS 32* v Yorks (Lord's) 1991. BB 3-27 v Hants (Lord's) 1991.

WILLIAMS, Neil FitzGerald (Acland Burghley CS), b Hope Well, St Vincent 2 Jul 1962. 5'11". RHB, RFM. Debut 1982. Cap 1984. Windward Is 1982-83 and 1989-91. Tasmania 1983-84. MCC Cricket Staff. **Tests:** 1 (1990); HS 38 and BB 2-148 v I (Oval) 1990. Tour: Z 1984-85 (EC). HS 77* v Warwks (Birmingham) 1991. 50 wkts (3); most – 63 (1983). BB 7-55 EC v Z (Harare) 1984-85. M BB 7-61 v Kent (Lord's) 1990. Award: BHC 1. **NWT:** HS 10 v Northumb (Jesmond) 1984. BB 4-36 v Derbys (Derby) 1983. **BHC:** HS 29* v Surrey (Lord's) 1985. BB 3-16 v Comb Us (Cambridge) 1982. **SL:** HS 43 v Somerset (Lord's) 1988. BB 4-39 v Sy (Oval) 1988.

NEWCOMERS and DEPARTURES – see p 154

MIDDLESEX 1991

RESULTS SUMMARY

	Place	Won	Lost	Drew	Abandoned
Britannic Assurance Championship	15th	3	9	10	
All First-class Matches		3	10	12	
Refuge Assurance League	11th	6	9		1
NatWest Trophy	2nd Round				
Benson and Hedges Cup	5th in Group B				

BRITANNIC ASSURANCE CHAMPIONSHIP AVERAGES
BATTING AND FIELDING

Cap		M	I	NO	HS	Runs	Avge	100	50	Ct/St
1977	M.W.Gatting	21	37	11	215*	2044	78.61	8	6	13
1990	M.R.Ramprakash	12	22	4	119	877	48.72	2	7	2
1990	K.R.Brown	21	36	6	143*	1069	35.63	1	6	33
1990	M.A.Roseberry	21	40	3	119*	1222	33.02	1	7	16
–	P.N.Weekes	6	11	1	86	249	24.90	–	2	5
–	I.J.F.Hutchinson	11	20	1	125	437	23.00	2	–	12
1977	J.E.Emburey	21	29	3	74	586	22.53	–	3	21
–	J.C.Pooley	11	20	0	88	390	19.50	–	2	8
–	M.Keech	14	22	2	58*	362	18.10	–	2	4
–	D.W.Headley	11	14	1	76	202	15.53	–	1	4
–	P.Farbrace	19	26	5	50	317	15.09	–	1	44/8
1984	N.F.Williams	16	24	3	77	296	14.09	–	1	4
–	C.W.Taylor	7	5	0	21	59	11.80	–	–	2
1984	N.G.Cowans	20	26	10	23*	146	9.12	–	–	5
1990	P.C.R.Tufnell	17	18	4	31*	120	8.57	–	–	7

Also played: A.A.Barnett (2 matches) 1*, 11*; P.R.Downton (3 matches – cap 1981) 51*, 38, 24* (8 ct, 1 st); R.M.Ellcock (3 matches) 26*; A.R.C.Fraser (2 matches – cap 1988) 12, 0 (2 ct); S.P.Hughes (3 matches – cap 1981) 1, 0*, 2 (2ct); S.A.Sylvester (1 match) 0 (1 ct).

BOWLING

	O	M	R	W	Avge	Best	5wI	10wM
P.C.R.Tufnell	733.4	199	1818	70	25.97	7-116	5	1
C.W.Taylor	147	30	480	18	26.66	3-35	–	–
J.E.Emburey	848.5	228	2031	64	31.73	7-71	1	–
A.A.Barnett	107.4	23	329	10	32.90	4-119	–	–
N.F.Williams	477.2	89	1474	41	35.95	5-89	1	–
N.G.Cowans	485.2	121	1370	34	40.29	4-42	–	–
D.W.Headley	309.2	44	1180	28	42.14	5-46	2	–

Also bowled: K.R.Brown 3-0-17-1; R.M.Ellcock 50-9-189-7; P.Farbrace 4.1-0-64-1; A.R.C.Fraser 39.5-12-91-6; M.W.Gatting 28-4-90-0; S.P.Hughes 70.5-14-270-5; I.J.F.Hutchinson 6-0-11-0; M.Keech 11-6-16-0; M.R.Ramprakash 5-1-25-1; M.A.Roseberry 9-1-36-0; S.A.Sylvester 20-2-98-0; P.N.Weekes 56.4-12-188-7.

The First-Class Averages (pp 164-179) give the records of Middlesex players in all first-class county matches (their other opponents being the West Indians, MCC and Cambridge U.), with the exception of:
M.R.Ramprakash 15-26-4-119-964-43.81-2-7-2ct. 19-3-88-1-88.00-1/0.
P.C.R.Tufnell 20-22-6-34-208-13.00-0-0-8ct. 801.4-229-1927-76-25.35-7/116-5-1.

MIDDLESEX RECORDS

FIRST-CLASS CRICKET

Highest Total	For	642-3d	v Hampshire	Southampton	1923
	V	665	by W Indians	Lord's	1939
Lowest Total	For	20	v MCC	Lord's	1864
	V	31	by Glos	Bristol	1924
Highest Innings	For	331* J.D.B.Robertson	v Worcs	Worcester	1949
	V	316* J.B.Hobbs	for Surrey	Lord's	1926

Highest Partnership for each Wicket

1st	367* G.D.Barlow/W.N.Slack	v Kent	Lord's	1981
2nd	380 F.A.Tarrant/J.W.Hearne	v Lancashire	Lord's	1914
3rd	424* W.J.Edrich/D.C.S.Compton	v Somerset	Lord's	1948
4th	325 J.W.Hearne/E.H.Hendren	v Hampshire	Lord's	1919
5th	338 R.S.Lucas/T.C.O'Brien	v Sussex	Hove	1895
6th	227 C.T.Radley/F.J.Titmus	v S Africans	Lord's	1965
7th	271* E.H.Hendren/F.T.Mann	v Notts	Nottingham	1925
8th	182* M.H.C.Doll/H.R.Murrell	v Notts	Lord's	1913
9th	160* E.H.Hendren/T.J.Durston	v Essex	Leyton	1927
10th	230 R.W.Nicholls/W.Roche	v Kent	Lord's	1899

Best Bowling	For	10-40 G.O.B.Allen	v Lancashire	Lord's	1929
(Innings)	V	9-38 R.C.Glasgow†	for Somerset	Lord's	1924
Best Bowling	For	16-114 G.Burton	v Yorkshire	Sheffield	1888
(Match)		16-114 J.T.Hearne	v Lancashire	Manchester	1898
	V	16-109 C.W.L.Parker	for Glos	Cheltenham	1930

Most Runs – Season	2,669	E.H.Hendren	(av 83.41)	1923
Most Runs – Career	40,302	E.H.Hendren	(av 48.81)	1907-1937
Most 100s – Season	13	D.C.S.Compton		1947
Most 100s – Career	119	E.H.Hendren		1907-1937
Most Wkts – Season	158	F.J.Titmus	(av 14.63)	1955
Most Wkts – Career	2,361	F.J.Titmus	(av 21.27)	1949-1982

LIMITED-OVERS CRICKET

Highest Total	NWT	296-4	v Lancashire	Manchester	1990
	BHC	303-7	v Northants	Northampton	1977
	SL	290-6	v Worcs	Lord's	1990
Lowest Total	NWT	41	v Essex	Westcliff	1972
	BHC	73	v Essex	Lord's	1985
	SL	23	v Yorkshire	Leeds	1974
Highest Innings	NWT	158 G.D.Barlow	v Lancashire	Lord's	1984
	BHC	143* M.W.Gatting	v Sussex	Hove	1985
	SL	147* M.Ramprakash	v Worcs	Lord's	1990
Best Bowling	NWT	6-15 W.W.Daniel	v Sussex	Hove	1980
	BHC	7-12 W.W.Daniel	v Minor C (E)	Ipswich	1978
	SL	6-6 R.W.Hooker	v Surrey	Lord's	1969

† R.C.Robertson-Glasgow

NORTHAMPTONSHIRE

Formation of Present Club: 31 July 1878
Colours: Maroon
Badge: Tudor Rose
Championships: (0) Second 1912, 1957, 1965, 1976
NatWest Trophy/Gillette Cup Winners: (1) 1976
Benson and Hedges Cup Winners: (1) 1980
Sunday League Champions: (0) Third 1991
Match Awards: NWT 38; BHC 39

Chief Executive: S.P.Coverdale, County Cricket Ground, Wantage Road, Northampton, NN1 4TJ (☎ 0604-32917)
Captain: A.J.Lamb
Scorer: A.C.Kingston
1992 Beneficiary: Target 2000

AMBROSE, Curtly Elconn Lynwall (All Saints Village SS), b Swetes Village, Antigua 21 Sep 1963. Cousin of R.M.Otto (Leeward Is 1979-91). 6'7". LHB, RF. Leeward Is 1985-91. Northamptonshire debut 1989. Cap 1990. Wisden 1991. **Tests** (WI): 33 (1987-88 to 1991); HS 53 v A (P-of-S) 1990-91; BB 8-45 v E (Bridgetown) 1989-90. LOI (WI): 46. Tours (WI): E 1988, 1991; A 1988-89; P 1990-91. HS 59 WI v Sussex (Hove) 1988. Nh HS 55* v Leics (Leicester) 1990. 50 wkts (2); most – 61 (1990). BB 8-45 (Tests). Nh BB 7-89 v Leics (Leicester) 1990. **NWT:** HS 48 v Lancs (Lord's) 1990. BB 3-31 v Suffolk (Bury St E) 1989. **BHC:** HS 17* v Kent (Northampton) 1989. BB 3-19 v Leics (Leicester) 1990. **SL:** HS 13* v Sussex (Hove) 1989. BB 3-15 v Notts (Finedon) 1989.

BAILEY, Robert John (Biddulph HS), b Biddulph, Staffs 28 Oct 1963. 6'3". RHB, OB. Debut 1982. Cap 1985. Staffordshire 1980. YC 1984. **Tests:** 4 (1988 to 1989-90); HS 43 v WI (Oval) 1988. LOI: 4. Tour: WI 1989-90. 1000 runs (8); most – 1987 (1990). HS 224* v Glam (Swansea) 1988. BB 3-27 v Glam (Wellingborough) 1988. Awards: NWT 2; BHC 5. **NWT:** HS 145 v Staffs (Stone) 1991. BB 3-47 v Notts (Northampton) 1989. **BHC:** HS 134 v Glos (Northampton) 1987. BB 1-22. **SL:** HS 125* v Derbys (Derby) 1987. BB 3-23 v Leics (Leicester) 1987.

CAPEL, David John (Roade CS), b Northampton 6 Feb 1963. 5'11". RHB, RMF. Debut 1981. Cap 1986. E Province 1985-87. **Tests:** 15 (1987 to 1989-90); HS 98 v P (Karachi) 1987-88; BB 3-88 v WI (Bridgetown) 1989-90. LOI: 23. Tours: A 1987-88; WI 1989-90; NZ 1987-88; P 1987-88. 1000 runs (3); most – 1311 (1989). HS 134 EP v W Province (Port Elizabeth) 1986-87. Nh HS 126 v Sussex (Hove) 1989. 50 wkts (3); most – 63 (1986). BB 7-46 v Yorks (Northampton) 1987. Awards: NWT 3. **NWT:** HS 101 v Notts (Northampton) 1990. BB 3-26 v Surrey (Oval) 1991. **BHC:** HS 97 v Yorks (Lord's) 1987. BB 4-29 v Warwks (Birmingham) 1986. **SL:** HS 121 v Glam (Northampton) 1990. BB 4-30 v Yorks (Middlesbrough) 1982.

COOK, Nicholas Grant Billson (Lutterworth GS), b Leicester 17 Jun 1956. 6'0". RHB, SLA. Leicestershire 1978-85 (cap 1982). Northamptonshire debut 1986. Cap 1987. **Tests:** 15 (1983 to 1989); HS 31 v A (Oval) 1989; BB 6-65 (11-83 match) v P (Karachi) 1983-84. LOI: 3. Tours: NZ 1979-80 (DHR) 1983-84; P 1983-84, 1987-88; SL 1985-86 (Eng B); Z 1980-81 (Leics), 1984-85 (EC). HS 75 Le v Somerset (Taunton) 1980. Nh HS 64 v Lancs (Manchester) 1987. 50 wkts (8); most – 90 (1982). BB 7-63 Le v Somerset (Taunton) 1982. Nh BB 6-56 v Essex (Chelmsford) 1988 and v Lancs (Southport) 1989. **NWT:** HS 13 v Middx (Northampton) 1986. BB 4-24 v Ire (Northampton) 1987. **BHC:** HS 23 Le v Warwks (Leicester) 1984. BB 3-35 v Kent (Northampton) 1989. **SL:** HS 17* v Surrey (Tring) 1991. BB 3-20 v Kent (Canterbury) 1989.

CURRAN, Kevin Malcolm (Marandellas HS), b Rusape, S Rhodesia 7 Sep 1959. Son of K.P. (Rhodesia 1947-54). 6′1″. RHB, RMF. Zimbabwe 1980-88. Natal 1988-89. Gloucestershire 1985-90 (cap 1985). Northamptonshire debut 1991. LOI (Z): 11. Tours (Z): E 1982; SL 1983-84. 1000 runs (5); most – 1353 (1986). HS 144* Gs v Sussex (Bristol) 1990. Nh HS 89* v Lancs (Lytham) 1991. 50 wkts (3); most – 65 (1988). BB 7-47 Natal v Transvaal (Johannesburg) 1988-89. BAC BB 7-54 Gs v Leics (Gloucester) 1988. Nh BB 5-60 v Notts (Wellingborough) 1991. Awards: NWT 2; BHC 2. **NWT:** HS 58* Gs v Leics (Leicester) 1988. BB 4-34 Gs v Northants (Bristol) 1985. **BHC:** HS 57 Gs v Derbys (Derby) 1987. BB 4-41 Gs v Notts (Bristol) 1989. **SL:** HS 92 Gs v Northants (Northampton) 1990. BB 5-15 Gs v Leics (Gloucester) 1988.

FELTON, Nigel Alfred (Millfield S; Loughborough U), b Guildford, Surrey 24 Oct 1960. 5′8″. LHB, OB. Somerset 1982-88 (cap 1986). Northamptonshire debut 1989. Cap 1990. 1000 runs (3); most – 1538 (1990). HS 173* Sm v Kent (Taunton) 1983. Nh HS 122 v Glam (Northampton) 1990. BB 1-48. Award: NWT 1. **NWT:** HS 87 Sm v Kent (Taunton) 1988. **BHC:** HS 50 Sm v Hants (Taunton) 1988. **SL:** HS 96 Sm v Essex (Chelmsford) 1986.

FORDHAM, Alan (Bedford Modern S; Durham U), b Bedford 9 Nov 1964. 6′1″. RHB, RM. Debut 1986. Cap 1990. Bedfordshire 1982-85. Comb Us (BHC) 1987. 1000 runs (2); most – 1840 (1991). HS 206* v Yorks (Leeds) 1990 sharing in Northants record stand of 393 for 3rd wkt with A.J.Lamb. BB 1-25. Nh 2nd XI record score: 236 (158 balls) v Worcs (Kidderminster) 1989. Awards: NWT 3; BHC 2. **NWT:** HS 132* v Leics (Northampton) 1991. BB 1-3. **BHC:** HS 93* v Comb Us (Northampton) 1991. **SL:** HS 76 v Yorks (Leeds) 1991.

HUGHES, John Gareth (Sir Christopher Hatton SS, Wellingborough; Sheffield City Polytechnic), b Wellingborough 3 May 1971. 6′1″. RHB, RM. Debut 1990. HS 2. BB 2-57 v Derbys (Chesterfield) 1990. **SL:** 1*.

LAMB, Allan Joseph (Wynberg HS; Abbotts C) b Langebaanweg, Cape Province, SA 20 Jun 1954. 5′8″. RHB, RM. W Province 1972-82. OFS 1987-88. Northamptonshire debut/cap 1978. Benefit 1988. Captain 1989-. Wisden 1980. **Tests:** 74 (1982 to 1991, 3 as captain); HS 139 v I (Lord's) 1990; BB 1-6. LOI: 110. Tours: A 1982-83, 1986-87, 1990-91; WI 1985-86, 1989-90; NZ 1983-84; I/SL 1984-85; P 1983-84. 1000 runs (10) inc 2000 (2): 2049 (1981). HS 294 OFS v E Province (Bloemfontein) 1987-88 – sharing record SA stand of 355 for 5th wkt with J.J.Strydom. Nh HS 235 v Yorks (Leeds) 1990 sharing in Northants record stand of 393 for 3rd wkt with A.Fordham. BB 2-29 v Lancs (Lytham) 1991. Awards: NWT 2; BHC 8. **NWT:** HS 103 v Suffolk (Bury St E) 1989. BB 1-4. **BHC:** HS 126* v Kent (Canterbury) 1987. BB 1-11. **SL:** HS 132* v Surrey (Guildford) 1985.

LOYE, Malachy Bernhard (Moulton S), b Northampton 27 Sep 1972. 6′2″. RHB, OB. Debut 1991. HS 3*.

MONTGOMERIE, Richard Robert (Rugby S; Worcester C, Oxford), b Rugby, Warwks 3 Jul 1971. 5′10½″. RHB, OB. Debut for Oxford U 1991 (blue 1991). Northamptonshire debut 1991. Rackets blue 1990. HS 88 OU v Hants (Oxford) 1991 – on debut. Nh HS 7.

NOON, Wayne Michael (Caistor S), b Grimsby, Lincs 5 Feb 1971. 5′9″. RHB, WK. Debut 1989. Worcs 2nd XI debut when aged 15yr 190d. HS 37 v A (Northampton) 1989. BAC HS 36 v Glos (Bristol) 1991. **SL:** HS 21 v Surrey (Oval) 1990.

PEARSON, Richard Michael (Batley GS; St John's, Cambridge), b Batley, Yorks 27 Jan 1972. 6′3″. RHB, OB. Cambridge U 1991 (blue 1991). No 1st XI appearances for Northamptonshire. HS 21 and BB 4-84 CU v Derbys (Cambridge) 1991.

PENBERTHY, Anthony Leonard (Camborne CS), b Troon, Cornwall 1 Sep 1969. 6'1". LHB, RM. Debut 1989. Cornwall 1987-89. HS 101* v CU (Cambridge) 1990. BAC HS 83 v Essex (Chelmsford) 1990. BB 4-91 v Warwks (Northampton) 1990. Dismissed M.A.Taylor with his first ball in f-c cricket. **BHC:** HS 10 v Notts (Nottingham) 1990. BB 2-22 v Comb Us (Northampton) 1991. **SL:** HS 41* v Worcs (Northampton) 1991. BB 3-26 v Essex (Northampton) 1989.

RIPLEY, David (Royds SS, Leeds), b Leeds, Yorks 13 Sep 1966. 5'9". RHB, WK. Debut 1984. Cap 1987. HS 134* v Yorks (Scarborough) 1986. BB 2-89 v Essex (Ilford) 1987. Award: BHC 1. NWT: HS 27* v Durham (Darlington) 1984. **BHC:** HS 36* v Glos (Bristol) 1991. **SL:** HS 36* v Hants (Southampton) 1986.

ROBERTS, Andrew Richard, b Kettering 16 Apr 1971. 5'5". RHB, LB. Debut 1989. HS 48 v Glos (Bristol) 1991. BB 6-72 v Lancs (Lytham) 1991. **SL:** HS 14 v Worcs (Northampton) 1991. BB 3-26 v Hants (Northampton) 1991.

SNAPE, Jeremy Nicholas (Denstone C), b Stoke-on-Trent, Staffs 27 Apr 1973. 5'8½". RHB, OB. No 1st XI appearances – joined staff 1990.

STANLEY, Neil Alan (Bedford Modern S), b Bedford 16 May 1968. 6'2". RHB, RM. Debut 1988. Bedfordshire 1987. HS 132 v Lancs (Lytham) 1991. **BHC:** HS 8. BB 1-3. **SL:** HS 18 v Warwks (Birmingham) 1988.

TAYLOR, Jonathan **Paul** (Pingle S, Swadlincote), b Ashby-de-la-Zouch 8 Aug 1964. 6'2". LHB, LFM. Derbyshire 1984-86. Northamptonshire debut 1991. Staffordshire 1989-90 (cap 1989). HS 11 D v Middx (Derby) 1984. Nh HS 5*. BB 5-42 v Lancs (Northampton) 1991. **NWT:** HS 9. BB 2-11 v Staffs (Stone) 1991. **BHC:** HS 1*. BB 2-30 v Worcs (Northampton) 1991. **SL:** HS 16 v Surrey (Tring) 1991. BB 3-14 D v Glos (Gloucester) 1986.

WALKER, Alan (Shelley HS), b Emley, Yorks 7 Jul 1962. 5'11". LHB, RFM. Debut 1983. Cap 1987. HS 41* v Warwks (Birmingham) 1987. 50 wkts (1): 54 (1988). BB 6-50 v Lancs (Northampton) 1986. Award: NWT 1. **NWT:** HS 11 v Surrey (Oval) 1991. BB 4-7 v Ire (Northampton) 1987. **BHC:** HS 15* v Notts (Nottingham) 1987. BB 4-46 v Glos (Northampton) 1985. **SL:** HS 13 v Yorks (Tring) 1983. BB 4-21 v Worcs (Worcester) 1985.

WALTON, Timothy Charles (Leeds GS), b Low Lead 8 Nov 1972. 6'0¾". RHB, RM. No 1st XI appearances – joined staff 1991.

WARREN, Russell John (Kingsthorpe Upper S), b Northampton 10 Sep 1971. 6'1". RHB, OB. No 1st XI appearances – joined staff 1990.

WILLIAMS, Richard Grenville (Ellesmere Port GS), Bangor, Caernarvonshire 10 Aug 1957. 5'6½". RHB, OB. Debut 1974. Cap 1979. Benefit 1989. Tours: NZ 1979-80 (DHR); Z 1984-85 (EC). 1000 runs (6); most – 1262 (1980). HS 175* v Leics (Leicester) 1980. BB 7-73 v CU (Cambridge) 1980. BAC HS 6-65 v Glos (Northampton) 1990. Hat-trick 1980. Awards: NWT 1; BHC 4. **NWT:** HS 94 v Worcs (Northampton) 1984. BB 4-10 v Leics (Leicester) 1987. **BHC:** HS 83 v Yorks (Bradford) 1980. BB 4-41 v Glos (Northampton) 1987. **SL:** HS 82 v Glos (Bristol) 1982. BB 5-30 v Warwks (Luton) 1983.

NEWCOMERS

GREEN, Simon James (Old Swinford Hospital S), b Bloxwich, Staffs 19 Mar 1970. 6'2". RHB, LM. Warwickshire 1988-91. HS 77* Wa v Somerset (Birmingham) 1991. **NWT:** HS 1. **BHC:** HS 0. **SL:** HS 25 Wa v Somerset (W-s-M) 1990.

INNES, Kevin, b Northampton 24 Sep 1975. RHB, RM. 2nd XI debut 1990 (aged 14yr 8mth – Northamptonshire record).

DEPARTURES – see p 155

NORTHAMPTONSHIRE 1991

RESULTS SUMMARY

	Place	Won	Lost	Drew	Abandoned
Britannic Assurance Championship	10th	5	6	11	
All First-class Matches		5	6	13	
Refuge Assurance League	3rd	10	4		2
NatWest Trophy	Semi-Finalist				
Benson and Hedges Cup	Quarter-Finalist				

BRITANNIC ASSURANCE CHAMPIONSHIP AVERAGES

BATTING AND FIELDING

Cap		M	I	NO	HS	Runs	Avge	100	50	Ct/St
1978	A.J.Lamb	14	23	2	194	993	47.28	3	5	13
1990	A.Fordham	22	40	2	165	1725	45.39	4	8	8
–	A.R.Roberts	14	15	9	48	244	40.66	–	–	7
1985	R.J.Bailey	19	34	4	117	1202	40.06	1	11	10
1976	W.Larkins	9	16	6	75	365	36.50	–	2	6
–	N.A.Stanley	8	13	0	132	470	36.15	1	2	5
–	K.M.Curran	19	30	7	89*	749	32.56	–	5	11
–	E.A.E.Baptiste	17	22	1	80	589	28.04	–	4	9
1987	D.Ripley	18	24	8	53*	429	26.81	1	37/2	
1986	D.J.Capel	20	32	2	71	692	23.06	–	7	10
1991	J.G.Thomas	10	12	3	64	206	22.88	–	1	3
1990	N.A.Felton	14	25	2	55	439	19.08	–	1	5
1979	R.G.Williams	7	10	2	35	123	15.37	–	–	1
–	A.L.Penberthy	11	14	2	52	184	15.33	–	1	6
–	W.M.Noon	6	9	2	36	93	13.71	–	–	11
1987	A.Walker	4	4	1	13	35	11.66	–	–	2
1987	N.G.B.Cook	16	15	5	29	114	11.40	–	–	6
–	J.P.Taylor	11	11	4	5*	22	3.14	–	–	4

Also played (1 match each): J.G.Hughes did not bat; M.B.Loye 3* (1 ct);
R.R.Montgomerie 2, 7 (2 ct).

BOWLING

	O	M	R	W	Avge	Best	5wI	10wM
K.M.Curran	410.2	101	1128	45	25.06	5-60	1	–
E.A.E.Baptiste	517.2	117	1418	49	28.93	7-95	3	–
J.P.Taylor	267.2	45	828	24	34.50	5-42	1	–
J.G.Thomas	248.4	33	829	24	34.54	5-62	2	–
A.R.Roberts	331.5	72	1032	29	35.58	6-72	1	–
R.J.Bailey	118.3	16	409	11	37.18	3-44	–	–
N.G.B.Cook	305.1	70	895	24	37.29	4-74	–	–
D.J.Capel	373.1	82	1099	28	39.25	4-83	–	–
A.L.Penberthy	163.4	26	531	13	40.84	3-27	–	–

Also bowled: N.A.Felton 6-0-66-0; A.Fordham 13-0-78-1; J.G.Hughes 12-1-43-1;
A.J.Lamb 3.4-0-29-2; W.Larkins 6-4-2-0; N.A.Stanley 10-2-19-0; A.Walker
103-20-296-6; R.G.Wiliams 87.3-17-256-4.

The First-Class Averages (pp 164-179) give the records of Northamptonshire
players in all first-class county matches (their other opponents being the West
Indians and Cambridge U.), with the exception of R.R.Montgomerie, whose full
county figures are as above, and:
    A.J.Lamb 15-23-2-194-993-47.28-3-5-14ct. 3.4-0-29-2-14.50-2/29.

NORTHAMPTONSHIRE RECORDS
FIRST-CLASS CRICKET

Highest Total	For 636-6d		v Essex	Chelmsford	1990
	V 670-9d		by Sussex	Hove	1921
Lowest Total	For 12		v Glos	Gloucester	1907
	V 33		by Lancashire	Northampton	1977
Highest Innings	For 300 R.Subba Row		v Surrey	The Oval	1958
	V 333 K.S.Duleepsinhji		for Sussex	Hove	1930

Highest Partnership for each Wicket

1st	361	N.Oldfield/V.Broderick	v Scotland	Peterborough	1953
2nd	344	G.Cook/R.J.Boyd-Moss	v Lancashire	Northampton	1986
3rd	393	A.Fordham/A.J.Lamb	v Yorkshire	Leeds	1990
4th	370	R.T.Virgin/P.Willey	v Somerset	Northampton	1976
5th	347	D.Brookes/D.W.Barrick	v Essex	Northampton	1952
6th	376	R.Subba Row/A.Lightfoot	v Surrey	The Oval	1958
7th	229	W.W.Timms/F.A.Walden	v Warwicks	Northampton	1926
8th	164	D.Ripley/N.G.B.Cook	v Lancashire	Manchester	1987
9th	156	R.Subba Row/S.Starkie	v Lancashire	Northampton	1955
10th	148	B.W.Bellamy/J.V.Murdin	v Glamorgan	Northampton	1925

Best Bowling	For 10-127 V.W.C.Jupp		v Kent	Tunbridge W	1932
(Innings)	V 10-30 C.Blythe		for Kent	Northampton	1907
Best Bowling	For 15-31 G.E.Tribe		v Yorkshire	Northampton	1958
(Match)	V 17-48 C.Blythe		for Kent	Northampton	1907

Most Runs – Season	2,198	D.Brookes	(av 51.11)		1952
Most Runs – Career	28,980	D.Brookes	(av 36.13)		1934-1959
Most 100s – Season	8	R.A.Haywood			1921
Most 100s – Career	67	D.Brookes			1934-1959
Most Wkts – Season	175	G.E.Tribe	(av 18.70)		1955
Most Wkts – Career	1,097	E.W.Clark	(av 21.31)		1922-1947

LIMITED-OVERS CRICKET

Highest Total	NWT	360-2	v Staffs	Northampton	1990
	BHC	300-9	v Derbyshire	Derby	1987
	SL	306-2	v Surrey	Guildford	1985
Lowest Total	NWT	62	v Leics	Leicester	1974
	BHC	85	v Sussex	Northampton	1978
	SL	41	v Middlesex	Northampton	1972
Highest Innings	NWT	145 R.J.Bailey	v Staffs	Stone	1991
	BHC	134 R.J.Bailey	v Glos	Northampton	1987
	SL	172* W.Larkins	v Warwicks	Luton	1983
Best Bowling	NWT	7-37 N.A.Mallender	v Worcs	Northampton	1984
	BHC	5-21 Sarfraz Nawaz	v Middlesex	Lord's	1980
	SL	7-39 A.Hodgson	v Somerset	Northampton	1976

NOTTINGHAMSHIRE

Formation of Present Club: March/April 1841
Substantial Reorganisation: 11 December 1866
Colours: Green and Gold
Badge: County Badge of Nottinghamshire
Championships (since 1890): (4) 1907, 1929, 1981, 1987
NatWest Trophy/Gillette Cup Winners: (1) 1987
Benson and Hedges Cup Winners: (1) 1989
Sunday League Champions: (1) 1991
Match Awards: NWT 32; BHC 55

Secretary/General Manager: B.Robson, Trent Bridge, Nottingham NG2 6AG
(☎ 0602-821525)
Captain: R.T.Robinson
Scorer: L.Beaumont
1992 Beneficiary: R.T.Robinson

AFFORD, John Andrew (Spalding GS; Stamford CFE), b Crowland, Lincs 12 May 1964. 6'1½". RHB, SLA. Debut 1984. Cap 1990. Tour: Z 1989-90 (Eng A). HS 22* v Leics (Nottingham) 1989. 50 wkts (2); most – 57 (1991). BB 6-81 v Kent (Nottingham) 1986. Award: BHC 1. **NWT:** HS 2*. BB 3-32 v Herts (Hitchin) 1989. **BHC:** HS 1*. BB 4-38 v Kent (Nottingham) 1989. **SL:** HS 0*. BB 2-39 v Glam (Nottingham) 1990.

BATES, Richard Terry (Bourne GS; Stamford CFE), b Stamford, Lincs 17 Jun 1972. 6'1". RHB, OB. No 1st XI appearances – joined staff 1991.

BROAD, Brian Christopher (Colston's S, Bristol; St. Paul's C, Cheltenham), b Knowle, Bristol 29 Sep 1957. 6'4". LHB, RM. Gloucestershire 1979-83 (cap 1981). Nottinghamshire debut/cap 1984. OFS 1985-86 (captain). **Tests:** 25 (1984 to 1989); HS 162 v A (Perth) 1986-87. LOI: 34. Tours: A 1986-87, 1987-88; SA 1989-90 (Eng XI); NZ 1987-88; P 1987-88; Z 1984-85 (EC). 1000 runs (9) inc 2000 (1): 2226 (1990). HS 227* v Kent (Tunbridge W) 1990. BB 2-14 Gs v WI (Bristol) 1980. Nt BB 2-23 v Derbys (Derby) 1984. Awards: NWT 4; BHC 2. **NWT:** HS 115 v Bucks (Marlow) 1990. **BHC:** HS 122 v Derbys (Derby) 1984. BB 2-73 v Lancs (Nottingham) 1984. **SL:** HS 108 v Glam (Cardiff) 1991. BB 3-46 Gs v Worcs (Bristol) 1982.

CAIRNS, Christopher Lance (Christchurch BHS), b Picton, NZ 13 Jun 1970. Son of B.L. (C Districts, Otago, N Districts and NZ 1971-86). 6'2". RHB, RFM. Nottinghamshire 1988-89. N Districts 1988-89. Canterbury 1990-91. **Tests:** 2 (1989-90 and 1990-91); HS 28 v A (Perth) 1989-90 – on debut; BB 5-75 v SL (Auckland) 1990-91. LOI: 2. Tour (NZ): A 1989-90. HS 110 N Districts v Auckland (Hamilton) 1988-89. Nt HS 58 v Kent (Nottingham) 1989. BB 7-39 Canterbury v CD (Napier) 1990-91. Nt BB 4-70 v Kent (Dartford) 1988 (on debut). **SL:** HS 4. DD 2-38 v Somerset (Nottingham) 1989.

COOPER, Kevin Edwin (Hucknall National SS), b Hucknall 27 Dec 1957. 6'1". LHB, RFM. Debut 1976. Cap 1980. Benefit 1990. HS 46 v Middx (Nottingham) 1985. 50 wkts (8) inc 100 wkts (1): 101 (1988). BB 8-44 v Middx (Lord's) 1984. Awards: NWT 1; BHC 2. **NWT:** HS 11 v Glos (Nottingham) 1982. BB 4-49 v Warwks (Nottingham) 1985. **BHC:** HS 25* v Lancs (Manchester) 1983. BB 4-9 v Yorks (Nottingham) 1989. **SL:** HS 31 v Glos (Nottingham) 1984. BB 4-25 v Hants (Nottingham) 1976.

CRAWLEY, Mark Andrew (Manchester GS; Oriel C, Oxford), b Newton-le-Willows, Lancs 16 Dec 1967. 6'3". RHB, RM. Oxford U 1987-90 (blue 1987-88-89-90; captain 1989). Lancashire 1990. Nottinghamshire debut 1991. HS 140 OU v CU (Lord's) 1987. Nt HS 112 v OU (Oxford) 1991 – on Nt debut. BAC HS 49* v Glos (Gloucester) 1991. BB 6-92 OU v Glam (Oxford) 1990. Nt BB 3-21 v Derbys

118

CRAWLEY – continued:
(Derby) 1991. Awards: NWT 1; BHC 1. **NWT:** HS 74* and 4-26 v Lincs (Nottingham) 1991 (on debut). **BHC:** HS 58 v Glam (Cardiff) 1991. BB 2-72 Comb Us v Worcs (Worcester) 1989. **SL:** HS 47* v Worcs (Nottingham) 1991. BB 2-13 v Leics (Leicester) 1991.

DESSAUR, Wayne Anthony (Loughborough GS), b Nottingham 4 Feb 1971. 6'0". RHB, RM. No 1st XI appearances – joined staff 1991.

EVANS, Kevin Paul (Colonel Frank Seely S) b Calverton 10 Sep 1963. Elder brother of R.J. (Notts 1987-90). 6'2". RHB, RMF. Debut 1984. Cap 1990. HS 100* v Somerset (W-s-M) 1990. BB 5-52 v Leics (Nottingham) 1991. **NWT:** HS 20 v Hants (Southampton) 1991. BB 4-30 v Kent (Nottingham) 1986. **BHC:** HS 31* v Northants (Northampton) 1988. BB 4-43 v Glam (Cardiff) 1991. **SL:** HS 30 v Kent (Canterbury) 1990. BB 4-28 v Derbys (Nottingham) 1989.

FIELD-BUSS, Michael Gwyn (Wanstead HS), b Mtarfa, Malta 23 Sep 1964. 5'10". RHB, OB. Essex 1987. Nottinghamshire debut 1989. HS 34* Ex v Middx (Lord's) 1987. Nt HS 25 v Middx (Lord's) 1991. BB 4-33 v Somerset (Nottingham) 1989. **SL:** HS 5. BB 2-22 v Yorks (Scarborough) 1991.

FRENCH, Bruce Nicholas (The Meden CS), b Warsop 13 Aug 1959. 5'6". RHB, WK. Debut 1976 (aged 16yr 287d). Cap 1980. Benefit 1991. **Tests:** 16 (1986 to 1987-88); HS 59 v P (Manchester) 1987. LOI: 13. Tours: A 1986-87, 1987-88; SA 1989-90 (Eng XI); WI 1985-86; NZ 1987-88; I/SL 1984-85; P 1987-88. HS 105* v Derbys (Derby) 1990. BB 1-37. Award: BHC 1. **NWT:** HS 49 v Staffs (Nottingham) 1985. **BHC:** HS 48* v Worcs (Nottingham) 1984. **SL:** HS 37 v Glos (Bristol) 1985.

HEMMINGS, Edward Ernest (Campion S), b Leamington Spa, Warwks 20 Feb 1949. 5'10". RHB, OB. Warwickshire 1966-78 (cap 1974). Nottinghamshire debut 1979. Cap 1980. Benefit 1987. **Tests:** 16 (1982 to 1990-91); HS 95 v A (Sydney) 1982-83; BB 6-58 v NZ (Birmingham) 1990. LOI: 33. Tours: A 1982-83, 1987-88, 1990-91; SA 1974-75 (DHR); WI 1982-83 (Int); 1989-90; NZ 1987-88; P 1981-82 (Int), 1987-88. HS 127* v Yorks (Worksop) 1982. 50 wkts (14); most – 94 (1984). BB 10-175 Int XI v WI XI (Kingston) 1982-83. Nt BB 7-23 v Lancs (Nottingham) 1983. 2 hat-tricks: 1977 (Wa), 1984. Awards: NWT 1; BHC 1. **NWT:** HS 31* v Staffs (Nottingham) 1985. BB 3-27 v Warwks (Nottingham) 1985. **BHC:** HS 61* Wa v Leics (Birmingham) 1974. BB 4-47 v Glos (Bristol) 1989. **SL:** HS 44* Wa v Kent (Birmingham) 1971. BB 5-22 Wa v Notts (Birmingham) 1974.

JOHNSON, Paul (Grove CS, Balderton), b Newark 24 Apr 1965. 5'7". RHB, RM. Debut 1982. Cap 1986. 1000 runs (5); most – 1518 (1990). HS 165* v Northants (Nottingham) 1990. BB 1-9. BAC 1-14. Awards: NWT 1; BHC 1. **NWT:** HS 101* v Staffs (Nottingham) 1985. **BHC:** HS 104* v Essex (Chelmsford) 1990. **SL:** HS 114 v Warwks (Birmingham) 1990.

MIKE, Gregory Wentworth, b Nottingham 14 Jul 1966. 6'0". RHB, RMF. Debut 1989. HS 56* and BB 2-62 v CU (Cambridge) 1989 (on debut). BAC HS 18* v Lancs (Nottingham) 1990. BAC BB 1-59. **BHC:** HS 29 v Kent (Nottingham) 1989. **SL:** HS 25* v Kent (Nottingham) 1989. BB 3-30 v Glos (Nottingham) 1990.

NEWELL, Michael (West Bridgford CS), b Blackburn, Lancs 25 Feb 1965. 5'8". RHB, LB. Debut 1984. Cap 1987. 1000 runs (1): 1054 (1987). HS 203* v Derbys (Derby) 1987. BB 2-38 v SL (Nottingham) 1988. BAC BB 1-0. **NWT:** HS 60 v Derbys (Derby) 1987. **BHC:** HS 39 v Somerset (Taunton) 1989. **SL:** HS 109* v Essex (Southend) 1990.

PICK, Robert Andrew (Alderman Derbyshire CS; High Pavement SFC), b Nottingham 19 Nov 1963. 5'10". LHB, RMF. Debut 1983. Cap 1987. Wellington 1989-90. Tour: SL 1990-91 (Eng A). HS 63 v Warwks (Nuneaton) 1985. 50 wkts (3); most – 67 (1991). BB 7-128 v Leics (Leicester) 1990. Awards: NWT 1; BHC 1. **NWT:** HS 34* v Sussex (Hove) 1983. BB 5-22 v Glos (Bristol) 1987. **BHC:** HS 25* v Hants (Southampton) 1991. BB 4-42 v Northants (Nottingham) 1987. **SL:** HS 24 v Yorks (Hull) 1986. BB 4-32 v Glos (Moreton) 1987.

POLLARD, Paul Raymond (Gedling CS), b Carlton, Nottingham, 24 Sep 1968. 5'11". LHB, RM. Debut 1987. 1000 runs (2); most – 1255 (1991). HS 153 v CU (Cambridge) 1989. BAC HS 145 v Lancs (Nottingham) 1991. BB 1-46. **NWT:** HS 23 v Middx (Uxbridge) 1989. **BHC:** HS 77 v Kent (Nottingham) 1989. **SL:** HS 123* v Surrey (Oval) 1989.

RANDALL, Derek William (Sir Frederick Milner SS), b Retford 24 Feb 1951. 5'9". RHB, RM. Debut 1972. Cap 1973. Benefit 1983. Wisden 1979. Tests: 47 (1976-77 to 1984); HS 174 v A (Melbourne) 1976-77. LOI: 49. Tours: A 1976-77, 1978-79, 1979-80, 1982-83; SA 1975-76 (DHR); NZ 1977-78, 1983-84; I/SL 1976-77; P 1977-78, 1983-84; Z 1985-86 (Eng B). 1000 runs (13) inc 2000 (1): 2151 (1985). HS 237 v Derbys (Nottingham) 1988. BB 3-15 v MCC (Lord's) 1982. BAC BB 3-43 v Sussex (Hove) 1984. Awards: NWT 7; BHC 6. **NWT:** HS 149* v Devon (Torquay) 1988. **BHC:** HS 103* v Minor C (N) (Nottingham) 1979. **SL:** HS 123 v Yorks (Nottingham) 1987.

ROBINSON, Robert Timothy (Dunstable GS; High Pavement SFC; Sheffield U), b Sutton in Ashfield 21 Nov 1958. 6'0". RHB, RM. Debut 1978. Cap 1983. Captain 1988-. Benefit 1992. Wisden 1985. Tests: 29 (1984-85 to 1989); HS 175 v A (Leeds) 1985. LOI: 26. Tours: A 1987-88; SA 1989-90 (Eng XI); NZ 1987-88; WI 1985-86; I/SL 1984-85; P 1987-88. 1000 runs (9) inc 2000 (1): 2032 (1984). HS 220* v Yorks (Nottingham) 1990. BB 1-22. Awards: NWT 4; BHC 6. **NWT:** HS 139 v Worcs (Worcester) 1985. **BHC:** HS 120 v Scot (Glasgow) 1985. **SL:** HS 116 v Derbys (Derby) 1990.

SAXELBY, Mark (Nottingham HS), b Worksop 4 Jan 1969. 6'3". LHB, RM. Younger brother of K. (Notts 1978-90). Debut 1989. HS 73 v CU (Cambridge) 1990. BAC HS 51 v Hants (Portsmouth) 1990. BB 3-41 v Derbys (Derby) 1991. **NWT:** HS 41 v Bucks (Marlow) 1990. BB 2-42 v Lincs (Nottingham) 1991. **BHC:** HS 32 v Hants (Southampton) 1991. BB 1-36. **SL:** HS 55 v Yorks (Scarborough) 1991. BB 4-29 v Leics (Leicester) 1991.

NEWCOMERS

ARCHER, Graeme Francis (King Edward VI S, Stafford), b Carlisle, Cumberland 26 Sep 1970. RHB, RM. Staffordshire 1990-91.

BRAMHALL, Stephen (Stockton Heath CHS; Newcastle U), b Warrington 26 Nov 1967. 6'1". RHB, WK. Lancashire 1990. Cheshire 1988-91. HS 1*. BAC HS 8*.

LEWIS, Clairmonte Christopher (Willesden HS, London), b Georgetown, Guyana 14 Feb 1968. 6'2½". RHB, RFM. Leicestershire 1987-91 (cap 1990). Tests: 7 (1990 to 1991); HS 65 and BB 6-111 v WI (Birmingham) 1991. LOI: 14. Tours: A 1990-91 (part); WI 1989-90 (part). HS 189* Le v Essex (Chelmsford) 1990. 50 wkts (1): 56 (1990). BB 6-22 Le v OU (Oxford) 1988. BAC BB 6-55 Le v Glam (Cardiff) 1990. **NWT:** HS 53 Le v Glos (Leicester) 1988. BB 3-28 Le v Salop (Leicester) 1991. **BHC:** HS 23* Le v Lancs (Manchester) 1989. BB 3-41 Le v Lancs (Leicester) 1988. **SL:** HS 93* Le v Essex (Leicester) 1990. BB 4-13 Le v Essex (Leicester) 1988.

DEPARTURES – see p 155

NOTTINGHAMSHIRE 1991

RESULTS SUMMARY

	Place	Won	Lost	Drew
Britannic Assurance Championship	4th	7	5	10
All First-class Matches		7	5	11
Refuge Assurance League	1st	13	3	
NatWest Trophy	Quarter-Finalist			
Benson and Hedges Cup	3rd in Group D			

BRITANNIC ASSURANCE CHAMPIONSHIP AVERAGES
BATTING AND FIELDING

Cap		M	I	NO	HS	Runs	Avge	100	50	Ct/St
1973	D.W.Randall	22	34	9	143*	1567	62.68	5	5	15
1983	R.T.Robinson	22	37	8	180	1673	57.68	3	10	18
1984	B.C.Broad	21	38	3	166	1739	49.68	5	7	9
1986	P.Johnson	22	36	6	124	1357	45.23	3	10	12
–	P.R.Pollard	22	40	3	145	1235	33.37	3	4	21
1990	K.P.Evans	14	17	7	56*	276	27.60	–	1	6
1988	F.D.Stephenson	22	27	7	58	423	21.15	–	1	6
–	M.A.Crawley	10	12	4	49*	160	20.00	–	–	14
–	M.Saxelby	6	9	1	44	136	17.00	–	–	–
1980	B.N.French	21	24	4	65	315	15.75	–	2	54/8
1987	R.A.Pick	21	16	5	46	142	12.90	–	–	7
1980	E.E.Hemmings	16	16	4	29*	143	11.91	–	–	4
1990	J.A.Afford	18	12	4	13	42	5.25	–	–	10

Also played: V.J.P.Broadley (1 match) 6; K.E.Cooper (1 match – cap 1980) did not bat; M.G.Field-Buss (2 matches) 25, 16 (1 ct); C.W.Scott (1 match – cap 1988) did not bat (3 ct).

BOWLING

	O	M	R	W	Avge	Best	5wI	10wM
F.D.Stephenson	719.1	158	2010	78	25.76	5-27	4	1
R.A.Pick	623.4	113	1985	65	30.53	5-17	3	–
J.A.Afford	670.3	207	1817	57	31.87	4-44	–	–
K.P.Evans	425	89	1278	40	31.95	5-52	–	–
E.E.Hemmings	638.3	171	1721	46	37.41	6-46	2	–
M.A.Crawley	176.5	53	463	11	42.09	3-21	–	–

Also bowled: V.J.P.Broadley 32-6-111-1; K.E.Cooper 17-3-54-1; M.G.Field-Buss 53-11-187-1; B.N.French 14-4-48-1; P.Johnson 12.2-1-62-2; P.R.Pollard 23.5-8-75-1; D.W.Randall 4-0-19-1; R.T.Robinson 8-0-39-1; M.Saxelby 97.2-17-423-4.

The First-Class Averages (pp 164-179) give the records of Nottinghamshire players in all first-class county matches (their other opponents being Oxford U.), with the exception of:
R.A.Pick 22-16-5-46-142-12.90-0-0-7ct. 623.4-113-1985-65-30.53-5/17-3-0.

NOTTINGHAMSHIRE RECORDS

FIRST-CLASS CRICKET

Highest Total	For 739-7d		v Leics	Nottingham	1903
	V 706-4d		by Surrey	Nottingham	1947
Lowest Total	For 13		v Yorkshire	Nottingham	1901
	V 16		by Derbyshire	Nottingham	1879
	16		by Surrey	The Oval	1880
Highest Innings	For 312*	W.W.Keeton	v Middlesex	The Oval	1939
	V 345	C.G.Macartney	for Australians	Nottingham	1921

Highest Partnership for each Wicket

1st	391	A.O.Jones/A.Shrewsbury	v Glos	Bristol	1899
2nd	398	A.Shrewsbury/W.Gunn	v Sussex	Nottingham	1890
3rd	369	W.Gunn/J.R.Gunn	v Leics	Nottingham	1903
4th	361	A.O.Jones/J.R.Gunn	v Essex	Leyton	1905
5th	266	A.Shrewsbury/W.Gunn	v Sussex	Hove	1884
6th	303*	F.H.Winrow/P.F.Harvey	v Derbyshire	Nottingham	1947
7th	204	M.J.Smedley/R.A.White	v Surrey	The Oval	1967
th	220	G.F.H.Heane/R.Winrow	v Somerset	Nottingham	1935
9th	165	W.McIntyre/G.Wootton	v Kent	Nottingham	1869
10th	152	E.B.Alletson/W.Riley	v Sussex	Hove	1911

Best Bowling (Innings)	For 10-66	K.Smales	v Glos	Stroud	1956
	V 10-10	H.Verity	for Yorkshire	Leeds	1932
Best Bowling (Match)	For 17-89	F.C.Matthews	v Northants	Nottingham	1923
	V 17-89	W.G.Grace	for Glos	Cheltenham	1877

Most Runs – Season	2,620	W.W.Whysall	(av 53.46)		1929
Most Runs – Career	31,592	G.Gunn	(av 35.69)		1902-1932
Most 100s – Season	9	W.W.Whysall			1928
	9	M.J.Harris			1971
	9	B.C.Broad			1990
Most 100s – Career	65	J.Hardstaff, jr			1930-1955
Most Wkts – Season	181	B.Dooland	(av 14.96)		1954
Most Wkts – Career	1,653	T.G.Wass	(av 20.34)		1896-1920

LIMITED-OVERS CRICKET

Highest Total	NWT	312-9		v Bucks	Marlow	1990
	BHC	296-6		v Kent	Nottingham	1989
	SL	283-6		v Yorkshire	Nottingham	1987
Lowest Total	NWT	123		v Yorkshire	Scarborough	1969
	BHC	74		v Leics	Leicester	1987
	SL	66		v Yorkshire	Bradford	1969
Highest Innings	NWT	149*	D.W.Randall	v Devon	Torquay	1988
	BHC	130*	C.E.B.Rice	v Scotland	Glasgow	1982
	SL	123*	P.R.Pollard	v Surrey	The Oval	1989
Best Bowling	NWT	6-18	C.E.B.Rice	v Sussex	Hove	1982
	BHC	6-22	M.K.Bore	v Leics	Leicester	1980
		6-22	C.E.B.Rice	v Northants	Northampton	1981
	SL	6-12	R.J.Hadlee	v Lancashire	Nottingham	1980

SOMERSET

Formation of Present Club: 18 August 1875
Colours: Black, White and Maroon
Badge: Somerset Dragon
Championships: (0) Third 1892, 1958, 1963, 1966, 1981
NatWest Trophy/Gillette Cup Winners: (2) 1979, 1983
Benson and Hedges Cup Winners: (2) 1981, 1982
Sunday League Champions: (1) 1979
Match Awards: NWT 40; BHC 52

Chief Executive: P.W.Anderson, The County Ground, Taunton TA1 1JT
(☎ 0823-272946)
Captain: C.J.Tavaré
Scorer: D.A.Oldam

BARTLETT, Richard James (Taunton S), b Ash Priors 8 Oct 1966. 5'9". RHB, OB. Debut 1986 scoring 117* v OU (Oxford). HS 117* (above). BAC HS 102* v Kent (Canterbury) 1988. BB: 1-9 (twice). **NWT:** HS 85 v Hants (Southampton) 1988. **BHC:** HS 36 v Comb Us (Taunton) 1989. **SL:** HS 55 v Lancs 1988 and 1990.

BURNS, Neil David (Moulsham HS, Chelmsford), b Chelmsford, Essex 19 Sep 1965. 5'10". LHB, WK, occ SLA. W Province B 1985-86. Essex 1986. Somerset debut/cap 1987. HS 166 v Glos (Taunton) 1990. **NWT:** HS 25* v Worcs (Taunton) 1990. **BHC:** HS 51 v Middx (Lord's) 1987. **SL:** HS 58 v Sussex (Hove) 1990.

CADDICK, Andrew Richard, b Christchurch, New Zealand 21 Nov 1968. Son of English emigrants – qualified for England 1992. 6'5". RHB, RFM. Debut 1991. Represented NZ in 1987-88 Youth World Cup. Took 96 wkts (av 12.84) in 1991 2nd XI Championship. Awaiting BAC debut. HS 0. BB 2-40 v SL (Taunton) 1991.

FLETCHER, Ian (Millfield S; Loughborough U), b Sawbridgeworth, Herts 31 Aug 1971. 5'11". RHB, RM. Debut 1991. Hertfordshire 1990. Comb Us (BHC) 1991. HS 56 v Hants (Southampton) 1991 – on debut. **NWT:** (Herts) HS 1. **BHC:** HS 9.

HALLETT, Jeremy Charles (Millfield S; Durham U), b Yeovil 18 Oct 1970. 6'2". RHB, RMF. Debut 1990. Comb Us (BHC) 1991. HS 15 v Glos (Bristol) 1991. BB 3-154 v Worcs (Worcester) 1991. **BHC:** HS 5. BB 3-36 Comb Us v Worcs (Cambridge) 1991. **SL:** HS 4*. BB 3-41 v Glam (Neath) 1990.

HARDEN, Richard John (King's C, Taunton), b Bridgwater 16 Aug 1965. 5'11". RHB, SLA. Debut 1985. Cap 1989. C Districts 1987-88. 1000 runs (3); most – 1460 (1990). HS 134 v Derbys (Derby) 1991. BB 2-7 CD v Canterbury (Blenheim) 1987-88. Sm BB 2-24 v Hants (Taunton) 1986. **NWT:** HS 39 v Middx (Taunton) 1991. **BHC:** HS 53* v Minor C (Taunton) 1990. **SL:** HS 79* v Notts (Nottingham) 1991.

HAYHURST, Andrew Neil (Worsley Wardley HS; Eccles SFC; Leeds Polytechnic), b Davyhulme, Manchester 23 Nov 1962. 5'11". RHB, RM. Lancashire 1985-89. Somerset debut/cap 1990. Tours: WI 1986-87 (Lancs); Z 1988-89 (Lancs). 1000 runs (1): 1559 (1990). HS 172* v Glos (Bath) 1991. BB 4-27 La v Middx (Manchester) 1987. Sm BB 3-58 v Sussex (Hove) 1990. Awards: NWT 1; BHC 1. **NWT:** HS 91* and BB 5-60 v Warwks (Birmingham) 1991. **BHC:** HS 76 v Minor C (Taunton) 1990. BB 4-50 La v Worcs (Worcester) 1987. **SL:** HS 84 La v Leics (Manchester) 1988. BB 4-37 La v Glam 1988 and Sm v Sussex 1990.

LATHWELL, Mark Nicholas (Braunton S, Devon), b Bletchley, Bucks 26 Dec 1971. 5'8". RHB, RM. Debut 1991. HS 43 v Worcs (Worcester) 1991. BB 1-29. **NWT:** HS 16 v Warwks (Birmingham) 1991. **SL:** HS 20 v Leics (W-s-M) 1991.

LEFEBVRE, Roland Philippe (Montessori Lyceum, Rotterdam; Hague Accademie of Physiotherapy), b Rotterdam, Holland 7 Feb 1963. 6'1". RHB, RMF. Debut 1990. Cap 1991. Holland 1983-90; ICC Trophy 1986 and 1989. Canterbury 1990-91. HS 100 v Worcs (W-s-M) 1991. BB 6-53 Canterbury v Auckland (Auckland) 1990-91. Sm BB 5-30 v Glos (Taunton) 1990. **NWT:** HS 21* v Warwks (Birmingham) 1991. BB 7-15 v Devon (Torquay) 1990. **BHC:** HS 37 v Middx (Lord's) 1990. BB 3-44 v Surrey (Taunton) 1991. **SL:** HS 28 v Yorks (Scarborough) 1990. BB 4-35 v Northants (Taunton) 1990.

MacLEAY, Kenneth Hervey (Scotch C, Perth; W Australia U), b Bradford-on-Avon, Wilts 2 Apr 1959. 6'4". RHB, RM. W Australia 1981-90. Somerset debut 1991. LOI (A) 16 – inc 1983 World Cup in England. Tours: I 1989-90 (WA); Z 1982-83 (Young A). HS 114* WA v NSW (Perth) 1986-87. Sm HS 63 v Warwks (Taunton) 1991. BB 6-93 WA v NSW (Perth) 1985-86. Sm BB 3-40 v Derbys (Derby) 1991. **NWT:** HS 25* v Middx (Taunton) 1991. BB 2-35 v Bucks (Bath) 1991. **SL:** HS 19 v Middx (Taunton) 1991. BB 3-31 v Notts (Nottingham) 1991.

MALLENDER, Neil Alan (Beverley GS), b Kirk Sandall, Yorks 13 Aug 1961. 6'0". RHB, RFM. Northamptonshire 1980-86 (cap 1984). Somerset debut/cap 1987. Otago 1983-91 (captain 1990-91). HS 88 Otago v C Districts (Oamaru) 1984-85. Sm HS 87* v Sussex (Hove) 1990 sharing in Somerset record stand of 183 for 9th wkt with C.J.Tavaré. 50 wkts (5); most – 56 (1983). BB 7-27 Otago v Auckland (Auckland) 1984-85. BAC BB 7-41 Nh v Derbys (Northampton) 1982. Sm BB 7-61 v Derbys (Taunton) 1987. Award: NWT 1. **NWT:** HS 11* Nh v Yorks (Leeds) 1983. BB 7-37 Nh v Worcs (Northampton) 1984. **BHC:** HS 16* v Hants (Taunton) 1988. BB 5-53 Nh v Leics (Northampton) 1986. **SL:** HS 24 v Glos (Bristol) 1990. BB 5-34 Nh v Middx (Tring) 1981.

ROSE, Graham David (Northumberland Park S, Tottenham), b Tottenham, London 12 Apr 1964. 6'4". RHB, RM. Middlesex 1985-86. Somerset debut 1987. Cap 1988. 1000 runs (1): 1000 (1990). HS 106 v Glos (Bristol) 1991. 50 wkts (2); most – 57 (1988). BB 6-41 M v Worcs (Worcester) 1985 – on debut. Sm BB 6-47 v Warwks (Bath) 1988. Award: BHC 1. **NWT:** HS 110 v Devon (Torquay) 1990. BB 2-30 v Bucks (High Wycombe) 1987. **BHC:** HS 64 v Derbys (Taunton) 1990. BB 4-37 v Sussex (Hove) 1990. **SL:** HS 148 v Glam (Neath) 1990. BB 4-28 v D (Derby) 1987.

TAVARÉ, Christopher James (Sevenoaks S; St John's, Oxford), b Orpington, Kent 27 Oct 1954. 6'1¼". RHB, RM. Kent 1974-88 (cap 1978; captain 1983-84; benefit 1988). Oxford U 1975-77 (blue 1975-76-77). Somerset debut/cap 1989. Captain 1990-. **Tests:** 31 (1980 to 1989); HS 149 v I (Delhi) 1981-82. LOI: 29. Tours: A 1982-83; NZ 1983-84; I/SL 1981-82; P 1983-84. 1000 runs (15); most – 1770 (1981). HS 219 v Sussex (Hove) 1990 sharing in Somerset record stand of 183 for 9th wkt with N.A.Mallender. BB 1-3. Awards: NWT 4; BHC 9. **NWT:** HS 162* v Devon (Torquay) 1990. **BHC:** HS 143 K v Somerset (Taunton) 1985. **SL:** HS 136* K v Glos (Canterbury) 1978.

TOWNSEND, Gareth Terence John (Tiverton S; Birmingham U), b Tiverton, Devon 28 Jun 1968. 6'0". RHB, RM. Debut 1990. HS 53 v SL (Taunton) 1991. BAC HS 29 v Hants (Southampton) 1991. **SL:** HS 27 v Worcs and v Yorks 1991.

TRUMP, Harvey Russell John (Millfield S), b Taunton 11 Oct 1968. 6'0". RHB, OB. Debut 1988. HS 48 v Notts (Taunton) 1988 – on debut. 50 wkts (1): 51 (1991). BB 6-48 v Worcs (W-s-M) 1991. **NWT:** HS 1. BB 2-44 v Essex (Taunton) 1989. **SL:** HS 19 v Kent (Taunton) 1991. BB 2-23 v Kent (Bath) 1989.

TURNER, Robert Julian (Millfield S; Magdalene C, Cambridge), b Malvern, Worcs 25 Nov 1967. 6'1½". RHB, WK. Brother of S.J. (Somerset 1984-85). Cambridge U 1988-91 (blue 1988-89-90-91; captain 1991). Somerset debut 1991. HS 69* CU v Middx (Cambridge) 1991. Sm HS 18* v SL (Taunton) 1991. Awaiting BAC debut. **BHC:** HS 25* Comb Us v Surrey (Oxford) 1990.

VAN TROOST, Adrianus Pelrus, b Schiedam, Holland 2 Oct 1972. RHB, RFM. Holland 1990 (opened bowling in ICC Trophy final v Zimbabwe). Debut 1991. HS 0*. BB 2-25 v Kent (Taunton) 1991.

WHITE, Giles William (Millfield S), b Barnstaple, Devon 23 Mar 1972. 6'0". RHB, LB. Debut 1991. Devon 1988-91. HS 42 and BB 1-30 v SL (Taunton) 1991 – on debut. Awaiting BAC debut.

NEWCOMERS

COTTAM, Andrew Colin (Axminster S), b Northampton 14 Jul 1973. Son of R.M.H. (Hants, Northants & England 1963-76). RHB, SLA.

KERR, Jason Ian Douglas, b Bolton, Lancs 7 Apr 1974. RHB, RM.

PARSONS, Kevin (Richard Huish's S), b Taunton 2 May 1973. Identical twin brother of Keith. RHB.

PARSONS, Keith Alan (Richard Huish's S), b Taunton 2 May 1973. Identical twin brother of Kevin. RHB, RM.

PAYNE, Andrew, b Rossendale, Lancs 20 Oct 1973. RHB, RM.

ROBINSON, Matthew FitzDavid (King's C, Taunton), b Cardiff 2 Apr 1973. RHB, RM.

SNELL, Richard Peter (Durban HS; Witwatersrand U), b Durban, SA 12 Sep 1968. RHB, RFM. Transvaal 1987-91. HS 31* Transvaal v N Transvaal (Verwoerdburg) 1989-90. BB 6-58 Transvaal v Natal (Johannesburg) 1990-91.

DEPARTURES

BEAL, David (Crispin S, Street), b Butleigh 17 Jul 1966. 6'1". RHB, RM. Debut 1991. HS 1. BB 1-37. **NWT:** HS 0. **BHC:** HS 1. BB 2-63 v Warwks (Birmingham) 1991. **SL:** BB 2-40 v Surrey (Oval) 1991.

CLEAL, Matthew William (Preston CS, Yeovil), b Yeovil 23 Jul 1969. 6'2". RHB, RMF. Somerset 1988-90. HS 30 v Leics (Taunton) 1989. BB 4-41 v WI (Taunton) 1988 (on debut). BAC BB 3-16 v Worcs (Worcester) 1988. **NWT:** HS 25 v Northants (Taunton) 1989. BB 1-42. **BHC:** HS 18 v Essex (Chelmsford) 1991. **SL:** HS 15 v Worcs (Worcester) 1989. BB 1-14.

COOK, Stephen James (Hyde Park HS; Witwatersrand U), b Jo'burg, SA 31 Jul 1953. 6'3". RHB. Transvaal 1972-91. Somerset 1989-91 (cap 1989). Wisden 1989. 1000 runs (3+2) inc 2000 (3); most – 2755 (1991). HS 313* v Glam (Cardiff) 1990. BB 2-25 v Derbys (Taunton) 1990. Awards: BHC 2. **NWT:** HS 45 v Worcs (Taunton) 1990. **BHC:** HS 177 v Sussex (Hove) 1990. **SL:** HS 136* v Glam (Neath) 1990.

GRAVENEY, D.A. – see DURHAM.

Continued on p 247

SOMERSET 1991

RESULTS SUMMARY

	Place	Won	Lost	Drew	Abandoned
Britannic Assurance Championship	17th	2	5	15	
All First-class Matches		2	6	16	
Refuge Assurance League	8th	7	7		2
NatWest Trophy	Quarter-Finalist				
Benson and Hedges Cup	3rd in Group B				

BRITANNIC ASSURANCE CHAMPIONSHIP AVERAGES

BATTING AND FIELDING

Cap		M	I	NO	HS	Runs	Avge	100	50	Ct/St
1989	S.J.Cook	22	39	6	210*	2370	71.81	9	8	13
1989	C.J.Tavaré	22	35	6	183	1482	51.10	4	7	20
1989	R.J.Harden	22	36	7	134	1242	42.82	2	9	19
1990	A.N.Hayhurst	18	30	5	172*	883	35.32	3	1	5
1978	P.M.Roebuck	16	27	3	101	820	34.16	1	5	3
–	I.G.Swallow	4	5	3	41*	67	33.50	–	–	3
1988	G.D.Rose	14	19	2	106	567	33.35	2	2	8
1987	N.D.Burns	22	32	8	108	794	33.08	1	4	35/8
–	K.H.MacLeay	14	19	6	63	388	29.84	–	2	5
–	R.J.Bartlett	5	7	1	71	177	29.50	–	1	3
1991	R.P.Lefebvre	15	16	3	100	361	27.76	1	1	6
–	G.T.J.Townsend	2	4	0	29	68	17.00	–	–	2
1987	N.A.Mallender	13	11	3	19	108	13.50	–	–	1
–	H.R.J.Trump	16	15	6	30*	79	8.77	–	–	11
–	J.C.Hallett	8	5	1	15	35	8.75	–	–	4
–	D.A.Graveney	20	13	7	17	51	8.50	–	–	10

Also played: D.Beal (2 matches) 1, 0; I.Fletcher (1 match) 56, 2*; M.N.Lathwell
(1 match) 4, 43; N.J.Pringle (1 match) 7, 17 (1 ct); A.P.van Troost (4 matches)
0* (1 ct).

BOWLING

	O	M	R	W	Avge	Best	5wI	10wM
N.A.Mallender	349.5	76	969	42	23.07	6-43	3	–
K.H.MacLeay	266.3	51	807	25	32.28	3-40	–	–
D.A.Graveney	673.2	148	2041	53	38.50	7-105	2	–
H.R.J.Trump	570.3	102	1826	47	38.85	6-48	4	–
G.D.Rose	307	51	1006	23	43.73	4-77	–	–
J.C.Hallett	178.3	31	637	12	53.08	3-154	–	–
R.P.Lefebvre	353	71	1048	18	58.22	3-51	–	–

Also bowled: D.Beal 44-3-209-1; S.J.Cook 4-0-26-0; R.J.Harden 23.5-0-122-3;
A.N.Hayhurst 191.3-30-715-9; M.N.Lathwell 17-6-55-0; P.M.Roebuck 128-32-309-9;
I.G.Swallow 100.1-16-354-8; A.P.van Troost 86.4-12-267-6.

The First-Class Averages (pp 164-179) give the records of Somerset players in all
first-class county matches (their other opponents being the West Indians and the Sri
Lankans), with the exception of:
  R.J.Turner 1-1-1-18*-18-∞-0-0-3ct. Did not bowl.

SOMERSET RECORDS
FIRST-CLASS CRICKET

Highest Total	For	675-9d		v Hampshire	Bath	1924
	V	811		by Surrey	The Oval	1899
Lowest Total	For	25		v Glos	Bristol	1947
	V	22		by Glos	Bristol	1920
Highest Innings	For	322	I.V.A.Richards	v Warwicks	Taunton	1985
	V	424	A.C.MacLaren	for Lancashire	Taunton	1895

Highest Partnership for each Wicket

1st	346	H.T.Hewett/L.C.H.Palairet	v Yorkshire	Taunton	1892
2nd	290	J.C.W.MacBryan/M.D.Lyon	v Derbyshire	Buxton	1924
3rd	319	P.M.Roebuck/M.D.Crowe	v Leics	Taunton	1984
4th	310	P.W.Denning/I.T.Botham	v Glos	Taunton	1980
5th	235	J.C.White/C.C.C.Case	v Glos	Taunton	1927
6th	265	W.E.Alley/K.E.Palmer	v Northants	Northampton	1961
7th	240	S.M.J.Woods/V.T.Hill	v Kent	Taunton	1898
8th	172	I.V.A.Richards/I.T.Botham	v Leics	Leicester	1983
9th	183	C.H.M.Greetham/H.W.Stephenson	v Leics	Weston-s-Mare	1963
	183	C.J.Tavaré/N.A.Mallender	v Sussex	Hove	1919
10th	143	J.J.Bridges/A.H.D.Gibbs	v Essex	Weston-s-Mare	1919

Best Bowling	For	10-49	E.J.Tyler	v Surrey	Taunton	1895
(Innings)	V	10-35	A.Drake	for Yorkshire	Weston-s-Mare	1914
Best Bowling	For	16-83	J.C.White	v Worcs	Bath	1919
(Match)	V	17-137	W.Brearley	for Lancashire	Manchester	1905

Most Runs – Season	2,761	W.E.Alley	(av 58.74)	1961
Most Runs – Career	21,142	H.Gimblett	(av 36.96)	1935-1954
Most 100s – Season	11	S.J.Cook		1991
Most 100s – Career	49	H.Gimblett		1935-1954
Most Wkts – Season	169	A.W.Wellard	(av 19.24)	1938
Most Wkts – Career	2,166	J.C.White	(av 18.02)	1909-1937

LIMITED-OVERS CRICKET

Highest Total	NWT	413-4		v Devon	Torquay	1990
	BHC	321-5		v Sussex	Hove	1990
	SL	360-3		v Glamorgan	Neath	1990
Lowest Total	NWT	59		v Middlesex	Lord's	1977
	BHC	98		v Middlesex	Lord's	1982
	SL	58		v Essex	Chelmsford	1977
Highest Innings	NWT	162*	C.J.Tavaré	v Devon	Torquay	1990
	BHC	177	S.J.Cook	v Sussex	Hove	1990
	SL	175*	I.T.Botham	v Northants	Wellingborough	1986
Best Bowling	NWT	7-15	R.P.Lefebvre	v Devon	Torquay	1990
	BHC	5-14	J.Garner	v Surrey	Lord's	1981
	SL	6-24	I.V.A.Richards	v Lancashire	Manchester	1983

127

SURREY

Formation of Present Club: 22 August 1845
Colours: Chocolate
Badge: Prince of Wales' Feathers
Championships (since 1890): (15) 1890, 1891, 1892, 1894, 1895, 1899, 1914, 1952, 1953, 1954, 1955, 1956, 1957, 1958, 1971. **Joint:** (1) 1950
NatWest Trophy/Gillette Cup Winners: (1) 1982
Benson and Hedges Cup Winners: (1) 1974
Sunday League Champions: (0) Fifth 1969, 1980
Match Awards: NWT 35; BHC 47

Secretary: D.G.Seward, Kennington Oval, London, SE11 5SS (☎ 071-582 6660)
Captain: A.J.Stewart
Scorer: M.R.L.W.Ayers
1992 Beneficiary: I.A.Greig

ALIKHAN, Rehan Iqbal ('**Ray**') (KCS, Wimbledon), b Westminster Hospital, London 28 Dec 1962. 6'1½". RHB, OB. Sussex 1986-88. PIA 1986-87. Surrey debut 1989. 1000 runs (1): 1055 (1991). HS 138 v Essex (Oval) 1990. BB 2-19 Sx v WI (Hove) 1988. Sy BB 2-43 v Northants (Northampton) 1991. **NWT:** HS 41 Sx v Worcs (Worcester) 1986. **BHC:** HS 71 Sx v Glam (Swansea) 1987. **SL:** HS 23 Sx v Essex (Chelmsford) 1987.

ATKINS, Paul David (Aylesbury G.S.), b Aylesbury, Bucks 11 Jun 1966. 6'1". RHB, OB. Debut 1988 v CU (Oval) scoring 114* and 8. Buckinghamshire 1985-90 (cap 1986). HS 114* (above). BAC HS 99 v Lancs (Southport) 1988. Award: NWT 1. **NWT:** HS 82 v Glam (Oval) 1988. **BHC:** HS 9. **SL:** HS 2.

BICKNELL, Darren John (Robert Haining SS; Guildford TC), b Guildford 24 Jun 1967. Elder brother of M.P. 6'4". LHB, LM. Debut 1987. Cap 1990. Tours: P 1990-91 (Eng A); SL 1990-91 (Eng A); Z 1989-90 (Eng A). 1000 runs (3); most – 1888 (1991). HS 186 v Kent (Canterbury) 1990 sharing in Surrey record stand of 413 for 3rd wkt with D.M.Ward. BB 2-62 v Northants (Northampton) 1991. Awards: NWT 1; BHC 1. **NWT:** HS 135* v Yorks (Oval) 1989. **BHC:** HS 119 v Hants (Oval) 1990. **SL:** HS 75 v Middx (Oval) 1990.

BICKNELL, Martin Paul (Robert Haining SS), b Guildford 14 Jan 1969. Younger brother of D.J. 6'3". RHB, RFM. Debut 1986. Cap 1989. LOI: 7. Tours: A 1990-91; Z 1989-90 (Eng A). HS 63 v Lancs (Manchester) 1991. Shared in Surrey record stand of 205 for 8th wkt with I.A.Greig v Lancs (Oval) 1990. 50 wkts (3); most – 67 (1990). BB 9-45 v CU (Oval) 1988. BAC BB 7-52 v Sussex (Oval) 1991. **NWT:** HS 66* v Northants (Oval) 1991. **BHC:** BB 4-49 v Yorks (Oval) 1989. **BHC:** HS 27* v Lancs (Manchester) 1990. BB 3-28 v Middx (Lord's) 1991. **SL:** HS 20* v Northants (Tring) 1991. BB 4-14 Middx (Oval) 1991.

BOILING, James (Rutlish S, Merton; Durham U), b New Delhi, India 8 Apr 1968. 6'4". RHB, OB. Debut 1988. Comb Us (BHC) 1988-90. HS 16 v Middx (Oval) 1991. BB 4-157 v Lancs (Manchester) 1991. Award: BHC 1. **NWT:** HS 22 and BB 2-22 v Northants (Oval) 1991. **BHC:** HS 9*. BB 3-9 Comb Us v Surrey (Cambridge) 1989. **SL:** HS 12* v Hants (Oval) 1991. BB 2-24 v Sussex (Oval) 1991.

BROWN, Alistair Duncan (Caterham S), b Beckenham, Kent 11 Feb 1970. 5'10". RHB, LB, occ WK. Awaiting f-c debut. **BHC:** HS 37 v Warwks (Oval) 1991. **SL:** HS 56 v Leics (Oval) 1991.

BUTCHER, Mark Alan (Archbishop Tenison's S, Croydon), b 23 Aug 1972. Son of A.R. (see GLAMORGAN). 5'11". LHB, RM. Awaiting f-c debut. SL 48* v Glam (Oval) 1991 (on debut and against team captained by his father).

128

FELTHAM, Mark Andrew (Tiffin S), b St John's Wood, London 26 June 1963. 6'2½". RHB, RMF. Debut 1983. Cap 1990. MCC Cricket Staff. HS 101 v Middx (Oval) 1990. 50 wkts (1): 56 (1988). BB 6-53 v Leics (Oval) 1990. Award: BHC 1. **NWT:** HS 19* v Hants (Oval) 1989. BB 2-27 v Cheshire (Birkenhead) 1986. **BHC:** HS 29 v Middx (Lord's) 1989. BB 5-28 v Comb Us (Cambridge) 1989. **SL:** HS 61 v Warwks (Oval) 1990. BB 4-35 v Sussex (Guildford) 1986.

GREIG, Ian Alexander (Queen's S, Queenstown; Downing C, Cambridge), b Queenstown, SA 8 Dec 1955. Brother of A.W. (Border, Sussex, E Province and England 1965-78). 5'11½". RHB, RM. Border 1974-75, 1979-80. GW 1975-76. Cambridge U 1977-79 (blue 1977-78-79; captain 1979). Sussex 1980-85 (cap 1981). Surrey debut/cap 1987. Captain 1987-91. Benefit 1992. **Tests:** 2 (1982); HS 14 and BB 4-53 v P (Birmingham) 1982. 1000 runs (2); most – 1259 (1990). HS 291 v Lancs (Oval) 1990 sharing in Surrey record stand of 205 for 8th wkt with M.P.Bicknell. 50 wkts (3); most – 76 (1981). BB 7-43 Sx v CU (Cambridge) 1981. BAC BB 6-21 Sx v Lancs (Hove) 1981. Sy BB 6-34 v CU (Cambridge) 1988. Awards: NWT 1; BHC 1. **NWT:** HS 82 and BB 4-31 Sx v Warwks (Birmingham) 1981. **BHC:** HS 51 and BB 5-35 Sx v Hants (Hove) 1981. **SL:** HS 68* v Middx (Lord's) 1991. BB 5-30 v Kent (Oval) 1988.

HOLLIOAKE, Adam John (Surrey Tutorial C, Guildford), b Melbourne, Australia 5 Sep 1971. 5'11". RHB, RMF. No 1st XI appearances – joined staff 1991.

KENDRICK, Neil Michael (Wilson's GS), b Bromley, Kent 11 Nov 1967. 5'11". RHB, SLA. Debut 1988. HS 52* v Middx (Lord's) 1990. BB 5-54 (10-174 match) v Lancs (Manchester) 1991. **SL:** HS 2*.

LYNCH, Monte Alan (Ryden's S, Walton-on-Thames), b Georgetown, British Guiana 21 May 1958. 5'8". RHB, OB. Debut 1977. Cap 1982. Benefit 1991. Guyana 1982-83. **LOI:** 3. Tours: SA 1983-84 (WI XI); P 1981-82 (Int). 1000 (7); most – 1714 (1985). HS 172* v Kent (Oval) 1989. BB 3-6 v Glam (Swansea) 1981. Awards: NWT 1; BHC 3. **NWT:** HS 129 v Durham (Oval) 1982. BB 1-11. **BHC:** HS 112* v Kent (Oval) 1987. **SL:** HS 136 v Yorks (Bradford) 1985. BB 2-2 v Northants 1987 and v Sussex 1990.

MEDLYCOTT, Keith Thomas (Parmiters GS, Wandsworth), b Whitechapel 12 May 1965. 5'11". RHB, SLA. Debut 1984 scoring 117* v CU (Banstead). Cap Natal. MCC Cricket Staff. Tour: WI 1989-90. HS 153 v Kent (Oval) 1987 – sharing Surrey record stand of 262 for 7th wkt with C.J.Richards. 50 wkts (3); most – 69 (1988). BB 8-52 v Sussex (Hove) 1988. **NWT:** HS 38 v Middx (Uxbridge) 1990. BB 1-45. **BHC:** HS 11 v Glos (Oval) 1989. BB 3-48 v Comb Us (Oxford) 1990. **SL:** HS 44* v Leics (Oval) 1990. BB 4-18 v Warwks (Birmingham) 1989.

MURPHY, Anthony John (Xaverian C, Swansea U), b Manchester 6 Aug 1962. 6'0". RHB, RMF. Lancashire 1985-88. Surrey debut 1989. Cheshire 1984-85. Tour: WI 1986-87 (Lancs). HS 38 v Glos (Oval) 1989. 50 wkts (1): 65 (1989). BB 6-97 v Derbys (Derby) 1989. **NWT:** HS 1*. BB 2-34 v Hants (Oval) 1989. **BHC:** HS 5*. BB 2-23 v Middx (Lord's) 1991. **SL:** HS 5*. BB 4-22 v Glos (Oval) 1989.

ROBINSON, Jonathan David (Lancing C; West Sussex IHE), b Epsom 3 Aug 1966. Son of P.M.H. (L.C.Stevens' XI 1961). 5'10". LHB, RM. Debut 1988. HS 79 v Lancs (Manchester) 1991. BB 2-37 v Leics (Leicester) 1989. Award: NWT 1. **NWT:** HS 47 v Essex (Oval) 1991. BB 3-46 v Kent (Oval) 1991. **BHC:** HS 38 v Warwks (Oval) 1991. BB 2-31 v Middx (Lord's) 1991. **SL:** HS 55* v Somerset (Oval) 1991. BB 2-32 v Glam (Oval) 1991.

SARGEANT, Neil Fredrick (Whitmore HS), b Hammersmith 8 Nov 1965. 5'8". RHB, WK. Debut 1989. HS 49 v Lancs (Manchester) 1991. BB 1-88. SL: HS 22 v Glos (Cheltenham) 1990.

SMITH, Andrew William (Sutton Manor S), b 30 May 1969. Son of W.A. (Surrey 1961-70). RHB, OB. No 1st XI appearances – joined staff 1990.

STEWART, Alec James (Tiffin S) b Merton 8 Apr 1963. Son of M.J. (Surrey and England 1954-72). 5'11". RHB, WK. Debut 1981. Cap 1985. Captain 1992. **Tests**: 14 (1989-90 to 1991); HS 113* v SL (Lord's) 1991. LOI: 23. Tours: A 1990-91; WI 1989-90. 1000 runs (6); most – 1665 (1986). HS 206* v Essex (Oval) 1989. BB 1-7. Held 11 catches (equalling world f-c match record) v Leics (Leicester) 1989. Awards: NWT 1; BHC 3. **NWT**: HS 107* v Middx (Oval) 1988. **BHC**: HS 110* v Somerset (Taunton) 1991. **SL**: HS 125 v Lancs (Oval) 1990.

THORPE, Graham Paul (Weydon CS; Farnham C), b Farnham 1 Aug 1969. 5'11". LHB, RM. Debut 1988. Cap 1991. Tours: P 1990-91 (Eng A); SL 1990-91 (Eng A); Z 1989-90 (Eng A). 1000 runs (2); most – 1203 (1991). HS 177 v Sussex (Oval) 1991. BB 2-31 v Essex (Oval) 1989. **NWT**: HS 93 v Hants (Lord's) 1991. **BHC**: HS 50* v Hants (Oval) 1990. BB 3-35 v Middx (Lord's) 1989. **SL**: HS 115* v Lancs (Manchester) 1991. BB 3-21 v Somerset (Oval) 1991.

WAQAR YOUNIS (Government C, Vehari), b Vehari, Pakistan 16 Nov 1971. 6'0". RHB, RF. Multan 1987-91. United Bank 1988-91. Surrey debut/cap 1990. Wisden 1991. **Tests** (P): 11 (1989-90 and 1990-91); HS 18 v A (Melbourne) 1989-90; BB 7-76 v NZ (Faisalabad) 1990-91. LOI (P): 31. Tour (P): A 1989-90. HS 51 United Bank v PIA (Lahore) 1989-90 Qaid-e-Azam Final. Sy HS 31 v Yorks (Guildford) 1991. 50 wkts (2) inc 100 wkts (1): 113 (1991). BB 7-64 United Bank v ADBP (Lahore) 1990-91. Sy BB 7-73 v Warwks (Oval) 1990. Awards: NWT 2. **NWT**: HS 26 v Essex (Oval) 1991. BB 5-40 v Northants (Oval) 1991. **BHC**: HS 5*. BB 3-29 v Somerset (Taunton) 1991. **SL**: HS 8. BB 5-26 v Kent (Oval) 1990.

WARD, David Mark (Haling Manor HS), b Croydon 10 Feb 1961. 6'1". RHB, OB. Debut 1985. Cap 1990. 1000 runs (2) inc 2000 runs (1): 2072 (1990). HS 263 v Kent (Canterbury) 1990 sharing in Surrey record stand of 413 for 3rd wkt with D.J.Bicknell. BB 2-66 v Glos (Guildford) 1991. Award: NWT 1. **NWT**: HS 97 v Northumb (Jesmond) 1989. **BHC**: HS 46* v Yorks (Oval) 1990. **SL**: HS 102* v Hants (Southampton) 1990.

NEWCOMERS

BAINBRIDGE, Mark R.

BENJAMIN, Joseph Emmanuel (Cayon HS, St Kitts; Mount Pleasant S, Highgate, Birmingham), b Christ Church, St Kitts 2 Feb 1961. 6'2". RHB, RMF. Warwickshire 1988-91. Staffordshire 1986-88. HS 41 Wa v Surrey (Oval) 1990. BB 5-29 Wa v CU (Cambridge) 1990. BAC BB 5-71 Wa v Middx (Lord's) 1990. **NWT**: HS 19 and BB 2-37 Staffs v Glam (Stone) 1986. **BHC**: HS 20 Wa v Worcs (Birmingham) 1990. BB 2-32 Wa v Glos (Bristol) 1990. **SL**: HS 24 Wa v Lancs (Manchester) 1990. BB 3-33 Wa v Derbys (Birmingham) 1991.

BRYSON, Rudi Edwin (Springs BHS), b Springs, SA 25 Jul 1968. RHB, RFM. N Transvaal 1987-88 to 1988-89. E Province 1988-89 to 1990-91. HS 31 EP v Transvaal (Jo'burg) 1989-90. BB 7-68 (12-133 match) EP B v GW (Kimberley) 1988-89.

LIGERTWOOD, David George Coutts (Adelaide U, Australia), b Oxford 16 May 1969. RHB, WK. Hertfordshire 1990-91. Awaiting f-c debut. **NWT**: HS 37* Herts v Warwks (Birmingham) 1991.

DEPARTURES – see p 155

SURREY 1991

RESULTS SUMMARY

	Place	Won	Lost	Drew	Abandoned
Britannic Assurance Championship	5th	8	6	8	
All First-class Matches		9	6	8	
Refuge Assurance League	8th	7	7		2
NatWest Trophy	Finalist				
Benson and Hedges Cup	4th in Group B				

BRITANNIC ASSURANCE CHAMPIONSHIP AVERAGES
BATTING AND FIELDING

Cap		M	I	NO	HS	Runs	Avge	100	50	Ct/St
1990	D.J.Bicknell	22	40	2	151	1762	46.36	5	8	10
1991	G.P.Thorpe	21	35	7	177	1164	41.57	4	4	8
1990	D.M.Ward	22	38	5	151	1304	39.51	1	9	9
1985	A.J.Stewart	17	30	6	109	936	39.00	1	6	20
–	J.D.Robinson	4	6	1	79	186	37.20	–	2	–
–	R.I.Alikhan	18	33	2	96*	963	31.06	–	7	9
1990	M.A.Feltham	12	16	4	69*	327	27.25	–	1	3
1987	I.A.Greig	19	29	4	72	593	23.72	–	3	7
1988	K.T.Medlycott	18	25	2	66	513	22.30	–	4	6
1982	M.A.Lynch	10	17	1	141*	342	21.37	1	1	13
–	N.M.Kendrick	2	4	1	24	58	19.33	–	–	1
1989	M.P.Bicknell	15	22	4	63	312	17.33	–	1	3
–	N.F.Sargeant	20	27	4	49	362	15.73	–	–	43/5
1990	Waqar Younis	17	20	8	31	177	14.75	–	–	3
–	A.J.Murphy	19	20	8	18	71	5.91	–	–	4
–	J.Boiling	4	7	1	16	22	3.66	–	–	6

Also played: A.G.Robson (2 matches) 0, 0, 3.

BOWLING

	O	M	R	W	Avge	Best	5wI	10wM
Waqar Younis	570.1	109	1623	113	14.36	7-87	13	3
N.M.Kendrick	105	26	262	12	21.83	5-54	2	1
M.P.Bicknell	470.5	118	1256	45	27.91	7-52	1	–
M.A.Feltham	328	56	996	35	28.45	4-36	–	–
K.T.Medlycott	458.5	98	1569	38	41.28	4-56	–	–
A.J.Murphy	546.4	118	1667	35	47.62	5-63	1	–

Also bowled: R.I.Alikhan 5-0-43-2; D.J.Bicknell 5.3-0-62-2; J.Boiling 149.1-37-420-9; I.A.Greig 154.2-31-398-9; M.A.Lynch 9-1-29-0; J.D.Robinson 28.3-110-2; A.G.Robson 39-14-103-1; N.F.Sargeant 5-0-88-1; A.J.Stewart 7-0-34-0; G.P.Thorpe 39.5-5-157-1; D.M.Ward 7.5-0-66-2.

The First-Class Averages (pp 164-179) give the records of Surrey players in all first-class county matches (their other opponents being Cambridge U.), with the exception of A.J.Stewart, whose full county figures are as above, and:
D.J.Bicknell 23-41-2-151-1844-47.28-5-9-10ct. 5.3-0-62-2-31.00-2/62.
G.P.Thorpe 22-37-8-177-1166-40.20-4-4-8ct. 49-8-194-2-97.00-1/37.

SURREY RECORDS

FIRST-CLASS CRICKET

Highest Total	For 811		v Somerset	The Oval	1899
	V 863		by Lancashire	The Oval	1990
Lowest Total	For 14		v Essex	Chelmsford	1983
	V 16		by MCC	Lord's	1872
Highest Innings	For 357*	R.Abel	v Somerset	The Oval	1899
	V 366	N.H.Fairbrother	for Lancashire	The Oval	1990

Highest Partnership for each Wicket

1st	428	J.B.Hobbs/A.Sandham	v Oxford U	The Oval	1926
2nd	371	J.B.Hobbs/E.G.Hayes	v Hampshire	The Oval	1909
3rd	413	D.J.Bicknell/D.M.Ward	v Kent	Canterbury	1990
4th	448	R.Abel/T.W.Hayward	v Yorkshire	The Oval	1899
5th	308	J.N.Crawford/F.C.Holland	v Somerset	The Oval	1908
6th	298	A.Sandham/H.S.Harrison	v Sussex	The Oval	1913
7th	262	C.J.Richards/K.T.Medlycott	v Kent	The Oval	1987
8th	205	I.A.Greig/M.P.Bicknell	v Lancashire	The Oval	1990
9th	168	E.R.T.Holmes/E.W.J.Brooks	v Hampshire	The Oval	1936
10th	173	A.Ducat/A.Sandham	v Essex	Leyton	1921

Best Bowling	For 10-43	T.Rushby	v Somerset	Taunton	1921
(Innings)	V 10-28	W.P.Howell	for Australians	The Oval	1899
Best Bowling	For 16-83	G.A.R.Lock	v Kent	Blackheath	1956
(Match)	V 15-57	W.P.Howell	for Australians	The Oval	1899

Most Runs – Season	3,246	T.W.Hayward	(av 72.13)		1906
Most Runs – Career	43,554	J.B.Hobbs	(av 49.72)		1905-1934
Most 100s – Season	13	T.W.Hayward			1906
	13	J.B.Hobbs			1925
Most 100s – Career	144	J.B.Hobbs			1905-1934
Most Wkts – Season	252	T.Richardson	(av 13.94)		1895
Most Wkts – Career	1,775	T.Richardson	(av 17.87)		1892-1904

LIMITED-OVERS CRICKET

Highest Total	NWT	313-5		v Northumb	Jesmond	1989
	BHC	331-5		v Hampshire	The Oval	1990
	SL	304-6		v Warwicks	The Oval	1985
Lowest Total	NWT	74		v Kent	The Oval	1967
	BHC	89		v Notts	Nottingham	1984
	SL	64		v Worcs	Worcester	1978
Highest Innings	NWT	146	G.S.Clinton	v Kent	Canterbury	1985
	BHC	121*	G.S.Clinton	v Kent	The Oval	1988
	SL	136	M.A.Lynch	v Yorkshire	Bradford	1985
Best Bowling	NWT	7-33	R.D.Jackman	v Yorkshire	Harrogate	1970
	BHC	5-21	P.H.L.Wilson	v Comb Univs	The Oval	1979
	SL	6-25	Intikhab Alam	v Derbyshire	The Oval	1974

SUSSEX

Formation of Present Club: 1 March 1839
Substantial Reorganisation: August 1857
Colours: Dark Blue, Light Blue and Gold
Badge: County Arms of Six Martlets
Championships: (0) Second 1902, 1903, 1932, 1933, 1934, 1953, 1981
NatWest Trophy/Gillette Cup Winners: (4) 1963, 1964, 1978, 1986
Benson and Hedges Cup Winners: (0) Semi-Finalists 1982
Sunday League Champions: (1) 1982
Match Awards: NWT 44; BHC 45

Secretary: N.Bett, County Ground, Eaton Road, Hove BN3 3AN (☎ 0273-732161)
Captain: A.P.Wells
Scorer: L.V.Chandler

DEAN, Jacob Winston (Chailey S; Haywards Heath SFC), b Cuckfield 23 Aug 1970. 5'10½". RHB, SLA. No 1st XI appearances – joined staff 1991.

DONELAN, Bradleigh Thomas Peter (Finchley Catholic HS), b Park Royal Hospital, Middx 3 Jan 1968. 6'1". RHB, OB. Debut 1989. MCC Cricket Staff. HS 61 v Kent (Hove) 1991. BB 6-62 (10-136 match) v Glos (Hove) 1991. **BHC:** HS 8*. **SL:** HS 19 and BB 1-35 v Glos (Hove) 1991.

GIDDINS, Edward Simon Hunter (Eastbourne C), b Eastbourne 20 Jul 1971. 6'4½". RHB, RMF. Debut 1991. HS 14* v Middx (Lord's) 1991. BB 1-29.

GREENFIELD, Keith (Falmer HS), b Brighton 6 Dec 1968. 6'0". RHB, RM. Debut 1987. HS 127* v CU (Hove) 1991. BAC HS 64 v Glos (Hove) 1991. **BHC:** HS 33 v Lancs (Manchester) 1991. BB 1-35. **SL:** HS 78* v Hants (Basingstoke) 1991.

HALL, James William (Chichester HS), b Chichester 30 Mar 1968. 6'3". RHB, OB. Debut 1990. 1000 runs (1): 1140 (1990 – debut season). HS 125 v Notts (Nottingham) 1990. **NWT:** HS 0. **BHC:** HS 71 v Lancs (Manchester) 1991. **SL:** HS 50 v Somerset (Taunton) 1991.

HANLEY, Robin (Willingdon S; Eastbourne SFC), b Tonbridge, Kent 5 Jan 1968. 6'2". RHB. Debut 1990. HS 28 v Warwks (Eastbourne) 1990. **SL:** HS 11 v Warwks (Eastbourne) 1990.

JONES, Adrian Nicholas (Seaford C), b Woking, Surrey 22 Jul 1961. 6'2". LHB, RFM. Sussex 1981-86 (cap 1986). Somerset 1987-90 (cap 1987). Border 1981-82. HS 43* Sm v Leics (Taunton) 1989. Sx HS 35 v Middx (Hove) 1984. 50 wkts (5); most – 71 (1989). BB 7-30 Sm v Hants (Southampton) 1988. Sx BB 5-29 v Glos (Hove) 1984. Awards: BHC 3. **NWT:** HS 7. BB 4-26 v Yorks (Leeds) 1986. **BHC:** HS 25 Sm v Essex (Taunton) 1989. BB 5-53 Sm v Notts (Taunton) 1989. **SL:** HS 37 Sm v Surrey (Oval) 1989. BB 7-41 v Notts (Nottingham) 1986.

LENHAM, Neil John (Brighton C), b Worthing 17 Dec 1965. Son of L.J. (Sussex 1956-70). 5'11". RHB, RMF. Debut 1984. Cap 1990. 1000 runs (2); most – 1663 (1990). HS 193 v Leics (Hove) 1991. BB 4-85 v Leics (Leicester) 1986. Awards: NWT 1; BHC 1. **NWT:** HS 66 v Scot (Edinburgh) 1991. BB 2-12 v Ire (Downpatrick) 1990. **BHC:** HS 82 v Somerset (Hove) 1986. BB 1-3. **SL:** HS 86 v Kent (Hove) 1991. BB 2-19 v Glos (Hove) 1989.

133

MOORES, Peter (King Edward VI S, Macclesfield), b Macclesfield, Cheshire 18 Dec 1962. 6'0". RHB, WK. Worcestershire 1983-84. Sussex debut 1985. Cap 1989. OFS 1988-89. HS 116 v Somerset (Hove) 1989. NWT: HS 26 v Scot (Edinburgh) 1991. BHC: HS 76 v Middx (Hove) 1990. SL: HS 34 v Derbys 1988 and v Glam 1991.

NORTH, John Andrew (Chichester HS), b Slindon 19 Nov 1970. 5'9". RHB, RM. Debut 1990. HS 63* v Hants (Hove) 1991. BB 4-47 v SL (Hove) 1991. BAC BB 3-54 v Somerset (Taunton) 1991. BHC: HS 22 v Scot (Hove) 1991. BB 2-80 v Lancs (Manchester) 1991. SL: HS 18 v Northants (Eastbourne) 1991. BB 3-29 v Kent (Hove) 1991.

PIGOTT, Anthony Charles Shackleton (Harrow S), b Fulham, London 4 Jun 1958. 6'1". RHB, RFM. Debut 1978. Cap 1982. Benefit 1991. Wellington 1982-84. **Tests**: 1 (1983-84); HS 8* and BB 2-75 v NZ (Christchurch) 1983-84. Tours: NZ 1979-80 (DHR), 1983-84 (part). HS 104* v Warwks (Birmingham) 1986. 50 wkts (5); most – 74 (1988). BB 7-74 v Northants (Eastbourne) 1982. Hat-trick 1978 (his first f-c wkts). **NWT:** HS 53 v Derbys (Hove) 1988. BB 3-4 v Ire (Hove) 1985. **BHC:** HS 49* v Essex (Hove) 1989. BB 3-29 v Leics (Hove) 1991. **SL:** HS 51* v Northants (Hove) 1989. BB 5-24 v Lancs (Manchester) 1986.

REMY, Carlos Charles (St Aloyous C; Haringey Cricket C), b Castries, St Lucia 24 Jul 1968. 5'9". RHB, RM. Debut 1989. HS 4*. BB 4-63 v CU (Hove) 1990. BAC BB 1-22. **NWT:** HS 1. **SL:** HS 12* v Leics (Leicester) 1990. BB 2-45 v Yorks (Hove) 1990.

SALISBURY, Ian David Kenneth (Moulton CS), b Northampton 21 Jan 1970. 5'11". RHB, LB. Debut 1989. Cap 1991. MCC Cricket Staff. Tours: P 1990-91 (Eng A); SL 1990-91 (Eng A). HS 68 v Derbys (Hove) 1990. BB 5-32 v Worcs (Worcester) 1990. **NWT:** HS 14* v Essex (Hove) 1991. BB 1-36. **BHC:** HS 17* and BB 3-40 v Kent (Canterbury) 1991. **SL:** HS 23 v Yorks (Middlesbrough) 1991. BB 3-10 v Glam (Swansea) 1991.

SMITH, David Mark (Battersea GS), b Balham, London 9 Jan 1956. 6'4". LHB, RM. Surrey 1973-83 and 1987-88 (cap 1980). Worcestershire 1984-86 (cap 1984). Sussex debut/cap 1989. **Tests**: 2 (1985-86); HS 47 v WI (P-of-S) 1985-86. LOI: 2. Tour: WI 1985-86. 1000 runs (6); most – 1305 (1989). HS 189* Wo v Kent (Worcester) 1984. Sx HS 184 v Notts (Eastbourne) 1989. BB 3-40 Sy v Sussex (Oval) 1976. Sx BB -. Awards: NWT 3; BHC 4. **NWT:** HS 109 Wo v Lancs (Manchester) 1985. BB 3-39 Sy v Derbys (Ilkeston) 1976. **BHC:** HS 126 Wo v Warwks (Worcester) 1985. BB 4-29 Sy v Kent (Oval) 1980. **SL:** HS 87* Sy v Hants (Oval) 1980. BB 2-21 Sy v Worcs (Byfleet) 1973.

SPEIGHT, Martin Peter (Hurstpierpoint C; Durham U), b Walsall, Staffs 24 Oct 1967. 5'9". RHB, WK. Debut 1986. Cap 1991. Comb Us (BHC) 1987-89. Wellington 1989-90. 1000 runs (1): 1375 (1990). HS 149 v CU (Hove) 1991. BAC HS 131 v Glam (Hove) 1990. BB 1-2. Award: BHC 1. **NWT:** HS 48 v Leics 1989 and v Essex 1991. **BHC:** HS 83 Comb Us v Glos (Bristol) 1988. **SL:** HS 106* v Worcs (Hove) 1991.

WELLS, Alan Peter (Tideway CS, Newhaven), b Newhaven 2 Oct 1961. Younger brother of C.M. 6'0". RHB, RM. Debut 1981. Cap 1986. Captain 1992. Border 1981-82. Tour: SA 1989-90 (Eng XI). 1000 runs (6); most – 1784 (1991). HS 253* v Yorks (Middlesbrough) 1991. BB 3-67 v Worcs (Worcester) 1987. **NWT:** HS 86* v Leics (Hove) 1989. **BHC:** HS 74 v Middx (Hove) 1990. BB 1-17. **SL:** HS 98 v Notts (Nottingham) 1990. BB 1-0.

WELLS, Colin Mark (Tideway CS, Newhaven), b Newhaven 3 Mar 1960. Elder brother of A.P. 5'11". RHB, RM. Debut 1979. Cap 1982. Border 1980-81. W Province 1984-85. LOI: 2. 1000 runs (6); most – 1456 (1987). HS 203 v Hants (Hove) 1984. 50 wkts (2); most – 59 (1984). BB 7-42 v Derbys (Derby) 1991. Awards: BHC 3. **NWT:** HS 76 v Ire (Hove) 1985. BB 3-16 v Scot (Edinburgh) 1991. **BHC:** HS 117 v Glam (Swansea) 1989. BB 4-21 v Middx (Lord's) 1980. **SL:** HS 104* v Warwks (Hove) 1983. BB 4-15 v Worcs (Worcester) 1983.

NEWCOMERS

ROBSON, Andrew George (Whitburn CS), b East Boldon, Co Durham 27 Apr 1971. 6'0". RHB, RFM. Surrey 1991. HS 3. BB 1-72. **SL:** BB 3-42 Sy v Hants (Oval) 1991.

STEPHENSON, Franklyn Dacosta (Samuel Jackson Prescod Polytechnic), b St James, Barbados 8 Apr 1959. 6'3½". RHB, RFM. Barbados 1981-82 and 1989-90. Tasmania 1981-82. Gloucestershire 1982-83. Nottinghamshire 1988-91 (cap 1988). Staffordshire 1980. Wisden 1988. Tour (WI XI): SA 1982-83, 1983-84. 1000 runs (1): 1018 (1988). HS 165 Barbados v Leeward Is (Basseterre) 1981-82. Nt HS 121 v Leics (Nottingham) 1990. 50 wkts (4) inc 100 wkts (1): 125 (1988). BB 8-47 (15-106 match) Nt v Essex (Nottingham) 1989. Scored 111 and 117 and took 11-222 Nt v Yorks (Nottingham) 1988. Double 1988. Awards: BHC 2. **NWT:** HS 29 Nt v Bucks (Marlow) 1990. BB 2-17 Gs v Notts (Nottingham) 1982. **BHC:** HS 98* Nt v Worcs (Nottingham) 1990. BB 4-14 Nt v Minor C (Nottingham) 1988. **SL:** HS 69 Nt v Hants (Nottingham) 1989. BB 4-23 Nt v Surrey (Nottingham) 1988.

DEPARTURES

BUNTING, Rodney Alan (King Edward VII GS, King's Lynn), b East Winch, Norfolk, 25 Apr 1965. 6'5". RHB, RFM. Sussex 1988-91 – taking 5-86 on debut v Glos (Bristol). Norfolk 1985-87 (cap 1986). HS 73 v CU (Hove) 1989. BAC HS 51* v Lancs (Manchester) 1991. BB 6-58 v Warwks (Hove) 1988. **NWT:** HS 6. BB 1-30. **BHC:** HS 2*. BB 2-43 Minor C v Glam (Oxford) 1987. **SL:** HS 5*. BB 4-35 v Middx (Hove) 1991.

DODEMAIDE, Anthony Ian Christopher (St John's/Chisholm C; Footscray Institute), b Williamstown, Melbourne, Australia 5 Oct 1963. 6'2". RHB, RFM. Victoria 1983-91. Sussex 1989-91 (cap 1989). **Tests** (A): 8 (1987-88 to 1988-89); HS 50 and BB 6-58 v NZ (Melbourne) 1987-88 (on debut). LOI (A): 12. Tour: Z 1985-86 (Young A). 1000 runs (1): 1001 (1990). HS 112 v Somerset (Hove) 1990. 50 wkts (3); most – 65 (1989). BB 6-58 (Tests). Sx BB 6-106 v Lancs (Horsham) 1990. Award: NWT 1. **NWT:** HS 32* v Scot (Edinburgh) 1991. BB 6-9 v Ire (Downpatrick) 1990. **BHC:** HS 38 v Essex (Hove) 1989. BB 3-26 v Glam (Swansea) 1989. **SL:** HS 40* v Warwks (Birmingham) 1989. BB 4-40 v Somerset (Hove) 1990.

PARKER, P.W. – see DURHAM.

THRELFALL, Philip Walter (Barrow GS; Parkview S), b Barrow-in-Furness, Lancs 11 Feb 1967. 6'3". RHB, RMF. Sussex 1988-91. Cumberland 1987. HS -. BB 3-45 v SL (Hove) 1990. BAC BB -.

SUSSEX 1991

RESULTS SUMMARY

	Place	Won	Lost	Tied	Drew	Abandoned
Britannic Assurance Championship	11th	4	3	1	14	
All First-class Matches		4	3	1	16	
Refuge Assurance League	12th	5	9			2
NatWest Trophy	2nd Round					
Benson and Hedges Cup	3rd in Group C					

BRITANNIC ASSURANCE CHAMPIONSHIP AVERAGES

BATTING AND FIELDING

Cap		M	I	NO	HS	Runs	Avge	100	50	Ct/St
–	R.A.Bunting	3	4	3	51*	106	106.00	–	1	–
1986	A.P.Wells	21	34	5	253*	1777	61.27	7	5	7
1989	D.M.Smith	19	33	5	126*	1130	40.35	1	8	14
1990	N.J.Lenham	18	31	3	193	1028	36.71	3	3	11
–	B.T.P.Donelan	12	15	5	61	353	35.30	–	2	3
1991	M.P.Speight	12	18	1	89	572	33.64	–	5	5
1982	C.M.Wells	12	19	5	76	451	32.21	–	2	2
1989	A.I.C.Dodemaide	19	28	9	100*	581	30.57	1	1	7
	J.W.Hall	14	25	2	117*	685	29.78	1	4	8
1989	P.Moores	22	27	3	86*	612	25.50	–	6	53/5
1979	P.W.G.Parker	16	26	1	111	607	24.28	1	3	8
–	J.A.North	5	7	1	63*	122	20.33	–	1	1
1982	A.C.S.Pigott	18	21	5	65	291	18.18	–	1	5
–	K.Greenfield	7	11	0	64	156	14.18	–	1	15
1991	I.D.K.Salisbury	20	20	7	34	179	13.76	–	–	12
1986	A.N.Jones	21	17	5	28	119	9.91	–	–	1

Also played: E.S.H.Giddins (2 matches) 14*; R.Hanley (1 match) 19, 0.

BOWLING

	O	M	R	W	Avge	Best	5wI	10wM
A.I.C.Dodemaide	555	110	1583	52	30.44	5-130	1	–
C.M.Wells	216.4	60	598	18	33.22	7-42	1	–
B.T.P.Donelan	426.3	112	1162	34	34.17	6-62	2	1
A.N.Jones	502.2	68	1829	53	34.50	5-46	2	–
J.A.North	129	20	507	14	36.21	3-54	–	–
A.C.S.Pigott	415.3	92	1293	35	36.94	5-37	1	–
I.D.K.Salisbury	605.2	144	1837	47	39.08	5-40	1	–

Also bowled: R.A.Bunting 62.2-7-260-8; E.S.H.Giddins 56.2-6-186-2; N.J.Lenham 29-5-79-2; P.W.G.Parker 2-0-10-0; D.M.Smith 2-0-15-0; A.P.Wells 8-1-21-1.

The First-Class Averages (pp 164-179) give the records of Sussex players in all first-class county matches (their other opponents being the Sri Lankans and Cambridge U.), with the exception of A.I.C.Dodemaide, whose full county figures are as above.

SUSSEX RECORDS

FIRST-CLASS CRICKET

Highest Total	For	705-8d	v	Surrey	Hastings	1902
	V	726	by	Notts	Nottingham	1895
Lowest Total	For	19	v	Surrey	Godalming	1830
		19	v	Notts	Hove	1873
	V	18	by	Kent	Gravesend	1867
Highest Innings	For	333	K.S.Duleepsinhji	v	Northants	Hove	1930
	V	322	E.Paynter	for	Lancashire	Hove	1937

Highest Partnership for each Wicket

1st	490	E.H.Bowley/J.G.Langridge	v	Middlesex	Hove	1933
2nd	385	E.H.Bowley/M.W.Tate	v	Northants	Hove	1921
3rd	298	K.S.Ranjitsinhji/E.H.Killick	v	Lancashire	Hove	1901
4th	326*	J.Langridge/G.Cox	v	Yorkshire	Leeds	1949
5th	297	J.H.Parks/H.W.Parks	v	Hampshire	Portsmouth	1937
6th	255	K.S.Duleepsinhji/M.W.Tate	v	Northants	Hove	1930
7th	344	K.S.Ranjitsinhji/W.Newham	v	Essex	Leyton	1902
8th	229*	C.L.A.Smith/G.Brann	v	Kent	Hove	1902
9th	178	H.W.Parks/A.F.Wensley	v	Derbyshire	Horsham	1930
10th	156	G.R.Cox/H.R.Butt	v	Cambridge U	Cambridge	1908

Best Bowling	For	10-48	C.H.G.Bland	v	Kent	Tonbridge	1899
(Innings)	V	9-11	A.P.Freeman	for	Kent	Hove	1922
Best Bowling	For	17-106	G.R.Cox	v	Warwicks	Horsham	1926
(Match)	V	17-67	A.P.Freeman	for	Kent	Hove	1922

Most Runs – Season	2,850	J.G.Langridge	(av 64.77)	1949
Most Runs – Career	34,152	J.G.Langridge	(av 37.69)	1928-1955
Most 100s – Season	12	J.G.Langridge		1949
Most 100s – Career	76	J.G.Langridge		1928-1955
Most Wkts – Season	198	M.W.Tate	(av 13.47)	1925
Most Wkts – Career	2,211	M.W.Tate	(av 17.41)	1912-1937

LIMITED-OVERS CRICKET

Highest Total	NWT	314-7	v	Kent	Tunbridge W	1963
	BHC	305-6	v	Kent	Hove	1982
	SL	293-4	v	Worcs	Horsham	1980
Lowest Total	NWT	49	v	Derbyshire	Chesterfield	1969
	BHC	61	v	Middlesex	Hove	1978
	SL	61	v	Derbyshire	Derby	1978
Highest Innings	NWT	141*	G.D.Mendis	v	Warwicks	Hove	1980
	BHC	117	R.D.V.Knight	v	Surrey	The Oval	1977
		117	C.M.Wells	v	Glamorgan	Swansea	1989
	SL	129	A.W.Greig	v	Yorkshire	Scarborough	1976
Best Bowling	NWT	6-9	A.I.Dodemaide	v	Ireland	Downpatrick	1990
	BHC	5-8	Imran Khan	v	Northants	Northampton	1978
	SL	7-41	A.N.Jones	v	Notts	Nottingham	1986

WARWICKSHIRE

Formation of Present Club: 8 April 1882
Substantial Reorganisation: 19 January 1884.
Colours: Dark Blue, Gold and Silver
Badge: Bear and Ragged Staff
Championships: (3) 1911, 1951, 1972
NatWest Trophy/Gillette Cup Winners: (3) 1966, 1968, 1989
Benson and Hedges Cup Winners: (0) Finalists 1984
Sunday League Champions: (1) 1980
Match Awards: NWT 41; BHC 43

General Secretary: D.M.W.Heath, County Ground, Edgbaston, Birmingham, B5 7QU (☎ 021-446 4422)
Captain: T.A.Lloyd
Scorer: A.Davies (home) and S.P.Austin (away)
1992 Beneficiary: G.C.Small

ASIF DIN, Mohamed (Ladywood CS, Birmingham), b Kampala, Uganda 21 Sep 1960. 5'9¼". RHB, LB. Debut 1981. Cap 1987. MCC Cricket Staff. 1000 (2); most – 1425 (1988). HS 158* v CU (Cambridge) 1988. BAC HS 140 v Leics (Leicester) 1991. BB 5-100 v Glam (Birmingham) 1982. Awards: NWT 2; BHC 1. **NWT:** HS 94* v Worcs (Birmingham) 1989. BB 5-40 v Herts (St Albans) 1990. **BHC:** HS 137 v Somerset (Birmingham) 1991. BB 1-26. **SL:** HS 113 v Somerset (W-s-M) 1990. BB 1-11.

BOOTH, Paul Antony (Honley HS), b Huddersfield, Yorks 5 Sep 1965. 5'10". LHB, SLA. Yorkshire 1982-89. Warwickshire debut 1990. HS 62 v Somerset (Taunton) 1991. BB 5-98 Y v Lancs (Manchester) 1988. Wa BB 4-55 v Yorks (Birmingham) 1990. **NWT:** HS 6*. **BHC:** HS 13* v Glam (Birmingham) 1990. BB 2-28 Y v Worcs (Bradford) 1985. **SL:** BB 1-33.

BROWN, Douglas Robert (West London IPE), b Stirling, Scotland 29 Oct 1969. RHB, RM. Scotland 1989. Awaiting Warwickshire f-c debut (SL debut 1991). HS 44* Scot v Ire (Dublin) 1989. **BHC:** HS 24 Scot v Notts (Glasgow) 1990. BB 3-50 Scot v Northants (Northampton) 1990. **SL:** HS -. BB 1-35.

BURNS, Michael (Walney CS), b Barrow-in-Furness, Lancs 2 Jun 1969. RHB, WK. Cumberland 1988-90. Awaiting f-c debut. **BHC:** HS 3.

DONALD, Allan Anthony (Grey College HS), b Bloemfontein, SA 20 Oct 1966. 6'2". RHB, RF. OFS 1985-91. Warwickshire debut 1987. Cap 1989. Wisden 1991. HS 46* OFS v W Province (Cape Town) 1990-91. Wa HS 40 v Yorks (Birmingham) 1989. 50 wkts (2); most – 86 (1989). BB 8-37 OFS v Transvaal (Johannesburg) 1986-87. Wa BB 7-66 v Middx (Birmingham) 1989. Awards: NWT 2. **NWT:** HS 2* v BB 5-12 v Wilts (Birmingham) 1989. **BHC:** HS 23* v Leics (Leicester) 1989. BB 4-28 v Scot (Perth) 1987. **SL:** HS 18* v Middx (Lord's) 1988. BB 4-32 v Middx (Birmingham) 1989.

HOLLOWAY, Piran Christopher Laity (Millfield S; Taunton S; Loughborough U), b Helston, Cornwall 1 Oct 1970. 5'8". LHB, WK. Debut 1988. Comb Us (BHC) 1991. HS 89* v Leics (Leicester) 1991. **NWT:** HS 2. **BHC:** HS 27 v Derbys (Oxford) 1991. **SL:** HS 34* v Northants (Northampton) 1991.

KHAN, Wasim Gulzar (Small Heath CS; Josiah Mason SFC, Erdington), b Birmingham 26 Feb 1971. 6'0". LHB, LB. No 1st XI appearances – joined staff 1991.

LLOYD, Timothy Andrew (Oswestry HS; Dorset CHE), b Oswestry, Salop 5 Nov 1956. 5'10". LHB, RM/OB. Debut 1977. Cap 1980. Captain 1988-. Benefit 1990. OFS 1978-80. Salop 1975. **Tests:** 1 (1984); HS 10* (rtd hurt) v WI (Birmingham) 1984. LOI: 3. Tour: Z 1984-85 (EC). 1000 runs (9); most – 1673 (1983). HS 208* v Glos (Birmingham) 1983. BB 3-62 v Surrey (Birmingham) 1985. Awards: NWT 3; BHC 2. **NWT:** HS 121 v Cambs (Birmingham) 1988. BB 1-4. **BHC:** HS 137* v Lancs (Birmingham) 1985. **SL:** HS 90 v Kent (Birmingham) 1980. BB 1-42.

MOLES, Andrew James (Finham Park CS; Butts CHE), b Solihull 12 Feb 1961. 5'10". RHB, RM. Debut 1986. Cap 1987. GW 1986-89. 1000 runs (4); most – 1854 (1990). HS 230* GW v N Transvaal B (Verwoerdburg) 1988-89. Wa HS 224* v Glam (Swansea) 1990. BB 3-21 v OU (Oxford) 1987. BAC BB 3-50 v Essex (Chelmsford) 1987. Awards: NWT 1; BHC 1. **NWT:** HS 127 v Bucks (Birmingham) 1987. **BHC:** HS 72 v Scot (Perth) 1987. BB 1-11. **SL:** HS 93* v Glam (Swansea) 1991. BB 2-24 v Worcs (Worcester) 1987.

MUNTON, Timothy Alan (Sarson HS; King Edward VII Upper S), b Melton Mowbray, Leics 30 Jul 1965. 6'5". RHB, RMF. Debut 1985. Cap 1989. Tours: P 1990-91 (Eng A); SL 1990-91 (Eng A). HS 38 v Yorks (Scarborough) 1987. 50 wkts (3); most – 78 (1990). BB 8-89 (11-128 match) v Middx (Birmingham) 1991. **NWT:** HS 5. BB 3-36 v Kent (Canterbury) 1989. **BHC:** HS 13 v Leics (Leicester) 1989. BB 4-35 v Surrey (Oval) 1991. **SL:** HS 10* v Northants (Northampton) 1991. BB 5-23 v Glos (Moreton) 1990.

OSTLER, Dominic Piers (Princethorpe C; Solihull TC), b Solihull 15 Jul 1970. 6'3". RHB, RM. Debut 1990. Cap 1991. 1000 runs (1): 1284 (1991). HS 120* v Kent (Tunbridge W) 1991. **NWT:** HS 34* v Yorks (Birmingham) 1991. **BHC:** HS 45 v Essex (Birmingham) 1991. **SL:** HS 62* v Derbys (Birmingham) 1991.

PIPER, Keith John (Haringey Cricket C), b Leicester 18 Dec 1969. 5'6". RHB, WK. Debut 1989. HS 111 v Somerset (Birmingham) 1990. **NWT:** HS 1. **BHC:** HS 11* v Surrey (Oval) 1991. **SL:** HS 30 v Lancs (Manchester) 1990.

RATCLIFFE, Jason David (Sharman's Cross SS; Solihull SFC), b Solihull 19 Jun 1969. Son of D.P. (Warwks 1957-68). 6'4". RHB, RM. Debut 1988. HS 127* v CU (Cambridge) 1989. BAC HS 94 v Middx (Birmingham) 1991. BB 1-15. Award: NWT 1. **NWT:** HS 113 68* v Herts (Birmingham) 1991. **BHC:** HS 29 v Surrey (Oval) 1991. **SL:** HS 37 v Somerset (Birmingham) 1989. BB 1-8.

REEVE, Dermot Alexander (King George V S, Kowloon), b Kowloon, Hong Kong 2 Apr 1963. 6'0". RHB, RMF. Sussex 1983-87 (cap 1986). Warwickshire debut 1988. Cap 1989. Hong Kong 1982 (ICCTrophy). MCC Cricket Staff. LOI: 1. 1000 runs (2); most – 1412 (1990). HS 202* v Northants (Northampton) 1990. 50 wkts (2); most – 55 (1984). BB 7-37 Sx v Lancs (Lytham) 1987. Wa BB 6-73 v Kent (Tunbridge W) 1991. Awards: NWT 3; BHC 1. **NWT:** HS 57* v Hants (Birmingham) 1991. BB 4-20 Sx v Lancs (Lord's) 1986. **BHC:** HS 80 v Essex (Birmingham) 1991. BB 4-42 Sx v Kent (Canterbury) 1987. **SL:** HS 100 v Lancs (Birmingham) 1991. BB 5-23 v Essex (Birmingham) 1988.

SMALL, Gladstone Cleophas (Moseley S; Hall Green TC), b St George, Barbados 18 Oct 1961. 5'11". RHB, RFM. Debut 1979-80 (DHR XI in NZ). Warwickshire debut 1980. Cap 1982. Benefit 1992. S Australia 1985-86. **Tests:** 17 (1986 to 1990); HS 59 v A (Oval) 1989; BB 5-48 v A (Melbourne) 1986-87. LOI: 46. Tours: A 1986-87, 1990-91; WI 1989-90; NZ 1979-80 (DHR); P 1981-82 (Int). HS 70 v Lancs (Manchester) 1988. 50 wkts (6); most – 80 (1988). BB 7-15 v Notts (Birmingham) 1988. NWT: HS 33 v Surrey (Lord's) 1982. BB 3-22 v Glam (Cardiff) 1982. **BHC:** HS 22 v Kent (Canterbury 1990. BB 4-22 v Glam (Birmingham) 1990. **SL:** HS 40* v Essex (Ilford) 1984. BB 5-29 v Surrey (Birmingham) 1980.

SMITH, Neil Michael Knight (Warwick S), b Birmingham 27 Jul 1967. Son of M.J.K. (Leics, Warwks and England 1951-75). 6'0". RHB, OB. Debut 1987. MCC Cricket Staff. HS 161 v Yorks (Leeds) 1989. BB 3-50 v Northants (Birmingham) 1991. **NWT:** HS 52 v Yorks (Leeds) 1990. BB 1-6. **BHC:** HS 30* v Worcs (Birmingham) 1990. BB 1-43. **SL:** HS 39 v Northants (Northampton) 1991. BB 3-36 v Hants (Birmingham) 1990.

SMITH, Paul Andrew (Heaton GS), b Jesmond, Northumb 15 Apr 1964. Son of K.D. sr (Leics 1950-51) and brother of K.D. jr (Warwks 1973-85). 6'2". RHB, RFM. Debut 1982. Cap 1986. MCC Cricket Staff. 1000 runs (2); most – 1508 (1986). HS 140 v Worcs (Worcester) 1989. BB 5-28 v Glos (Birmingham) 1991. 2 hat-tricks: 1989, 1990. Awards: BHC 2. **NWT:** HS 79 v Durham (Birmingham) 1986. BB 3-10 v Salop (Birmingham) 1984. **BHC:** HS 74 v Northants (Birmingham) 1989. BB 3-28 v Middx (Lord's) 1991. **SL:** HS 93* v Middx (Birmingham) 1989. BB 4-21 v Somerset (Birmingham) 1991.

TWOSE, Roger Graham (King's C, Taunton), b Torquay, Devon 17 Apr 1968. Nephew of R.W.Tolchard (Leics and England 1965-83). 6'0". LHB, RM. Debut 1989. N Districts 1989-90. Devon 1988-89. MCC Cricket Staff. HS 64* v SL (Birmingham) 1990. BAC HS 51 v Kent (Birmingham) 1990. BB 1-31. **NWT:** HS 56 Devon v Notts (Torquay) 1988. BB 1-31. **BHC:** HS 17 v Worcs (Birmingham) 1990. **SL:** HS 40 v Surrey (Oval) 1990. BB 2-11 v Derbys (Derby) 1990.

USHER, Benjamin Che (Malvern C), b Wycliffe, Barnard Castle, Co Durham 3 Feb 1970. Grandson of C.U.Peat (OU & Middlesex 1913-22). 6'3". RHB, RM. No 1st XI appearances – joined staff 1991.

WELCH, Graeme (Hetton CS), b Durham 21 Mar 1972. RHB, RM. No 1st XI appearances – joined staff 1990.

NEWCOMERS

GILES, Ashley F., b Ripley, Surrey. SLA.

PENNEY, Trevor Lionel, b Salisbury, Rhodesia 12 Jun 1968. Qualified 1992. RHB, LB.

DEPARTURES

BENJAMIN, J.E. – see SURREY.

GREEN, S.J. – see NORTHAMPTONSHIRE.

PIERSON, Adrian Roger Kirshaw (Kent C, Canterbury; Hatfield Polytechnic), b Enfield, Middx 21 Jul 1963. 6'4". RHB, OB. Warwickshire 1985-91. MCC Cricket Staff. HS 42* v Northants (Northampton) 1986. BB 6-82 v Derbys (Nuneaton) 1989. Award: BHC 1. **NWT:** HS 1*. BB 3-20 v Wilts (Birmingham) 1989. **BHC:** HS 11 v Minor C (Walsall) 1986. BB 3-34 v Lancs (Birmingham) 1988. **SL:** HS 21* v Hants (Birmingham) 1987. BB 3-21 v Leics (Birmingham) 1988.

WARWICKSHIRE 1991

RESULTS SUMMARY

	Place	Won	Lost	Tied	Drew	Abandoned
Britannic Assurance Championship	2nd	11	4		7	
All First-class Matches		11	4		7	
Refuge Assurance League	5th	8	4	1		3
NatWest Trophy	Semi-Finalist					
Benson and Hedges Cup	Quarter-Finalist					

BRITANNIC ASSURANCE CHAMPIONSHIP AVERAGES

BATTING AND FIELDING

Cap		M	I	NO	HS	Runs	Avge	100	50	Ct/St
	P.C.L.Holloway	6	9	5	89*	263	65.75	–	2	9
1989	D.A.Reeve	20	33	7	99*	1260	48.46	–	14	10
1991	D.P.Ostler	22	40	5	120*	1284	36.68	1	10	20
1987	A.J.Moles	22	39	2	133	1246	33.67	1	10	10
1980	T.A.Lloyd	21	35	2	97	1076	32.60	–	10	10
–	J.D.Ratcliffe	17	31	1	94	953	31.76	–	8	15
–	N.M.K.Smith	5	9	2	70	209	29.85	–	2	–
–	A.R.K.Pierson	5	6	4	35	55	27.50	–	–	1
1987	Asif Din	15	27	1	140	685	26.34	2	1	9
1986	P.A.Smith	14	23	1	68	411	18.68	–	2	2
–	K.J.Piper	16	23	3	55	349	17.45	–	1	48
1982	G.C.Small	20	29	7	58	370	16.81	–	1	5
–	P.A.Booth	10	13	0	62	175	13.46	–	1	5
1989	T.A.Munton	22	24	7	31	226	13.29	–	–	14
1989	A.A.Donald	21	21	9	18	96	8.00	–	–	10
–	J.E.Benjamin	3	4	0	11	12	3.00	–	–	1

Also played: S.J.Green (1 match) 77*; R.G.Twose (2 matches) 41, 1*.

BOWLING

	O	M	R	W	Avge	Best	5wI	10wM
A.A.Donald	522.3	91	1634	83	19.68	6-69	8	2
D.A.Reeve	402.1	117	957	45	21.26	6-73	1	–
T.A.Munton	662	177	1795	71	25.28	8-89	5	2
G.C.Small	498	126	1347	45	29.93	4-36	–	–
P.A.Smith	157.1	31	513	15	34.20	5-28	1	–
P.A.Booth	226.1	47	690	18	38.33	4-103	–	–

Also bowled: Asif Din 53-9-206-2; J.E.Benjamin 76.4-11-257-7; T.A.Lloyd 16-13-26-0; A.J.Moles 33-13-65-1; D.P.Ostler 2-1-7-0; A.R.K.Pierson 73-11-279-4; J.D.Ratcliffe 3-1-14-0; N.M.K.Smith 111-32-321-8; R.G.Twose 9-0-27-1.

The First-Class Averages (pp 164-179) give the records of Warwickshire players in all first-class county matches, with the exception of T.M.Munton, whose full county figures are as above.

WARWICKSHIRE RECORDS

FIRST-CLASS CRICKET

Highest Total	For	657-6d	v Hampshire	Birmingham	1899
	V	887	by Yorkshire	Birmingham	1896
Lowest Total	For	16	v Kent	Tonbridge	1913
	V	15	by Hampshire	Birmingham	1922
Highest Innings	For	305* F.R.Foster	v Worcs	Dudley	1914
	V	322 I.V.A.Richards	for Somerset	Taunton	1985

Highest Partnership for each Wicket

1st	377* N.F.Horner/K.Ibadulla	v Surrey	The Oval	1960
2nd	465* J.A.Jameson/R.B.Kanhai	v Glos	Birmingham	1974
3rd	327 S.P.Kinneir/W.G.Quaife	v Lancashire	Birmingham	1901
4th	470 A.I.Kallicharran/G.W.Humpage	v Lancashire	Southport	1982
5th	268 W.Quaife/W.G.Quaife	v Essex	Leyton	1900
6th	220 H.E.Dollery/J.Buckingham	v Derbyshire	Derby	1938
7th	250 H.E.Dollery/J.S.Ord	v Kent	Maidstone	1953
8th	228 A.J.W.Croom/R.E.S.Wyatt	v Worcs	Dudley	1925
9th	154 G.W.Stephens/A.J.W.Croom	v Derbyshire	Birmingham	1925
10th	128 F.R.Santall/W.Sanders	v Yorkshire	Birmingham	1930

Best Bowling	For	10-41 J.D.Bannister	v Comb Servs	Birmingham	1959
(Innings)	V	10-36 H.Verity	for Yorkshire	Leeds	1931
Best Bowling	For	15-76 S.Hargreave	v Surrey	The Oval	1903
(Match)	V	17-92 A.P.Freeman	for Kent	Folkestone	1932

Most Runs – Season	2,417	M.J.K.Smith	(av 60.42)	1959
Most Runs – Career	35,146	D.L.Amiss	(av 41.64)	1960-1987
Most 100s – Season	9	A.I.Kallicharran		1984
Most 100s – Career	78	D.L.Amiss		1960-1987
Most Wkts – Season	180	W.E.Hollies	(av 15.13)	1946
Most Wkts – Career	2,201	W.E.Hollies	(av 20.45)	1932-1957

LIMITED-OVERS CRICKET

Highest Total	NWT	392-5	v Oxfordshire	Birmingham	1984
	BHC	308-4	v Scotland	Birmingham	1988
	SL	301-6	v Essex	Colchester	1982
Lowest Total	NWT	109	v Kent	Canterbury	1971
	BHC	96	v Leics	Leicester	1972
	SL	65	v Kent	Maidstone	1979
Highest Innings	NWT	206 A.I.Kallicharran	v Oxfordshire	Birmingham	1984
	BHC	137* T.A.Lloyd	v Lancashire	Birmingham	1985
	SL	123* J.A.Jameson	v Notts	Nottingham	1973
Best Bowling	NWT	6-32 K.Ibadulla	v Hampshire	Birmingham	1965
		6-32 A.I.Kallicharran	v Oxfordshire	Birmingham	1984
	BHC	7-32 R.G.D.Willis	v Yorkshire	Birmingham	1981
	SL	6-20 N.Gifford	v Northants	Birmingham	1985

WORCESTERSHIRE

Formation of Present Club: 11 March 1865
Colours: Dark Green and Black
Badge: Shield Argent a Fess between three Pears Sable
Championships: (5) 1964, 1965, 1974, 1988, 1989
NatWest Trophy/Gillette Cup Winners: (0) Finalists 1963, 1966, 1988
Benson and Hedges Cup Winners: (1) 1991
Sunday League Champions: (3) 1971, 1987, 1988
Match Awards: NWT 35; BHC 51

Secretary: Revd M.D.Vockins, County Ground, New Road, Worcester, WR2 4QQ
(☎ 0905-422694)
Captain: T.S.Curtis
Scorer: J.W.Sewter

BEVINS, Stuart Roy (Solihull S; Solihull TC), b Solihull, Warwks 8 Mar 1967. 5'6½". RHB, WK. Debut 1989. HS 10 v NZ (Worcester) 1990. BAC HS 6*. **BHC:** HS 0*. **SL:** HS -.

CURTIS, Timothy Stephen (Worcester RGS; Durham U; Magdalene C, Cambridge), b Chislehurst, Kent 15 Jan 1960. 5'11". RHB, LB. Debut 1979. Cap 1984. Captain 1992. Cambridge U 1983 (blue). **Tests:** 5 (1988 and 1989), HS 41 v A (Birmingham) 1989. Tour: Z 1990-91 (Wo). 1000 runs (8); most – 1731 (1990). HS 248 v Somerset (Worcester) 1991. Shared record Worcs stand of 287* for 2nd wkt with G.A.Hick v Glam (Neath) 1986. BB 2-17 v OU (Oxford) 1991. BAC BB 2-72 v Warwks (Worcester) 1987. Awards: NWT 5; BHC 2. **NWT:** HS 120 v Notts (Nottingham) 1988. BB 1-6. **BHC:** HS 97 v Warwks (Birmingham) 1990. **SL:** HS 124 v Somerset (Taunton) 1990.

DILLEY, Graham Roy (Dartford West SS), b Dartford, Kent 18 May 1959. 6'3". LHB, RF. Kent 1977-86 (cap 1980). Worcestershire debut/cap 1987. Natal 1985-86. YC 1980. **Tests:** 41 (1979-80 to 1989); HS 56 v A (Leeds) 1981; BB 6-38 v NZ (Christchurch) 1987-88. LOI: 36. Tours: A 1979-80, 1986-87, 1987-88; SA 1989-90 (Eng XI); WI 1980-81; NZ 1983-84, 1987-88; I 1979-80, 1981-82; P 1983-84, 1987-88; SL 1981-82. HS 81 K v Northants (Northampton) 1979. Wo HS 45* v Glam (Worcester) 1990. 50 wkts (3); most – 64 (1982). BB 7-63 Natal v Transvaal (Johannesburg) 1985-86. Wo/BAC BB 6-43 v Leics (Worcester) 1987. 2 hat-tricks (Kent): 1985, 1986. Awards: NWT 1; BHC 1. **NWT:** HS 25 v Essex (Chelmsford) 1987. BB 5-29 K v Scot 1986 and Wo v Middx 1988. **BHC:** HS 37* K v Hants (Canterbury) 1983. BB 4-14 K v Comb Us (Canterbury) 1981. **SL:** HS 33 K v Northants (Northampton) 1982. BB 4-20 K v Glos (Canterbury) 1980.

D'OLIVEIRA, Damian Basil (Blessed Edward Oldcorne SS), b Cape Town, SA 19 Oct 1960. Son of B.L. (Worcs and England 1964-80). 5'9". RHB, OB. Debut 1982. Cap 1985. MCC Cricket Staff. Tours: Z 1984-85 (EC), 1990-91 (Wo). 1000 runs (4); most – 1263 (1990). HS 237 v OU (Oxford) 1991. BAC HS 155 v Lancs (Manchester) 1990. BB 2-17 v Glos (Bristol) 1986. Awards: NWT 2; BHC 2. **NWT:** HS 99 v Oxon (Worcester) 1986. BB 2-17 v Suffolk (Bury St E) 1990. **BHC:** HS 66 v Yorks (Leeds) 1986. BB 3-12 v Scot (Glasgow) 1986. **SL:** HS 103 v Surrey (Worcester) 1985. BB 3-23 v Derbys (Derby) 1983.

HAYNES, Gavin Richard (High Park S; King Edward VI S, Stourbridge), b Wordsley Hospital, Stourbridge 29 Sep 1969. 5'10". RHB, RM. Debut 1991. HS 16 v Notts and v SL (Worcester) 1991.

HICK, Graeme Ashley (Prince Edward HS, Salisbury), b Salisbury, Rhodesia 23 May 1966. 6'3". RHB, OB. Zimbabwe 1983-86. Worcestershire debut 1984. Cap 1986. N Districts 1987-89. Queensland 1990-91. Wisden 1986. **Tests:** 4 (1991); HS 43 v WI (Nottingham) 1991; BB 2-77 v WI (Lord's) 1991. **LOI:** 3. Tours (Z): E 1985; SL 1983-84; Z 1990-91 (Wo). 1000 runs (7+1) inc 2000 runs (3); most – 2713 (1988); youngest to score 2000 (1986). 1019 runs before June 1988. HS 405* (Worcs record and 2nd-highest in UK f-c matches) v Somerset (Taunton) 1988. Shared in 4 record Worcs stands: 287* (2nd) with T.S.Curtis; 265 (6th) with S.J.Rhodes; 205 (7th) with P.J.Newport and 177* (8th) with R.K.Illingworth. BB 5-37 v Glos (Worcester) 1990. Awards: NWT 2; BHC 7. **NWT:** HS 172* v Devon (Worcester) 1987. BB 4-54 v Hants (Worcester) 1988. **BHC:** HS 109 v Comb Us (Worcester) 1989. BB 3-36 v Warwks (Birmingham) 1990. **SL:** HS 114* v Notts (Worcester) 1990. BB 4-42 v Sussex (Worcester) 1988.

ILLINGWORTH, Richard Keith (Salts GS), b Bradford, Yorks 23 Aug 1963. 5'11". RHB, SLA. Debut 1982. Cap 1986. Natal 1988-89. **Tests:** 2 (1991); HS 13 (twice) and BB 3-110 (including wicket of P.V.Simmons with first ball) v WI (Nottingham) 1991 – on debut. **LOI:** 3. Tours: P 1990-91 (Eng A); SL 1990-91 (Eng A); Z 1989-90 (Eng A), 1990-91 (Wo). HS 120* v Warwks (Worcester) 1987. Shared record Worcs stand of 177* for 8th wkt with G.A.Hick v Somerset (Taunton) 1988. 50 wkts (3); most – 75 (1990). BB 7-50 v OU (Oxford) 1985. BAC BB 5-23 v Hants (Bournemouth) 1989. **NWT:** HS 22 v Northants (Northampton) 1984. BB 4-20 v Devon (Worcester) 1987. **BHC:** HS 36* v Kent (Worcester) 1990. BB 4-36 v Yorks (Bradford) 1985. **SL:** HS 25* v Essex (Ilford) 1991. BB 5-24 v Somerset (Worcester) 1983.

LAMPITT, Stuart Richard (Kingswinford S; Dudley TC), b Wolverhampton, Staffs 29 Jul 1966. 5'11". RHB, RM. Debut 1985. Cap 1989. Tour: Z 1990-91 (Wo). HS 93 v Derbys (Kidderminster) 1991. Shared record Worcs stand of 184 for 8th wkt with S.J.Rhodes v Derbys (Kidderminster) 1991. 50 wkts (2); most – 58 (1990). BB 5-32 v Kent (Worcester) 1989. Awards: NWT 1; BHC 1. **NWT:** HS 9*. BB 5-22 v Suffolk (Bury St E) 1990. **BHC:** HS 41 v Glam (Worcester) 1990. BB 4-46 v Glos (Worcester) 1991. **SL:** HS 25* and BB 5-67 v Middx (Lord's) 1990.

LEATHERDALE, David Anthony (Pudsey Grangefield S), b Bradford, Yorks 26 Nov 1967. 5'10½". RHB, RM. Debut 1988. HS 157 v Somerset (Worcester) 1991. BB 1-12. **NWT:** HS 43 v Hants (Worcester) 1988. **SL:** HS 62* v Kent (Folkestone) 1988.

MOODY, Thomas Masson (Guildford GS, WA), b Adelaide, Australia 2 Oct 1965. 6'6⅜". RHB, RM. W Australia 1985-91. Warwickshire 1990 (cap 1990). Worcestershire debut/cap 1991. **Tests** (A): 4 (1989-90); HS 106 v SL (Brisbane) 1989-90; BB 1-23. **LOI** (A): 13. Tours (A): E 1989; I 1989-90 (WA). 1000 runs (2+1); most – 1887 (1991). HS 210 v Warwks (Worcester) 1991. Scored 26-minute 100 for Wa v Glam (Swansea) 1990. BB 7-43 (10-109 match) WA v Victoria (Perth) 1990-91. BAC BB 1-7. Wo BB 1-19. Awards: BHC 3. **NWT:** HS 58 Wa v Herts (St Albans) 1990. BB 1-7. **BHC:** HS 110* v Derbys (Worcester) 1991. BB 2-2 v Glos (Worcester) 1991. **SL:** HS 160 v Kent (Worcester) 1991 (on Wo debut in all competitions). BB 2-42 Wa v Northants (Birmingham) 1990.

NEALE, Phillip Anthony (Frederick Gough CS; John Leggott SFC; Leeds U), b Scunthorpe, Lincs 5 Jun 1954. 5'11". RHB, RM. Debut 1975. Cap 1978. Captain 1982-91. Benefit 1988. Lincolnshire 1972. Wisden 1988. Tour: Z 1990-91 (Wo – captain). 1000 runs (8); most – 1706 (1984). HS 167 v Sussex (Kidderminster) 1988. BB 1-15. Awards: NWT 1; BHC 2. **NWT:** HS 98 v Cumberland (Worcester) 1988. **BHC:** HS 128 v Lancs (Manchester) 1980. **SL:** HS 102 v Northants (Luton) 1982. BB 2-46 v Warwks (Worcester) 1976.

NEWPORT, Philip John (High Wycombe RGS; Portsmouth Polytechnic), b High Wycombe, Bucks 11 Oct 1962. 6'3". RHB, RFM. Debut 1982. Cap 1986. Boland 1987-88. Buckinghamshire 1981-82. **Tests:** 3 (1988 to 1990-91); HS 40* v A (Perth) 1990-91; BB 4-87 v SL (Lord's) 1988. Tours: A 1990-91 (part); P 1990-91 (Eng A); SL 1990-91 (Eng A). HS 98 v NZ (Worcester) 1990. BAC HS 96 v Essex (Worcester) 1990. Shared record Worcs stand of 205 for 7th wkt with G.A.Hick v Yorks (Worcester) 1988. 50 wkts (4); most – 93 (1988). BB 8-52 v Middx (Lord's) 1988. **NWT:** HS 25 v Northants (Northampton) 1984. BB 4-46 v Northants (Northampton) 1990. **BHC:** HS 28 v Kent (Worcester) 1990. BB 5-22 v Warwks (Birmingham) 1987. **SL:** HS 26* v Leics (Leicester) 1987. BB 4-18 v Glam (Worcester) 1989.

RADFORD, Neal Victor (Athlone BHS, Johannesburg), b Luanshya, N Rhodesia 7 Jun 1957. Brother of W.R. (OFS). 5'11". RHB, RFM. Transvaal 1978-89. Lancashire 1980-84. Worcestershire debut/cap 1985. Wisden 1985. **Tests:** 3 (1986 and 1987-88); HS 12* v NZ (Lord's); BB 2-131 v I (Birmingham). LOI: 6. Tours: NZ 1987-88; Z 1990-91 (Wo). HS 76* La v Derbys (Blackpool) 1981. Wo HS 66* v Sussex (Hove) 1989. 50 wkts (5) inc 100 wkts (2); most – 109 (1987). BB 9-70 v Somerset (Worcester) 1986. Award: NWT 1. **NWT:** HS 37 v Essex (Chelmsford) 1987. BB 7-19 v Beds (Bedford) 1991. **BHC:** HS 40 v Glam (Worcester) 1990. BB 4-25 v Northants (Northampton) 1988. **SL:** HS 48* La v Glam (Cardiff) 1981. BB 5-32 v Warwks (Worcester) 1987.

RHODES, Steven John (Lapage Middle S; Carlton-Bolling S, Bradford), b Bradford, Yorks 17 Jun 1964. Son of W.E. (Notts 1961-64). 5'7". RHB, WK. Yorkshire 1981-84. Worcestershire debut 1985. Cap 1986. LOI: 3. Tours: SL 1985-86 (Eng B), 1990-91 (Eng A); Z 1989-90 (Eng A), 1990-91 (Wo). HS 108 v Derbys (Derby) 1988. Shared in 2 record Worcs stands: 265 (6th) with G.A.Hick and 184 (8th) with S.R.Lampitt. Award: BHC 1. **NWT:** HS 61 v Derbys (Worcester) 1989. **BHC:** HS 51* v Warwks (Birmingham) 1987. **SL:** HS 48* v Kent (Worcester) 1989.

STEMP, Richard David (Brittania HS, Rowley Regis), b Erdington, Birmingham 11 Dec 1967. 6'0". RHB, SLA. Debut 1990. HS 15* v Notts (Worcester) 1991. BB 4-62 v Yorks (Leeds) 1991. **SL:** HS 3*. BB 3-18 v Derbys (Worcester) 1991.

TOLLEY, Christopher Mark (King Edward VI C, Stourbridge; Loughborough U), b Kidderminster 30 Dec 1967. 5'9". RHB, LMF. Debut 1989. Comb Us (BHC) 1989-90. Tour: Z 1990-91 (Wo). HS 37 v Kent (Worcester) 1989. BB 4-69 v SL (Worcester) 1991. BAC BB 3-40 v Middx (Worcester) 1991. Award: BHC 1. **BHC:** HS 77 Comb Us v Lancs (Cambridge) 1990. BB 1-12. **SL:** HS 1*. BB 1-18.

WESTON, Martin John (Samuel Southall SS), b Worcester 8 Apr 1959. 6'1". RHB, RM. Debut 1979. Cap 1986. 1000 runs (1): 1061 (1984). HS 145* v Northants (Worcester) 1984. BB 4-24 v Warwks (Birmingham) 1988. Awards: NWT 1; BHC 1. **NWT:** HS 98 v Somerset (Taunton) 1990. BB 4-30 v Suffolk (Worcester) 1984. **BHC:** HS 99* v Notts (Nottingham) 1990. BB 2-27 v Yorks (Bradford) 1985. **SL:** HS 109 v Somerset (Taunton) 1982. BB 4-11 v Hants (Worcester) 1984.

WESTON, William Philip Christopher (Durham S), b Durham City 16 Jun 1973. Son of M.P. (Durham; England RF(1). 6'3". LHB, LM. Debut 1991. HS 15 v Notts (Nottingham) 1991.

NEWCOMERS

SEYMOUR, Adam Charles Hylton (Millfield S), b Royston, Cambs 7 Dec 1967. 6'2". LHB, RM. Essex 1988-91. HS 157 Ex v Glam (Cardiff) 1991. **NWT:** HS 0. **SL:** HS 25 Ex v Lancs (Manchester) 1991.

WYLIE, Alex (Bromsgrove S), b Tamworth, Staffs 20 Feb 1973. LHB, RFM.

DEPARTURES – see p 155

WORCESTERSHIRE 1991

RESULTS SUMMARY

	Place	Won	Lost	Tied	Drew	Abandoned
Britannic Assurance Championship	6th	6	4		12	
All First-class Matches		8	4		13	
Refuge Assurance League	4th	9	4	1		2
NatWest Trophy	2nd Round					
Benson and Hedges Cup	Winners					

BRITANNIC ASSURANCE CHAMPIONSHIP AVERAGES

BATTING AND FIELDING

Cap		M	I	NO	HS	Runs	Avge	100	50	Ct/St
1991	T.M.Moody	19	31	4	210	1770	65.55	6	8	29
–	D.A.Leatherdale	3	4	0	157	219	54.75	1	–	2
1984	T.S.Curtis	22	37	3	248	1555	45.73	3	8	14
1986	G.A.Hick	16	27	2	186	975	39.00	3	4	17
1987	I.T.Botham	10	17	2	104	567	37.80	1	4	7
1986	S.J.Rhodes	22	32	6	90	907	34.88	–	8	48/7
1989	S.R.Lampitt	19	20	5	93	447	29.80	–	3	5
–	P.Bent	7	12	1	100*	285	25.90	1	1	3
1978	P.A.Neale	13	20	4	69*	385	24.06	–	1	5
1986	R.K.Illingworth	17	23	4	56*	442	23.26	–	1	14
–	C.M.Tolley	6	9	3	36	137	22.83	–	–	4
1986	P.J.Newport	22	24	9	48	340	22.66	–	–	4
1990	G.J.Lord	9	16	0	85	356	22.25	–	3	2
1985	D.B.D'Oliveira	15	22	2	79	335	16.75	–	1	21
1985	N.V.Radford	17	16	6	45	157	15.70	–	–	4
–	R.D.Stemp	8	8	5	15*	30	10.00	–	–	4
1987	G.R.Dilley	10	10	4	15*	37	6.16	–	–	3

Also played: G.R.Haynes (3 matches) 13*, 16, 6; M.J.Weston (2 matches – cap 1986) 9, 5; W.P.C.Weston (2 matches) 8, 15.

BOWLING

	O	M	R	W	Avge	Best	5wI	10wM
G.R.Dilley	281	56	752	35	21.48	5-91	2	–
I.T.Botham	279.1	55	886	38	23.31	7-54	3	–
R.D.Stemp	141.1	30	382	15	25.46	4-62	–	–
C.M.Tolley	105	21	292	11	26.54	3-40	–	–
N.V.Radford	434.1	92	1363	46	29.63	7-43	2	–
S.R.Lampitt	422.4	74	1358	45	30.17	5-70	3	–
P.J.Newport	609.4	115	1840	54	34.07	4-44	–	–
R.K.Illingworth	430.4	132	971	26	37.34	5-49	2	–

Also bowled: P.Bent 3-1-5-0; T.S.Curtis 21-2-95-0; D.B.D'Oliveira 31-7-116-1; G.R.Haynes 19.2-2-82-0; G.A.Hick 123.4-29-379-8; T.M.Moody 8.4-3-25-0; P.A.Neale 17.5-1-86-1; S.J.Rhodes 1-0-30-0; M.J.Weston 5-1-27-1.

The First-Class Averages (pp 164–179) give the records of Worcestershire players in all first-class county matches (their other opponents being the West Indians, the Sri Lankans and Oxford U.), with the exception of:
I.T.Botham 11-18-2-161-728-45.50-2-4-7ct. 308.1-60-969-40-24.22-7/54-3-0.
G.A.Hick 17-28-2-186-986-37.92-3-4-17ct. 123.4-29-379-8-47.37-5/42-1-0.
R.K.Illingworth 19.25-5-56*-493-24.65-0-1-7ct. 472.3-143-1083-33-32.81-5/43-3-0.
S.J.Rhodes 23-33-6-90-942-34.88-0-8-53ct/8st. 1-0-30-0.

WORCESTERSHIRE RECORDS

FIRST-CLASS CRICKET

Highest Total	For	633	v Warwicks	Worcester	1906
	V	701-4d	by Leics	Worcester	1906
Lowest Total	For	24	v Yorkshire	Huddersfield	1903
	V	30	by Hampshire	Worcester	1903
Highest Innings	For	405* G.A.Hick	v Somerset	Taunton	1988
	V	331* J.D.B.Robertson	for Middlesex	Worcester	1949

Highest Partnership for each Wicket

1st	309	F.L.Bowley/H.K.Foster	v Derbyshire	Derby	1901
2nd	287*	T.S.Curtis/G.A.Hick	v Glamorgan	Neath	1986
3rd	314	M.J.Horton/T.W.Graveney	v Somerset	Worcester	1962
4th	281	J.A.Ormrod/Younis Ahmed	v Notts	Nottingham	1979
5th	393	E.G.Arnold/W.B.Burns	v Warwicks	Birmingham	1909
6th	265	G.A.Hick/S.J.Rhodes	v Somerset	Taunton	1988
7th	205	G.A.Hick/P.J.Newport	v Yorkshire	Worcester	1988
8th	184	S.J.Rhodes/S.R.Lampitt	v Derbyshire	Kidderminster	1991
9th	181	J.A.Cuffe/R.D.Burrows	v Glos	Worcester	1907
10th	119	W.B.Burns/G.A.Wilson	v Somerset	Worcester	1906

Best Bowling	For	9-23 C.F.Root	v Lancashire	Worcester	1931
(Innings)	V	10-51 J.Mercer	for Glamorgan	Worcester	1936
Best Bowling	For	15-87 A.J.Conway	v Glos	Moreton-in-M	1914
(Match)	V	17-212 J.C.Clay	for Glamorgan	Swansea	1937

Most Runs – Season	2,654	H.H.I.Gibbons	(av 52.03)	1934
Most Runs – Career	33,490	D.Kenyon	(av 33.19)	1946-1967
Most 100s – Season	10	G.M.Turner		1970
	10	G.A.Hick		1988
Most 100s – Career	72	G.M.Turner		1967-1982
Most Wkts – Season	207	C.F.Root	(av 17.52)	1925
Most Wkts – Career	2,143	R.T.D.Perks	(av 23.73)	1930-1955

LIMITED-OVERS CRICKET

Highest Total	NWT	404-3	v Devon	Worcester	1987
	BHC	314-5	v Lancashire	Manchester	1980
	SL	307-4	v Derbyshire	Worcester	1975
Lowest Total	NWT	98	v Durham	Chester-le-St	1968
	BHC	81	v Leics	Worcester	1983
	SL	86	v Yorkshire	Leeds	1969
Highest Innings	NWT	172* G.A.Hick	v Devon	Worcester	1987
	BHC	143* G.M.Turner	v Warwicks	Birmingham	1976
	SL	160 T.M.Moody	v Kent	Worcester	1991
Best Bowling	NWT	7-19 N.V.Radford	v Beds	Bedford	1991
	BHC	6-8 N.Gifford	v Minor C (S)	High Wycombe	1979
	SL	6-26 A.P.Pridgeon	v Surrey	Worcester	1978

YORKSHIRE

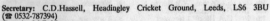

Formation of Present Club: 8 January 1863
Substantial Reorganisation: 10 December 1891
Colours: Dark Blue, Light Blue and Gold
Badge: White Rose
Championships (since 1890): (29) 1893, 1896, 1898, 1900,
1901, 1902, 1905, 1908, 1912, 1919, 1922, 1923, 1924,
1925, 1931, 1932, 1933, 1935, 1937, 1938, 1939, 1946,
1959, 1960, 1962, 1963, 1966, 1967, 1968. Joint: (1) 1949
NatWest Trophy/Gillette Cup Winners: (2) 1965, 1969
Benson and Hedges Cup Winners: (1) 1987
Sunday League Champions: (1) 1983
Match Awards: NWT 25; BHC 54

Secretary: C.D.Hassell, Headingley Cricket Ground, Leeds, LS6 3BU
(☎ 0532-787394)
Captain: M.D.Moxon
Scorer: E.I.Lester (home) and J.T.Potter (away)
1992 Beneficiary: S.N.Hartley

BATTY, Jeremy David (Bingley GS; Horsforth C), b Bradford 15 May 1971. 6'1".
RHB, OB. Debut 1989. HS 51 v SL (Leeds) 1991. BAC HS 31 v Northants (Leeds)
1991. BB 6-48 v Notts (Worksop) 1991. **NWT:** HS 4. BB 1-17. **BHC:** BB 1-34. **SL:**
HS 13* and BB 4-33 v Kent (Scarborough) 1991.

BLAKEY, Richard John (Rastrick GS), b Huddersfield 15 Jan 1967. 5'9". RHB,
WK. Debut 1985. Cap 1987. YC 1987. Tours: WI 1986-87 (Y); P 1990-91 (Eng A);
SL 1990-91 (Eng A); Z 1989-90 (Eng A). 1000 runs (3); most – 1361 (1987). HS 221
Eng A v Z (Bulawayo) 1989-90. Y HS 204* v Glos (Leeds) 1987. BB 1-68. Award:
BHC 1. **NWT:** HS 22 v Surrey (Oval) 1989. **BHC:** HS 79 v Surrey (Oval) 1990. **SL:**
HS 130* v Kent (Scarborough) 1991.

BROADHURST, Mark (Kingstone S, Barnsley) , b Worsborough Common,
Barnsley 20 Jun 1974. 6'0". RHB, RFM. Debut 1991. Awaiting BAC debut. HS 1.
BB 3-61 v OU (Oxford) 1991. **SL:** HS -.

BYAS, David (Scarborough C), b Kilham 26 Aug 1963. 6'4". LHB, RM. Debut 1986.
Cap 1991. HS 153 v Notts (Worksop) 1991. 1000 runs (1): 1557 (1991). BB 3-55 v
Derbys (Chesterfield) 1990. **NWT:** HS 54 v Scot (Leeds) 1989. BB 1-23. **BHC:** HS 92
v Hants (Leeds) 1991. BB 2-38 v Somerset (Leeds) 1989. **SL:** HS 74* v Leics
(Leicester) 1988. BB 3-19 v Notts (Leeds) 1989.

CARRICK, Phillip (Bramley SS; Intake SS; Park Lane CPE), b Armley 16 Jul 1952.
5'11½". RHB, SLA. Debut 1970. Cap 1976. Captain 1987-89. Benefit 1985. E
Province 1976-77. N Transvaal 1982-83. Tours: SA 1975-76 (DHR); WI 1986-87
(Y – capt); SL 1977-78 (DHR). HS 131* v Northants (Northampton) 1980. 50
wkts (11); most – 79 (1975). BB 8-33 v CU (Cambridge) 1973. BAC BB 8-72 v
Derbys (Scarborough) 1975. Awards: NWT 1; BHC 1. **NWT:** HS 54 v Sussex (Leeds)
1986. BB 3-8 v Norfolk (Leeds) 1990. **BHC:** HS 53 v Warwks (Leeds) 1985. BB 3-22
v Warwks (Leeds) 1991. **SL:** HS 48* Worcs (Scarborough) 1989. BB 5-22 v Glam
(Leeds) 1991.

CHAPMAN, Colin Anthony (Beckfoot GS, Bingley; Bradford & Ilkley Art C), b
Bradford 8 Jun 1971. 5'8½". RHB, WK. Debut 1990. HS 20 v Middx (Uxbridge)
1990. **SL:** HS 36* v Middx (Scarborough) 1990.

DOIDGE, Matthew James (Benton Park S, Rawdon), b Horsforth 2 Jul 1970. 6'0".
LHB, SLA. Debut 1990. HS -.

GOUGH, Darren (Priory CS, Lundwood), b Barnsley 18 Sep 1970. 5'11". RHB, RMF. Debut 1989. HS 72 v Northants (Northampton) 1991. BB 5-41 v Lancs (Scarborough) 1991. **NWT:** HS 2. BB 2-22 v Norfolk (Leeds) 1990. **BHC:** HS 1 and BB 2-41 v Lancs (Manchester) 1991. **SL:** HS 72* v Leics (Leicester) 1991. BB 2-32 v Kent (Scarborough) 1991.

GRAYSON, Adrian Paul (Bedale CS), b Ripon 31 Mar 1971. 6'1". RHB, SLA. Debut 1990. HS 44* v Somerset (Scarborough) 1990. BB 1-3. **SL:** BB 1-32.

HARTLEY, Peter John (Greenhead GS; Bradford C), b Keighley 18 Apr 1960. 6'0". RHB, RMF. Warwickshire 1982. Yorkshire debut 1985. Cap 1987. Tour: WI 1986-87 (Y). HS 127* v Lancs (Manchester) 1988. 50 wkts (2); most – 52 (1990). BB 6-57 v Warwks (Sheffield) 1990. Awards: NWT 1; BHC 1. **NWT:** HS 52 and BB 5-46 v Hants (Southampton) 1990. **BHC:** HS 29* v Notts (Nottingham) 1986. BB 5-43 v Scot (Leeds) 1986. **SL:** HS 51 v Northants (Tring) 1990. BB 5-38 v Worcs (Worcester) 1990.

HOUSEMAN, Ian James (Harrogate GS, Loughborough U), b Harrogate 12 Oct 1969. 5'10". RHB, RFM. Debut 1989. HS 18 v Sussex (Middlesbrough) 1989. BB 2-26 v I (Leeds) 1990. **BAC** BB -.

JARVIS, Paul William (Bydales CS, Marske), b Redcar 29 Jun 1965. 5'10". RHB, RFM. Debut 1981 aged 16yr 75d (youngest Yorkshire player). Cap 1986. **Tests:** 6 (1987-88 to 1989); HS 29* and BB 4-107 v WI (Lord's) 1988. **LOI:** 5. Tours: SA 1989-90 (Eng XI); WI 1986-87 (Y); NZ 1987-88; P 1987-88. HS 59* v Notts (Nottingham) 1989. 50 wkts (3); most – 81 (1987). BB 7-55 v Surrey (Leeds) 1986. **NWT:** HS 16 v Somerset (Leeds) 1985. BB 4-41 v Leics (Leeds) 1987. **BHC:** HS 42 v Lancs (Leeds) 1990. BB 4-43 v Northants (Lord's) 1987. **SL:** HS 29* v Somerset (Taunton) 1987. BB 6-27 v Somerset (Taunton) 1989.

KELLETT, Simon Andrew (Whitcliffe Mount S), b Mirfield 16 Oct 1967. 6'2". RHB. Debut 1989. 1000 runs (1): 1266 (1991). HS 125* v Derbys (Chesterfield) 1991. **BHC:** HS 45 v Surrey (Oval) 1990. **SL:** HS 32 v Derbys (Leeds) 1990.

METCALFE, Ashley Anthony (Bradford GS; University C, London), b Horsforth 25 Dec 1963. 5'8". RHB, OB. Debut 1983 scoring 122 v Notts (Bradford). Cap 1986. YC 1986. OFS 1988-89. Tour: WI 1986-87 (Y). 1000 runs (6) inc 2000 runs (1): 2047 (1990). HS 216* v Middx (Leeds) 1991. BB 2-18 v Warwks (Scarborough) 1987. Awards: NWT 1; BHC 5. **NWT:** HS 127* v Warwks (Leeds) 1990. BB 2-44 v Wilts (Trowbridge) 1987. **BHC:** HS 114 v Lancs (Manchester) 1991. **SL:** HS 116 v Middx (Lord's) 1991.

MOXON, Martyn Douglas (Holgate GS, Barnsley), b Barnsley 4 May 1960. 6'0". RHB, RM. Debut 1981 scoring 5 and 116 v Essex (Leeds). Cap 1984. Captain 1990-. GW 1982-84. **Tests:** 10 (1986 to 1989); HS 99 v NZ (Auckland) 1987-88. LOI: 8. Tours: A 1987-88; WI 1986-87 (Y); NZ 1987-88; I 1984-85; SL 1984-85, 1985-86 (Eng B). 1000 runs (7); most – 1669 (1991). HS 218* v Sussex (Eastbourne) 1990. BB 3-24 v Hants (Southampton) 1989. Awards: NWT 4; BHC 7. **NWT:** HS 107* v Warwks (Leeds) 1990. BB 2-19 v Norfolk (Leeds) 1990. **BHC:** HS 141* v Glam (Cardiff) 1991. BB 5-31 v Warwks (Leeds) 1991. **SL:** HS 129* v Surrey (Oval) 1991. BB 3-29 v Sussex (Hove) 1990.

PICKLES, Christopher Stephen (Whitcliffe Mount CS), b Mirfield 30 Jan 1966. 6'1". RHB, RM. Debut 1985. HS 66 v Somerset (Taunton) 1989. BB 4-92 v Northants (Northampton) 1989. **NWT:** HS 12 and BB 1-30 v Warwks (Birmingham) 1991. **BHC:** HS 13* v Scot (Glasgow) 1987. BB 2-49 v Minor C (Leeds) 1991. **SL:** HS 30* v Worcs (Sheffield) 1991. BB 4-36 v Somerset (Scarborough) 1990.

ROBINSON, Mark Andrew (Hull GS), b Hull 23 Nov 1966. 6'3". RHB, RFM. Northamptonshire 1987-90 (cap 1990). Canterbury 1988-89. Yorkshire debut 1991. Failed to score in 12 successive f-c innings 1990 – world record. HS 19* Nh v Essex (Chelmsford) 1988. Y HS 8. BB 4-19 Nh v Glam (Wellingborough) 1988. Y BB 3-43 v Lancs (Manchester) 1991. Award: BHC 1. NWT: HS 3*. BB 4-32 Nh v Somerset (Taunton) 1989. **BHC:** HS 1*. BB 3-20 Nh v Scot (Glasgow) 1989. **SL:** HS 2*. BB 4-33 v Surrey (Oval) 1991.

SHARP, Kevin (Abbey Grange HS), b Leeds 6 Apr 1959. 5'9". LHB, OB. Debut 1976. Cap 1982. Benefit 1991. 2nd XI captain 1992. GW 1981-84. Tour: WI 1986-87 (Y); NZ 1979-80 (DHR). 1000 runs (1): 1445 (1984). HS 181 v Glos (Harrogate) 1986. BB 2-13 v Glam (Bradford) 1984. **NWT:** HS 50 v Leics (Leeds) 1987. BB 4-40 v Wilts (Trowbridge) 1987. **BHC:** HS 105* v Scot (Leeds) 1986. **SL:** HS 114 v Essex (Chelmsford) 1985.

WHITE, Craig (Flora Hill HS, Bendigo, Australia; Bendigo HS), b Morley Hall 16 Dec 1969. 6'0". RHB, OB. Debut 1990. Victoria 1990-91. Scored 209* and 115* for Yorks II v Worcs II (Worcester) 1990. HS 38 v Northants (Northampton) 1990. BB 5-74 v Surrey (Harrogate) 1990. **BHC:** HS 17* v Hants (Southampton) 1990. BB 1-31. **SL:** HS 37 v Notts (Scarborough) 1991. BB 2-49 v Kent (Canterbury) 1990.

NEWCOMERS

BARTLE, Steven (Backfoot GS), b Shipley 5 Aug 1971. LHB, RFM.

BETHEL, Steven b Sheffield 28 Nov 1970. RHB.

McDERMOTT, Craig John (Ipswich GS), b Ipswich, Australia 14 Apr 1965. 6'3¼". RHB, RF. Queensland 1983-91. **Tests** (A): 31 (1984-85 to 1990-91); HS 42* v E (Adelaide) 1990-91; BB 8-97 v E (Perth) 1990-91. LOI (A): 70. Tours (A): E 1985; WI 1990-91; NZ 1985-86; I 1986-87; P 1988-89. HS 74 Queensland v WA (Perth) 1990-91. BB 8-44 Queensland v Tasmania (Brisbane) 1989-90.

PARKER, Bradley, b Mirfield 23 Jun 1970. RHB, RM.

DEPARTURES

BERRY, P.J. – see DURHAM.

FLETCHER, S.D. – see LANCASHIRE.

ROBINSON, Phillip Edward (Greenhead GS, Keighley), b Keighley 3 Aug 1963. 5'9". RHB, LM. Yorkshire 1984-91 (cap 1988). 1000 runs (3); most – 1402 (1990). HS 189 v Lancs (Scarborough) 1991. BB 1-10. Award: BHC 1. **NWT:** HS 66 v Middx (Leeds) 1986. **BHC:** HS 73* v Hants (Southampton) 1990. **SL:** HS 78* v Leics (Leicester) 1985.

SIDEBOTTOM, Arnold (Broadway GS, Barnsley), b Barnsley 1 Apr 1954. 6'1". RHB, RMF. Yorkshire 1973-91 (cap 1980; benefit 1988). OFS 1981-84. **Tests:** 1 (1985); HS 2 and BB 1-65 v A (Nottingham) 1985. Tours: SA 1981-82 (SAB); WI 1986-87 (Y). HS 124 v Glam (Cardiff) 1977. 50 wkts (3); most – 68 (1989). BB 8-72 v Leics (Middlesbrough) 1986. Awards: NWT 1; BHC 3. **NWT:** HS 45 v Hants (Bournemouth) 1977. BB 5-27 v Glam (Leeds) 1987. **BHC:** HS 32 v Notts (Leeds) 1983. BB 5-27 v Worcs (Bradford) 1985. **SL:** HS 52* v Northants (Middlesbrough) 1982. BB 4-22 v Worcs (Worcester) 1987.

YORKSHIRE 1991

RESULTS SUMMARY

	Place	Won	Lost	Drew
Britannic Assurance Championship	14th	4	6	12
All First-class Matches		4	6	14
Refuge Assurance League	7th	9	7	
NatWest Trophy	1st Round			
Benson and Hedges Cup	Semi-Finalist			

BRITANNIC ASSURANCE CHAMPIONSHIP AVERAGES
BATTING AND FIELDING

Cap		M	I	NO	HS	Runs	Avge	100	50	Ct/St
1984	M.D.Moxon	21	37	1	200	1669	46.36	3	12	17
1991	D.Byas	22	37	4	153	1413	42.81	4	2	20
1986	P.W.Jarvis	4	5	2	37*	114	38.00	–	–	–
1988	P.E.Robinson	22	38	6	189	1136	35.50	1	8	19
–	S.A.Kellett	22	36	4	125*	992	31.00	1	6	17
1976	P.Carrick	21	32	9	67	662	28.78	–	4	3
1986	A.A.Metcalfe	22	39	2	123	1060	28.64	2	5	12
–	D.Gough	12	14	3	72	307	27.90	–	2	3
1987	P.J.Hartley	20	24	10	50*	322	23.00	–	1	3
–	C.S.Pickles	11	16	3	51	284	21.84	–	2	2
1987	R.J.Blakey	22	36	2	97	739	21.73	–	6	35/4
–	J.D.Batty	16	16	6	31	151	15.10	–	–	7
1988	S.D.Fletcher	12	11	2	9*	48	5.33	–	–	5
–	M.A.Robinson	15	13	4	8	17	1.88	–	–	4

BOWLING

	O	M	R	W	Avge	Best	5wI	10wM
P.W.Jarvis	95	26	235	12	19.58	4-28	–	–
P.Carrick	701.2	231	1748	61	28.65	5-13	2	–
J.D.Batty	399.4	91	1230	37	33.24	6-48	1	–
P.J.Hartley	522.3	100	1751	50	35.02	6-151	3	–
S.D.Fletcher	230.1	45	738	20	36.90	6-70	1	–
M.A.Robinson	377.1	78	1126	23	48.95	3-43	–	–
D.Gough	252	52	890	16	55.62	5-41	1	–

Also bowled: D.Byas 2-0-7-0; S.A.Kellett 4-0-7-0; A.A.Metcalfe 3-0-23-0; M.D.Moxon 11-2-27-2; C.S.Pickles 138-19-468-6; P.E.Robinson 10-1-49-0.

The First-Class Averages (pp 164-179) give the records of Yorkshire players in all first-class county matches (their other opponents being the Sri Lankans and Oxford U.).

YORKSHIRE RECORDS

FIRST-CLASS CRICKET

Highest Total	For 887		v Warwicks	Birmingham	1896
	V 630		by Somerset	Leeds	1901
Lowest Total	For 23		v Hampshire	Middlesbrough	1965
	V 13		by Notts	Nottingham	1901
Highest Innings	For 341	G.H.Hirst	v Leics	Leicester	1905
	V 318*	W.G.Grace	for Glos	Cheltenham	1876

Highest Partnership for each Wicket

1st	555	P.Holmes/H.Sutcliffe	v Essex	Leyton	1932
2nd	346	W.Barber/M.Leyland	v Middlesex	Sheffield	1932
3rd	323*	H.Sutcliffe/M.Leyland	v Glamorgan	Huddersfield	1928
4th	312	D.Denton/G.H.Hirst	v Hampshire	Southampton	1914
5th	340	E.Wainwright/G.H.Hirst	v Surrey	The Oval	1899
6th	276	M.Leyland/E.Robinson	v Glamorgan	Swansea	1926
7th	254	W.Rhodes/D.C.F.Burton	v Hampshire	Dewsbury	1919
8th	292	R.Peel/Lord Hawke	v Warwicks	Birmingham	1896
9th	192	G.H.Hirst/S.Haigh	v Surrey	Bradford	1898
10th	149	G.Boycott/G.B.Stevenson	v Warwicks	Birmingham	1982

Best Bowling (Innings)	For 10-10	H.Verity	v Notts	Leeds	1932
	V 10-37	C.V.Grimmett	for Australians	Sheffield	1930
Best Bowling (Match)	For 17-91	H.Verity	v Essex	Leyton	1933
	V 17-91	H.Dean	for Lancashire	Liverpool	1913

Most Runs – Season	2,883	H.Sutcliffe	(av 80.08)		1932
Most Runs – Career	38,561	H.Sutcliffe	(av 50.20)		1919-1945
Most 100s – Season	12	H.Sutcliffe			1932
Most 100s – Career	112	H.Sutcliffe			1919-1945
Most Wkts – Season	240	W.Rhodes	(av 12.72)		1900
Most Wkts – Career	3,608	W.Rhodes	(av 16.00)		1898-1930

LIMITED-OVERS CRICKET

Highest Total	NWT	317-4		v Surrey	Lord's	1965
	BHC	317-5		v Scotland	Leeds	1986
	SL	274-8		v Sussex	Middlesbrough	1991
Lowest Total	NWT	76		v Surrey	Harrogate	1970
	BHC	111		v Notts	Nottingham	1989
	SL	74		v Warwicks	Birmingham	1972
Highest Innings	NWT	146	G.Boycott	v Surrey	Lord's	1965
	BHC	142	G.Boycott	v Worcs	Worcester	1980
	SL	130*	R.J.Blakey	v Kent	Scarborough	1991
Best Bowling	NWT	6-15	F.S.Trueman	v Somerset	Taunton	1965
	BHC	6-27	A.G.Nicholson	v Minor C (N)	Middlesbrough	1972
	SL	7-15	R.A.Hutton	v Worcs	Leeds	1969

EAST, David Edward (Hackney Downs S; E Anglia U), b Clapton 27 Jul 1959. 5'9". RHB, WK. Essex 1981-90 (cap 1982; benefit 1991). HS 134 v Glos (Ilford) 1988. Set world f-c record by catching the FIRST eight wickets to fall in an innings (v Somerset at Taunton 1985 on his 26th birthday). Award: NWT 1. **NWT:** HS 28 v Northumb (Jesmond) 1986. **BHC:** HS 33 v Glos (Chelmsford) 1984. **SL:** HS 43 v Derbys (Derby) 1982.

SALIM MALIK (Government C, Lahore), b Lahore, Pakistan 16 Apr 1963. 5'9". RHB, RSM. Lahore 1978-86. Habib Bank 1982-91. Essex 1991 (cap 1991). **Tests** (P): 63 (1981-82 to 1990-91); HS 119* v NZ (Karachi) 1984-85; BB 1-3. LOI (P): 125. Tours (P): E 1982, 1987; A 1981-82, 1983-84, 1989-90; WI 1987-88; NZ 1984-85, 1988-89; I 1983-84, 1986-87; SL 1984-85 (P U-23), 1985-86. 1000 runs (1+1); most – 1972 (1991). HS 215 v Leics (Ilford) 1991. Shared Essex record stand of 314 for 4th wkt with N.Hussain v Surrey (Oval) 1991. BB 5-19 Habib Bank v Karachi (Karachi) 1985-86. Ex BB 3-26 v Northants (Colchester) 1991. Award: BHC 1. **NWT:** HS 26 v Surrey (Oval) 1991. **BHC:** HS 90* v Surrey (Oval) 1991. BB 1-7. **SL:** HS 89 v Worcs (Ilford) 1991. BB 1-25.

SEYMOUR, A.C.H. – see WORCESTERSHIRE.

GLAMORGAN – DEPARTURES (continued from p 79)

DERRICK, John (Blaengwawr CS), b Cwmaman 15 Jan 1963. 6'1". RHB, RM. Glamorgan 1983-91 (cap 1988). MCC Cricket Staff. Tour: Z 1990-91 (Gm). HS 78* v Derbys (Abergavenny) 1986. BB 6-54 v Leics (Leicester) 1988. **NWT:** HS 4. BB 4-14 v Scot (Edinburgh) 1985. **BHC:** HS 42 v Kent (Cardiff) 1985. BB 4-53 v Comb Us (Cardiff) 1988. **SL:** HS 26 v Northants (Northampton) 1983 and 26 v Kent (Maidstone) 1986. BB 5-32 v Middx (Lord's) 1987.

HOLMES, Geoffrey Clark (West Denton HS), b Newcastle-upon-Tyne, Northumb 16 Sep 1958. 5'10". RHB, RM. Glamorgan 1978-91 (cap 1985; benefit 1991). Border 1989-90. MCC Cricket Staff. 1000 runs (3); most – 1129 (1985). HS 182 Border v W Province B (East London) 1989-90. Gm HS 125* v Somerset (Cardiff) 1990. BB 5-38 v Essex (Colchester) 1988. Awards: NWT 2. **NWT:** HS 57 v Cheshire (Cardiff) 1987. BB 5-24 v Scot (Edinburgh) 1985. **BHC:** HS 70 v Somerset (Taunton) 1985. BB 3-26 v Minor C (Swansea) 1985. **SL:** HS 73 v Warwks (Birmingham) 1984. BB 5-2 v Derbys (Ebbw Vale) 1984.

ROBERTS, Martin Leonard (Helston CS), b Mullion, Cornwall 12 Apr 1966. 6'1". RHB, WK. Glamorgan 1985-91. Cornwall 1983-84. Tour: Z 1990-91 (Gm). HS 25 v SL (Ebbw Vale) 1990. BAC HS 13 v Lancs (Colwyn Bay) 1990. **BHC:** HS 1*. **SL:** HS 12* v Sussex (Hove) 1990.

SHASTRI, Ravishankar Jayadritha (Don Bosco HS, Bombay), b Bombay, India 27 May 1962. 6'3". RHB, SLA. Bombay 1979-91 (capt 1987-88). Glamorgan 1987-91 (cap 1988). **Tests** (I): 73 (1980-81 to 1990-91 – 1 as captain); HS 187 v E (Oval) 1990. BB 5-75 v P (Nagpur) 1983-84. LOI (I): 128. Tours (I): E 1982, 1986, 1990; A 1985-86; WI 1982-83, 1988-89; NZ 1980-81; P 1982-83, 1984-85, 1989-90; SL 1985-86. 1000 runs (2+1); most – 1108 (1991). HS 217 Rest of India v Bengal (Bangalore) 1990-91. Scored 200* in 113 min, inc 6 sixes off one over – world records – for Bombay v Baroda (Bombay) 1984-85. Gm HS 157 v Somerset (Cardiff) 1988. BB 9-101 Bombay v Rest (Indore) 1981-82. Gm BB 7-49 v Lancs (Swansea) 1988. Awards: NWT 1; BHC 1. **NWT:** HS 59* v Surrey (Oval) 1988. BB 5-13 v Scot (Edinburgh) 1988. **BHC:** HS 138* v Minor C (Trowbridge) 1991. BB 1-17. **SL:** HS 92 and BB 3-26 v Hants (Ebbw Vale) 1991.

SMITH, I. – see DURHAM.

GLOUCESTERSHIRE – DEPARTURES (continued from p 84)

LLOYDS, Jeremy William (Blundell's S), b Penang, Malaya 17 Nov 1954. 6'0". LHB, OB. Somerset 1979-84 (cap 1982). OFS 1983-88. Gloucestershire 1985-91 (cap 1985). MCC Cricket Staff. Tour: SL 1986-87 (Gs). 1000 runs (3); most – 1295 (1986). HS 132* Sm v Northants (Northampton) 1982. Gs HS 130 v Glam (Swansea) 1987. BB 7-88 Sm v Essex (Chelmsford) 1982. Gs BB 7-134 v Somerset (Bath) 1989. NWT: HS 73* v Lincs (Gloucester) 1990. BB 2-35 v Berks (Reading) 1986. BHC: HS 53* v Warwks (Bristol) 1990. BB 3-14 v Comb Us (Bristol) 1991. SL: HS 65 v Yorks (Leeds) 1989. BB 2-1 Sm v Hants (Taunton) 1981.

MILBURN, Edward Thomas (King Edward VI C, Nuneaton), b Nuneaton 15 Sep 1967. 6'1¼". RHB, RM. Warwickshire 1987. Gloucestershire 1990-91. HS 35 v I (Bristol) 1990. BAC HS 24 Wa v Hants (Birmingham) 1987. BB 3-43 v I (Bristol) 1990. BAC BB 1-26. BHC: BB 1-23. SL: HS 21 v Essex (Cheltenham) 1991. BB 2-34 v Surrey (Cheltenham) 1990.

ROMAINES, Paul William (Leeholm S), b Bishop Auckland, Co Durham 25 Dec 1955. 6'0". RHB, occ OB. Northants 1975-76. Gloucestershire 1982-91 (cap 1983; benefit 1991). GW 1984-85. Durham 1977-81. Tour: SL 1986-87 (Gs). 1000 runs (3); most – 1844 (1984). HS 186 v Warwks (Nuneaton) 1982. BB 3-42 v Surrey (Oval) 1985. Awards: BHC 2. NWT: HS 82 v Hants (Bristol) 1983. BHC: HS 125 v Notts (Bristol) 1985. SL: HS 105 v Northants (Northampton) 1985. Appointed commercial manager Durham CCC.

HAMPSHIRE – DEPARTURES (continued from p 89)

AQIB JAVED, b Sheikhupura, Pakistan 5 Aug 1972. RHB, RFM. Lahore Div 1986-87. PACO 1989-90. Hampshire 1991. **Tests** (P): 5 (1988-89 to 1990-91); HS 7; BB 3-57 v NZ (Faisalabad) 1990-91. LOI (P): 35. Tours (P): A 1988-89, 1989-90; NZ 1988-89. HS 32* PACO v PIA (Lahore) 1989-90. H HS 15* v Somerset (Bath) 1991. 50 wkts (1): 53 (1991). BB 6-91 v Notts (Nottingham) 1991. NWT: BB 4-51 v Notts (Southampton) 1991. BHC: HS 3. BB 3-43 v Minor C (Trowbridge) 1991. SL: HS 4*. BB 3-50 v Worcs (Southampton) 1991.

SMITH, Christopher Lyall ('Kippy') (Northlands HS, Durban), b Durban, SA 15 Oct 1958. Brother of R.A. and grandson of Dr V.L.Shearer (Natal). 5'10". RHB, OB. Natal 1977-83. Glamorgan 1979. Hampshire 1980 (cap 1981; benefit 1990). Wisden 1984. **Tests:** 8 (1983 to 1986); HS 91 v NZ (Auckland) 1983-84; BB 2-31 v NZ (Nottingham) 1983. LOI: 4. Tours: NZ 1983-84; P 1983-84; SL 1985-86 (Eng B). 1000 runs (10) inc 2000 (1): 2000 (1985). HS 217 v Warwks (Birmingham) 1987 – sharing record Hants stand of 347 for 1st wkt with V.P.Terry. BB 5-69 v Sussex (Southampton) 1988. Awards: NWT 8 (equal record); BHC 5. NWT: HS 159 v Cheshire (Chester) 1989. BB 3-32 v Berks (Southampton) 1985. BHC: HS 154* v Comb Us (Southampton) 1990. SL: HS 114 v Worcs (Southampton) 1991. BB 2-3 v Glos (Bristol) 1984. Appointed W.A.C.A. assistant marketing manager 1991.

MIDDLESEX – NEWCOMERS (continued from p 110)

HARRISON, Jason Christian, b Amersham, Bucks 15 Jan 1972. RHB, OB.
JOHNSON, Richard Leonard, b Chertsey, Surrey 29 Dec 1974. RHB, RM.
WALKER, David Anthony, b Hampstead, London 18 Jun 1975. RHB, LMF.

DEPARTURES

BARNETT, A.A. – see LANCASHIRE.

DOWNTON, Paul Rupert (Sevenoaks S; Exeter U), b Farnborough, Kent 4 Apr 1957. Son of G.C. (Kent 1948). 5'10". RHB, WK, OB. Kent 1977-79 (cap 1979). Middlesex 1980-91 (cap 1981; benefit 1990). **Tests:** 30 (1980-81 to 1988); HS 74 v I (Delhi) 1984-85. LOI: 28. Tours: WI 1980-81, 1985-86; NZ 1977-78; I/SL 1984-85; P 1977-78; Z 1980-81 (Middx). 1000 runs (1): 1120 (1987). HS 126* v OU (Oxford) 1986. BAC HS 120 v Lancs (Manchester) 1990. BB 1-4. Award: NWT 1. NWT: HS 69 v Notts (Uxbridge) 1989. BHC: HS 80* v Hants (Southampton) 1987. SL: HS 70 v Notts (Nottingham) 1989.

HUGHES, S.P. – see DURHAM.

NORTHAMPTONSHIRE – DEPARTURES (continued from p 115)

BAPTISTE, Eldine Ashworth Elderfield (All Saints SS, Liberta), b Liberta, Antigua 12 Mar 1960. 6'0". RHB, RFM. Leeward Is 1981-91. Kent 1981-87 (cap 1983). Northamptonshire 1991. **Tests** (WI): 10 (1983-84 to 1989-90); HS 87* v E (Birmingham) 1984; BB 3-31 v E (Manchester) 1984. **LOI** (WI): 43. Tours (WI): E 1984; A 1984-85; I 1983-84, 1987-88; Z 1986-87 (WI B). HS 136* K v Yorks (Sheffield) 1983. Nh HS 80 v Notts (Wellingborough) 1991. 50 wkts (1): 50 (1991). BB 8-76 K v Warwks (Birmingham) 1987. Nh BB 7-95 v Yorks (Northampton) 1991. Awards: NWT 1; BHC 1. **NWT:** HS 34 v Surrey (Oval) 1991. BB 5-20 K v Hants (Canterbury) 1983. **BHC:** HS 43* K v Somerset (Taunton) 1985. BB 5-30 K v Glam (Cardiff) 1985. **SL:** HS 60 K v Warwks (Canterbury) 1985. BB 4-22 K v Surrey (Canterbury) 1986.

LARKINS, W. – see DURHAM.

THOMAS, John Gregory (Cwmtawe HS; Cardiff CE), b Trebanos, Glam 12 Aug 1960. 6'3". RHB, RF. Glamorgan 1979-88 (cap 1986). Border 1983-87. E Province 1987-89. Northamptonshire 1989-91 (cap 1991). **Tests:** 5 (1985-86 and 1986); HS 31* v WI (P-of-S) 1985-86; BB 4-70 v WI (Bridgetown) 1985-86. **LOI:** 3. Tours: SA 1989-90 (Eng XI); WI 1985-86. HS 110 Gm v Warwks (Birmingham) 1988. Nh HS 64 v Derbys (Northampton) 1991. 50 wkts (1): 67 (1989). BB 7-75 v Glam (Northampton) 1990. Awards: NWT 1; BHC 2. **NWT:** HS 34 Gm v Cheshire (Cardiff) 1987. BB 5-17 Gm v Sussex (Cardiff) 1985. **BHC:** HS 32 Gm v Kent 1987 and Nh v Scot 1990. BB 5-29 v Derbys (Derby) 1991. **SL:** HS 37 Gm v Notts (Nottingham) 1983. BB 5-38 Gm v Yorks (Cardiff) 1983.

NOTTINGHAMSHIRE – DEPARTURES (continued from p 120)

BROADLEY, Vaughan John Pascal (Dukeries CS; Sheffield U), b Sutton in Ashfield 4 Apr 1972. 6'0". RHB, RFM. Nottinghamshire 1991. HS 6. BB 1-92.

MARTINDALE, Duncan John Richardson (Lymm GS; Trent Polytechnic), b Harrogate, Yorks 13 Dec 1963. 5'11". RHB, OB. Nottinghamshire 1985-91. HS 138 v CU (Cambridge) 1990. BAC HS 108* v Northants (Nottingham) 1990. **NWT:** HS 47 v Herts (Hitchin) 1989. **BHC:** HS 0. **SL:** HS 53 v Northants (Finedon) 1989.

SCOTT, C.W. – see DURHAM.

STEPHENSON, F.D. – see SUSSEX.

SURREY – DEPARTURES (continued from p 130)

BULLEN, Christopher Keith (Rutlish S, Merton) b Clapham 5 Nov 1962. 6'4½". RHB, OB. Surrey 1982 (cap 1990). HS 65 v P (Oval) 1987. BAC HS 57 v Glos (Cheltenham) 1987. BB 6-119 v Middx (Lord's) 1987. Award: NWT 1. **NWT:** HS 93* v Wilts (Trowbridge) 1990. BB 2-55 v Middx (Oval) 1988. **BHC:** HS 35* and BB 2-14 v Comb Us (Cambridge) 1989. **SL:** HS 28* v Middx (Lord's) 1989. BB 5-31 v Yorks (Oval) 1989.

ROBSON, A.G. – see SUSSEX.

WORCESTERSHIRE – DEPARTURES (continued from p 145)

BENT, Paul (Worcester RGS), b Worcester 1 May 1965. 6'0". RHB, OB. Worcestershire 1985-91. MCC Cricket Staff. HS 144 v Kent (Worcester) 1989. **SL:** HS 36 v Sussex (Worcester) 1988.

BOTHAM, I.T. – see DURHAM.

LORD, Gordon John (Warwick S; Durham U), b Edgbaston, Birmingham 25 Apr 1961. 5'10". LHB, SLA. Warwickshire 1983-86. Worcestershire 1987-91 (cap 1990). Tour: Z 1990-91 (Wo). 1000 runs (1): 1003 (1990). HS 199 Wa v Yorks (Birmingham) 1985. Wo HS 190 v Hants (Worcester) 1990. **NWT:** HS 0. **BHC:** HS 26 v Glos (Bristol) 1990. **SL:** HS 103 Wa v Derbys (Birmingham) 1985.

McEWAN, S.M. – see DURHAM.

UNIVERSITY MATCH RESULTS

Played: 146. Wins: Cambridge 54; Oxford 46. Drawn: 46. Abandoned: 1.
This, the oldest surviving first-class fixture, dates from 1827 and, wartime interruptions apart, it has been played annually since 1838. With the exception of five matches played in the area of Oxford (1829, 1843, 1846, 1848 and 1850), all the fixtures have been played at Lord's.

1827	Drawn	1884	Oxford	1937	Oxford
1829	Oxford	1885	Cambridge	1938	Drawn
1836	Oxford	1886	Oxford	1939	Oxford
1838	Oxford	1887	Oxford	1946	Oxford
1839	Cambridge	1888	Drawn	1947	Drawn
1840	Cambridge	1889	Cambridge	1948	Oxford
1841	Cambridge	1890	Cambridge	1949	Cambridge
1842	Cambridge	1891	Cambridge	1950	Drawn
1843	Cambridge	1892	Oxford	1951	Oxford
1844	Drawn	1893	Cambridge	1952	Drawn
1845	Cambridge	1894	Oxford	1953	Cambridge
1846	Oxford	1895	Cambridge	1954	Drawn
1847	Cambridge	1896	Oxford	1955	Drawn
1848	Oxford	1897	Cambridge	1956	Drawn
1849	Cambridge	1898	Oxford	1957	Cambridge
1850	Oxford	1899	Drawn	1958	Cambridge
1851	Cambridge	1900	Drawn	1959	Oxford
1852	Oxford	1901	Drawn	1960	Drawn
1853	Oxford	1902	Cambridge	1961	Drawn
1854	Oxford	1903	Oxford	1962	Drawn
1855	Oxford	1904	Drawn	1963	Drawn
1856	Cambridge	1905	Cambridge	1964	Drawn
1857	Oxford	1906	Cambridge	1965	Drawn
1858	Oxford	1907	Cambridge	1966	Oxford
1859	Cambridge	1908	Oxford	1967	Drawn
1860	Cambridge	1909	Drawn	1968	Drawn
1861	Cambridge	1910	Oxford	1969	Drawn
1862	Cambridge	1911	Oxford	1970	Drawn
1863	Oxford	1912	Cambridge	1971	Drawn
1864	Oxford	1913	Cambridge	1972	Cambridge
1865	Oxford	1914	Oxford	1973	Drawn
1866	Oxford	1919	Oxford	1974	Drawn
1867	Cambridge	1920	Drawn	1975	Drawn
1868	Cambridge	1921	Cambridge	1976	Oxford
1869	Cambridge	1922	Cambridge	1977	Drawn
1870	Cambridge	1923	Oxford	1978	Drawn
1871	Oxford	1924	Cambridge	1979	Cambridge
1872	Cambridge	1925	Drawn	1980	Drawn
1873	Oxford	1926	Cambridge	1981	Drawn
1874	Oxford	1927	Cambridge	1982	Cambridge
1875	Oxford	1928	Drawn	1983	Drawn
1876	Cambridge	1929	Drawn	1984	Oxford
1877	Cambridge	1930	Cambridge	1985	Drawn
1878	Cambridge	1931	Oxford	1986	Cambridge
1879	Cambridge	1932	Drawn	1987	Drawn
1880	Cambridge	1933	Drawn	1988	Abandoned
1881	Oxford	1934	Drawn	1989	Drawn
1882	Cambridge	1935	Cambridge	1990	Drawn
1883	Cambridge	1936	Cambridge	1991	Drawn

CAMBRIDGE v OXFORD
(146th UNIVERSITY MATCH)

Played at Lord's, on 2, 3, 4 July.
Toss: Cambridge. Result: MATCH DRAWN.

CAMBRIDGE UNIVERSITY

A.M.Hooper c Lovell b Gerrans	89	b Wood	4
R.I.Clitheroe c Lovell b Wood	6	c Sandiford b Gerrans	0
J.P.Crawley b Wood	66	not out	59
*†R.J.Turner lbw b Oppenheimer	27	lbw b Wood	0
M.J.Morris c Lovell b Gerrans	6	b Oppenheimer	27
M.J.Lowrey c Morris b Turner	25	lbw b MacDonald	0
J.P.Arscott c Pfaff b Turner	14	run out	10
R.M.Pearson c Montgomerie b Turner	10	c Sandiford b Gerrans	10
R.H.J.Jenkins c Sandiford b MacDonald	9	not out	17
S.W.Johnson c Gupte b MacDonald	7		
R.B.Waller not out	6		
Extras (B1, LB11, W1, NB11)	24	(LB5, W3, NB11)	19
	—		—
Total	**279**	(7 wickets declared)	**146**

OXFORD UNIVERSITY

R.R.Montgomerie not out	50	not out	53
R.E.Morris c Arscott b Waller	71	c Arscott b Jenkins	18
G.B.T.Lovell not out	15	not out	30
*G.J.Turner			
D.B.Pfaff			
C.M.Gupte			
P.S.Gerrans	did not bat		
†D.C.Sandiford			
R.H.MacDonald			
J.M.E.Oppenheimer			
B.S.Wood			
Extras (B6, LB2, NB1)	9	(B3, LB2, W1, NB1)	7
	—		—
Total (1 wicket declared)	**145**	(1 wicket)	**108**

OXFORD	O	M	R	W	O	M	R	W	FALL OF WICKETS			
										CU	OU	CU	OU
MacDonald	24.2	6	73	2	8	3	16	1		1st	1st	2nd	2nd
Wood	21	7	41	2	7	2	24	2	Wkt				
Turner	8	2	32	3	8	1	25	0	1st	12	125	5	30
Gerrans	23	5	73	2	13	1	65	2	2nd	172	—	10	—
Oppenheimer	19	4	48	1	4	2	11	1	3rd	182	—	20	—
									4th	198	—	72	—
CAMBRIDGE									5th	228	—	81	—
Johnson	12	2	47	0	3	0	25	0	6th	253	—	111	—
Jenkins	10	2	29	0	8	0	25	1	7th	253	—	126	—
Waller	9.5	2	33	1	4	0	16	0	8th	256	—	—	—
Pearson	8	1	28	0	11	2	24	0	9th	267	—	—	—
Arscott					1	0	13	0	10th	279	—	—	—

Umpires: J.C.Balderstone and K.J.Lyons.

CAMBRIDGE UNIVERSITY

ARSCOTT, Jonathan Paul (Tonbridge S; Magdalene C), b Tooting, London 4 Jul 1970. 5'10". RHB, RM, WK. Debut 1990; blue 1991. HS 74 v Derbys (Cambridge) 1991. BB 1-17.

BUSH, Damien Jonathon (King Edward VI S, Birmingham; St Catharine's C), b Solihull, Warwks 19 May 1968. 6'3". LHB, LM. Debut/blue 1989. HS 28 v Kent (Cambridge) 1989. BB 3-64 v Essex (Cambridge) 1989.

CLITHEROE, Roger Ian (Bury GS; Monmouth S; Christ's C), b Radcliffe, Lancs 18 Nov 1966. 5'11". RHB, WK. Debut 1987; blue 1991. HS 36 v Northants (Cambridge) 1987 and v Derbys (Cambridge) 1991.

COTTON, Daniel Charles (Merchant Taylor's S, Northwood; St Catharine's C), b Bletchley, Bucks 3 Sep 1968. 6'3". RHB, RMF. Debut 1989. HS 4. BB 1-43.

CRAWLEY, John Paul (Manchester GS; Trinity C), b Maldon, Essex 21 Sep 1971. Brother of M.A. (see NOTTS). 6'1". RHB, RM. Lancashire 1990-91. CU debut/blue 1991; captain 1992. HS 130 La v Surrey (Manchester) 1991. CU HS 83 v Lancs (Cambridge) 1991 – on debut.

FENTON, Nigel Charles Windsor (Rugby S; Durham U; Magdalene C), b Bradford, Yorks 22 Jun 1965. 6'5". RHB, RFM. Debut/blue 1988. HS 7*. BB 4-64 v Middx (Cambridge) 1988.

HOOPER, Anthony Mark (Latymer Upper S; St John's C), b Perivale, Middx 5 Sep 1967. 5'7". RHB, RM. Debut 1987; blue 1987-91. HS 125 v Surrey (Cambridge) 1991. BB 1-30.

JENKINS, Rory Harry John (Oundle S; Downing C), b Leicester 29 Jun 1970. 6'2". RHB, RM. Debut 1990; blue 1990-91. HS 20 v Northants (Cambridge) 1991. BB 5-100 v Middx (Cambridge) 1990.

JOHNSON, Simon Wolseley (Newcastle RGS; Magdalene C), b Newcastle upon Tyne, Northumb 29 Jan 1970. 6'2". RHB, RMF. Debut 1990; blue 1990-91. HS 20 v Northants (Cambridge) 1991. BB 2-86 v Northants (Cambridge) 1990.

JONES, Garri Wyn (King's S, Chester; Gonville & Caius C), b Birmingham 1 May 1970. 5'7". LHB, OB. Debut 1991. HS 13* v Leics (Cambridge) 1991.

LOWREY, Mark John (Radley C; Homerton C), b Hampstead, London 13 Sep 1971. 5'8". RHB, OB. Debut 1990; blue 1990-91. HS 72 v Sussex (Hove) 1990. BB 3-31 v Surrey (Cambridge) 1991.

LYONS, Russell John (King Edward VII S, Jo'burg; Witwatersrand U; Downing C), b Johannesburg, SA 6 Dec 1967. 5'11". RHB, LB. Debut 1991. HS 20 and BB 1-26 v Essex (Cambridge) 1991.

MORRIS, Michael John (Cherwell S, Oxford; Pembroke C), b Melbourne, Australia 8 Mar 1969. 5'10". RHB. Debut 1989; blue 1990-91. HS 60 v Leics (Cambridge) 1991.

PEARSON, Richard Michael (Batley GS; St John's C), b Batley, Yorks 27 Jan 1972. 6'3". RHB, OB. Debut/blue 1991. Northants II 1991. HS 21 and BB 4-84 v Derbys (Cambridge) 1991.

PYMAN, Richard Anthony (Harrow S; Pembroke C), b Changi, Singapore 17 Apr 1968. 5'10". RHB, RM. Debut 1988; blue 1989-90. Eton fives half-blue. HS 69 v Notts (Cambridge) 1989. BB 5-43 v OU (Lord's) 1989.

THWAITES, Guy Edward (Eastbourne C; Girton C), b Brighton, Sussex 19 Jan 1971. Son of I.G. (CU 1963-64). 5'9". RHB. Debut 1991. HS 32 v Derbys (Cambridge) 1991.

TURNER, Robert Julian (Millfield S; Magdalene C), b Malvern, Worcs 25 Nov 1967. 6'1½". RHB, WK. Brother of S.J. (Somerset 1984-85). Debut 1988; blue 1988-89-90-91; captain 1991. Somerset 1991. HS 69* CU v Middx (Cambridge) 1991.

VILJOEN, Jan Neil (Stellenbosch U; Darwin C), b Wepener, SA 4 Jul 1962. 6'2". RHB, RSM. Debut 1991. Rugby for W Province. HS 1*. BB 1-34.

WALLER, Richard Beaumont (Radley C; Trinity C), b London 5 Dec 1969. 6'0". RHB, RMF. Debut/blue 1991. HS 6*. BB 3-31 v Glam (Cambridge) 1991.

CAMBRIDGE UNIVERSITY 1991

RESULTS SUMMARY

	Played	Won	Lost	Drew
All first-class matches	10	0	3	7

FIRST-CLASS AVERAGES
BATTING AND FIELDING

	M	I	NO	HS	Runs	Avge	100	50	Ct/St
J.P.Crawley	10	16	2	83	619	44.21	–	7	6
A.M.Hooper	7	12	1	125	458	41.63	1	2	–
R.J.Turner	8	12	3	69*	231	25.66	–	1	9/1
S.W.Johnson	7	8	3	20	85	17.00	–	–	3
M.J.Lowrey	10	16	2	51	234	16.71	–	1	2
R.I.Clitheroe	10	17	2	36	228	15.20	–	–	3
J.P.Arscott	9	12	1	74	157	14.27	–	1	7
G.E.Thwaites	3	5	0	32	68	13.60	–	–	2
M.J.Morris	9	13	0	60	171	13.15	–	1	2
R.B.Waller	5	4	3	6*	12	12.00	–	–	1
D.J.Bush	7	7	2	24*	58	11.60	–	–	3
R.H.J.Jenkins	6	8	1	20	64	9.14	–	–	2
R.A.Pyman	2	4	1	8*	20	6.66	–	–	1
R.M.Pearson	10	12	1	21	70	6.36	–	–	2
G.W.Jones	3	5	1	13*	19	4.75	–	–	–

Also played (1 match each): D.C.Cotton 0*, 0; N.C.W.Fenton 7*; R.J.Lyons 20, 18; J.N.Viljoen 1*.

BOWLING

	O	M	R	W	Avge	Best	5wI	10wM
J.P.Arscott	48	4	252	7	36.00	1-17	–	–
R.B.Waller	85.2	16	363	7	51.85	3-31	–	–
M.J.Lowrey	136	17	496	9	55.11	3-31	–	–
R.M.Pearson	332	59	1098	15	73.20	4-84	–	–
R.H.J.Jenkins	150	20	514	7	73.42	2-46	–	–
D.J.Bush	131.3	22	540	6	90.00	1-14	–	–

Also bowled: D.C.Cotton 21-4-85-1; J.P.Crawley 2-0-14-0; N.C.W.Fenton 25-5-95-0; A.M.Hooper 43-6-187-2; S.W.Johnson 131.1-17-608-3; R.J.Lyons 4-0-26-1; M.J.Morris 3-1-15-0; R.A.Pyman 65-15-216-4; J.N.Viljoen 22-2-99-1.

The following appeared in other first-class matches in 1991:
J.P.Crawley in two matches for Lancashire; R.J.Turner in one match for Somerset. Their records in all first-class matches appear on pp 164-179.

OXFORD UNIVERSITY

DAVIES, Henry Richard (St Dunstan's C; Christ Church), b Camberwell, London 2 Sep 1970. 5'10". LHB, OB. Debut 1990. HS 38 v Worcs (Oxford) 1991. BB 3-93 v Hants (Oxford) 1990 – on debut.

GERRANS, Philip Simon (Daramalau C; Canberra U; Worcester C), Melbourne, Australia 14 Oct 1959. 6'0". RHB, RSM. Debut 1990; blue 1990-91. Golf blue. HS 39 v Lancs (Oxford) 1990. BB 3-86 v Surrey (Oxford) 1990.

GUPTE, Chinmay Madhukar (John Lyon S, Harrow; Pembroke C), b Poona, India 5 Jul 1972. Son of M.S. (Maharashtra). 5'7". RHB, SLA. Debut/blue 1991. HS 55* v Glos (Oxford) 1991. BB 2-41 v Notts (Oxford) 1991.

HAGAN, David Andrew (Trinity S, Leamington Spa; St Edmund Hall and Linacre C), b Wide Open, Northumb 25 Jun 1966. 5'9". RHB, OB. Debut 1985; blue 1986-88-89-90. HS 88 v Lancs (Oxford) 1986.

JONES, Christopher David (Hartford HS; Sir John Deane's SFC; Brasenose C), b Maidstone, Kent 30 Apr 1971. 6'2". RHB, RM. Debut 1991. Hockey blue 1991. HS 23 v Kent (Oxford) 1991.

LOVELL, Geoffrey Bruce Tasman (Sydney C of E GS; Sydney U; Exeter C), b Sydney, Australia 11 Jul 1966. 5'10½". RHB, RM. Debut/blue 1991. Captain 1992. Inaugural Bradman Scholarship. HS 49 v Glos (Oxford) 1991. BB 1-13.

MACDONALD, Robert Hepburn (Rondebosch BHS; Cape Town U; Durham U; Keble C), b Cape Town, South Africa 18 Jul 1965. 6'2". RHB, RMF. Debut/blue 1991. Squash blue 1990. HS 20 v Hants (Oxford) 1991. BB 3-66 v Glos (Oxford) 1991.

MONTGOMERIE, Richard Robert (Rugby S; Worcester C), b Rugby, Warwicks 3 Jul 1971. 5'10½". RHB, OB. Debut/blue 1991. Northamptonshire 1991. Rackets blue 1990. HS 88 OU v Hants (Oxford) 1991 – on debut.

MORRIS, James George (Nottingham HS; Birmingham U; Wadham C), b Nottingham 4 Feb 1967. 6'2". RHB. Debut 1991. HS 28 v Worcs (Oxford) 1991.

MORRIS, Russell Edward (Dyffryn Conwy S, Llanrwst; Oriel C), b St Asaph, Flintshire, 8 Jun 1967. 5'8". RHB, RM. Debut 1987; blue 1987-89-90-91; captain 1990. Soccer blue. HS 96 v Surrey (Oxford) 1990. BB 2-82 v Yorks (Oxford) 1991.

OPPENHEIMER, Jonathan Maximillian Ernest (Harrow S; Christ Church), b Johannesburg, SA 18 Nov 1970. 5'11". RHB, RM. Debut 1989; blue 1991. HS 7. BB 3-51 v Derbys (Oxford) 1989.

PFAFF, David Brian (Hilton C; Cape Town U; Keble C), b Cape Town, SA 26 Jun 1965. Son of B.D. (W Province 1952-57); brother of M.W. (N Transvaal 1983-88). 5'10". LHB, RM. Debut/blue 1991. Hockey for South Africa 1985-90. HS 50 v Hants (Oxford) 1991 – on debut.

RUSSELL, Mark John (Medina HS, IOW; Pembroke C), b Lincoln 18 Nov 1970. 5'10". RHB, RSM. Debut 1990. HS 30 and BB 4-31 v Kent (Oxford) 1991.

SANDIFORD, David Charles (Bolton S; St Edmund Hall), b Bolton, Lancs 24 Dec 1970. 5'9". RHB, WK. Debut/blue 1991. HS 83 v Yorks (Oxford) 1991.

TURNER, Graeme John (St Stithian's; Cape Town U; St Anne's C), b Bulawayo, Rhodesia 5 Aug 1964. 6'2". LHB, OB. W Province 1984-86. N Transvaal B 1986-88. SADF 1988-89. OU debut 1990; blue 1990-91; captain 1991. HS 101* v Lancs (Oxford) 1991. BB 4-94 SADF v Boland (Windhoek) 1988-89. OU BB 3-32 v CU (Lord's) 1991.

WARLEY, Simon Nicholas (Kent C, Canterbury; Oriel C), b Sittingbourne, Kent 6 Jan 1972. 6'4". RHB, RMF. Debut 1991. HS 11 v Kent (Oxford) 1991.

WOOD, Benjamin Shaw (Batley GS; Worcester C), b Dewsbury, Yorks 25 Jan 1971. 6'0". RHB, RMF. Debut/blue 1991. HS 6. BB 2-24 v CU (Lord's) 1991.

OXFORD UNIVERSITY 1991

RESULTS SUMMARY

	Played	Won	Lost	Drew
All first-class matches	9	0	2	7

FIRST-CLASS AVERAGES
BATTING AND FIELDING

	M	I	NO	HS	Runs	Avge	100	50	Ct/St
G.J.Turner	8	8	2	101*	349	58.16	1	2	1
D.B.Pfaff	8	7	2	50	231	46.20	–	1	4
R.R.Montgomerie	8	11	2	88	300	33.33	–	4	7
C.M.Gupte	8	9	1	55*	200	25.00	–	1	2
G.B.T.Lovell	9	13	3	49	250	25.00	–	–	5
D.C.Sandiford	9	9	1	83	189	23.62	–	1	11/1
R.E.Morris	8	11	1	71	236	23.60	–	2	3
M.J.Russell	3	6	0	30	91	15.16	–	–	–
R.H.MacDonald	7	6	3	20	41	13.66	–	–	–
H.R.Davies	7	9	3	38	80	13.33	–	–	–
J.G.Morris	3	5	0	28	63	12.60	–	–	3
B.S.Wood	9	6	1	6	8	1.60	–	–	–

Also played: P.S.Gerrans (3 matches) 17*, 14, 4; D.A.Hagan (1 match) did not bat; C.D.Jones (1 match) 4, 23; J.M.E.Oppenheimer (5 matches) 0* (1 ct); S.N.Warley (2 matches) 3, 11, 1 (1 ct).

BOWLING

	O	M	R	W	Avge	Best	5wI	10wM
R.H.MacDonald	157	49	457	10	45.70	3-66	–	–
J.M.E.Oppenheimer	107	19	385	8	48.12	2-51	–	–
B.S.Wood	187.5	34	665	12	55.41	2-24	–	–
P.S.Gerrans	77.3	12	308	5	61.60	2-65	–	–
G.J.Turner	169	36	564	9	62.66	3-32	–	–

Also bowled: C.M.Gupte 24.1-3-120-3; H.R.Davies 107.1-16-476-4; G.B.T.Lovell 32-3-141-1; R.E.Morris 24-3-129-2; D.B.Pfaff 2-0-6-0; M.J.Russell 8-2-31-4.

The following appeared in other first-class matches in 1991:
R.R.Montgomerie in one match for Northamptonshire.
His record in all first-class matches appears on pp 164-179.

CAMBRIDGE UNIVERSITY RECORDS

FIRST-CLASS CRICKET

Highest Total	For	703-9d	v	Sussex	Hove	1890
	V	730-3		by W Indians	Cambridge	1950
Lowest Total	For	30	v	Yorkshire	Cambridge	1928
	V	32		by Oxford U	Lord's	1878

Highest Innings	For	254* K.S.Duleepsinhji	v	Middlesex	Cambridge	1927
	V	304* E.de C.Weekes	for	W Indians	Cambridge	1950

Highest Partnership for each Wicket

1st	349	J.G.Dewes/D.S.Sheppard	v	Sussex	Hove	1950
2nd	429*	J.G.Dewes/G.H.G.Doggart	v	Essex	Cambridge	1949
3rd	284	E.T.Killick/G.C.Grant	v	Essex	Cambridge	1929
4th	275	R.de W.K.Winlaw/J.H.Human	v	Essex	Cambridge	1934
5th	220	R.Subba Row/F.C.M.Alexander	v	Notts	Nottingham	1953
6th	245	J.L.Bryan/C.T.Ashton	v	Surrey	The Oval	1921
7th	289	G.Goonesena/G.W.Cook	v	Oxford U	Lord's	1957
8th	145	H.Ashton/A.E.R.Gilligan	v	F Foresters	Cambridge	1920
9th	200	G.W.Cook/C.S.Smith	v	Lancashire	Liverpool	1957
10th	177	A.E.R.Gilligan/J.H.Naumann	v	Sussex	Hove	1919

Best Bowling	For	10-69	S.M.J.Woods	v	C.I.T's XI†	Cambridge	1890
(Innings)	V	10-38	S.E.Butler	for	Oxford U	Lord's	1871
Best Bowling	For	15-88	S.M.J.Woods	v	C.I.T's XI†	Cambridge	1890
(Match)	V	15-95	S.E.Butler	for	Oxford U	Lord's	1871

Most Runs – Season	1,581	D.S.Sheppard	(av 79.05)	1952
Most Runs – Career	4,310	J.M.Brearley	(av 38.48)	1961-1968
Most 100s – Season	7	D.S.Sheppard		1952
Most 100s – Career	14	D.S.Sheppard		1950-1952
Most Wkts – Season	80	O.S.Wheatley	(av 17.63)	1958
Most Wkts – Career	208	G.Goonesena	(av 21.82)	1954-1957

UNIVERSITY MATCH RECORDS

Highest Total	432-9d	1936
Lowest Total	39	1858
Highest Innings	211 G.Goonesena	1957
Hundred in each Innings	139,124 R.J.Boyd-Moss	1983
Best Bowling (Innings)	8-44 G.E.Jeffery	1873
Best Bowling (Match)	13-73 A.G.Steel	1878
Hat-Tricks	F.C.Cobden (1870), A.G.Steel (1879), P.H.Morton (1880), J.F.Ireland (1911), R.G.H.Lowe (1926)	
Match Double	No instance	

† C.I.Thornton's XI

OXFORD UNIVERSITY RECORDS

FIRST-CLASS CRICKET

Highest Total	For	651	v Sussex	Hove	1895
	V	679-7d	by Australians	Oxford	1938
Lowest Total	For	12	v MCC	Oxford	1877
	V	24	by MCC	Oxford	1846

Highest Innings	For	281	K.J.Key	v Middlesex	Chiswick Park	1887
	V	338	W.W.Read	for Surrey	The Oval	1888

Highest Partnership for each Wicket

1st	338	T.Bowring/H.Teesdale	v Gentlemen	Oxford	1908
2nd	226	W.G.Keighley/H.A.Pawson	v Cambridge U	Lord's	1947
3rd	273	F.C.de Saram/N.S.M-Innes†	v Glos	Oxford	1934
4th	276	P.G.T.Kingsley/N.M.Ford	v Surrey	The Oval	1930
5th	256*	A.A.Baig/C.A.Fry	v I Foresters	Oxford	1959
6th	270	D.R.Walsh/S.A.Westley	v Warwicks	Oxford	1969
7th	340	K.J.Key/H.Philipson	v Middlesex	Chiswick Park	1887
8th	160	H.Philipson/A.C.M.Croome	v MCC	Lord's	1889
9th	157	H.M.G.Wells‡/C.K.H.Hill-Wood	v Kent	Oxford	1928
10th	149	F.H.Hollins/B.A.Collins	v MCC	Oxford	1901

Best Bowling	For	10-38	S.E.Butler	v Cambridge U	Lord's	1871
(Innings)	V	10-49	W.G.Grace	for MCC	Oxford	1886
Best Bowling	For	15-65	B.J.T.Bosanquet	v Sussex	Oxford	1900
(Match)	V	16-225	J.E.Walsh	for Leics	Oxford	1953

Most Runs – Season	1,307	Nawab of Pataudi, sr	(av 93.35)	1931
Most Runs – Career	3,319	N.S.Mitchell-Innes	(av 47.41)	1934-1937
Most 100s – Season	6	Nawab of Pataudi, sr		1931
Most 100s – Career	9	A.M.Crawley		1927-1930
	9	Nawab of Pataudi, sr		1928-1931
	9	N.S.Mitchell-Innes		1934-1937
	9	M.P.Donnelly		1946-1947
Most Wkts – Season	70	I.A.R.Peebles	(av 18.15)	1930
Most Wkts – Career	182	R.H.B.Bettington	(av 19.38)	1920-1923

UNIVERSITY MATCH RECORDS

Highest Total	503		1900
Lowest Total	32		1878
Highest Innings	238*	Nawab of Pataudi, sr	1931
Best Bowling (Innings)	10-38	S.E.Butler	1871
Best Bowling (Match)	15-95	S.E.Butler	1871
Hat-Trick	No instance		
Match Doubles	160 and 11-66	P.R.le Couteur	1910
	149 and 10-93	G.J.Toogood	1985

† N.S.Mitchell-Innes   ‡ H.M.Garland-Wells

1991 FIRST-CLASS AVERAGES

These averages include performances in all first-class matches played in the British Isles in 1991.

'Cap' denotes the season in which the player was awarded a 1st XI cap by the county he represented in 1991.

Team abbreviations: CU – Cambridge University: D – Derbyshire; E – England; Ex – Essex; Gm – Glamorgan; Gs – Gloucestershire; H – Hampshire; Ire – Ireland; K – Kent; La – Lancashire; Le – Leicestershire; M – Middlesex; MCC – Marylebone Cricket Club; Nh – Northamptonshire; Nt – Nottinghamshire; OU – Oxford University; Sc – Scotland; SL – Sri Lanka(ns); Sm – Somerset; Sy – Surrey; Sx – Sussex; V – Victoria; W – World XI; Wa – Warwickshire; WI – West Indies(ians); WIX – West Indies XI; Wo – Worcestershire; Y – Yorkshire.

† Left-handed batsman.

BATTING AND FIELDING

	Cap	M	I	NO	HS	Runs	Avge	100	50	Ct/St
Adams, C.J.(D)	—	15	24	2	134	691	31.40	2	1	15
Afford, J.A.(Nt)	1990	19	12	4	13	42	5.25	—	—	10
†Ahangama, F.S.(SL)	—	3	4	1	7	7	2.33	—	—	—
Alikhan, R.I.(Sy)	—	19	34	2	96*	1055	32.96	—	8	10
Allen, I.B.A.(WI)	—	10	5	4	8	16	16.00	—	—	8
Alleyne, M.W.(Gs)	1990	25	40	5	165	1121	32.02	1	6	12/1
Allott, P.J.W.(La)	1981	8	8	2	26	63	10.50	—	—	6
†Ambrose, C.E.L.(WI)	—	10	8	1	17	53	7.57	—	—	1
Andrew, S.J.W.(Ex)	—	15	9	2	13	30	4.28	—	—	5
Anthony, H.A.G.(WI)	—	11	8	3	33*	76	15.20	—	—	7
Anurasiri, S.D.(SL)	—	4	3	1	16	17	8.50	—	—	1
Aqib Javed(H)	—	18	12	8	15*	25	6.25	—	—	—
Arscott, J.P.(CU)	—	9	12	1	74	157	14.27	—	1	7
Asif Din(Wa)	1987	15	27	1	140	685	26.34	2	1	9
Atapattu, M.S.(SL)	—	5	6	2	52*	132	33.00	—	1	2
Atherton, M.A.(La/E)	1989	14	23	3	138	820	41.00	3	2	9
Athey, C.W.J.(Gs)	1985	25	40	6	127	1522	44.76	5	9	18
†Austin, I.D.(La)	1990	12	16	4	101*	315	26.25	1	1	4
Ayling, J.R.(H)	1991	10	14	3	58	321	29.18	—	2	3
Aymes, A.N.(H)	1991	24	30	7	53	644	28.00	—	2	51/2
Azharuddin, M.(D)	1991	22	39	5	212	2016	59.29	7	10	24
†Babington, A.M.(Gs)	—	18	20	7	58	176	13.53	—	1	7
Bailey, K.R.(Ire)	—	1	—	—	—	—	—	—	—	1/1
Bailey, R.J.(Nh)	1985	21	36	5	117	1224	39.48	1	11	10
Bakker, P-J.(H)	1989	10	6	2	6*	17	4.25	—	—	2
Ball, M.C.J.(Gs)	—	6	9	0	28	106	11.77	—	—	8
Baptiste, E.A.E.(Nh)	—	18	22	1	80	589	28.04	—	4	9
Barnes, S.N.(Gs)	—	1	1	1	0*	0	—	—	—	—
Barnett, A.A.(M)	—	2	2	2	11*	12	—	—	—	—
Barnett, K.J.(D)	1982	24	39	2	217	1399	37.81	2	9	25
Bartlett, R.J.(Sm)	—	5	7	1	71	177	29.50	—	1	3
Barwick, S.R.(Sm)	1987	12	10	1	24*	64	7.11	—	—	1
Base, S.J.(D)	1990	15	18	4	36	151	10.78	—	—	14
Bastien, S.(Gm)	—	13	6	3	22*	26	8.66	—	—	1
Batty, J.D.(Y)	—	18	17	6	51	202	18.36	—	1	7
Beal, D.(Sm)	—	3	2	0	1	1	0.50	—	—	1
Bell, R.M.H.(Gs)	—	1	—	—	—	—	—	—	—	—
Benjamin, J.E.(Wa)	—	3	4	0	11	12	3.00	—	—	1

	Cap	M	I	NO	HS	Runs	Avge	100	50	Ct/St
Benson, J.D.R.(Le)	—	9	12	1	133*	393	35.72	1	1	9
†Benson, M.R.(K)	1981	20	30	2	257	1329	47.46	4	6	9
Bent, P.(Wo)	—	8	13	1	100*	288	24.00	1	—	3
Berry, D.S.(V)	—	1	2	0	4	5	2.50	—	—	3
Bevins, S.R.(Wo)	—	2	1	0	6	6	6.00	—	—	5
†Bicknell, D.J.(Sy/MCC)	1990	24	42	2	151	1888	47.20	5	9	11
Bicknell, M.P.(Sy)	1989	15	22	4	63	312	17.33	—	1	3
Bishop, I.R.(WIX)	—	1	—	—	—	—	—	—	—	—
Blakey, R.J.(Y)	1987	24	38	2	196	941	26.13	1	6	40/5
Boiling, J.(Sy)	—	5	7	1	16	22	3.66	—	—	7
Boon, T.J.(Le)	1986	22	40	2	108	1185	31.18	2	6	11
†Booth, P.A.(Wa)	—	10	13	0	62	175	13.46	—	1	5
Botham, I.T.(Wo/E)	1987	13	21	3	161	785	43.61	2	4	12
Bowler, P.D.(D)	1989	24	44	3	104*	1458	35.56	2	11	15
Briers, N.E.(Le)	1981	24	43	5	160	1485	39.07	4	7	19
†Broad, B.C.(Nt)	1984	21	38	3	166	1739	49.68	5	7	9
Broadhurst, M.(Y)	—	2	1	0	1	1	1.00	—	—	—
Broadley, V.J.P.(Nt)	—	1	1	0	6	6	6.00	—	—	—
Brown, A.M.(D)	—	1	1	0	3	3	3.00	—	—	—
Brown, K.R.(M)	1990	24	41	6	143*	1184	33.82	1	6	36
Bullen, C.K.(Sy)	1990	1	1	1	37*	37	—	—	—	4
Bunting, R.A.(Sx)	—	4	4	3	51*	106	106.00	—	1	1
†Burns, N.D.(Sm)	1987	23	34	8	108	808	31.07	1	4	35/8
†Bush, D.J.(CU)	—	7	7	2	24*	58	11.60	—	—	3
†Butcher, A.R.(Gm)	1987	23	39	2	147	1677	45.32	4	13	13
†Byas, D.(Y)	1991	24	41	6	153	1557	44.48	5	2	21
Caddick, A.R.(Sm)	—	2	1	0	0	0	0.00	—	—	1
†Cann, M.J.(Gm)	—	1	1	1	29*	29	—	—	—	1
Capel, D.J.(Nh)	1986	22	33	2	100	792	25.54	1	7	10
Carrick, P.(Y)	1976	21	32	9	67	662	28.78	—	4	3
Childs, J.H.(Ex)	1986	22	15	7	41*	120	15.00	—	—	6
Clitheroe, R.I.(CU)	—	10	17	2	36	228	15.20	—	—	3
Cohen, M.F.(Ire)	—	1	2	0	44	48	24.00	—	—	—
Connor, C.A.(H)	1988	16	16	0	30	148	9.25	—	—	3
Cook, N.G.B.(Nh)	1987	18	15	5	29	114	11.40	—	—	10
Cook, S.J.(Sm)	1989	24	42	8	210*	2755	81.02	11	8	16
†Cooper, K.E.(Nt)	1980	1	—	—	—	—	—	—	—	—
Cork, D.G.(D)	—	18	28	5	44	423	21.15	—	—	9
Cottey, P.A.(Gm)	—	14	20	7	55	299	23.00	—	1	9
Cotton, D.C.(CU)	—	1	2	1	0*	0	0.00	—	—	—
Cowan, D.(Sc)	—	1	1	1	2*	2	—	—	—	1
Cowans, N.G.(M)	1984	23	29	11	35	186	10.33	—	—	5
Cowdrey, C.S.(K)	1979	3	4	0	97	154	38.50	—	1	1
Cowdrey, G.R.(K)	1988	22	34	4	114	1175	39.16	3	5	17
†Cox, R.M.F(H)	—	2	2	0	26	41	20.50	—	—	1
Crawley, J.P.(CU/La)	—	12	20	2	130	849	47.16	1	8	13
Crawley, M.A.(Nt)	—	11	13	4	112	272	30.22	1	—	14
Croft, R.D.B.(Gm)	—	25	27	4	50	345	15.00	—	1	12
Curran, K.M.(Nh)	—	21	31	7	89*	828	34.50	—	6	11
Curtis, T.S.(Wo)	1984	25	40	3	248	1653	44.67	3	9	15
Dale, A.(Gm)	—	17	26	5	140	869	41.38	1	5	8
†Davies, H.R.(OU)	—	7	9	3	38	80	13.33	—	—	—
Davis, R.P.(K)	1990	20	26	4	44	383	17.40	—	—	23
Davis, W.W.(W)	1987	1	1	1	54*	54	—	—	1	—
DeFreitas, P.A.J.(La/E)	1989	18	26	2	60	499	20.79	—	3	2

	Cap	M	I	NO	HS	Runs	Avge	100	50	Ct/St
De la Pena, J.M.(Gs)	—	2	2	1	1*	1	1.00	—	—	—
Dennis, S.J.(Gm)	—	3	2	0	3	3	1.50	—	—	—
Derrick, J.(Gm)	1988	1	1	1	12*	12	—	—	—	1
De Silva, P.A.(SL)	—	5	7	1	57*	198	33.00	—	1	4
†Dilley, G.R.(Wo)	1987	11	11	5	15*	37	6.16	—	—	3
Dobson, M.C.(K)	—	1	2	1	50	63	63.00	—	1	1
Dodemaide, A.I.C.(Sx/V)	1989	20	30	9	100*	602	28.66	1	1	8
D'Oliveira, D.B.(Wo)	1985	17	24	2	237	586	26.63	1	1	21
Donald, A.A.(Wa)	1989	21	21	9	18	96	8.00	—	—	10
Donelan, B.T.P.(Sx)	—	13	15	5	61	353	35.30	—	2	3
Downton, P.R.(M)	1981	5	6	2	51*	189	47.25	—	1	11/1
Dujon, P.J.L.(WI)	—	11	14	3	142*	439	39.90	1	2	21
Duthie, P.G.(Sc)	—	1	1	0	0	0	0.00	—	—	1
Ealham, M.A.(K)	—	4	7	1	37	135	22.50	—	—	3
Ellcock, R.M.(M)	—	4	1	1	26*	26	—	—	—	1
†Ellison, R.M.(K)	1983	17	26	7	61*	415	21.84	—	3	10
Emburey, J.E.(M)	1977	24	33	4	74	630	21.72	—	3	25
Evans, K.P.(Nt)	1990	15	18	7	56*	289	26.27	—	1	6
†Fairbrother, N.H.(La/MCC)	1985	19	29	6	121	1064	46.26	5	3	19
Farbrace, P.(M)	—	20	27	5	50	326	14.81	—	1	46/8
Feltham, M.A.(Sy)	1990	13	18	5	69*	375	28.84	—	1	4
†Felton, N.A.(Nh)	1990	16	28	3	55	497	19.88	—	1	5
Fenton, N.C.W.(CU)	—	1	1	1	7*	7	—	—	—	—
Field-Buss, M.G.(Nt)	—	3	2	0	25	41	20.50	—	—	1
†Fitton, J.D.(La)	—	8	11	1	60	217	21.70	—	1	—
Fleming, D.W.(V)	—	1	1	0	8	8	8.00	—	—	—
Fleming, M.V.(K)	1990	20	32	3	116	917	31.62	2	6	14
Fletcher, I.(Sm)	—	1	2	1	56	58	58.00	—	1	—
Fletcher, S.D.(Y)	1988	13	11	2	9*	48	5.33	—	—	5
Folley, I.(D)	—	4	5	1	17*	20	5.00	—	—	1
Fordham, A.(Nh)	1990	24	42	3	165	1840	47.17	4	9	8
Foster, D.J.(Gm)	—	9	9	3	13*	35	5.83	—	—	3
Foster, N.A.(Ex)	1983	22	22	4	107*	513	28.50	1	1	11
†Fowler, G.(La)	1981	19	33	2	113	953	30.74	2	3	2
Fraser, A.G.J.(Ex)	—	3	2	1	52*	75	75.00	—	1	—
Fraser, A.R.C.(M)	1988	2	2	0	12	12	6.00	—	—	2
French, B.N.(Nt)	1980	21	24	4	65	315	15.75	—	2	54/8
Frost, M.(Gm)	1991	20	12	5	8*	19	2.71	—	—	4
Garnham, M.A.(Ex)	1990	25	29	8	123	986	46.95	3	5	62
Gatting, M.W.(M)	1977	22	39	11	215*	2057	73.46	8	6	14
Gerrans, P.S.(OU)	—	3	3	1	17*	35	17.50	—	—	1
Gerrard, M.J.(Gs)	—	8	9	5	42	49	12.25	—	—	2
Giddins, E.S.H.(Sx)	—	2	1	1	14*	14	—	—	—	—
†Gidley, M.I.(Le)	—	6	9	2	80	107	15.28	—	1	4
Gilbert, D.R.(Gs)	—	22	28	7	28*	303	14.42	—	—	5
Goldsmith, S.C.(D)	—	16	26	3	127	610	26.52	1	2	2
Gooch, G.A.(Ex/E)	1975	20	31	4	259	1911	70.77	6	6	22
†Goram, A.L.(Sc)	—	1	1	0	5	5	5.00	—	—	—
Gough, D.(Y)	—	13	14	3	72	307	27.90	—	2	3
Govan, J.W.(Sc)	—	1	1	0	1	1	1.00	—	—	1
†Gower, D.I.(H)	1990	23	38	5	80*	1142	34.60	—	8	13
Graveney, D.A.(Sm)	—	21	14	7	17	59	8.42	—	—	10
Grayson, A.P.(Y)	—	2	2	1	18*	18	18.00	—	—	1
Green, S.J.(Wa)	—	1	1	1	77*	77	—	—	1	—
Greenfield, K.(Sx)	—	9	14	1	127*	394	30.30	2	1	15

	Cap	M	I	NO	HS	Runs	Avge	100	50	Ct/St
Greenidge, C.G.(WI/WIX)	—	3	6	2	55*	141	35.25	–	1	3
Greig, I.A.(Sy)	1987	20	31	4	72	610	22.59	–	3	7
Griffith, F.A.(D)	—	2	3	0	6	11	3.66	–	–	–
Gupte, C.M.(OU)	—	8	9	1	55*	200	25.00	–	1	2
†Gurusinha, A.P.(SL)	—	6	10	0	98	292	29.20	–	1	2
Hagan, D.A.(OU)	—	1	–	–	–	–	–	–	–	–
Haggo, D.J.(Sc)	—	1	1	0	25	25	25.00	–	–	1/1
Hall, J.W.(Sx)	—	15	26	2	117*	686	28.58	1	4	8
Hallett, J.C.(Sm)	—	8	5	1	15	35	8.75	–	–	4
Hancock, T.H.C.(Gs)	—	5	9	2	51	93	13.28	–	1	7
Hanley, R.(Sx)	—	2	2	0	19	19	9.50	–	–	–
Harden, R.J.(Sm)	1989	24	39	8	134	1355	43.70	3	9	21
†Hardy, J.J.E.(Gs)	—	10	15	2	52	242	18.61	–	1	–
Harper, R.A.(WIX)	—	1	2	2	63*	87	–	–	1	–
†Harrison, G.D.(Ire)	—	1	2	0	77	98	49.00	–	1	1
Hartley, P.J.(Y)	1987	20	24	10	50*	322	23.00	–	1	3
Hathurusinghe, U.C.(SL)	—	6	11	1	74*	311	31.10	–	3	2
Hayhurst, A.N.(Sm)	1990	19	32	5	172*	910	33.70	3	1	5
Haynes, D.L.(WI)	—	13	22	5	151	721	42.41	1	4	4
Haynes, G.R.(Wo)	—	4	4	1	16	51	17.00	–	–	2
Headley, D.W.(M)	—	12	15	1	76	202	14.42	–	1	5
Hegg, W.K.(La)	1989	22	32	8	97	784	32.66	–	3	43/3
Hemmings, E.E.(Nt)	1980	16	16	4	29*	143	11.91	–	–	4
†Hemp, D.L.(Gm)	—	1	2	1	8	12	12.00	–	–	–
†Henry, O.(Sc)	—	1	1	0	22	22	22.00	–	–	–
Hepworth, P.N.(Le)	—	23	38	4	115	1119	32.91	2	4	19
Hick, G.A.(Wo/MCC/E)	1986	22	36	2	186	1119	32.91	3	5	26
†Hinks, S.G.(K)	1985	9	14	2	61*	275	22.91	–	2	6
Hodgson, G.D.(Gs)	—	23	39	2	105	1101	29.75	1	7	8
Hoey, C.J.(Ire)	—	1	1	1	1*	1	–	–	–	–
†Holloway, P.C.L.(Wa)	—	6	9	5	89*	263	65.75	–	2	9
Holmes, G.C.(Gm)	1985	7	8	1	54	136	19.42	–	1	1
Hooper, A.M.(CU)	—	7	12	1	125	458	41.63	1	2	–
Hooper, C.L.(WI/WIX)	—	16	25	9	196	1501	93.81	5	8	20
Houseman, I.J.(Y)	—	1	–	–	–	–	–	–	–	–
Hughes, D.P.(La)	1970	8	9	3	51	111	18.50	–	1	4
Hughes, J.G.(Nh)	—	1	–	–	–	–	–	–	–	–
Hughes, M.G.(V)	—	1	2	2	60*	72	–	–	1	–
Hughes, S.P.(M)	1981	5	5	2	5	11	3.66	–	–	2
Hunt, A.J.(Gs)	—	1	2	0	12	15	7.50	–	–	–
Hussain, N.(Ex/MCC)	1989	25	33	8	196	1354	54.16	3	8	38
Hutchinson, I.J.F.(M)	—	14	24	1	125	656	28.52	2	2	15
Igglesden, A.P.(K)	1989	19	17	4	16*	101	7.76	–	–	4
Illingworth, R.K.(Wo/MCC/E)	1986	22	29	7	56*	524	23.81	–	1	8
†Ilott, M.C.(Ex)	—	1	–	–	–	–	–	–	–	–
Irani, R.C.(La)	—	1	1	1	31*	31	–	–	–	–
Jackson, P.W.(V)	—	1	1	0	4	4	4.00	–	–	–
†James, K.D.(H)	1989	24	37	10	134*	1274	47.18	2	6	9
James, S.P.(Gm)	—	11	19	3	70	461	28.81	–	2	8
Jarvis, P.W.(Y)	1986	4	5	2	37*	114	38.00	–	–	1
Javed Miandad (W)	—	1	2	0	88	110	55.00	–	1	1
†Jayasuriya, S.T.(SL)	—	6	11	2	100*	482	53.55	1	3	–
Jean-Jacques, M.(D)	—	5	7	1	28	35	5.83	–	–	–
Jenkins, R.H.J.(CU)	—	6	8	1	20	64	9.14	–	1	2
Jesty, T.E.(La)	1989	1	2	2	122*	126	–	1	–	–

167

	Cap	M	I	NO	HS	Runs	Avge	100	50	Ct/St
Johnson, P.(Nt)	1986	23	37	7	124	1454	48.46	3	11	12
Johnson, S.W.(CU)	—	7	8	3	20	85	17.00	–	–	3
†Jones, A.N.(Sx)	1986	23	18	6	28	128	10.66	–	–	1
Jones, C.D.(OU)	—	1	2	0	23	27	13.50	–	–	–
Jones, D.M.(V)	—	1	2	0	25	34	17.00	–	–	–
†Jones, G.W.(CU)	—	3	5	1	13*	19	4.75	–	–	–
Kaluwitharana, R.S.(SL)	—	3	5	0	34	73	14.60	–	–	2
Kapil Dev(W)	—	1	2	1	22	27	27.00	–	–	1
Keech, M.(M)	—	15	24	3	58*	420	20.00	–	2	4
Kelleher, D.J.M.(K)	—	1	2	1	29*	39	39.00	–	–	–
Kellett, S.A.(Y)	—	24	40	5	125*	1266	36.17	2	8	19
Kendrick, N.M.(Sy)	—	2	4	1	24	58	19.33	–	–	1
Kersey, G.J.(K)	—	2	1	1	27*	27	–	–	–	7
†Knight, N.V.(Ex)	—	7	10	1	101*	441	49.00	1	3	5
Krikken, K.M.(D)	—	24	38	8	65	697	23.23	–	2	58/3
Kuruppu, D.S.B.P.(SL)	—	7	12	0	86	389	32.41	–	4	4
Lamb, A.J.(Nh/E)	1978	19	30	2	194	1081	38.60	3	5	21
Lambert, C.B.(WI/WIX)	—	7	13	2	116	551	50.09	1	4	5
Lampitt, S.R.(Wo)	1989	22	23	6	93	523	30.76	–	4	6
†Lara, B.C.(WI/WIX)	—	9	14	0	93	344	24.57	–	3	9
Larkins, W.(Nh)	1976	9	16	6	75	365	36.50	–	2	6
Lathwell, M.N.(Sm)	—	2	3	0	43	63	21.00	–	–	–
Lawrence, D.V.(Gs/E)	1985	18	26	1	66	433	17.32	–	1	4
Leatherdale, D.A.(Wo)	—	5	6	0	157	379	63.16	1	2	4
Lefebvre, R.P.(Sm)	1991	16	18	4	100	366	26.14	1	1	6
†Lehmann, D.S.(V)	—	1	2	0	15	23	11.50	–	–	–
Lenham, N.J.(Sx)	1990	19	33	3	193	1091	36.36	3	4	11
Lewis, C.C.(Le/E)	1990	16	20	2	73	621	34.50	–	4	9
Lewis, D.A.(Ire)	—	1	2	0	44	58	29.00	–	–	–
Lewis, J.J.B.(Ex)	—	2	2	0	48	73	36.50	–	–	1
†Llong, N.J.(K)	—	4	7	2	42*	63	12.60	–	–	4
Lloyd, G.D.(La)	—	18	30	0	96	829	27.63	–	6	11
†Lloyd, T.A.(Wa)	1980	21	35	2	97	1076	32.60	–	10	10
†Lloyds, J.W.(Gs)	1985	24	35	6	71*	803	27.68	–	8	21
Logie, A.L.(WI)	—	12	17	1	78	433	27.06	–	3	7
†Lord, G.J.(Wo)	1990	11	18	0	85	378	21.00	–	3	2
Lovell, G.B.T.(OU)	—	9	13	3	49	250	25.00	–	–	5
Lowrey, M.J.(CU)	—	10	16	2	51	234	16.71	–	1	2
Loye, M.B.(Nh)	—	1	1	1	3*	3	–	–	–	1
Lynch, M.A.(Sy)	1982	10	17	1	141*	342	21.37	1	1	13
Lyons, R.J.(CU)	—	1	2	0	20	38	19.00	–	–	–
McCague, M.J.(K)	—	8	10	2	29	142	17.75	–	–	7
McCray, E.(D)	—	2	2	0	37	68	34.00	–	–	1
MacDonald, R.H.(OU)	—	7	6	3	20	41	13.66	–	–	–
MacLeay, K.H.(Sm)	—	15	21	6	63	417	27.80	–	2	5
Madan Lal (W)	—	1	2	0	16	25	12.50	–	–	2
†Madurasinghe, A.W.R.(SL)	—	3	4	2	17*	28	14.00	–	–	1
Maguire, J.N.(Le)	—	24	24	7	44*	237	13.94	–	–	7
Mahanama, R.S.(SL)	—	6	9	0	65	146	16.22	–	1	8
Maher, B.J.M.(D)	1987	1	1	0	5	5	5.00	–	–	–
Malcolm, D.E.(D/E)	1989	13	17	3	18	93	6.64	–	–	1
Mallender, N.A.(Sm)	1987	13	11	3	19	108	13.50	–	–	1
Maninder Singh (W)	—	1	1	0	0	0	0.00	–	–	–
Manjrekar, S.V.(W)	—	1	2	1	154*	199	199.00	1	–	1
Marsh, S.A.(K)	1986	23	32	5	113*	910	33.70	2	5	66/4

168

	Cap	M	I	NO	HS	Runs	Avge	100	50	Ct/St
Marshall, M.D.(WI/WIX)	—	11	11	2	67	196	21.77	–	1	–
Martin, P.J.(La)	—	16	13	8	29	85	17.00	–	–	5
Martindale, D.J.R.(Nt)	—	1	1	1	4*	4	–	–	–	–
Martyn, D.R.(Le)	—	1	2	1	60*	95	95.00	–	1	–
†Maru, R.J.(H)	1986	22	26	3	61	392	17.04	–	1	31
Maynard, M.P.(Gm)	1987	23	36	6	243	1803	60.10	7	5	18
Medlycott, K.T.(Sy)	1988	19	27	2	109	624	24.96	1	4	6
Mendis, G.D.(La)	1986	23	43	5	127*	1394	36.68	4	3	8
Merrick, T.A.(K)	—	19	23	6	36	204	12.00	–	–	4
Metcalfe, A.A.(Y)	1986	24	43	2	123	1210	29.51	2	6	12
Metson, C.P.(Gm)	1987	24	26	3	84	543	23.60	–	2	73/3
Middleton, T.C.(H)	1990	18	31	2	102	864	29.79	1	3	15
Milburn, E.T.(Gs)	—	1	–	–	–	–	–	–	–	–
†Millns, D.J.(Le)	1991	20	24	8	44	306	19.12	–	–	9
Moles, A.J.(Wa)	1987	22	39	2	133	1246	33.67	1	10	10
Montgomerie, R.R.(OU/Nh)	—	9	13	2	88	309	28.09	–	4	9
Moody, T.M.(Wo)	1991	30	34	4	210	1887	62.90	6	9	36
Moores, P.(Sx)	1989	23	28	3	102	714	28.56	1	6	56/6
†Morris, H.(Gm/MCC/E)	1986	23	41	7	156*	1803	53.02	5	8	17
Morris, J.E.(D)	1986	21	36	2	131	1398	41.11	2	8	8
Morris, J.G.(OU)	—	3	5	0	28	63	12.60	–	–	3
Morris, M.J.(CU)	—	9	13	0	60	171	13.15	–	1	2
Morris, R.E.(OU)	—	8	11	1	71	236	23.60	–	2	3
Morrison, D.K.(W)	—	1	1	0	1	1	1.00	–	–	2
Mortensen, O.H.(D)	1986	19	17	9	8	32	4.00	–	–	5
Moxon, M.D.(Y)	1984	21	37	1	200	1669	46.36	3	12	17
Mudassar Nazar (W)	—	1	1	0	3	3	3.00	–	–	1
Mullally, A.D.(Le)	—	2	–	–	–	–	–	–	–	–
Munton, T.A.(Wa/MCC)	1989	23	24	7	31	226	13.29	–	–	14
Muralitharan, M.(SL)	—	3	4	1	22*	27	9.00	–	–	2
Murphy, A.J.(Sy)	—	19	20	8	18	71	5.91	–	–	4
Neale, P.A.(Wo)	1978	14	21	4	69*	419	24.64	–	1	5
Nelson, A.N.(Ire)	—	1	–	–	–	–	–	–	–	1
Newell, M.(Nt)	1987	1	1	0	91	91	91.00	–	1	–
Newport, P.J.(Wo)	1986	25	26	9	48	353	20.76	–	–	4
Nicholas, M.C.J.(H)	1982	22	37	10	107*	826	30.59	1	5	10
†Nixon, P.A.(Le)	—	4	4	1	31	54	18.00	–	–	8/1
Noon, W.M.(Nh)	—	6	9	2	36	96	13.71	–	–	11
North, J.A.(Sx)	—	7	8	1	63*	163	23.28	–	1	1
O'Donnell, S.P.(V)	—	1	2	0	12	17	8.50	–	–	–
O'Gorman, T.J.G.(D)	—	25	44	4	148	1116	27.90	2	4	21
Oppenheimer, J.M.E.(OU)	—	5	1	1	0*	0	–	–	–	1
Orrell, T.M.(La)	—	1	2	0	16	21	10.50	–	–	–
Ostler, D.P.(Wa)	1991	22	40	5	120*	1284	36.68	1	10	10
Parker, G.R.(V)	—	1	2	0	1	1	0.50	–	–	–
Parker, P.W.G.(Sx)	1979	16	26	1	111	607	24.28	1	3	8
†Parsons, G.J.(Le)	1984	2	4	1	63	78	26.00	–	1	–
Patel, M.M.(K)	—	5	7	2	43	76	15.20	–	–	2
Patterson, B.M.W.(Sc)	—	1	2	0	108	114	57.00	1	–	1
Patterson, B.P.(WI)	—	11	5	3	5*	11	5.50	–	–	4
†Patterson, T.J.T.(Ire)	—	1	2	1	73*	76	76.00	–	1	–
Pearson, R.M.(CU)	—	10	12	1	21	70	6.36	–	–	2
†Penberthy, A.L.(Nh)	—	12	15	3	52	186	15.50	–	1	6
†Penn, C.(K)	1987	18	22	4	52	311	17.27	–	1	6
†Pfaff, D.B.(OU)	—	8	7	2	50	231	46.20	–	1	4

	Cap	M	I	NO	HS	Runs	Avge	100	50	Ct/St
Philip, I.L.(Sc)	—	1	2	1	116*	123	123.00	1	–	1
Phillips, W.N.(V)	—	1	2	0	11	13	6.50	–	–	–
†Pick, R.A.(Nt/MCC)	1987	23	16	5	46	142	12.90	–	–	7
Pickles, C.S.(Y)	–	11	16	3	51	284	21.84	–	2	2
Pierson, A.R.K.(Wa)	–	5	6	4	35	55	27.50	–	–	1
Pigott, A.C.S.(Sx)	1982	19	22	5	65	320	18.82	–	1	5
Piper, K.J.(Wa)	–	16	23	3	55	349	17.45	–	1	48
†Pollard, P.R.(Nt)	–	23	41	3	145	1255	33.02	3	4	21
†Pooley, J.C.(M)	–	12	21	0	88	407	19.38	–	2	8
Potter, L.(Le)	1988	24	37	4	89	1027	31.12	–	7	21
Prichard, P.J.(Ex)	1986	24	38	7	190	1124	36.25	4	3	19
Pringle, D.R.(Ex/E)	1982	19	21	7	78*	607	43.35	–	4	9
Pringle, N.J.(Sm)	–	2	4	0	20	45	11.25	–	–	1
Pyman, R.A.(CU)	–	2	4	1	8*	20	6.66	–	–	1
Radford, N.V.(Wo)	1985	17	16	6	45	157	15.70	–	–	4
Ramanayake, C.P.H.(SL)	–	6	8	2	41*	152	25.33	–	–	1
Ramprakash, M.R.(M/E)	1990	21	36	4	119	1174	36.68	2	7	6
Ramshaw, D.J.(V)	–	1	2	0	11	11	5.50	–	–	–
Randall, D.W.(Nt)	1973	22	34	9	143*	1567	62.68	5	5	15
Ratcliffe, J.D.(Wa)	–	17	31	1	94	953	31.76	–	8	15
Ratnayake, R.J.(SL)	–	4	5	1	68*	193	48.25	–	2	3
Rea, M.P.(Ire)	–	1	2	0	27	39	19.50	–	–	–
Reeve, D.A.(Wa)	1989	20	33	7	99*	1260	48.46	–	14	10
Rhodes, S.J.(Wo/MCC)	1986	24	33	6	90	942	34.88	–	8	54/8
Richards, I.V.A.(WI)	–	12	18	4	131	817	58.35	1	6	8
Richardson, R.B.(WI/WIX)	–	15	26	5	135*	1403	66.81	6	6	14
Ripley, D.(Nh)	1987	20	25	9	53*	467	29.18	–	1	41/2
Roberts, A.R.(Nh)	–	14	15	9	48	244	40.66	–	–	7
Roberts, B.(D)	1986	1	2	2	44*	80	–	–	–	1
Roberts, M.L.(Gm)	–	1	–	–	–	–	–	–	–	1/2
†Robinson, J.D.(Sy)	–	4	6	1	79	186	37.20	–	2	–
Robinson, M.A.(Y)	–	17	13	4	8	17	1.88	–	–	4
Robinson, P.E.(Y)	1988	24	41	7	189	1293	38.02	2	8	20
Robinson, R.T.(Nt)	1983	22	37	8	180	1673	57.68	3	10	14
Robson, A.G.(Sy)	–	2	3	0	3	3	1.00	–	–	–
Roebuck, P.M.(Sm)	1978	17	29	3	101	833	32.03	1	5	4
Romaines, P.W.(Gs)	1983	3	5	0	28	35	7.00	–	–	1
Rose, G.D.(Sm)	1988	15	20	3	106	590	34.70	2	2	8
Roseberry, M.A.(M)	1990	24	44	4	123*	1511	37.77	2	8	19
Russell, A.B.(Sc)	–	1	1	0	16	16	16.00	–	–	–
Russell, M.J.(OU)	–	3	6	0	30	91	15.16	–	–	–
†Russell, R.C.(Gs/E)	1985	20	32	5	111	627	23.22	1	2	48/4
Salim Malik (Ex)	1991	24	36	9	215	1972	73.03	6	8	25
Salisbury, I.D.K.(Sx)	1991	22	21	8	34	188	14.46	–	–	12
†Salmond, G.(Sc)	–	1	1	0	66	66	66.00	–	1	1
Sandiford, D.C.(OU)	–	9	9	1	83	189	23.62	–	1	11/1
Sargeant, N.F.(Sy)	–	21	28	4	49	391	16.29	–	–	46/8
†Saxelby, M.(Nt)	–	7	10	1	44	149	16.55	–	–	–
Scott, C.W.(Nt)	1988	2	–	–	–	–	–	–	–	3
†Scott, R.J.(Gs)	–	20	34	1	127	848	25.69	2	3	6
†Seymour, A.C.H.(Ex)	–	10	18	1	157	533	31.35	1	3	7
Shahid, N.(Ex)	–	8	9	1	83	147	18.37	–	1	6
†Sharp, M.A.(La)	–	1	–	–	–	–	–	–	–	–
Shastri, R.J.(Gm)	1988	22	32	9	133*	1108	48.17	2	7	9
Shine, K.J.(H)	–	16	18	8	25	92	9.20	–	–	2

	Cap	M	I	NO	HS	Runs	Avge	100	50	Ct/St
Sidebottom, A.(Y)	1980	1	1	1	18*	18	–	–	–	1
Simmons, P.V.(WI/WIX)	—	15	28	1	136	1031	38.18	3	4	13
Sladdin, R.W.(D)	—	8	9	4	18	68	13.60	–	–	6
Sleep, P.R.(W)	—	1	2	0	37	50	25.00	–	–	1/1
Small, G.C.(Wa)	1982	20	29	7	58	370	16.81	–	1	5
Smith, A.M.(Gs)	—	14	13	2	22	60	5.45	–	–	–
Smith, B.F.(Le)	—	15	23	5	71	674	37.44	–	3	3
Smith, C.L.(H)	1981	16	27	3	200	1553	64.70	6	7	4
†Smith, D.M.(Sx)	1989	20	35	6	126*	1238	42.68	2	8	14
Smith, I.(Gm)	—	10	13	2	47	245	22.27	–	–	7
Smith, N.M.K.(Wa)	—	5	9	2	70	209	29.85	–	2	–
Smith, P.A.(Wa)	1986	14	23	1	68	411	18.68	–	2	2
Smith, R.A.(H/E)	1985	16	30	4	148*	1397	53.73	3	11	15
†Smyth, S.G.(Ire)	—	1	2	1	14	21	21.00	–	–	–
Speak, N.J.(La)	—	18	33	3	153	844	28.13	1	2	8
Speight, M.P.(Sx)	1991	14	20	1	149	754	39.68	1	5	6
Stanley, N.A.(Nh)	—	8	13	0	132	470	36.15	1	2	5
Stanworth, J.(La)	1989	2	–	–	–	–	–	–	–	2/1
Staple, R.W.(WIX)	—	1	2	0	56	96	48.00	–	1	2
Stemp, R.D.(Wo)	—	9	8	5	15*	30	10.00	–	–	–
Stephenson, F.D.(Nt)	1988	22	27	7	58	423	21.15	–	1	6
Stephenson, J.P.(Ex)	1989	25	41	3	116	1421	37.39	3	8	8
Stewart, A.J.(Sy/E)	1985	19	34	8	113*	1161	44.65	2	6	24
Such, P.M.(Ex)	1991	14	6	4	23*	31	15.50	–	–	3
Swallow, I.G.(Sm)	—	4	5	3	41*	67	33.50	–	–	3
Swan, R.G.(Sc)	—	1	1	0	15	15	15.00	–	–	1
Sylvester, S.A.(M)	—	1	1	0	0	0	0.00	–	–	1
Tavaré, C.J.(Sm)	1989	23	37	7	183	1601	53.36	5	7	20
†Taylor, C.W.(M)	—	7	5	0	21	59	11.80	–	–	2
†Taylor, J.P.(Nh)	—	13	11	4	5*	22	3.14	–	–	4
Taylor, N.R.(K)	1982	23	36	4	203*	1806	56.43	7	7	14
Tendulkar, S.R.(W)	—	1	2	0	61	75	37.50	–	1	–
Tennant, L.(Le)	—	6	9	3	23*	94	15.66	–	–	–
Terry, V.P.(H)	1983	20	35	3	171	1244	38.87	2	7	24
Thomas, J.G.(Nh)	1991	12	12	3	64	206	22.88	–	1	3
Thompson, N.E.(Ire)	—	1	2	1	21*	21	21.00	–	–	–
†Thorpe, G.P.(Sy/MCC)	1991	23	38	9	177	1203	41.48	4	4	8
Threlfall, P.W.(Sx)	—	1	–	–	–	–	–	–	–	–
Thwaites, G.E.(CU)	—	3	5	0	32	68	13.60	–	–	2
†Tillekeratne, H.P.(SL)	—	5	6	1	80*	155	31.00	–	1	9
Titchard, S.P.(La)	—	8	15	1	135	546	39.00	1	2	8
Tolley, C.M.(Wo)	—	8	10	4	36	144	24.00	–	–	3
Topley, T.D.(Ex)	1988	20	19	4	50*	320	21.33	–	2	15
Townsend, G.T.J.(Sm)	—	3	5	0	53	121	24.20	–	1	2
Tremlett, T.M.(H)	1983	1	1	0	2	2	2.00	–	–	–
Trump, H.R.J.(Sm)	—	18	17	7	30*	108	10.80	–	–	12
Tufnell, P.C.R. (M/E)	1990	22	24	6	34	210	11.66	–	–	9
†Turner, G.J.(OU)	—	8	8	2	101*	349	58.16	1	2	1
Turner, I.J.(H)	—	8	10	4	39*	87	14.50	–	–	3
Turner, R.J.(CU/Sm)	—	9	13	4	69*	249	27.66	–	1	12/1
†Twose, R.G.(Wa)	—	2	2	1	41	42	42.00	–	–	–
Udal, S.D.(H)	—	1	1	0	0	0	0.00	–	–	–
Van Troost, A.P.(Sm)	—	4	1	1	0*	0	0.00	–	–	1
Viljoen, J.N.(CU)	—	1	1	1	1*	1	–	–	–	–
†Walker, A.(Nh(	1987	4	4	1	13	35	11.66	–	–	2

171

	Cap	M	I	NO	HS	Runs	Avge	100	50	Ct/St
Waller, R.B.(CU)	—	5	4	3	6*	12	12.00	–	–	1
Walsh, C.A.(WI)	—	11	8	1	18	66	9.42	–	–	1
Waqar Younis (Sy)	1990	18	20	8	31	177	14.75	–	–	4
Ward, D.M.(Sy)	1990	23	40	6	151	1372	40.35	1	10	10
Ward, M.J.P.(La)	—	1	–	–	–	–	–	–	–	–
Ward, T.R.(K)	1989	22	34	2	235*	1493	46.65	5	6	10
Warke, S.J.S.(Ire)	—	1	2	0	78	110	55.00	–	1	–
Warley, S.N.(OU)	—	2	3	0	11	15	5.00	–	–	–
Warner, A.E.(D)	1987	17	24	3	53	410	19.52	–	2	4
†Wasim Akram (La)	1989	14	19	2	122	471	27.70	1	1	5
Wassan, A.S.(W)	—	1	2	1	22	33	16.50	–	–	1
Watkin, S.L.(Gm/MCC/E)	1989	22	19	8	25*	136	12.36	–	–	2
Watkinson, M.(La)	1987	21	35	4	114*	758	24.45	1	3	8
Weekes, P.N.(M)	—	6	11	1	86	249	24.90	–	2	5
Wells, A.P.(Sx)	1986	22	36	6	253*	1784	59.46	7	5	7
Wells, C.M.(Sx)	1982	14	21	6	76	503	33.53	–	3	3
Wells, V.J.(K)	—	3	4	0	58	87	21.75	–	1	1
Weston, M.J.(Wo)	1986	3	3	0	9	15	5.00	–	–	1
†Weston, W.P.C.(Wo)	—	2	3	0	15	28	9.33	–	–	–
Whitaker, J.J.(Le)	1986	23	37	3	105	1289	37.91	1	8	13
White, G.W.(Sm)	—	1	1	0	42	42	42.00	–	–	–
Whitticase, P.(Le)	1987	20	25	5	114*	620	31.00	1	4	44/3
Wijegunawardene, K.I.W.(SL)	—	5	6	2	26	52	13.00	–	–	–
Wilkinson, C.W.(Le)	—	14	13	2	41	138	12.54	–	–	7
Willey, P.(Le)	1984	12	18	5	42*	217	16.69	–	–	6
Williams, D.(WI/WIX)	—	7	6	1	35	102	20.40	–	–	24/3
Williams, N.F.(M)	1984	18	27	3	77	351	14.62	–	1	5
Williams, R.C.(Gs)	—	1	2	0	13	13	6.50	–	–	–
†Williams, R.C.J.(Gs)	—	10	12	2	55*	95	9.50	–	1	18/3
Williams, R.G.(Nh)	1979	8	11	3	101*	224	28.00	1	–	1
Wood, B.S.(OU)	—	9	6	1	6	8	1.60	–	–	–
†Wood, J.R.(H)	—	2	2	0	25	25	12.50	–	–	–
Wren, T.N.(K)	—	1	–	–	–	–	–	–	–	–
Wright, A.J.(Gs)	1987	25	41	6	120	1596	45.60	3	10	19
Yates, G.(La)	—	20	26	13	100*	315	24.23	1	–	9

BOWLING

See BATTING and FIELDING section for details of caps and teams.

	Cat	O	M	R	W	Avge	Best	5 wI	10 wM
Adams, C.J.	OB	19.4	3	59	6	9.83	4-29	-	-
Afford, J.A.	SLA	670.3	207	1817	57	31.87	4-44	-	-
Ahangama, F.S.	RMF	64	20	189	2	94.50	1-41	-	-
Alikhan, R.I.	OB	5	0	43	2	21.50	2-43	-	-
Allen, I.B.A.	RF	217.4	35	811	16	50.68	2-61	-	-
Alleyne, M.W.	RM	144.1	27	474	11	43.09	3-35	-	-
Allott, P.J.W.	RFM	192.1	49	516	14	36.85	4-56	-	-
Ambrose, C.E.L.	RF	390	122	869	51	17.03	6-52	3	-
Andrew, S.J.W.	RMF	399.3	74	1352	43	31.44	4-38	-	-
Anthony, H.A.G.	RF	223.3	30	878	26	33.76	3-28	-	-
Anurasiri, S.D.	SLA	208.1	51	560	9	62.22	3-122	-	-
Aqib Javed	RFM	510.1	84	1656	53	31.24	6-91	3	-
Arscott, J.P.	RM	48	4	252	7	36.00	1-17	-	-
Asif Din	LB	53	9	206	2	103.00	1-37	-	-

	Cat	O	M	R	W	Avge	Best	5 wI	10 wM
Athey, C.W.J.	RM	66	10	189	2	94.50	1-18	-	-
Austin, I.D.	RM	237.2	42	787	12	65.58	3-58	-	-
Ayling, J.R.	RM	211.1	49	595	25	23.80	4-47	-	-
Azharuddin, M.	LB	86.4	18	252	3	84.00	1-35	-	-
Babington, A.M.	RFM	483.3	89	1487	42	35.40	4-33	-	-
Bailey, R.J.	OB	122.3	16	419	11	38.09	3-44	-	-
Bakker, P-J.	RMF	239.3	65	655	20	32.75	4-66	-	-
Ball, M.C.J.	OB	186	36	582	19	30.63	5-128	1	-
Baptiste, E.A.E.	RFM	529.2	122	1443	50	28.86	7-95	3	-
Barnes, S.N.	RM	12	4	23	0	-	-	-	-
Barnett, A.A.	SLA	107.4	23	329	10	32.90	4-119	-	-
Barnett, K.J.	LB	211.1	47	496	20	24.80	6-28	1	-
Barwick, S.R.	RMF	307.5	86	767	28	27.39	4-46	-	-
Base, S.J.	RMF	433.4	69	1344	36	37.33	-34	-	-
Bastien, S.	RMF	356.2	96	1023	22	46.50	5-39	1	-
Batty, J.D.	OB	459.4	106	1439	41	35.09	6-48	1	-
Beal, D.	RM	71	6	320	3	106.66	1-37	-	-
Bell, R.M.H.	RM	5	2	9	0	-	-	-	-
Benjamin, J.E.	RMF	76.4	11	257	7	36.71	2-62	-	-
Benson, J.D.R.	RM	35.1	7	145	1	145.00	1-18	-	-
Benson, M.R.	OB	13	0	44	0	-	-	-	-
Bent, P.	OB	3	1	5	0	-	-	-	-
Bicknell, D.J.	LM	5.3	0	62	2	31.00	2-62	-	-
Bicknell, M.P.	RFM	470.5	118	1256	45	27.91	7-52	1	-
Bishop, I.R.	RF	17	3	58	2	29.00	2-58	-	-
Boiling, J.	OB	181.3	44	505	12	42.08	4-157	-	-
Boon, T.J.	RM	10	3	21	1	21.00	1-11	-	-
Booth, P.A.	SLA	226.1	47	690	18	38.33	4-103	-	-
Botham, I.T.	RMF	351.1	73	1077	44	24.47	7-54	3	-
Bowler, P.D.	OB	114	20	464	9	51.55	3-41	-	-
Broadhurst, M.	RFM	38	7	130	6	21.66	3-61	-	-
Broadley, V.J.P.	RFM	32	6	111	1	111.00	1-92	-	-
Brown, K.R.	RSM	5.5	1	33	1	33.00	1-17	-	-
Bullen, C.K.	OB	17	2	48	4	12.00	4-48	-	-
Bunting, R.A.	RFM	62.2	7	260	8	32.50	4-99	-	-
Bush, D.J.	LM	131.3	22	540	6	90.00	1-14	-	-
Butcher, A.R.	LM	2	1	1	0	-	-	-	-
Byas, D.	RM	9	2	14	0	-	-	-	-
Caddick, A.R.	RFM	64.5	13	251	5	50.20	2-40	-	-
Cann, M.J.	OB	8	0	37	0	-	-	-	-
Capel, D.J.	RMF	383.1	83	1127	28	40.25	4-83	-	-
Carrick, P.	SLA	701.2	231	1748	61	28.65	5-13	2	-
Childs, J.H.	SLA	751.1	248	1907	65	29.33	6-61	4	-
Connor, C.A.	RFM	390	69	1306	34	38.41	4-49	-	-
Cook, N.G.B.	SLA	336.3	79	994	28	35.50	4-74	-	-
Cook, S.J.	OB	4	0	26	0	-	-	-	-
Cooper, K.E.	RFM	17	3	54	1	54.00	1-54	-	-
Cork, D.G.	RFM	494.3	84	1460	57	25.61	8-53	1	1
Cotton, D.C.	RMF	21	4	85	1	85.00	1-43	-	-
Cowan, D.	RFM	53	13	133	5	26.60	3-41	-	-
Cowans, N.G.	RF	542.1	145	1500	44	34.09	4-42	-	-
Cowdrey, G.R.	RM	2	1	6	0	-	-	-	-
Crawley, J.P.	RM	2	0	14	0	-	-	-	-
Crawley, M.A.	RM	176.5	53	463	11	42.09	3-21	-	-
Croft, R.D.B.	OB	704.2	168	1930	38	50.78	5-62	1	-

	Cat	O	M	R	W	Avge	Best	5 wI	10 wM
Curran, K.M.	RMF	436.2	110	1204	48	25.08	5-60	1	-
Curtis, T.S.	LB	28	3	112	2	56.00	2-17	-	-
Dale, A.	RM	120.1	24	436	9	48.44	2-33	-	-
Davies, H.R.	OB	107.1	16	476	4	119.00	2-46	-	-
Davis, R.P.	SLA	513.2	142	1531	37	41.37	4-81	-	-
Davis, W.W.	RF	20	5	79	0	-	-	-	-
DeFreitas, P.A.J.	RFM	657.1	173	1780	73	24.38	7-70	3	-
De la Pena, J.M.	RFM	25	0	138	3	46.00	2-69	-	-
Dennis, S.J.	LFM	36.3	9	98	3	32.66	3-31	-	-
Derrick, J.	RM	7	3	16	0	-	-	-	-
De Silva, P.A.	RM	9	2	27	0	-	-	-	-
Dilley, G.R.	RF	305.2	62	823	37	22.24	5-91	1	-
Dobson, M.C.	SLA	8	1	17	0	-	-	-	-
Dodemaide, A.I.C.	RFM	579	116	1637	54	30.31	5-130	1	-
D'Oliveira, D.B.	OB	51	16	146	1	146.00	1-36	-	-
Donald, A.A.	RF	522.3	91	1634	83	19.68	6-69	8	2
Donelan, B.T.P.	OB	426.3	112	1162	34	34.17	6-62	2	1
Duthie, P.G.	RM	47	15	115	2	57.50	2-80	-	-
Ealham, M.A.	RMF	118.1	24	354	17	20.82	5-39	2	-
Ellcock, R.M.	RF	62	15	204	8	25.50	4-60	-	-
Ellison, R.M.	RMF	484.1	102	1480	47	31.48	7-33	2	-
Emburey, J.E.	OB	899.3	246	2170	68	31.91	7-71	1	-
Evans, K.P.	RMF	425	89	1278	40	31.95	5-52	2	-
Farbrace, P.	(WK)	4.1	0	64	1	64.00	1-64	-	-
Feltham, M.A.	RMF	349	57	1075	35	30.71	4-36	-	-
Felton, N.A.	OB	6	0	66	0	-	-	-	-
Fenton, N.C.W.	RFM	25	5	95	0	-	-	-	-
Field-Buss, M.G.	OB	53	11	187	1	187.00	1-73	-	-
Fitton, J.D.	OB	237.1	39	829	12	69.08	2-42	-	-
Fleming, D.W.	RFM	25	5	88	2	44.00	2-88	-	-
Fleming, M.V.	RM	214	46	573	16	35.81	3-28	-	-
Fletcher, S.D.	RMF	238.1	45	765	20	38.25	6-70	1	-
Folley, I.	SLA	127	14	469	3	156.33	1-60	-	-
Fordham, A.	RM	13	0	78	1	78.00	1-42	-	-
Foster, D.J.	RFM	223.5	35	814	25	32.56	6-84	1	-
Foster, N.A.	RFM	757.2	185	2138	102	20.96	8-99	7	1
Fowler, G.	RM	7	0	41	1	41.00	1-41	-	-
Fraser, A.G.J.	RFM	19	5	44	0	-	-	-	-
Fraser, A.R.C.	RFM	39.5	12	91	6	15.16	4-24	-	-
French, B.N.	(WK)	14	4	48	1	48.00	1-37	-	-
Frost, M.	RMF	533.2	90	1868	65	28.73	7-99	1	1
Garnham, M.A.	(WK)	4	0	39	0	-	-	-	-
Gatting, M.W.	RM	30.2	5	99	0	-	-	-	-
Gerrans, P.S.	RM	77.3	12	308	5	61.60	2-65	-	-
Gerrard, M.J.	LMF	131.5	21	415	15	27.66	6-40	1	1
Giddins, E.S.H.	RMF	56.2	6	186	2	93.00	1-29	-	-
Gidley, M.I.	OB	107.4	29	323	4	80.75	2-58	-	-
Gilbert, D.R.	RFM	648.5	135	1865	64	29.14	8-55	1	-
Goldsmith, S.C.	RM	187	32	607	18	33.72	3-42	-	-
Gooch, G.A.	RM	63.1	22	215	4	53.75	2-16	-	-
Goram, A.L.	RM	23	6	62	2	31.00	1-16	-	-
Gough, D.	RMF	270	55	945	18	52.50	5-41	1	-
Govan, J.W.	OB	24	5	76	1	76.00	1-47	-	-
Gower, D.I.	OB	0.1	0	4	0	-	-	-	-
Graveney, D.A.	SLA	708.2	153	2160	55	39.27	7-105	2	-

174

	Cat	O	M	R	W	Avge	Best	5 wI	10 wM
Grayson, A.P.	SLA	27	10	56	1	56.00	1-3	-	-
Greenfield, K.	RM	6	0	30	0	-	-	-	-
Greenidge, C.G.	RM	2	0	7	1	7.00	1-7	-	-
Greig, I.A.	RM	165.3	34	426	10	42.60	3-30	-	-
Griffith, F.A.	RM	31	6	125	2	62.50	1-16	-	-
Gupte, C.M.	SLA	24.1	3	120	3	40.00	2-41	-	-
Gurusinha, A.P.	RM	18	5	41	2	20.50	2-16	-	-
Hallett, J.C.	RMF	178.3	31	637	12	53.08	3-154	-	-
Harden, R.J.	SLA	23.5	0	122	3	40.66	2-70	-	-
Harper, R.A.	OB	17	1	77	1	77.00	1-77	-	-
Harrison, G.D.	RFM	26	6	93	1	93.00	1-43	-	-
Hartley, P.J.	RMF	522.3	100	1751	50	35.02	6-151	3	-
Hathurusinghe, U.C.	RM	39.3	10	110	3	36.66	2-18	-	-
Hayhurst, A.N.	RM	205.3	32	780	11	70.90	2-42	-	-
Haynes, G.R.	RM	19.2	2	82	0	-	-	-	-
Headley, D.W.	RFM	329.3	51	1258	29	43.37	5-46	2	-
Hemmings, E.E.	OB	638.3	171	1721	46	37.41	6-46	2	-
Henry, O.	SLA	41	13	85	1	85.00	1-43	-	-
Hepworth, P.N.	OB	119.2	20	463	14	33.07	3-51	-	-
Hick, G.A.	OB	151.4	34	492	10	49.20	5-42	1	-
Hoey, C.J.	LB	25.2	7	85	3	28.33	3-38	-	-
Hooper, A.M.	RM	43	6	187	2	93.50	1-30	-	-
Hooper, C.L.	OB	336.2	71	837	31	27.00	5-94	1	-
Houseman, I.J.	RFM	21	4	52	1	52.00	1-52	-	-
Hughes, D.P.	SLA	85.2	21	245	5	49.00	2-7	-	-
Hughes, J.G.	RM	12	1	43	1	43.00	1-43	-	-
Hughes, M.G.	RF	30.3	7	85	1	85.00	1-85	-	-
Hughes, S.P.	RFM	107.5	25	388	6	64.66	2-44	-	-
Hussain, N.	LB	8.3	0	50	0	-	-	-	-
Hutchinson, I.J.F.	RMF	12	0	29	1	29.00	1-18	-	-
Igglesden, A.P.	RF	471	94	1351	50	27.02	5-36	1	-
Illingworth, R.K.	SLA	551.1	155	1342	38	35.31	5-43	3	-
Ilott, M.C.	LMF	21.4	7	62	3	20.66	2-30	-	-
Irani, R.C.	RM	32.2	5	82	0	-	-	-	-
Jackson, P.W.	SLA	18	11	50	2	25.00	2-50	-	-
James, K.D.	LMF	442.5	99	1354	41	33.02	4-32	-	-
Jarvis, P.W.	RFM	95	26	235	12	19.58	4-28	-	-
Jayasuriya, S.T.	SLA	12.5	2	53	0	-	-	-	-
Jean-Jacques, M.	RMF	141.3	26	496	12	41.33	4-54	-	-
Jenkins, R.H.J.	RM	150	20	514	7	73.42	2-46	-	-
Johnson, P.	RM	12.2	1	62	2	31.00	1-26	-	-
Johnson, S.W.	RMF	131.1	17	608	3	202.66	1-34	-	-
Jones, A.N.	RFM	527.2	74	1918	57	33.64	5-46	2	-
Kapil Dev	RFM	13	0	65	2	32.50	2-42	-	-
Keech, M.	RM	14	6	36	0	-	-	-	-
Kelleher, D.J.M.	RMF	26	5	47	3	15.66	3-25	-	-
Kellett, S.A.	-	4	0	7	0	-	-	-	-
Kendrick, N.M.	SLA	105	26	262	12	21.83	5-54	2	1
Knight, N.V.	-	5	0	32	0	-	-	-	-
Lamb, A.J.	RM	3.4	0	29	2	14.50	2-29	-	-
Lambert, C.B.	RSM	11.4	3	37	3	12.33	2-33	-	-
Lampitt, S.R.	RMF	503.4	84	1643	56	29.33	5-70	4	-
Lara, B.C.	LB	11	1	59	0	-	-	-	-
Larkins, W.	RM	6	4	2	0	-	-	-	-
Lathwell, M.N.	RM	28	9	99	1	99.00	1-29	-	-
Lawrence, D.V.	RF	515.1	79	1790	74	24.18	6-67	4	1

175

	Cat	O	M	R	W	Avge	Best	5 wI	10 wM
Leatherdale, D.A.	RM	2	0	6	0	-	-	-	-
Lefebvre, R.P.	RMF	365	74	1075	18	59.72	3-51	-	-
Lenham, N.J.	RMF	29	5	79	2	39.50	2-5	-	-
Lewis, C.C.	RFM	471.4	127	1213	48	25.27	6-111	3	-
Lewis, D.A.	RM	16	1	63	1	63.00	1-40	-	-
Llong, N.J.	OB	5	1	28	0	-	-	-	-
Lloyd, G.D.	RM	10	0	57	1	57.00	1-57	-	-
Lloyd, T.A.	RM/OB	16	13	26	0	-	-	-	-
Lloyds, J.W.	OB	541.2	122	1650	34	48.52	6-94	1	-
Lovell, G.B.T.	RM	32	3	141	1	141.00	1-13	-	-
Lowrey, M.J.	OB	136	17	496	9	55.11	3-31	-	-
Lynch, M.A.	OB	9	1	29	0	-	-	-	-
Lyons, R.J.	LB	4	0	26	1	26.00	1-26	-	-
McCague, M.J.	RFM	153.3	23	481	16	30.06	6-88	1	-
McCray, E.	RM	42	16	87	0	-	-	-	-
MacDonald, R.H.	RMF	157	49	457	10	45.70	3-66	-	-
MacLeay, K H.	RM	284.3	54	872	25	34.88	3-40	-	-
Madan Lal	RFM	9	0	47	1	47.00	1-25	-	-
Madurasinghe,A.W.R.	OB	82	15	252	5	50.40	1-13	-	-
Maguire, J.N.	RFM	786	168	2437	77	31.64	7-57	4	-
Malcolm, D.E.	RF	388.5	54	1451	42	34.54	5-45	1	-
Mallender, N.A.	RFM	349.5	76	969	42	23.07	6-43	3	-
Maninder Singh	SLA	44	5	208	4	52.00	2-86	-	-
Marsh, S.A.	(WK)	5	0	28	0	-	-	-	-
Marshall, M.D.	RF	282.1	57	782	30	26.06	4-33	-	-
Martin, P.J.	RFM	454.4	107	1323	36	36.75	4-30	-	-
Maru, R.J.	SLA	625.1	178	1641	40	41.02	5-128	1	-
Maynard, M.P.	RM	4.5	0	34	0	-	-	-	-
Medlycott, K.T.	SLA	510.4	115	1703	49	34.75	6-98	2	1
Merrick, T.A.	RFM	539	101	1787	61	29.29	7-99	1	-
Metcalfe, A.A.	OB	3	0	23	0	-	-	-	-
Middleton, T.C.	SLA	12	2	77	3	25.66	2-41	-	-
Milburn, E.T.	RM	7	1	29	0	-	-	-	-
Millns, D.J.	RMF	550.1	95	1957	63	31.06	9-37	3	1
Moles, A.J.	RM	33	13	65	1	65.00	1-14	-	-
Moody, T.M.	RM	26.4	11	47	1	47.00	1-19	-	-
Morris, J.E.	RM	2	0	30	0	-	-	-	-
Morris, M.J.	-	3	1	15	0	-	-	-	-
Morris, R.E.	RM	24	3	129	2	64.50	2-82	-	-
Morrison, D.K.	RFM	17	2	113	2	56.50	2-82	-	-
Mortensen, O.H.	RFM	559.1	143	1384	58	23.86	6-101	2	-
Moxon, M.D.	RM	11	2	27	2	13.50	1-10	-	-
Mullally, A.D.	LFM	37.4	10	99	1	99.00	1-35	-	-
Munton, T.A.	RMF	693.1	184	1863	73	25.52	8-89	5	2
Muralitharan, M.	OB	70.1	8	209	0	-	-	-	-
Murphy, A.J.	RMF	546.4	118	1667	35	47.62	5-63	1	-
Neale, P.A.	RM	17.5	1	86	1	86.00	1-81	-	-
Nelson, A.N.	RFM	27	6	79	4	19.75	4-30	-	-
Newport, P.J.	RFM	712.4	138	2140	66	32.42	4-27	-	-
Nicholas, M.C.J.	RM	67.5	6	288	4	72.00	3-25	-	-
North, J.A.	RM	156.3	26	597	20	29.85	4-47	-	-
O'Donnell, S.P.	RFM	13	6	47	1	47.00	1-47	-	-
O'Gorman, T.J.G.	OB	15	0	59	1	59.00	1-17	-	-
Oppenheimer, J.M.E.	RM	107	19	385	8	48.12	2-51	-	-
Ostler, D.P.	RM	2	1	7	0	-	-	-	-

176

	Cat	O	M	R	W	Avge	Best	5 wI	10 wM
Parker, P.W.G.	RM	2	0	10	0	-	-	-	-
Parsons, G.J.	RMF	40	10	116	3	38.66	2-44	-	-
Patel, M.M.	SLA	183.2	43	458	13	35.23	3-33	-	-
Patterson, B.P.	RF	287.4	68	912	32	28.50	5-81	2	-
Pearson, R.M.	OB	332	59	1098	15	73.20	4-84	-	-
Penberthy, A.L.	RM	174.2	29	555	15	37.00	3-37	-	-
Penn, C.	RFM	429.4	82	1323	52	25.44	5-43	3	-
Pfaff, D.B.	RM	2	0	6	0	-	-	-	-
Pick, R.A.	RMF	650.4	117	2080	67	31.04	5-17	3	-
Pickles, C.S.	RM	138	19	468	6	78.00	2-8	-	-
Pierson, A.R.K.	OB	73	11	279	4	69.75	3-45	-	-
Pigott, A.C.S.	RFM	444.2	98	1402	36	38.94	5-37	1	-
Pollard, P.R.	RM	23.5	8	75	1	75.00	1-46	-	-
Potter, L.	SLA	457.2	105	1338	28	47.78	4-116	-	-
Prichard, P.J.	-	13.3	0	158	1	158.00	1-28	-	-
Pringle, D.R.	RMF	533.5	146	1308	47	27.82	5-70	2	-
Pyman, R.A.	RM	65	15	216	4	54.00	2-74	-	-
Radford, N.V.	RFM	434.1	92	1363	46	29.63	7-43	2	-
Ramanayake,C.P.H.	RMF	166	29	594	12	49.50	3-83	-	-
Ramprakash, M.R.	RM	19	3	88	1	88.00	1-0	-	-
Randall, D.W.	RM	4	0	19	1	19.00	1-19	-	-
Ratcliffe, J.D.	RM	3	1	14	0	-	-	-	-
Ratnayake, R.J.	RFM	137.3	15	447	17	26.29	6-97	2	-
Reeve, D.A.	RMF	402.1	117	957	45	21.26	6-73	1	-
Rhodes, S.J.	(WK)	1	0	30	0	-	-	-	-
Richards, I.V.A.	OB	47	9	161	2	80.50	1-32	-	-
Richardson, R.B.	RM	10	2	42	0	-	-	-	-
Roberts, A.R.	LB	331.5	72	1032	29	35.58	6-72	1	-
Robinson, J.D.	RM	28	3	110	2	55.00	1-18	-	-
Robinson, M.A.	RFM	416.1	85	1241	25	49.64	3-43	-	-
Robinson, P.E.	LM	10	1	49	0	-	-	-	-
Robinson, R.T.	RM	8	0	39	1	39.00	1-30	-	-
Robson, A.G.	RFM	39	14	103	1	103.00	1-72	-	-
Roebuck, P.M.	RM/LB	130	33	315	9	35.00	3-10	-	-
Rose, G.D.	RM	323	53	1075	25	43.00	4-77	-	-
Roseberry, M.A.	RM	14	1	63	0	-	-	-	-
Russell, A.B.	RM	5	2	10	0	-	-	-	-
Russell, M.J.	RSM	8	2	31	4	7.75	4-31	-	-
Russell, R.C.	(WK)	1.2	0	14	1	14.00	1-4	-	-
Salim Malik	RSM	118.2	10	473	15	31.53	3-26	-	-
Salisbury, I.D.K.	LB	638.2	148	2001	48	41.68	5-40	1	-
Sargeant, N.F.	(WK)	5	0	88	1	88.00	1-88	-	-
Saxelby, M.	RM	97.2	17	423	4	105.75	3-41	-	-
Scott, R.J.	RM	199	40	614	15	40.93	3-43	-	-
Seymour, A.C.H.	RM	4	0	27	0	-	-	-	-
Sharp, M.A.	RM	15	7	21	1	21.00	1-21	-	-
Shastri, R.J.	SLA	307.5	88	724	31	23.35	5-71	1	-
Shine, K.J.	RFM	343.5	48	1454	38	38.26	5-43	2	-
Sidebottom, A.	RMF	11	4	26	1	26.00	1-26	-	-
Simmons, P.V.	RM	100	22	346	8	43.25	2-34	-	-
Sladdin, R.W.	SLA	368.5	101	965	27	35.74	5-186	1	-
Small, G.C.	RFM	498	126	1347	45	29.93	4-36	-	-
Smith, A.M.	LM	310.2	55	983	29	33.89	4-41	-	-
Smith, B.F.	RM	13	2	91	1	91.00	1-5	-	-
Smith, C.L.	OB	19	3	63	0	-	-	-	-

	Cat	O	M	R	W	Avge	Best	5 wI	10 wM
Smith, D.M.	RM	2	0	15	0	-	-	-	-
Smith, I.	RM	42.1	8	156	4	39.00	1-7	-	-
Smith, N.M.K.	OB	111	32	321	8	40.12	3-50	-	-
Smith, P.A.	RFM	157.1	31	513	15	34.20	5-28	1	-
Smith, R.A.	LB	18	3	97	3	32.33	2-20	-	-
Smyth, S.G.	LM	1	0	7	0	-	-	-	-
Speak, N.J.	RM/OB	0.1	0	0	1	0.00	1-0	-	-
Stanley, N.A.	RM	10	2	19	0	-	-	-	-
Staple, R.W.	-	8	1	56	0	-	-	-	-
Stemp, R.D.	SLA	172.1	43	425	17	25.00	4-62	-	-
Stephenson, F.D.	RFM	719.1	158	2010	78	25.76	5-27	4	1
Stephenson, J.P.	RM	106.4	19	399	17	23.47	4-30	-	-
Stewart, A.J.	RSM	7	0	34	0	-	-	-	-
Such, P.M.	OB	370.1	101	933	34	27.44	3-7	-	-
Swallow, I.G.	OB	100.1	16	354	8	44.25	3-43	-	-
Sylvester, S.A.	LFM	20	2	98	0	-	-	-	-
Taylor, C.W.	LMF	147	30	480	18	26.66	3-35	-	-
Taylor, J.P.	LFM	295.2	50	920	27	34.07	5-42	1	-
Taylor, N.R.	OB	3	0	26	0	-	-	-	-
Tendulkar, S.R.	RSM	4	0	35	0	-	-	-	-
Tennant, L.	RMF	99	20	393	12	32.75	4-54	-	-
Thomas, J.G.	RF	278.4	39	937	28	33.46	5-62	2	-
Thompson, N.E.	RM	19.3	6	67	0	-	-	-	-
Thorpe, G.P.	RM	64	10	242	4	60.50	2-48	-	-
Threlfall, P.W.	RMF	4	1	10	2	5.00	2-10	-	-
Tolley, C.M.	LMF	161	39	413	18	22.94	4-69	-	-
Topley, T.D.	RMF	498.3	86	1767	55	32.12	5-58	3	-
Tremlett, T.M.	RMF	10	3	39	1	39.00	1-39	-	-
Trump, H.R.J.	OB	637.2	111	2113	51	41.43	6-48	4	-
Tufnell, P.C.R.	SLA	903.4	254	2219	88	25.21	7-116	7	1
Turner, G.J.	OB	169	36	564	9	62.66	3-32	-	-
Turner, I.J.	SLA	238.5	65	637	14	45.50	4-28	-	-
Twose, R.G.	RM	9	0	27	1	27.00	1-27	-	-
Udal, S.D.	OB	22	3	117	2	58.50	2-117	-	-
Van Troost, A.P.	RMF	86.4	12	267	6	44.50	2-25	-	-
Viljoen, J.N.	RSM	22	2	99	1	99.00	1-34	-	-
Walker, A.	RFM	103	20	296	6	49.33	3-84	-	-
Waller, R.B.	RMF	85.2	16	363	7	51.85	3-31	-	-
Walsh, C.A.	RF	324.4	75	915	29	31.55	4-39	-	-
Waqar Younis	RF	582	112	1656	113	14.65	7-87	13	3
Ward, D.M.	OB	7.5	0	66	2	33.00	2-66	-	-
Ward, M.J.P.	OB	2	0	6	0	-	-	-	-
Ward, T.R.	OB	17	4	40	1	40.00	1-20	-	-
Warner, A.E.	RFM	446.4	101	1215	37	32.83	4-42	-	-
Wasim Akram	LFM	429.3	99	1251	56	22.33	6-66	7	1
Wassan, A.S.	RFM	49	4	220	4	55.00	3-114	-	-
Watkin, S.L.	RMF	728.5	155	2175	74	29.39	6-55	4	-
Watkinson, M.	RMF	629.2	115	2173	53	41.00	4-45	-	-
Weekes, P.N.	OB	56.4	12	188	7	26.85	3-57	-	-
Wells, A.P.	RM	8	1	21	1	21.00	1-21	-	-
Wells, C.M.	RM	230.4	62	644	18	35.77	7-42	1	-
Wells, V.J.	RM	22.4	8	45	4	11.25	3-21	-	-
Weston, M.J.	RM	12	2	52	1	52.00	1-27	-	-
Whitaker, J.J.	OB	1	0	14	0	-	-	-	-
White, G.W.	LB	6	1	30	1	30.00	1-30	-	-

	Cat	O	M	R	W	Avge	Best	5 wI	10 wM
Wijegunawardene, K.I.W.	RMF	124.3	14	537	15	35.80	4-97	-	-
Wilkinson, C.W.	RM	315	64	1009	23	43.86	4-59	-	-
Willey, P.	OB	157.4	36	441	5	88.20	2-15	-	-
Williams, N.F.	RFM	524.5	99	1668	47	35.48	5-89	1	-
Williams, R.C.	RM	26	4	81	1	81.00	1-81	-	-
Williams, R.G.	OB	91.3	19	259	4	64.75	2-29	-	-
Wood, B.S.	RMF	187.5	34	665	12	55.41	2-24	-	-
Wood, J.R.	RM	6	0	17	0	-	-	-	-
Wren, T.N.	LM	19.3	3	48	4	12.00	3-14	-	-
Wright, A.J.	RM	0.3	0	4	0	-	-	-	-
Yates, G.	OB	591	117	1914	31	61.74	3-39	-	-

YOUNG CRICKETER OF THE YEAR

The Cricket Writers' Club (founded in 1946) makes an annual award to the best England-qualified cricketer who was under 23 on 1st April. In 1986 their ballot resulted in a dead heat. Only five of their selections have ended their first-class careers without playing Test cricket.

1950	R.Tattersall	1972	D.R.Owen-Thomas
1951	P.B.H.May	1973	M.Hendrick
1952	F.S.Trueman	1974	P.H.Edmonds
1953	M.C.Cowdrey	1975	A.Kennedy
1954	P.J.Loader	1976	G.Miller
1955	K.F.Barrington	1977	I.T.Botham
1956	B.Taylor	1978	D.I.Gower
1957	M.J.Stewart	1979	P.W.G.Parker
1958	A.C.D.Ingleby-Mackenzie	1980	G.R.Dilley
1959	G.Pullar	1981	M.W.Gatting
1960	D.A.Allen	1982	N.G.Cowans
1961	P.H.Parfitt	1983	N.A.Foster
1962	P.J.Sharpe	1984	R.J.Bailey
1963	G.Boycott	1985	D.V.Lawrence
1964	J.M.Brearley	1986 {	A.A.Metcalfe
1965	A.P.E.Knott		J.J.Whitaker
1966	D.L.Underwood	1987	R.J.Blakey
1967	A.W.Greig	1988	M.P.Maynard
1968	R.M.H.Cottam	1989	N.Hussain
1969	A.Ward	1990	M.A.Atherton
1970	C.M.Old	1991	M.R.Ramprakash
1971	J.Whitehouse		

179

LEADING CURRENT PLAYERS

The leading career records of players currently registered for first-class county cricket. All figures are to the end of the 1991 English season.

BATTING
(Qualification: 100 innings)

	Runs	Avge
G.A.Hick	17184	59.46
M.E.Waugh	8210	55.10
I.V.A.Richards	34255	50.00
M.W.Gatting	26512	49.18
A.J.Lamb	26472	47.86
T.M.Moody	7822	47.69
G.A.Gooch	33897	47.40
D.M.Jones	9363	47.28
D.L.Haynes	19147	46.47
R.A.Smith	12993	45.27
N.Hussain	4265	44.89
M.A.Atherton	6826	44.32
R.T.Robinson	18662	41.93
A.J.Moles	9364	41.43
N.H.Fairbrother	11465	41.24
M.P.Maynard	9250	41.11
C.L.Hooper	5136	41.08
M.R.Benson	14553	40.99
R.J.Bailey	12071	40.78
G.P.Thorpe	3529	40.56
D.M.Ward	5551	40.51
T.S.Curtis	13482	40.48
D.J.Bicknell	5819	40.13
M.D.Moxon	13849	39.91
D.I.Gower	23978	39.69
M.R.Ramprakash	4759	39.65
J.J.Whitaker	11173	39.48
A.Fordham	4917	39.33
C.J.Tavaré	23121	39.32
N.R.Taylor	14114	39.09
B.C.Broad	19107	38.60
D.W.Randall	27294	38.44
J.E.Morris	11448	38.16
A.J.Stewart	10824	38.11

BOWLING
(Qualification: 100 wickets)

	Wkts	Avge
M.D.Marshall	1475	18.41
Waqar Younis	302	20.09
I.R.Bishop	261	21.23
C.E.L.Ambrose	354	21.87
O.H.Mortensen	388	22.88
A.A.Donald	450	23.09
F.D.Stephenson	471	23.39
C.A.Walsh	847	23.68
Wasim Akram	360	23.75
N.A.Foster	869	23.78
T.M.Tremlett	450	23.99
A.R.C.Fraser	332	24.40
N.G.Cowans	620	24.56
W.K.M.Benjamin	289	25.01
P.J.W.Allott	652	25.55
K.M.Curran	359	25.66
N.V.Radford	840	25.95
J.E.Emburey	1285	26.09
T.A.Munton	337	26.14
D.R.Pringle	673	26.22
T.D.Topley	327	26.58
I.T.Botham	1128	26.70
G.R.Dilley	648	26.75
P.A.J.DeFreitas	497	26.92
D.A.Reeve	352	27.09
M.P.Bicknell	312	27.16
P-J.Bakker	182	27.28
K.E.Cooper	705	27.33
C.J.McDermott	421	27.34
P.W.Jarvis	417	27.35
J.N.Maguire	463	27.75
N.A.Mallender	738	27.75
A.P.Igglesden	282	27.87
S.J.Base	297	27.94

WICKET-KEEPING

	Total	Ct	St
B.N.French	822	731	91
R.J.Parks	687	617	70
R.C.Russell	585	505	80
S.J.Rhodes	496	444	52
C.P.Metson	363	338	25
D.Ripley	355	305	50
M.A.Garnham	348	320	28
S.A.Marsh	347	324	23
P.Whitticase	296	284	12

FIELDING

	Ct
G.A.Gooch	456
I.V.A.Richards	429
J.E.Emburey	382
C.J.Tavaré	381
M.W.Gatting	360
C.W.J.Athey	350
D.W.Randall	344
I.T.Botham	336
A.J.Lamb	305

FIRST-CLASS CAREER RECORDS

Compiled by Paul Cartwright in association with Philip Bailey

The following career records are for all players who appeared in first-class cricket during the 1991 season, and are complete to the end of that season. Some players who did not appear in 1991 but may do so in 1992, are also included.

BATTING AND FIELDING

'1000' denotes instances of scoring 1000 runs in a season. Where these have been achieved outside the UK, they are shown after a plus sign.

	M	I	NO	HS	Runs	Avge	100	1000	Ct/St
Adams, C.J.	46	70	7	134	1905	30.23	4	-	51
Afford, J.A.	97	82	35	22*	166	3.53	-	-	32
Ahangama, F.S.	31	25	9	51	197	12.31	-	-	6
Alikhan, R.I.	99	170	14	138	4482	28.73	8	1	54
Allen, I.B.A.	28	32	15	35	227	13.35	-	-	14
Alleyne, M.W.	102	158	22	256	4017	29.53	5	1	80/2
Allott, P.J.W.	245	262	64	88	3360	16.96	-	-	136
Ambrose, C.E.L.	89	115	26	59	1360	15.28	-	-	20
Andrew, S.J.W.	90	57	27	35	254	8.46	-	-	21
Anthony, H.A.G.	27	31	4	82	386	14.29	-	-	13
Anurasiri, S.D.	44	48	10	74	517	13.60	-	-	17
Aqib Javed	34	28	13	32*	101	6.73	-	-	3
Arscott, J.P.	11	16	2	74	232	16.57	-	-	7/2
Asif Din	196	321	43	158*	8244	29.65	8	2	107
Atapattu, M.S.	29	40	10	110*	1262	42.06	2	-	22
Atherton, M.A.	102	174	20	191	6826	44.32	21	3	84
Athey, C.W.J.	367	607	62	184	19107	35.05	40	9	350/2
Atkins, P.D.	10	18	3	114*	471	31.40	1	-	3
Austin, I.D.	43	56	15	101*	1019	24.85	1	-	7
Ayling, J.R.	38	58	10	88*	1400	29.16	-	-	10
Aymes, A.N.	32	40	12	75*	1043	37.25	-	-	74/5
Azharuddin, M.	121	184	23	226	9038	56.13	30	1+2	104
Babington, A.M.	78	81	33	58	400	8.33	-	-	28
Bailey, K.R.	1	-	-	-	-	-	-	-	1/1
Bailey, R.J.	209	349	53	224*	12071	40.78	27	8	144
Bainbridge, P.	257	424	60	169	12353	33.93	22	8	110
Bakker, P-J.	63	47	18	22	264	9.10	-	-	9
Ball, M.C.J.	20	23	3	28	178	8.90	-	-	17
Baptiste, E.A.E.	173	242	31	136*	5907	27.99	3	-	85
Barnes, S.N.	11	10	3	12*	23	3.28	-	-	3
Barnett, A.A.	3	3	2	11*	22	22.00	-	-	-
Barnett, K.J.	314	504	42	239*	17225	37.28	34	9	211
Bartlett, R.J.	43	69	6	117*	1504	23.87	2	-	30
Barwick, S.R.	155	147	58	30	693	7.78	-	-	31
Base, S.J.	96	119	31	58	1076	12.22	-	-	42
Bastien, S.	34	23	10	36*	131	10.07	-	-	3
Batty, J.D.	26	24	9	51	236	15.73	-	-	11
Beal, D.	3	2	0	1	1	0.50	-	-	1
Bell, R.M.H.	3	2	1	0*	0	0.00	-	-	-
Benjamin, J.E.	25	22	8	41	225	16.07	-	-	7
Benjamin, W.K.M.	102	120	30	101*	2130	23.66	1	-	44
Benson, J.D.R.	32	48	7	133*	1231	30.02	2	-	22
Benson, M.R.	227	384	29	257	14553	40.99	38	10	105
Bent, P.	32	54	2	144	1289	24.78	2	-	4

	M	I	NO	HS	Runs	Avge	100	1000	Ct/St
Berry, D.S.	25	34	4	98	481	16.03	-	-	81/4
Berry, P.J.	7	7	6	31*	76	76.00	-	-	6
Bevins, S.R.	6	6	2	10	34	8.50	-	-	18
Bicknell, D.J.	93	162	17	186	5819	40.13	15	3	39
Bicknell, M.P.	100	107	32	63	1116	14.88	-	-	31
Bishop, I.R.	68	94	30	103*	954	14.90	1	-	13
Blakey, R.J.	135	220	26	221	6110	31.49	7	3	205/18
Boden, D.J.P.	1	-	-	-	-	-	-	-	1
Boiling, J.	9	13	4	16	60	6.66	-	-	8
Boon, T.J.	184	309	36	144	8669	31.75	10	6	91
Booth, P.A.	43	58	11	62	608	12.93	-	-	15
Botham, I.T.	373	573	43	228	18254	34.44	36	4	336
Bowler, P.D.	104	185	15	210	6212	36.54	12	4	69/1
Briers, N.E.	311	505	49	201*	14605	32.02	23	8	132
Broad, B.C.	297	530	35	227*	19107	38.60	42	9	167
Broadhurst, M.	2	1	0	1	1	1.00	-	-	-
Broadley, V.J.P.	1	1	0	6	6	6.00	-	-	-
Brown, A.M.	15	23	3	139*	671	33.55	1	-	12
Brown, D.R.	1	2	1	44*	49	49.00	-	-	-
Brown, G.K.	2	.4	1	103	209	69.66	1	-	2
Brown, K.R.	111	175	29	200*	5283	36.18	9	2	141
Brown, S.J.E.	15	14	6	25*	70	8.75	-	-	5
Bryson, R.E.	21	23	8	31	269	17.93	-	-	6
Bullen, C.K.	30	35	7	65	663	23.67	-	-	30
Bunting, R.A.	38	40	14	73	366	14.07	-	-	5
Burns, N.D.	121	178	38	166	4098	29.27	4	-	237/25
Bush, D.J.	16	15	5	28	115	11.50	-	-	6
Butcher, A.R.	398	679	59	216*	22543	36.35	46	12	183
Butler, K.A.	1	1	1	10*	10	-	-	-	-
Byas, D.	78	129	13	153	3697	31.87	7	1	69
Caddick, A.R.	2	1	0	0	0	0.00	-	-	1
Cairns, C.L.	30	36	6	110	789	26.30	1	-	13
Cann, M.J.	45	71	6	141	1916	29.47	4	-	17
Capel, D.J.	238	360	54	134	9176	29.98	11	3	110
Carr, J.D.	113	184	21	156	5395	33.09	10	2	82
Carrick, P.	421	541	97	131*	9987	22.49	3	-	189
Chapman, C.A.	2	4	0	20	47	11.75	-	-	2
Childs, J.H.	304	273	128	41*	1281	8.83	-	-	98
Clitheroe, R.I.	13	21	2	36	291	15.31	-	-	8/2
Cobb, R.A.	122	195	15	91	4388	24.37	-	1	73
Cohen, M.F.	9	16	0	60	282	17.62	-	-	4
Connor, C.A.	144	116	33	46	762	9.18	-	-	42
Cook, G.	460	793	65	203	23277	31.97	37	12	419/3
Cook, N.G.B.	320	333	88	75	2871	11.71	-	-	188
Cook, S.J.	239	421	49	313*	18696	50.25	55	3+2	132
Cooper, K.E.	271	279	67	46	2139	10.08	-	-	85
Cork, D.G.	20	30	9	44	432	20.57	-	-	9
Cottey, P.A.	63	101	17	156	2253	26.82	3	1	31
Cotton, D.C.	4	6	2	4	4	1.00	-	-	-
Cowan, D.	1	1	1	2*	2	-	-	-	1
Cowans, N.G.	220	228	61	66	1531	9.16	-	-	59
Cowdrey, C.S.	297	451	68	159	12202	31.85	21	4	290
Cowdrey, G.R.	103	162	21	145	4718	33.46	8	2	60
Cox, R.M.F.	6	9	2	104*	261	37.28	1	-	4
Crawley, J.P.	15	23	3	130	952	47.60	1	-	14

	M	I	NO	HS	Runs	Avge	100	1000	Ct/St
Crawley, M.A.	37	50	10	140	1603	40.07	4	-	31
Croft, R.D.B.	47	63	17	91*	1213	26.36	-	-	18
Curran, K.M.	189	290	52	144*	8711	36.60	18	5	108
Curtis, T.S.	226	382	49	248	13482	40.48	23	8	124
Dale, A.	31	50	7	140	1350	31.39	2	-	15
Davies, H.R.	11	13	5	38	116	14.50	-	-	-
Davies, M.	1	1	1	5*	5	-	-	-	1
Davis, R.P.	92	112	26	67	1308	15.20	-	-	83
Davis, W.W.	180	225	61	77	2332	14.21	-	-	57
DeFreitas, P.A.J.	149	206	22	113	3959	21.51	4	-	42
De la Pena, J.M.	2	2	1	1*	1	1.00	-	-	-
Dennis, S.J.	104	100	29	53*	669	9.42	-	-	26
Derrick, J.	95	125	38	78*	1995	22.93	-	-	40
De Silva, P.A.	75	114	13	267	4575	45.29	12	-	53
Dilley, G.R.	232	249	92	81	2278	14.50	-	-	75
Dobson, M.C.	9	14	2	52	206	17.16	-	-	1
Dodemaide, A.I.C.	140	214	52	112	4711	29.08	3	1	71
Doidge, M.J.	1	-	-	-	-	-	-	-	-
D'Oliveira, D.B.	199	312	21	237	8132	27.94	9	4	174
Donald, A.A.	126	150	57	46*	1033	11.10	-	-	38
Donelan, B.T.P.	33	37	14	61	605	26.30	-	-	11
Downton, P.R.	314	405	76	126*	8270	25.13	6	1	690/89
Dujon, P.J.L.	190	282	43	151*	9179	38.40	19	-	422/17
Duthie, P.G.	5	6	1	54*	122	24.40	-	-	5
Ealham, M.A.	8	12	3	45	204	22.66	-	-	3
Ellcock, R.M.	46	47	13	45*	424	12.47	-	-	9
Ellison, R.M.	185	258	63	108	4631	23.74	1	-	72
Emburey, J.E.	423	535	106	133	9762	22.75	4	-	382
Evans, K.P.	70	99	26	100*	1936	26.52	1	-	57
Fairbrother, N.H.	207	325	47	366	11465	41.24	25	8	132
Farbrace, P.	36	47	10	79	643	17.37	-	-	81/12
Feltham, M.A.	101	123	32	101	2089	22.95	1	-	45
Felton, N.A.	160	273	15	173*	7601	29.46	12	3	81
Fenton, N.C.W.	8	10	4	7*	11	1.83	-	-	1
Field-Buss, M.G.	10	11	2	34*	109	12.11	-	-	2
Fitton, J.D.	44	52	13	60	736	18.87	-	-	10
Fleming, D.W.	21	24	8	63*	225	14.06	-	-	13
Fleming, M.V.	47	76	12	116	2101	32.82	3	-	21
Fletcher, I.	1	2	1	56	58	58.00	-	-	-
Fletcher, S.D.	107	91	31	28*	414	6.90	-	-	25
Folley, I.	140	163	50	69	1485	13.14	-	-	60
Fordham, A.	79	139	14	206*	4917	39.33	10	2	51
Foster, D.J.	37	35	14	20	161	7.66	-	-	7
Foster, N.A.	210	243	56	107*	3782	20.22	2	-	103
Fothergill, A.R.	1	1	0	3	3	3.00	-	-	-
Fowler, G.	263	444	25	226	15180	36.22	34	8	136/5
Fraser, A.G.J.	8	7	4	52*	126	42.00	-	-	-
Fraser, A.R.C.	101	114	27	92	1022	11.74	-	-	16
French, B.N.	323	424	84	105*	6461	19.00	1	-	731/91
Frost, M.	54	43	14	12	83	2.86	-	-	5
Garnham, M.A.	147	193	42	123	4387	29.05	4	-	320/28
Gatting, M.W.	408	640	101	258	26512	49.18	66	13+1	360
Gerrans, P.S.	12	12	1	39	137	12.45	-	-	4
Gerrard, M.J.	8	9	5	42	49	12.25	-	-	2
Giddins, E.S.H.	2	1	1	14*	14	-	-	-	-

183

	M	I	NO	HS	Runs	Avge	100	1000	Ct/St
Gidley, M.I.	16	22	5	80	416	24.47	-	-	9
Gilbert, D.R.	117	137	50	117	1298	14.91	1	-	28
Goldsmith, S.C.	65	107	9	127	2373	24.21	1	1	34
Gooch, G.A.	459	777	62	333	33897	47.40	89	15+1	456
Goram, A.L.	2	3	0	32	48	16.00	-	-	3
Gough, D.	29	33	10	72	441	19.17	-	-	4
Govan, J.W.	9	12	1	17	81	7.36	-	-	5
Gower, D.I.	412	666	62	228	23978	39.69	48	11	255/1
Graveney, D.A.	404	501	149	119	6168	17.52	2	-	211
Grayson, A.P.	7	10	5	44*	163	32.60	-	-	3
Green, S.J.	5	8	1	77*	168	24.00	-	-	2
Greenfield, K.	19	32	3	127*	790	27.24	3	-	22
Greenidge, C.G.	522	888	75	273*	37330	45.91	92	15+2	516
Greig, I.A.	253	339	50	291	8301	28.72	8	2	152
Griffith, F.A.	13	21	1	37	219	10.95	-	-	6
Gupte, C.M.	8	9	1	55*	200	25.00	-	-	2
Gurusinha, A.P.	57	87	10	121	3353	43.54	10	-	43
Hagan, D.A.	41	65	4	88	1242	20.36	-	-	18
Haggo, D.J.	5	7	0	45	140	20.00	-	-	6/4
Hall, J.W.	35	63	4	125	1826	30.94	3	1	14
Hallett, J.C.	11	6	1	15	35	7.00	-	-	4
Hancock, T.H.C.	5	9	2	51	93	13.28	-	-	7
Hanley, R.	4	6	0	28	51	8.50	-	-	-
Harden, R.J.	135	212	36	134	6515	37.01	12	3	86
Hardy, J.J.E.	142	236	31	119	6120	29.85	4	1	80
Harper, R.A.	170	220	38	234	5899	32.41	8	-	210
Harrison, G.D.	9	15	1	86	413	29.50	-	-	2
Hartley, P.J.	104	115	32	127*	1894	22.81	1	-	35
Hathurusinghe, U.C.	42	67	5	136	2077	33.50	3	-	23
Hawkes, C.J.	1	2	1	3	5	5.00	-	-	1
Hayhurst, A.N.	83	130	19	172*	3654	32.91	8	1	25
Haynes, D.L.	274	468	56	255*	19147	46.47	45	2+4	152/1
Haynes, G.R.	4	4	1	16	51	17.00	-	-	2
Headley, D.W.	12	15	1	76	202	14.42	-	-	5
Hegg, W.K.	109	155	27	130	3080	24.06	2	-	251/29
Hemmings, E.E.	475	616	141	127*	9165	19.29	1	-	194
Hemp, D.L.	1	2	1	8	12	12.00	-	-	-
Henry, O.	107	166	30	125	3739	27.49	4	-	110
Hepworth, P.N.	36	60	6	115	1499	27.75	2	1	23
Hick, G.A.	202	327	38	405*	17184	59.46	60	7+1	229
Hinks, S.G.	154	267	15	234	7569	30.03	11	3	96
Hodgson, G.D.	50	83	6	126	2481	32.22	3	2	20
Hoey, C.J.	1	1	0	1*	1	-	-	-	-
Holloway, P.C.L.	9	14	5	89*	303	33.66	-	-	17/1
Holmes, G.C.	209	335	51	182	8092	28.49	11	3	85
Hooper, A.M.	14	22	1	125	580	27.61	1	-	1
Hooper, C.L.	95	142	17	196	5136	41.08	10	1	92
Houseman, I.J.	5	2	1	18	18	18.00	-	-	-
Hughes, D.P.	447	587	109	153	10419	21.79	8	2	325
Hughes, J.G.	5	7	0	2	4	0.57	-	-	-
Hughes, M.G.	113	134	32	72*	1665	16.32	-	-	37
Hughes, S.P.	179	193	63	53	1509	11.60	-	-	43
Hunt, A.J.	1	2	0	12	15	7.50	-	-	1
Hussain, N.	78	114	19	197	4265	44.89	9	1	95
Hutchinson, I.J.F.	27	46	4	201*	1435	34.16	5	-	29
Igglesden, A.P.	87	93	32	41	603	9.88	-	-	24

184

	M	I	NO	HS	Runs	Avge	100	1000	Ct/St
Illingworth, R.K.	222	244	64	120*	3800	21.11	3	-	97
Ilott, M.C.	19	17	7	42*	167	16.70	-	-	3
Irani, R.C.	2	1	1	31*	31	-	-	-	-
Jack, S.D.	12	14	5	26	143	15.88	-	-	4
Jackson, P.W.	35	36	12	31	191	7.95	-	-	11
James, K.D.	117	160	34	162	4230	33.57	7	1	37
James, S.P.	53	92	7	151*	2691	31.65	7	1	33
Jarvis, P.W.	128	148	47	59*	1522	15.06	-	-	34
Javed Miandad	379	598	90	311	27468	54.07	78	5+9	328/3
Jayasuriya, S.T.	47	72	14	207*	2605	44.91	6	-	20
Jean-Jacques, M.	51	64	14	73	581	11.62	-	-	11
Jenkins, R.H.J.	15	20	6	20	122	8.71	-	-	3
Jesty, T.E.	490	777	107	248	21916	32.71	35	10	265/1
Johnson, P.	192	317	33	165*	10099	35.55	20	5	131/1
Johnson, S.W.	13	14	7	20	120	17.14	-	-	5
Jones, A.N.	160	138	57	43*	942	11.62	-	-	41
Jones, C.D.	1	2	0	23	27	13.50	-	-	-
Jones, D.M.	133	217	19	248	9363	47.28	25	1+2	96
Jones, G.W.	3	5	1	13*	19	4.75	-	-	-
Kaluwitharana, R.S.	12	19	1	63	433	24.05	-	-	22/3
Kapil Dev	248	353	37	193	10332	32.69	16	-	178
Keech, M.	15	24	3	58*	420	20.00	-	-	4
Kelleher, D.J.M.	34	43	6	53*	565	15.27	-	-	8
Kellett, S.A.	42	71	8	125*	2045	32.46	2	1	28
Kendrick, N.M.	19	20	7	52*	207	15.92	-	-	19
Kersey, G.J.	2	1	1	27*	27	-	-	-	7
Knight, N.V.	7	10	1	101*	441	49.00	1	-	5
Krikken, K.M.	51	77	13	77*	1293	20.20	-	-	123/7
Kuruppu, D.S.B.P.	48	79	7	201*	2671	37.09	5	-	47/10
Lamb, A.J.	389	648	95	294	26472	47.86	72	10	305
Lambert, C.B.	55	94	10	219	3814	45.40	9	-	80
Lampitt, S.R.	70	70	17	93	1100	20.75	-	-	29
Lara, B.C.	39	62	2	182	2546	42.43	6	-	47
Larkins, W.	414	721	48	252	22848	33.94	49	11	244
Lathwell, M.N.	2	3	0	43	63	21.00	-	-	-
Lawrence, D.V.	178	203	35	66	1809	10.76	-	-	44
Leatherdale, D.A.	26	35	2	157	881	26.69	-	-	22
Lefebvre, R.P.	40	40	10	100	645	21.50	1	-	17
Lehmann, D.S.	31	53	1	228	2279	43.82	7	0+1	16
Lenham, N.J.	108	184	19	193	5294	32.08	9	2	44
Lewis, C.C.	70	101	12	189*	2262	25.41	1	-	51
Lewis, D.A.	4	7	0	44	134	19.14	-	-	1
Lewis, J.J.B.	3	3	1	116*	189	94.50	1	-	2
Llong, N.J.	5	7	2	42*	63	12.60	-	-	5
Lloyd, G.D.	40	64	3	117	2089	34.24	3	-	23
Lloyd, T.A.	288	506	43	208*	16256	35.11	29	9	142
Lloyds, J.W.	267	408	64	132*	10679	31.04	10	3	229
Logie, A.L.	152	237	25	171	7478	35.27	13	-	101/1
Longley, J.I.	4	8	0	17	42	5.25	-	-	-
Lord, G.J.	85	137	10	199	3406	26.81	5	1	22
Lovell, G.B.T.	9	13	3	49	250	25.00	-	-	5
Lowrey, M.J.	20	34	4	72	597	19.90	-	-	3
Loye, M.B.	1	1	1	3*	3	-	-	-	1
Lynch, M.A.	277	443	52	172*	13912	35.58	31	7	265
Lyons, R.J.	1	2	0	20	38	19.00	-	-	-
McCague, M.J.	12	15	4	29	170	15.45	-	-	4

	M	I	NO	HS	Runs	Avge	100	1000	Ct/St
McCray, E.	2	2	0	37	68	34.00	-	-	1
McDermott, C.J.	108	134	22	74	1882	16.80	-	-	33
MacDonald, R.H.	7	6	3	20	41	13.66	-	-	-
McEwan, S.M.	55	35	16	54	348	18.31	-	-	17
MacLeay, K.H.	116	152	31	114*	3298	27.25	3	-	72
Madan Lal	232	327	89	223	10204	42.87	22	-	142
Madurasinghe, A.W.R.	36	43	12	65	497	16.03	-	-	20
Maguire, J.N.	134	152	46	65*	1162	10.96	-	-	43
Mahanama, R.S.	54	82	10	114	2361	32.79	2	-	47
Maher, B.J.M.	128	200	35	126	3667	22.22	4	-	280/14
Malcolm, D.E.	108	122	34	51	675	7.67	-	-	20
Mallender, N.A.	281	307	97	88	3408	16.22	-	-	100
Maninder Singh	115	107	46	61*	622	10.19	-	-	41
Manjrekar, S.V.	67	99	16	377	5026	60.55	15	-	36/1
Marsh, S.A.	150	210	41	120	4596	27.19	5	-	324/23
Marshall, M.D.	347	439	57	117	9350	24.47	6	-	120
Martin, P.J.	28	22	11	29	149	13.54	-	-	11
Martindale, D.J.R.	55	85	10	138	1861	24.81	4	-	23
Martyn, D.R.	7	13	3	68*	353	35.30	-	-	3
Maru, R.J.	192	179	43	74	2234	16.42	-	-	201
Maynard, M.P.	155	257	32	243	9250	41.11	19	6	130
Medlycott, K.T.	141	180	38	153	3684	25.94	3	-	90
Mendis, G.D.	343	601	60	209*	20192	37.32	40	12	140/1
Merrick, T.A.	88	111	23	74*	1265	14.37	-	-	30
Metcalfe, A.A.	165	288	17	216*	9683	35.73	23	6	62
Metson, C.P.	143	184	40	96	2564	17.80	-	-	338/25
Middleton, T.C.	54	90	9	127	2742	33.85	6	1	40
Mike, G.W.	5	7	2	56*	116	23.20	-	-	4
Milburn, E.T.	6	8	4	35	86	21.50	-	-	2
Millns, D.J.	44	49	19	44	365	12.16	-	-	18
Moles, A.J.	140	253	27	230*	9364	41.43	21	4	98
Montgomerie, R.R.	9	13	2	88	309	28.09	-	-	9
Moody, T.M.	109	179	15	210	7822	47.69	24	2+1	75
Moores, P.	115	158	20	116	3082	22.33	3	-	238/27
Morris, H.	188	321	35	160*	10539	36.84	24	5	104
Morris, J.E.	195	326	26	191	11448	38.16	26	6	85
Morris, J.G.	3	5	0	28	63	12.60	-	-	3
Morris, M.J.	25	39	5	60	452	13.29	-	-	10
Morris, R.E.	35	52	4	96	1109	23.10	-	-	8
Morrison, D.K.	73	72	25	36	357	7.59	-	-	28
Mortensen, O.H.	130	146	79	74*	592	8.83	-	-	40
Moxon, M.D.	217	373	26	218*	13849	39.91	28	7	176
Mudassar Nazar	218	354	33	241	14078	43.85	42	0+4	140
Mullally, A.D.	38	32	11	34	196	9.33	-	-	9
Munton, T.A.	124	124	48	38	700	9.21	-	-	42
Muralitharan, M.	6	8	2	22*	56	9.33	-	-	2
Murphy, A.J.	67	66	26	38	180	4.50	-	-	12
Neale, P.A.	352	568	93	167	17366	36.56	28	8	134
Nelson, A.N.	4	5	2	23*	56	18.66	-	-	2
Newell, M.	100	175	24	203*	4561	30.20	6	1	90/1
Newport, P.J.	172	187	60	98	3253	25.61	-	-	50
Nicholas, M.C.J.	300	494	71	206*	13949	32.97	29	7	186
Nixon, P.A.	29	34	12	46	552	25.09	-	-	69/4
Noon, W.M.	10	14	2	37	139	11.58	-	-	19/2
North, J.A.	11	13	2	63*	204	18.54	-	-	2
O'Donnell, S.P.	64	103	15	130	3620	41.13	7	-	43

186

	M	I	NO	HS	Runs	Avge	100	1000	Ct/St
O'Gorman, T.J.G.	47	83	8	148	2197	29.29	5	1	34
Oppenheimer, J.M.E.	10	7	2	7	7	1.40	-	-	2
Orrell, T.M.	1	2	0	16	21	10.50	-	-	-
Ostler, D.P.	33	59	7	120*	1794	34.50	1	1	29
Parker, G.R.	16	27	2	76*	598	23.92	-	-	16
Parker, P.W.G.	332	566	76	215	17164	35.02	41	8	228
Parks, R.J.	248	274	79	89	3775	19.35	-	-	617/70
Parsons, G.J.	246	327	75	76	4787	18.99	-	-	72
Patel, M.M.	15	20	7	43	183	14.07	-	-	5
Patterson, B.M.W.	4	6	0	108	373	62.16	2	-	8
Patterson, B.P.	154	154	57	29	596	6.14	-	-	31
Patterson, T.J.T.	3	4	1	84	183	61.00	-	-	2
Pearson, R.M.	10	12	1	21	70	6.36	-	-	2
Penberthy, A.L.	28	40	6	101*	696	20.47	1	-	18
Penn, C.	116	136	34	115	1959	19.20	1	-	51
Pfaff, D.B.	8	7	2	50	231	46.20	-	-	4
Philip, I.L.	6	9	1	145	467	58.37	3	-	5
Phillips, W.N.	30	52	6	134	1856	40.34	3	-	9
Pick, R.A.	126	119	34	63	1272	14.96	-	-	31
Pickles, C.S.	52	67	20	66	1205	25.63	-	-	22
Pierson, A.R.K.	57	64	29	42*	427	12.20	-	-	17
Pigott, A.C.S.	217	263	56	104*	4261	20.58	1	-	110
Piper, K.J.	44	59	6	111	1018	19.20	1	-	114/5
Pollard, P.R.	62	110	4	153	3156	29.77	6	2	55
Pooley, J.C.	14	24	0	88	442	18.41	-	-	9
Potter, L.	188	301	36	165*	7789	29.39	7	3	168
Prichard, P.J.	171	268	34	245	8125	34.72	12	4	107
Pringle, D.R.	260	360	68	128	8061	27.60	8	-	136
Pringle, N.J.	27	48	6	79	707	16.83	-	-	15
Pyman, R.A.	23	31	6	49	340	13.60	-	-	7
Radford, N.V.	235	234	55	76*	2879	16.08	-	-	117
Ramanayake, C.P.H.	51	62	16	69	961	20.89	-	-	14
Ramprakash, M.R.	88	146	26	158	4759	39.65	9	3	34
Ramshaw, D.J.	6	10	0	44	106	10.60	-	-	8
Randall, D.W.	464	788	78	237	27294	38.44	51	13	344
Ratcliffe, J.D.	46	86	8	127*	2335	29.93	1	-	29
Ratnayake, R.J.	48	65	13	68*	893	17.17	-	-	14
Rea, M.P.	5	10	1	53	192	21.33	-	-	-
Reeve, D.A.	166	212	57	202*	5445	35.12	5	2	111
Remy, C.C.	3	2	1	4*	4	4.00	-	-	1
Rhodes, S.J.	184	235	76	108	5044	31.72	1	-	444/52
Richards, I.V.A.	476	741	56	322	34255	50.00	111	13+3	429/1
Richardson, R.B.	148	246	22	194	9750	43.52	29	1+2	141
Ripley, D.	155	196	47	134*	3349	22.47	4	-	305/50
Roberts, A.R.	18	21	10	48	271	24.63	-	-	9
Roberts, B.	205	333	34	184	9182	30.70	13	3	166/1
Roberts, M.L.	10	10	2	25	100	12.50	-	-	16/4
Robinson, J.D.	22	32	5	79	591	21.88	-	-	4
Robinson, M.A.	82	81	36	19*	89	1.97	-	-	18
Robinson, P.E.	132	217	31	189	6668	35.84	7	3	96
Robinson, R.T.	293	511	66	220*	18662	41.93	42	9	186
Robson, A.G.	2	3	0	3	3	1.00	-	-	-
Roebuck, P.M.	335	552	81	221*	17552	37.26	33	9	162
Romaines, P.W.	173	309	23	186	8120	28.39	13	3	68
Rose, G.D.	100	125	32	106	2796	30.06	2	1	46
Roseberry, M.A.	95	160	20	135	4738	33.84	6	2	69

	M	I	NO	HS	Runs	Avge	100	1000	Ct/St
Russell, A.B.	5	6	0	51	138	23.00	-	-	5
Russell, M.J.	7	9	0	30	101	11.22	-	-	1
Russell, R.C.	224	309	68	128*	6107	25.34	4	-	505/80
Salim Malik	170	261	40	215	10435	47.21	28	1+1	117
Salisbury, I.D.K.	56	58	23	68	565	16.14	-	-	34
Salmond, G.	1	1	0	66	66	66.00	-	-	1
Sandiford, D.C.	9	9	1	83	189	23.62	-	-	11/1
Sargeant, N.F.	27	33	5	49	436	15.57	-	-	56/10
Saxelby, M.	16	27	6	73	520	24.76	-	-	3
Scott, C.W.	63	72	18	78	1263	23.38	-	-	135/9
Scott, R.J.	47	80	5	127	1765	23.53	3	-	26
Seymour, A.C.H.	14	24	4	157	697	34.85	1	-	8
Shahid, N.	34	47	10	125	1405	37.97	1	1	34
Sharp, K.	218	361	38	181	9962	30.84	14	1	107
Sharp, M.A.	1	-	-	-	-	-	-	-	-
Shastri, R.J.	221	318	54	217	11650	44.12	29	2+1	127
Shine, K.J.	25	21	10	26*	145	13.18	-	-	3
Sidebottom, A.	228	263	62	124	4508	22.42	1	-	63
Simmons, P.V.	80	144	6	136	4496	32.57	8	1	78
Sladdin, R.W.	8	9	4	18	68	13.60	-	-	6
Sleep, P.R.	155	253	42	146*	7118	33.73	13	-	89/1
Small, G.C.	255	334	76	70	3852	14.93	-	-	77
Smith, A.M.	14	13	2	22	60	5.45	-	-	-
Smith, B.F.	17	25	6	71	693	36.47	-	-	4
Smith, C.L.	269	466	60	217	18028	44.40	47	10	176
Smith, D.M.	278	443	85	189*	13061	36.48	25	6	171
Smith, I.	63	83	13	116	1723	24.61	3	-	25
Smith, N.M.K.	27	39	7	161	886	27.68	1	-	7
Smith, P.A	173	282	33	140	6945	27.89	4	2	47
Smith, R.A.	206	352	65	209*	12993	45.27	31	6	134
Smyth, S.G.	1	2	1	14	21	21.00	-	-	-
Snell, R.P.	21	25	5	31*	204	10.20	-	-	5
Speak, N.J.	31	56	4	153	1488	28.61	2	-	17
Speight, M.P.	60	97	10	149	2984	34.29	3	1	42
Stanley, N.A.	19	31	2	132	920	31.72	1	-	9
Stanworth, J.	39	38	11	50*	236	8.74	-	-	56/9
Staple, R.W.	4	8	0	56	147	18.37	-	-	4
Stemp, R.D.	11	10	7	15*	33	11.00	-	-	1
Stephenson, F.D.	118	181	24	165	3998	25.46	4	1	49
Stephenson, J.P.	129	219	24	202*	7161	36.72	12	3	68
Stewart, A.J.	196	323	39	206*	10824	38.11	18	6	243/6
Such, P.M.	117	92	37	27	202	3.67	-	-	44
Swallow, I.G.	88	104	28	114	1550	20.39	1	-	43
Swan, R.G.	12	18	1	77	374	22.00	-	-	8
Sylvester, S.A.	1	1	0	0	0	0.00	-	-	1
Tavaré, C.J.	397	660	72	219	23121	39.32	44	15	381
Taylor, C.W.	9	7	1	21	72	12.00	-	-	2
Taylor, J.P.	20	18	6	11	51	4.25	-	-	7
Taylor, N.R.(H)	2	2	0	0	0	0.00	-	-	1
Taylor, N.R.(K)	243	415	54	204	14114	39.09	37	8	133
Tendulkar, S.R.	38	61	8	159	3129	59.03	7	-	13
Tennant, L.	10	13	5	23*	110	13.75	-	-	1
Terry, V.P.	216	362	36	190	11515	35.32	24	8	243
Thomas, J.G.	192	253	45	110	3419	16.43	2	-	74
Thompson, N.E.	3	6	1	38	79	15.80	-	-	1
Thorpe, G.P.	68	109	22	177	3529	40.56	7	2	39

188

	M	I	NO	HS	Runs	Avge	100	1000	Ct/St
Threlfall, P.W.	3	-	-	-	-	-	-	-	-
Thursfield, M.J.	2	-	-	-	-	-	-	-	-
Thwaites, G.E.	3	5	0	32	68	13.60	-	-	2
Tillekeratne, H.P.	54	75	16	128*	2250	38.13	7	-	74/3
Titchard, S.P.	11	20	1	135	675	35.52	1	-	8
Tolley, C.M.	20	22	7	37	343	22.86	-	-	7
Topley, T.D.	100	113	26	66	1436	16.50	-	-	59
Townsend, G.T.J.	5	9	1	53	142	17.75	-	-	6
Tremlett, T.M.	207	250	66	102*	3864	21.00	1	-	73
Trump, H.R.J.	48	48	11	48	275	7.43	-	-	28
Tufnell, P.C.R.	93	94	34	37	657	10.95	-	-	43
Turner, G.J.	42	67	5	101*	1741	28.08	1	-	26
Turner, I.J.	14	15	6	39*	111	12.33	-	-	5
Turner, R.J.	34	54	9	69*	959	21.31	-	-	36/12
Twose, R.G.	21	36	7	64*	819	28.24	-	-	10
Udal, S.D.	9	7	2	28*	79	15.80	-	-	2
Van Troost, A.P.	4	1	1	0*	0	-	-	-	1
Viljoen, J.N.	1	1	1	1*	1	-	-	-	-
Walker, A.	94	89	45	41*	624	14.18	-	-	37
Waller, R.B.	5	4	3	6*	12	12.00	-	-	1
Walsh, C.A.	225	267	67	63*	2560	12.80	-	-	58
Waqar Younis	67	67	26	51	532	12.97	-	-	17
Ward, D.M.	103	162	25	263	5551	40.51	11	2	97/3
Ward, M.J.P.	1	-	-	-	-	-	-	-	-
Ward, T.R.	72	123	9	235*	4035	35.39	8	2	46
Warke, S.J.S.	10	18	2	144*	815	50.93	2	-	5
Warley, S.N.	2	3	0	11	15	5.00	-	-	3
Warner, A.E.	146	206	38	91	2954	17.58	-	-	36
Wasim Akram	103	134	20	123	2525	22.14	3	-	34
Wassan, A.S.	31	23	5	53	314	17.44	-	-	14
Watkin, S.L.	92	95	28	31	585	8.73	-	-	18
Watkinson, M.	180	267	35	138	5710	24.61	3	-	89
Waugh, M.E.	111	175	26	229*	8210	55.10	28	2+2	129
Weekes, P.N.	9	14	1	86	324	24.92	-	-	8
Wells, A.P.	212	351	59	253*	11016	37.72	21	6	107
Wells, C.M.	270	429	68	203	12070	33.43	20	6	85
Wells, V.J.	14	25	1	58	482	20.08	-	-	11
Weston, M.J.	152	242	20	145*	5294	23.84	3	1	72
Weston, W.P.C.	2	3	0	15	28	9.33	-	-	-
Whitaker, J.J.	203	323	40	200*	11173	39.48	24	8	129
White, C.	12	13	2	38	155	14.09	-	-	6
White, G.W.	1	1	0	42	42	42.00	-	-	-
Whitticase, P.	121	159	36	114*	2901	23.58	1	-	284/12
Wijegunewardene, K.I.W	35	34	13	26	218	10.38	-	-	13
Wilkinson, C.W.	14	13	2	41	138	12.54	-	-	7
Willey, P.	559	918	121	227	24361	30.56	44	10	235
Williams, D.	68	91	9	57	1389	16.93	-	-	135/20
Williams, N.F.	176	207	43	77	3320	20.24	-	-	42
Williams, R.C.	1	2	0	13	13	6.50	-	-	-
Williams, R.C.J.	18	20	6	55*	227	16.21	-	-	45/7
Williams, R.G.	282	444	65	175*	11788	31.10	18	6	99
Wood, B.S.	9	6	1	6	8	1.60	-	-	-
Wood, J.R.	16	22	2	96	641	32.05	-	-	7
Wren, T.N.	6	5	2	16	23	7.66	-	-	2
Wright, A.J.	186	319	23	161	8565	28.93	11	4	129
Yates, G.	25	30	15	106	480	32.00	2	-	10

BOWLING

'100wS' denotes instances of taking 100 or more wickets in a season.

	Runs	Wkts	Avge	Best	5wI	10wM	100wS
Adams, C.J.	115	8	14.37	4-29	-	-	-
Afford, J.A.	8301	245	33.88	6-81	7	1	-
Ahangama, F.S.	2082	109	19.10	7-30	6	2	-
Alikhan, R.I.	274	7	39.14	2-19	-	-	-
Allen, I.B.A.	2380	64	37.18	7-48	2	-	-
Alleyne, M.W.	2003	48	41.72	4-48	-	-	-
Allott, P.J.W.	16665	652	25.55	8-48	30	-	-
Ambrose, C.E.L.	7744	354	21.87	8-45	18	3	-
Andrew, S.J.W.	7500	236	31.77	7-92	5	-	-
Anthony, H.A.G.	2227	77	28.92	5-23	2	-	-
Anurasiri, S.D.	3115	129	24.14	8-53	8	3	-
Aqib Javed	2923	78	37.47	6-91	3	-	-
Arscott, J.P.	252	7	36.00	1-17	-	-	-
Asif Din	4162	70	59.45	5-100	1	-	-
Atapattu, M.S.	159	6	26.50	3-19	-	-	-
Atherton, M.A.	4323	102	42.38	6-78	3	-	-
Athey, C.W.J.	2155	43	50.11	3-3	-	-	-
Austin, I.D.	2397	66	36.31	5-79	1	-	-
Ayling, J.R.	2265	83	27.28	4-47	-	-	-
Azharuddin, M.	533	7	76.14	2-33	-	-	-
Babington, A.M.	6158	177	34.79	5-37	2	-	-
Bailey, R.J.	2037	46	44.28	3-27	-	-	-
Bainbridge, P.	9985	273	36.57	8-53	7	-	-
Bakker, P-J.	4965	182	27.28	7-31	7	-	-
Ball, M.C.J.	1377	42	32.78	5-128	1	-	-
Baptiste, E.A.E.	12672	494	25.65	8-76	21	3	-
Barnes, S.N.	625	16	39.06	4-51	-	-	-
Barnett, A.A.	394	10	39.40	4-119	-	-	-
Barnett, K.J.	5074	133	38.15	6-28	2	-	-
Bartlett, R.J.	145	4	36.25	1-9	-	-	-
Barwick, S.R.	11304	342	33.05	8-42	9	1	-
Base, S.J.	8300	297	27.94	7-60	10	1	-
Bastien, S.	2761	77	35.85	6-75	4	-	-
Batty, J.D.	2354	61	38.59	6-48	2	-	-
Beal, D.	320	3	106.66	1-37	-	-	-
Bell, R.M.H.	123	3	41.00	2-38	-	-	-
Benjamin, J.E.	2020	64	31.56	5-29	4	-	-
Benjamin, W.K.M.	7230	289	25.01	7-54	17	2	-
Benson, J.D.R.	346	3	115.33	1-18	-	-	-
Benson, M.R.	468	4	117.00	2-55	-	-	-
Bent, P.	5	0			-	-	-
Berry, P.J.	401	7	57.28	2-35	-	-	-
Bicknell, D.J.	175	3	58.33	2-62	-	-	-
Bicknell, M.P.	8475	312	27.16	9-45	9	-	-
Bishop, I.R.	5542	261	21.23	6-39	14	1	-
Blakey, R.J.	68	1	68.00	1-68	-	-	-
Boden, D.J.P.	26	4	6.50	4-11	-	-	-
Boiling, J.	707	17	41.58	4-157	-	-	-
Boon, T.J.	350	7	50.00	3-40	-	-	-
Booth, P.A.	2843	66	43.07	5-98	1	-	-
Botham, I.T.	30126	1128	26.70	8-34	59	8	1
Bowler, P.D.	1357	20	67.85	3-41	-	-	-

190

	Runs	Wkts	Avge	Best	5wI	10wM	100wS
Briers, N.E.	988	32	30.87	4-29	-	-	-
Broad, B.C.	1036	16	64.75	2-14	-	-	-
Broadhurst, M.	130	6	21.66	3-61	-	-	-
Broadley, V.J.P.	111	1	111.00	1-92	-	-	-
Brown, D.R.	46	0	-	-	-	-	-
Brown, G.K.	39	1	39.00	1-39	-	-	-
Brown, K.R.	162	5	32.40	2-7	-	-	-
Brown, R.E.	1719	72	23.87	7-68	5	1	-
Brown, S.J.E.	814	25	32.56	3-20	-	-	-
Bryson, R.E.	1719	72	23.87	7-68	5	1	-
Bullen, C.K.	1078	38	28.36	6-119	1	-	-
Bunting, R.A.	3047	80	38.08	5-44	3	-	-
Burns, N.D.	8	0	-	-	-	-	-
Bush, D.J.	1111	15	74.06	3-64	-	-	-
Butcher, A.R.	5433	141	38.53	6-48	1	-	-
Byas, D.	612	10	61.20	3-55	-	-	-
Caddick, A.R.	251	5	50.20	2-40	-	-	-
Cairns, C.L.	2773	89	31.15	7-39	2	1	-
Cann, M.J.	1226	19	64.52	3-30	-	-	-
Capel, D.J.	13136	391	33.59	7-46	11	-	-
Carr, J.D.	2742	59	46.47	6-61	3	-	-
Carrick, P.	30626	1024	29.90	8-33	45	5	-
Childs, J.H.	23273	773	30.10	9-56	42	8	-
Cobb, R.A.	49	0	-	-	-	-	-
Connor, C.A.	11940	373	32.01	7-31	9	1	-
Cook, G.	806	15	53.73	3-47	-	-	-
Cook, N.G.B.	23441	816	28.72	7-63	30	3	-
Cook, S.J.	107	3	35.66	2-25	-	-	-
Cooper, K.E.	19269	705	27.33	8-44	25	1	1
Cork, D.G.	1583	59	26.83	8-53	1	1	-
Cottey, P.A.	122	1	122.00	1-49	-	-	-
Cotton, D.C.	273	4	68.25	1-43	-	-	-
Cowan, D.	133	5	26.60	3-41	-	-	-
Cowans, N.G.	15232	620	24.56	6-31	23	1	-
Cowdrey, C.S.	7962	200	39.81	5-46	2	-	-
Cowdrey, G.R.	536	9	59.55	1-5	-	-	-
Cox, R.M.F.	1	0	-	-	-	-	-
Crawley, J.P.	14	0	-	-	-	-	-
Crawley, M.A.	2035	38	53.55	6-92	1	-	-
Croft, R.D.B.	3796	70	54.22	5-62	1	-	-
Curran, K.M.	9213	359	25.66	7-47	11	4	-
Curtis, T.S.	541	9	60.11	2-17	-	-	-
Dale, A.	903	18	50.16	3-21	-	-	-
Davies, H.R.	737	7	105.28	3-93	-	-	-
Davies, M.	16	0	-	-	-	-	-
Davis, R.P.	8401	206	40.78	6-40	6	1	-
Davis, W.W.	17236	607	28.39	7-52	28	7	-
DeFreitas, P.A.J.	13384	497	26.92	7-21	26	2	-
De la Pena, J.M.	138	3	46.00	2-69	-	-	-
Dennis, S.J.	8426	254	33.17	5-35	7	-	-
Derrick, J.	5213	137	38.05	6-54	2	-	-
De Silva.P.A.	750	11	68.18	2-16	-	-	-
Dilley, G.R.	17338	648	26.75	7-63	34	3	-
Dobson, M.C.	441	8	55.12	2-20	-	-	-
Dodemaide, A.I.C.	12978	393	33.02	6-58	11	-	-
Doidge, M.J.	106	0	-	-	-	-	-

	Runs	Wkts	Avge	Best	5wI	10wM	100wS
D'Oliveira, D.B.	1176	27	43.55	2-17	-	-	-
Donald, A.A.	10393	450	23.09	8-37	24	3	-
Donelan, B.T.P.	2795	68	41.10	6-62	2	1	-
Downton, P.R.	9	1	9.00	1-4	-	-	-
Dujon, P.J.L.	45	1	45.00	1-43	-	-	-
Duthie, P.G.	448	11	40.72	3-99	-	-	-
Ealham, M.A.	592	21	28.19	5-39	2	-	-
Ellcock, R.M.	3395	117	29.01	5-35	1	-	-
Ellison, R.M.	12400	442	28.05	7-33	16	2	-
Emburey, J.E.	33530	1285	26.09	7-27	60	9	1
Evans, K.P.	4682	134	34.94	5-52	2	-	-
Fairbrother, N.H.	423	5	84.60	2-91	-	-	-
Farbrace, P.	64	1	64.00	1-64	-	-	-
Feltham, M.A.	8141	267	30.49	6-53	6	-	-
Felton, N.A.	252	2	126.00	1-48	-	-	-
Fenton, N.C.W.	821	21	39.09	4-64	-	-	-
Field-Buss, M.G.	414	11	37.63	4-33	-	-	-
Fitton, J.D.	3894	69	56.43	6-59	3	-	-
Fleming, D.W.	1934	68	28.44	6-37	2	-	-
Fleming, M.V.	2090	44	47.50	3-28	-	-	-
Fletcher, S.D.	7966	234	34.04	8-58	5	-	-
Folley, I.	9359	287	32.60	7-15	10	1	-
Fordham, A.	127	2	63.50	1-25	-	-	-
Foster, D.J.	3024	74	40.86	6-84	1	-	-
Foster, N.A.	20667	869	23.78	8-99	49	8	2
Fowler, G.	306	9	34.00	2-34	-	-	-
Fraser, A.G.J.	291	9	32.33	3-46	-	-	-
Fraser, A.R.C.	8103	332	24.40	7-77	16	1	-
French, B.N.	70	1	70.00	1-37	-	-	-
Frost, M.	4992	149	33.50	7-99	4	2	-
Garnham, M.A.	39	0	-	-	-	-	-
Gatting, M.W.	4428	154	28.75	5-34	2	-	-
Gerrans, P.S.	1003	17	59.00	3-86	-	-	-
Gerrard, M.J.	415	15	27.66	6-40	1	1	-
Giddins, E.S.H.	186	2	93.00	1-29	-	-	-
Gidley, M.I.	868	14	62.00	3-51	-	-	-
Gilbert, D.R.	10765	339	31.75	8-55	11	1	-
Goldsmith, S.C.	1152	26	44.30	3-42	-	-	-
Gooch, G.A.	7644	219	34.90	7-14	3	-	-
Goram, A.L.	78	2	39.00	1-16	-	-	-
Gough, D.	2155	52	41.44	5-41	1	-	-
Govan, J.W.	690	26	26.53	5-54	1	-	-
Gower, D.I.	227	4	56.75	3-47	-	-	-
Graveney, D.A.	26113	884	29.53	8-85	38	7	-
Grayson, A.P.	326	2	163.00	1-3	-	-	-
Greenfield, K.	49	0	-	-	-	-	-
Greenidge, C.G.	479	18	26.61	5-49	1	-	-
Greig, I.A.	13023	419	31.08	7-43	10	2	-
Griffith, F.A.	644	18	35.77	4-47	-	-	-
Gupte, C.M.	120	3	40.00	2-41	-	-	-
Gurusinha, A.P.	1017	44	23.11	5-54	1	-	-
Hagan, D.A.	31	0	-	-	-	-	-
Hallett, J.C.	875	18	48.61	3-154	-	-	-
Harden, R.J.	921	19	48.47	2-7	-	-	-
Hardy, J.J.E.	26	0	-	-	-	-	-
Harper, R.A.	12874	466	27.62	6-57	19	2	-

	Runs	Wkts	Avge	Best	5wI	10wM	100wS
Harrison, G.D.	474	19	24.94	9-113	2	-	-
Hartley, P.J.	9083	258	35.20	6-57	9	-	-
Hathurusinghe, U.C.	1451	58	25.01	5-44	1	-	-
Hawkes, C.J.	40	0	-	-	-	-	-
Hayhurst, A.N.	3511	77	45.59	4-27	-	-	-
Haynes, D.L.	196	6	32.66	1-2	-	-	-
Haynes, G.R.	82	0	-	-	-	-	-
Headley, D.W.	1258	29	43.37	5-46	2	-	-
Hegg, W.K.	7	0	-	-	-	-	-
Hemmings, E.E.	40859	1386	29.47	10-175	66	14	-
Henry, O.	9305	385	24.16	7-22	19	3	-
Hepworth, P.N.	463	14	33.07	3-51	-	-	-
Hick, G.A.	4848	129	37.58	5-37	4	1	-
Hinks, S.G.	367	8	45.87	2-18	-	-	-
Hoey, C.J.	85	3	28.33	3-38	-	-	-
Holmes, G.C.	3963	88	45.03	5-38	2	-	-
Hooper, A.M.	187	2	93.50	1-30	-	-	-
Hooper, C.L.	4611	146	31.58	5-33	5	-	-
Houseman, I.J.	311	3	103.66	2-26	-	-	-
Hughes, D.P.	19858	655	30.31	7-24	20	2	-
Hughes, J.G.	336	4	84.00	2-57	-	-	-
Hughes, M.G.	11776	393	29.96	8-87	17	3	-
Hughes, S.P.	12915	424	30.45	7-35	9	-	-
Hussain, N.	160	0	-	-	-	-	-
Hutchinson, I.J.F.	29	1	29.00	1-18	-	-	-
Igglesden, A.P.	7862	282	27.87	6-34	11	2	-
Illingworth, R.K.	15116	482	31.36	7-50	19	4	-
Ilott, M.C.	1716	53	32.37	5-34	2	-	-
Irani, R.C.	155	2	77.50	1-12	-	-	-
Jack, S.D.	1072	60	17.86	8-51	3	1	-
Jackson, P.W.	3125	82	38.10	6-55	1	-	-
James, K.D.	6447	205	31.44	6-22	7	-	-
Jarvis, P.W.	11407	417	27.35	7-55	18	3	-
Javed Miandad	6395	191	33.48	7-39	6	-	-
Jayasuriya, S.T.	675	19	35.52	2-6	-	-	-
Jean-Jacques, M.	3956	110	35.96	8-77	2	1	-
Jenkins, R.H.J.	1473	22	66.95	5-100	1	-	-
Jesty, T.E.	16075	585	27.47	7-75	19	-	-
Johnson, P.	480	5	96.00	1-9	-	-	-
Johnson, S.W.	1060	6	176.66	2-86	-	-	-
Jones, A.N.	12398	397	31.22	7-30	12	1	-
Jones, D.M.	848	12	70.66	1-0	-	-	-
Kapil Dev	20754	766	27.09	9-83	37	3	-
Keech, M.	36	0	-	-	-	-	-
Kelleher, D.J.M.	2533	77	32.89	6-109	2	-	-
Kellett, S.A.	7	0	-	-	-	-	-
Kendrick, N.M.	1692	44	38.45	5-54	2	1	-
Knight, N.V.	32	0	-	-	-	-	-
Krikken, K.M.	40	0	-	-	-	-	-
Lamb, A.J.	193	8	24.12	2-29	-	-	-
Lambert, C.B.	101	4	25.25	2-33	-	-	-
Lampitt, S.R.	4416	151	29.24	5-32	8	-	-
Lara, B.C.	76	0	-	-	-	-	-
Larkins, W.	1854	42	44.14	5-59	1	-	-
Lathwell, M.N.	99	1	99.00	1-29	-	-	-
Lawrence, D.V.	15962	497	32.11	7-47	20	1	-

	Runs	Wkts	Avge	Best	5wI	10wM	100wS
Leatherdale, D.A.	26	1	26.00	1-12	-	-	-
Lefebvre, R.P.	2849	69	41.28	6-53	2	-	-
Lehmann, D.S.	48	3	16.00	2-15	-	-	-
Lenham, N.J.	1033	23	44.91	4-85	-	-	-
Lewis, C.C.	5743	204	28.15	6-22	10	2	-
Lewis, D.A.	151	2	75.50	1-33	-	-	-
Llong, N.J.	52	0	-	-	-	-	-
Lloyd, G.D.	141	1	141.00	1-57	-	-	-
Lloyd, T.A.	1384	17	81.41	3-62	-	-	-
Lloyds, J.W.	12943	333	38.86	7-88	13	1	-
Logie, A.L.	128	3	42.66	1-2	-	-	-
Lord, G.J.	61	0	-	-	-	-	-
Lovell, G.B.T.	141	1	141.00	1-13	-	-	-
Lowrey, M.J.	979	19	51.52	3-31	-	-	-
Lynch, M.A.	127	25	51.00	3-6	-	-	-
Lyons, R.J.	26	1	26.00	1-26	-	-	-
McCague, M.J.	933	31	30.09	6-88	2	-	-
McCray, E.	87	0	-	-	-	-	-
McDermott, C.J.	11513	421	27.34	8-44	24	2	-
MacDonald, R.H.	457	10	45.70	3-66	-	-	-
McEwan, S.M.	4069	139	29.27	6-34	3	-	-
MacLeay, K.H.	8708	291	29.92	6-93	6	-	-
Madan Lal	15938	625	25.50	9-31	27	5	-
Madurasinghe, A.W.R.	2765	86	32.15	5-19	3	1	-
Maguire, J.N.	12851	463	27.75	7-46	26	3	-
Mahanama, R.S.	3	0	-	-	-	-	-
Maher, B.J.M.	234	4	58.50	2-69	-	-	-
Malcolm, D.E.	10573	341	31.00	7-74	8	1	-
Mallender, N.A.	20483	738	27.75	7-27	24	3	-
Maninder Singh	11656	460	25.33	8-48	32	10	-
Manjrekar, S.V.	213	3	71.00	1-4	-	-	-
Marsh, S.A.	101	2	50.50	2-20	-	-	-
Marshall, M.D.	27163	1475	18.41	8-71	82	13	2
Martin, P.J.	2324	59	39.38	4-30	-	-	-
Martindale, D.J.R.	8	0	-	-	-	-	-
Martyn, D.R.	44	1	44.00	1-22	-	-	-
Maru, R.J.	15094	462	32.67	8-41	15	1	-
Maynard, M.P.	491	4	122.75	3-21	-	-	-
Medlycott, K.T.	11517	357	32.26	8-52	18	6	-
Mendis, G.D.	158	1	158.00	1-65	-	-	-
Merrick, T.A.	7918	311	25.45	7-45	15	2	-
Metcalfe, A.A.	316	4	79.00	2-18	-	-	-
Middleton, T.C.	180	5	36.00	2-41	-	-	-
Mike, G.W.	370	4	92.50	2-62	-	-	-
Milburn, E.T.	307	5	61.40	3-43	-	-	-
Millns, D.J.	3701	121	30.58	9-37	5	1	-
Moles, A.J.	1582	34	46.52	3-21	-	-	-
Moody, T.M.	1761	51	34.52	7-43	1	1	-
Moores, P.	16	0	-	-	-	-	-
Morris, H.	323	2	161.50	1-6	-	-	-
Morris, J.E.	740	4	185.00	1-13	-	-	-
Morris, M.J.	15	0	-	-	-	-	-
Morris, R.E.	145	2	72.50	2-82	-	-	-
Morrison, D.K.	6990	210	33.28	7-82	8	-	-
Mortensen, O.H.	8878	388	22.88	6-27	15	1	-

	Runs	Wkts	Avge	Best	5wI	10wM	100wS
Moxon, M.D.	1467	28	52.39	3-24	-	-	-
Mudassar Nazar	5221	152	34.34	6-32	2	-	-
Mullally, A.D.	3216	77	41.76	4-59	-	-	-
Munton, T.A.	8810	337	26.14	8-89	12	2	-
Muralitharan, M.	441	10	44.10	5-81	1	-	-
Murphy, A.J.	6310	163	38.71	6-97	5	-	-
Neale, P.A.	369	2	184.50	1-15	-	-	-
Nelson, A.N.	316	14	22.57	5-27	1	-	-
Newell, M.	282	7	40.28	2-38	-	-	-
Newport, P.J.	13987	500	27.97	8-52	23	3	-
Nicholas, M.C.J.	3107	70	44.38	6-37	2	-	-
North, J.A.	833	26	32.03	4-47	-	-	-
O'Donnell, S.P.	4592	123	37.33	6-54	2	-	-
O'Gorman, T.J.G.	59	1	59.00	1-17	-	-	-
Oppenheimer, J.M.E.	928	13	71.38	3-51	-	-	-
Ostler, D.P.	7	0	-	-	-	-	-
Parker, G.R.	80	4	20.00	2-30	-	-	-
Parker, P.W.G.	668	11	60.72	2-21	-	-	-
Parks, R.J.	166	0	-	-	-	-	-
Parsons, G.J.	17481	567	30.83	9-72	16	1	-
Patel, M.M.	1328	34	39.05	6-57	2	1	-
Patterson, B.P.	12906	478	27.00	7-24	24	2	-
Patterson, T.J.T.	96	3	32.00	2-54	-	-	-
Pearson, R.M.	1098	15	73.20	4-84	-	-	-
Penberthy, A.L.	1508	40	37.70	4-91	-	-	-
Penn, C.	9016	278	32.43	7-70	12	-	-
Pfaff, D.B.	6	0	-	-	-	-	-
Phillips, W.N.	65	0	-	-	-	-	-
Pick, R.A.	10512	328	32.04	7-128	11	3	-
Pickles, C.S.	3251	69	47.11	4-92	-	-	-
Pierson, A.R.K.	3753	85	44.15	6-82	3	-	-
Pigott, A.C.S.	17363	573	30.30	7-74	23	1	-
Pollard, P.R.	80	1	80.00	1-46	-	-	-
Pooley, J.C.	11	0	-	-	-	-	-
Potter, L.	5046	126	40.04	4-52	-	-	-
Prichard, P.J.	309	1	309.00	1-28	-	-	-
Pringle, D.R.	17651	673	26.22	7-18	24	3	-
Pringle, N.J.	551	5	110.20	2-35	-	-	-
Pyman, R.A.	1753	32	54.78	5-43	1	-	-
Radford, N.V.	21799	840	25.95	9-70	41	6	2
Ramanayake, C.P.H.	4556	137	33.25	7-21	3	-	-
Ramprakash, M.R.	466	5	93.20	1-0	-	-	-
Randall, D.W.	405	13	31.15	3-15	-	-	-
Ratcliffe, J.D.	96	1	96.00	1-15	-	-	-
Ratnayake, R.J.	4436	164	27.04	6-57	11	-	-
Reeve, D.A.	9538	352	27.09	7-37	6	-	-
Remy, C.C.	257	6	42.83	4-63	-	-	-
Rhodes, S.J.	30	0	-	-	-	-	-
Richards, I.V.A.	9801	219	44.75	5-88	1	-	-
Richardson, R.B.	204	5	40.80	5-40	1	-	-
Ripley, D.	89	2	44.50	2-89	-	-	-
Roberts, A.R.	1396	34	41.05	6-72	1	-	-
Roberts, B.	2948	89	33.12	5-68	1	-	-
Robinson, J.D.	811	15	54.06	2-37	-	-	-
Robinson, M.A.	6434	176	36.55	4-19	-	-	-

	Runs	Wkts	Avge	Best	5wI	10wM	100wS
Robinson, P.E.	238	1	238.00	1-10	-	-	-
Robinson, R.T.	250	3	83.33	1-22	-	-	-
Robson, A.G.	103	1	103.00	1-72	-	-	-
Roebuck, P.M.	3540	72	49.16	6-50	1	-	-
Romaines, P.W.	247	4	61.75	3-42	-	-	-
Rose, G.D.	7090	236	30.04	6-41	4	-	-
Roseberry, M.A.	311	4	77.75	1-1	-	-	-
Russell, A.B.	56	1	56.00	1-23	-	-	-
Russell, M.J.	31	4	7.75	4-31	-	-	-
Russell, R.C.	33	1	33.00	1-4	-	-	-
Salim Malik	1621	53	30.58	5-19	2	-	-
Salisbury, I.D.K.	5264	109	48.29	5-32	3	-	-
Sargeant, N.F.	88	1	88.00	1-88	-	-	-
Saxelby, M.	743	9	82.55	3-41	-	-	-
Scott, C.W.	10	0	-	-	-	-	-
Scott, R.J.	871	20	43.55	3-43	-	-	-
Seymour, A.C.H.	27	0	-	-	-	-	-
Shahid, N.	780	15	52.00	3-91	-	-	-
Sharp, K.	887	12	73.91	2-13	-	-	-
Sharp, M.A.	21	1	21.00	1-21	-	-	-
Shastri, R.J.	15684	466	33.65	9-101	16	3	-
Shine, K.J.	2094	55	38.07	5-43	2	-	-
Sidebottom, A.	14558	596	24.42	8-72	23	3	-
Simmons, P.V.	1321	33	40.03	5-24	1	-	-
Sladdin, R.W.	965	27	35.74	5-186	1	-	-
Sleep, P.R.	12975	328	39.55	8-133	8	-	-
Small, G.C.	20494	720	28.46	7-15	27	2	-
Smith, A.M.	983	29	33.89	4-41	-	-	-
Smith, B.F.	91	1	91.00	1-5	-	-	-
Smith, C.L.	2685	50	53.70	5-69	1	-	-
Smith, D.M.	1556	30	51.86	3-40	-	-	-
Smith, I.	2450	52	47.11	3-48	-	-	-
Smith, N.M.K.	1455	30	48.50	3-50	-	-	-
Smith, P.A.	7336	198	37.05	5-28	3	-	-
Smith, R.A.	617	12	51.41	2-11	-	-	-
Smyth, S.G.	7	0	-	-	-	-	-
Snell, R.P.	1755	79	22.21	6-58	5	-	-
Speak, N.J.	26	2	13.00	1-0	-	-	-
Speight, M.P.	2	1	2.00	1-2	-	-	-
Stanley, N.A.	19	0	-	-	-	-	-
Staple, R.W.	56	0	-	-	-	-	-
Stemp, R.D.	548	18	30.44	4-62	-	-	-
Stephenson, F.D.	11021	471	23.39	8-47	29	7	1
Stephenson, J.P.	1789	47	38.06	4-30	-	-	-
Stewart, A.J.	329	3	109.66	1-7	-	-	-
Such, P.M.	8019	261	30.72	6-123	6	-	-
Swallow, I.G.	5798	106	54.69	7-95	1	-	-
Swan, R.G.	0	0	-	-	-	-	-
Sylvester, S.A.	98	0	-	-	-	-	-
Tavaré, C.J.	687	5	137.40	1-3	-	-	-
Taylor, C.W.	619	24	25.79	5-33	1	-	-
Taylor, J.P.	1407	37	38.02	5-42	1	-	-
Taylor, N.R. (H)	131	4	32.75	3-44	-	-	-
Taylor, N.R. (K)	891	16	55.68	2-20	-	-	-
Tendulkar, S.R.	873	9	97.00	3-60	-	-	-

	Runs	Wkts	Avge	Best	5wI	10wM	100wS
Tennant, L.	503	15	33.53	4-54	-	-	-
Terry, V.P.	58	0	-	-	-	-	-
Thomas, J.G.	16303	525	31.05	7-75	18	1	-
Thompson, N.E.	193	3	64.33	2-67	-	-	-
Thorpe, G.P.	659	13	50.69	2-31	-	-	-
Threlfall, P.W.	130	7	18.57	3-45	-	-	-
Thursfield, M.J.	130	2	65.00	1-24	-	-	-
Tillekeratne, H.P.	142	3	47.33	1-9	-	-	-
Tolley, C.M.	915	24	38.72	4-69	-	-	-
Topley, T.D.	8694	327	26.58	7-75	14	2	-
Tremlett, T.M.	10798	450	23.99	6-53	11	-	-
Trump, H.R.J.	4454	109	40.86	6-48	4	-	-
Tufnell, P.C.R.	9826	306	32.11	7-116	15	1	-
Turner, G.J.	1539	27	57.00	4-94	-	-	-
Turner, I.J.	1109	27	41.07	4-28	-	-	-
Twose, R.G.	499	7	71.28	1-10	-	-	-
Udal, S.D.	1038	24	43.25	4-139	-	-	-
Van Troost, A.P.	267	6	44.50	2-25	-	-	-
Viljoen, J.N.	99	1	99.00	1-34	-	-	-
Walker, A.	6757	218	30.99	6-50	2	-	-
Waller, R.B.	363	7	51.85	3-31	-	-	-
Walsh, C.A.	20059	847	23.68	9-72	44	9	1
Waqar Younis	6069	302	20.09	7-64	26	8	1
Ward, D.M.	97	2	48.50	2-66	-	-	-
Ward, M.J.P.	6	0	-	-	-	-	-
Ward, T.R.	426	6	71.00	2-48	-	-	-
Warner, A.E.	9703	297	32.67	5-27	2	-	-
Wasim Akram	8553	360	23.75	7-42	28	5	-
Wassan, A.S.	3560	114	31.22	7-36	7	3	-
Watkin, S.L.	9193	301	30.54	8-59	15	3	-
Watkinson, M.	13308	394	33.77	7-25	17	-	-
Waugh, M.E.	2953	76	38.85	5-37	1	-	-
Weekes, P.N.	452	11	41.09	3-57	-	-	-
Wells, A.P.	596	9	66.22	3-67	-	-	-
Wells, C.M.	13087	382	34.25	7-42	7	-	-
Wells, V.J.	414	18	23.00	5-43	1	-	-
Weston, M.J.	3050	79	38.60	4-24	-	-	-
Whitaker, J.J.	182	1	182.00	1-41	-	-	-
White, C.	678	15	45.20	5-74	1	-	-
White, G.W.	30	1	30.00	1-30	-	-	-
Whitticase, P.	7	0	-	-	-	-	-
Wijegunewardene, K.I.W.	2588	103	25.12	6-42	4	-	-
Wilkinson, C.W.	1009	23	43.86	4-59	-	-	-
Willey, P.	23400	756	30.95	7-37	26	3	-
Williams, N.F.	13552	457	29.65	7-55	13	1	-
Williams, R.C.	81	1	81.00	1-81	-	-	-
Williams, R.G.	12639	372	33.97	7-73	9	-	-
Wood, B.S.	665	12	55.41	2-24	-	-	-
Wood, J.R.	38	1	38.00	1-5	-	-	-
Wren, T.N.	537	10	53.70	3-14	-	-	-
Wright, A.J.	41	1	41.00	1-16	-	-	-
Yates, G.	2334	39	59.84	4-94	-	-	-

LIMITED-OVERS INTERNATIONALS
CAREER RECORDS

These career records for players currently registered for first-class county cricket are complete to 17 October 1991 and have been compiled by **Philip Bailey**.

BATTING AND FIELDING

	M	I	NO	HS	Runs	Avge	100	50	Ct/St
Allott, P.J.W.	13	6	1	8	15	3.00	–	–	2
Ambrose, C.E.L.	46	25	15	26*	176	17.60	–	–	14
Atherton, M.A.	10	10	1	74	335	37.22	–	3	3
Athey, C.W.J.	31	30	3	142*	848	31.40	2	4	16
Bailey, R.J.	4	4	2	43*	137	68.50	–	–	1
Barnett, K.J.	1	1	0	84	84	84.00	–	1	–
Benjamin, W.K.M.	47	27	3	31	118	4.91	–	–	6
Benson, M.R.	1	1	0	24	24	24.00	–	–	–
Bicknell, M.P.	7	6	2	31*	96	24.00	–	–	2
Bishop, I.R.	29	11	7	33*	73	18.25	–	–	7
Botham, I.T.	99	90	12	72	1738	22.28	–	7	30
Broad, B.C.	34	34	0	106	1361	40.02	1	11	10
Butcher, A.R.	1	1	0	14	14	14.00	–	–	–
Cairns, C.L.	2	2	0	6	11	5.50	–	–	2
Capel, D.J.	23	19	2	50*	327	19.23	–	1	6
Cook, N.G.B.	3	–	–	–	–	–	–	–	2
Cowans, N.G.	23	8	3	4*	13	2.60	–	–	5
Cowdrey, C.S.	3	3	1	46*	51	25.50	–	–	–
Curran, K.M.	11	11	0	73	287	25.09	–	2	1
DeFreitas, P.A.J.	62	44	17	49*	473	17.51	–	–	16
Dilley, G.R.	36	18	8	31*	114	11.40	–	–	4
Ellison, R.M.	14	12	4	24	86	10.75	–	–	4
Emburey, J.E.	58	43	10	34	471	14.27	–	–	19
Fairbrother, N.H.	14	14	3	113	354	32.18	1	2	7
Foster, N.A.	48	25	12	24	150	11.53	–	–	12
Fowler, G.	26	26	2	81*	744	31.00	–	4	4/2
Fraser, A.R.C.	24	10	4	38*	69	11.50	–	–	–
French, B.N.	13	8	3	9*	34	6.80	–	–	13/3
Gatting, M.W.	85	82	17	115*	2049	31.52	1	9	22
Gooch, G.A.	96	94	5	142	3641	40.91	8	20	34
Gower, D.I.	114	111	8	158	3170	30.77	7	12	44
Haynes, D.L.	182	181	23	152*	6780	42.91	16	39	42
Hemmings, E.E.	33	12	6	8*	30	5.00	–	–	5
Hick, G.A.	3	3	1	86*	129	64.50	–	1	–
Hooper, C.L.	56	47	14	113*	1037	31.42	1	3	23
Hussain, N.	2	2	1	15*	17	17.00	–	–	1
Illingworth, R.K.	3	1	1	9*	9	–	–	–	4
Jarvis, P.W.	5	2	1	5*	5	5.00	–	–	–
Jones, D.M.	115	113	21	145	4576	49.73	7	33	40
Lamb, A.J.	110	106	16	118	3710	41.22	4	24	30
Larkins, W.	25	24	0	124	591	24.62	1	–	8
Lawrence, D.V.	1	–	–	–	–	–	–	–	–
Lewis, C.C.	14	8	0	7	28	3.50	–	–	6
Lloyd, T.A.	3	3	0	49	101	33.66	–	–	–
Lynch, M.A.	3	3	0	6	8	2.66	–	–	1
McDermott, C.J.	70	48	11	37	329	8.89	–	–	18

	M	I	NO	HS	Runs	Avge	100	50	Ct/St
MacLeay, K.H.	16	13	2	41	139	12.63	–	–	2
Malcolm, D.E.	4	2	1	4	7	7.00	–	–	–
Marshall, M.D.	121	70	17	66	888	16.75	–	2	12
Moody, T.M.	13	13	2	89	281	25.54	–	2	4
Morris, J.E.	8	8	1	63*	167	23.85	–	1	2
Moxon, M.D.	8	8	0	70	174	21.75	–	1	5
Pringle, D.R.	29	22	9	49*	370	28.46	–	–	8
Radford, N.V.	6	3	2	0*	0	0.00	–	–	2
Ramprakash, M.R.	2	2	2	6*	6	–	–	–	–
Randall, D.W.	49	45	5	88	1067	26.67	–	5	25
Reeve, D.A.	1	–	–	–	–	–	–	–	–
Rhodes, S.J.	3	2	1	8	9	9.00	–	–	3
Richards, I.V.A.	187	167	24	189*	6721	47.00	11	45	101
Robinson, R.T.	26	26	0	83	597	22.96	–	3	6
Russell, R.C.	26	19	6	50	261	20.07	–	1	26/5
Small, G.C.	46	23	9	18*	93	6.64	–	–	6
Smith, D.M.	2	2	1	10*	15	15.00	–	–	–
Smith, R.A.	31	30	3	128	933	34.55	2	5	12
Stewart, A.J.	23	21	3	61	497	27.61	–	2	11
Tavaré, C.J.	29	28	2	83*	720	27.69	–	4	7
Tufnell, P.C.R.	9	5	4	5*	10	10.00	–	–	3
Walsh, C.A.	96	33	14	29*	166	8.73	–	–	13
Waqar Younis	31	10	6	20*	40	10.00	–	–	3
Wasim Akram	99	70	14	86	776	13.85	–	1	19
Waugh, M.E.	23	22	2	67	477	23.85	–	2	11
Wells, C.M.	2	2	0	17	22	11.00	–	–	–
Whitaker, J.J.	2	2	1	44*	48	48.00	–	–	1

BOWLING

	Balls	Runs	Wkts	Avge	Best	4w
Allott, P.J.W.	819	552	15	36.80	3-41	–
Ambrose, C.E.L.	2519	1518	79	19.21	5-17	6
Athey, C.W.J.	6	10	0	–	–	–
Bailey, R.J.	36	25	0	–	–	–
Benjamin, W.K.M.	2491	1763	53	33.26	3-21	–
Bicknell, M.P.	413	347	13	26.69	3-55	–
Bishop, I.R.	1477	974	52	18.73	5-27	5
Botham, I.T.	5335	3556	122	29.14	4-45	2
Broad, B.C.	6	6	0	–	–	–
Cairns, C.L.	114	96	6	16.00	4-55	1
Capel, D.J.	1038	805	17	47.35	3-38	–
Cook, N.G.B.	144	95	5	19.00	2-18	–
Cowans, N.G.	1282	913	23	39.69	3-44	–
Cowdrey, C.S.	52	55	2	27.50	1-3	–
Curran, K.M.	506	398	9	44.22	3-65	–
DeFreitas, P.A.J.	3533	2303	71	32.43	4-35	1
Dilley, G.R.	2043	1291	48	26.89	4-23	3
Ellison, R.M.	696	510	12	42.50	3-42	–
Emburey, J.E.	3281	2226	75	29.68	4-37	2
Foster, N.A.	2627	1836	59	31.11	3-20	–
Fraser, A.R.C.	1336	797	23	34.65	3-22	–
Gatting, M.W.	386	334	10	33.40	3-32	–
Gooch, G.A.	1946	1423	36	39.52	3-19	–
Gower, D.I.	5	14	0	–	–	–

	Balls	Runs	Wkts	Avge	Best	4w
Haynes, D.L.	30	24	0	–	–	–
Hemmings, E.E.	1752	1294	37	34.97	4-52	1
Hooper, C.L.	1788	1408	43	32.74	3-22	–
Illingworth, R.K.	192	115	3	38.33	2-53	–
Jarvis, P.W.	287	187	6	31.16	4-33	1
Jones, D.M.	106	81	3	27.00	2-34	–
Lamb, A.J.	6	3	0	–	–	–
Larkins, W.	15	22	0	–	–	–
Lawrence, D.V.	66	67	4	16.75	4-67	1
Lewis, C.C.	720	552	19	29.05	4-35	1
McDermott, C.J.	3783	2773	103	26.92	5-44	4
MacLeay, K.H.	857	626	15	41.73	6-39	1
Malcolm, D.E.	234	171	6	28.50	2-19	–
Marshall, M.D.	6413	3735	142	26.30	4-23	5
Moody, T.M.	102	81	1	81.00	1-21	–
Pringle, D.R.	1601	1209	25	48.36	3-21	–
Radford, N.V.	348	230	2	115.00	1-32	–
Randall, D.W.	2	2	1	2.00	1-2	–
Reeve, D.A.	66	43	0	–	–	–
Richards, I.V.A.	5644	4228	118	35.83	6-41	3
Small, G.C.	2504	1741	51	34.13	4-31	1
Tavaré, C.J.	12	3	0	–	–	–
Tufnell, P.C.R.	498	347	9	38.55	3-40	–
Walsh, C.A.	5115	3326	108	30.79	5-1	5
Waqar Younis	1410	905	59	15.33	6-26	7
Wasim Akram	4941	3131	133	23.54	5-21	5
Waugh, M.E.	459	337	20	16.85	4-37	1

TEST CAREER RECORDS

(To the end of the 1991 season)

ENGLAND

BATTING AND FIELDING
	Tests	I	NO	HS	Runs	Avge	100	50	Ct/St
Allott, P.J.W.	13	18	3	52*	213	14.20	–	1	4
Atherton, M.A.	18	34	1	151	1166	35.33	3	7	15
Athey, C.W.J.	23	41	1	123	919	22.97	1	4	13
Bailey, R.J.	4	8	0	43	119	14.87	–	–	–
Barnett, K.J.	4	7	0	80	207	29.57	–	2	1
Benson, M.R.	1	2	0	30	51	25.50	–	–	–
Botham, I.T.	99	157	6	208	5176	34.27	14	22	117
Broad, B.C.	25	44	2	162	1661	39.54	6	6	10
Butcher, A.R.	1	2	0	20	34	17.00	–	–	–
Capel, D.J.	15	25	1	98	374	15.58	–	2	6
Childs, J.H.	2	4	4	2*	2	–	–	–	1
Cook, N.G.B.	15	25	4	31	179	8.52	–	–	5
Cowans, N.G.	19	29	7	36	175	7.95	–	–	9
Cowdrey, C.S.	6	8	1	38	101	14.42	–	–	5

	Tests	I	NO	HS	Runs	Avge	100	50	Ct/St
Curtis, T.S.	5	9	0	41	140	15.55	–	–	3
DeFreitas, P.A.J.	26	40	3	55*	513	13.86	–	1	6
Dilley, G.R.	41	58	19	56	521	13.35	–	2	10
Ellison, R.M.	11	16	1	41	202	13.46	–	–	2
Emburey, J.E.	60	89	18	75	1540	21.69	–	8	33
Fairbrother, N.H.	7	9	1	33*	64	8.00	–	–	4
Foster, N.A.	28	43	7	39	410	11.38	–	–	7
Fowler, G.	21	37	0	201	1307	35.32	3	8	10
Fraser, A.R.C.	11	14	1	29	88	6.76	–	–	1
French, B.N.	16	21	4	59	308	18.11	–	1	38/1
Gatting, M.W.	68	117	14	207	3870	37.57	9	18	51
Gooch, G.A.	91	166	6	333	7028	43.92	15	39	94
Gower, D.I.	114	199	16	215	8081	44.15	18	38	73
Greig, I.A.	2	4	0	14	26	6.50	–	–	–
Hemmings, E.E.	16	21	4	95	383	22.52	–	2	5
Hick, G.A.	4	7	0	43	75	10.71	–	–	8
Hussain, N.	3	5	0	35	100	20.00	–	–	1
Igglesden, A.P.	1	1	1	2*	2	–	–	–	1
Illingworth, R.K.	2	4	2	13	31	15.50	–	–	1
Jarvis, P.W.	6	9	2	29*	109	15.57	–	–	–
Lamb, A.J.	74	131	10	139	4264	35.23	13	16	73
Larkins, W.	13	25	1	64	493	20.54	–	3	8
Lawrence, D.V.	4	5	0	34	54	10.80	–	–	–
Lewis, C.C.	7	9	1	65	206	25.75	–	1	9
Lloyd, T.A.	1	1	1	10*	10	–	–	–	–
Malcolm, D.E.	18	24	8	15*	99	6.18	–	–	2
Maynard, M.P.	1	2	0	10	13	6.50	–	–	–
Morris, H.	3	6	0	44	115	19.16	–	–	3
Morris, J.E.	3	5	2	32	71	23.66	–	–	3
Moxon, M.D.	10	17	1	99	455	28.43	–	3	10
Newport, P.J.	3	5	1	40*	110	27.50	–	–	1
Parker, P.W.G.	1	2	0	13	13	6.50	–	–	–
Pigott, A.C.S.	1	2	1	8*	12	12.00	–	–	–
Pringle, D.R.	25	43	3	63	640	16.00	–	1	8
Radford, N.V.	3	4	1	12*	21	7.00	–	–	–
Ramprakash, M.R.	6	10	0	29	210	21.00	–	–	4
Randall, D.W.	47	79	5	174	2470	33.37	7	12	31
Robinson, R.T.	29	49	5	175	1601	36.38	4	6	8
Russell, R.C.	25	40	7	128*	869	26.33	1	3	66/6
Small, G.C.	17	24	7	59	263	15.47	–	1	9
Smith, D.M.	2	4	0	47	80	20.00	–	–	–
Smith, R.A.	28	53	13	148*	2118	52.95	6	15	14
Stephenson, J.P.	1	2	0	25	36	18.00	–	–	–
Stewart, A.J.	14	27	3	113*	766	31.91	1	3	19
Tavaré, C.J.	31	56	2	149	1755	32.50	2	12	20
Terry, V.P.	2	3	0	8	16	5.33	–	–	2
Tufnell, P.C.R.	6	8	4	8	15	3.75	–	–	2
Watkin, S.L.	2	3	0	6	8	2.66	–	–	–
Whitaker, J.J.	1	1	0	11	11	11.00	–	–	1
Willey, P.	26	50	6	102*	1184	26.90	2	5	3
Williams, N.F.	1	1	0	38	38	38.00	–	–	–

BOWLING

	Balls	Runs	Wkts	Avge	Best	5wI	10wM
Allott, P.J.W.	2225	1084	26	41.69	6-61	1	–
Atherton, M.A.	366	282	1	282.00	1-60	–	–
Barnett, K.J.	36	32	0	–	–	–	–
Botham, I.T.	21539	10741	380	28.26	8-34	27	4
Broad, B.C.	6	4	0	–	–	–	–
Butcher, A.R.	12	9	0	–	–	–	–
Capel, D.J.	2000	1064	21	50.66	3-88	–	–
Childs, J.H.	516	183	3	61.00	1-13	–	–
Cook, N.G.B.	4174	1689	52	32.48	6-65	4	1
Cowans, N.G.	3452	2003	51	39.27	6-77	2	–
Cowdrey, C.S.	399	309	4	77.25	2-65	–	–
Curtis, T.S.	18	7	0	–	–	–	–
DeFreitas, P.A.J.	5634	2603	78	33.37	7-70	3	–
Dilley, G.R.	8192	4107	138	29.76	6-38	6	–
Ellison, R.M.	2264	1048	35	29.94	6-77	3	1
Emburey, J.E.	14227	5105	138	36.99	7-78	6	–
Fairbrother, N.H.	12	9	0	–	–	–	–
Foster, N.A.	6081	2797	88	31.78	8-107	5	1
Fowler, G.	18	11	0	–	–	–	–
Fraser, A.R.C.	3106	1255	47	26.70	6-82	4	–
Gatting, M.W.	752	317	4	79.25	1-14	–	–
Gooch, G.A.	1989	800	17	47.05	2-12	–	–
Gower, D.I.	36	20	1	20.00	1-1	–	–
Greig, I.A.	188	114	4	28.50	4-53	–	–
Hemmings, E.E.	4437	1825	43	42.44	6-58	1	–
Hick, G.A.	144	95	2	47.50	2-77	–	–
Igglesden, A.P.	222	146	3	48.66	2-91	–	–
Illingworth, R.K.	340	213	4	53.25	3-110	–	–
Jarvis, P.W.	1347	708	14	50.57	4-107	–	–
Lamb, A.J.	30	23	1	23.00	1-6	–	–
Lawrence, D.V.	914	605	17	35.58	5-106	1	–
Lewis, C.C.	1368	727	20	36.35	6-111	1	–
Malcolm, D.E.	4204	2293	61	37.59	6-77	3	1
Moxon, M.D.	48	30	0	–	–	–	–
Newport, P.J.	669	417	10	41.70	4-87	–	–
Pigott, A.C.S.	102	75	2	37.50	2-75	–	–
Pringle, D.R.	4519	2129	60	35.48	5-95	3	–
Radford, N.V.	678	351	4	87.75	2-131	–	–
Randall, D.W.	16	3	0	–	–	–	–
Robinson, R.T.	6	0	0	–	–	–	–
Small, G.C.	3927	1871	55	34.01	5-48	2	–
Tavaré, C.J.	30	11	0	–	–	–	–
Tufnell, P.C.R.	1452	637	21	30.33	6-25	3	–
Watkin, S.L.	216	153	5	30.60	3-38	–	–
Willey, P.	1091	456	7	65.14	2-73	–	–
Williams, N.F.	246	148	2	74.00	2-148	–	–

AUSTRALIA

BATTING AND FIELDING

	Tests	I	NO	HS	Runs	Avge	100	50	Ct/St
Alderman, T.M.	41	53	22	26*	203	6.54	–	–	27
Boon, D.C.	58	106	10	200	3982	41.47	10	18	54
Border, A.R.	125	215	38	205	9257	52.29	23	52	130
Campbell, G.D.	4	4	0	6	10	2.50	–	–	1
Healy, I.A.	31	44	2	69	859	20.45	–	3	89/2
Hughes, M.G.	32	41	5	72*	534	14.83	–	2	13
Jones, D.M.	44	75	9	216	3045	46.13	9	11	27
McDermott, C.J.	31	43	4	42*	424	10.87	–	–	8
Marsh, G.R.	46	85	6	138	2669	33.78	4	14	36
Matthews, G.R.J.	28	44	8	130	1411	39.19	4	6	14
Moody, T.M.	4	6	0	106	234	39.00	1	1	3
O'Donnell, S.P.	6	10	3	48	206	29.42	–	–	4
Rackemann, C.G.	12	14	4	15*	53	5.30	–	–	2
Reid, B.A.	24	30	13	13	88	5.17	–	–	4
Sleep, P.R.	14	21	1	90	483	24.15	–	3	4
Taylor, M.A.	25	46	3	219	2272	52.83	7	14	31
Taylor, P.L.	11	17	3	87	389	27.78	–	2	10
Veletta, M.R.J.	8	11	0	39	207	18.81	–	–	12
Waugh, M.E.	7	11	2	139*	554	61.55	2	2	11
Waugh, S.R.	44	67	11	177*	2097	37.44	3	13	32
Whitney, M.R.	6	10	4	4	11	1.83	–	–	–

BOWLING

	Balls	Runs	Wkts	Avge	Best	5wI	10wM
Alderman, T.M.	10181	4616	170	27.15	6-47	14	1
Boon, D.C.	12	5	0	–	–	–	–
Border, A.R.	3331	1292	37	34.91	7-46	2	1
Campbell, G.D.	951	503	13	38.69	3-79	–	–
Hughes, M.G.	7224	3643	122	29.86	8-87	5	1
Jones, D.M.	198	64	1	64.00	1-5	–	–
McDermott, C.J.	6770	3659	122	29.99	8-97	6	1
Matthews, G.R.J.	4957	2402	49	49.02	5-103	2	1
Moody, T.M.	234	53	1	53.00	1-23	–	–
O'Donnell, S.P.	940	504	6	84.00	3-37	–	–
Rackemann, C.G.	2719	1137	39	29.15	6-86	3	1
Reid, B.A.	5570	2497	94	26.56	7-51	2	1
Sleep, P.R.	2982	1397	31	45.06	5-72	1	–
Taylor, P.L.	2017	952	26	36.61	6-78	1	–
Waugh, M.E.	426	209	8	26.12	4-80	–	–
Waugh, S.R.	4076	1980	44	45.00	5-69	2	–
Whitney, M.R.	1485	748	18	41.55	7-89	1	–

WEST INDIES

BATTING AND FIELDING

	Tests	I	NO	HS	Runs	Avge	100	50	Ct/St
Allen, I.B.A.	2	2	2	4*	5	–	–	–	1
Ambrose, C.E.L.	33	49	8	53	501	12.21	–	1	6
Arthurton, K.L.T.	5	8	2	37	105	17.50	–	–	2
Baptiste, E.A.E.	10	11	1	87*	233	23.30	–	1	2
Benjamin, W.K.M.	8	10	1	40*	124	13.77	–	–	3
Best, C.A.	8	13	1	164	342	28.50	1	1	8
Bishop, I.R.	11	17	7	30*	156	15.60	–	–	1
Dujon, P.J.L.	81	115	11	139	3322	31.94	5	16	267/5
Greenidge, C.G.	108	185	16	226	7558	44.72	19	34	96
Haynes, D.L.	102	178	21	184	6644	42.31	16	36	59
Hooper, C.L.	32	54	4	134	1409	28.18	3	7	29
Lambert, C.B.	1	2	0	39	53	26.50	–	–	2
Lara, B.C.	1	2	0	44	49	24.50	–	–	1
Logie, A.L.	52	78	9	130	2470	35.79	2	16	57
Marshall, M.D.	81	107	11	92	1810	18.85	–	10	25
Moseley, E.A.	2	4	0	26	35	8.75	–	–	1
Patterson, B.P.	26	35	16	21*	134	7.05	–	–	5
Richards, I.V.A.	121	182	12	291	8540	50.23	24	45	122
Richardson, R.B.	62	107	10	194	4647	47.90	14	18	70
Simmons, P.V.	7	14	0	38	230	16.42	–	–	5
Walsh, C.A.	50	67	22	30*	437	9.71	–	–	6

BOWLING

	Balls	Runs	Wkts	Avge	Best	5wI	10wM
Allen, I.B.A.	282	180	5	36.00	2-69	–	–
Ambrose, C.E.L.	7855	3239	140	23.13	8-45	5	1
Arthurton, K.L.T.	84	38	0	–	–	–	–
Baptiste, E.A.E.	1362	563	16	35.18	3-31	–	–
Benjamin, W.K.M.	1248	564	26	21.69	4-52	–	–
Best, C.A.	30	21	0	–	–	–	–
Bishop, I.R.	2425	1091	53	20.58	6-87	3	–
Greenidge, C.G.	26	4	0	–	–	–	–
Haynes, D.L.	18	8	1	8.00	1-2	–	–
Hooper, C.L.	2914	1247	15	83.13	2-28	–	–
Lambert, C.B.	4	4	1	4.00	1-4	–	–
Logie, A.L.	7	4	0	–	–	–	–
Marshall, M.D.	17584	7876	376	20.94	7-22	22	4
Moseley, E.A.	522	261	6	43.50	2-70	–	–
Patterson, B.P.	4493	2643	91	29.04	5-24	5	–
Richards, I.V.A.	5170	1964	32	61.37	2-17	–	–
Richardson, R.B.	60	14	0	–	–	–	–
Simmons, P.V.	18	7	0	–	–	–	–
Walsh, C.A.	9827	4342	174	24.95	6-62	5	1

NEW ZEALAND

BATTING AND FIELDING

	Tests	I	NO	HS	Runs	Avge	100	50	Ct/St
Bradburn, G.E.	4	7	2	30*	97	19.40	–	–	3
Cairns, C.L.	2	3	0	28	46	15.33	–	–	2
Crowe, M.D.	56	92	9	299	3993	48.10	13	13	56
Franklin, T.J.	21	37	1	101	828	23.00	1	4	8
Greatbatch, M.J.	19	31	5	146*	1105	42.50	2	5	12
Horne, P.A.	4	7	0	27	71	10.14	–	–	3
Jones, A.H.	20	36	5	186	1703	54.93	5	6	15
Morrison, D.K.	22	30	8	27*	126	5.72	–	–	7
Parore, A.C.	1	2	1	20	32	32.00	–	–	4/1
Patel, D.N.	13	26	2	62	443	20.13	–	1	3
Priest, M.W.	1	1	0	26	26	26.00	–	–	–
Pringle, C.	5	8	1	24*	69	9.85	–	–	–
Rutherford, K.R.	28	45	3	107*	763	18.16	1	5	18
Smith, I.D.S.	61	85	17	173	1773	26.07	2	6	164/8
Thomson, S.A.	3	6	2	80*	237	59.25	–	2	3
Watson, W.	9	12	4	11	47	5.87	–	–	2
Wright, J.G.	74	132	6	185	4706	37.34	11	20	35

BOWLING

	Balls	Runs	Wkts	Avge	Best	5wI	10wM
Bradburn, G.E.	372	194	2	97.00	1-32	–	–
Cairns, C.L.	426	271	9	30.11	5-75	1	–
Crowe, M.D.	1341	651	14	46.50	2-25	–	–
Greatbatch, M.J.	6	0	0	–	–	–	–
Jones, A.H.	192	111	1	111.00	1-40	–	–
Morrison, D.K.	4495	2650	70	37.85	5-69	5	–
Patel, D.N.	1231	587	5	117.40	2-90	–	–
Priest, M.W.	72	26	1	26.00	1-26	–	–
Pringle, C.	1110	568	15	37.86	7-52	1	1
Rutherford, K.R.	256	161	1	161.00	1-38	–	–
Smith, I.D.S.	18	5	0	–	–	–	–
Thomson, S.A.	436	235	6	39.16	3-63	–	–
Watson, W.	2388	1000	27	37.03	6-78	1	–
Wright, J.G.	30	5	0	–	–	–	–

INDIA

BATTING AND FIELDING

	Tests	I	NO	HS	Runs	Avge	100	50	Ct/St
Ankola, S.A.	1	1	0	6	6	6.00	–	–	–
Arshad Ayub	13	19	4	57	257	17.13	–	1	2
Azharuddin, M.	41	61	3	199	2976	51.31	10	10	32
Gursharan Singh	1	1	0	18	18	18.00	–	–	2
Hirwani, N.D.	14	18	10	17	45	5.62	–	–	5
Kapil Dev	110	159	13	163	4525	30.99	7	23	54
Kumble, A.	1	1	0	2	2	2.00	–	–	–
Maninder Singh	34	38	12	15	99	3.80	–	–	9
Manjrekar, S.V.	16	25	2	218	1106	48.08	3	5	11
More, K.S.	35	47	11	73	961	26.69	–	5	72/15
Prabhakar, M.	13	21	6	95	652	43.46	–	4	3
Raju, S.L.V.	3	4	1	31	69	23.00	–	–	1
Raman, W.V.	6	10	1	96	303	33.66	–	3	3
Razdan, V.	2	2	1	6	6	6.00	–	–	–
Sharma, G.	5	4	1	10*	11	3.66	–	–	2
Sharma, S.K.	2	3	1	38	56	28.00	–	–	1
Shastri, R.J.	73	110	14	187	3460	36.04	10	12	36
Sidhu, N.S.	17	28	2	116	792	30.46	2	4	2
Srikkanth, K.	39	64	3	123	1927	31.59	2	12	33
Tendulkar, S.R.	11	16	1	119*	588	39.20	1	4	5
Vengsarkar, D.B.	111	176	22	166	6710	43.57	17	33	74
Wassan, A.S.	4	5	1	53	94	23.50	–	1	1

BOWLING

	Balls	Runs	Wkts	Avge	Best	5wI	10wM
Ankola, S.A.	180	128	2	64.00	1-35	–	–
Arshad Ayub	3663	1438	41	35.07	5-50	3	–
Azharuddin, M.	6	8	0	–	–	–	–
Hirwani, N.D.	3872	1799	58	31.01	8-61	3	1
Kapil Dev	23263	11249	376	29.91	9-83	21	2
Kumble, A.	360	170	3	56.66	3-105	–	–
Maninder Singh	7816	3143	81	38.80	7-27	3	2
Manjrekar, S.V.	6	7	0	–	–	–	–
More, K.S.	12	12	0	–	–	–	–
Prabhakar, M.	3051	1651	34	48.55	6-132	2	–
Raju, S.L.V.	599	150	11	13.63	6-12	1	–
Raman, W.V.	258	66	2	33.00	1-7	–	–
Razdan, V.	240	141	5	28.20	5-79	1	–
Sharma, G.	1307	418	10	41.80	4-88	–	–
Sharma, S.K.	414	247	6	41.16	3-37	–	–
Shastri, R.J.	15103	5913	143	41.34	5-75	2	–
Sidhu, N.S.	6	9	0	–	–	–	–
Srikkanth, K.	210	109	0	–	–	–	–
Tendulkar, S.R.	30	25	0	–	–	–	–
Vengsarkar, D.B.	47	36	0	–	–	–	–
Wassan, A.S.	712	504	10	50.40	4-108	–	1

PAKISTAN

BATTING AND FIELDING

	Tests	I	NO	HS	Runs	Avge	100	50	Ct/St
Aamer Malik	13	17	3	117	489	34.92	2	2	15/1
Abdul Qadir	67	77	11	61	1029	15.59	–	3	15
Akram Raza	2	2	0	5	5	2.50	–	–	2
Aqib Javed	5	5	1	7	11	2.75	–	–	1
Ijaz Ahmed	19	25	0	122	743	29.72	2	3	16
Imran Khan	85	123	24	136	3692	37.29	6	17	28
Javed Miandad	109	165	18	280*	8064	54.85	22	39	87/1
Masood Anwar	1	2	0	37	39	19.50	–	–	–
Moin Khan	2	3	0	32	63	21.00	–	–	5/1
Mushtaq Ahmed	3	5	2	5*	14	4.66	–	–	–
Naved Anjum	2	3	0	22	44	14.66	–	–	–
Ramiz Raja	36	58	3	122	1617	29.40	2	10	25
Saeed Anwar	1	2	0	0	0	0.00	–	–	1
Salim Jaffer	12	13	5	10*	34	4.25	–	–	2
Salim Malik	63	90	16	119*	3146	42.51	8	18	46
Salim Yousuf	32	44	5	91*	1055	27.05	–	5	91/13
Shoaib Mohammad	35	53	6	203*	2307	49.08	7	9	18
Tausif Ahmed	33	37	19	35*	297	16.50	–	–	9
Waqar Younis	11	13	2	18	69	6.27	–	–	1
Wasim Akram	37	46	7	123	766	19.64	1	3	12
Zahid Fazal	3	6	0	32	75	12.50	–	–	2

BOWLING

	Balls	Runs	Wkts	Avge	Best	5wI	10wM
Aamer Malik	126	73	1	73.00	1-0	–	–
Abdul Qadir	17126	7742	236	32.80	9-56	15	5
Akram Raza	266	147	2	73.50	2-52	–	–
Aqib Javed	1075	502	10	50.20	3-57	–	–
Ijaz Ahmed	54	18	1	18.00	1-9	–	–
Imran Khan	19404	8242	362	22.76	8-58	23	6
Javed Miandad	1470	682	17	40.11	3-74	–	–
Masood Anwar	161	102	3	34.00	2-59	–	–
Mushtaq Ahmed	516	241	4	60.25	2-56	–	–
Naved Anjum	342	162	4	40.50	2-57	–	–
Salim Jaffer	2381	1084	33	32.84	5-40	1	–
Salim Malik	260	106	5	21.20	1-3	–	–
Shoaib Mohammad	252	113	5	22.60	2-8	–	–
Tausif Ahmed	7604	2888	93	31.05	6-45	3	–
Waqar Younis	2248	1072	55	19.49	7-76	5	2
Wasim Akram	8126	3427	142	24.13	6-62	9	2

SRI LANKA

BATTING AND FIELDING

	Tests	I	NO	HS	Runs	Avge	100	50	Ct/St
Ahangama, F.S.	3	3	1	11	11	5.50	–	–	1
Anurasiri, S.D.	5	7	2	16	30	6.00	–	–	–
Atapattu, M.S.	1	2	0	0	0	0.00	–	–	–
De Silva, E.A.R.	10	16	4	50	185	15.41	–	1	4
De Silva, P.A.	22	40	2	267	1539	40.50	5	4	15
Gurusinha, A.P.	14	24	3	119	874	41.61	3	3	9
Hathurusinghe, U.C.	3	6	0	81	282	47.00	–	3	1
Jayasuriya, S.T.	3	5	1	66	142	35.50	–	1	1
Kuruppu, D.S.B.P.	4	7	1	201*	320	53.33	1	–	1
Labrooy, G.F.	9	14	3	70*	158	14.36	–	1	3
Madurasinghe, A.W.R.	2	4	0	11	19	4.75	–	–	–
Mahanama, R.S.	9	14	0	85	309	22.07	–	1	6
Ramanayake, C.P.H.	8	14	5	34*	100	11.11	–	–	3
Ranatunga, A.	30	53	3	135*	1824	36.48	2	13	15
Ranatunga, D.	2	3	0	45	87	29.00	–	–	–
Ratnayake, R.J.	20	33	5	56	411	14.67	–	2	8
Samarasekera, M.A.R.	3	5	0	57	93	18.60	–	1	3
Senanayake, C.P.	3	5	0	64	97	19.40	–	1	2
Tillekeratne, H.P.	6	11	0	55	190	17.27	–	1	21
Warnaweera, K.P.J.	3	5	1	3	6	1.50	–	–	–
Wickremasinghe, A.G.D.	1	1	0	2	2	2.00	–	–	3
Wijegunawardene, K.I.W.	1	2	1	6*	10	10.00	–	–	–

BOWLING

	Balls	Runs	Wkts	Avge	Best	5wI	10wM
Ahangama, F.S.	801	348	18	19.33	5-52	1	–
Anurasiri, S.D.	805	339	10	33.90	4-71	–	–
De Silva, E.A.R.	2328	1032	8	129.00	2-67	–	–
De Silva, P.A.	294	207	3	69.00	2-65	–	–
Gurusinha, A.P.	454	252	8	31.50	2-25	–	–
Hathurusinghe, U.C.	114	55	1	55.00	1-40	–	–
Jayasuriya, S.T.	42	19	0	–	–	–	–
Labrooy, G.F.	2158	1194	27	44.22	5-133	1	–
Madurasinghe, A.W.R.	252	101	3	33.66	3-60	–	–
Mahanama, R.S.	6	3	0	–	–	–	–
Ramanayake, C.P.H.	1832	1025	19	53.94	2-39	–	–
Ranatunga, A.	1826	809	14	57.78	2-17	–	–
Ratnayake, R.J.	4562	2341	70	33.44	6-66	5	–
Samarasekera, M.A.R.	192	104	3	34.66	2-38	–	–
Warnaweera, K.P.J.	567	205	4	51.25	3-90	–	–
Wijegunawardene, K.I.W.	72	49	0	–	–	–	–

FIRST-CLASS CRICKET RECORDS

UPDATED TO THE END OF THE 1991 SEASON

TEAM RECORDS

HIGHEST INNINGS TOTALS

1107	Victoria v New South Wales	Melbourne	1926-27
1059	Victoria v Tasmania	Melbourne	1922-23
951-7d	Sind v Baluchistan	Karachi	1973-74
918	New South Wales v South Australia	Sydney	1900-01
912-8d	Holkar v Mysore	Indore	1945-46
910-6d	Railways v Dera Ismail Khan	Lahore	1964-65
903-7d	England v Australia	The Oval	1938
887	Yorkshire v Warwickshire	Birmingham	1896
863	Lancashire v Surrey	The Oval	1990
860-6d	Tamil Nadu v Goa	Panjim	1988-89

There have been 26 instances of a team scoring 800 runs or more in an innings, the most recent being by Bombay (855-6d, including 48 penalty runs) v Hyderabad at Bombay in 1990-91. Tamil Nadu's total of 860-6d was boosted to 912 by 52 penalty runs.

HIGHEST SECOND INNINGS TOTAL

770	New South Wales v South Australia	Adelaide	1920-21

HIGHEST FOURTH INNINGS TOTAL

654-5	England v South Africa	Durban	1938-39

HIGHEST MATCH AGGREGATE

2376	Maharashtra v Bombay	Poona	1948-49

RECORD MARGIN OF VICTORY

Innings and 851 runs: Railways v Dera Ismail Khan	Lahore	1964-65

MOST RUNS IN A DAY

721	Australians v Essex	Southend	1948

MOST HUNDREDS IN AN INNINGS

6	Holkar v Mysore	Indore	1945-46

LOWEST INNINGS TOTALS

12	† Oxford University v MCC and Ground	Oxford	1877
12	Northamptonshire v Gloucestershire	Gloucester	1907
13	Auckland v Canterbury	Auckland	1877-78
13	Nottinghamshire v Yorkshire	Nottingham	1901

14	Surrey v Essex	Chelmsford	1983
15	MCC v Surrey	Lord's	1839
15	† Victoria v MCC	Melbourne	1903-04
15	† Northamptonshire v Yorkshire	Northampton	1908
15	Hampshire v Warwickshire	Birmingham	1922

† Batted one man short

There have been 26 instances of a team being dismissed for under 20, the most recent being by Surrey in 1983 (above).

LOWEST MATCH AGGREGATE BY ONE TEAM

| 34 | (16 and 18) Border v Natal | East London | 1959-60 |

LOWEST COMPLETED MATCH AGGREGATE BY BOTH TEAMS

| 105 | MCC v Australians | Lord's | 1878 |

FEWEST RUNS IN AN UNINTERRUPTED DAY'S PLAY

| 95 | Australia (80) v Pakistan (15-2) | Karachi | 1956-57 |

TIED MATCHES

Before 1948 a match was considered to be tied if the scores were level after the fourth innings, even if the side batting last had wickets in hand when play ended. Law 22 was amended in 1948 and since then a match has been tied only when the scores are level after the fourth innings has been completed. There have been 49 tied first-class matches, five of which would not have qualified under the current law. The most recent is:

| Kent (381/408-7d) v Sussex (353/436) | Hove | 1991 |

BATTING RECORDS

HIGHEST INDIVIDUAL INNINGS

499	Hanif Mohammad	Karachi v Bahawalpur	Karachi	1958-59
452*	D.G.Bradman	New South Wales v Queensland	Sydney	1929-30
443*	B.B.Nimbalkar	Maharashtra v Kathiawar	Poona	1948-49
437	W.H.Ponsford	Victoria v Queensland	Melbourne	1927-28
429	W.H.Ponsford	Victoria v Tasmania	Melbourne	1922-23
428	Aftab Baloch	Sind v Baluchistan	Karachi	1973-74
424	A.C.MacLaren	Lancashire v Somerset	Taunton	1895
405*	G.A.Hick	Worcestershire v Somerset	Taunton	1988
385	B.Sutcliffe	Otago v Canterbury	Christchurch	1952-53
383	C.W.Gregory	New South Wales v Queensland	Brisbane	1906-07
377	S.V.Manjrekar	Bombay v Hyderabad	Bombay	1990-91
369	D.G.Bradman	South Australia v Tasmania	Adelaide	1935-36
366	N.H.Fairbrother	Lancashire v Surrey	The Oval	1990
365*	C.Hill	South Australia v NSW	Adelaide	1900-01
365*	G.St A.Sobers	West Indies v Pakistan	Kingston	1957-58
364	L.Hutton	England v Australia	The Oval	1938
359*	V.M.Merchant	Bombay v Maharashtra	Bombay	1943-44
359	R.B.Simpson	New South Wales v Queensland	Brisbane	1963-64
357*	R.Abel	Surrey v Somerset	The Oval	1899

357	D.G.Bradman	South Australia v Victoria	Melbourne	1935-36
356	B.A.Richards	S Australia v W Australia	Perth	1970-71
355*	G.R.Marsh	W Australia v S Australia	Perth	1989-90
355	B.Sutcliffe	Otago v Auckland	Dunedin	1949-50
352	W.H.Ponsford	Victoria v New South Wales	Melbourne	1926-27
350	Rashid Israr	Habib Bank v National Bank	Lahore	1976-77

There have been 105 triple hundreds in first-class cricket, W.V.Raman (313) and
Arjan Kripal Singh (302*) for Tamil Nadu v Goa at Panjim in 1988-89 providing the
only instance of two batsmen scoring 300 in the same innings.

MOST HUNDREDS IN SUCCESSIVE INNINGS

6	C.B.Fry	Sussex and Rest of England	1901
6	D.G.Bradman	South Australia and D.G.Bradman's XI	1938-39
6	M.J.Procter	Rhodesia	1970-71

TWO DOUBLE HUNDREDS IN A MATCH

244	202* A.E.Fagg	Kent v Essex	Colchester	1938

TRIPLE HUNDRED AND HUNDRED IN A MATCH

333	123 G.A.Gooch	England v India	Lord's	1990

DOUBLE HUNDRED AND HUNDRED IN A MATCH MOST TIMES

4	Zaheer Abbas	Gloucestershire	1976-81

TWO HUNDREDS IN A MATCH MOST TIMES

8	Zaheer Abbas	Gloucestershire and PIA	1976-82
7	W.R.Hammond	Gloucestershire, England and MCC	1927-45

MOST HUNDREDS IN A SEASON

18	D.C.S.Compton	1947
16	J.B.Hobbs	1925

MOST HUNDREDS IN A CAREER

(The season in which his 100th hundred was scored is given in brackets)

197	J.B.Hobbs (1923)	117	D.G.Bradman (1947-48)
170	E.H.Hendren (1928-29)	111	I.V.A.Richards (1988-89)
167	W.R.Hammond (1935)	108	Zaheer Abbas (1982-83)
153	C.P.Mead (1927)	107	A.Sandham (1935)
151	G.Boycott (1977)	107	M.C.Cowdrey (1973)
149	H.Sutcliffe (1932)	104	T.W.Hayward (1913)
145	F.E.Woolley (1929)	103	J.H.Edrich (1977)
129	L.Hutton (1951)	103	G.M.Turner (1982)
126	W.G.Grace (1895)	102	G.E.Tyldesley (1934)
123	D.C.S.Compton (1952)	102	L.E.G.Ames (1950)
122	T.W.Graveney (1964)	102	D.L.Amiss (1986)

MOST RUNS IN A MONTH

1294   (avge 92.42)   L.Hutton   Yorkshire   June 1949

MOST RUNS IN A SEASON

Runs			I	NO	HS	Avge	100	Season
3816	D.C.S.Compton	Middlesex	50	8	246	90.85	18	1947
3539	W.J.Edrich	Middlesex	52	8	267*	80.43	12	1947
3518	T.W.Hayward	Surrey	61	8	219	66.37	13	1906

The feat of scoring 3000 runs in a season has been achieved on 28 occasions, the most recent instance being by W.E.Alley (3019) in 1961. The highest aggregate in a season since 1969, when the number of County Championship matches was substantially reduced, is 2755 by S.J.Cook in 1991.

1000 RUNS IN A SEASON MOST TIMES

28   W.G.Grace (Gloucestershire), F.E.Woolley (Kent)

HIGHEST BATTING AVERAGE IN A SEASON

(Qualification: 12 innings)

Avge			I	NO	HS	Runs	100	Season
115.66	D.G.Bradman	Australians	26	5	278	2429	13	1938
102.53	G.Boycott	Yorkshire	20	5	175*	1538	6	1979
102.00	W.A.Johnston	Australians	17	16	28*	102	–	1953
101.70	G.A.Gooch	Essex	30	3	333	2746	12	1990
100.12	G.Boycott	Yorkshire	30	5	233	2503	13	1971

FASTEST HUNDRED AGAINST GENUINE BOWLING

35 min   P.G.H.Fender   Surrey v Northamptonshire   Northampton   1920

FASTEST DOUBLE HUNDRED

113 min   R.J.Shastri   Bombay v Baroda   Bombay   1984-85

FASTEST TRIPLE HUNDRED

181 min   D.C.S.Compton   MCC v NE Transvaal   Benoni   1948-49

MOST SIXES IN AN INNINGS

15	J.R.Reid	Wellington v N Districts	Wellington	1962-63
14	Shakti Singh	Himachal Pradesh v Haryana	Dharmsala	1990-91
13	Majid Khan	Pakistanis v Glamorgan	Swansea	1967
13	C.G.Greenidge	D.H.Robins' XI v Pakistanis	Eastbourne	1974
13	C.G.Greenidge	Hampshire v Sussex	Southampton	1975
13	G.W.Humpage	Warwickshire v Lancashire	Southport	1982
13	R.J.Shastri	Bombay v Baroda	Bombay	1984-85

MOST SIXES IN A MATCH

17   W.J.Stewart   Warwickshire v Lancashire   Blackpool   1959

MOST SIXES IN A SEASON

80 I.T.Botham   Somerset and England   1985

MOST BOUNDARIES IN AN INNINGS

68 P.A.Perrin   Essex v Derbyshire   Chesterfield   1904

MOST RUNS OFF ONE OVER

36 G.St A.Sobers   Nottinghamshire v Glamorgan   Swansea   1968
36 R.J.Shastri   Bombay v Baroda   Bombay   1984-85

Both batsmen hit all six balls in an over (bowled by M.A.Nash and Tilak Raj respectively) for six.

MOST RUNS IN A DAY

345 C.G.Macartney   Australians v Nottinghamshire   Nottingham   1921

There have been 18 instances of a batsman scoring 300 or more runs in a day, the most recent being by N.H.Fairbrother (311*) for Lancashire v Surrey at The Oval in 1990.

HIGHEST PARTNERSHIPS

First Wicket
561	Waheed Mirza/Mansoor Akhtar	Karachi W v Quetta	Karachi	1976-77
555	P.Holmes/H.Sutcliffe	Yorkshire v Essex	Leyton	1932
554	J.T.Brown/J.Tunnicliffe	Yorkshire v Derbys	Chesterfield	1898

Second Wicket
465*	J.A.Jameson/R.B.Kanhai	Warwickshire v Glos	Birmingham	1974
455	K.V.Bhandarkar/B.B.Nimbalkar	Maha'tra v Kathiawar	Poona	1948-49
451	D.G.Bradman/W.H.Ponsford	Australia v England	The Oval	1934

Third Wicket
467	A.H.Jones/M.D.Crowe	N Zealand v Sri Lanka	Wellington	1990-91
456	Khalid Irtiza/Aslam Ali	United Bank v Multan	Karachi	1975-76
451	Mudassar Nazar/Javed Miandad	Pakistan v India	Hyderabad	1982-83
445	P.E.Whitelaw/W.N.Carson	Auckland v Otago	Dunedin	1936-37
434	J.B.Stollmeyer/G.E.Gomez	Trinidad v Br Guiana	Port-of-Spain	1946-47
424*	W.J.Edrich/D.C.S.Compton	Middlesex v Somerset	Lord's	1948

Fourth Wicket
577	V.S.Hazare/Gul Mahomed	Baroda v Holkar	Baroda	1946-47
574*	C.L.Walcott/F.M.M.Worrell	Barbados v Trinidad	Port-of-Spain	1945-46
502*	F.M.M.Worrell/J.D.C.Goddard	Barbados v Trinidad	Bridgetown	1943-44
470	A.I.Kallicharran/G.W.Humpage	Warwickshire v Lancs	Southport	1982

Fifth Wicket
464*	M.E.Waugh/S.R.Waugh	NSW v W Australia	Perth	1990-91
405	S.G.Barnes/D.G.Bradman	Australia v England	Sydney	1946-47
397	W.Bardsley/C.Kelleway	NSW v S Australia	Sydney	1920-21
393	E.G.Arnold/W.B.Burns	Worcs v Warwickshire	Birmingham	1909

Sixth Wicket

487*	G.A.Headley/C.C.Passailaigue	Jamaica v Tennyson's	Kingston	1931-32
428	W.W.Armstrong/M.A.Noble	Australians v Sussex	Hove	1902
411	R.M.Poore/E.G.Wynyard	Hampshire v Somerset	Taunton	1899

Seventh Wicket

347	D.St E.Atkinson/C.C.Depeiza	W Indies v Australia	Bridgetown	1954-55
344	K.S.Ranjitsinhji/W.Newham	Sussex v Essex	Leyton	1902
340	K.J.Key/H.Philipson	Oxford U v Middlesex	Chiswick Park	1887

Eighth Wicket

433	A.Sims/V.T.Trumper	Australians v C'bury	Christchurch	1913-14
292	R.Peel/Lord Hawke	Yorkshire v Warwicks	Birmingham	1896
270	V.T.Trumper/E.P.Barbour	NSW v Victoria	Sydney	1912-13

Ninth Wicket

283	J.Chapman/A.Warren	Derbys v Warwicks	Blackwell	1910
251	J.W.H.T.Douglas/S.N.Hare	Essex v Derbyshire	Leyton	1921
245	V.S.Hazare/N.D.Nagarwalla	Maharashtra v Baroda	Poona	1939-40

Tenth Wicket

307	A.F.Kippax/J.E.H.Hooker	NSW v Victoria	Melbourne	1928-29
249	C.T.Sarwate/S.N.Banerjee	Indians v Surrey	The Oval	1946
235	F.E.Woolley/A.Fielder	Kent v Worcs	Stourbridge	1909

MOST RUNS IN A CAREER

	Career	I	NO	HS	Runs	Avge	100
J.B.Hobbs	1905-34	1315	106	316*	61237	50.65	197
F.E.Woolley	1906-38	1532	85	305*	58969	40.75	145
E.H.Hendren	1907-38	1300	166	301*	57611	50.80	170
C.P.Mead	1905-36	1340	185	280*	55061	47.67	153
W.G.Grace	1865-1908	1493	105	344	54896	39.55	126
W.R.Hammond	1920-51	1005	104	336*	50551	56.10	167
H.Sutcliffe	1919-45	1088	123	313	50138	51.95	149
G.Boycott	1962-86	1014	162	261*	48426	56.83	151
T.W.Graveney	1948-71/72	1223	159	258	47793	44.91	122
T.W.Hayward	1893-1914	1138	96	315*	43551	41.79	104
D.L.Amiss	1960-87	1139	126	262*	43423	42.86	102
M.C.Cowdrey	1950-76	1130	134	307	42719	42.89	107
A.Sandham	1911-1937/38	1000	79	325	41284	44.82	107
L.Hutton	1934-60	814	91	364	40140	55.51	129
M.J.K.Smith	1951-75	1091	139	204	39832	41.84	69
W.Rhodes	1898-1930	1528	237	267*	39802	30.83	58
J.H.Edrich	1956-78	979	104	310*	39790	45.47	103
R.E.S.Wyatt	1923-57	1141	157	232	39405	40.04	85
D.C.S.Compton	1936-64	839	88	300	38942	51.85	123
G.E.Tyldesley	1909-36	961	106	256*	38874	45.46	102
J.T.Tyldesley	1895-1923	994	62	295*	37897	40.60	86
K.W.R.Fletcher	1962-88	1167	170	228*	37665	37.77	63
C.G.Greenidge	1970-92	888	75	273*	37330	45.91	92
J.W.Hearne	1909-36	1025	116	285*	37252	40.98	96
L.E.G.Ames	1926-51	951	95	295	37248	43.51	102
D.Kenyon	1946-67	1159	59	259	37002	33.63	74
W.J.Edrich	1934-58	964	92	267*	36965	42.39	86
J.M.Parks	1949-76	1227	172	205*	36673	34.76	51

	Career	I	NO	HS	Runs	Avge	100
D.Denton	1894-1920	1163	70	221	36479	33.37	69
G.H.Hirst	1891-1929	1215	151	341	36323	34.13	60
A.Jones	1957-83	1168	72	204*	36049	32.89	56
W.G.Quaife	1894-1928	1203	185	255*	36012	35.37	72
R.E.Marshall	1945/46-72	1053	59	228*	35725	35.94	68
G.Gunn	1902-32	1061	82	220	35208	35.96	62

BOWLING RECORDS

ALL TEN WICKETS IN AN INNINGS

This feat has been achieved on 72 occasions at first-class level.
Three Times: A.P.Freeman (1929, 1930, 1931)
Twice: V.E.Walker (1859, 1865); H.Verity (1931, 1932); J.C.Laker (1956)

Instances since 1945:

W.E.Hollies	Warwickshire v Notts	Birmingham	1946
J.M.Sims	East v West	Kingston on Thames	1948
J.K.R.Graveney	Gloucestershire v Derbyshire	Chesterfield	1949
T.E.Bailey	Essex v Lancashire	Clacton	1949
R.Berry	Lancashire v Worcestershire	Blackpool	1953
S.P.Gupte	President's XI v Combined XI	Bombay	1954-55
J.C.Laker	Surrey v Australians	The Oval	1956
K.Smales	Nottinghamshire v Glos	Stroud	1956
G.A.R.Lock	Surrey v Kent	Blackheath	1956
J.C.Laker	England v Australia	Manchester	1956
P.M.Chatterjee	Bengal v Assam	Jorhat	1956-57
J.D.Bannister	Warwicks v Combined Services	Birmingham	1959
A.J.G.Pearson	Cambridge U v Leicestershire	Loughborough	1961
N.I.Thomson	Sussex v Warwickshire	Worthing	1964
P.J.Allan	Queensland v Victoria	Melbourne	1965-66
I.J.Brayshaw	Western Australia v Victoria	Perth	1967-68
Shahid Mahmood	Karachi Whites v Khairpur	Karachi	1969-70
E.E.Hemmings	International XI v W Indians	Kingston	1982-83
P.Sunderam	Rajasthan v Vidarbha	Jodhpur	1985-86
S.T.Jefferies	Western Province v OFS	Cape Town	1987-88
Imran Adil	Bahawalpur v Faisalabad	Faisalabad	1989-90

MOST WICKETS IN A MATCH

19	J.C.Laker	England v Australia	Manchester	1956

MOST WICKETS IN A SEASON

Wkts		Season	Matches	Overs	Mdns	Runs	Avge
304	A.P.Freeman	1928	37	1976.1	423	5489	18.05
298	A.P.Freeman	1933	33	2039	651	4549	15.26

The feat of taking 250 wickets in a season has been achieved on 12 occasions, the last instance being by A.P.Freeman in 1933. 200 or more wickets in a season have been taken on 59 occasions, the last being by G.A.R.Lock (212 wickets, average 12.02) in 1957.

The highest aggregates of wickets taken in a season since the reduction of the County Championship matches in 1969 are as follows:

215

Wkts		Season	Matches	Overs	Mdns	Runs	Avge
134	M.D.Marshall	1982	22	822	225	2108	15.73
131	L.R.Gibbs	1971	23	1024.1	295	2475	18.89
125	F.D.Stephenson	1988	22	819.1	196	2289	18.31
121	R.D.Jackman	1980	23	746.2	220	1864	15.40

Since 1969 there have been 46 instances of bowlers taking 100 wickets in a season.

MOST HAT-TRICKS IN A CAREER

7 D.V.P.Wright
6 T.W.J.Goddard, C.W.L.Parker
5 S.Haigh, V.W.C.Jupp, A.E.G.Rhodes, F.A.Tarrant

MOST WICKETS IN A CAREER

	Career	Runs	Wkts	Avge	100w
W.Rhodes	1898-1930	69993	4187	16.71	23
A.P.Freeman	1914-36	69577	3776	18.42	17
C.W.L.Parker	1903-35	63817	3278	19.46	16
J.T.Hearne	1888-1923	54352	3061	17.75	15
T.W.J.Goddard	1922-52	59116	2979	19.84	16
W.G.Grace	1865-1908	51545	2876	17.92	10
A.S.Kennedy	1907-36	61034	2874	21.23	15
D.Shackleton	1948-69	53303	2857	18.65	20
G.A.R.Lock	1946-70/71	54709	2844	19.23	14
F.J.Titmus	1949-82	63313	2830	22.37	16
M.W.Tate	1912-37	50571	2784	18.16	13+1
G.H.Hirst	1891-1929	51282	2739	18.72	15
C.Blythe	1899-1914	42136	2506	16.81	14
D.L.Underwood	1963-87	49993	2465	20.28	10
W.E.Astill	1906-39	57783	2431	23.76	9
J.C.White	1909-37	43759	2356	18.57	14
W.E.Hollies	1932-57	48656	2323	20.94	14
F.S.Trueman	1949-69	42154	2304	18.29	12
J.B.Statham	1950-68	36995	2260	16.36	13
R.T.D.Perks	1930-55	53770	2233	24.07	16
J.Briggs	1879-1900	35430	2221	15.95	12
D.J.Shepherd	1950-72	47302	2218	21.32	12
E.G.Dennett	1903-26	42571	2147	19.82	12
T.Richardson	1892-1905	38794	2104	18.43	10
T.E.Bailey	1945-67	48170	2082	23.13	9
R.Illingworth	1951-83	42023	2072	20.28	10
F.E.Woolley	1906-38	41066	2068	19.85	8
N.Gifford	1960-88	48731	2068	23.56	4
G.Geary	1912-38	41339	2063	20.03	11
D.V.P.Wright	1932-57	49307	2056	23.98	10
J.A.Newman	1906-30	51111	2032	25.15	9
A.Shaw	1864-97	24579	2027†	12.12	9
S.Haigh	1895-1913	32091	2012	15.94	11

† Excluding one wicket for which no analysis is available.

ALL-ROUND RECORDS

THE 'DOUBLE'

3000 runs and 100 wickets: J.H.Parks (1937)
2000 runs and 200 wickets: G.H.Hirst (1906)
2000 runs and 100 wickets: F.E.Woolley (4), J.W.Hearne (3), W.G.Grace (2), G.H.Hirst (2), W.Rhodes (2), T.E.Bailey, D.E.Davies, G.L.Jessop, V.W.C.Jupp, James Langridge, F.A.Tarrant, C.L.Townsend, L.F.Townsend
1000 runs and 200 wickets: M.W. Tate (3), A.E.Trott (2), A.S.Kennedy

Most Doubles: W.Rhodes (16), G.H.Hirst (14), V.W.C.Jupp (10)

Double in Debut Season: D.B.Close (1949) – aged 18, he is the youngest to achieve this feat

The feat of scoring 1000 runs and taking 100 wickets in a season has been achieved on 305 occasions, R.J.Hadlee (1984) and F.D.Stephenson (1988) being the only players to complete the 'double' since the reduction of Championship matches in 1969.

WICKET-KEEPING RECORDS

MOST DISMISSALS IN AN INNINGS

8 (8ct)	A.T.W.Grout	Queensland v W Australia	Brisbane	1959-60
8 (8ct)	D.E.East	Essex v Somerset	Taunton	1985
8 (8ct)	S.A.Marsh	Kent v Middlesex	Lord's	1991

MOST DISMISSALS IN A MATCH

12 (8ct, 4st)	E.Pooley	Surrey v Sussex	The Oval	1868
12 (9ct, 3st)	D.Tallon	Queensland v NSW	Sydney	1938-39
12 (9ct, 3st)	H.B.Taber	NSW v South Australia	Adelaide	1968-69

MOST CATCHES IN A MATCH

11	A.Long	Surrey v Sussex	Hove	1964
11	R.W.Marsh	W Australia v Victoria	Perth	1975-76
11	D.L.Bairstow	Yorkshire v Derbyshire	Scarborough	1982
11	W.K.Hegg	Lancashire v Derbyshire	Chesterfield	1989
11	A.J.Stewart	Surrey v Leicestershire	Leicester	1989
11	E.J.Nielson	S Australia v W Australia	Perth	1990-91

MOST DISMISSALS IN A SEASON

128 (79ct, 49st)   L.E.G.Ames   1929

MOST DISMISSALS IN A CAREER

	Career	Dismissals	Ct	St
R.W.Taylor	1960-88	1649	1473	176
J.T.Murray	1952-75	1527	1270	257
H.Strudwick	1902-27	1497	1242	255
A.P.E.Knott	1964-85	1344	1211	133
F.H.Huish	1895-1914	1310	933	377
B.Taylor	1949-73	1294	1083	211
D.Hunter	1889-1909	1253	906	347

	Career	Dismissals	Ct	St
H.R.Butt	1890-1912	**1228**	953	275
J.H.Board	1891-1914/15	**1207**	852	355
H.Elliott	1920-47	**1206**	904	302
J.M.Parks	1949-76	**1181**	1088	93
R.Booth	1951-70	**1126**	948	178
L.E.G.Ames	1926-51	**1121**	703	418
D.L.Bairstow	1970-90	**1099**	961	138
G.Duckworth	1923-47	**1096**	753	343
H.W.Stephenson	1948-64	**1082**	748	334
J.G.Binks	1955-75	**1071**	895	176
T.G.Evans	1939-69	**1066**	816	250
A.Long	1960-80	**1046**	922	124
G.O.Dawkes	1937-61	**1043**	895	148
R.W.Tolchard	1965-83	**1037**	912	125
W.L.Cornford	1921-47	**1017**	675	342

FIELDING RECORDS

MOST CATCHES IN AN INNINGS

7	M.J.Stewart	Surrey v Northamptonshire	Northampton	1957
7	A.S.Brown	Gloucestershire v Nottinghamshire	Nottingham	1966

MOST CATCHES IN A MATCH

10	W.R.Hammond	Gloucestershire v Surrey	Cheltenham	1928

MOST CATCHES IN A SEASON

78	W.R.Hammond	(1928)	77	M.J.Stewart	(1957)

MOST CATCHES IN A CAREER

1018	F.E.Woolley	(1906-38)	784	J.G.Langridge	(1928-55)
887	W.G.Grace	(1865-1908)	764	W.Rhodes	(1898-1930)
830	G.A.R.Lock	(1946-70/71)	758	C.A.Milton	(1948-74)
819	W.R.Hammond	(1920-51)	754	E.H.Hendren	(1907-38)
813	D.B.Close	(1949-86)			

TEST CRICKET RECORDS

(UPDATED TO THE END OF THE 1991 SEASON)

TEAM RECORDS

HIGHEST INNINGS TOTALS

903-7d	England v Australia	The Oval	1938
849	England v West Indies	Kingston	1929-30
790-3d	West Indies v Pakistan	Kingston	1957-58
758-8d	Australia v West Indies	Kingston	1954-55
729-6d	Australia v England	Lord's	1930
708	Pakistan v England	The Oval	1987
701	Australia v England	The Oval	1934
699-5	Pakistan v India	Lahore	1989-90
695	Australia v England	The Oval	1930
687-8d	West Indies v England	The Oval	1976
681-8d	West Indies v England	Port-of-Spain	1953-54
676-7	India v Sri Lanka	Kanpur	1986-87
674-6	Pakistan v India	Faisalabad	1984-85
674	Australia v India	Adelaide	1947-48
671-4	New Zealand v Sri Lanka	Wellington	1990-91
668	Australia v West Indies	Bridgetown	1954-55
659-8d	Australia v England	Sydney	1946-47
658-8d	England v Australia	Nottingham	1938
657-8d	Pakistan v West Indies	Bridgetown	1957-58
656-8d	Australia v England	Manchester	1964
654-5	England v South Africa	Durban	1938-39
653-4d	England v India	Lord's	1990
652-7d	England v India	Madras	1984-85
652-8d	West Indies v England	Lord's	1973
652	Pakistan v India	Faisalabad	1982-83
650-6d	Australia v West Indies	Bridgetown	1964-65

The highest innings for South Africa and Sri Lanka are:

622-9d	South Africa v Australia	Durban	1969-70
497	Sri Lanka v New Zealand	Wellington	1990-91

LOWEST INNINGS TOTALS

26	New Zealand v England	Auckland	1954-55
30	South Africa v England	Port Elizabeth	1895-96
30	South Africa v England	Birmingham	1924
35	South Africa v England	Cape Town	1898-99
36	Australia v England	Birmingham	1902
36	South Africa v Australia	Melbourne	1931-32
42	Australia v England	Sydney	1887-88
42	New Zealand v Australia	Wellington	1945-46
42	India v England	Lord's	1974
43	South Africa v England	Cape Town	1888-89
44	Australia v England	The Oval	1896
45	England v Australia	Sydney	1886-87
45	South Africa v Australia	Melbourne	1931-32
47	South Africa v England	Cape Town	1888-89
47	New Zealand v England	Lord's	1958

The lowest innings for other countries are:

53	West Indies v Pakistan	Faisalabad	1986-87
62	Pakistan v Australia	Perth	1981-82
82	Sri Lanka v India	Chandigarh	1990-91

BATTING RECORDS

HIGHEST INDIVIDUAL INNINGS

365*	G.St A.Sobers	WI v P	Kingston	1957-58
364	L.Hutton	E v A	The Oval	1938
337	Hanif Mohammad	P v WI	Bridgetown	1957-58
336*	W.R.Hammond	E v NZ	Auckland	1932-33
334	D.G.Bradman	A v E	Leeds	1930
333	G.A.Gooch	E v I	Lord's	1990
325	A.Sandham	E v WI	Kingston	1929-30
311	R.B.Simpson	A v E	Manchester	1964
310*	J.H.Edrich	E v NZ	Leeds	1965
307	R.M.Cowper	A v E	Melbourne	1965-66
304	D.G.Bradman	A v E	Leeds	1934
302	L.G.Rowe	WI v E	Bridgetown	1973-74
299*	D.G.Bradman	A v SA	Adelaide	1931-32
299	M.D.Crowe	NZ v SL	Wellington	1990-91
291	I.V.A.Richards	WI v E	The Oval	1976
287	R.E.Foster	E v A	Sydney	1903-04
285*	P.B.H.May	E v WI	Birmingham	1957
280*	Javed Miandad	P v I	Hyderabad	1982-83
278	D.C.S.Compton	E v P	Nottingham	1954
274	R.G.Pollock	SA v A	Durban	1969-70
274	Zaheer Abbas	P v E	Birmingham	1971
271	Javed Miandad	P v NZ	Auckland	1988-89
270*	G.A.Headley	WI v E	Kingston	1934-35
270	D.G.Bradman	A v E	Melbourne	1936-37
268	G.N.Yallop	A v P	Melbourne	1983-84
267	P.A.De Silva	SL v NZ	Wellington	1990-91
266	W.H.Ponsford	A v E	The Oval	1934
262*	D.L.Amiss	E v WI	Kingston	1973-74
261	F.M.M.Worrell	WI v E	Nottingham	1950
260	C.C.Hunte	WI v P	Kingston	1957-58
260	Javed Miandad	P v E	The Oval	1987
259	G.M.Turner	NZ v WI	Georgetown	1971-72
258	T.W.Graveney	E v WI	Nottingham	1957
258	S.M.Nurse	WI v NZ	Christchurch	1968-69
256	R.B.Kanhai	WI v I	Calcutta	1958-59
256	K.F.Barrington	E v A	Manchester	1964
255*	D.J.McGlew	SA v NZ	Wellington	1952-53
254	D.G.Bradman	A v E	Lord's	1930
251	W.R.Hammond	E v A	Sydney	1928-29
250	K.D.Walters	A v NZ	Christchurch	1976-77
250	S.F.A.F.Bacchus	WI v I	Kanpur	1978-79

The highest individual innings for India is:

236*	S.M.Gavaskar	I v WI	Madras	1983-84

MOST RUNS IN A SERIES

Runs			Series	M	I	NO	HS	Avge	100	50
974	D.G.Bradman	A v E	1930	5	7	0	334	139.14	4	–
905	W.R.Hammond	E v A	1928-29	5	9	1	251	113.12	4	–
839	M.A.Taylor	A v E	1989	6	11	1	219	83.90	2	5
834	R.N.Harvey	A v SA	1952-53	5	9	0	205	92.66	4	3
829	I.V.A.Richards	WI v E	1976	4	7	0	291	118.42	3	2
827	C.L.Walcott	WI v A	1954-55	5	10	0	155	82.70	5	2
824	G.St A.Sobers	WI v P	1957-58	5	8	2	365*	137.33	3	3
810	D.G.Bradman	A v E	1936-37	5	9	0	270	90.00	3	1
806	D.G.Bradman	A v SA	1931-32	5	5	1	299*	201.50	4	–
779	E.de C.Weekes	WI v I	1948-49	5	7	0	194	111.28	4	2
774	S.M.Gavaskar	I v WI	1970-71	4	8	3	220	154.80	4	3
761	Mudassar Nazar	P v I	1982-83	6	8	2	231	126.83	4	1
758	D.G.Bradman	A v E	1934	5	8	0	304	94.75	2	1
753	D.C.S.Compton	E v SA	1947	5	8	0	208	94.12	4	2
752	G.A.Gooch	E v I	1990	3	6	0	333	125.33	3	2

HIGHEST PARTNERSHIP FOR EACH WICKET

1st	413	V.Mankad/Pankaj Roy	I v NZ	Madras	1955-56
2nd	451	W.H.Ponsford/D.G.Bradman	A v E	The Oval	1934
3rd	467	A.H.Jones/M.D.Crowe	NZ v SL	Wellington	1990-91
4th	411	P.B.H.May/M.C.Cowdrey	E v WI	Birmingham	1957
5th	405	S.G.Barnes/D.G.Bradman	A v E	Sydney	1946-47
6th	346	J.H.W.Fingleton/D.G.Bradman	A v E	Melbourne	1936-37
7th	347	D.St E.Atkinson/C.C.Depeiza	WI v A	Bridgetown	1954-55
8th	246	L.E.G.Ames/G.O.B.Allen	E v NZ	Lord's	1931
9th	190	Asif Iqbal/Intikhab Alam	P v E	The Oval	1967
10th	151	B.F.Hastings/R.O.Collinge	NZ v P	Auckland	1972-73

WICKET PARTNERSHIPS OF OVER 300

467	3rd	A.H.Jones/M.D.Crowe	NZ v SL	Wellington	1990-91
451	2nd	W.H.Ponsford/D.G.Bradman	A v E	The Oval	1934
451	3rd	Mudassar Nazar/Javed Miandad	P v I	Hyderabad	1982-83
446	2nd	C.C.Hunte/G.St A.Sobers	WI v P	Kingston	1957-58
413	1st	V.Mankad/Pankaj Roy	I v NZ	Madras	1955-56
411	4th	P.B.H.May/M.C.Cowdrey	E v WI	Birmingham	1957
405	5th	S.G.Barnes/D.G.Bradman	A v E	Sydney	1946-47
399	4th	G.St A.Sobers/F.M.M.Worrell	WI v E	Bridgetown	1959-60
397	3rd	Qasim Omar/Javed Miandad	P v SL	Faisalabad	1985-86
388	4th	W.H.Ponsford/D.G.Bradman	A v E	Leeds	1934
387	1st	G.M.Turner/T.W.Jarvis	NZ v WI	Georgetown	1971-72
382	2nd	L.Hutton/M.Leyland	E v A	The Oval	1938
382	1st	W.M.Lawry/R.B.Simpson	A v WI	Bridgetown	1964-65
370	3rd	W.J.Edrich/D.C.S.Compton	E v SA	Lord's	1947
369	2nd	J.H.Edrich/K.F.Barrington	E v NZ	Leeds	1965
359	1st	L.Hutton/C.Washbrook	E v SA	Jo'burg	1948-49
351	2nd	G.A.Gooch/D.I.Gower	E v A	The Oval	1985
350	4th	Mushtaq Mohammad/Asif Iqbal	P v NZ	Dunedin	1972-73
347	7th	D.St E.Atkinson/C.C.Depeiza	WI v A	Bridgetown	1954-55
346	6th	J.H.W.Fingleton/D.G.Bradman	A v E	Melbourne	1936-37
344*	2nd	S.M.Gavaskar/D.B.Vengsarkar	I v WI	Calcutta	1978-79
341	3rd	E.J.Barlow/R.G.Pollock	SA v A	Adelaide	1963-64

Runs									
338	3rd	E.de C.Weekes/F.M.M.Worrell	WI v E	Port-of-Spain	1953-54
336	4th	W.M.Lawry/K.D.Walters	A v WI	Sydney	1968-69
331	2nd	R.T.Robinson/D.I.Gower	E v A	Birmingham	1985
329	1st	G.R.Marsh/M.A.Taylor	A v A	Nottingham	1989
323	1st	J.B.Hobbs/W.Rhodes	E v A	Melbourne	1911-12
319	3rd	A.Melville/A.D.Nourse	SA v E	Nottingham	1947
316 †	3rd	G.R.Viswanath/Yashpal Sharma	I v E	Madras	1981-82
308	7th	Waqar Hassan/Imtiaz Ahmed	P v NZ	Lahore	1955-56
308	3rd	R.B.Richardson/I.V.A.Richards	WI v A	St John's	1983-84
308	3rd	G.A.Gooch/A.J.Lamb	E v I	Lord's	1990
303	3rd	I.V.A.Richards/A.I.Kallicharran	WI v E	Nottingham	1976
301	2nd	A.R.Morris/D.G.Bradman	A v E	Leeds	1948

† 415 runs were added for this wicket in two separate partnerships.
D.B. Vengsarkar retired hurt and was replaced by Yashpal Sharma after 99 runs had been added.

4000 RUNS IN TESTS

Runs			M	I	NO	HS	Avge	100	50
10122	S.M.Gavaskar	I	125	214	16	236*	51.12	34	45
9257	A.R.Border	A	125	215	38	205	52.29	23	52
8540	I.V.A.Richards	WI	121	182	12	291	50.23	24	45
8114	G.Boycott	E	108	193	23	246*	47.72	22	42
8081	D.I.Gower	E	114	199	16	215	44.15	18	38
8064	Javed Miandad	P	109	165	18	280*	54.85	22	39
8032	G.St A.Sobers	WI	93	160	21	365*	57.78	26	30
7624	M.C.Cowdrey	E	114	188	15	182	44.06	22	38
7558	C.G.Greenidge	WI	108	185	16	226	44.72	19	34
7515	C.H.Lloyd	WI	110	175	14	242*	46.67	19	39
7249	W.R.Hammond	E	85	140	16	336*	58.45	22	24
7110	G.S.Chappell	A	87	151	19	247*	53.86	24	31
7028	G.A.Gooch	E	91	166	6	333	43.92	15	39
6996	D.G.Bradman	A	52	80	10	334	99.94	29	13
6971	L.Hutton	E	79	138	15	364	56.67	19	33
6806	K.F.Barrington	E	82	131	15	256	58.67	20	35
6710	D.B.Vengsarkar	I	111	176	22	166	43.57	17	33
6644	D.L.Haynes	WI	102	178	21	184	42.31	16	36
6227	R.B.Kanhai	WI	79	137	6	256	47.53	15	28
6149	R.N.Harvey	A	79	137	10	205	48.41	21	24
6080	G.R.Viswanath	I	91	155	10	222	41.93	14	35
5807	D.C.S.Compton	E	78	131	15	278	50.06	17	28
5410	J.B.Hobbs	E	61	102	7	211	56.94	15	28
5357	K.D.Walters	A	74	125	14	250	48.26	15	33
5345	I.M.Chappell	A	75	136	10	196	42.42	14	26
5234	W.M.Lawry	A	67	123	12	210	47.15	13	27
5176	I.T.Botham	E	99	157	6	208	34.27	14	22
5138	J.H.Edrich	E	77	127	9	310*	43.54	12	24
5062	Zaheer Abbas	P	78	124	11	274	44.79	12	20
4882	T.W.Graveney	E	79	123	13	258	44.38	11	20
4869	R.B.Simpson	A	62	111	7	311	46.81	10	27
4737	I.R.Redpath	A	66	120	11	171	43.45	8	31
4706	J.G.Wright	NZ	74	132	6	185	37.34	11	20
4647	R.B.Richardson	WI	62	107	10	194	47.90	14	18
4555	H.Sutcliffe	E	54	84	9	194	60.73	16	23
4537	P.B.H.May	E	66	106	9	285*	46.77	13	22

Runs			M	I	NO	HS	Avge	100	50
4525	Kapil Dev	I	110	159	13	163	30.99	7	23
4502	E.R.Dexter	E	62	102	8	205	47.89	9	27
4455	E.de C.Weekes	WI	48	81	5	207	58.61	15	19
4415	K.J.Hughes	A	70	124	6	213	37.41	9	22
4399	A.I.Kallicharran	WI	66	109	10	187	44.43	12	21
4389	A.P.E.Knott	E	95	149	15	135	32.75	5	30
4378	M.Amarnath	I	69	113	10	138	42.50	11	24
4334	R.C.Fredericks	WI	59	109	7	169	42.49	8	26
4264	A.J.Lamb	E	74	131	10	139	35.23	13	16
4114	Mudassar Nazar	P	76	116	8	231	38.09	10	17

MOST HUNDREDS

34	S.M.Gavaskar	I	22	G.Boycott	E
29	D.G.Bradman	A	22	M.C.Cowdrey	E
26	G.St A.Sobers	WI	22	W.R.Hammond	E
24	G.S.Chappell	A	22	Javed Miandad	P
24	I.V.A.Richards	WI	21	R.N.Harvey	A
23	A.R.Border	A	20	K.F.Barrington	E

BOWLING RECORDS

MOST WICKETS IN AN INNINGS

10-53	J.C.Laker	E v A	Manchester	1956
9-28	G.A.Lohmann	E v SA	Johannesburg	1895-96
9-37	J.C.Laker	E v A	Manchester	1956
9-52	R.J.Hadlee	NZ v A	Brisbane	1985-86
9-56	Abdul Qadir	P v E	Lahore	1987-88
9-69	J.M.Patel	I v A	Kanpur	1959-60
9-83	Kapil Dev	I v WI	Ahmedabad	1983-84
9-86	Sarfraz Nawaz	P v A	Melbourne	1978-79
9-95	J.M.Noreiga	WI v I	Port-of-Spain	1970-71
9-102	S.P.Gupte	I v WI	Kanpur	1958-59
9-103	S.F.Barnes	E v SA	Johannesburg	1913-14
9-113	H.J.Tayfield	SA v E	Johannesburg	1956-57
9-121	A.A.Mailey	A v E	Melbourne	1920-21

MOST WICKETS IN A TEST

19-90	J.C.Laker	E v A	Manchester	1956
17-159	S.F.Barnes	E v SA	Johannesburg	1913-14
16-136	N.D.Hirwani	I v WI	Madras	1987-88
16-137	R.A.L.Massie	A v E	Lord's	1972
15-28	J.Briggs	E v SA	Cape Town	1888-89
15-45	G.A.Lohmann	E v SA	Port Elizabeth	1895-96
15-99	C.Blythe	E v SA	Leeds	1907
15-104	H.Verity	E v A	Lord's	1934
15-123	R.J.Hadlee	NZ v A	Brisbane	1985-86
15-124	W.Rhodes	E v A	Melbourne	1903-04

MOST WICKETS IN A SERIES

Wkts			Series	M	Balls	Runs	Avge	5 wI	10 wM
49	S.F.Barnes	E v SA	1913-14	4	1356	536	10.93	7	3
46	J.C.Laker	E v A	1956	5	1703	442	9.60	4	2
44	C.V.Grimmett	A v SA	1935-36	5	2077	642	14.59	5	3
42	T.M.Alderman	A v E	1981	6	1950	893	21.26	4	–
41	R.M.Hogg	A v E	1978-79	6	1740	527	12.85	5	2
41	T.M.Alderman	A v E	1989	6	1616	712	17.36	6	1
40	Imran Khan	P v I	1982-83	6	1339	558	13.95	4	2
39	A.V.Bedser	E v A	1953	5	1591	682	17.48	5	1
39	D.K.Lillee	A v E	1981	6	1870	870	22.30	2	1
38	M.W.Tate	E v A	1924-25	5	2528	881	23.18	5	1
37	W.J.Whitty	A v SA	1910-11	5	1395	632	17.08	2	–
37	H.J.Tayfield	SA v E	1956-57	5	2280	636	17.18	4	1
36	A.E.E.Vogler	SA v E	1909-10	5	1349	783	21.75	4	1
36	A.A.Mailey	A v E	1920-21	5	1465	946	26.27	4	2
35	G.A.Lohmann	E v SA	1895-96	3	520	203	5.80	4	2
35	B.S.Chandrasekhar	I v E	1972-73	5	1747	662	18.91	4	1
35	M.D.Marshall	WI v E	1988	5	1219	443	12.65	3	1

200 WICKETS IN TESTS

Wkts			M	Balls	Runs	Avge	5 wI	10 wM
431	Sir R.J.Hadlee	NZ	86	21918	9611	22.29	36	9
380	I.T.Botham	E	99	21539	10741	28.26	27	4
376	M.D.Marshall	WI	81	17584	7876	20.94	22	4
376	Kapil Dev	I	110	23263	11249	29.91	21	2
362	Imran Khan	P	85	19404	8242	22.76	23	6
355	D.K.Lillee	A	70	18467	8493	23.92	23	7
325	R.G.D.Willis	E	90	17357	8190	25.20	16	–
309	L.R.Gibbs	WI	79	27115	8989	29.09	18	2
307	F.S.Trueman	E	67	15178	6625	21.57	17	3
297	D.L.Underwood	E	86	21862	7674	25.83	17	6
266	B.S.Bedi	I	67	21364	7637	28.71	14	1
259	J.Garner	WI	58	13169	5433	20.97	7	–
252	J.B.Statham	E	70	16056	6261	24.84	9	1
249	M.A.Holding	WI	60	12680	5898	23.68	13	2
248	R.Benaud	A	63	19108	6704	27.03	16	1
246	G.D.McKenzie	A	60	17681	7328	29.78	16	3
242	B.S.Chandrasekhar	I	58	15963	7199	29.74	16	2
236	A.V.Bedser	E	51	15918	5876	24.89	15	5
236	Abdul Qadir	P	67	17126	7742	32.80	15	5
235	G.St A.Sobers	WI	93	21599	7999	34.03	6	–
228	R.R.Lindwall	A	61	13650	5251	23.03	12	–
216	C.V.Grimmett	A	37	14513	5231	24.21	21	7
202	A.M.E.Roberts	WI	47	11136	5174	25.61	11	2
202	J.A.Snow	E	49	12021	5387	26.66	8	1
200	J.R.Thomson	A	51	10535	5601	28.00	8	–

HAT-TRICKS

F.R.Spofforth	Australia v England	Melbourne	1878-79
W.Bates	England v Australia	Melbourne	1882-83
J.Briggs	England v Australia	Sydney	1891-92
G.A.Lohmann	England v South Africa	Port Elizabeth	1895-96
J.T.Hearne	England v Australia	Leeds	1899

H.Trumble	Australia v England	Melbourne	1901-02
H.Trumble	Australia v England	Melbourne	1903-04
T.J.Matthews (2)*	Australia v South Africa	Manchester	1912
M.J.C.Allom †	England v New Zealand	Christchurch	1929-30
T.W.J.Goddard	England v South Africa	Johannesburg	1938-39
P.J.Loader	England v West Indies	Leeds	1957
L.F.Kline	Australia v South Africa	Cape Town	1957-58
W.W.Hall	West Indies v Pakistan	Lahore	1958-59
G.M.Griffin	South Africa v England	Lord's	1960
L.R.Gibbs	West Indies v Australia	Adelaide	1960-61
P.J.Petherick	New Zealand v Pakistan	Lahore	1976-77
C.A.Walsh ‡	West Indies v Australia	Brisbane	1988-89
M.G.Hughes ‡	Australia v West Indies	Perth	1988-89

*Hat-trick in each innings † Four wickets in five balls
‡ Involving both innings

WICKET-KEEPING RECORDS

MOST DISMISSALS IN AN INNINGS

7	Wasim Bari	Pakistan v New Zealand	Auckland	1978-79
7	R.W.Taylor	England v India	Bombay	1979-80
7	I.D.S.Smith	New Zealand v Sri Lanka	Hamilton	1990-91
6	A.T.W.Grout	Australia v South Africa	Johannesburg	1957-58
6	D.T.Lindsay	South Africa v Australia	Johannesburg	1966-67
6	J.T.Murray	England v India	Lord's	1967
6 †	S.M.H.Kirmani	India v New Zealand	Christchurch	1975-76
6	R.W.Marsh	Australia v England	Brisbane	1982-83
6	S.A.R.Silva	Sri Lanka v India	Colombo (SSC)	1985-86
6	R.C.Russell	England v Australia	Melbourne	1990-91

† Including one stumping

MOST STUMPINGS IN AN INNINGS

| 5 | K.S.More | India v West Indies | Madras | 1987-88 |

MOST DISMISSALS IN A TEST

10	R.W.Taylor	England v India	Bombay	1979-80
9 †	G.R.A.Langley	Australia v England	Lord's	1956
9	D.A.Murray	West Indies v Australia	Melbourne	1981-82
9	R.W.Marsh	Australia v England	Brisbane	1982-83
9	S.A.R.Silva	Sri Lanka v India	Colombo (SSC)	1985-86
9 †	S.A.R.Silva	Sri Lanka v India	Colombo (PSS)	1985-86

† Including one stumping

MOST DISMISSALS IN A SERIES

28	R.W.Marsh	Australia v England	1982-83
26 (inc 3st)	J.H.B.Waite	South Africa v New Zealand	1961-62
26	R.W.Marsh	Australia v West Indies (6 Tests)	1975-76
24 (inc 2st)	D.L.Murray	West Indies v England	1963
24	D.T.Lindsay	South Africa v Australia	1966-67
24 (inc 3st)	A.P.E.Knott	England v Australia (6 Tests)	1970-71
24	I.A.Healy	Australia v England	1990-91

100 DISMISSALS IN TESTS

Total			Tests	Ct	St
355	R.W.Marsh	Australia	96	343	12
272 †	P.J.L.Dujon	West Indies	81	267	5
269	A.P.E.Knott	England	95	250	19
228	Wasim Bari	Pakistan	81	201	27
219	T.G.Evans	England	91	173	46
198	S.M.H.Kirmani	India	88	160	38
189	D.L.Murray	West Indies	62	181	8
187	A.T.W.Grout	Australia	51	163	24
174	R.W.Taylor	England	57	167	7
172	I.D.S.Smith	New Zealand	61	164	8
141	J.H.B.Waite	South Africa	50	124	17
130	W.A.S.Oldfield	Australia	54	78	52
114 †	J.M.Parks	England	46	103	11
104	Salim Yousuf	Pakistan	32	91	13

† Including two catches taken in the field

FIELDING RECORDS
(Excluding Wicket-Keepers)

MOST CATCHES IN AN INNINGS

5	V.Y.Richardson	Australia v South Africa	Durban	1935-36
5	Yajurvindra Singh	India v England	Bangalore	1976-77
5	M.Azharuddin	India v Pakistan	Karachi	1989-90

MOST CATCHES IN A TEST

7	G.S.Chappell	Australia v England	Perth	1974-75
7	Yajurvindra Singh	India v England	Bangalore	1976-77

MOST CATCHES IN A SERIES

15	J.M.Gregory	Australia v England	1920-21

100 CATCHES IN TESTS

Total			Tests
130	A.R.Border	Australia	125
122	G.S.Chappell	Australia	87
122	I.V.A.Richards	West Indies	121
120	M.C.Cowdrey	England	114
117	I.T.Botham	England	99
110	R.B.Simpson	Australia	62
110	W.R.Hammond	England	85
109	G.St A.Sobers	West Indies	93
108	S.M.Gavaskar	India	125
105	I.M.Chappell	Australia	75

MOST TEST APPEARANCES

England	M.C.Cowdrey, D.I.Gower	114
Australia	A.R.Border	125
South Africa	J.H.B.Waite	50
West Indies	I.V.A.Richards	121
New Zealand	R.J.Hadlee	86
India	S.M.Gavaskar	125
Pakistan	Javed Miandad	109
Sri Lanka	A.Ranatunga	30

122	A.R.Border	Australia	March 1979 to May 1991
106	S.M.Gavaskar	India	January 1975 to February 1987

MOST MATCHES BETWEEN APPEARANCES

104	Younis Ahmed	Pakistan	November 1969 to February 1987
103	D.Shackleton	England	November 1951 to June 1963

SUMMARY OF ALL TEST MATCHES

To end of 1991 season in England

		Tests	E	A	SA	WI	NZ	I	P	SL	Tied	Drawn
							Won by					
England	v Australia	274	88	104	–	–	–	–	–	–	–	82
	v South Africa	102	46	–	18	–	–	–	–	–	–	38
	v West Indies	104	24	–	–	43	–	–	–	–	–	37
	v New Zealand	69	31	–	–	–	4	–	–	–	–	34
	v India	78	31	–	–	–	–	11	–	–	–	36
	v Pakistan	47	13	–	–	–	–	–	5	–	–	29
	v Sri Lanka	4	3	–	–	–	–	–	–	0	–	1
Australia	v South Africa	53	–	29	11	–	–	–	–	–	–	13
	v West Indies	72	–	29	–	24	–	–	–	–	1	18
	v New Zealand	26	–	10	–	–	6	–	–	–	–	10
	v India	45	–	20	–	–	–	8	–	–	1	16
	v Pakistan	34	–	12	–	–	–	–	9	–	–	13
	v Sri Lanka	4	–	3	–	–	–	–	–	0	–	1
South Africa	v New Zealand	17	–	–	9	–	2	–	–	–	–	6
West Indies	v New Zealand	24	–	–	–	8	4	–	–	–	–	12
	v India	62	–	–	–	26	–	6	–	–	–	30
	v Pakistan	28	–	–	–	10	–	–	7	–	–	11
New Zealand	v India	31	–	–	–	–	6	12	–	–	–	13
	v Pakistan	32	–	–	–	–	3	–	13	–	–	16
	v Sri Lanka	9	–	–	–	–	4	–	–	0	–	5
India	v Pakistan	44	–	–	–	–	–	4	7	–	–	33
	v Sri Lanka	8	–	–	–	–	–	3	–	1	–	4
Pakistan	v Sri Lanka	9	–	–	–	–	–	–	5	1	–	3
		1176	236	207	38	111	29	44	46	2	2	461

	Tests	Won	Lost	Drawn	Tied	Toss Won
England	678	236	185	257	–	335
Australia	508	207	146	153	2	256
South Africa	172	38	77	57	–	80
West Indies	290	111	70	108	1	151
New Zealand	208	29	83	96	–	103
India	268	44	91	132	1	134
Pakistan	194	46	43	105	–	100
Sri Lanka	34	2	18	14	–	17

To 16 October 1991

	Matches	E	A	I	NZ	P	SL	WI	B	C	EA	Z	Tied	NR
England v Australia	51	24	25	–	–	–	–	–	–	–	–	–	1	1
v India	22	12	–	10	–	–	–	–	–	–	–	–	–	–
v New Zealand	36	17	–	–	16	–	–	–	–	–	–	–	–	3
v Pakistan	29	19	–	–	–	10	–	–	–	–	–	–	–	–
v Sri Lanka	8	7	–	–	–	–	1	–	–	–	–	–	–	–
v West Indies	42	17	–	–	–	–	–	23	–	–	–	–	–	2
v Canada	1	1	–	–	–	–	–	–	–	0	–	–	–	–
v East Africa	1	1	–	–	–	–	–	–	–	–	0	–	–	–
Australia v India	33	–	18	12	–	–	–	–	–	–	–	–	–	3
v New Zealand	49	–	34	–	13	–	–	–	–	–	–	–	–	2
v Pakistan	33	–	15	–	–	16	–	–	–	–	–	–	–	2
v Sri Lanka	20	–	15	–	–	–	3	–	–	–	–	–	–	2
v West Indies	58	–	21	–	–	–	–	36	–	–	–	–	1	–
v Bangladesh	1	–	1	–	–	–	–	–	0	–	–	–	–	–
v Canada	1	–	1	–	–	–	–	–	–	0	–	–	–	–
v Zimbabwe	4	–	3	–	–	–	–	–	–	–	–	1	–	–
India v New Zealand	28	–	–	16	12	–	–	–	–	–	–	–	–	–
v Pakistan	34	–	–	10	–	22	–	–	–	–	–	–	–	2
v Sri Lanka	25	–	–	17	–	–	7	–	–	–	–	–	–	1
v West Indies	33	–	–	6	–	–	–	27	–	–	–	–	–	–
v Bangladesh	2	–	–	2	–	–	–	–	0	–	–	–	–	–
v East Africa	1	–	–	1	–	–	–	–	–	–	0	–	–	–
v Zimbabwe	4	–	–	4	–	–	–	–	–	–	–	0	–	–
N Zealand v Pakistan	23	–	–	–	11	11	–	–	–	–	–	–	–	1
v Sri Lanka	22	–	–	–	18	–	4	–	–	–	–	–	–	–
v West Indies	13	–	–	–	1	–	–	11	–	–	–	–	–	1
v Bangladesh	1	–	–	–	1	–	–	–	0	–	–	–	–	–
v East Africa	1	–	–	–	1	–	–	–	–	–	0	–	–	–
v Zimbabwe	2	–	–	–	2	–	–	–	–	–	–	0	–	–
Pakistan v Sri Lanka	30	–	–	–	–	23	6	–	–	–	–	–	–	1
v West Indies	51	–	–	–	–	16	–	35	–	–	–	–	–	–
v Bangladesh	2	–	–	–	–	2	–	–	0	–	–	–	–	–
v Canada	1	–	–	–	–	1	–	–	–	0	–	–	–	–
Sri Lanka v West Indies	11	–	–	–	–	–	1	10	–	–	–	–	–	–
v Bangladesh	3	–	–	–	–	–	3	–	0	–	–	–	–	–
W Indies v Zimbabwe	2	–	–	–	–	–	–	2	–	–	–	0	–	–
	678	98	133	78	75	101	25	144	0	0	0	1	2	21

	Matches	Won	Lost	Tied	No Result	% Won (exc NR)
West Indies	210	144	62	1	3	69.56
Australia	250	133	105	2	10	55.41
England	190	98	85	1	6	53.26
Pakistan	203	101	96	–	6	51.26
New Zealand	175	75	93	–	7	44.64
India	182	78	98	–	6	44.31
Sri Lanka	119	25	90	–	4	21.73
Zimbabwe	12	1	11	–	–	8.33
Bangladesh	9	–	9	–	–	–
Canada	3	–	3	–	–	–
East Africa	3	–	3	–	–	–

LIMITED-OVERS INTERNATIONALS RECORDS

Compiled by Philip Bailey to 16 October 1991

TEAM RECORDS

HIGHEST TOTALS

360-4 (50 overs)	West Indies v Sri Lanka	Karachi	1987-88
338-4 (50 overs)	New Zealand v Bangladesh	Sharjah	1989-90
338-5 (60 overs)	Pakistan v Sri Lanka	Swansea	1983
334-4 (60 overs)	England v India	Lord's	1975
333-8 (45 overs)	West Indies v India	Jamshedpur	1983-84
333-9 (60 overs)	England v Sri Lanka	Taunton	1983
332-3 (50 overs)	Australia v Sri Lanka	Sharjah	1989-90
330-6 (60 overs)	Pakistan v Sri Lanka	Nottingham	1975

HIGHEST TOTAL BATTING SECOND

298-6 (54.5 overs)	New Zealand v England	Leeds	1990

HIGHEST MATCH AGGREGATE

626-14 (120 overs)	Pakistan v Sri Lanka	Swansea	1983

LOWEST TOTALS
(Excluding abbreviated matches)

45 (40.3 overs)	Canada v England	Manchester	1979
55 (28.3 overs)	Sri Lanka v West Indies	Sharjah	1986-87
63 (25.5 overs)	India v Australia	Sydney	1980-81
64 (35.5 overs)	New Zealand v Pakistan	Sharjah	1985-86
70 (25.2 overs)	Australia v England	Birmingham	1977
70 (26.3 overs)	Australia v New Zealand	Adelaide	1985-86

LOWEST MATCH AGGREGATE

91-12 (54.2 overs)	England v Canada	Manchester	1979

LARGEST MARGINS OF VICTORY

232 runs	Australia beat Sri Lanka	Adelaide	1984-85
206 runs	New Zealand beat Australia	Adelaide	1985-86
202 runs	England beat India	Lord's	1975
10 wickets	India beat East Africa	Leeds	1975
10 wickets	New Zealand beat India	Melbourne	1980-81
10 wickets	West Indies beat Zimbabwe	Birmingham	1983
10 wickets	India beat Sri Lanka	Sharjah	1983-84
10 wickets	West Indies beat New Zealand	Port-of-Spain	1984-85
10 wickets	Pakistan beat New Zealand	Sharjah	1985-86
10 wickets	West Indies beat New Zealand	Christchurch	1986-87

TIED MATCHES

Australia	222-9	West Indies	222-5	Melbourne	1983-84
England	226-5	Australia	226-8	Nottingham	1989

BATTING RECORDS

HIGHEST INDIVIDUAL INNINGS

189*	I.V.A.Richards	West Indies v England	Manchester	1984
181	I.V.A.Richards	West Indies v Sri Lanka	Karachi	1987-88
175*	Kapil Dev	India v Zimbabwe	Tunbridge Wells	1983
171*	G.M.Turner	New Zealand v East Africa	Birmingham	1975
158	D.I.Gower	England v New Zealand	Brisbane	1982-83
153*	I.V.A.Richards	West Indies v Australia	Melbourne	1979-80
152*	D.L.Haynes	West Indies v India	Georgetown	1988-89

HUNDRED ON DEBUT

103	D.L.Amiss	England v Australia	Manchester	1972
148	D.L.Haynes	West Indies v Australia	St John's	1977-78

HIGHEST PARTNERSHIP FOR EACH WICKET

1st	212	G.R.Marsh/D.C.Boon	A v I	Jaipur	1986-87
2nd	221	C.G.Greenidge/I.V.A.Richards	WI v I	Jamshedpur	1983-84
3rd	224*	D.M.Jones/A.R.Border	A v SL	Adelaide	1984-85
4th	173	D.M.Jones/S.R.Waugh	A v P	Perth	1986-87
5th	152	I.V.A.Richards/C.H.Lloyd	WI v SL	Brisbane	1984-85
6th	144	Imran Khan/Shahid Mahboob	P v SL	Leeds	1983
7th	115	P.J.L.Dujon/M.D.Marshall	WI v P	Gujranwala	1986-87
8th	117	D.L.Houghton/I.P.Butchart	Z v NZ	Hyderabad (Ind)	1987-88
9th	126*	Kapil Dev/S.M.H.Kirmani	I v Z	Tunbridge Wells	1983
10th	106*	I.V.A.Richards/M.A.Holding	WI v E	Manchester	1984

MOST RUNS IN A CAREER

		I	NO	HS	Runs	Avge	100	50
D.L.Haynes	WI	181	23	152*	6780	42.91	16	39
I.V.A.Richards	WI	167	24	189*	6721	47.00	11	45
Javed Miandad	P	167	32	119*	5654	41.88	6	38
A.R.Border	A	208	30	127*	5620	31.57	3	36
C.G.Greenidge	WI	127	13	133*	5134	45.03	11	31
D.M.Jones	A	113	21	145	4576	49.73	7	33
R.B.Richardson	WI	134	17	110	4206	35.94	3	34
G.R.Marsh	A	101	6	126*	3924	41.30	9	19
J.G.Wright	NZ	140	1	101	3767	27.10	1	23
A.J.Lamb	E	106	16	118	3710	41.22	4	24
G.A.Gooch	E	94	5	142	3641	40.91	8	20
K.Srikkanth	I	125	3	123	3541	29.02	4	22
D.B.Vengsarkar	I	120	19	105	3508	34.73	1	23
M.D.Crowe	NZ	108	9	105*	3428	34.62	2	24
Salim Malik	P	117	15	102	3407	33.40	4	21

BOWLING RECORDS

MOST WICKETS IN AN INNINGS

7-51	W.W.Davis	West Indies v Australia	Leeds	1983
6-14	G.J.Gilmour	Australia v England	Leeds	1975
6-14	Imran Khan	Pakistan v India	Sharjah	1984-85
6-15	C.E.H.Croft	West Indies v England	Kingston	1980-81
6-26	Waqar Younis	Pakistan v Sri Lanka	Sharjah	1989-90
6-29	B.P.Patterson	West Indies v India	Nagpur	1987-88
6-39	K.H.MacLeay	Australia v India	Nottingham	1983
6-41	I.V.A.Richards	West Indies v India	Delhi	1989-90
6-50	A.H.Gray	West Indies v Australia	Port-of-Spain	1990-91

HAT-TRICKS

Jalaluddin	Pakistan v Australia	Hyderabad	1982-83
B.A.Reid	Australia v New Zealand	Sydney	1985-86
C.Sharma	India v New Zealand	Nagpur	1987-88
Wasim Akram	Pakistan v West Indies	Sharjah	1989-90
Wasim Akram	Pakistan v Australia	Sharjah	1989-90
Kapil Dev	India v Sri Lanka	Calcutta	1990-91

MOST WICKETS IN A CAREER

		Balls	Runs	Wkts	Avge	Best	4w
Kapil Dev	I	8225	5150	197	26.14	5-43	3
Imran Khan	P	6553	4209	167	25.20	6-14	4
R.J.Hadlee	NZ	6182	3407	158	21.56	5-25	6
J.Garner	WI	5330	2752	146	18.84	5-31	5
M.A.Holding	WI	5473	3034	142	21.36	5-26	6
M.D.Marshall	WI	6413	3735	142	26.30	4-23	5
E.J.Chatfield	NZ	6065	3621	140	25.86	5-34	4
Wasim Akram	P	4941	3131	133	23.54	5-21	5
Abdul Qadir	P	4996	3364	131	25.67	5-44	6
I.T.Botham	E	5335	3556	122	29.14	4-45	2
I.V.A.Richards	WI	5644	4228	118	35.83	6-41	3
R.J.Shastri	I	5810	4068	115	35.37	4-38	2
M.C.Snedden	NZ	4519	3235	114	28.37	4-34	1
Mudassar Nazar	P	4855	3431	111	30.90	5-28	2
C.A.Walsh	WI	5115	3326	108	30.79	5-1	5
S.P.O'Donnell	A	4248	3028	107	28.29	5-13	6
D.K.Lillee	A	3593	2145	103	20.82	5-34	4
C.J.McDermott	A	3783	2773	103	26.92	5-44	4
S.R.Waugh	A	4255	3191	100	31.91	4-33	2

WICKET-KEEPING RECORDS

MOST DISMISSALS IN AN INNINGS

5 (5ct)	R.W.Marsh	Australia v England	Leeds	1981
5 (5ct)	R.G.de Alwis	Sri Lanka v Australia	Colombo (PSS)	1982-83
5 (5ct)	S.M.H.Kirmani	India v Zimbabwe	Leicester	1983
5 (3ct, 2st)	S.Viswanath	India v England	Sydney	1984-85
5 (3ct, 2st)	K.S.More	India v New Zealand	Sharjah	1987-88
5 (5ct)	H.P.Tillekeratne	Sri Lanka v Pakistan	Sharjah	1990-91

MOST DISMISSALS IN A CAREER

200 (181ct, 19st) P.J.L.Dujon (West Indies) in 165 matches

FIELDING RECORDS

MOST CATCHES IN AN INNINGS

4	Salim Malik	Pakistan v New Zealand	Sialkot	1984-85
4	S.M.Gavaskar	India v Pakistan	Sharjah	1984-85
4	R.B.Richardson	West Indies v England	Birmingham	1991

MOST CATCHES IN A CAREER

A.R.Border	Australia	102 in 223 matches
I.V.A.Richards	West Indies	101 in 187 matches

ALL-ROUND RECORDS

1000 RUNS AND 100 DISMISSALS

I.T.Botham	England	1738 runs	122 wickets
P.J.L.Dujon	West Indies	1877 runs	200 dismissals (181ct, 19st)
R.J.Hadlee	New Zealand	1749 runs	158 wickets
Imran Khan	Pakistan	3255 runs	167 wickets
Kapil Dev	India	3132 runs	197 wickets
R.W.Marsh	Australia	1225 runs	124 dismissals (120ct, 4st)
Mudassar Nazar	Pakistan	2624 runs	111 wickets
S.P.O'Donnell	Australia	1232 runs	107 wickets
I.V.A.Richards	West Indies	6721 runs	118 wickets
R.J.Shastri	India	2567 runs	115 wickets
S.R.Waugh	Australia	2295 runs	100 wickets

TOURS PROGRAMME

1992

Apr	South Africa to West Indies
Apr/Aug	Pakistan to England

1992-93

Aug/Sep	Australia to Sri Lanka
Oct/Feb	West Indies to Australia
Nov/Jan	India to South Africa*
Nov/Dec	New Zealand to Sri Lanka
Dec/Mar	England to India*
Dec/Feb	Pakistan to Australia
Feb/Mar	Australia to New Zealand
Mar	England to Sri Lanka*
Mar/Apr	Pakistan to West Indies
Apr	West Indies to Sri Lanka*

1993

May/Aug	Australia to England

1993-94

Aug/Sep	South Africa to Sri Lanka*
Oct/Jan	New Zealand to Australia
Nov/Jan	India to Pakistan
Dec/Feb	Sri Lanka to Australia
Feb/Mar	England to West Indies
Feb/Mar	India to Sri Lanka
Feb/Mar	Pakistan to New Zealand

Mar/Apr	Australia to Pakistan*

1994

May/Jul	India to England*
July/Sep	New Zealand to England*

1994-95

Oct/Feb	West Indies to Australia
Nov/Dec	West Indies to India*
Jan/Mar	West Indies to New Zealand
Jan/Mar	Pakistan to India
Mar/May	Australia to West Indies*

1995-96

Nov/Dec	Sri Lanka to India
Nov/Feb	Pakistan to Australia*
Dec/Feb	West Indies to Australia*
Jan/Feb	England to New Zealand
Mar/Apr	New Zealand to West Indies

1996-97

Nov/Dec	New Zealand to India
Feb/Apr	India to West Indies*

1997-98

Jan/Mar	India to New Zealand

* unconfirmed

ENGLAND v PAKISTAN
1954 to 1987-88

Season	England	Captains Pakistan	P	Eng	Pak	D
1954	L.Hutton[1]	A.H.Kardar	4	1	1	2
1961-62	E.R.Dexter	Imtiaz Ahmed	3	1	–	2
1962	E.R.Dexter[2]	Javed Burki	5	4	–	1
1967	D.B.Close	Hanif Mohammad	3	2	–	1
1968-69	M.C.Cowdrey	Saeed Ahmed	3	–	–	3
1971	R.Illingworth	Intikhab Alam	3	1	–	2
1972-73	A.R.Lewis	Majid Khan	3	–	–	3
1974	M.H.Denness	Intikhab Alam	3	–	–	3
1977-78	J.M.Brearley[3]	Wasim Bari	3	–	–	3
1978	J.M.Brearley	Wasim Bari	3	2	–	1
1982	R.G.D.Willis[4]	Imran Khan	3	2	1	–
1983-84	R.G.D.Willis[5]	Zaheer Abbas	3	–	1	2
1987	M.W.Gatting	Imran Khan	5	–	1	4
1987-88	M.W.Gatting	Javed Miandad	3	–	1	2

	P	Eng	Pak	D
At Lord's	8	2	1	5
At Nottingham	3	2	–	1
At Manchester	2	–	–	2
At The Oval	5	2	1	2
At Birmingham	5	3	–	2
At Leeds	6	3	1	2
At Lahore	6	1	1	4
At Dacca	2	–	–	2
At Karachi	6	–	1	5
At Hyderabad	2	–	–	2
At Faisalabad	2	–	–	2
In England	29	12	3	14
In Pakistan	18	1	2	15
Totals	47	13	5	29

The following deputised for the official touring captain or were appointed by the home authority for only a minor proportion of the series:
[1] D.S.Sheppard (2nd and 3rd). [2] M.C.Cowdrey (3rd). [3] G.Boycott (3rd). [4] D.I.Gower (2nd). [5] D.I.Gower (2nd and 3rd).

HIGHEST INNINGS TOTALS

England	in England	558-6d	Nottingham	1954
	in Pakistan	546-8d	Faisalabad	1983-84
Pakistan	in England	708	The Oval	1987
	in Pakistan	569-9d	Hyderabad	1972-73

LOWEST INNINGS TOTALS

England	in England	130	The Oval	1954
	in Pakistan	130	Lahore	1987-88
Pakistan	in England	87	Lord's	1954
	in Pakistan	191	Faisalabad	1987-88

HIGHEST MATCH AGGREGATE

1274 for 25 wickets	Hyderabad	1972-73
1274 for 37 wickets	Birmingham	1987

LOWEST MATCH AGGREGATE

509 for 28 wickets	Nottingham	1967

HIGHEST INDIVIDUAL INNINGS

England	in England	278 D.C.S.Compton	Nottingham	1954
		183 D.L.Amiss	The Oval	1974
		182 M.C.Cowdrey	The Oval	1962
		172 E.R.Dexter	The Oval	1962
		166 R.T.Robinson	Manchester	1987
		159 M.C.Cowdrey	Birmingham	1962
		153 T.W.Graveney	Lord's	1962
		150* M.W.Gatting	The Oval	1987
	in Pakistan	205 E.R.Dexter	Karachi	1961-62
		173* D.I.Gower	Lahore	1983-84
		165 G.Pullar	Dacca	1961-62
		158 D.L.Amiss	Hyderabad	1972-73
		152 D.I.Gower	Faisalabad	1983-84
Pakistan	in England	274 Zaheer Abbas	Birmingham	1971
		260 Javed Miandad	The Oval	1987
		240 Zaheer Abbas	The Oval	1974
		200 Mohsin Khan	Lord's	1982
		187* Hanif Mohammad	Lord's	1967
	in Pakistan	157 Mushtaq Mohammad	Hyderabad	1972-73

71 hundreds have been scored in this series (England 41, Pakistan 30). At Karachi in 1972-73, three batsmen – Majid Khan, Mushtaq Mohammad and D.L.Amiss – each scored 99, a coincidence unique in Test cricket.

HUNDRED IN EACH INNINGS

Pakistan	111	104 Hanif Mohammad	Dacca	1961-62

HUNDREDS ON DEBUT IN SERIES

England (6)	139 K.F.Barrington	Lahore	1961-62
	159 M.C.Cowdrey	Birmingham	1962
	108* B.W.Luckhurst	Birmingham	1971
	106 C.T.Radley	Birmingham	1978
	100 I.T.Botham	Birmingham	1978
	166 R.T.Robinson	Manchester	1987
Pakistan (4)	138 Javed Burki	Lahore	1961-62
	274 Zaheer Abbas	Birmingham	1971
	122 Haroon Rashid	Lahore	1977-78
	114 Mudassar Nazar	Lahore	1977-78

HIGHEST AGGREGATE OF RUNS IN A SERIES

England	in England	453 (av 90.60)	D.C.S.Compton	1954
	in Pakistan	449 (av 112.25)	D.I.Gower	1983-84
Pakistan	in England	401 (av 44.55)	Mushtaq Mohammad	1962
	in Pakistan	407 (av 67.83)	Hanif Mohammad	1961-62

RECORD WICKET PARTNERSHIPS – ENGLAND

1st	198	G.Pullar (165), R.W.Barber (86)	Dacca	1961-62
2nd	248	M.C.Cowdrey (182), E.R.Dexter (172)	The Oval	1962
3rd	201	K.F.Barrington (148), T.W.Graveney (81)	Lord's	1967
4th	188	E.R.Dexter (205), P.H.Parfitt (111)	Karachi	1961-62
5th	192	D.C.S.Compton (278), T.E.Bailey (36*)	Nottingham	1954
6th	153*	P.H.Parfitt (101*), D.A.Allen (79*)	Birmingham	1962
7th	167	D.I.Gower (152), V.J.Marks (83)	Faisalabad	1983-84
8th	99	P.H.Parfitt (119), D.A.Allen (62)	Leeds	1962
9th	76	T.W.Graveney (153), F.S.Trueman (29)	Lord's	1962
10th	79	R.W.Taylor (54), R.G.D.Willis (28*)	Birmingham	1982

RECORD WICKET PARTNERSHIPS – PAKISTAN

1st	173	Mohsin Khan (104), Shoaib Mohammad (80)	Lahore	1983-84
2nd	291	Zaheer Abbas (274), Mushtaq Mohammad (100)	Birmingham	1971
3rd	180	Mudassar Nazar (114), Haroon Rashid (122)	Lahore	1977-78
4th	234	Javed Miandad (260), Salim Malik (102)	The Oval	1987
5th	197	Javed Burki (101), Nasim-ul-Ghani (101)	Lord's	1962
6th	145	Mushtaq Mohammad (157), Intikhab Alam (138)	Hyderabad	1972-73
7th	89	Ijaz Ahmed (69), Salim Yousuf (42)	The Oval	1987
8th	130	Hanif Mohammad (187*), Asif Iqbal (76)	Lord's	1967
9th	190	Asif Iqbal (146), Intikhab Alam (51)	The Oval	1967
10th	62	Sarfraz Nawaz (53), Asif Masood (4*)	Leeds	1974

BEST INNINGS BOWLING ANALYSIS

England	in England	8-34	I.T.Botham	Lord's	1978
	in Pakistan	7-66	P.H.Edmonds	Karachi	1977-78
Pakistan	in England	7-40	Imran Khan	Leeds	1987
	in Pakistan	9-56	Abdul Qadir	Lahore	1987-88

BEST MATCH BOWLING ANALYSIS

England	in England	13-71	D.L.Underwood	Lord's	1974
	in Pakistan	11-83	N.G.B.Cook	Karachi	1983-84
Pakistan	in England	12-99	Fazal Mahmood	The Oval	1954
	in Pakistan	13-101	Abdul Qadir	Lahore	1987-88

HIGHEST AGGREGATE OF WICKETS IN A SERIES

England	in England	22 (av 19.95)	F.S.Trueman	1962
	in Pakistan	14 (av 31.71)	N.G.B.Cook	1983-84
Pakistan	in England	{ 21 (av 18.57)	Imran Khan	1982
		21 (av 21.66)	Imran Khan	1987
	in Pakistan	30 (av 14.56)	Abdul Qadir	1987-88

FIRST-CLASS UMPIRES 1992

BALDERSTONE, John **Christopher** (Paddock Council S, Huddersfield), b Longwood, Huddersfield, Yorks 16 Nov 1940. RHB, SLA. Yorkshire 1961-69. Leicestershire 1971-86 (cap 1973; testimonial 1984). **Tests:** 2 (1976); HS 35 v WI (Leeds) 1976; BB 1-80. Tour: Z 1980-81 (Le). 1000 runs (11); most – 1482 (1982). Hat-trick 1976. HS 181* Le v Glos (Leicester) 1984. BB 6-25 Le v Hants (Southampton) 1978. F-c career: 390 matches; 19,034 runs @ 34.11, 32 hundreds; 310 wickets @ 26.32; 210 ct. Soccer for Huddersfield Town, Carlisle United, Doncaster Rovers and Queen of the South. Appointed 1988.

*BIRD, Harold Dennis (**'Dickie'**) (Raley SM, Barnsley), b Barnsley, Yorks 19 Apr 1933. RHB, RM. Yorkshire 1956-59. Leicestershire 1960-64 (cap 1960). MBE 1986. 1000 runs (1): 1028 (1960). HS 181* Y v Glam (Bradford) 1959. F-c career: 93 matches; 3314 runs @ 20.71, 2 hundreds. Appointed 1970. Umpired 46 Tests (1973 to 1991); only F.Chester (48 – 1924 to 1955) has stood in more. Officiated in 61 LOI (1973 to 1991), including 1975, 1979, 1983 and 1987 World Cup Finals and 6 Sharjah tournaments.

BOND, John David (**'Jack'**) (Bolton S), b Kearsley, Lancs 6 May 1932. RHB, LB. Lancashire 1955-72 (cap 1955; captain 1968-72; coach 1973; manager 1980-86; benefit 1970). Nottinghamshire 1974 (captain/coach 1974). 1000 (2); most – 2125 (1963). HS 157 La v Hants (Manchester) 1962. Test selector 1974. F-c career: 362 matches; 12,125 runs @ 25.90, 14 hundreds; 222 ct. Appointed 1988.

BURGESS, Graham Iefvion (Millfield S), b Glastonbury, Somerset 5 May 1943. RHB, RM. Somerset 1966-79 (cap 1968; testimonial 1977). HS 129 v Glos (Taunton) 1973. BB 7-43 (13-75 match) v OU (Oxford) 1975. F-c career: 252 matches; 7,129 runs @ 18.90, 2 hundreds; 474 wickets @ 28.57. Appointed 1991.

CONSTANT, David John, b Bradford-on-Avon, Wilts 9 Nov 1941. LHB, SLA. Kent 1961-63. Leicestershire 1965-68. HS 80 Le v Glos (Bristol) 1966. F-c career: 61 matches; 1517 runs @ 19.20; 1 wicket @ 36.00. Appointed 1969. Umpired 36 Tests (1971 to 1988) and 29 LOI (1972 to 1990). Represented Gloucestershire at bowls 1984-86.

*DUDLESTON, Barry (Stockport S), b Bebington, Cheshire 16 Jul 1945. RHB, SLA. Leicestershire 1966-80 (cap 1969; benefit 1980). Gloucestershire 1981-83. Rhodesia 1976-80. 1000 (8); most – 1374 (1970). HS 202 Le v Derbys (Leicester) 1979. BB 4-6 Le v Surrey (Leicester) 1972. F-c career: 295 matches; 14,747 runs @ 32.48, 32 hundreds; 47 wickets @ 29.04. Appointed 1984. Umpired 1 Test (1991).

HAMPSHIRE, John Harry (Oakwood THS, Rotherham), b Thurnscoe, Yorks 10 Feb 1941. RHB, LB. Son of J. (Yorks 1937); brother of A.W. (Yorks 1975). Yorkshire 1961-81 (cap 1963; benefit 1976; captain 1979-80). Derbyshire 1982-84 (cap 1982). Tasmania 1967-69, 1977-79. Tests: 8 (1969 to 1975); 403 runs @ 26.86, HS 107 v WI (Lord's) 1969 on debut (only England player to score hundred at Lord's on debut in Tests). Tours: Aus 1970-71; SA 1972-73 (DHR), 1974-75 (DHR); WI 1964-65 (Cav); NZ 1970-71; Pak 1967-68 (Cwlth XI); SL 1969-70; Z 1980-81 (Le XI). 1000 runs (15); most – 1596 (1978). HS 183 Y v Sussex (Hove) 1971. BB 7-52 Y v Glam (Cardiff) 1963. F-c career: 577 matches; 28,059 runs @ 34.55, 43 hundreds; 30 wickets @ 54.56; 445 ct. Appointed 1985. Umpired 9 Tests (1989 to 1991), including 4 in Pakistan 1989-90, and 4 LOI (1989 to 1991).

HARRIS, John Henry, b Taunton, Somerset 13 Feb 1936. LHB, RFM. Somerset 1952-59. Suffolk 1960-62. Devon 1975. HS 41 v Worcs (Taunton) 1957. BB 3-29 v Worcs (Bristol) 1959. F-c career: 15 matches; 154 runs @ 11.00; 19 wickets @ 32.57. Appointed 1983.

HOLDER, John Wakefield (Combermere S, Barbados), b St George, Barbados 19 Mar 1945. RHB, RFM. Hampshire 1968-72. Hat-trick 1972. HS 33 v Sussex (Hove) 1971. BB 7-79 v Glos (Gloucester) 1972. F-c career: 47 matches; 374 runs @ 10.68; 139 wickets @ 24.56. Appointed 1983. Umpired 10 Tests (1988 to 1991), including 4 in Pakistan 1989-90, and 8 LOI (1988 to 1990) including 1989-90 Nehru Cup.

HOLDER, Vanburn Alonza (Richmond SM, Barbados), b Bridgetown, Barbados 8 Oct 1945. RHB, RFM. Barbados 1966-78. Worcestershire 1968-80 (cap 1970; benefit 1979). Shropshire 1981. **Tests** (WI): 40 (1969 to 1978-79); HS 42 v NZ (P-o-S) 1971-72; BB 6-28 v A (P-o-S) 1977-78. LOI: 13. Tours (WI): E 1969, 1973, 1976; A 1975-76; I 1974-75, 1978-79; P 1973-74 (RW), 1974-75; SL 1974-75, 1978-79. HS 122 Barbados v Trinidad (Bridgetown) 1973-74. Wo HS 52 v Glos (Dudley) 1970. BB 7-40 v Glam (Cardiff) 1974. F-c career: 311 matches; 3,559 runs @ 13.03, 1 hundred; 947 wickets @ 24.48. Appointed 1992.

JONES, Allan Arthur (St John's C, Horsham), b Horley, Surrey 9 Dec 1947. RHB RFM. Sussex 1966-69. Somerset 1970-75 (cap 1972). Northern Transvaal 1972-73. Middlesex 1976-79 (cap 1976). Orange Free State 1976-77. Glamorgan 1980-81. HS 33 M v Kent (Canterbury) 1978. BB 9-51 Sm v Sussex (Hove) 1972. F-c career: 214 matches; 799 runs @ 5.39; 549 wickets @ 28.07. Appointed 1985.

JULIAN, Raymond (Wigston SM), b Cosby, Leics 23 Aug 1936. RHB, WK. Leicestershire 1953-71 (cap 1961). HS 51 v Worcs (Worcester) 1962. F-c career: 192 matches; 2581 runs @ 9.73; 421 dismissals (382 ct, 39 st). Appointed 1972.

*KITCHEN, Mervyn John (Backwell SM, Nailsea), b Nailsea, Somerset 1 Aug 1940. LHB, RM. Somerset 1960-79 (cap 1966; testimonial 1973). Tour: Rhodesia 1972-73 (Int W). 1000 runs (7); most – 1730 (1968). HS 189 v Pakistanis (Taunton) 1967. BB 1-4. F-c career: 354 matches; 15,230 runs @ 26.25, 17 hundreds; 2 wickets @ 54.50. Appointed 1982. Umpired 3 Tests (1990 to 1991) and 7 LOI (1983 to 1991).

LEADBEATER, Barrie (Harehills SS), b Harehills, Leeds, Yorks 14 Aug 1943. RHB, RM. Yorkshire 1966-79 (cap 1969; joint benefit with G.A.Cope 1980). Tour: WI 1969-70 (DN). HS 140* v Hants (Portsmouth) 1976. F-c career: 147 matches; 5373 runs @ 25.34, 1 hundred; 1 wicket @ 5.00. Appointed 1981. Umpired 4 LOI (1983).

*MEYER, Barrie John (Boscombe S), b Bournemouth, Hants 21 Aug 1932. RHB, WK. Gloucestershire 1957-71 (cap 1958; benefit 1971). HS 63 v Indians (Cheltenham) 1959, v OU (Bristol) 1962, and v Sussex (Bristol) 1964. F-c career: 406 matches; 5367 runs @ 14.16; 826 dismissals (707 ct, 119 st). Soccer for Bristol Rovers, Plymouth Argyle, Newport County and Bristol City. Appointed 1973. Umpired 23 Tests (1978 to 1991) and 21 LOI (1977 to 1990), including 1979 and 1983 World Cup finals.

OSLEAR, Donald Osmund, b Cleethorpes, Lincs 3 Mar 1929. No first-class appearances. Appointed 1975. Umpired in 5 Tests (1980 to 1984) and 8 LOI (1980 to 1984).

*PALMER, Kenneth Ernest (Southbroom SM, Devizes), b Winchester, Hants 22 Apr 1937. RHB, RFM. Brother of R. (below) and father of G.V. (Somerset 1982-88). Somerset 1955-69 (cap 1958; testimonial 1968). Tours: WI 1963-64 (Cav); Pak 1963-64 (Cwlth XI). **Tests**: 1 (1964-65; while coaching in South Africa); 10 runs; 1 wicket. 1000 runs (1): 1036 (1961). 100 wickets (4); most – 139 (1963). HS 125* v Northants (Northampton) 1961. BB 9-57 v Notts (Nottingham) 1963. F-c career: 314 matches; 7,761 runs @ 20.64, 2 hundreds; 866 wickets @ 21.34. Appointed 1972. Umpired 19 Tests (1978 to 1991) and 16 LOI (1977 to 1988).

*PALMER, Roy (Southbroom SM), b Devizes, Wilts 12 Jul 1942. RHB, RFM. Brother of K.E. (above). Somerset 1965-70. HS 84 v Leics (Taunton) 1967. BB 6-45 v Middx (Lord's) 1967. F-c career: 74 matches; 1037 runs @ 13.29; 172 wickets @ 31.62. Appointed 1980. Umpired 4 LOI (1983).

PLEWS, Nigel Trevor, b Nottingham 5 Sep 1934. Former policeman (Fraud Squad). No first-class appearances. Appointed 1982. Umpired 5 Tests (1988 to 1990) and 4 LOI (1986 to 1990).

SHARP, George (Elwick Road SS, Hartlepool), b West Hartlepool, Co Durham 12 Mar 1950. RHB, WK, occ LM. Northamptonshire 1968-85 (cap 1973; benefit 1982). HS 98 v Yorks (Northampton) 1983. BB 1-47. F-c career: 306 matches; 6,254 runs @ 19.85; 1 wicket @ 70.00; 565 ct, 90 st. Appointed 1992.

*SHEPHERD, David Robert (Barnstaple GS; St Luke's C, Exeter), b Bideford, Devon 27 Dec 1940. RHB, RM. Gloucestershire 1965-79 (cap 1969; joint benefit with J. Davey 1978). Scored 108 on debut (v OU). Devon 1959-64. 1000 runs (2); most – 1079 (1970). HS 153 v Middlesex (Bristol) 1968. F-c career: 282 matches; 10,672 runs @ 24.47, 12 hundreds; 2 wickets @ 53.00. Appointed 1981. Umpired 13 Tests (1985 to 1991) and 40 LOI (1983 to 1991), including 1987 World Cup in India and Pakistan and 4 Sharjah tournaments.

STICKLEY, Gerald Albert (Holly Lodge GS, Smethwick), b St Chad's Hospital, Birmingham 24 Sep 1938. No first-class appearances. Appointed 1992.

TOLCHARD, Raymond Charles (Malvern C), b Torquay, Devon 13 Oct 1953. Brother of J.G. (Leics and Devon) and R.W. (Leics, Devon and England 1965-83). LHB. Devon 1975-84. No first-class appearances. Appointed 1991.

WHITE, Robert Arthur (Chiswick GS), b Fulham, London 6 Oct 1936. LHB, OB. Middlesex 1958-65 (cap 1963). Nottinghamshire 1966-80 (cap 1966; benefit 1974). 1000 runs (1): 1355 (1963). HS 116* Nt v Surrey (Oval) 1967. BB 7-41 Nt v Derbys (Ilkeston) 1971. F-c career: 413 matches; 12,452 runs @ 23.18, 5 hundreds; 693 wickets @ 30.50. Appointed 1983.

WHITEHEAD, Alan Geoffrey Thomas, b Butleigh, Somerset 28 Oct 1940. LHB, SLA. Somerset 1957-61. HS 15 v Hants (Southampton) 1959 and v Leics (Leicester) 1960. BB 6-74 v Sussex (Eastbourne) 1959. F-c career: 38 matches; 137 runs @ 5.70; 67 wickets @ 34.41. Appointed 1970. Umpired 5 Tests (1982 to 1987) and 12 LOI (1979 to 1987).

WIGHT, Peter Bernard, b Georgetown, British Guiana 25 Jun 1930. RHB, OB. Brother of G.L. (West Indies 1949-53), H.A. and N. (all British Guiana). British Guiana 1950-51. Somerset 1953-65 (cap 1954; benefit 1963). Canterbury 1963-64. 1000 runs (10); most – 2375 (1960). HS 222* v Kent (Taunton) 1959. BB 6-29 v Derbyshire (Chesterfield) 1957. F-c career: 333 matches; 17,773 runs @ 33.09, 28 hundreds; 68 wickets @ 33.26. Appointed 1966.

RESERVE LIST

P.ADAMS, A.CLARKSON, Dr D.FAWKNER-CORBETT, M.J.HARRIS, P.WILLEY

* On Test Match and Texaco Trophy Panel for 1992
See page 63 for key to abbreviations.

PRINCIPAL FIXTURES 1992

* Includes Sunday play

† Reserve day Sunday

Monday 13 April

Lord's: England 'A' v Britannic
   Assurance Champions (Essex) (Four
   days)

Tuesday 14 April

Fenner's: Cambridge U v Leics
The Parks: Oxford U v Durham

Friday 17 April

Fenner's: Cambridge U v Middx
The Parks: Oxford U v Worcs

Sunday 19 April

Sunday League
Derby: Derbys v Essex
Durham University: Durham v Lancs
Southampton: Hants v Glos
Canterbury: Kent v Somerset
Leicester: Leics v Middx
Trent Bridge: Notts v Sussex
The Oval: Surrey v Northants
Edgbaston: Warwicks v Glam
Worcester: Worcs v Yorks

Tuesday 21 April

Benson & Hedges Cup
Durham University: Durham v Glam
Chelmsford: Essex v Lancs
Cheltenham (Dowty Arle Court): Glos
   v Leics
Canterbury: Kent v Somerset
Lord's: Middx v Minor Counties
Forfar: Scotland v Northants
Hove: Sussex v Surrey
Edgbaston: Warwicks v Yorks
Worcester: Worcs v Derbys
Other Match
Headingley: Rapid Cricketline
   Champions (Yorkshire 2nd XI) v
   England Under-19 (Four days)

Thursday 23 April

Benson & Hedges Cup
Derby: Derbys v Glam
Cheltenham (Dowty Arle Court): Glos
   v Minor Counties
Southampton: Hants v Essex

Old Trafford: Lancs v Scotland
Leicester: Leics v Sussex
Trent Bridge: Notts v Kent
Taunton: Somerset v Yorks
The Oval: Surrey v Middx
The Parks: Combined Us v Worcs

Saturday 25 April

*Britannic Assurance Championship
   (Four days)*
Durham University: Durham v Leics
Southampton: Hants v Sussex
*Old Trafford: Lancs v Kent
Lord's: Middx v Glam
*Trent Bridge: Notts v Warwicks
*Taunton: Somerset v Glos
The Oval: Surrey v Yorks
Worcester: Worcs v Northants
Other Match
Fenner's: Cambridge U v Essex

Sunday 26 April

Sunday League
Gateshead Fell: Durham v Leics
Chelmsford: Essex v Surrey
Lord's: Middx v Glam
Hove: Sussex v Yorks
Worcester: Worcs v Northants

Thursday 30 April

Benson & Hedges Cup
Derby: Derbys v Combined Us
Chelmsford: Essex v Scotland
Southampton: Hants v Northants
Leicester: Leics v Surrey
Lord's: Middx v Glos
Marlow: Minor Counties v Sussex
Edgbaston: Warwicks v Notts
Worcester: Worcs v Durham
Headingley: Yorks v Kent

Saturday 2 May

Benson & Hedges Cup
†Fenner's: Combined Us v Durham
Cardiff: Glam v Worcs
Old Trafford: Lancs v Hants
Leicester: Leics v Middx
Northampton: Northants v Essex
Taunton: Somerset v Warwicks

†The Oval: Surrey v Minor Counties
Hove: Sussex v Glos
Headingley: Yorks v Notts

Sunday 3 May

Sunday League
Cardiff: Glam v Worcs
Old Trafford: Lancs v Hants
Leicester: Leics v Essex
Lord's: Middx v Glos
Northampton: Northants v Kent
Taunton: Somerset v Warwicks
Headingley: Yorks v Notts
Tourist Match
Arundel: Lavinia, Duchess of Norfolk's
XI v Pakistanis (One day)

Monday 4 May

Tourist Match
Canterbury: Kent v Pakistanis (One
day)

Tuesday 5 May

Benson & Hedges Cup
Jesmond: Durham v Derbys
Cardiff: Glam v Combined Us
Glasgow (Hamilton Crescent):
  Scotland v Hants
Canterbury: Kent v Warwicks
Stone: Minor Counties v Leics
Northampton: Northants v Lancs
Trent Bridge: Notts v Somerset
The Oval: Surrey v Glos
Hove: Sussex v Middx

Wednesday 6 May

Tetley Bitter Challenge
Worcester: Worcs v Pakistanis

Thursday 7 May

Britannic Assurance Championship
(Four days)
Chelmsford: Essex v Leics
Canterbury: Kent v Durham
*Lord's: Middx v Lancs
Northampton: Northants v Surrey
Hove: Sussex v Somerset
Edgbaston: Warwicks v Derbys
Headingley: Yorks v Hants

Other Match
The Parks: Oxford U v Notts

Saturday 9 May

Tetley Bitter Challenge
*Cardiff: Glam v Pakistanis

Sunday 10 May

Sunday League
Derby: Derbys v Glos
Chelmsford: Essex v Northants
Canterbury: Kent v Durham
Trent Bridge: Notts v Surrey
Hove: Sussex v Somerset
Worcester: Worcs v Warwicks

Tuesday 12 May

Fenner's: Cambridge U v Warwicks
The Parks: Oxford U v Middx

Wednesday 13 May

Tetley Bitter Challenge
Taunton: Somerset v Pakistanis

Thursday 14 May

Britannic Assurance Championship
(Four days)
Derby: Derbys v Worcs
Chelmsford: Essex v Kent
*Cardiff: Glam v Durham
Leicester: Leics v Lancs
Northampton: Northants v Notts
*Headingley: Yorks v Glos

Friday 15 May

Fenner's: Cambridge U v Surrey
The Parks: Oxford U v Hants

Saturday 16 May

Tourist Match
Hove: Sussex v Pakistanis (One day)

Sunday 17 May

Sunday League
Derby: Derbys v Worcs
Northampton: Northants v Lancs
Trent Bridge: Notts v Middx
Taunton: Somerset v Hants
The Oval: Surrey v Kent
Edgbaston: Warwicks v Leics
Tourist Match
Hove: Sussex v Pakistanis (One day)

Tuesday 19 May

*Britannic Assurance Championship
(Four days)*
Gloucester: Glos v Worcs
Southampton: Hants v Surrey
Leicester: Leics v Middx

Wednesday 20 May

TEXACO TROPHY
Lord's: ENGLAND v PAKISTAN
(First One-day International)
Britannic Assurance Championship
Swansea: Glam v Warwicks
Canterbury: Kent v Yorks
Blackpool: Lancs v Derbys
Trent Bridge: Notts v Sussex
Taunton: Somerset v Essex

Friday 22 May

TEXACO TROPHY
The Oval: ENGLAND v PAKISTAN
(Second One-day International)

Saturday 23 May

Britannic Assurance Championship
Derby: Derbys v Notts
Stockton: Durham v Northants
Gloucester: Glos v Somerset
Old Trafford: Lancs v Hants
Lord's: Middx v Surrey
Hove: Sussex v Kent
Edgbaston: Warwicks v Worcs
Tetley Bitter Challenge
*Leicester: Leics v Pakistanis

Sunday 24 May

Sunday League
Derby: Derbys v Notts
Stockton: Durham v Northants
Chelmsford: Essex v Glam
Gloucester: Glos v Somerset
Canterbury: Kent v Middx
The Oval: Surrey v Sussex
Edgbaston: Warwicks v Lancs
Headingley: Yorks v Hants

Wednesday 27 May

Benson & Hedges Cup
Quarter-Finals

Tourist Match
Luton: England Amateur XI v
Pakistanis (Two days)

Friday 29 May

Britannic Assurance Championship
Swansea: Glam v Leics
Southampton: Hants v Durham
Old Trafford: Lancs v Somerset
Northampton: Northants v Derbys
The Oval: Surrey v Sussex
Worcester: Worcs v Glos
Other Match
The Parks: Oxford U v Yorks

Saturday 30 May

Tetley Bitter Challenge
*Lord's: Middx v Pakistanis

Sunday 31 May

Sunday League
Swansea: Glam v Leics
Southampton: Hants v Durham
Canterbury: Kent v Yorks
Old Trafford: Lancs v Somerset
Northampton: Northants v Derbys
Trent Bridge: Notts v Glos
Hove: Sussex v Warwicks
Worcester: Worcs v Essex

Tuesday 2 June

Britannic Assurance Championship
Darlington: Durham v Somerset
Chelmsford: Essex v Glam
Basingstoke: Hants v Yorks
Tunbridge Wells: Kent v Worcs
Northampton: Northants v Leics
Trent Bridge: Notts v Middx
The Oval: Surrey v Derbys
Hove: Sussex v Warwicks
Other Match
The Parks: Oxford U v Lancs

Thursday 4 June

FIRST CORNHILL INSURANCE
TEST MATCH
*Edgbaston: ENGLAND v PAKISTAN

Friday 5 June

Britannic Assurance Championship
Chesterfield: Derbys v Durham
Tunbridge Wells: Kent v Essex
Old Trafford: Lancs v Glos
Lord's: Middx v Leics
Middlesbrough: Yorks v Somerset

Sunday 7 June

Sunday League
Chesterfield: Derbys v Durham
Chelmsford: Essex v Kent
Basingstoke: Hants v Surrey
Old Trafford: Lancs v Glos
Lord's: Middx v Warwicks
Hove: Sussex v Glam
Middlesbrough: Yorks v Somerset

Tuesday 9 June

Harrogate: Tilcon Trophy (Three days)

Wednesday 10 June

Benson & Hedges Cup
Semi-Finals
Tetley Bitter Challenge
Trent Bridge or Canterbury: Notts or
Kent v Pakistanis

Friday 12 June

Britannic Assurance Championship
Hartlepool: Durham v Essex
Colwyn Bay: Glam v Lancs
Leicester: Leics v Sussex
The Oval: Surrey v Worcs
Edgbaston: Warwicks v Hants
Harrogate: Yorks v Derbys

Saturday 13 June

Tetley Bitter Challenge
*Northampton: Northants v Pakistanis

Sunday 14 June

Sunday League
Hartlepool: Durham v Essex
Colwyn Bay: Glam v Lancs
Swindon: Glos v Kent
Leicester: Leics v Sussex
Bath: Somerset v Notts
The Oval: Surrey v Worcs
Edgbaston: Warwicks v Hants
Headingley: Yorks v Derbys

Tuesday 16 June

Britannic Assurance Championship
Bristol: Glos v Kent
Leicester: Leics v Hants
Trent Bridge: Notts v Lancs
Bath: Somerset v Northants
Coventry: Warwicks v Middx
Worcester: Worcs v Glam
Headingley: Yorks v Essex
Other Match
Fenner's: Cambridge U v Derbys

Thursday 18 June

**SECOND CORNHILL INSURANCE
TEST MATCH
*Lord's: ENGLAND v PAKISTAN**

Friday 19 June

Britannic Assurance Championship
Bristol: Glos v Warwicks
Bournemouth: Hants v Essex
Old Trafford: Lancs v Middx
Trent Bridge: Notts v Northants
Bath: Somerset v Durham
Horsham: Sussex v Durham
Worcester: Worcs v Yorks
Other Matches
*Fenner's: Cambridge U v Kent
The Parks: Oxford U v Glam

Saturday 20 June

*Dundee (Broughty Ferry): Scotland v
Ireland (Three days)

Sunday 21 June

Sunday League
Derby: Derbys v Middx
Ebbw Vale: Glam v Yorks
Bristol: Glos v Warwicks
Bournemouth: Hants v Essex
Old Trafford: Lancs v Leics
Trent Bridge: Notts v Northants
Bath: Somerset v Surrey
Horsham: Sussex v Durham

Wednesday 24 June

NatWest Trophy
First Round
Beaconsfield: Bucks v Sussex
Derby: Derbys v Berks
Chelmsford: Essex v Cumberland

Swansea: Glam v Surrey
Bristol: Glos v Cheshire
Southampton: Hants v Dorset
Dublin (Castle Ave): Ireland v Durham
Canterbury: Kent v Devon
Leicester: Leics v Norfolk
Northampton: Northants v Cambs
Trent Bridge: Notts v Worcs
Oxford (Christ Church): Oxon v Lancs
Telford (St Georges): Shrops v Middx
Taunton: Somerset v Scotland
Edgbaston: Warwicks v Staffs
Headingley: Yorks v Northd
Tourist Match
Fenner's: Oxbridge v Pakistanis (Three
  days)

Friday 26 June

Britannic Assurance Championship
Derby: Derbys v Warwicks
Ilford: Essex v Lancs
Bristol: Glos v Surrey
Lord's: Middx v Somerset
Luton: Northants v Glam
Worcester: Worcs v Sussex

Saturday 27 June

Britannic Assurance Championship
*Gateshead Fell: Durham v Kent
Tetley Bitter Challenge
*Southampton: Hants v Pakistanis
Other Match
*Trent Bridge: Notts v Cambridge U

Sunday 28 June

Sunday League
Derby: Derbys v Leics
Ilford: Essex v Lancs
Bristol: Glos v Surrey
Lord's: Middx v Somerset
Luton: Northants v Glam
Worcester: Worcs v Sussex
Scarborough: Yorks v Warwicks

Tuesday 30 June

Britannic Assurance Championship
Derby: Derbys v Glos
Ilford: Essex v Middx
Maidstone: Kent v Notts
Leicester: Leics v Worcs
The Oval: Surrey v Northants

Arundel: Sussex v Hants
Other Match
Lord's: Oxford U v Cambridge U

Thursday 2 July

**THIRD CORNHILL INSURANCE
  TEST MATCH**
Old Trafford: ENGLAND v PAKISTAN

Friday 3 July

Britannic Assurance Championship
Stockton: Durham v Glos
Neath: Glam v Surrey
Southampton: Hants v Notts
Maidstone: Kent v Lancs
Northampton: Northants v Sussex
Taunton: Somerset v Derbys
Edgbaston: Warwicks v Essex
Sheffield: Yorks v Leics

Sunday 5 July

Sunday League
Stockton: Durham v Glos
Llanelli: Glam v Surrey
Southampton: Hants v Notts
Maidstone: Kent v Lancs
Lord's: Middx v Worcs
Tring: Northants v Sussex
Taunton: Somerset v Derbys
Edgbaston: Warwicks v Essex
Sheffield: Yorks v Leics

Thursday 9 July

NatWest Trophy
Second Round
Derby or Finchampstead: Derbys or
  Berks v Leics or Norfolk
Chelmsford or Netherfield: Essex or
  Cumberland v Oxon or Lancs
Southampton or Bournemouth (Dean
  Park): Hants or Dorset v Kent
  or Devon
Northampton or March: Northants or
  Cambs v Yorks or Northd
Trent Bridge or Worcester: Notts v
  Worcs v Glam or Surrey
Telford (St Georges) or Uxbridge:
  Shrops or Middx v Ireland or Durham
Taunton or Glasgow (Hamilton
  Crescent): Somerset or Scotland v
  Glos or Cheshire

243

Edgbaston or Stone: Warwicks or Staffs
  v Bucks or Sussex
Tourist Match
Haslingden: League Cricket
  Conference v Pakistanis (One day)

Saturday 11 July

Lord's: *Benson & Hedges Cup Final*
Tourist Match
Glasgow (Titwood): Scotland v
  Pakistanis (One day)

Sunday 12 July

‡*Sunday League*
Moreton-in-Marsh: Glos v Northants
Canterbury: Kent v Notts
Old Trafford: Lancs v Middx
Leicester: Leics v Worcs
Taunton: Somerset v Durham
The Oval: Surrey v Derbys
Hove: Sussex v Hants
Scarborough: Yorks v Essex
Tourist Match
Glasgow (Titwood): Scotland v
  Pakistanis (One day)

‡ Matches involving B & H Cup Finalists
  to be rearranged

Tuesday 14 July

Britannic Assurance Championship
Southend: Essex v Glos
Portsmouth: Hants v Derbys
Southport: Lancs v Leics
Uxbridge: Middx v Northants
Trent Bridge: Notts v Worcs
Guildford: Surrey v Kent
Sheffield: Yorks v Warwicks
Tetley Bitter Challenge
Chester le Street: Durham v Pakistanis

Friday 17 July

Britannic Assurance Championship
Southend: Essex v Sussex
Cheltenham College: Glos v Yorks
Portsmouth: Hants v Glam
Leicester: Leics v Somerset
Uxbridge: Middx v Worcs
Northampton: Northants v Lancs
Trent Bridge: Notts v Durham
Guildford: Surrey v Warwicks

Saturday 18 July

Tetley Bitter Challenge
*Derby: Derbys v Pakistanis

Sunday 19 July

Sunday League
Southend: Essex v Sussex
Cheltenham College: Glos v Yorks
Portsmouth: Hants v Glam
Canterbury: Kent v Worcs
Leicester: Leics v Somerset
Northampton: Northants v Middx
Trent Bridge: Notts v Durham
The Oval: Surrey v Warwicks

Tuesday 21 July

Britannic Assurance Championship
Derby: Derbys v Middx
Cardiff: Glam v Yorks
Cheltenham College: Glos v Hants
Canterbury: Kent v Somerset
Leicester: Leics v Durham
Northampton: Northants v Warwicks
The Oval: Surrey v Notts
Hove: Sussex v Lancs
Kidderminster: Worcs v Essex

Thursday 23 July

**FOURTH CORNHILL INSURANCE
TEST MATCH**
*Headingley: ENGLAND v PAKISTAN

Friday 24 July

Britannic Assurance Championship
Abergavenny: Glam v Somerset
Cheltenham College: Glos v Sussex
Leicester: Leics v Essex
Lord's: Middx v Durham
Edgbaston: Warwicks v Notts
Worcester: Worcs v Derbys

Sunday 26 July

Sunday League
Pontypridd: Glam v Derbys
Cheltenham College: Glos v Sussex
Old Trafford: Lancs v Surrey
Leicester: Leics v Kent
Lord's: Middx v Durham
Taunton: Somerset v Northants
Edgbaston: Warwicks v Notts
Worcester: Worcs v Hants

Wednesday 29 July

NatWest Trophy
Quarter-Finals
Tourist Match
Marlow: Minor Counties v Pakistanis
  (Two days)
Other Match
Jesmond: England XI v Rest of the
  World XI (One day)
  (Heritage Homes Festival)

Thursday 30 July

Jesmond: England XI v Rest of the
  World XI (One day)
  (Heritage Homes Festival)

Friday 31 July

Britannic Assurance Championship
Durham University: Durham v Surrey
Swansea: Glam v Kent
*Taunton: Somerset v Sussex
Edgbaston: Warwicks v Leics
Headingley: Yorks v Lancs

Saturday 1 August

Tetley Bitter Challenge
*Chelmsford: Essex v Pakistanis

Sunday 2 August

Sunday League
Leek: Derbys v Warwicks
Durham University: Durham v Surrey
Swansea: Glam v Kent
Southampton: Hants v Middx
Trent Bridge: Notts v Leics
Worcester: Worcs v Glos
Headingley: Yorks v Lancs

Tuesday 4 August

Britannic Assurance Championship
Ilkeston: Derbys v Leics
Durham University: Durham v Yorks
Chelmsford: Essex v Northants
Canterbury: Kent v Middx
Lytham: Lancs v Surrey
Worksop: Notts v Glos
Taunton: Somerset v Warwicks
Eastbourne: Sussex v Glam
Worcester: Worcs v Hants

Thursday 6 August

**FIFTH CORNHILL INSURANCE
TEST MATCH**
*The Oval: ENGLAND v PAKISTAN

Friday 7 August

Britannic Assurance Championship
Canterbury: Kent v Hants
Old Trafford: Lancs v Worcs
Lord's: Middx v Glos
Northampton: Northants v Yorks
Trent Bridge: Notts v Glam
Eastbourne: Sussex v Derbys
Edgbaston: Warwicks v Durham

Sunday 9 August

Sunday League
Bristol: Glos v Leics
Canterbury: Kent v Hants
Old Trafford: Lancs v Worcs
Lord's: Middx v Essex
Northampton: Northants v Yorks
Trent Bridge: Notts v Glam
Eastbourne: Sussex v Derbys
Edgbaston: Warwicks v Durham

Monday 10 or Tuesday 11 August

Bain Clarkson Trophy
Semi-Finals (One day)

Wednesday 12 August

NatWest Trophy
Semi-Finals
Tourist Match
‡Edgbaston: Warwicks v Pakistanis
  (One day)

Thursday 13 August

Tourist Match
‡Edgbaston: Warwicks v Pakistanis
  (One day)

‡ Or another first-class County if
  Warwickshire involved in NWT Semi-
  Finals

Friday 14 August

Britannic Assurance Championship
Chesterfield: Derbys v Kent
Hartlepool: Durham v Glam
Colchester: Essex v Notts
Bournemouth: Hants v Northants
Uxbridge: Middx v Yorks
The Oval: Surrey v Leics
Bull Under-19 International Series
*Headingley: England Under-19 v Sri
  Lanka Under-19
  (First Youth Test Match) (Four days)

Saturday 15 August

Tetley Bitter Challenge
*Bristol: Glos v Pakistanis

Sunday 16 August

Sunday League
Chesterfield: Derbys v Kent
Hartlepool: Durham v Glam
Colchester: Essex v Notts
Bournemouth: Hants v Northants
Uxbridge: Middx v Yorks
Taunton: Somerset v Worcs
The Oval: Surrey v Leics
Hove: Sussex v Lancs

Tuesday 18 August

Britannic Assurance Championship
Chesterfield: Derbys v Glam
Colchester: Essex v Surrey
Bristol: Glos v Northants
Bournemouth: Hants v Middx
Leicester: Leics v Kent
Weston-super-Mare: Somerset v
  Worcs
Edgbaston: Warwicks v Lancs
Scarborough: Yorks v Notts

Thursday 20 August

TEXACO TROPHY
Trent Bridge: ENGLAND v PAKISTAN
  (Third One-day International)

Friday 21 August

Britannic Assurance Championship
Swansea: Glam v Glos
Leicester: Leics v Notts
Northamton: Northants v Kent
Weston-super-Mare: Somerset v Hants
Hove: Sussex v Middx
Worcester: Worcs v Durham
Bradford: Yorks v Surrey

Saturday 22 August

TEXACO TROPHY
Lord's: ENGLAND v PAKISTAN
  (Fourth One-day International)

Sunday 23 August

Sunday League
Bristol or Lydney: Glos v Glam
Southampton: Hants v Derbys
Leicester: Leics v Northants
Trent Bridge: Notts v Lancs
Weston-super-Mare: Somerset v Essex
Hove: Sussex v Middx
Edgbaston: Warwicks v Kent
Worcester: Worcs v Durham
Scarborough: Yorks v Surrey

Monday 24 August

TEXACO TROPHY
Old Trafford: ENGLAND v PAKISTAN
  (Fifth One-day International)

Tuesday 25 August

Bull Under-19 International Series
Taunton: England Under-19 v Sri
  Lanka Under-19
  (Second Youth Test Match) (Four
  days)

Wednesday 26 August

Britannic Assurance Championship
(Four days)
Derby: Derbys v Somerset
Darlington: Durham v Hants
Canterbury: Kent v Glos
Old Trafford: Lancs v Yorks
Northampton: Northants v Middx
Hove: Sussex v Essex
Edgbaston: Warwicks v Glam
Worcester: Worcs v Notts
Other Match
Scarborough: World XI v Pakistanis
  (Tesco International) (Three days)

Sunday 30 August

Sunday League
Darlington: Durham v Yorks
Chelmsford: Essex v Glos
Cardiff: Glam v Somerset
Canterbury: Kent v Sussex
Old Trafford: Lancs v Derbys
Leicester: Leics v Hants
Northampton: Northants v Warwicks
The Oval: Surrey v Middx
Worcester: Worcs v Notts

Monday 31 August

*Britannic Assurance Championship
(Four days)*
Chelmsford: Essex v Hants
Cardiff: Glam v Sussex
Bristol: Glos v Leics
Trent Bridge: Notts v Derbys
The Oval: Surrey v Somerset
Worcester: Worcs v Warwicks
Scarborough: Yorks v Northants

Friday 4 September

Scarborough: Joshua Tetley Festival
Trophy (Three days)

Saturday 5 September

Lord's: *NatWest Trophy Final*
Reserve days Sunday and Monday

Monday 7 September

‡*Britannic Assurance Championship
(Four days)*
Derby: Derbys v Essex
Canterbury: Kent v Glam
Old Trafford: Lancs v Sussex
Trent Bridge: Notts v Surrey
Taunton: Somerset v Durham

Bull Under-19 International Series
Worcester: England Under-19 v Sri
Lanka Under-19
(Third Youth Test Match) (Four
days)
Bain Clarkson Trophy Final (One day)

‡ Matches involving NWT Finalists to be
played Tue 8–Fri 11 Sept

Tuesday 8 September

*Britannic Assurance Championship
(Four days)*
Lord's: Middx v Warwicks

Saturday 12 September

*Britannic Assurance Championship
(Four days)*
*Gateshead Fell: Durham v Lancs
*Cardiff: Glam v Derbys
*Bristol: Glos v Essex
*Southampton: Hants v Worcs
*Leicester: Leics v Northants
*Taunton: Somerset v Notts
*The Oval: Surrey v Middx
*Hove: Sussex v Yorks
*Edgbaston: Warwicks v Kent

SOMERSET DEPARTURES (continued from p 125)

PRINGLE, Nicholas John (Taunton S), b Weymouth, Dorset 20 Sep 1966. 5'10½".
RHB, RMF. Somerset 1986-91. MCC Cricket Staff. HS 79 v Warwks (Birmingham)
1987. BB 2-35 v Glam (W-s-M) 1987. **NWT:** HS 17 v Hants (Southampton) 1988. **SL:**
HS 22 v Glam (W-s-M) 1987.

ROEBUCK, Peter Michael (Millfield S; Emmanuel C, Cambridge), b Oxford 6 Mar
1956. Brother of P.G.P. (CU, Glos and Glam 1983-88). 6'0". RHB, LB. Somerset
1974-91 (cap 1978; captain 1986-88; benefit 1990). 2nd XI debut 1969 (aged 13).
Cambridge U 1975-77 (blue 1975-76-77). Wisden 1987. 1000 runs (9); most – 1702
(1984). HS 221* v Notts (Nottingham) 1986. Shared record Somerset stand of 319 for
3rd wkt with M.D.Crowe v Leics (Taunton) 1984. BB 6-50 CU v Kent (Canterbury)
1977. Sm BB 3-10 v Leics (W-s-M) 1991. Awards: NWT 2; BHC 2. **NWT:** HS 102 v
Essex (Taunton) 1989. BB 1-21. **BHC:** HS 120 v Comb Us (Taunton) 1987. BB 2-13
v Comb Us 1982 and v Middx 1990. **SL:** HS 105 v Glos (Bath) 1983. BB 4-11 v Derbys
(Derby) 1991.

SWALLOW, Ian Geoffrey (Hoyland Kirk CS, Balk), b Barnsley, Yorks 18 Dec
1962. 5'7¼". RHB, OB. Yorkshire 1983-89. Somerset 1990-91. HS 114 Y v MCC
(Scarborough) 1987. BAC HS 64 Y v Derbys (Leeds) 1989. Sm HS 41* v Glam
(Taunton) 1991. BB 7-95 Y v Notts (Nottingham) 1987. Sm BB 3-43 v Sussex
(Taunton) 1991. **NWT:** HS 17* Y v Surrey (Oval) 1989. **BHC:** HS 18 v Middx
(Taunton) 1990. BB 2-32 v Minor C (Taunton) 1990. **SL:** HS 31 v Yorks
(Scarborough) 1990. BB 2-44 v Middx (Lord's) 1990.

SECOND XI FIXTURES 1992

(R)   Rapid Cricketline Championship (Three days)
(BC) Bain Clarkson Trophy (One day)

APRIL

Mon 20	(BC)	Old Trafford	Lancashire v Derbyshire
Tue 21	(R)	Liverpool	Lancashire v Derbyshire
	(R)	Taunton (King's College)	Somerset v Kent
		Headingley	Yorkshire v England Under 19 (Four days)
Fri 24	(BC)	Birkbeck College	MCC YCs v Middlesex
Mon 27	(R)	Portsmouth	Hampshire v Somerset
	(R)	Canterbury	Kent v Lancashire
	(R)	Leicester	Leicestershire v Durham
	(R)	Hove	Sussex v Worcestershire
	(R)	Headingley	Yorkshire v Surrey
Tue 28	(R)	Ilkeston (Shipley Hall)	Derbyshire v Gloucestershire
Thu 30	(BC)	Canterbury	Kent v Middlesex
	(BC)	Uppingham School	Leicestershire v Durham

MAY

Fri 1	(BC)	Chesterfield	Derbyshire v Durham
	(BC)	Bristol	Gloucestershire v Worcestershire
	(BC)	Canterbury	Kent v MCC YCs
	(BC)	Bingley	Yorkshire v Lancashire
Mon 4	(BC)	Norton CC	Durham v Nottinghamshire
	(BC)	Bristol	Gloucestershire v Somerset
	(BC)	Hove	Sussex v Middlesex
Tue 5	(R)	Bristol	Gloucestershire v Somerset
	(R)	Uxbridge	Middlesex v Yorkshire
	(BC)	Chesterfield	Derbyshire v Nottinghamshire
	(BC)	Leicester	Leicestershire v Lancashire
Wed 6	(R)	Sunderland	Durham v Sussex
	(R)	Leicester	Leicestershire v Lancashire
	(R)	Knowle & Dorridge	Warwickshire v Derbyshire
Fri 8	(BC)	Taunton	Somerset v Hampshire
	(BC)	The Oval	Surrey v Kent
Mon 11	(R)	Colchester	Essex v Nottinghamshire
	(BC)	Chesterfield	Derbyshire v Leicestershire
	(BC)	Bristol	Gloucestershire v Warwickshire
	(BC)	Old Trafford	Lancashire v Yorkshire
	(BC)	The Oval	Surrey v Middlesex
	(BC)	Worcester	Worcestershire v Hampshire
Tue 12	(R)	Old Trafford	Lancashire v Yorkshire
	(R)	Harrow	Middlesex v Kent
	(R)	The Oval	Surrey v Durham
	(R)	Horsham	Sussex v Derbyshire
	(R)	Old Hill	Worcestershire v Hampshire
	(BC)	Bristol	Gloucestershire v Glamorgan
	(BC)	Leicester	Leicestershire v Northamptonshire
Wed 13	(R)	North Perrott	Somerset v Northamptonshire
Thu 14	(BC)	Trent Bridge	Nottinghamshire v Leicestershire
Fri 15	(BC)	Harrow	Middlesex v Kent

Mon 18	(BC)	Wickford	Essex v Middlesex
	(BC)	Bridgend	Glamorgan v Gloucestershire
	(BC)	Norbury	MCC YCs v Sussex
	(BC)	Worcester	Worcestershire v Somerset
	(BC)	Bingley	Yorkshire v Nottinghamshire
Tue 19	(R)	Felling	Durham v Derbyshire
	(R)	Cheltenham	Gloucestershire v Leicestershire
		(Dowty Arle Court)	
	(R)	Harrogate	Yorkshire v Nottinghamshire
	(R)	Chelmsford	Essex v Kent
	(BC)	Bournemouth	Hampshire v Warwickshire
		Hove	Sussex v England Under 19
Wed 20	(R)	Chelmsford	Essex v Kent
	(R)	Bournemouth	Hampshire v Warwickshire
	(R)	Old Trafford	Lancashire v Middlesex
	(R)	Northampton	Northamptonshire v Glamorgan
	(R)	Worcester	Worcestershire v Surrey
Fri 22	(BC)	Philadelphia CC	Durham v Derbyshire
Mon 25	(BC)	Trent Bridge	Nottinghamshire v Lancashire
	(BC)	Sheffield (Bawtry Road)	Yorkshire v Derbyshire
Tue 26	(R)	Bournemouth	Hampshire v Sussex
	(R)	Kibworth	Leicestershire v Somerset
	(R)	Oundle School	Northamptonshire v Warwickshire
	(R)	Worthington Simpson	Nottinghamshire v Lancashire
	(R)	Todmorden	Yorkshire v Gloucestershire
	(BC)	Ealing	Middlesex v Surrey
Wed 27	(R)	Boldon	Durham v Essex
	(R)	Maidstone	Kent v Glamorgan
	(R)	Uxbridge	Middlesex v Surrey
Fri 29	(BC)	Leicester	Leicestershire v Nottinghamshire
	(BC)	Solihull	Warwickshire v Somerset

JUNE

Mon 1	(BC)	Canterbury	Kent v Surrey
	(BC)	Wigan	Lancashire v Northamptonshire
	(BC)	Leicester	Leicestershire v Derbyshire
	(BC)	Uxbridge (RAF Vine Lane)	Middlesex v Sussex
	(BC)	Farnsfield	Nottinghamshire v Durham
	(BC)	Taunton	Somerset v Gloucestershire
Tue 2	(R)	Ammanford	Glamorgan v Essex
	(R)	Bristol	Gloucestershire v Lancashire
	(R)	Canterbury	Kent v Surrey
	(R)	Loughborough GS	Leicestershire v Derbyshire
	(R)	Shireoaks (Steetley)	Nottinghamshire v Durham
	(R)	Stratford-upon-Avon	Warwickshire v Sussex
	(R)	York	Yorkshire v Hampshire
Wed 3	(R)	Oundle School	Northamptonshire v Middlesex
Fri 5	(BC)	Winscombe	Somerset v Glamorgan
	(BC)	The Oval	Surrey v MCC YCs
	(BC)	Worcester	Worcestershire v Warwickshire
Mon 8	(BC)	Southampton	Hampshire v Somerset
	(BC)	Lancaster	Lancashire v Nottinghamshire
	(BC)	The Oval	Surrey v Sussex
	(BC)	Sheffield (Abbeydale Park)	Yorkshire v Durham

Tue 9	(R)	Chester-le-Street	Durham v Lancashire
	(R)	Abergavenny	Glamorgan v Middlesex
	(R)	Sittingbourne	Kent v Gloucestershire
	(R)	Old Northamptonians	Northamptonshire v Leicestershire
	(R)	Glastonbury	Somerset v Derbyshire
	(R)	Banstead	Surrey v Sussex
	(R)	Nuneaton (Griff & Coton)	Warwickshire v Essex
	(R)	Barnt Green	Worcestershire v Nottinghamshire
Fri 12	(BC)	Bishop Auckland	Durham v Lancashire
	(BC)	Eastbourne	Sussex v MCC YCs
	(BC)	Old Edwardians	Warwickshire v Gloucestershire
Mon 15	(BC)	Southampton	Hampshire v Gloucestershire
	(BC)	Maidstone	Kent v Essex
	(BC)	Uxbridge	Middlesex v MCC YCs
	(BC)	Worksop College	Nottinghamshire v Yorkshire
Tue 16	(R)	Southend	Essex v Yorkshire
	(R)	Cardiff	Glamorgan v Derbyshire
	(R)	Dartford	Kent v Leicestershire
	(R)	Old Trafford	Lancashire v Worcestershire
	(R)	Uxbridge (RAF Vine Lane)	Middlesex v Warwickshire
	(R)	Northampton	Northamptonshire v Durham
	(R)	Taunton	Somerset v Surrey
	(R)	Hastings	Sussex v Nottinghamshire
		Southampton	Hampshire v England Under 19
Fri 19	(BC)	Checkley	Derbyshire v Lancashire
	(BC)	Northampton	Northamptonshire v Durham
	(BC)	Edgbaston	Warwickshire v Worcestershire
Sun 21	(BC)	Worcester	Worcestershire v Gloucestershire
Mon 22	(BC)	Worthington Simpson	Nottinghamshire v Derbyshire
	(BC)	The Oval	Surrey v Essex
	(BC)	Bradford (Park Avenue)	Yorkshire v Leicestershire
Tue 23	(R)	Abbotsholme S, Rocester	Derbyshire v Kent
	(R)	Shildon	Durham v Warwickshire
	(R)	Leigh on Sea	Essex v Hampshire
	(R)	Pontardulais	Glamorgan v Sussex
	(R)	Harrow	Middlesex v Worcestershire
	(R)	Bradford (Park Avenue)	Yorkshire v Leicestershire
Wed 24	(R)	Worksop CC	Nottinghamshire v Northamptonshire
	(R)	The Oval	Surrey v Gloucestershire
Fri 26	(BC)	Durham City	Durham v Leicestershire
	(BC)	Panteg	Glamorgan v Somerset
	(BC)	Bournemouth	Hampshire v Worcestershire
Mon 29	(BC)	Leicester	Leicestershire v Yorkshire
	(BC)	Northampton	Northamptonshire v Lancashire
	(BC)	Hove	Sussex v Essex
Tue 30	(R)	Eppleton	Durham v Somerset
	(R)	Bournemouth	Hampshire v Glamorgan
	(R)	Southgate	Middlesex v Derbyshire
	(R)	Oundle School	Northamptonshire v Lancashire
	(R)	Trent Bridge	Nottinghamshire v Gloucestershire
	(R)	Hove	Sussex v Essex
	(R)	Studley	Warwickshire v Kent
	(R)	Worcester	Worcestershire v Yorkshire

JULY

Fri 3	(BC)	Knypersley	Derbyshire v Northamptonshire
	(BC)	Bournemouth	Hampshire v Glamorgan
	(BC)	Norbury	MCC YCs v Surrey
Mon 6	(R)	Oakham	Leicestershire v Warwickshire
	(BC)	Chesterfield	Derbyshire v Yorkshire
	(BC)	Norbury	MCC YCs v Kent
	(BC)	Trent Bridge	Nottinghamshire v Northamptonshire
	(BC)	Hove	Sussex v Surrey
	(BC)	Worcester	Worcestershire v Glamorgan
Tue 7	(R)	Chesterfield	Derbyshire v Yorkshire
	(R)	Bristol	Gloucestershire v Hampshire
	(R)	Crosby (Northern)	Lancashire v Somerset
	(R)	The Oval	Surrey v Nottinghamshire
	(R)	Hove	Sussex v Kent
	(R)	Kidderminster	Worcestershire v Northamptonshire
Thu 9	(BC)	Birkbeck College	MCC YCs v Essex
Fri 10	(BC)	Cardiff	Glamorgan v Warwickshire
	(BC)	Bristol	Gloucestershire v Hampshire
	(BC)	Harrow	Middlesex v Essex
	(BC)	Lewes Priory	Sussex v Kent
Mon 13	(BC)	Newbury Park	Essex v Sussex
	(BC)	Cardiff	Glamorgan v Hampshire
	(BC)	Northampton	Northamptonshire v Leicestershire
Tue 14	(R)	Ebbw Vale	Glamorgan v Somerset
	(R)	Maidstone	Kent v Durham
	(R)	Hinckley	Leicestershire v Middlesex
	(R)	Bedford School	Northamptonshire v Sussex
	(R)	Collingham	Nottinghamshire v Hampshire
	(R)	Leamington Spa	Warwickshire v Yorkshire
	(R)	Worcester	Worcestershire v Gloucestershire
		The Oval	Surrey v England Under 19
Fri 17	(BC)	Maidstone	Kent v Sussex
	(BC)	Bedford Modern School	Northamptonshire v Yorkshire
	(BC)	Taunton	Somerset v Warwickshire
Mon 20	(BC)	Durham School	Durham v Yorkshire
	(BC)	Newbury Park	Essex v MCC YCs
	(BC)	Old Trafford	Lancashire v Leicestershire
	(BC)	Banbury	Northamptonshire v Nottinghamshire
	(BC)	Edgbaston	Warwickshire v Glamorgan
Tue 21	(R)	Seaton Carew	Durham v Middlesex
	(R)	Chelmsford	Essex v Gloucestershire
	(R)	Wellingborough School	Northamptonshire v Hampshire
	(R)	Worksop College	Nottinghamshire v Glamorgan
	(R)	Mitchells & Butlers	Warwickshire v Surrey
	(R)	Worcester (Flagge Meadow)	Worcestershire v Kent
Fri 24	(BC)	Northampton	Northamptonshire v Derbyshire
	(BC)	Taunton	Somerset v Worcestershire
	(BC)	Coventry & North Warwicks	Warwickshire v Hampshire
Mon 27	(BC)	Durham School	Durham v Northamptonshire
	(BC)	Southend	Essex v Surrey
	(BC)	Swansea	Glamorgan v Worcestershire

Tue 28	(R)	Belper Meadow	Derbyshire v Worcestershire
	(R)	Southend	Essex v Surrey
	(R)	Cardiff	Glamorgan v Leicestershire
	(R)	Gloucester (Kings School)	Gloucestershire v Middlesex
	(R)	Folkestone	Kent v Hampshire
	(R)	Liverpool	Lancashire v Sussex
	(R)	Clevedon	Somerset v Nottinghamshire
	(R)	Marske-by-Sea	Yorkshire v Northamptonshire
Fri 31	(BC)	Crosby (Northern)	Lancashire v Durham
	(BC)	Marske-by-Sea	Yorkshire v Northamptonshire

AUGUST

Tue 4	(R)	Derby	Derbyshire v Surrey
	(R)	Bristol	Gloucestershire v Glamorgan
	(R)	Southampton	Hampshire v Durham
	(R)	Old Trafford	Lancashire v Essex
	(R)	Leicester	Leicestershire v Worcestershire
	(R)	Southgate	Middlesex v Somerset
	(R)	Trent Bridge	Nottinghamshire v Warwickshire
	(R)	Hove	Sussex v Yorkshire
Mon 10	(BC)		Bain Clarkson Trophy
or Tue 11			Semi-Finals
Wed 12	(R)	Ilkeston (Shipley Hall)	Derbyshire v Nottinghamshire
	(R)	Enfield	Middlesex v Essex
	(R)	Guildford	Surrey v Northamptonshire
	(R)	Walmley	Warwickshire v Somerset
	(R)	Halesowen	Worcestershire v Glamorgan
	(R)	Elland	Yorkshire v Kent
Mon 17	(R)	Northampton	Northamptonshire v Gloucestershire
Tue 18	(R)	Heanor	Derbyshire v Essex
	(R)	Boldon	Durham v Yorkshire
	(R)	Southampton	Hampshire v Middlesex
	(R)	Blackpool	Lancashire v Warwickshire
	(R)	Market Harborough	Leicestershire v Sussex
	(R)	Taunton	Somerset v Worcestershire
	(R)	The Oval	Surrey v Glamorgan
Sat 22	(R)	BP Llandarcy	Glamorgan v Durham
	(R)	Bournemouth	Hampshire v Leicestershire
Tue 25	(R)	Cheltenham	Gloucestershire v Durham
		(Dowty Arle Court)	
	(R)	Folkestone	Kent v Northamptonshire
	(R)	The Oval	Surrey v Leicestershire
Wed 26	(R)	Colchester	Essex v Worcestershire
	(R)	Usk	Glamorgan v Warwickshire
	(R)	Southampton	Hampshire v Lancashire
	(R)	Trent Bridge	Nottinghamshire v Middlesex
	(R)	Eastbourne	Sussex v Somerset

SEPTEMBER

Tue 1	(R)	Chesterfield	Derbyshire v Northamptonshire
	(R)	Pontymister	Glamorgan v Lancashire
	(R)	Cheltenham Town CC	Gloucestershire v Sussex
	(R)	Canterbury	Kent v Nottinghamshire
	(R)	Leicester	Leicestershire v Essex
	(R)	Taunton	Somerset v Yorkshire
	(R)	Guildford	Surrey v Hampshire

Wed 2	(R)	Moseley	Warwickshire v Worcestershire
Mon 7	(BC)		Bain Clarkson Trophy Final
			(Reserve Day Tuesday 8)
Wed 9	(R)	Seaton Carew	Durham v Worcestershire
	(R)	Chelmsford	Essex v Northamptonshire
	(R)	Bristol	Gloucestershire v Warwickshire
	(R)	Southampton	Hampshire v Derbyshire
	(R)	Shireoaks (Steetley)	Nottinghamshire v Leicestershire
	(R)	The Oval	Surrey v Lancashire
	(R)	Horsham	Sussex v Middlesex
	(R)	Bradford (Park Avenue)	Yorkshire v Glamorgan
Wed 16	(R)	Taunton	Somerset v Essex

MINOR COUNTIES FIXTURES 1992

APRIL   *Benson & Hedges Cup*

Tue 21	Lord's	Middlesex v Minor Counties
Thu 23	Dowty Arle, Cheltenham	Gloucestershire v Minor Counties
Thu 30	Marlow	Minor Counties v Sussex

MAY

| Sat 2 | The Oval | Surrey v Minor Counties |
| Tue 5 | Stone | Minor Counties v Leicestershire |

Holt Cup Qualifying Round

Sun 17	Barrow	Cumberland v Lincolnshire
	Chester, Boughton Hall	Cheshire v Northumberland
	Northop Hall, Nr. Mold	Wales v Staffordshire
	Perkins, Shrewsbury	Shropshire v Herefordshire

Championship

Sun 24	Falkland C.C., Newbury	(W) Berkshire v Oxfordshire
	Brockhampton C.C.	(W) Herefordshire v Wales
	Sleaford	(E) Lincolnshire v Bedfordshire
Mon 25	Sherborne School	(W) Dorset v Shropshire
Tue 26	Carlisle	(E) Cumberland v Suffolk
Thu 28	Meir Heath	(E) Staffordshire v Suffolk

Holt Cup First Round

Sun 31	Burneside	Cumberland or Lincolnshire
	or Sleaford	v Cheshire or Northumberland
	Neath	Wales or Staffordshire
	or Longton	v Shropshire or Herefordshire
	Aylesbury	Buckinghamshire v Berkshire
	Christ Church	Oxfordshire v Hertfordshire
	Framlingham College	Suffolk v Bedfordshire
	Ley's School	Cambridgeshire v Norfolk
	Truro	Cornwall v Devon
	Devizes	Wiltshire v Dorset

JUNE

Wed 3	March	*Championship* (E) Cambridgeshire v Staffordshire
Sun 7	Bedford School	(E) Bedfordshire v Norfolk
	Kidmore End C.C.	(W) Berkshire v Herefordshire
	Pressed Steel	(W) Oxfordshire v Wales
	St Georges	(W) Shropshire v Wiltshire
	St Albans	(E) Hertfordshire v Buckinghamshire
	Burghley Park	(E) Lincolnshire v Northumberland
Mon 8	Redruth	(W) Cornwall v Cheshire
Wed 10	Wisbech	(E) Cambridgeshire v Suffolk
	Torquay	(W) Devon v Cheshire
Sun 14		*Holt Cup Quarter-Finals* *Championship*
Tue 16	Jesmond	(E) Northumberland v Hertfordshire
	Brewood	(E) Staffordshire v Buckinghamshire
Thu 18	Millom	(E) Cumberland v Hertfordshire
Sun 21	Henlow	(E) Bedfordshire v Northumberland
	Neston	(W) Cheshire v Wales
	Camborne	(W) Cornwall v Devon
	Bourne	(E) Lincolnshire v Cambridgeshire
	Shrewsbury	(W) Shropshire v Herefordshire
	Swindon (B.R.)	(W) Wiltshire v Oxfordshire
Wed 24		*NatWest Trophy, Round 1*
Sun 28		*Holt Cup Semi-Finals* *Championship*
Sun 28	Hereford City S.C.	*(W) Herefordshire v Devon
	Trowbridge	*(W) Wiltshire v Berkshire
Mon 29	Penrith	(E) Cumberland v Norfolk

JULY

Wed 1	Norton	(E) Staffordshire v Norfolk
Sun 5	Truro	(W) Cornwall v Wiltshire
	Sidmouth	(W) Devon v Dorset
	Stevenage	(E) Hertfordshire v Lincolnshire
	Colwyn Bay	(W) Wales v Shropshire
	Jesmond	(E) Northumberland v Bucks
Tue 7	Barrow	(E) Cumberland v Buckinghamshire
Thu 9		*NatWest Trophy, Round 2* *Championship*
Sun 12	Warrington	(W) Cheshire v Shropshire
	Brockhampton	(W) Herefordshire v Dorset
Mon 13	Ashington	(E) Northumberland v Staffordshire
Wed 15	Fenner's	(E) Cambridgeshire v Bucks
	Netherfield	(E) Cumberland v Staffordshire
	Mildenhall	(E) Suffolk v Lincolnshire
Sun 19	Reading C.C.	(W) Berkshire v Devon
	Weymouth	(W) Dorset v Oxfordshire
	Cleethorpes	(E) Lincolnshire v Cumberland
	Penarth	(W) Wales v Cornwall
	Trowbridge	(W) Wiltshire v Cheshire
Tue 21	Dorchester	(W) Dorset v Cheshire
	Dales C.C., Leominster	(W) Herefordshire v Cornwall
Wed 22	Luton	(E) Bedfordshire v Hertfordshire
	Fenner's	(E) Cambridgeshire v Northumberland

Sun 26	Exmouth	(W) Devon v Wiltshire
	Lakenham	(E) Norfolk v Lincolnshire
	Leek	(E) Staffordshire v Hertfordshire
Mon 27	Christ Church	(W) Oxfordshire v Cornwall
Tue 28	Ipswich School	(E) Suffolk v Bedfordshire

Representative Match

| Wed 29 | Marlow | Minor Counties v Pakistanis (two days) |

Championship

| Wed 29 | Reading C.C. | (W) Berkshire v Cornwall |
| | Lakenham | (E) Norfolk v Cambridgeshire |

AUGUST

Sun 2	Bedford Town	(E) Bedfordshire v Cumberland
	Slough	(E) Buckinghamshire v Lincolnshire
	Stalybridge	(W) Cheshire v Herefordshire
	Dorchester	(W) Dorset v Berkshire
	Lakenham	(E) Norfolk v Hertfordshire
	Bury St Edmunds	(E) Suffolk v Northumberland
	Marlborough College	(W) Wiltshire v Wales
Mon 3	Falmouth	(W) Cornwall v Shropshire
Tue 4	March	(E) Cambridgeshire v Cumberland
	Lakenham	(E) Norfolk v Northumberland
Wed 5	Bovey Tracey	(W) Devon v Shropshire
Sun 9	Finchampstead C.C.	(W) Berkshire v Wales
	Bowdon	(W) Cheshire v Oxfordshire
	Hertford	(E) Hertfordshire v Cambridgeshire
	Lincoln Lindum	(E) Lincolnshire v Staffordshire
	Devizes	(W) Wiltshire v Dorset
Tue 11	Beaconsfield	(E) Buckinghamshire v Norfolk
	Oswestry	(W) Shropshire v Oxfordshire
Sun 16	Toft	(W) Cheshire v Berkshire
	St Austell	(W) Cornwall v Dorset
	Letchworth	(E) Hertfordshire v Suffolk
	Jesmond	(E) Northumberland v Cumberland
	Aston Rowant	(W) Oxfordshire v Herefordshire
	Stone	(E) Staffordshire v Bedfordshire
	Ebbw Vale	(W) Wales v Devon
Tue 18	Leighton Buzzard	(E) Bedfordshire v Cambridgeshire
	Wellington	(W) Shropshire v Berkshire
Sun 23	Marlow	(E) Buckinghamshire v Suffolk
	Banbury XX	(W) Oxfordshire v Devon
Wed 26	Lord's	*Holt Cup Final*
Sun 30	Amersham	(E) Buckinghamshire v Bedfordshire
	Copdock, Ipswich	(E) Suffolk v Norfolk
Mon 31	Pontardulais	(W) Wales v Dorset
	Hereford City S.C.	(W) Herefordshire v Wiltshire

SEPTEMBER

| Sun 13 | Worcester | *Championship Final* |

* These matches could be affected by progress in the Holt Cup.

© Queen Anne Press 1992

First published in Great Britain in 1992 by
Queen Anne Press/Headline Book Publishing plc
Headline House
79 Great Titchfield
London W1P 7FN

Cover photograph: Phillip DeFreitas (Lancashire and England)
by Allsport/Shaun Botterill

A CIP catalogue record for this book
is available from the British Library

ISBN 0–356–20571–1 (Paperback)
ISBN 0–356–20574–6 (Hardback)

Typeset by
J&L Composition Ltd, Filey, North Yorkshire

Printed and bound in Great Britain by
BPCC Hazells Ltd
Member of BPCC Ltd.